HUMAN SEXUALITY 91/92

D1473616

Sixteenth Edition

Editor

Ollie Pocs
Illinois State University

Ollie Pocs is a professor in the Department of Sociology, Anthropology, and Social Work at Illinois State University. He received his B.A. and M.A. in sociology from the University of Illinois, and a Ph.D. in family studies from Purdue University. His primary areas of interest are marriage and family, human sexuality and sexuality education, sex roles, and counseling/therapy. He has published several books and articles in these areas.

Cover illustration by Mike Eagle

The Dushkin Publishing Group, Inc.
Sluice Dock, Guilford, Connecticut 06437

The Annual Editions Series

Annual Editions is a series of over fifty volumes designed to provide the reader with convenient, low-cost access to a wide range of current, carefully selected articles from some of the most important magazines, newspapers, and journals published today. Annual Editions are updated on an annual basis through a continuous monitoring of over 200 periodical sources. All Annual Editions have a number of features designed to make them particularly useful, including topic guides, annotated tables of contents, unit overviews, and indexes. For the teacher using Annual Editions in the classroom, an Instructor's Resource Guide with test questions is available for each volume.

VOLUMES AVAILABLE

Africa
Aging
American Government
American History, Pre-Civil War
American History, Post-Civil War
Anthropology
Biology
Business and Management
Business Ethics
Canadian Politics
China
Comparative Politics
Computers in Education
Computers in Business
Computers in Society
Criminal Justice
Drugs, Society, and Behavior
Early Childhood Education
Economics
Educating Exceptional Children
Education
Educational Psychology
Environment
Geography
Global Issues
Health
Human Development
Human Resources
Human Sexuality

Latin America
Macroeconomics
Management
Marketing
Marriage and Family
Microeconomics
Middle East and the Islamic World
Money and Banking
Nutrition
Personal Growth and Behavior
Psychology
Public Administration
Race and Ethnic Relations
Social Problems
Sociology
Soviet Union and Eastern Europe
State and Local Government
Third World
Urban Society
Violence and Terrorism
Western Civilization,
  Pre-Reformation
Western Civilization,
  Post-Reformation
Western Europe
World History, Pre-Modern
World History, Modern
World Politics

Library of Congress Cataloging in Publication Data
Main entry under title: Annual Editions: Human sexuality. 1991/92.
    1. Sexual behavior—Addresses, essays, lectures—Periodicals. 2. Sexual hygiene—Addresses, essays, lectures—Periodicals. 3. Sex education—Addresses, essays, lectures—Periodicals. 4. Human relations—Addresses, essays, lectures—Periodicals. I. Pocs, Ollie, comp. II. Title: Human sexuality.
ISBN 1–56134–024–3   155.3′05   75-20756

Sixteenth Edition

Manufactured by The Banta Company, Harrisonburg, Virginia 22801

Editors/ Advisory Board

To The Reader

In publishing ANNUAL EDITIONS we recognize the enormous role played by the magazines, newspapers, and journals of the *public press* in providing current, first-rate educational information in a broad spectrum of interest areas. Within the articles, the best scientists, practitioners, researchers, and commentators draw issues into new perspective as accepted theories and viewpoints are called into account by new events, recent discoveries change old facts, and fresh debate breaks out over important controversies.

Many of the articles resulting from this enormous editorial effort are appropriate for students, researchers, and professionals seeking accurate, current material to help bridge the gap between principles and theories and the real world. These articles, however, become more useful for study when those of lasting value are carefully *collected, organized, indexed,* and *reproduced* in a *low-cost format,* which provides easy and permanent access when the material is needed. That is the role played by *Annual Editions.* Under the direction of each volume's *Editor,* who is an expert in the subject area, and with the guidance of an *Advisory Board,* we seek each year to provide in each *ANNUAL EDITION* a current, well-balanced, carefully selected collection of the best of the public press for your study and enjoyment. We think you'll find this volume useful, and we hope you'll take a moment to let us know what you think.

> Sex lies at the root of life, and we can never learn to reverence life until we know how to understand sex.
>
> —Havelock Ellis

The above quote by one of the first sexologists highlights the objective of this book. Learning about sex is a lifelong process that can occur informally and formally. With knowledge comes the understanding that we are all born sexual, and that sex, per se, is neither good nor bad, beautiful nor ugly, moral nor immoral.

While we are all born with basic sexual interests, drives, and desires, human sexuality is a dynamic and complex force that involves psychological and sociocultural dimensions in addition to the physiological ones. Sexuality includes an individual's whole body and personality. We are not born with a fully developed body or mind, but instead grow and learn; so it is with respect to our sexuality. Sexuality is learned. We learn what "appropriate" sexual behavior is, how to express it, when to do so, and under what circumstances. We also learn sexual feelings: positive feelings such as acceptance of sexuality, or negative and repressive feelings such as guilt and shame.

Sexuality, which affects human life so basically and powerfully, has, until recently, received little attention in scientific research, and even less attention within higher education communities. Yet our contemporary social environment is expanding its sexual and social horizons toward greater freedom for the individual, especially for women and for people who deviate from societal norms: those who are somehow handicapped and those who make less common sexual or relationship choices. Without proper understanding, this expansion in sexual freedom can lead to new forms of sexual bondage as easily as to increased joy and pleasure. The celebration of sexuality today is most likely found somewhere between the traditional, rigid, repressive morality that is our sociosexual heritage, and a new performance-oriented, irresponsible, self-seeking mentality.

In trying to understand sexuality, our goal is to seek a joyful acceptance of being sexual, and to express this awareness in the most considerate way for ourselves and our sexual partners, while at the same time taking personal and social consequences into account. This anthology is aimed at helping all of us achieve this goal.

The articles selected for this edition cover a wide range of important topics and were written primarily by professionals for a nonprofessional audience. In them, health educators, psychologists, sociologists, sexologists, and sex therapists writing for professional journals and popular magazines present their views on how and why sexual attitudes and behaviors are developed, maintained, and changed. This edition of *Annual Editions: Human Sexuality* is organized into six sections. *Sexuality and Society* notes historical and cross-cultural views, and analyzes our constantly changing society and sexuality. *Sexual Biology and Health* explains the functioning and responses of the human body, and a range of common, and not-so-common, sexual behaviors and practices. *Interpersonal Relationships* provides suggestions for establishing and maintaining intimate, responsible, quality relationships. *Reproduction* discusses some recent trends related to pregnancy and child-bearing, and deals with reproductive topics including conception, contraception, and abortion. *Sexuality Through the Life Cycle* looks at what happens sexually throughout one's lifetime—from childhood to the later years. Finally, *Old/New Sexual Concerns* deals with such topics as sexual hygiene and functioning, sexual abuse and violence, and gender differences and similarities.

The articles in this anthology have been carefully reviewed and selected for their quality, currency, and interest. They present a variety of viewpoints. Some you will agree with, some you will not, but you will learn from all of them.

Appreciation and a thank-you go to Susan Bunting for her work and expertise. We feel that *Human Sexuality 91/92* is one of the most useful and up-to-date books available. Please let us know what you think. Return the article rating form on the last page of this book with your suggestions and comments. Any book can be improved. This one will continue to be—annually.

Ollie Pocs

Ollie Pocs
Editor

Contents

Unit 1

Sexuality and Society

Eight selections consider sexuality from historical and cross-cultural perspectives, and examine today's changing attitudes toward human sexual interaction.

The concepts in bold italics are developed in the article. For further expansion please refer to the Topic Guide, the Index, and the Glossary.

Unit 2

Sexual Biology and Health

Eleven selections examine the biological aspects of human sexuality and emphasize the importance of understanding sexual hygiene.

The concepts in bold italics are developed in the article. For further expansion please refer to the Topic Guide, the Index, and the Glossary.

Unit 3

Interpersonal Relationships

Seven selections examine the dynamics of establishing sexual relationships and the need to make these relationships responsible and effective.

Unit 4

Reproduction

Eleven articles discuss the roles of both males and females in pregnancy and childbirth, and consider the influences of the latest birth control methods and practices on individuals and society as a whole.

The concepts in bold italics are developed in the article. For further expansion please refer to the Topic Guide, the Index, and the Glossary.

Unit 5

Sexuality Through the Life Cycle

Seven articles consider human sexuality as an important element throughout the life cycle. Topics include responsible adolescent sexuality, sex in and out of marriage, and sex in old age.

The concepts in bold italics are developed in the article. For further expansion please refer to the Topic Guide, the Index, and the Glossary.

CHLAMYDIA IS NOT A FLOWER.
It's a Sexually Transmitted Disease with Devastating Effects.

Unit
6

Old/New Sexual Concerns

Fourteen selections discuss ongoing sexual concerns of sexual hygiene, sexual harassment and violence, and gender roles.

The concepts in bold italics are developed in the article. For further expansion please refer to the Topic Guide, the Index, and the Glossary.

Topic Guide

This topic guide suggests how the selections in this book relate to topics of traditional concern to human sexuality students and professionals. It can be very useful in locating articles that relate to each other for reading and research. The guide is arranged alphabetically according to topic. Articles may, of course, treat topics that do not appear in the topic guide. In turn, entries in the topic guide do not necessarily constitute a comprehensive listing of all the contents of each selection.

TOPIC AREA	TREATED IN:	TOPIC AREA	TREATED IN:
Abortion	7. Abortion Policy and Medical Policy 14. Sexuality Attitudes of Black Adults 31. Reluctant Crusader 32. "She Died Because of a Law" 33. Abortion in a New Light	**Children**	2. Latino Culture and Sex Education 5. Sexuality Education in the 1990s 14. Sexuality Attitudes of Black Adults 18. Variations on a Theme 28. Curbing Teen Pregnancy 38. My Body, My Self 39. Double Vision 45. Risky Adolescent Sexual Behavior 49. AIDS: The Next Ten Years 51. Adolescent Female Prostitutes
Abuse, Sexual/Incest	2. Latino Culture and Sex Education 8. Censorship and Fear of Sexuality 17. Homosexuality: Who and Why? 27. Adolescent Pregnancy Prevention Program 51. Adolescent Female Prostitutes	**Health**	4. AIDS News, Highlights 7. Abortion Policy and Medical Practice 10. Man's Greatest Reflex 13. Men Who Fake Orgasm 16. Life-Threatening Autoerotic Behavior 29. Birth Control 44. Death of a Sex Life 46. Dangerous Liaison 47. PMS: Proof or Promises? 48. Chronic Disease and Impotence 49. AIDS: The Next Ten Years
Acquired Immuno-deficiency Syndrome (AIDS)	4. AIDS News, Highlights 6. AIDS and STD Education 15. Americans and Their Sexual Partners 30. Can You Rely on Condoms? 49. AIDS: The Next Ten Years		
Aging	10. Man's Greatest Reflex 41. Sex: Better After 35 42. Erotic Play 43. Most-Asked Sex Questions 44. Death of a Sex Life 48. Chronic Disease and Impotence	**Homosexuality**	1. Sex in China 2. Latino Culture and Sex Education 8. Censorship and Fear of Homosexuality 15. Americans and Their Sexual Partners 17. Homosexuality: Who and Why? 18. Variations on a Theme 19. Should Gays Have Marriage Rights? 49. AIDS: The Next Ten Years
Attitudes/Values	1. Sex in China 2. Latino Culture and Sex Education 3. Manhood 5. Sexuality Education in the 1990s 7. Abortion Policy and Medical Practice 8. Censorship and Fear of Sexuality 11. Women and Sexuality 14. Sexuality Attitudes of Black Adults 15. Americans and Their Sexual Partners 19. Should Gays Have Marriage Rights? 25. Sexual Pursuit 28. Curbing Teenage Pregnancy 31. Reluctant Crusader 33. Abortion in a New Light 38. My Body, My Self 39. Double Vision 45. Risky Adolescent Sexual Behavior 49. AIDS: The Next Ten Years 50. Sexual Harrassment '80s-Style 54. Conflict Between the Sexes 56. Sexuality Scale 58. Mind Sex	**Intimacy, Sexual**	11. Women and Sexuality 13. Men Who Fake Orgasm 15. Americans and Their Sex Partners 17. Homosexuality: Who and Why? 20. Looking for Love 22. How Do You Build Intimacy? 23. Friends and Lovers? 25. Sexual Pursuit 26. Art of Sex 36. Sex During Pregnancy 37. Sex After the Baby 41. Sex: Better After 35 42. Erotic Play 43. Most-Asked Sex Questions 54. Conflict Between the Sexes 56. Sensuality Scale 57. Sexual Secrets
Birth/Control/Contraception	1. Sex in China 2. Latino Culture and Sex Education 5. Sexuality Education in the 1990s 11. Women and Sexuality 14. Sexuality Attitudes of Black Adults 27. Adolescent Pregnancy Prevention Program 29. Birth Control 30. Can You Rely on Condoms? 31. Reluctant Crusader 34. Teenage Birth's New Conceptions 35. Teenage Pregnancy in New York 45. Risky Adolescent Sexual Behavior	**Men**	2. Latino Culture and Sex Education 3. Manhood 10. Men's Greatest Reflex 12. Premature Ejaculation 13. Men Who Fake Orgasm 14. Sexuality Attitudes of Black Adults 17. Homosexuality: Who and Why? 18. Variations on a Theme 26. Art of Sex 43. Most-Asked Sex Questions

Sexuality and Society

- **Historical and Cross-Cultural Perspectives (Articles 1-4)**
- **Changing Society/Changing Sexuality (Articles 5-8)**

People of different civilizations in different historical periods have engaged in a variety of modes of sexual expression and behavior. Despite this cultural and historical diversity, one important principle should be kept in mind: Sexual awareness, attitudes, and behaviors are learned within sociocultural contexts that define appropriate sexuality for society's members. Our sexual attitudes and behaviors are in large measure social and cultural phenomena.

For several centuries, Western civilization has been characterized by an "anti-sex ethic" that has normatively limited sexual behavior to the confines of monogamous heterosexual pair bonds (marriages) for the sole purpose of procreation. Today, changes in our social environment—the widespread availability of effective contraception, the liberation of women from the home and kitchen, and the reconsideration of democratic values of "individual freedom" and the "pursuit of happiness"—are strengthening our concept of ourselves as sexual beings and posing a challenge to the "anti-sex ethic" that has traditionally served to orient sexuality.

As a rule, social change is not easily accomplished. Sociologists generally acknowledge that changes in the social environment are accompanied by the presence of interest groups that offer competing versions of what "is" or "should be" appropriate social behavior. The contemporary sociocultural changes with respect to sexuality are highly illustrative of such social dynamics. Many of the articles in this section document changes in the social environment and the beliefs of different groups about what are or should be our social policies regarding sexuality. The articles also illustrate the diversity of beliefs regarding what was beneficial or detrimental about the past, and what needs to be preserved or changed for a better future.

The fact that human sexuality is primarily a learned behavior can be both a blessing and a curse. The learning process enables humans to achieve a range of sexual expression and meaning that far exceeds their biological programming. Unfortunately, however, our society's lingering "anti-sex ethic" tends to foreclose constructive learning experiences and contexts, often driving learning underground. What is needed for the future is high-quality, pervasive sex education to counteract the locker room, commercial sex, and the trial-and-error contexts in which

most individuals in our society acquire misinformation, anxiety, and fear—as opposed to knowledge, reassurance, and comfort—about themselves as sexual people.

A view of the past illustrates the connectedness of our values and perceptions of sexuality with other sociopolitical events and beliefs. Cross-cultural perspectives provide common human patterns and needs with respect to sexuality and other interpersonal issues. Several of the articles in this section describe and examine patterns of change in political, economic, medical, and educational spheres as they relate to sexuality including beliefs, values, behaviors, relationships, and health. They also discuss and challenge present sociocultural, educational, medical, and legal practices in controversial areas related to sexuality such as sex education in school and public media, sex roles and expectations, AIDS, abortion, and censorship. Although the authors may not agree on the desirability of the changes they describe nor advocate the same future directions, they do emphasize the necessity for people to have information and awareness about a wide range of sexual topics. They also share another belief: we as individuals and as a world society have a vital interest in the translation of social consciousness and sexuality into a meaningful and rewarding awareness and expression for all of society's members.

The first subsection, *Historical and Cross-Cultural Perspectives*, contains four fascinating articles that address sexuality related issues in settings as varied as China, the South Pacific, and ethnic and mainstream America. Each article challenges the reader with questions of why cultures dictate and/or proscribe certain beliefs, values, or practices. They also link misinformation and lack of access to accurate or complete information about sexuality to problematic personal, interpersonal, and societal consequences. Each calls for increased awareness, understanding, and acceptance as avenues for more positive sexual experiences for individuals and improved sexual health in the era of AIDS.

The four articles that make up the second subsection, *Changing Society/Changing Sexuality*, provide an in-depth look at three controversies of this and recent decades—sex education, abortion, and censorship. In informative and thought-provoking fashion each article presents today's debate on these issues in a broader sociocultural

content. Trends and mistakes of past commentaries on the ethics and acceptability of various alternative positions, and predictions and recommendations for the future provide readers with ample food for thought and lively discussion.

Looking Ahead: Challenge Questions

What surprised you about the questions asked by the Chinese people about sex?

Which characteristics of the Latino culture seem the most different from those your family/ethnic group taught you about sexuality and family life? What questions would you like to ask an age-mate raised in this culture?

How strong do you think the pressure to prove one's manhood is for today's men? Is it beneficial or detrimental to them, their families, and/or their lovers?

Looking back on your sex education in elementary and secondary school, what was done well, and what was done poorly? How would you like to see it changed for this generation of school children?

What did you learn about the history of the abortion policy and medical practice that was most surprising to you? What was most upsetting?

How do you *feel* about Klein's assertion that much of people's position on the censorship of sexual materials is fear-based?

Sex in China

Unable for many years to learn the answers to their questions about sex, the Chinese people can now find the information they have long been forbidden to seek.

Fang Fu Ruan, MD,
and Vern L. Bullough, PhD, RN

Fang Fu Ruan was a professor of medicine at Beijing University, and is currently Adjunct Professor of Nursing, State University of New York at Buffalo. Vern L. Bullough is Dean of Natural and Social Sciences, State University of New York College at Buffalo, and SUNY Distinguished Professor.

For more than 30 years, the Chinese Republic permitted virtually no information concerning sex to reach the Chinese people, either via publications or any other source, such as classroom instruction. Certain regulations concerning reproductive behavior were strictly enforced. For example, abortions were mandatory for unauthorized pregnancies.

In 1980, health and other publications were once again allowed to publish sexuality-related materials, and the senior author (Ruan) spent five years (1980–1985) writing a health column for several popular national publications in China.

Readers of medical columns in lay newspapers were encouraged for the first time in decades to submit questions about sexuality, and receive answers published in these media. Such information had always been scarce and virtually unobtainable, since the Chinese emphasis on propriety made it almost impossible to discuss sex even in private.

Traditionally, Chinese parents have not explained the facts of life to their children until just before they marry. Since marriage between 1949 and 1980 was not officially sanctioned until young people reached their mid-20s, sexual ignorance was widespread. Many Chinese girls had no idea what was happening to them when they began to menstruate. Inevitably, when

people first learned that they could ask (and receive answers to) questions about sex, numerous readers submitted questions to the media. Not surprisingly, many of these questions were rather naïve.

Newpaper and magazine health columns also provided new and valuable sources of research information, which had been forbidden in earlier years. For example, it was now possible to contact a number of homosexuals and transsexuals, and gather important data about them. It also became possible to perform transsexual gender-change surgery in at least one case.

The naïveté of many questions obviously reflected the long period in which there had been absolutely no sex education in China. For example, several women wrote to ask whether they could become pregnant as a result of merely being touched by a man. More than one couple inquired how the wife could become pregnant since "nothing had happened" despite several years of marriage. Correspondence with some of these couples revealed that a number of them had never engaged in sexual intercourse and did not even know what it was! Acutely aware of the need for sex information, the Chinese government officials were at last persuaded to call a national conference on sex education in 1985. In the course of the conference, sex education classes were recommended for all Chinese youth, and the government finally set up such a program in 1988.

The following are typical questions answered in Chinese newspapers' health columns from 1980 to 1985. (Additional information has been added in some instances to aid American readers in understanding the context in which some of the questions were asked and answered.)

Sexual frequency

Question: I read in the booklet *Knowledge of Sex* that the normal frequency for intercourse is once every week or every other week. I have sex with my wife every night and I worry that I am not normal. Am I wrong to have intercourse so often? Should we limit our frequency?

Comment: This booklet, issued after the ravages of the Cultural Revolution had ended, marked the Chinese government's first effort to respond to its citizens' demands for information about sex. The booklet's authors, however, mindful of the forced confessions of wrongdoing by those few professionals who had written about sexual activity before the Cultural Revolution, took a very cautious approach in discussing sexuality. Dr. Ruan's columns marked a new level of frankness.

Answer: China has a long tradition of opinions concerning how often individuals should engage in sexual intercourse. The famous Tang dynasty physician Sun Si-mao (AD 581–682) stated that 20-year-old men should engage in sex at least once every four days; 30-year-old men, once every eight days; 40-year-old men, once every 16 days; and 50-year-old men, once every 21 days. Today we know that this is neither right nor wrong, but depends on the individual. Every person has different sexual needs and the frequency of intercourse therefore needs to be decided by the sexual partners. Thus, if you and your wife enjoy having sex every night, that's fine. There is nothing wrong with this. Your own feelings and wishes about sex are important, but at the same time, you also need to consider those of your wife. Each of you should try to satisfy the other.

Masturbation

Question: I have been told that one drop of semen equals 20 drops of blood, and that the loss of semen, especially through masturbation, will cause neurosis, insomnia, impotence, impaired ejaculation, and other severe disorders. Is this true?

Comment: In China there is much misinformation about masturbation. Several male correspondents were so worried about their practice of masturbation that they had attempted to cut off their penis. Some parents wrote in to say that their sons had committed suicide due to their inability to stop masturbating. Thus, it was imperative to answer this type of question by allaying fear as well as providing factual information.

Answer: No. Semen can be stored by the body only for about a month and is then either absorbed by the body or used up. The loss of semen is therefore not harmful. Masturbation is a normal physiological phenomenon. According to the studies of such internationally known sex researchers as Alfred Kinsey and William Masters (as well as others), masturbation can actually be helpful in certain circumstances. Unfortunately, many people experience totally unwarranted fears and guilt feelings because of false, misleading, and unscientific beliefs and teachings; such fears and guilt feelings often cause needless suffering.

Female sexual arousal

Question: How can I tell when my wife is sexually aroused, and how can I satisfy her?

Answer: This is an old question, but it is just as important today as it was years ago. In one of the classic handbooks on sex, *Yu Fang Pi Chueh (Secret Instructions Concerning the Jade Chamber),* which predates the modern era, the Yellow Emperor asked: "How can I become aware of the joyfulness [arousal] of the woman?" The answer was given by the character called the Plain Girl, who said: "There are five signs, five desires, and ten movements. By looking at these changes you will become aware of what is happening to the woman's body." She identified these signs: flushing of her face, hardening of her breasts, a growing dryness of her throat, a moist vagina, and finally a transmission of fluid through the vagina. She said that intercourse should begin during the second phase; after the fifth phase, you should slowly withdraw from her.

The Plain Girl also mentioned other signals that indicate a woman's sexual feelings: If she bates her breath, it means that she wants to have sex with you. If her nose and mouth are dilated, she wants to begin sexual activity, and if she embraces you tightly, you will know that she is excited and aroused. If perspiration flows, it means that she is approaching orgasm, and lastly, if her body straightens out and her eyes close, it means that she has been satisfied.

According to a well-known scholar of ancient Chinese sex customs, the five signs described in classical Chinese sexual writings are comparable to those discussed by Kinsey.[1,2] It is clear that ancient Chinese sexologists were observant and that Chinese culture attached great importance to orgasm. Therefore, pay attention to your partner's responses, gain her full cooperation, and you and your partner will discover what works best for you as you both try to attain orgasm.

Sex change

Question: I read that some women want to change their sex to become a man, and vice versa. Is this true? Is it normal? Do we have such people in our country?

Answer: Yes, there are such people and some live in China. This phenomenon, called "transsexualism" in the West, became widespread there during the 1950s and 1960s. The number of transsexuals in China is estimated to be very small, perhaps one in every 40,000 to 400,000 individuals. "Normal" is not a good word to use in discussing these people, for we need to understand and accept them.

Homosexuality

Question: I was surprised to learn that there are men who love other men sexually, and that this is also true of certain women. A newspaper said that this phenomenon is called "homosexuality" in the West, and I believe it just emphasizes the corrupt, rotten, decayed, and degenerate life-style encouraged by capitalism. But more recently, I heard that there are also homosexuals in China. Is this true? Is homosexuality a disease?

Answer: Homosexuality is not a phenomenon that can be labeled as "Western" or "capitalist." Neither is it a disease. People who are attracted to the same sex are found in every country, every culture, every historical period, and every social class. Since China currently forbids any overt display of homosexuality, these people have to live a closeted life—and therefore are not generally recognized.

China, like every other country in the world, has always had homosexuals. Ji Yun, the eminent scholar of the Ch'ing dynasty (AD 1644–1911), stated in his famous *Yuwei Caotang Biji (Notes of the Yuewei Heritage)* that the position of "catamite," a young boy who serves as the sex partner for an adult man, existed at the court of Huang-ti (Yellow Emperor)—the reputed first Emperor of China—more than 4,600 years ago. The surviving literature of the Spring-Autumn period (770–745 BC), and the Warring States period (475–221 BC) of the Chou and Han dynasties (206 BC–AD 220) indicates that homosexuality was accepted by the royal courts. The official dynastic histories show that in the Western Han dynasty alone, all 10 male emperors either had homosexual lovers or at least tolerated and accepted homosexuality. In view of this documented historical information, no one in China can claim that homosexuality was imported from a Western capitalist country.

Teenage sex and pregnancy

Question: I have heard that many teenagers now have sex and that a lot of teenage girls become pregnant. Is this true? Should we teach a teenage son or daughter how to use contraceptives?

Answer: Yes, it is true that many teenagers have sex, and teenage pregnancy is very common. We know this from several kinds of data: In 1985, for example, in a major hospital in Shantong province, 38% of the women who had abortions were teenagers. Healthcare professionals believe that this figure will soon rise to 60%. A survey in this same city showed that 80% of the

women have had sexual intercourse before they marry, usually without using any contraceptives.

A rural area in Zhejiang province reported that 66% of the women had had intercourse before they married. The number of abortions performed on girls in Shanghai, the largest city in China, rose from 39,000 in 1982 to 65,000 in 1984. This is the reality that we must face. Traditionally many groups in China opposed any sex education or instruction in the use of contraceptives. They believed that "words relating to sex should never be mentioned." It is time to change this attitude.

The problem of teenage pregnancy needs attention since most of these girls are too young to be responsible mothers, and their male partners are too young to be responsible fathers. Both need time to grow and mature physically and psychologically, and they need more education. Although we can advise them not to engage in sex before they reach adulthood, they tend to ignore what we say. Since they have the right to decide how they will use their bodies, we must teach them about contraceptives and encourage them to use these methods. This will benefit the teenagers and their families, as well as the nation.

Female anorgasmia

Question: I have heard that many women fail to have orgasm. Could you tell me how many? Do Western women have more orgasms than Chinese women? How can a woman achieve an orgasm?

Comment: Many Chinese women do not know what an orgasm is. An American journalist who recently visited Beijing wrote that he had asked a Chinese woman whether she had ever experienced an orgasm, a question never yet asked by a Chinese sex researcher.[3] Upon hearing this question, the woman frowned, puzzled by the question. The journalist then used a more technical expression (common in Hong Kong) to describe what he meant—*gao-chao* (literally, "high tide"). She did not know what this meant either, but once the journalist explained it, she said she had never had any such sensation. When asked about intercourse, the woman explained that it usually lasted three or four minutes, and then her husband would withdraw.

A survey concerning orgasm, taken of a small sample of Chinese women, was conducted by the newly formed group of sex educators and published in 1987. This survey revealed that some 35% of the respondents either had never had an orgasm or had one only occasionally.

Answer: Chinese women can enjoy orgasm as readily as Western women. But first they need to know what it is. The male sex partner must pay greater attention to arousing the woman by engaging in longer foreplay, and by letting her reach orgasm first. Finally, both should enjoy the experience, and stop being concerned about orgasm.

Conclusion

Many changes have taken place in recent years. For example, in 1988 the Chinese government authorized a second pregnancy for families whose first child is a girl. Contraception, in general, is practiced by means of a modified version of the Lippes loop, voluntary sterilizations, or abortion. These methods, however, may be available only to married women in many instances.

In reviewing the questions submitted to the media, it is worth noting that most of the questions came from male readers. Chinese women rarely inquire about sexual matters, unless they relate to pregnancy or menstruation—the only types of sexually related questions Chinese women believe are appropriate to ask.

It is obvious that despite the many questions submitted, much remains to be done in the near future before Chinese men and women have the sexual knowledge necessary to understand and cope with questions regarding sexual functioning. As sex education becomes widely available for young people in China, it will increase their understanding of sexuality and sexual problems. It will also help to provide solutions via sexual counseling and sex therapy.

References

1. Van Gulik RH: *Sexual Life in Ancient China*. Leiden, Holland, EJ Brill, 1961.
2. Kinsey AC: *Sexual Behavior in the Human Female*. Philadelphia, WB Saunders, 1953.
3. Butterfield F; *China: Alive in the Bitter Sea*. New York, New York Times Books, 1982.

LATINO CULTURE AND SEX EDUCATION

Carmen Medina, MPH

Director, Latino Family Life Education Project
New York, New York

As a group, Latinos are wonderfully unique and diverse. They have traditions and espouse values which long ago combined the indigenous Indians, the cultures of Spain, blacks from Africa, and many other European ancestors.

Latinos are not only the fastest growing minority in the U.S., but to date census figures show that close to 15 million documented as well as between 5 and 6 million undocumented Latinos are living in the U.S. While we inundate the Latino populous with pills, diaphragms, intrauterine devices, condoms, marked calendars, and unnecessary sterilizations, forecasts warn us that by the year 2000, the Latino population will exceed that of 25 million black Americans in this country.

As family life educators, we are responsible for learning and integrating the dynamics of Latino cultural patterns into the programs we provide. In order to be effective educators—especially family life educators—we must become sensitive to the differences that exist among Latino groups, respond appropriately to nuances of Latino behavior, and, most importantly, become aware of perceptions Latinos have about human sexuality and their own sexuality. It is our obligation as educators to account for and respect the significance that Latino culture plays in the lives of the Latinos to whom we are providing services.

This article will point out important facets of Latino culture to which family life educators must be sensitive. But health and human service providers should continue to pursue and integrate knowledge about the various Latino histories, heritages, cultures, and lifestyles into their programs in order to provide effective and responsible programming for this community.

Social Integration

Many social scientists and ideology makers in this country argue in defense of the educational, medical, and social service systems that historically have failed Latinos, contending that Latinos are socially, culturally, economically, and politically marginal. It is easier to say, whether naively or by calculation, that Latinos do not take advantage of services offered them because they are apathetic and indifferent, rather than to reexamine and redesign the conceptual framework in which these services were invented.

Latinos are not marginal but in fact fully integrated into this society, albeit in a manner not fully reciprocated by the society of which they are a vital part, and in many respects detrimental to Latino interests. Latinos contribute their hard work, their high hopes, and their loyalties to this system as much as any other group or culture.

Language

If a family life education program is to prove successful for any Latino community, it must be bilingual. Workshop facilitators and the individuals doing community outreach must speak Spanish. Although many Latinos understand English, they may still find it difficult or impossible to talk about intimate and sexual matters in this second language. Human sexuality is still one of the least talked about topics within the Latino household, in either language. Just saying sexual words out loud will be difficult; the family life educator will have to dedicate great efforts to enhancing participants' comfort with hearing and using sexual language.

Confianza, the breaking down of barriers and the building of trust, can rarely be established with Latinos if the language barrier remains uncrossed. Many Latinos who are proficient in the use of the English language frequently choose Spanish to convey intimate and personal feelings. The Spanish language is cherished and respected in the Latino community, and the family life educator who understands and can integrate this unique issue into a program increases the chances of its success.

Religion

The practice of religion is deeply imbedded in the Latino culture. Approximately 85% of all Latinos are Catholic. The initiatives directed at Latino concerns on behalf of the Catholic church have been minimal. In addition to Catholicism, many Latinos belong to Protestant sects, such as Baptist, Jehovah's Witness, Church of Jesus Christ of Latter-Day Saints (Mormons), and the Pentecostal church (Charismatic Movement), in addition to alternate religions like "espiritsmo" and "Santerismo."

Family

As family life educators and workshop facilitators, it is necessary to understand the dynamics of the family in Latino culture and how it relates to family life education. Latinos are not accustomed to extensive support from the world outside the family; the cultural pattern is to rely on support from the extended family.

Although the nuclear family is becoming a more prevalent family unit, the Latino conception of family has always implied the extended family of aunts, uncles, cousins, and grandparents, stretching over great distances and generations. Latinos feel intensely close with a wide circle of family members, and maintaining these ties through all phases of life is considered normal and necessary.

Of particular concern to family life educators is the extent to which this concept of family has a practical impact on how children in the Latino community are reared. Unlike in other American families, Latino child-rearing practices are generally characterized by a greater emphasis on support from within the family unit and less emphasis on self reliance, more authoritarian parenting models, close maternal relationships, and more expression of parental affection.

Family ties serve to unburden certain members of the family—particularly single parents, who are rarely ostracized by the family or the community anymore. The pregnant adolescent is more often than not assured a home for her and her baby during and after pregnancy. It is not surprising to find Latino families caring for small children other than and in addition to their own. These additional *hijos de crianza* (children raised by relatives or close friends) appear when a child is thought to be better off with adoptive parents who can provide a better future for the child than can the natural parents.

Besides the *hijos de crianza*, there are those adults who are like family: *como familia*. These individuals have through the years proved their willingness to engage in important family matters. There are also the *compadres* (Godparents), the adults who would assure responsibility for the child's welfare should tragedy befall the child's natural parents, and who are looked upon as members of the family. Assignment of the *compadres* is confirmed by the Catholic church and involves a traditional religious ceremony. It would not be unusual for such individuals to take part in a family life education program on behalf of a particular child. Adults other than the child's natural parents are interested in and concerned with the child's well being.

Parental Attitudes

Latino parents deal with the same realistic fears as do any parents. In addition to the fear that drugs and crime will harm their children, traditional Latino parents are especially concerned that differing sexual mores, values, and customs will corrupt their children. For these reasons, Latino parents living in the U.S. may seem to be overprotective of their children and probably will not allow their children to take part in family life education programs that are not culturally appropriate.

The school based comprehensive health care programs that are popping up all over the country must invest time to sensitize Latino parents and their children to the meaning of preventive health care and health maintenance. Opponents to these clinics are working on the fears of Latino parents that school based health care means contraception, promiscuity, and corruption of their youth. Anything that may threaten traditional family stability and challenge parental authority will be rejected by Latino parents; therefore, time spent educating Latinos about these programs will not only provide them with accurate information but also increase the chances of it being accepted and supported.

Latino parents place a high value on the ideal of cultural preservation or conservation. Family life educators need to understand how and why these cultural factors play such an essential role in the lives of Latinos. Incest and child sexual abuse prevention programs, for example, may be too frightening to a Latino community; therefore, a family life educator must be alert enough to promote this type of program under the guise of child safety. Also important to bear in mind is that the punitive attitude of the church may result in Latino children underreporting or not reporting at all (to parents or other trusted adults) acts of incest and child sexual abuse committed against them. Feeling guilt ridden and believing that punishment from God is impending may leave a child feeling helpless.

Any family life educator who hopes to have an impact must begin by considering the following issues. Are traditional values entrenched? Are there different, perhaps conflicting, values in some or many families? Are there intergenerational cultural strains? To what extent do families rely on outside support systems? What kinds of support systems are utilized? What is the degree of religiosity? Which are appropriate resources for program planners to tap?

1. SEXUALITY AND SOCIETY: Historical and Cross-Cultural Perspectives

Gender Roles

To better understand the interrelationships within the Latino family, it is important to look at male-female relationships as they exist and have existed for many generations. Although these roles are in a state of transition, the traditional roles must still be considered.

MACHISMO. In American usage, this term, pirated from the Spanish language, has taken on the derogatory connotation of the chauvinistic and tyrannical male character. The fact that the direct translation of this word simply means "male pride" in Spanish has been lost in its application as a negative label for men regardless of ethnicity. This bastardization can have troublesome implications for the Latino male self-image and his interpersonal dynamics.

The macho concept or the exaggerated importance of being a man is inculcated in a male child from a very early age. One way the male child is socialized and reminded of his maleness is by his parents and other adults admiring and fondling the baby's penis. Little boys are valued for being male from the moment they are born into the family; even if there are older sisters, the male sibling is the dominant figure, both in the eyes of the parents and in sibling interactions. Mothers train their daughters early on to play "little women" to their fathers, brothers, and husbands; and train their sons to be dominant and independent in relationships with their wives as well as other women.

ETIQUETA. Little girls are also socialized early on, but quite differently. To begin with, her genitals are always kept from the public gaze and never handled by anyone but her mother. She is usually taught not to focus very much attention on her vagina and not to touch it. From the moment she is born, she is adorned with earrings, bracelets and special spiritual amulets, and is dressed in exaggeratedly feminine outfits. As she grows older, her liberty is severely curtailed, her virginity emphasized and guarded, and she is carefully supervised by male and female members of the family. Girls are constantly reminded of their inferiority and weakness and usually praised for their docility and submissiveness, in addition to their physical attractiveness. The fact that Latina women are oppressed both as women and as Latinas makes their grip on this feminine ideal even stronger.

MARIANISMO. Marianismo, the submissive and obedient female character, pervades the traditional role of wife bestowed upon the Latina. Latino opinion holds that a good woman centers her life around her husband and children. She is expected to avoid self-indulgence and sensuality. To display sexual pleasures, even in marriage, may suggest a lack of virtue. Sex is for procreation, and not to be sought after or enjoyed by women. *Una buena mujer,* a good woman, is always ready for her man and should not exhibit comfort with sexuality issues or ease with the sex act itself. This fear of unbridled sexual emotion holds true for Latino men but in another dimension, such as homophobia.

Homosexuality

Male and female homosexuality is not looked upon favorably in the Latino community. Training for appropriate heterosexuality is started very early in life. Besides the obvious religious taboo, homosexuality represents a dishonor to the family. Homosexuality, both male and female, also threatens the male Latino's sexual identity. Homosexuals are not only ridiculed and rejected by the community, but "coming-out" for a homosexual male or female could mean losing all of his or her status in the family and the community. Frequently, discrimination of male homosexuals is not as severe if the individual is an accomplished artist.

Latinos have little interest in or awareness of gay issues, which has caused them to ignore and ridicule the problem of AIDS. Due to homophobic attitudes, educating the Latino community on this issue has been problematic. In order for this issue to be recognized, it must be presented in the context of heterosexuality and the preservation of the family.

Formalidad

Latinos generally utilize a certain degree of formality when dealing with outsiders, professionals, and community leaders. Doctors, lawyers, political leaders, and educators are considered authorities and experts. This expectation can be interpreted mistakenly as dependence, docility, or submissiveness, when in fact the Latino behaving in this manner may be demonstrating politeness or respect. It is important for educators to be sensitive to Latino vulnerability to authority. Latinos will frequently keep true feelings to themselves out of respect for authority. If, however, feelings of trust, acceptance, and *confianza* can be gained for the outsider by the family, Latinos will become less formal and more open.

It is necessary to transcend the bounds of *respeto* (respect) when dealing with the family unit and controversial issues. A family life educator who does not engage the father in community workshops with children or relates only to the mother and child risks displaying a lack of respect or *falta de respeto* and losing any chance of impact. In preparing programs, the family life educator must keep in mind that direct questioning of authority is discouraged and would create discomfort.

Fatalismo

Fatalismo, or fatalism, a phenomenon that has plagued Latinos for centuries, is particularly to blame for Latinos' apparent deference to others and yielding to authorities. The Latino tendency to be fatalistic about his/her destiny is a direct result of the tremendous influence religion has had and continues to have on the lives of Latinos.

This obstacle is often difficult to overcome, though not impossible. While one Latino family might have little sense of power to affect its destiny, a family life educator might help families join forces with other families and community leaders to produce change within their communities. Family life educators must learn to examine the total social field within which an individual family is embedded.

The Community

Latinos have social clubs and "town-clubs," where people from the same hometown form a club for socializing and networking. These clubs, in addition to the *bodega* or ethnic grocery store, are key gathering places. Besides the merchants and social club leaders, there are traditional folk healers in every Latino community who can be called upon to assist in developing community based projects for parents and their children.

Many times starting family life education workshops right in someone's house or initiating simple conversations in a local *bodega* or *botanica* (religious items store) could prove to be a successful beginning towards a community's acceptance of a family life education program. Once a Latino community has recognized a family life education project that is culturally sensitive and whose staff has made an effort to extend itself, it will naturally and probably enthusiastically reciprocate.

Conclusion

We hope that this brief review of some cultural considerations will be helpful to health and human service providers who have little knowledge and information about Latino culture and traditions. Once these basic characteristics are understood, providers can pick up on the forces operating to modify this traditional outline, such as social class, education, socioeconomic status, country of origin, religiosity, the changing role of women, and the impact of the media, as well as the potential beneficial impact of family life education programs.

Many factors will influence the degree to which individual Latino families adhere to traditional values, like extended family, marianismo and machismo, fatalismo, formalidad, and so on. One very important fact to remember is that although Latinos share many commonalities—language, religion, respect, concept of family, etc.—there are also many differences among them. However vast or subtle the cultural differences between Latinos are, with regard to their values, traditions, and practices, family life educators must make a concerted effort to identify and collaborate with cultural strengths within individual groups. It is vital that educators create programs which will enhance and strengthen Latino parents' understanding and feeling of pride in their culture and parenting abilities. It is precisely this self-esteem, or lack thereof, which will be transmitted to the next generation.

Manhood

Why is being a "real man" so often a prize to be won?

by David D. Gilmore

David D. Gilmore is a professor of anthropology at the State University of New York at Stony Brook.

Masculinity is not something given to you, something you're born with, but something you gain.... And you gain it by winning small battles with honor.
— Norman Mailer,
"Cannibals and Christians"

We Westerners have always been concerned with manhood as a matter of personal identity or reputation, but this concern is not confined to the West. On Truk Island, a little atoll in the South Pacific, for example, men are also obsessed with being masculine. Echoing Lady Macbeth, a common challenge there is: "Are you a man? Come, I will take your life now." In East Africa, young boys from cattle-herding tribes, including the Masai, Rendille, Jie, and Samburu, are taken away from their mothers and subjected to painful circumcision rites by which they become men. If the Samburu boy cries out while his flesh is being cut, if he so much as blinks an eye, he is shamed for life as unworthy of manhood. The Amhara, an Ethiopian tribe, have a passionate belief in masculinity called *wand-nat*. To show their *wand-nat,* Amhara youths are forced to engage in bloody whipping contests known as *buhe*. Far away, in the high mountains of Melanesia, young boys undergo similar trials before being admitted into the select club of manhood. They are torn from their mothers and forced to undergo a series of brutal rituals. These include whipping, bloodletting, and beating, all of which the boys must endure stoically. The Tewa people of New Mexico also believe that boys must be "made"

into men. Tewa boys are taken away from their homes, purified by ritual means, and then whipped mercilessly by the kachina spirits (their fathers in disguise). Each boy is lashed on the back with a crude yucca whip that draws blood and leaves permanent scars. "You are made a man," the elders tell them afterward.

Why must manhood be vindicated in so many cultures through tests and challenges? And how widespread are such rites of masculinity? My own interest in this subject arose through experiences in the field—in my case, a rural *pueblo* (town or village) in Andalusia, a region of southern Spain. There I noticed a heavy emphasis on being manly, or *macho* as Andalusians say, using the Spanish word for "male" (a word that, significantly, has worked its way into many languages as *machismo*). Hardly a day passed by when this subject went unmentioned. I found that it was hard to measure up in this regard. Indeed, it became a minor personal crisis when some male friends requested my company—rather insistently—on a nocturnal visit to a whorehouse so that I could prove that I was a "man."

Trained to see each culture as unique, cultural anthropologists emphasize human differences, but sometimes common themes draw them ineluctably to the contemplation of human similarities. As I pondered my friends' invitation, I experienced a curious sense of familiarity. I sensed affinity not only with the cultures described above but also with my own. I had grown up absorbing the manly fiction of Ernest Hemingway, Jack London, Norman Mailer, Tom McGuane, and James Dickey. Like many of my friends I, too, had gone to Pamplona to run with the

bulls in imitation of Jake Barnes in *The Sun Also Rises,* a typical, if ersatz, rite of passage for college-age Americans. Later, when I returned home, I found the topic of manliness cropping up in discussions with colleagues. Almost every society, I found, has some specific notion about "true" manhood.

Sometimes, as in Andalusia, virility or potency is paramount; elsewhere, as among the Trukese and Amhara, physical toughness is more important. Sometimes economic "go-getting," athletic ability, or heavy drinking is the measure of a man. The ingredients vary, but in all these places a man has to pass some sort of test, measure up, accomplish something. Why is manhood a test in so many cultures? My quests for answers started in Spain.

There was a young man in the *pueblo* named Lorenzo. He was a perennial student and bachelor. A gentle character of outstanding native intelligence, Lorenzo was the only person from the *pueblo* ever to have gone to graduate school to pursue a doctorate, in this case in literature. But he was unable for various reasons ever to complete his dissertation, so he remained in a kind of occupational limbo, indecisive and feckless. Because of his erudition, Lorenzo was generally acknowledged as a sort of locally grown genius. Many people had high hopes for him. But the more traditionally minded were not among his admirers. In the very important matter of gender appropriateness, Lorenzo was eccentric, even deviant. "A grave case," as one man put it.

First, there were his living arrangements. Oddly, Lorenzo stayed indoors with his widowed mother, studying, reading books, rarely leaving his scholar's cloister. He had no discernible job. He lived off his uncomplaining old mother, hardworking but poor. Withdrawn and secretive, Lorenzo made no visible efforts to change this state of affairs; nor did he often, as men are supposed to do, enter the masculine world of the bars to drink or engage in the usual convivial banter. Rarely did he enter into the aggressive card games or the drunken bluster that men in his *pueblo* enjoy and expect.

Perhaps most bizarre, Lorenzo avoided women. He was actually intensely shy with girls. This is a very unusual dereliction indeed, one that is always greeted with real dismay by both men and women in Spain. Sexual shyness is more than a casual flaw; it is a serious, even tragic inadequacy. The entire village bemoans shyness as a personal calamity and collective disgrace. People said that Lorenzo was "afraid" of girls, afraid to try his luck. They believe that a real man must break down the wall of female resistance that separates the sexes. Otherwise there will be no children—God's gift to family, community, and nation. Being a sensitive soul, Lorenzo keenly felt the pressure to go out and run after women. He knew he was supposed to target a likely wife, get a paying job, and start a family. A cultural rebel by default, he felt himself to be a man of modern, "European" sensibilities, and he resisted.

One evening, after we had spent a pleasant hour talking about Cervantes, Lorenzo looked up at me with his great, melancholy eyes and confessed his cultural transgressions. He began by confiding his anxieties about the aggressive courting that is a man's presumed function. "I know you have to throw yourself violently at women," he said glumly, "but I prefer not to." Taking up a book, he shook his head with a shrug, awaiting a comforting word. It was obvious he was pathologically afraid of rejection.

Because he was a decent and honest man, Lorenzo had a small circle of friends in the town, all educated people, and he was the subject of much concern among them. They feared he would never marry, bachelorhood being accounted the most lamentable fate outside of blatant homosexuality. With the best intentions in mind, these people often asked me if I did not think it was sad that Lorenzo was so withdrawn and what should be done about him? Finally, one perceptive friend, discussing Lorenzo's case at length as we often did, summed up the problem in an unforgettable phrase. He noted his friend's debilitating unhappiness and so-

cial estrangement, and he told me in all seriousness that Lorenzo's problem was his failure "to be a man." When I asked him what he meant, he explained that in pursuing arcane knowledge, Lorenzo had "forgotten" how to be a man. Shaking his head sadly, he uttered a lapidary diagnosis: *como hombre, no sirve* (literally, as a man he just doesn't "serve," or work).

Spoken by a concerned friend in a tone of commiseration rather than reproach, the phrase *no sirve* has much meaning. Loosely translated, it means that as a man Lorenzo fails muster in some practical way, the Spanish verb *servir* meaning getting things done, "working" in the sense of proficiency: serviceability. This emphasis on serviceability, on efficiency and competence, provides a common thread in manly imagery and a clue to its deeper meanings. How does Lorenzo fail the test of manhood?

I had the good fortune, also, to encounter the model man. The opposite of Lorenzo was Juan, known to everyone by his nickname, Robustiano, "the robust one." He was tall and energetic, a worker who toiled hard in the fields from dawn till dusk, "sacrificed," as they say, to support his huge family. He was a fearless labor organizer, too, and during the dark days of the Franco dictatorship he had kept the faith alive among the town's workers and peasants by openly defying the police. He went to jail often and suffered many beatings, but even the tough Civil Guards could not break his spirit. They said that he resembled a mule in stubbornness, but that he had more *cojones* (balls) than a mountain of ministers—a begrudging way of complimenting a political opponent. *Muy hombre,* they admitted as they beat him, "a lot of man." In addition, Robustiano had fathered many children, with five sons among his brood. Only in his forties, Robustiano was a kind of culture hero.

These negative and positive examples sum up the qualities of manliness in Andalusia. A real man is one who provides for his family, protects dependents, and produces babies. He is not a bully, never a wife beater. On the contrary, he is a supporting prop of his community; above all, he is competent, a doer. He is willing to absorb punishment in pursuit of approved civic goals. He is fearless. On a more abstract level, one might summarize by saying he reproduces and augments the highest values of his culture by force of will. He creates something from nothing. In this way, he serves. Lorenzo's main fail-

ure, by contrast, is his fickle recessiveness, his timidity.

How can we conceptualize this composite image of manhood in Spain? It seems a threefold threshold: "man the protector" is also "man the provider" and, of course, "man the impregnator." This trinity of competencies is a recurrent image of communal hope. The emphasis on productivity and on omnicompetence is a common denominator that unites men and women in the re-creation of core values. It is this deeper function of creating and buttressing, not the specifics of form, that opens the door to cross-cultural comparison. Let us take a few brief examples from other cultures, far from Spain.

Among the aboriginal Mehinaku, a Stone Age tribe of farmers and fishermen living in the Amazon Basin in Brazil, there are "real men" and there are effeminate "trash yard men." A real man is one who displays efficiency in all walks of life. He gets up early to go on long, arduous fishing expeditions over dangerous terrain, ignoring hostile tribes that wait in ambush. When he returns, sometimes days later, he marches ostentatiously to the middle of the village where he throws down his catch for everyone to share. He is a fierce competitor in games and sports, especially wrestling—a favorite tribal pastime. He fathers many children, has many lovers, and satisfies his wife sexually. An incompetent man, one who is stingy, weak, or impotent, is scorned as effeminate.

Among the nonviolent Bushmen of the Kalahari Desert in southwest Africa, boys are not granted their manhood until they stalk and kill a large antelope single-handedly. In this way they show that they are capable of providing meat for the entire band. Among the Sambia people of highland New Guinea, a boy cannot be a man until he has learned to disdain the sight of his own blood—basic training for the warrior's life that awaits him and upon which the security of the tribe depends. To be really a man, the Sambia tribesman must also father at least two children. Among the Masai of Kenya, a boy is not a man until he has stood up to a charging lion, established an independent household, and fathered more than one child. Among the Mende of West Africa, a boy is only a man when he shows he can survive unaided in the bush. In all these cases, the tests and accomplishments involved are those that will prepare boys and youths specifically for the skills needed in adult life to support, protect, and expand the living community. And it is only when these skills are mastered and displayed communally, in public, that manhood is conferred consensually upon the youth.

But still, we ask: why the stress and drama of manhood? Why is all this indoctrination needed, why the trials and tribulations? Why must males be literally pushed into such displays of performance? Here, as in most cases of human behavior where strong emotions are involved, we need a little guidance from psychological theory, and here, too, is where there is agreement with what feminists have said about the plasticity of gender roles. The key, I think, lies in the inherent weaknesses of human nature, in the inborn tendency of all human beings, male and female, to run from danger, to retreat from challenges, to return to the safety of the hearth and home. In psychoanalytic thinking, this tendency, exemplified perhaps by Lorenzo, is called psychic regression. It is defined as the tidal pull back toward the world of childhood, the pull back to the mother, the wish to return to the blissful, traumaless idyll of infancy.

Seen from this psychological perspective, we can interpret manhood as a moral instigation for performance—the moral force that culture erects against the eternal child in men, that makes retreat impossible by creating a cultural sanction literally worse than death: the theft of one's sexual identity.

Interestingly, manhood is not just a call to aggression. The brutal *machismo* of violent men is not real manhood in these cultures, but a meretricious counterfeit—the sign of weakness. A curious commonality is that true manhood is a call to nurturing. "Real" men are those who give more than they take, who, like "the robust one," serve others by being brave and protective. This "manly" nurturing is different from the female. It is less direct, more obscure; the "other" involved may be society in general rather than specific persons. Yet real men do nurture. They do this by shedding their blood, their sweat, their semen; by bringing home food, producing children, or dying if necessary in far away places to provide security for their families. But this masculine nurturing is paradoxical. To be supportive, a man must first be tough in order to ward off enemies; to be generous, he must first be selfish in order to amass goods; to be tender, he must be aggressive enough to court, seduce, "win" a wife.

Finally, with all this said, why should the challenges (and rewards) of these manhood codes be confined to males? We have seen that true manhood often means serving society: accepting challenges, taking risks, being expendable in the service of society. So why aren't women allowed to be "real men" too? Why can't women also earn the glory of a risk successfully taken? But here we have to stop, for this is a question for the philosopher, not the cultural anthropologist.

AIDS NEWS

Number of cases in U.S.: Over 97,000

HIGHLIGHTS: FIFTH INTERNATIONAL AIDS CONFERENCE: Montreal, June 4-9

Patricia Kloser, MD

Patricia Kloser is Clinical Coordinator, AIDS Services, University Hospital, Newark, NJ, and Attending Physician, Department of Infectious Diseases, University of Medicine and Dentistry of New Jersey, Newark.

More than 12,000 scientists, physicians, health workers, and people with AIDS (PWA) convened in Montreal to share their ideas and data regarding HIV. This very intense conference drew participants from all over the globe, with a major focus on the management of AIDS as a chronic illness rather than as an infectious disease that can be readily cured. AIDS patients in developed countries today are living longer as clinicians have become more experienced in treating AIDS-related opportunistic infections and the HIV-infected patient.

All of the news, however, was not upbeat. New cases continue to increase, both in the United States and worldwide; the current total number of cases in the United States (97,000) is projected to double by the year 1991. The possibility of a longer than heretofore recognized HIV incubation period during which time serum antibody cannot be detected is particularly worrisome. While HIV antibody is detectable within 6-10 weeks after infection in most cases, this time period can exceed two years in some individuals.

The following highlights represent the developments of greatest interest to the primary care physician, who may diagnose and treat HIV-infected patients in office practice.

EPIDEMIOLOGY

Prevalence

- The World Health Organization (WHO) reports more than 150,000 cases of AIDS from 145 countries, with an estimated 5–10 million HIV-infected people worldwide.

- In the US, more than 97,000 AIDS cases have been reported as of June 1989, with 14,137 new AIDS cases occurring in 1989 alone.

Profile of AIDS in the US

The following figures represent the current distribution of AIDS:

- Adults: Men, 91% (61% in homosexual men); women, 9%.

- Of these cases, 46% are in the 30–39 year age group and 88% are in the 20–49 year group.

- Racial composition: White, 57%; Black, 27%; Hispanic, 15%; other/unknown, 1%.

- Children: As of May 31, 1989, 1,632 cases have been reported in children; 79% of these children have a parent at risk for AIDS.

HIV seroprevalence in the US

- Early randomized studies show 0.6% seropositivity in a general population, outpatient primary care setting.

- Up to 30% of randomly selected males 25–44 years old in two inner city urban hospitals were seropositive.

• In 1987 in New York City, 53% of intravenous drug users (IVDU) tested positive for HIV. Seropositivity was found to be related positively to injection frequency, length of time of drug use, cocaine use, certain ethnic backgrounds, and certain geographic locations.

Trends

• AIDS is now one of the 10 leading causes of death among 1–4 year olds and 15–24 year olds in the US. (Source: Centers for Disease Control [CDC].)

• Among women with AIDS nationwide, 25.6% contracted their disease via sexual contact in 1988, up from 14.8% in 1983.

• The perinatal HIV transmission rate (seropositive mothers to their offspring) is at least 33%.

• At least one in every 1,000 women of childbearing age in the US is HIV seropositive.

• Every state in the US has reported AIDS cases.

• In a recent CDC study, 0.2% of university students tested HIV positive.

• The largest number of AIDS cases currently are in urban areas of New York, California, Florida, New Jersey, and Texas.

• HIV infection rates have been stable among military recruits.

• The incidence of AIDS is increasing among younger and older adults, women and children, and in minority groups.

• The incidence of infection is decreasing among homosexual men.

• The growth in condom sales is up from a 0.6% increase between 1982 and 1983 to a 20.3% increase between 1986 and 1987.

New developments in patterns of infection

• Pattern I. North America, Europe, Australia, New Zealand, South/Central America, Southeast Asia: Homosexual/bisexual men, IV drug-abusers, heterosexual spread

• Pattern II. Africa, Caribbean areas: Heterosexual spread, blood products

• Pattern III. Asia, Middle East: Low numbers, but increasing in high-risk groups (male/female prostitutes)

TRANSMISSION

Heterosexual: The incidence of cases attributed to heterosexual transmission is rising. These cases remain confined to those whose sexual partners belong to a known high-risk group. The highest rate of HIV seropositivity due to presumed heterosexual transmission is in drug treatment centers (35%) and sexually transmitted disease (STD) clinics (0.4%–5.6%).

Homosexual: Anorectal trauma appears to be associated more frequently than symptomatic genital ulceration with HIV transmission, according to one study. Another study indicates that simultaneous nitrite inhalation and receptive anal intercourse increase the likelihood of HIV transmission.[1]

Hemophiliac: HIV progression with opportunistic infection and decreased T4 levels is more rapid in older adults (age greater than 34).[2]

IVDU: Coinfection with HTLV-1 is associated with risk for progression to AIDS among HIV-positive users. The number of cases directly or indirectly associated with IVDU represents the area of greatest growth now and in the future. Behavior modification in this group is difficult, due to social, political, legal, and economic problems that are not easily solved. Drug rehabilitation on demand, needle exchange, and early education are being attempted in some areas.[3]

VIROLOGY

Each year scientists present new information about retroviruses and about HIV in particular. Much knowledge has been acquired in a short time with the help of our "high-tech" society.

HIV-1: This virulent retrovirus remains the most common cause of AIDS in the US. The virus is heterogeneous (consists of several different strands) in each individual and is even heterogeneous in individual infected cells. It can vary during disease progression in the patient. Selection of more virulent strains may be responsible for disease progression in the individual.

HIV-2: This virus remains the infective agent in Central/West African AIDS, with sporadic cases occurring throughout the world. It is less virulent than HIV-1.

HTLV-1: This virus is endemic in the Caribbean and occurs more frequently in the older age groups. Coinfection with this virus and with HIV-1 is associated with disease progression.

AIDS-RELATED DISEASES

Pneumocystis carinii pneumonia (PCP): This is the most common opportunistic infection that occurs with AIDS, and is associated with the most morbidity and mortality in the AIDS patient. Encouraging treatment results were reported at this conference concerning PCP prevention and treatment, and the increasing rate and period of survival of patients with PCP.

• Prophylaxis: Preventive treatment is recommended for all patients who have had one episode of PCP or whose T4 count is less than $200/mm^3$. Oral trimethoprim/sulfamethoxazole (TMP/SMX) may be used. Recently the Food and Drug Administration (FDA) approved aerosolized pentamidine for prophylaxis. The suggested dose: 300 mg by the Respigard II nebulizer every four weeks. Studies continue on the use of dapsone, 50 mg/day.[4]

• Treatment: Intravenous treatment with either pentamidine or TMP/SMX is the "gold standard," and most patients respond well to two to three weeks of therapy. Concurrent treatment with steroids has been found useful in some studies. Aerosolized pentamidine has been studied as a treatment modality for mild to moderate PCP, with final results pending.

● Salvage treatment: When PCP is refractory or usual treatments cannot be tolerated, other drugs are available for compassionate or experimental use. Trimetrexate with leucovorin rescue has been used successfully in some cases. Eflornithine shows promise and is being studied. The oral anti-infectives clindamycin and primaquine have also shown early positive results and are being investigated.

Intestinal pathogens: In addition to other diarrhea-causing pathogens, microsporidia and HIV itself have been described as intestinal pathogens. Cryptosporidium is often refractory to treatment, but spiramycin may be of help in up to 40% of patients. Investigational treatment with hyperimmune colostrum may be beneficial. *Isospora belli* may respond to TMP/SMX, sulfadoxine plus pyrimethamine, or metronidazole hydrochloride. In the most difficult cases, parenteral hyperalimentation may be required.

Cytomegalovirus (CMV) infection: Retinitis secondary to CMV infection often responds to treatment with ganciclovir (now approved by the FDA for general use). The drug must be given intravenously for life. Due to bone marrow toxicity, patients may not tolerate this drug long-term. Another drug, trisodium phosphonoformate, or foscarnet, has also shown promise in the treatment of CMV.

Cryptococcus infection: Amphotericin B with or without fluorocytosine (5FC) has been the mainstay in acute and maintenance therapy for cryptococcal infection. Another drug, fluconazole, given orally, has recently shown excellent results in the treatment of acute and chronic infection. This medication is expected to reduce morbidity associated with intravenous drug therapy. Currently this drug is available for the treatment of patients who cannot tolerate amphotericin B. Suppressive therapy for cryptococcal meningitis with ketoconazole, 400 mg/day, has shown encouraging early results.

Anemia: Many patients with AIDS and HIV infection are anemic, either because of their disease or because of side effects associated with toxic reactions to drugs used to treat their illness. Recently, the FDA approved erythropoietin, which stimulates bone marrow production of red blood cells, for use in dialysis patients. The drug has now been approved by the FDA for use in AIDS patients. Similarly, colony-stimulating factor (CSF), which stimulates granulocyte production, but which has not yet been approved by the FDA, may be of benefit for the leukopenia frequently present in these patients. Both agents may be given subcutaneously, are under study at this time, and may become generally available in the near future.

Kaposi's sarcoma (KS): This malignancy in its aggressive form is most common in the homosexual man with HIV disease. Treatment with full-dose zidovudine (AZT) and interferon has been successful, given subcutaneously at induction doses followed by maintenance doses.

The patient, or a family member, can be taught to administer the medication at home. Intralesional vinblastine given for oral KS lesions has also been of therapeutic benefit. In advanced cases, more aggressive chemotherapy with multiple agents has yielded positive salvage results.

ANTIVIRALS

AZT: AZT has shown and continues to show benefit as a suppressive treatment for HIV infection. The usual dosage of 200 mg every four hours is tolerated by many patients, but bone marrow toxicity is common. The greatest drug benefit occurs during the first 6–18 months of treatment. Good treatment results continue at a somewhat lower percentage for up to 30 months—the length of time in which it has been studied to date. Newer studies show that AZT may not be entirely effective after prolonged use, since the development of some AZT-resistant HIV strains has been noted. For the present, however, AZT remains the mainstay of treatment for HIV infection as a single agent or in combination with other agents such as acyclovir, ganciclovir, 2′3′dideoxycytidine (DDC) or 2′3′dideoxyinosine (DDI).

INVESTIGATIONAL ANTIVIRALS

DDC: This drug is of the same family as AZT. Possible toxicity: neuropathy. Effectiveness may be enhanced by alternating treatment cycles with AZT therapy.

DDI: This drug has effective antiviral properties, can be given orally, appears to have low toxicity, and thus shows therapeutic promise.

CD4: Given intravenously, CD4 is well tolerated, but still under investigation. Intramuscular and subcutaneous dosage and administration are currently under study.

Colchicine: Generally used in the treatment of gout, this drug has been shown to have antiviral activity *in vitro*. Further studies are under way.

VACCINES

The study of vaccines has yielded exciting news. Jonas Salk, MD, described the results of his vaccine research at the Salk Institute (La Jolla, CA), and the clinical trials to be carried out in HIV-seropositive asymptomatic patients in 1989–1990. The vaccine under investigation appears to be of low toxicity, with promise of becoming an immune enhancer in this population, thus prolonging the asymptomatic state. While a vaccine to prevent HIV infection is considered to be years away, these preliminary studies are seen as a first step toward achieving that goal early in the next century. The French physician Daniel Zagury has continued to produce HIV antibodies in his laboratory at Université Pierre et Marie Curie, Paris; the volunteers who have been injected with his vaccine, gp 160, have shown few toxic effects. The next step in testing this vaccine will be to administer it to selected populations at risk, in order to determine its protective effect.

EDUCATION

General education remains the key to the prevention of HIV disease. All-out campaigns on safe sexual practices, safe IVDU, and safe blood products are being mandated worldwide. AIDS-prevention education now starts in many parts of the world with *pre*-schoolers. It has become obvious that preventive education is a continuous process into adulthood. Never before has it been so important yet so difficult to modify life-style, and reduce high-risk behavior. Preventive education is difficult to implement because it must cross religious, political, economic, language and cultural barriers to be effective. Numerous presentations and posters made a convincing case for the critical importance of worldwide AIDS education. Without it, the survival of entire populations may be at stake.

References

1. Van Raden M, et al: The role of ulcerative genital diseases in promoting acquisition of HIV-1 by homosexual men. Abstract ThAO 17. Multicenter AIDS Cohort.
2. Goedert J, et al: The effect of age on HIV progression in hemophiliacs. Abstract ThAO 26. NCI for the Multicenter Study of AIDS in Hemophiliacs.
3. Weiss S, et al: HTLV I/II co-infection is significantly associated with risk for progression to AIDS among HIV+ IVDU. Abstract ThAO 23. New Jersey, UMDNJ.
4. Guidelines for prophylaxis against PCP in AIDS. *MMWR* 38 (S-5); June 16, 1989.

Sexuality Education in the 1990s

Sol Gordon

We sex educators didn't accomplish very much in the '80s—teen pregnancy rates slowed a bit, but still rose alarmingly above one million each year. There has been no reduction in sexually transmitted diseases, especially among youth. The devastation of AIDS is the most tragic example of this trend. Sex is still a critical factor. Getting married primarily for sex is still a primary reason why one-half of all contemporary marriages fail. And to make matters worse, reactionary elements in our society (now in ascendency) are more often than not the power brokers in our government who are criticizing sex educators for the "prevailing moral decadence."

We are supposed to be the purveyors of the philosophy "If it feels good, do it." Yet I do not know of a single sex educator of prominence in this country who embraces such a position (and certainly not any of our professional organizations). Comparing the rise of teen pregnancies with the increase of sex education in our schools is nonsense. Sex education is not taught in the vast majority of American schools. Most courses that do exist can be described as courses in plumbing—a relentless pursuit of the Fallopian Tubes. We estimate that less than 10 percent of American school children are exposed to anything approaching a reasonably good sex education. (For facts and figures amplifying all positions taken in this personal essay, refer to *Raising A Child Conservatively in a Sexually Permissive World* by Sol and Judith Gordon, 1989 edition, Fireside Books (Simon and Schuster) and *Personal Issues in Human Sexuality* by Sol Gordon and Craig Snyder, 1989 edition, Allyn and Bacon.)

Even though all major public opinion polls in the '80s (Gallup, Roper, *New York Times, Time*) reveal that 83 percent of the American public favors sex education in public schools, we probably have fewer substantive programs now than were available 25 years ago. All you need is three or four extremists in virtually any school district to stop development of such programs. These fanatics protest to school administrators, "We don't want you to impose your values on our children." And how does the "average" administration respond? "Don't worry, Mrs. Jones, we have no values."

This is the heart of the matter. We sex educators are to blame in one sense. We have not figured out how to get our messages across. To us it is so obvious that knowledge is not harmful, that we have not bothered to map out an effective strategy to combat the outrageous notions that if you tell kids about sex, they'll do it. Yet all research reveals that young people who are knowledgeable are the ones most likely to delay their first sexual experience. Further, if they do have sex, they generally are the ones who use contraceptives.

The crucial points we have not gotten across to the American public is that we sex educators firmly believe in values and morals . . . but whose values? . . . ours! We endorse and represent the highest aspirations of the democratic society we live in. We are against exploitation and seduction. We are opposed to sexism and racism. We favor equal opportunities for men and women—equal opportunities for career choice, for leisure and decision making (as well as equal pay for equal work). There is a difference between moral and moralistic—a moralistic position favors a particular religious or personal viewpoint that cannot be taught in a public school due to the constitutional separation of church and state. There is a critical difference between encouraging teenagers not to impregnate or to become pregnant (a sound moral position) and proselytizing that if you have sex before marriage, you'll go to hell (a moralistic view which has no place in a public school but can legitimately be taught in a church or a parochial school).

However, this does not mean we can't discuss controversial issues—abortion, for example, can be discussed in the context of presenting both (or several) points of view.

Sex educators are, by definition, moralists. We, however, when working within the context of the public school, should be careful not to present our own special brand of religion or ethics. This does not mean that we cannot present a controversial view when, for example, we are invited to address a school assembly. Another speaker can be invited to present an alternate view if it seems pertinent.

The next crucial message is not to be fooled by simplistic and ineffectual slogans such as "Just Say No." It is up to us and our colleagues in education to get across the idea that vulnerable, at-risk youth are not responsive to ridiculous propaganda. The youth who may be responsive do

This article is reprinted with permission from *Health Education,* January/February 1990, pp. 4-5. *Health Education* is a publication of the American Alliance for Health, Physical Education, Recreation and Dance, 1900 Association Drive, Reston, VA 22091.

not need our crude slogans. Youth are getting what they need at home and in established religions. We need also to know that separate programs dealing with drugs, sex, and violence only divide our energies and dissipate our scarce resources. We need programs that relate to young people who are depressed and desperate and who respond to high levels of anxiety with drugs, sex, and violence (instant gratification). Imagine dealing with severe problem youth by giving them "Just Say No" buttons!

Sex educators need to unite with drug educators and dropout counselors to begin programming youth for self-esteem. (Already, substance abuse programs are beginning to notice that they don't work unless they are able to deal with relationship issues—including sexual difficulties. Programs for promotion of self-esteem are the same for all vulnerable groups, but some of the specific messages are not. (The definition of self-esteem that I favor was developed by the California Commission on Self-Esteem in 1989: "Appreciating my own worth and importance and having the character to be accountable for myself and to act reasonable towards others." Write to me for a gratis copy of my article entitled "Promoting Self-Esteem Among 'At Risk' Youth" at 28 Her-

itage Court, Belmont, CA 94002, and enclose a 45-cent stamp for the postage.) For example, we always oppose drugs—they are dangerous (no double message here). But regarding alcohol, we must face the fact that most people drink. So we must get the message across that if you drink, you shouldn't drive, since even one drink can severely affect perception. And if you intend to get pregnant, you shouldn't drink at all.

Sex—70 percent of all high school students will have had sex before graduation whether we like it or not and whether they like it or not and even though we don't think teenagers should have sex—they are too young, too vulnerable, and too readily available for exploitation. They don't know that the first experience of sex is often grim. Few teenage girls will experience an orgasm the first time and the typical teenage boy will experience his "orgasm" three days later when he tells the guys about his sexual encounters. But we must teach that if kids are going to have sex regardless of our warnings, they should use contraceptives. My 30-second birth control message to the majority of teenagers who are going to have sex anyway is for the girls to use contraceptive foam if they are not on the pill and for the boys to use condoms (especially in an age of

AIDS). If a boy cannot afford a 50-cent condom, he is too cheap to be allowed in!

Finally, we sex educators need to put sex into perspective. My recent book, *Why Love is Not Enough,* says it clearly—Don't marry for sex or love alone. Love and sex are fine, but the decision to marry should be a rational, intellectual one. Friendship, intimacy, caring, and trusting are more important than love and sex. If I were to list the 10 most important aspects of a relationship, I would present the following list (in order of importance):

1. Intimacy (this is the real turn-on in a long-term relationship)
2. A sense of humor (it is suggested that you do not have teen-age children unless you have this trait)
3. Open communication
9. Sex
10. Sharing household tasks together

What happened to 4, 5, 6, 7 and 8? Well, we need room for curriculum development!

In short, my messages for the '90s are exactly the same as they were for the '80s and the '70s and the '60s. Hopefully we'll be more successful this next decade in getting our message across.

AIDS and STD Education: What's Really Happening in Our Schools?

Elizabeth G. Calamidas, PhD

Stockton State College

A recent study revealed that, in the school districts surveyed, AIDS and STD educational programs have been incorporated into the curricula only minimally. In addition, educational objectives for the programs varied greatly across the curricula. Lack of sufficient time, resources, preparation, and support were noted as hindrances to effective teacher performance in implementing the educational programs.

INTRODUCTION

It is estimated that 270,000 cases of acquired immune deficiency syndrome (AIDS) will have occurred by 1991 (Koop, 1986). With respect to children, however, a recent report from the Department of Health and Human Services Special Initiative on Pediatric HIV Disease ("AIDS", 1989) projects that approximately 10,000 to 20,000 children in the United states will be infected with the human immunodeficiency virus (HIV) by 1991. The fact that the report also states that aids is currently the ninth leading cause of death among children between 1 and 4 years of age, and the seventh leading cause of death among individuals between 15 and 24 years of age appears to support the initiative's projection that by 1991 1 out of 10 pediatric beds will be occupied by a child infected with HIV. According to Samuels, Mann, and Koop (1986), the threat of HIV infection among the young is so great that "AIDS can roll back the global child survival efforts of both UNICEF and the World Health Organization and undermine the hard-won victories in reducing infant mortality" (p. 221).

The DHHS Special Initiative on Pediatric HIV Disease ("AIDS", 1989) made several recommendations with respect to managing the current epidemic. It was stated that efforts should be targeted specifically toward the nation's population of adolescents and that care and treatment should be readily available to all children infected with HIV.

In order to decrease the potential number of youths who may become infected with the HIV, Koop (1986) espoused that educational efforts must be directed toward adolescents and preadolescents. During this developmental stage, individuals are particularly vulnerable because of their heightened sexual awareness and exploration. Influencing their behavior at an early age will enable the youths to protect themselves from exposure to the HIV. Kegeles, Adler, and Irwin (1988) stress the importance of addressing the adolescents' sense of personal vulnerability in an effort to have them partake in behaviors that would reduce the possibility of contracting any sexually transmitted diseases (STDs).

Educators in the public schools play a key role in shaping and influencing the behavior of adolescents. In light of the current AIDS epidemic and the incidence of other STDs (Becker, Blount, & Guinan, 1985; Centers for Disease Control, 1985, 1989), the role must not be taken lightly. The information that educators provide, or fail to provide, in helping young people make choices, could mean the difference between life and death. The difficult task of broaching the issue of AIDS, as compared to other educational issues, is compounded by the fact that in order to address the mode of transmission of the HIV, educators must also address behaviors that historically have proven to be sensitive and problematic areas for intervention (Becker & Joseph, 1988). The educators must be adept at dealing with sexual, reproductive, needle sharing, and addictive behaviors in order to be successful in their endeavors.

The role of teachers in the State of New Jersey is particularly critical since the population affected is unique when it is compared to other states in the nation. According to a report from the State of New Jersey (Department of Health, November 1988), New Jersey has the unfortunate distinction of ranking second among states in the nation with respect to the number of children with AIDS. Overall, the state ranks 4th with regard to the number of AIDS cases in adults,

From *Journal of Sex Education & Therapy*, Vol. 16, No. 1, Spring 1990, pp. 54-63. Copyright © 1990 by the American Association for Sex Education, Counselors, and Therapists.

preceded only by New York, California, and Florida. Fifty-four percent of adults with AIDS in New Jersey are believed to have received the virus via intravenous drug use, while nationally only 20% of persons with AIDS (PWAS) are reported to have contracted the virus by sharing needles. Sixty-six percent of those infected via intravenous drug use are women and 51% are men. Twenty-seven percent of the women in New Jersey who have AIDS are believed to have acquired it through heterosexual transmission. Ninety-four percent of the female children and 88% of the male children diagnosed with AIDS before the age of 13 are believed to have become infected during the prenatal period.

New Jersey is also unique in that 80% of its children with AIDS are either Black or Hispanic (Department of Health, November 1988). This is particularly significant since the pregnancy rate among minority adolescent women (15 to 19 years of age) in New Jersey is twice the national average (Singh, 1986). Because the majority of children infected with HIV are Black or Hispanic and because a significant proportion of the minority adolescent females in New Jersey are at risk for becoming pregnant, one may surmise that the current possibility of increasing the population of infants with AIDS is very real. Therefore, additional educational efforts must be targeted at this very high risk population.

PURPOSE

In light of the aforementioned statistics concerning the number of youths affected by AIDS, of Dr Koop's (1986) conviction that education is a primary defense in the prevention of the transmission of HIV, and of the recommendation that efforts be targeted at the adolescent population ("AIDS", 1989; Koop, 1986) the present descriptive study was developed. It was designed to assess the extent to which AIDS and STD education programs have been incorporated into the curriculum. Factors concerning STD education were included to determine if issues concerning AIDS were being addressed differently than other STDs. In addition, educational objectives, strengths and weaknesses of the curricula, and teacher preparation were assessed.

PROCEDURE

During the late fall in 1987 and early winter in 1988, questionnaires were mailed to supervisors of high school health education classes in 50 school districts in southern New Jersey. The school districts surveyed encompassed an eight-county region, including Camden and Atlantic counties, which rank 11th and 12th, respectively, with respect to the incidence of AIDS in the 21 counties of the state. The questionnaire was designed to assess (1) school size; (2) degree to which AIDS education and STD education have been incor-

porated into the curriculum; (3) AIDS educator area of certification; (4) objectives of AIDS and STD education; (5) strengths and weaknesses of the programs; and (6) helpful educational resources.

Twenty-two (44%) of the supervisors completed and returned the survey. In an effort to gain as much information as possible, a second mailing was sent to those who had not responded and, subsequently, 10 additional completed questionnaires were returned. The overall response rate was 64% ($N = 32$), and it was on this final 64% that the data analysis was conducted.

RESULTS

The 32 schools from which the supervisors responded are responsible for educating a rather sizable population. School sizes ranged from 250 to almost 5,000 students. It is estimated that 35,000 to 40,000 students attend the schools from which responses were received. Therefore, despite the limited number of respondents, it is evident that a significant proportion of youths in New Jersey are being reached by the educational programs in the schools sampled.

Of these high schools, 37.5% have incorporated AIDS and STD education units within two grades, 21.9% have incorporated them within three grades, and 25% within four grades. Despite the fact that 85% of the respondents indicated that their students receive aids and STD instruction in more than one grade, the number of hours of instruction was minimal in most cases. Eighteen percent of the respondents indicated that their students receive a total of 1 to 5 hours of combined instruction in AIDS and STD during their high school careers. Six to ten hours of instruction is given in 34% of the districts and 25% offer 11 to 15 hours of combined instruction.

The majority of respondents (75%) indicated that the topics are taught by individuals who are certified in both health and physical education. None of the respondents indicated that the teachers responsible for teaching the units on AIDS and STD education are specialists in sex education.

In order to allow for differences within the course curricula among the different schools, rather than having respondents indicate their educational objectives by selecting from an established list of items, an open-ended question was asked. Each respondent was requested to list the educational objectives that their particular curriculum emphasizes with respect to AIDS and STD educational units. Not unexpectedly, a wide variety of responses was received. Table 1 summarizes the objectives the respondents indicated that their respective schools have incorporated into their AIDS and STD education programs.

Dissemination of accurate and complete information in order to dispel myths and misconceptions was a primary objective for both AIDS and STD programs,

TABLE 1. Objectives for AIDS and STD Education Programs

Objective	% of Respondents Indicating Objective for Each Program	
	AIDS	STDs
Dispel myths; disseminate accurate information	56.3	37.5
Discuss prevention and transmission of pathogen(s)	50.0	50.0
Discuss signs and symptoms of illness	47.0	53.0
Discuss treatment regimens	31.0	47.0
Discuss personal responsibility, behavior change, and/or decision making	15.0	15.0
Discuss availability of services for treatment and intervention	9.4	9.4
Discuss social ramifications of disease(s)	9.0	0.0
Emphasize need for mandatory testing	3.1	0.0
Emphasize need to humanize public attitudes toward care and treatment of affected individuals	3.1	0.0
Create a safe, comfortable learning environment	3.1	3.1

but this was mentioned more frequently with respect to AIDS. However, the need to discuss the methods of transmission and prevention was mentioned equally for both programs. However, only 15% indicated the need to address personal responsibility, behavior change, and/or decision making. Knowing that behavior change is one of the primary means by which transmission can be decreased, it was interesting to note that such a small percentage of respondents specifically indicated the need to address personal responsibility as an objective.

Understanding treatment regimens for both AIDS and STDs was regarded as a relatively important objective; however, very few indicated the need to discuss the availability of services for intervention and/or treatment purposes. Based on the data, one may surmise that students are being helped by being informed of the various health conditions, but hindered by the failure to inform them of the available services. More specifically, students may be taught what the conditions are and how they are manifested, but not how to truly avoid them or how to get help if they suspect that they have been exposed.

It is estimated that each year in the United States alone, there are 3 to 4 million new cases of chlamydia (Centers for Disease Control, 1985) and 300,000 to 600,000 new cases of genital herpes (Becker, Blount, & Guinan, 1985). Despite the incidence and prevalence of these STDs, none of the respondents indicated the need to discuss the social ramifications of them. However, several indicated that the social ramifications of AIDS must be addressed. No explanation or rationale was given for the difference, and one can only speculate on the reason for the conspicuous absence of the objective with respect to STDs in general and its obvious presence with respect to AIDS.

Perhaps it was the same rationale that led one respondent to indicate the importance of emphasizing the need for testing for AIDS. The objective was volunteered despite the fact that the Surgeon General has reported that mandatory testing is not necessary, not truly helpful (Koop, 1986).

Only a small percentage of the respondents indicated the need to either create a comfortable educational environment or emphasize the importance of fostering a humane attitude toward PWAS. In light of these findings and the fact that very few indicated the need to discuss personal behavior and decision making, perhaps it may be speculated that teachers are uncomfortable or somewhat reticent in discussing these issues on an effective level.

In an effort to become familiar with the resources that the teachers utilize, those completing the survey were asked to list any educational resources that they found to be particularly helpful in addressing the issue of AIDS or other STDs. Twenty-eight percent stated that current television programs and news documentaries are most helpful. Among those programs listed were television productions entitled *An enemy among us* (White, 1987) and *AIDS: Everything you and your family need to know . . . but were afraid to ask* (Barclay, 1987). Many respondents (19%) revealed that state, federal, and/or local publications were helpful resources. Two documents released jointly by the New Jersey Department of Health and New Jersey Department of Education, *AIDS: Instructional guide for teachers—grades 6 through 8* (Saunders, DeMaio, & Fonte, 1987a) and *AIDS: Instructional guide for teachers—grades 9 through 12* (Saunders, DeMaio, & Fonte, 1987b), were repeatedly referred to by the respondents. Speakers, written publications, and audiovisual materials from the American Red Cross, American Cancer Society, and local family planning centers were utilized by 15% of the respondents. Finally, 18% of the respondents indicated that the teacher-created classroom activities designed to relay accurate information serve as the most beneficial resource in the educational curricula.

One of the most comprehensive sources of sexuality-related information in the country, the Sex Information and Education Council of the United States (SIECUS), was mentioned by only one person as being a valuable resource. The conspicuous absence of SIECUS, as well as AASECT [American Association of Sex Educators, Counselors and Therapists], from the list of resources for teachers may suggest a need for more efficient networking among professional educational organizations.

Strengths and weaknesses of the existing programs, as perceived by the health education supervisors, were assessed. Two strengths were most commonly noted. First, almost two thirds of the individuals (65%) prided themselves in affording students with complete and accurate information. In addition, teachers, with their keen sensitivity and thorough preparation, were regarded as the major strength of the AIDS and STD programs by 34% of the supervisors. On the other hand, 16% felt that teachers were inadequately prepared and, in reality, a weakness in the program. The disparity may be attributed to the fact that 22% of the faculty received no special training in these issues and 12% relied on information obtained only through self-initiated information searches.

Insufficient time allotment in the curriculum was most frequently reported as the major weakness in the AIDS and STDs curricula. In order to compensate for the insufficient time allotted, some individuals suggested that AIDS and STD educational units should be started at earlier grade levels. Several respondents believed that too much time was given to drug and alcohol education, and suggested that the time allotment for AIDS and STD education be switched with drug and alcohol education. Recent literature has suggested, however, that alcohol or drug use of any kind is significantly associated with partaking in behaviors that put one at risk for exposure to the HIV (Stall, Muckusic, Wiley, Coates, & Ostrow, 1986). Therefore, in light of the fact that in New Jersey intravenous drug users account for the largest number of PWAS (Department of Health, 1988), this option may not be appropriate.

The inherent problem of conflicting information concerning AIDS and STDs was regarded as a weakness in the educational programs in 13% of the cases. Finally, insufficient community support and insufficient or outdated materials were noted to be weaknesses in 6% and 9% of the cases, respectively.

With respect to strengths and weaknesses of the programs, suggestions were solicited for changes that, if implemented, would strengthen the existing programs. Suggestions for change included: (1) increase in the availability and quantity of material resources, (2) increase the time allotment, (3) increase the number of teaching staff, and (4) increase public awareness. One individual recommended conducting a carefully controlled evaluation study of the existing programs in order to accurately measure their effectiveness. It was suggested that particular attention be paid, not only to changes in student knowledge, but to changes in student attitude as well.

It was evident that the majority of the individuals responsible for supervising AIDS and STD education believe that additional continuing education workshops addressing these issues are necessary. Despite the fact that 65% of the respondents indicated that the teachers have attended either professional conferences or in-service workshops, 81% felt that additional workshops are necessary. Only 12% of the respondents did not believe that additional workshops would be helpful. One of those opposed stated that additional workshops are not necessary and wrote, "we are being saturated by this information."

The primary issues the respondents would like to see addressed at future conferences are: (1) current information concerning the prevention, transmission, and treatment of STDs and AIDS; and (2) new and innovative ways to teach students about these important issues. Several requested assistance in handling delicate moral issues. Recognizing the importance of discussing explicit sexual practices, yet being aware of the conflict this may create within individuals or groups of individuals, places teachers in a precarious position. The need to discuss these issues was exemplified by one person who claimed experiencing difficulty in fostering an understanding among students of the need to accept and care for PWAS. Finally, the need to further understand the legal issues, such as AIDS testing and patients rights, as well as the appropriate precautions for nurses, coaches, and teachers to take when caring for an injured student were expressed by a few respondents.

Ninety percent of the respondents indicated that a representative from their district would attend any conference or workshop that would meet the serious educational task at hand. However, there is evidence that more needs to be done to assist educators in attaining the support and information they need. For example, one individual expressed a desire to attend future AIDS and STD conferences but indicated that it would not be possible. The reason given for the inability to attend was that previous requests to attend such conferences in the past were denied because, according to the administration, attendance at such conferences is not warranted since enough information concerning AIDS and STDs is available elsewhere.

CONCLUSION

It must be stated that the State of New Jersey has attempted to address many health-related issues including AIDS and STD education by establishing a statewide mandate for Family Life Education (FLE) in the schools. A comprehensive discussion of the actual effectiveness of FLE programs is beyond the scope of this paper. However, a recent report on the implementation of FLE programs in 354 districts indicated that the manner in which FLE is implemented is determined at the local level (Flamer & Dougherty, 1986). FLE is taught either as a separate course, using an interdisciplinary instructional approach, or as a combination of the two techniques. In addition, many of the school districts follow state FLE guidelines and, therefore, do not perceive a need to improve the programs in their districts. However, with respect to staff training, Flamer and Dougherty (1986) noted:

More districts provide their own training, rather than acquiring it by other means. For slightly more than half, no training needs are reported. For the remainder, there are a variety of topics, including awareness and prevention of child abuse and neglect, curriculum development, and drugs and alcohol abuse, as well as training for new staff and retraining for continuing staff. (p. iii)

No mention was made of the specific need for staff training in AIDS and/or STD education. Finally, it was also stated that "Some districts, however, perceive problems of inadequate staff knowledge, lack of materials, and insufficient time for staff training" (Flamer & Dougherty, 1986, p. iii).

Therefore, in light of the aforementioned information, and the data gathered from the study, several conclusions can be drawn. First, it is evident that teachers are genuinely concerned, but there are a number of obstacles with which they must contend. The issue of AIDS and STDs is emotionally charged and thereby inherently more difficult to broach within a classroom. This difficulty is compounded by the influx of new and changing information. Teachers need to and want to have access to this information, and must be encouraged and facilitated in seeking it.

Second, there is a need for candid communication among school administrators, community members, teachers, and students despite the differences in beliefs concerning the appropriateness of sex education and the discussion of diverse, explicit sexual behavior in the classroom. An inherent facet of being human is being sexual. We must acknowledge this sexual component in our students, just as we acknowledge it in ourselves. To deny their sexuality is to deny an integral part of their existence.

Third, a more efficient network among professional educators must be created to allow for the quick exchange of information and material resources. Perhaps the improved networking should originate from the organizations possessing the ability to network more efficiently instead of from individual teachers.

Finally, the monumental importance of these issues must be made manifest to faculty and students by creating sufficient time within the curriculum to appropriately and thoroughly address them. Just as the "3Rs" will serve as the building blocks students will use to create the futures they envision for themselves, the information and skills they learn about AIDS and STDs will ensure their survival to enjoy and prosper in those futures.

REFERENCES

AIDS may soon be among top 5 killers of US children. (January, 1989). *Nations Health*, p. 15.

Barclay, R. (Producer), & Stafford, V. (Director). (1987). *AIDS: Everything you and your family need to know . . . but were afraid to ask* [Film]. New York: Concepts Unlimited Productions.

Becker, T., Blount, J., & Guinan, M. (1985). Genital herpes infections in private practice in the United States: 1966 to 1981. *Journal of the American Medical Association, 253*, 1601–1603.

Becker, M., & Joseph, J. (1988). AIDS and behavioral change to reduce risk: A review. *American Journal of Public Health, 78*(4), 394–410.

Centers for Disease Control. (1985). Chlamydia Trachomatis infections. *Morbidity and Mortality Weekly Report, 34*(3s), 535–745.

Centers for Disease Control. (1989). Summary: Cases of specified notifiable diseases, United States. *Morbidity and Mortality Weekly Report, 37*(51 & 52), 802.

Department of Health. (1988, November). *AIDS cases State of New Jersey as of November 30, 1988*. Trenton: State of New Jersey Department of Health.

Flamer, M. & Dougherty, J. (1986). *A report on the implementation of family life education in New Jersey public schools*. Trenton: New Jersey State Department of Education.

Kegeles, S., Adler, N., & Irvin, C. (1988). Sexually active adolescents and condoms: Changes over one year in knowledge, attitude, and use. *American Journal of Public Health, 78*(4), 460–461.

Koop, C. (1986). *United States Department of Health and Human Services Surgeon General's report on Acquired Immune Deficiency Syndrome*. Washington, DC: Public Health Service.

Samuels, M., Mann, J., & Koop, C. (1988, May-June). Containing the spread of HIV infection: A world health priority. *Public Health Reports, 103*(3), 221–223.

Saunders, E., DeMaio, J., & Fonte, D. (1987a). *AIDS: Instructional guide for teachers—grades 6 through 8*. Trenton: New Jersey Department of Health and New Jersey Department of Education.

Saunders, E., DeMaio, J., & Fonte, D. (1987b). *AIDS: Instructional guide for teachers—grades 9 through 12*. Trenton: New Jersey Department of Health and New Jersey Department of Education.

Singh, S. (1986). Adolescent pregnancy in the United States: An interstate analysis. *Family Planning Perspectives, 18*(5), 210–220.

Stall, R., Muckusic, L., Wiley, J., Coates, T., & Ostrow, D. (1986). Alcohol and drug use during sexual activity and compliance with safe sex guidelines for AIDS: The AIDS behavioral research project. *Health Education Quarterly, 13*, 359–371.

White, D. (Producer), & Seidelman, A. (Director). (1987). *An enemy among us* [Film]. Helios Productions.

Abortion Policy and Medical Practice

Jonathan B. Imber

Jonathan B. Imber is Whitehead Associate Professor of Sociology at Wellesley College. He is author of Abortion and the Private Practice of Medicine *and editor of* The Feeling Intellect: Selected Writings of Philip Rieff. *He is presently at work on a study of the idea of vocation in three professions: ministering, doctoring, and teaching.*

In its 1989 ruling *Webster* v. *Reproductive Health Services,* the Supreme Court of the United States agreed that states may propose certain restrictions on the performance of abortion, while, in principle, they may not close off access to the procedure completely. The reaction to this dramatic, but not unexpected, turn of events has been complex, but it is clear already that neither side in the abortion controversy can fully anticipate what the consequences of *Webster* and any subsequent rulings will be for the future of abortion practice in America.

With states struggling over what kinds of restrictions to enact, and with politicians scrutinizing public sentiments toward such restrictions, some pause ought to be taken to remember how abortion is made available in this country. The historical and contemporary part played by medicine in shaping this peculiarly American controversy has largely been ignored by those who are presently struggling to determine when the procedure should be performed. In no other Western nation have the politics of abortion been so far removed from, and at the same time, so dependent upon, the scientific and technical expertise of the medical profession.

Few struggles have more symbolic importance for understanding the nature of modern technical elites than the abortion debate in medicine. Legalization of abortion has not resolved what the profession's medical and moral responsibilities are, and to this extent, such uncertainty now appears to be entirely a matter for either judicial review or legislative action.

The American medical profession's response to abortion has been consistently enigmatic, defying any simple formulation about how social policy about abortion can be constructed. With the overwhelming approval of formal organizations such as the American Medical Association and the American College of Obstetricians and Gynecologists, several important innovations in the medical uses of abortion have intensified the contradiction between a technical routinization of the procedure and a moral uncertainty about how routine an abortion can ever be.

Since 1973, more than 20 million clinically documented abortions have been performed in the United States. For nearly ten years after that time, the Abortion Surveillance Division of the Centers for Disease Control kept careful track of the numbers, types, and outcomes of abortion procedures performed in physicians' offices, hospitals, and freestanding clinics. The Division was closed during the early years of the Reagan administration. Some may wish to regard this closing as more evidence of that administration's commitment to overturn the Supreme Court's ruling on abortion. But it could be argued, in retrospect, that the Division accomplished what its chief investigators set out to do, namely to routinize the medical procedures of abortion in the first and second trimesters of pregnancy. The epidemiological study of abortion methods and outcomes was as central to establishing the relative safety of abortion (as compared to other types of surgery) as the epidemiological study of cancer was to establishing the harm of cigarette smoking. The federal government played an instrumental part in assuring the highest quality assessment of abortion procedures.

In what follows, I trace out historically how physicians, who remain the only legal providers of abortion, conducted themselves amidst changing norms of medical practice and changing interpretations of the law. The pragmatic nature of medical practice has always served to preserve and protect the autonomy of doctors. Yet the same pragmatism that preserves autonomy may also undermine it, especially as new forms of knowledge are applied to medical practice.

From *Society*, Vol. 27, No. 5, July/August 1990, pp. 27-34. Published by permission of Transaction Publishers. Copyright © 1990 by Transaction Publishers.

As social policy evolves in terms of understanding what the new uses may be to which abortion can be put, the unintended consequences of legal choice, for physicians and women, will become clearer. It should already by clear that no choice, legal or otherwise, is without consequences. The reluctance to explore the social consequences of legal abortion is no credit to a constructive social science. The ideology of legal choice has not freed women and men to determine their future as much as it has determined what those choices will be.

The American public debate over abortion may be divided historically into four parts. Between 1820 and 1900, the debate centered on who should have legal authority to perform the procedure. Between the years 1900 and 1950, the abortion debate shifted to one about how best to instruct in the responsible control of conception. By 1950, an increased scrutiny of what constituted a "therapeutic" abortion directed medical attention to the health of the unborn. And after 1973, the debate became centered on how the rights that pertain to pregnant women, unborn children, physicians and biological fathers should be defined and distributed. It is important to remember that as distinctive as all of these debates were to their particular historical circumstances, the character of the present debate about abortion policy conceals much of what remained unresolved in the older debates. In the brief overview that follows, an attempt is made to recount the ways in which such unresolved matters continue to shape our understanding of and bafflement with the abortion issue.

Physicians and Abortion, 1820-1900

By today's medical, legal, and regulatory standards, the restraints of trade enacted in the nineteenth and early twentieth centuries by physicians and those supporting medical interests can hardly appear unreasonable. Ethical drug manufacture has spawned its own unintended consequences, as in the case of DES (Diethylstilbestrol). But there is little dispute presently, with the exception of treatments for a disease such as AIDS, about the rightfulness of determining drug safety and efficacy before mass distribution is permitted. In the same way, concern about the safety and efficacy of abortion procedures was raised by those physicians who led various state efforts to outlaw the procedure except under the authority of a licensed physician.

The elite physicians who established state licensing for medical practice underscored their resolve to control abortion by asserting that human life was a continuous development from the moment of conception to birth. The history of embryology makes clear that scientific knowledge about conception and pregnancy informed the nineteenth-century physician's belief that abortion was the taking of a human life. Scientific training was conducted in institutional settings that linked scientific, medical, and eventually epidemiological research with medical practice. Those opposed to abortion presently may view the nineteenth-century physician's view of unborn life as consistent with their own views, but it is important to remember that opposition to abortion in the nineteenth century did not turn on contemporary arguments such as the one about the nature of "personhood." The dovetailing of nineteenth-century medical and professional practices with twentieth-century theological and political convictions has led to a certain confusion about how to understand the role of medicine in the abortion debate. James Mohr's book, *Abortion in America,* has inspired many opposed to abortion. A careful reading of his book, especially its conclusion, suggests that Mohr would hardly approve of this use of his historiography.

Yet historiography cannot remain neutral in the struggle to determine who will, at any present moment, be given authority to decide when abortions should be performed. If Mohr laments the misinterpretations of the facts he presents in his book, there is nevertheless an important lesson to be learned: nineteenth-century physician authority, as distinct from the professional power asserted on the basis of that authority, was founded on the belief that abortion was a morally and medically problematic matter. Abortion was not simply a convenient target for regulation, it was an inevitable one. The professional claim about medical and surgical efficacy and the scientific finding about the continuous and developmental nature of human life combined to form a new basis for medical practice. Physicians were not to offer ineffective treatments, and they were not to destroy life needlessly. Of course, such exhortations, like oaths, did not bind all in like ways. But the recent and decided emphasis of social scientists and historians on market formation and professional dominance has overshadowed the factors distinctive to medical practice itself, factors that not only enabled doctors to better their lot but also to secure their professional authority.

The Birth Control Movement and Its Opponents

The social reality of abortion practice in the United States after 1900 was not as remarkably different from 50 years earlier as one might imagine, despite the fact that by that time every state in the union had passed some type of restriction on its performance. Women continued to seek out abortions, but state-licensed physicians rarely, if ever, agreed to perform them. What these physicians often saw and treated were the sequelae of badly performed procedures. Medical knowledge about abortion was first improved in the course of treating the sequelae of spontaneous, incomplete, or illegally performed abortions.

From the medical perspective, the laws on abortion were sufficient to deny any abortion request unless the physician could reason that it might be effective in treating a disease exacerbated by pregnancy itself. In the medical literature of the first half of the twentieth century, *early* termination of pregnancy did not mean during the first trimester, but rather during the last trimester of pregnancy. In other words, in the United States, at least, the medical prerogative was to maintain pregnancy unless it became life-threatening to the mother or unborn child.

A dramatic exception to this medical view of pregnancy and abortion occurred in the Soviet Union starting in 1920 when the government permitted abortion more or less on demand. The first modern clinics devoted almost entirely to the provision of abortions operated legally and under medical supervision until 1936 when access to the procedure was restricted. American medical responses to the legalization of abortion in the Soviet Union were, with few exceptions, negative. In part, American physicians' disapproval of this particular Soviet experiment can be seen as a legacy of the medical profession's move against abortion in the nineteenth century.

The growing public demand for other forms of birth control also contributed to a general disapproval about abortion in the United States. Precisely because the American medical profession did not routinely and could not legally offer abortion services, the leaders of the Birth Control Movement, led by Margaret Sanger, argued that more and better instruction in other and safer methods would reduce the resort to illegal abortion.

The rhetoric of the Birth Control Movement was elegant and powerful: abortion was dangerous (because it was illegal) and was in any case a far cruder way to control birth than the use of mechanical forms of birth control such as the diaphragm and condom. Sanger even visited the Soviet Union where she chided health officials about their tolerance of abortion as a routine form of birth control.

It is unimaginable that the rhetorical strategies of the Birth Control Movement could have been otherwise, if one assumes that a major aim of the Movement was to persuade the medical profession to embrace the principles of birth control, if not each and every method. To advocate abortion as a method would have doomed any effort to defend the use of contraception. A brilliant strategy was developed that has had lasting consequences for the abortion debate in the United States. That strategy asserted a moral claim about the practice of birth control itself, not unlike the strategy that physicians had used fifty years earlier to obtain legal control over abortion. Not only was abortion unsafe and crude, it was said to be *morally* inferior to contraception. Resort to abortion thus became in its present moral rendering, a last resort. Women who resorted to it were characterized as having no other means at their disposal and doctors who resorted to it, in order to save the life of the mother, regarded it as symptomatic of their own inability to treat effectively.

Abortion was a symbol of failure, and remains so despite all changes in rhetoric and law. This symbol of failure is culturally embedded in the word itself and as such suggests why euphemism (*e.g.*, pregnancy termination) has for so long played an important part in the American dispute. Arguments about how an act should be named are themselves reflective of the cultural struggle over the meaning of such acts. This cultural struggle over abortion is best understood in terms of how moralizing priorities are established and maintained. Abortion cannot be condemned as a failure and at the same time praised as a routinely accepted form of birth control without some struggle to determine which view shall prevail.

By the 1940s, the active leadership of the Birth Control Movement was joined by the medical profession in relegating abortion to the moral underworld in which lurked abortionists, infection, and death. Nevertheless, the practice of birth control, including abortion, continued. The social reality of abortion practice without a rhetoric that condemned it in the mid-nineteenth century was replaced by a strongly stated rhetoric that condemned it but that showed little regard for or response to the social reality of its practice in the mid-twentieth century. In many respects, physicians were more rather than less aware of the social realities in both periods. Efforts to reform restrictive abortion laws were of little consequence until the rhetoric contrasting abortion with birth control began to lose its moral force.

Abortion and Medicine After 1950

Two things were becoming clear about the medical practice of abortion in the United States by mid-century: First, the surgical procedure, D & C (dilatation and curettage), was by most standards, a relatively safe and efficient way to perform an abortion in the early stages of pregnancy. Second, the medical indications for when a "therapeutic" abortion should be performed were considerably reduced, supplanted by more effective treatments of disease and by an optimism about the tremendous progress of medicine. Caught in this optimism in the 1950s, an expectant mother sometimes had to argue with her less than optimistic doctor about continuing a pregnancy that the doctor believed was better interrupted. The improvement of abortion procedures and the loss of reasons to use them set the stage for a conflict over rights that has effectively concealed the role that medicine played in bringing it about.

Opposition to abortion, based on the claim that it had once been provided in an ineffective and dangerous way, could no longer be used against the physicians who could perform them efficiently and safely. The rapid decline of medical indications created a vacuum for decision making that was gradually filled by hospital-run therapeutic abortion committees and by the use (and abuse) of psychiatric indications to justify the procedure. The result was that there were no medical reasons to perform abortions and no medical reasons not to perform them. From the medical standpoint, it appeared that the status of the unborn child would become the major factor in determining whether any reasons, for or against, could be found.

New medical reasons for abortion were formulated as a result of improved knowledge of the effects of disease (in this instance, rubella) upon the unborn. "Fetal" or "eugenic" indications for abortion were established on the basis of epidemiological research that led to the incorporation of statistical reasoning into the abortion decision-making process. Unlike previous statistical arguments that attempted to predict the chances of whether one would live or die by submitting or not submitting to a particular medical treatment, epidemiological knowledge about exposure to disease presented doctors, expectant mothers, and families with statistical arguments about whether or not a particular pregnancy in question would produce a "normal" and healthy infant.

The implications of this shift in the use of epidemiological knowledge to predict other than ultimate outcomes (i.e., whether a child would be born "normal" and healthy rather than live or die) can only by mentioned here. One important sociological consequence of this shift is that a new model for medical/scientific decision making was beginning to take shape, the implications of which have yet to be fully appreciated. This model calls for the gathering of aggregate data, the establishing of a range of probabilities associated with those data, and the presenting of those probabilities to physicians and patients. The pervasiveness of the idea of risk in American society is as much a cultural preoccupation as it is a consequence of the growing prestige of epidemiological knowledge about the incidence and distribution of disease in the human population.

"Quality of life" arguments are based upon diagnostic reasoning that first broadly determines risk to a population and then, by refinement in diagnostic techniques, endeavors to establish whether a particular person is at risk. The consistent aims of assessing the risks of exposure to rubella, screening for genetic anomalies, and relying on the nearly definitive results of amniocentesis and chorionic villus sampling, has been to map the probabilities of normalcy and health of the unborn in order to determine whether any particular pregnancy should be interrupted. Unlike the 1950s, medicine today is no longer without elaborately constructed and technologically informed rationales for abortion.

If these rationales were not sufficient to assure medical participation in abortion, then the case of Sherri Finkbine who took Thalidomide and who was unable to obtain an abortion in the state of Arizona in 1962 helps to explain how physician authority over the procedure was finally disestablished from within the profession by the growing limitations inherent in its knowledge about the myriad and uncertain effects of medication on pregnancy. It may be that, at one time, with a more limited knowledge about the developing condition of the unborn, the medical profession was able to perform "therapeutic" abortions without having to address either directly or probabilistically the physical condition of the unborn, in large part because the risks of continuing a pregnancy focussed entirely on maternal health even as those risks changed.

The symbolic importance of the Finkbine case was that it was a case of iatrogenically induced harm. From that point on, epidemiological knowledge about the effects of disease on the unborn would be supplemented by a review of the effects of medical treatment on all diseases and on all patients. At the same time the profession was seeking to inform itself about the possible effects of untreated diseases upon the unborn, it also assumed the added responsibility of determining the possible effects (or side-effects) of all of its own treatments for all diseases.

The tragedies of Thalidomide and exposure to rubella had the unintended effect of further medicalizing pregnancy insofar as they became symptomatic of a lack of medical attention to the potential dangers of exposure to all disease and to all kinds of substances ingested during pregnancy. For physicians the inevitable rise in expectations about achieving "normal" and healthy births in all cases was linked on the one hand with the character of epidemiological uncertainty and on the other hand with an enormous increase in diagnostic procedures to reduce that uncertainty.

The number of abortions performed for fetal reasons has never been large when compared, particularly after 1973, with the number performed for reasons not related to medical diagnoses. If state laws in the United States had only been changed to include fetal indications, the demand for further liberalization would obviously have persisted. The safety of the abortion procedure early in pregnancy had considerable bearing on how it was regarded as a form of birth control. Epidemiological arguments marshalled to demonstrate that interrupting a pregnancy was safer than following it through to term, however disingenuous, were rhetorically useful in putting to rest the older claims of the birth controllers. The rhetoric that distinguished among different forms of birth control was recast to include abortion as a constitutional right.

Constitutional Rights and Private Practices

American physicians were the first entrepreneurs against abortion in the United States. They were willing to accommodate themselves to the rhetoric of early birth controllers precisely because abortion was condemned; and they were tireless in their efforts to save any and all pregnancies, if medically possible. Taken together, these three conditions underlying the medical approach to abortion were part of the profession's ideal-ethical stance toward, if not consistently practical response to, requests for the procedure.

In other words, charges of hypocrisy became the prevailing criticism against a profession that was unable to formulate a consistent stand about abortion in practice. The rich were said to be able to obtain safely performed abortions while the poor were not; psychiatrists could diagnose "symptoms" that then became "indications" for the procedure; and many states were highly selective in their efforts to enforce their laws on abortion. Against this backdrop, the movement to reform state abortion laws called upon outspoken physicians to take a stand. Physicians played a prominent role in that reform in Hawaii, New York, and California. Yet the emergence of abortion politics resulted in more than professional

and legal reform. Access to abortion became a central demand in the call for social reform by the women's movement of the late 1960s and 1970s.

In 1973, the United States Supreme Court rulings on abortion (*Roe* v. *Wade* and *Doe* v. *Bolton*) were surprising to all sides. The argument that the United States Constitution revealed a special "right" to privacy that included a right to abortion has been rather consistently criticized by strict and broad constructionists alike. Therapeutic abortion committees were dismantled, and physicians were no longer required to justify to anyone *their* reasons for performing abortions. Abortion remained in the hands of licensed practitioners, but it no longer had to be thought of as a medically indicated operation. This does not mean that physicians suddenly stopped thinking of it in this way.

The medical profession had little difficulty in adapting to the Court's rulings because the Court neither prevented nor required physicians to perform abortions. This meant, in effect, that a woman's right to obtain an abortion was constrained by a physician's right not to perform one. The result of this potential conflict of rights is reflected in the present social organization of the delivery of abortion services in the United States. The vast majority of physicians perform a relatively small number of the procedures, while a small number of physicians perform the vast majority of abortions.

The responsibility for the provision of abortion services has fallen to one medical specialty in particular, obstetrics and gynecology. Numerous consequences have followed for the specialty as a result.. Beneath the publicly defined contexts of abortion politics is a more complex historical, cultural, and social reality of medical confrontation with a medical procedure that remains in the hidden hands of medicine despite all the rhetoric to the contrary.

Obstetrician/gynecologists have been the ones consistently faced with the actual requests for the procedure. It should not be surprising that of all medical specialties surveyed during the last thirty years, ob/gyn has consistently ranked among the most conservative on abortion. This conservatism reflects both the historical and cultural reality out of which modern obstetrics and gynecology have emerged. When looking at medical practice in contrast to legal assessments of that practice, several generalizations about abortion services can be made. First, the vast majority of abortions are performed in clinic settings by physicians who have been hired for that specific purpose. The remaining abortions are performed by physicians in private practice either in hospital or office settings. Second, the physician in private practice handles abortion requests in essentially two ways: by accepting to do them or by referring requests for them elsewhere. The result is that free-standing clinics have assumed the major responsibility for abortions in the United States. Third, abortions have been technically routinized, but physicians have not generally accommodated them to their practice of medicine. In other words, abortion has not been morally routinized within the profession of medicine.

One reason for this lack of accommodation can be found by examining the typical career patterns of obstetrician/gynecologists. Since *Roe* v. *Wade* in 1973, a practitioner's first encounter with abortion is most likely to occur during residency, when a well-established teaching hierarchy determines who will be assigned the responsibilities for performing first-trimester abortions in particular. (The only obvious exception to this rule is the case of Catholic teaching hospitals.) In the United States, 90 percent of all abortions are performed between the ninth and twelfth weeks of pregnancy. The medical risks associated with the abortion procedure at this stage of pregnancy are relatively minor when compared with other forms of surgery. Residents in ob/gyn can acquire some useful surgical skills by performing such procedures but not necessarily by performing large numbers of them. Once in private practice, physicians are typically expected to acquire skills and document their experiences for Board Certification in order to remain on a hospital staff. This expectation reduces even more the likelihood that they will perform large numbers of these procedures since their performance does not demonstrate any degree of surgical or medical specialization within ob/gyn.

The private physician's reluctance to perform abortions also depends on how medicine is practiced in a community where reputation and expertise are important factors for attracting and retaining patients. Abortion remains stigmatized in private medical practice largely because of lingering public perceptions that those who perform them have been or will be discredited among their professional peers. The stigma of abortionist has powerful resonances in communities that still exhibit strong feelings about *who* does such work as distinct from the work itself. In a community of medical practice, reputation cannot be so easily separated from what physicians are known to do.

Physicians reduce or stop performing abortions once in private practice on account of their personal beliefs about why they chose obstetrics/gynecology as a medical specialty. The generation who began residency after *Roe* v. *Wade* has been most dramatically affected by the changing character of this specialty. By looking more systematically at this generation's personal reasons for avoiding and referring requests for abortion, it appears that family and religion play an important part in explaining what for some doctors is a journey from a strong support for a woman's right to choose to an equally strong defense of a physician's right not to have to perform. In some cases, a physician's spouse contributes to the view that private practice is a refuge from the political wars over abortion in which no one is a winner. At the same time, physicians' recounting of their own experiences with performing the procedure, particularly after the first trimester, adds to the conviction that political conflict is deeply tied to the moral and medical uncertainty about the status of the fetus and the meaning of its active destruction through abortion. In the second trimester, the recognition of the human form of the fetus becomes literally a source of revulsion, especially when the fetus is morselated (cut up) and removed from the uterus.

The public image of abortion practice in the United States suggests that physicians are reluctant to accommodate women's requests for abortion. Since 1973, most efforts to restrict access to abortion have sought to frame the pregnant woman's right to the procedure in terms of the competing rights of spouse, parents, and biological father. Yet little attention has been given to the Supreme Court's initial framing of the pregnant woman's right in its relation to medicine. From this perspective, there are really two types of abortions performed. On the one hand, abortions requested for what are construed to be "personal" reasons have been largely handed over to the clinics. These procedures are viewed in medicine as "dirty work." On the other hand, abortions performed for what are construed to be "medical" and "eugenic" reasons have been largely undertaken by physicians practicing outside the clinic setting. These procedures are now considered integral to the practice of medicine.

Two implications follow for abortion practice generally. Abortions that cannot be subsumed under any medical rubric are presumed to be a "private choice" and therefore are thought to require no justification. Nevertheless, in private practice, moralizing, that is, seeking justifications for such a choice, is still widely practiced. Even in the culture of clinics where family planning workers typically mediate between requests for abortions and their performance by staff physicians, abortion remains a negotiated encounter. On the other hand, a much smaller number of abortions are performed, generally after 18 weeks as the result of amniocentesis, for reasons that have strictly speaking been medicalized along the same trajectory that followed from the rubella outbreaks and the Thalidomide tragedy in the 1960s. With carrier and prenatal screening gradually put in place, that trajectory promises to offer what could theoretically be an infinite range of "indications" to evaluate in deciding whether or not to conceive or to bring a particular conception to birth. And with the development of prenatal screening methods such as chorionic villus sampling, the clinics providing the vast majority of first-trimester abortions could offer much the same information that is now only available through amniocentesis.

The medical elite necessary to accomplish the performance of both types of abortions does not need to be very large. The legal struggle over abortion rights in the United States has consistently taken for granted that so long as abortion is legal, physicians will be trained and available to perform them. The cultural pressures to assure "normal" and healthy births will depend evermore on a medical-technical elite that guarantees its work. Yet because eugenic abortions constitute in sheer numbers so small a percentage of all the abortions performed, it is difficult to predict how the profession will respond once a first-trimester method comparable to amniocentesis is available on a mass basis.

In recent years, the use of a so-called "abortion pill" has been heralded as the kind of technological innovation that will inevitably defuse the contentious politics of abortion. But such optimism is excessive, if not naive, given the nature of abortion politics but also given the medical consequences that could follow the widespread use of such a pill. RU 486, the latest addition to pharmaceutically induced abortion methods, has been celebrated as the innovation in "late" birth control methods for which everyone has been waiting. Yet anyone familiar with the medical uses of this drug will not deny that it may actually prove more cumbersome to use than the epidemiologically reliable and efficient method of suction D & C and that its possible long-term effects on women's health are much more difficult to predict. In other words, despite the periodic optimism that ensues about technological innovations that directly affect the health of women, the epidemiological debates over surgical versus pharmaceutical intervention remain the most important indicator of how extensive the diffusion of any innovation will be. The rush to achieve "private" control is inevitably a denial

of the complex medical consequences that underlie any form of control whatsoever.

The Future of Abortion Policy in Light of Medicine

The abortion issue has largely been framed in the United States in the absence of a recognition of the medical profession's strategic place in the provision of abortion services. But "policy" about abortion cannot be separated from the role that medicine has played in making abortion technically safe, yet morally unclear. Political debates have proceeded on the assumption that the protection of rights (of women and of the unborn) is central to the struggle over whether abortions should be permitted or prohibited. Philosophical debates have attempted to explore the ways in which such rights can be defined and defended. The lack of political consensus about abortion has been characterized in terms of how people think, for example, about whether the fetus is a person. Depending on which criteria one uses, the conflict appears resolvable only in terms of the rights that pertain to a pregnant woman or an unborn child.

The philosophical definitions of personhood are entirely divorced from the practice of medicine as it grows out of specific encounters between physicians and patients. The reluctance of physicians to perform abortions after the first trimester suggests that human form, not personhood, is a basic element in an aesthetics of medical practice which draws a line between ushering life into the world and destroying it before birth. The use of abortion turns on the relation between doctor and patient, and always has since Hippocrates. The licit practice of abortion, taken over now largely by clinics, has resulted in a transformation of how the physician's responsibilities are to be construed. The doctor is seen as an instrument of competing wills, each one shaped in terms of rights. If the unborn may be seen as the third will in this competition, it becomes clear that medicine's historic refusal to perform abortions, except in well-defined circumstances, has resulted until very recently in the protection of the third will.

In the clinic, there is no third will. And now, in what may be its most radical departure from itself, the medical profession has begun by diagnostic refinement to adopt an epidemiological perspective on what is "normal" human life. Obstetrical science has medicalized the womb in such a way that "choice" takes on an entirely new cast: no longer is the choice whether or not to have a child but rather whether or not to have this child with these diagnosed "qualities." Philosophers who have labored on personhood have been content with ignoring how selective the criteria may be for establishing whether a life is worth living. That selectivity is social in its essence, but not, by that virtue, arbitrary. In this sense, the uses of abortion are changing in ways that radically depart from the cultural struggles over whether abortion is a morally inferior or constitutionally protected form of birth control. The rhetoric of the early birth controllers and the chorus of rights that has superseded that rhetoric are being replaced by a far more powerful set of justifications for abortion practice informed by epidemiology and prenatal diagnostic tests.

In the near future, as the abortion issue is hammered out in individual states, the rhetoricians of pro-choice will no doubt transform their style of affirmation, accepting certain restrictions while opposing others. The disestablishment of judicial hegemony will require that choice not be framed in absolute terms, as it has been for nearly twenty years. Yet it is doubtful that "choice" will be reframed in terms of moral valuations of different forms of birth control. Rather, the defense of choice is bound to be medicalized in special ways that will depend on the kinds of diagnostic technologies developed and diffused. There is ample precedent for the medical profession encouraging this diffusion because, in effect, it has already accepted the principle that definitions of what is "normal" human life can be used for determining when a pregnancy can be interrupted: all of this has flowed quite innocently and appropriately from the confidential physician-patient relation.

As new abortion restrictions seriously challenge the process by which negotiation for the procedure is made, a new testing of conviction will appear, this time in the rhetorical establishment of competing rights among all interested parties, including parents, husbands, and the unborn. Regulations will be promulgated that test the limits of how far such convictions may be imposed on a woman's right to decide for herself. There will inevitably be cynical and sincere responses to such convictions. In this sense, the medical profession may go through the motions of imposing such convictions without being forced legally to act upon them, so long as they are legally permitted to perform abortions. The role of medicine in this struggle may thus become an impor-

tant target for pro-life efforts precisely because the future of abortion restrictions will focus less on those seeking abortions than on those performing them.

Abortion policy in American society now appears to turn entirely on the ability of law to shape, guide, and deter certain options regarding the use of abortion. The absence of debate about how medicine has systematically made certain options possible over the course of time has allowed physicians to appear as if they were merely the instruments of others' decisions, whether those others are women, the courts, or state legislatures. As abortion becomes more medically controversial by virtue of the extraordinary improvement in its diagnostic powers, even more physicians will be reluctant to perform them than those already deterred by the legal conflict. Yet as long as the confidentiality of the physician-patient relation is legally protected, the only way the abortion decision could be interfered with would be by outlawing the diagnostic tests themselves. What this portends for the practice of abortion in the next century is the rise of new types of social movements that contest the new diagnostic environments created by medical knowledge. Medicine will remain a major player in abortion politics, despite all appearances to the contrary.

READINGS SUGGESTED BY THE AUTHOR

Kass, Leon R. "Perfect Babies: Prenatal Diagnosis and the Equal Right to LIfe." In *Toward a More Natural Science: Biology and Human Affairs.* New York: Free Press, 1985.

Keown, John. A*bortion, Doctors, and the Law: Some Aspects of the Legal Regulation of Abortion in England from 1803 to 1982.* Cambridge: Cambridge University Press, 1988.

Luker, Kristin. *Abortion and the Politics of Motherhood.* Berkeley: University of California Press, 1984.

Mohr, James C. *Abortion in America: The Origins and Evolution of National Policy.* New York: Oxford University Press, 1978.

Ramsey, Paul. *Ethics at the Edges of Life: Medical and Legal Intersections.* New Haven: Yale University Press, 1978.

Censorship and the Fear of Sexuality

Marty Klein

Marty Klein is a licensed marriage counselor and sex therapist in Palo Alto, California. His new book is Your Sexual Secrets: When to Keep Them, How to Share Them. *The author gratefully acknowledges the support of Humanists of Washington and the Northwest Feminist Anti-Censorship Taskforce in the preparation of this article.*

By treating censorship as an exclusively political issue, we fail to address the psychological factors that typically underlie the desire to suppress sexually explicit materials

In 1986, Ronald Reagan created the Meese Commission with the express purpose of destroying the pornography industry. It was widely expected that the commission would issue a report linking pornography to sexual violence. As often happened during the Reagan Administration, however, things did not go exactly as planned. The Meese Commission could find no causal link between sexually explicit materials and sexually aggressive behavior. To its surprise, the commission also found that less than one percent of the imagery in the most popular porn magazines was of "force, violence, or weapons." And yet, despite these and other well-known findings, a surprising number of people—many of them otherwise staunch defenders of our First Amendment rights—

wish to censor pornography in the interests of some greater social good.

I will not address the pornography issue from the standpoint of civil liberties, although there is overwhelming evidence from this point of view that the censorship of sexually explicit materials is harmful. Nor will I address the argument that pornography degrades women. Proponents of censorship almost invariably want to suppress pornography by and for lesbians and gay men as well—which shows that, although some censors may sincerely wish to uphold the dignity of women, this is not their real motive.

Finally, I will not discuss the dangerous way that censorship strengthens the hand of America's political and religious right wing. Conservatives such as Citizens Against Pornography candidly admit that they also

want to criminalize abortion, restore prayer in school, and destroy anti-discrimination programs. Humanists and feminists who align themselves with these people are making a profound mistake.

Instead, I wish to address the psychological issues that typically lie behind the desire to censor sexually explicit materials.

What does every child learn about sex? Simple: sex is bad. We all learn this as children when we are rudely discouraged from touching ourselves, when we are forbidden to play "doctor," when we are punished for asking certain questions, or when we experience our parents' discomfort while bathing us.

So, although no one ever explains *why* sex is bad, we come to believe that it is. But we also know that *we* are sexual beings—which makes *us* bad. All children know that their sexual feelings and behavior put them in constant danger of being punished, leading inescapably to the fear that their sexuality will cause them to be rejected or even abandoned by their parents. This is what Freud's "latency period" is really about: children hiding their sexuality to avoid punishment, rejection, and abandonment.

This article first appeared in *The Humanist,* July/August 1990, pp. 15-17, 38, and is reprinted by permission.

This early terror of sex stays with us, and the fear of sexuality getting out of control becomes a part of every adult's unconscious. The fear that "bad" sexuality can lead to destruction or abandonment means that trusting one's own sexuality or the sexuality of others feels *very* dangerous. And this is what a lot of the desire to censor pornography is: an expression of our fear of "dangerous" sexuality.

Our basic, archaic fear, then, is that our sexual impulses will invite punishment and destroy others. This is an irrational fear that people do not admit to themselves, much less talk about with each other. Thus, both individuals and the society they constitute develop myths that are taken as fact, myths that are easier to deal with than the irrational fear. Jimmy Swaggart, for example, could not accept the reality of his own sexual desires, and so instead spent a lot of time decrying the "perversions" of others. Pornography, of course, does not depict *real* sex—only fantasy. But some people want to censor it because pornography is a *symbol* of the "bad" sexuality that we unconsciously fear.

What distinguishes this kind of sexuality? First, it is pleasure-centered. Second, it does not feel constrained to conform to roles or polite rules. Third, it is not bound or controlled by notions of "love." And fourth, it places value on losing control (although within a secure environment).

This kind of sexuality admits to being a form of self-expression, self-exploration, and self-healing. From this perspective, sex is the most personal of art forms. And, as a way of plugging into the cosmic battery, it can be intensely spiritual, because it allows people to interface with the universe directly, instead of through a person, ritual, or institution.

Yet, because our culture has traditionally depicted sex as beyond our control and therefore dangerous, anything which threatens our ability to maintain that con-

People fear that even something as profoundly basic as their sexual identity is not safe from intrusion and unwanted change. Therefore . . . controlling the influences on one's sexuality is critical.

trol is also seen as dangerous. And pornography, since it is designed to be sexually arousing, does exactly that. Moreover, the sexuality it depicts is itself frequently out of control (that is, driven by passion instead of reason), which can be frightening. Censorship, then, is an attempt to reestablish some crucial sense of control over sexuality.

There are many ways in which pornography triggers people's fear of losing control of sexuality. Pornography depicts sex outside the context of love—which, in our culture, is the most important boundary separating "bad," uncivilized sex from "good," sane sex. As depicted in romance novels and other media, love conquers sexuality, making it wholesome and restoring control to its wild, unpredictable expression.

When sex is separated from love, a wide range of choices suddenly appears. These choices include multiple partners, sex with those of "inappropriate" age, class, or race, sex that is (consensually) rough rather than gentle, and sex for pleasure rather than intimacy.

In other activities, such as shopping and eating, a high degree of choice is considered positive rather than problematic. But in the context of our sexual fears and our desire for sexual simplicity, a high degree of choice is threatening. For example, many men unconsciously fear that exposure to homosexuals and homosexual culture will seduce them away from heterosexuality. That is, people fear that even something as profoundly basic as their sexual identity is not safe from intrusion

and unwanted change. Therefore, according to this "reasoning," controlling the influences on one's sexuality is critical.

Pornography is also an invitation to get in touch with one's fantasies and desires. Since most people fear that their desires are weird (or worse), this invitation is frightening. Many people look at their mates and think, "If you *really* knew me, you couldn't love me." Therefore, some people desire to remove the temptation of pornography so they can stay hidden—from themselves as well as their mates.

Interestingly, our culture suggests that the "wrong" kind of sexual experience will undermine people's *nonsexual* values and "morality." Our culture fears that sexual pleasure-seeking will be so rewarding that it will soon overwhelm us, destroying our ability to defer it. Sexual pleasure is thus seen as something that must not get a foothold in our consciousness.

There is much truth to the fear that the unfettered pursuit of sexual pleasure will force us to examine our choices and our reality. This does not mean, however, that we will subordinate everything else in our lives to the quest for sexual gratification. In reality, when people accept their desire to seek pleasure, they can also leave it at will and return to it when appropriate. As proof, look at an extreme: in even the most "immoral" pleasure-seeking activity—extramarital affairs—people *do* go back to work, remain with their families, and so on. The illicit sex doesn't necessarily control them.

Finally, censorship often appeals to people who were sexually abused as children. Being molested is an experience of powerlessness for a child, and depictions of sex without the conventional constraints of love and politeness can trigger fear, shame, anger, or traumatic memories for these people. Some claim that the child molester is "motivated" or "instructed" by pornography. We know, however, that this is rarely true; as even the FBI admits, most child molesters are into power, not pedophilia.

The unconscious fear of punishment can also lead to the desire to limit "bad" sexuality. Most of us are or have been ashamed that we masturbate and associate the activity with the possibility or experience of punishment. Since pornography is primarily designed to enhance masturbation, it feels to many like dangerous stuff.

Some of us also experience an unconscious feeling of shame or fear over the voyeurism involved in consuming pornography. People who had no privacy as children may overidentify with porn actors being "violated" by the viewing public, forgetting that filmmaking is a consensual business arrangement. And people with voyeuristic fantasies they can't acknowledge may react by condemning pornography especially harshly. Psychodynamically, sexuality can be seen as the dangerous, "child" part of the self, while the censor is the "parent" reassuring the child that everything is under control—whether it actually is or not.

Virtually no one has enough accurate, judgment-free information about sex. We don't watch other people do it, we can't find many accurate representations of it in the media, and few of us talk honestly about it with each other. It's almost impossible to know the full range of sexual thoughts and behavior of the people around us—and, therefore, impossible to know how much we have in common.

This is difficult enough to handle, but much of American advertising is based upon exploiting this fact. Its message is: "Are you sexually adequate or normal? Why take a chance that you're not? Buy this product and feel secure." Of course, religion, government, and medicine are also involved in persuading people that their sexuality may not be "normal" or "acceptable" in some abstract, theoretical sense. As a result, people learn to distrust their own sexuality and to trust only those with the "authority" to judge it. The fear of sexual abnormality easily leads to censorship—to suppressing that abnormal sexuality out *there.*

We Americans like things neat and

> **There is no reason that sex cannot or should not express our ignoble side: aggression, lust, greed, selfishness, hedonism (all with the consent of one's partner, of course).**

tidy; the problem is, real sex isn't. Nor is sex clean and wholesome. Pornography holds up a mirror of what sex is like on a broad level—not in terms of the content (which is an exaggeration of common experience, just like major league sports and PBS cooking shows), but in terms of the passion and the willingness to relinquish control. It shows a part of the reality of sex that many of us wish to avoid.

By portraying lust as acceptable, pornography also increases some people's fears about aggression: "Will I lose control of my lust and hurt myself? Will I 'use' someone and later regret it?" Some censors complain that pornography cheapens sex—that is, shows it without love or "meaning." But what's wrong with "meaningless" sex if both partners agree to it? There is no reason that sex cannot or should not express our ignoble side: aggression, lust, greed, selfishness, hedonism (all with the consent of one's partner, of course). Sex is the most harmless arena of all in which to play out, express, and investigate this side of being human. Sexuality can be our sandbox, if we simply set down some basic ground rules.

These same critics also tend to attack pornography because it treats people as sexual objects. So long as this is done with the consent of both viewer and viewed, this is a reasonable activity as well. Unfortunately, some people fear that they won't be adequate sex objects. They don't understand that *just being emotionally present* makes one sexually adequate.

Our culture depends on a symbiotic system of male-female sexual incapacity and miscommunication; the authentic sexuality represented by pornography transcends and shatters this unholy alliance.

The idea of female sexual power being unblocked (that is, not bound by love, commitment, or the need of a male's expertise) is frightening to both men and women; our society clearly fears that this power will be expressed by voracious female sexual appetites, the abandonment of the family, or the judgment of some men as simply not good enough. Contrast, for example, the way a woman with a strong sexual appetite is called a "nympho"—someone out of control—while a man with a similar appetite is called a "stud"—someone who is skilled and selective, clearly in control. The portrayals of female lust and sexual enthusiasm in pornography confront us with our modern double standard: seeing women as competent, powerful equals in the workplace, but as weak, vulnerable creatures needing protection and guidance in the bedroom.

Thus, pornography is the symbol of a threatening kind of sexuality that places value on losing control and separates sex from love. We can also describe this as "authentic" sexuality—sex valued for its own sake, with its own subjective logic.

To the extent that we are attached to the status quo, the fear of this kind of sex *is* rational. Authentic sexuality is ultimately revolutionary. It challenges gender roles by depicting women as lusty without being bad. It enfranchises us all as sexual beings—but for who we are, not for what we do. It returns to us the right and means to own and evaluate our own sexuality, rather than referring us to social definitions of what is "normal." It challenges the role of monogamy and the nuclear family as the exclusive source of emotional comfort. It undermines traditional religions by refusing to make procreation the primary purpose of sex. It also challenges the basis of advertising, which creates sexual insecurity in order to sell products. It trusts people to take care of themselves and others during sexual encounters. Finally, it sees sex as a positive force we can use to explore and expand our human horizons, rather than as a negative force we must control and restrict to protect ourselves.

Contrast this with the kind of sexual expression that is *not* generally subject to censorship—the kind that connects sex with either love or guilt and punishment. Clearly, these forms of sexual expression pose no threat to the status quo. Examples include teen magazines featuring male heartthrobs, Barbie and Ken dolls, romance novels ("women's pornography" that routinely depicts rape leading to love), sexually titillating yet moralistic television shows like *Dynasty,* and even sexual harassment in the workplace. Of course, would-be censors do not admit that fear motivates them. No one says, "Sex scares me," because such a statement would not be considered a valid foundation for public policy (nor should it be). Instead, people hide behind social fables about the supposedly "objective"

dangers of uncontrolled sexuality such as rape and child molestation.

hat can be done about the dangerous, anti-democratic censorship that stems from the fear of sexuality? We can affirm that many people are afraid of sex and empower them to find the solution to their fear. We can work to separate this fear from valid public policy considerations. While acknowledging the difficulties in changing such deeply rooted attitudes, we must remind people that they already know how to handle their anger and fear without acting it out in their significant relationships. We also need to identify and develop programs dealing with sexuality in a positive light, programs which the public can support. These may include educating young women about date rape; teaching young men to use

condoms; providing accurate sexual information through respected figures like Ann Landers; training medical students in sexuality; and teaching people how to discuss sexual values and anxieties with their children.

Two thousand years ago, the Roman senate considered a law requiring slaves to wear distinctive clothing. "This is a bad idea," protested one citizen. "They may look around and realize just how large their numbers are." If only enough people had the courage to wear X-rated hat pins or armbands—because the reality is that millions and millions of Americans consume various kinds of sexually explicit materials every month. If you're one of them, know that your numbers are large—and that your rights are under attack in virtually every segment of society.

Now, more than ever, it is time—emotionally and spiritually—to just say yes.

Sexual Biology and Health

- **The Body and Its Responses (Articles 9-13)**
- **Sexual Attitudes and Practice (Articles 14-16)**
- **Sexual Orientation (Articles 17-19)**

Human bodies are miraculous things. Most of us, however, have a less than complete understanding of how they work. This is especially true of our bodily responses and functioning during sexual activity. Efforts to develop a healthy sexual awareness are severely hindered by misconceptions and lack of quality information about sexual physiology. The first portion of this section directs attention to the development of a clearer understanding and appreciation of the workings of the human body.

As you read through the articles in this section, you will be able to see more clearly that matters of sexual biology and behavior are not merely physiological in origin. The articles in the first two subsections demonstrate clearly the psychological, social, and cultural origins of sexual behavior as well. Why we humans choose to behave sexually can be quite complex.

A final topic in this section is sexual orientation. Perhaps no other area of sexual behavior is as misunderstood as this one. Even experts do not agree to what extent someone's sexual orientation—homosexual, heterosexual, or bisexual—is genetically determined, environmentally influenced, and/or of free choice. In the early years of this century, sexologist Alfred Kinsey's seven-point continuum of sexual orientation was introduced. It placed exclusive heterosexual orientation at one end, exclusive homosexual orientation at the other, and identified the middle range as where most people would fall if society and culture were unprejudiced. Since Kinsey, many others have developed other theories or refinements, but the case remains that there is probably more not known than known about our sexual orientation.

That the previous paragraph may have been upsetting, even distasteful to some readers, emphasizes the connectedness of psychological, social, and cultural issues with those of sexuality. Human sexual functioning is biology and far more. What behaviors and choices are socially and culturally prescribed and proscribed are also part of human sexuality. This section attempts to address all of these issues.

The subsection *The Body and Its Responses* opens with a review of research into the effects of hormones on women's behavior. That sounds simple, maybe even a little boring, but these findings have reignited the long-standing fervor of medical, social, and political groups,

especially feminists. The second article, "Man's Greatest Reflex," provides an abundance of factual information about a topic rarely talked, but often joked, about—erection. "Women and Sexuality" provides discussion of historical and present day views of the importance (or unimportance) of orgasm in women. The last two articles in this section emphasize the interaction of couples that involve sexual functioning and dysfunctioning. The first looks at what is usually viewed as a male problem—premature ejaculation, and discusses possible contributions of female partners to this dysfunction. The final article examines what for some readers might be a paradox—men who fake orgasms.

The *Sexual Attitudes and Practices* subsection opens with an overview of the research into the sexuality related attitudes of a little-studied group—black middle-class adults. The second article challenges popular conceptions about American attitudes and behaviors toward and about monogamy. The final article explains and profiles a group of sexual behaviors that are rarely written about—life-threatening masturbatory behaviors. Each of these articles and their authors seek to increase our understanding of why we think, feel, and behave as we do sexually. Amidst the surprises, intrigue, and even shock, readers will find much new information and insight.

The *Sexual Orientation* subsection opens with an article that overviews homosexuality as an orientation. Its coverage of who and why illustrates that there can be no one definition of homosexuality. It suggests that sexualities would be a preferable term.

"Variations on a Theme" examines some nontraditional families. Single, gay, lesbian, and skip-generation families are real today, and they are expected to increase as the last decade of the century draws to a close. The extent to which these families, and homosexual relationships, are accepted by society is yet to be determined. The final article examines the heated debate for and against any marital-like legitimization of gay unions.

Looking Ahead: Challenge Questions

What makes it hard for us to talk objectively and seriously about orgasms, erections, and dysfunctions? How has this class affected this situation for you?

What surprised you most about the attitudes of black adults? Did you expect there to be more or less of a difference between your attitude and the ones reported?

How important is monogamy to you? What would it mean if your partner or spouse was not monogamous?

How would you rate yourself on a risk-taking continuum?

It is rare for people to wonder why someone is hetero-sexual in the same ways that we wonder why someone is homosexual. What do you think has contributed to your sexual orientation?

In the society of the future, what consequences do you foresee if people choose a life partner on the basis of their feelings, needs, interests, and characteristics, and gender was not an issue? What do you expect relationships and families to look like? Why?

How Sex Hormones Boost - or Cut - Intellectual Ability

Doreen Kimura

Doreen Kimura is a professor of psychology at the University of Western Ontario in London, Ontario.

There is arguably no area of scientific inquiry as political and controversial as research on sex differences. So it should not have been surprising last November— when two biological psychologists reported landmark work on fluctuations in intellectual abilities linked to hormone changes—that the findings made national headlines that infuriated many who read them. Harvard professor of biology Ruth Hubbard, for example, who has written extensively on the subject of gender differences, dismissed the reports as "absurd."

Here, for the first time, the chief investigator on that study explains in her own words the details of the extensive research behind those headlines—and her personal interpretation of the findings.

—THE EDITORS

Most people accept the idea that hormones influence how we behave in explicitly sexual situations, and even that they can affect our moods. But evidence is growing that sex hormones influence a wider range of behaviors, including problem-solving or intellectual activities. Some of the observed male-female differences in cognitive ability appear to be determined by sex hormones working on brain systems.

Much of what we know about hormonal control of behavior has been discovered in nonhuman animals, mostly rats and mice. The parallel between human and animal mechanisms has been good enough that we can often fill in the knowledge gaps about human beings by looking at studies in rodents. They tell us that fetal hormones not only determine whether male or female sexual genitalia will be formed, but also whether the adult will act sexually like a male or female. Merely having an XY (male) or XX (female) chromosome does not in itself ensure male or female development. If no male sex hormones (androgens) are present in the fetal life of an XY individual, or if there is a serious abnormality of androgen systems, a female will be formed.

Monthly fluctuations in sex hormones affect women's cognitive skills.

Similarly, we may have XY individuals who do not merely look like females, but appear to have many "sex-typical" female behavioral characteristics, show female play preferences, and the like. In another kind of hormonal anomaly, XX individuals may be mildly androgenized by early exposure to natural or synthetic androgens. Even if they are raised as girls, report Melissa Hines at UCLA and June Reinisch at the Kinsey Institute in Indiana, such individuals are tomboyish, engage in rough and tumble play, and show masculine preferences in toys and other matters. This illustrates the general principle that early exposure to sex hormones has lifelong effects on behavior of both men and women. This type of influence is referred to as an "organizational" effect, in contrast to "activational" effects—the short-term influence of fluctuations in hormones.

One way to observe organizational effects on cognitive function is to look at the differences which exist, on average, between men and women. Men excel on certain spatial tasks, especially those requiring accurate orientation of a line or pattern, imaginal rotation, or discerning a figure embedded in a background pattern. Men are also better on tests of mathematical reasoning. Women, on the other hand, are better at certain verbal tasks, particularly verbal fluency and articulation as well as some fine manual skills. They also appear to be faster in scanning a perceptual array, especially to make an identity match.

How Hormones Affect Average Gender Differences

One problem with attributing these differences to early hormonal influences is that men and women are also treated differently all their lives. Many people would argue vociferously that the cognitive differences are not large, that they can be diminished by intensive training, and that there is great overlap between men and women in each ability. Without denying any of this, it is nevertheless true that sex hormones have been shown to influence cognitive function in ways not readily explained by differential experience.

For example, Daniel Hier and William Crowley in Chicago found that males in whom puberty did not develop at normal age — a condition related to abnormally low testosterone levels and reduced testicular size — were poor on spatial tasks. The researchers compared them to a group of males who had developed puberty normally, but who subsequently suffered lowered testosterone levels as a result of disease. The males with early testosterone deficiency performed worse on tasks of spatial construction and orientation, and on disembedding. The groups were equal on several verbal intelligence tests.

Rat studies offer direct evidence that manipulating the hormonal environment can affect spatial problem-solving ability. Christina Williams and her coworkers at Barnard College found that in running a radial-arm maze, male rats used only geometry cues while females employed both geometry and landmark cues. In rats, sex hormones can still alter brain organization in the immediate postnatal period, when the genitals have already been formed.

Williams found that castrating males during this period, so that gonadal hormones could no longer affect the brain, caused the males when adults to adopt a more "female" strategy on mazes. Since the rats were neither reared differently by their parents nor exposed differently to mazes, hormones clearly had a powerful, lasting effect on a nonreproductive behavior.

Hier and Crowley's study might appear to suggest that the higher the androgen levels, the higher the spatial ability, but keep in mind that they were comparing normal and subnormal levels. Within the normal range of androgens, it appears that males with lower levels actually perform better on spatial tasks. Valerie Shute and coworkers at the University of California, Santa Barbara, found that, comparing men in the bottom and top 25% in terms of testosterone levels, those with lower levels scored higher on spatial tests. We have recently confirmed this in our laboratory.

Findings from these and other studies suggest a curvilinear rather than a direct relationship between androgen levels and spatial ability. This is consistent with the finding that in females — who of course have lower levels of testosterone than males — those with higher levels of testosterone score higher in spatial ability. The situation is complicated by the fact that testosterone is probably converted to estradiol in the brain before it affects the nervous system. Helmuth Nyborg of the University of Aarhus in Denmark has proposed that

Women had better "male" skills when their estrogen levels were low.

estrogen actually is the critical determinant of spatial ability.

Does Ability Fluctuate During Menstrual Cycles?

All these studies were probably sampling the organizational (chronic) effects of sex hormones among groups of people. About six years ago, I decided to examine the possibility that fluctuations in hormones *within* an individual might also be reflected in cognitive changes. The most readily available subjects for this approach were women — young women undergoing natural fluctuations in the course of the menstrual cycle, and older post-menopausal women who were taking hormone replacement therapy.

To maximize the likelihood of finding intellectual changes, we selected tests that measured either abilities favoring males or those favoring females. We assumed that higher levels of female sex hormones (estrogen and progesterone) might enhance "female" abilities, such as verbal fluency and manual skill, but have no effect, or even a negative effect, on "male" abilities such as spatial skill.

The menstrual-cycle study was done with Elizabeth Hampson, a doctoral student in my laboratory. Initially, we did not have the capacity to analyze blood from our subjects, so we picked periods in the menstrual cycle which could be identified without such assays — the midluteal, about 7 to 10 days before onset of menstruation, when both estrogen and progesterone were high; and days 3 to 5 after onset of menstruation, when levels of all sex hormones are low. (Days 1 and 2 were avoided because some women experience physical discomfort then.) Half the women (we studied 45 in all) were tested first in the

high or midluteal phase, and half in the low, or menstrual phase. About 6 weeks elapsed between the two test periods.

We used tests that had previously shown sex differences, either in overall score or in brain organization: spatial tasks, perceptual speed tasks, verbal fluency (saying as many words as possible beginning with a particular letter), rapid articulation and speeded manual learning tasks (see illustration). I had found that the latter two, although dependent on the left hemisphere in both men and women, showed a different intrahemispheric organization in the two sexes (see "Male Brain, Female Brain: The Hidden Difference," *Psychology Today,* November 1985). We also administered a mood inventory, since it is known that there are some mood changes throughout the month, though these are usually greatest in the immediate premenstrual period, which we deliberately avoided.

Female Hormones Make "Female" Skills Better, "Male" Skills Worse

The results were definitive. Comparing women with themselves on tests usually done better by women than men, they did significantly better in speeded articulation and manual skill tasks in the high or midluteal phase than in the low phase. Verbal fluency and perceptual speed were also generally better in the high phase.

In contrast, performance on the spatial tests, in which men are usually better, showed the reverse trend: The women did better in the low phase than in the high. This effect was significant for the Rod-and-Frame test, in which the subject simply makes a judgment about whether a rod is vertical or not. Since practice effects from the first to the second session sometimes obscured the finding, Hampson then looked only at the first test-session results of individuals who were in either the high or low phase. This produced a clearer difference between tests favoring males and tests favoring females: The paper-and-pencil spatial tests now also showed a significant enhancement in the low phase.

The fact that scores went in opposite directions on the two types of tasks suggests very strongly that we are seeing more than a generalized change in ability during one phase or the other. The same was true of the mood inventory. We saw no significant changes in mood between the two phases, and only one significant correlation between any of the mood components — which sample, among other things, depression, fatigue and vigor, and performance on the various tasks.

These were exciting findings, but we were concerned that the spontaneous fluctuations of hormones during the menstrual cycle might be secondary effects; perhaps the cognitive changes were due to concomitant fluctuations in other systems.

The Effects of Hormone Therapy

Fortunately, I had already begun to look into the possible effects of exogenous hormones in post-menopausal women. With them, sex hormones don't fluctuate spontaneously but are administered on a regular basis to relieve discomfort during or after menopause and lessen the risk of osteoporosis. Most of the various regimes of hormone therapy now include progesterone along with estrogen. This treatment can raise plasma estradiol levels into the midluteal range of the natural menstrual cycle, and often improves the feeling of well-being—but we know almost nothing of its intellectual effects.

The 33 women we studied were all over 50 years of age and had not menstruated for at least a year. Twenty-two of them were on estrogen alone, the rest on combined estrogen and medroxyprogesterone. They all took estrogen alone (orally) for at least the first 15 days of the month. Some then took progesterone as well for 5 to 10 days. For the rest of the month they took nothing.

We tested them twice, once 10 days after they had begun estrogen (but before any progesterone was taken), and again when they had been off all medication for at least 4 days. To reduce the effect of practice, we tested half of the women first in the "on" phase, and half in the "off" phase, with approximately 6 weeks between testing. Any effects we saw should have been due primarily to estrogen, since the few who took progesterone took it immediately before the off period.

We again gave a variety of tests, including vocabulary to provide a measure of general intelligence; a manual skill task in which a sequence of hand movements had to be carried out quickly on a Manual Sequence Box (see below); an articulatory task—a tongue twister; perceptual speed tests; and two spatial tasks.

The Selective Effects of Estrogen

We found that estrogen affected the motor skills strongly: In the manual task and to a lesser degree the tongue twister, perfor-

mance was significantly better under the "on estrogen" condition than in the off period. On the perceptual speed tasks, one of the comparisons showed improvement under estrogen; on the other there was no effect. On the spatial tasks, there were no significant changes related to hormonal status. The results of these studies confirmed that the effects of estrogen, even when administered orally, were selective, in that not all the speeded tasks were improved, but we did not replicate all the findings from the menstrual study.

One reason for the differences might be that, since exogenous estrogen in post-menopausal women is detectable in plasma even several weeks after treatment has ended, the difference in estrogen level between our so-called on and off phases may be quite small. It may be too small to produce changes in spatial ability, though clearly large enough to produce changes in motor and articulatory skill. That suggests that motor programming skills are more sensitive to fluctuating estrogen levels than is spatial skill. We have some indications from the menstrual study as well that this might be the case.

Another reason for the difference might be that older and younger women have different baseline levels of spatial ability, in which case changes in sex hormones would

not have the same effects. Unfortunately, we didn't use identical spatial tests, so we couldn't compare our two samples.

How Hormones Affect the Brain

We can only guess what mechanism enhances motor skill during high estrogen states, since we have no direct information on what is happening in the brain then. Here again, however, the animal literature is suggestive. Jill Becker and coworkers at the University of Michigan in Ann Arbor found that female rats were better at walking a narrow plank in the estrus phase of their cycle, when estrogen and progesterone levels are high. She also found that implanting estradiol directly into the basal ganglia enhanced performance. The precise mechanism for this change has still to be worked out, but Becker suggested that estrogen might induce changes in the firing of dopamine neurons. And estrogen may affect other brain areas as well.

In our human studies, estrogen seems to have a strongly positive effect on functions which we know depend critically on the left hemisphere. Performance on the Manual Sequence Box and on speech articulation tasks requires an intact left hemisphere. What's more, these functions are carried out differently in the left hemi-

How Hormones Affect Manual Dexterity

Because women tend to have better manual dexterity than men, we decided to investigate what aspects of dexterity might be affected by fluctuations in estrogen levels. The aspect most sensitive to estrogen turned out to be organizing several movements into a pattern, which we measure using the Manual Sequence Box (below).

The task is to press the top button with your index finger; pull the verti-

cal handle toward you with all four fingers; and press down on the bottom bar with the thumb. Each woman did a learning sequence and five timed trials during both her high-estrogen and low-estrogen periods. On average, each woman did markedly better with high estrogen levels. Women undergoing hormone therapy also did the task faster when they were on estrogen.

sphere of males and females: The left anterior part of the brain is more critical in females, suggesting that estrogen somehow facilitates activity of the frontal regions, of the left hemisphere, or of both.

Further evidence that the left hemisphere may be favored by high estrogen levels comes from Hampson's finding that the right-ear superiority on dichotic listening is increased during the preovulatory estrogen surge that occurs in normally cycling women. We are currently also investigating the possibility that frontal and posterior regions of the brain are differently affected by estrogen levels.

People often ask why hormonal changes affect adult abilities, since such effects would seem to serve no useful function. We don't really know the answer, but it seems reasonable that, whatever hormonal mechanism originally establishes these individual variations, it may simply continue to be sensitive to changes in the critical hormones throughout life. Although the fluctuations may merely be ripples on a preestablished baseline, they are sufficient to suggest that the adult human brain continues to be sensitive to such influences.

Hormones Affect Men as Well as Women

The question of how androgens and estrogen interact, both in originally organizing male and female behaviors, and in their adult effects, is being studied extensively. Roger Gorski of the University of California, Los Angeles, has shown that estradiol

For most women, normal hormone fluctuations don't affect everyday life.

produces some aspects of brain sexual differentiation related to perinatal testosterone. Bruce McEwen at Rockefeller University, however, points out that estrogen can have different effects in male and female brains. Perhaps different programs are activated by the same hormone.

We need a great deal more information about the basic action of sex hormones before we can work out their specific contributions to cognitive patterns. For example, knowing the current blood levels of testosterone in either men or women is just one step in a chain of information which ultimately must include how much testosterone reaches the brain, what proportion is converted to estradiol, where the estradiol has its effects, and so on.

How Important Are These Differences?

What do our studies on the apparent fluidity of certain abilities mean for the day-to-day functioning of women? While the fluctuations we find are interesting and significant—they tell us something about how cognitive ability patterns are formed—they are not large. Also, up to now they seem most consistent for the kinds of things women already do well. So for most women, they aren't an important factor. Of course, women vary widely in their sensitivity to these influences. For some, the changes may make them feel clumsier at some periods of the month than at others.

It's important to remember that we studied women because it was easy to do. It turns out that men also undergo hormonal fluctuations, both daily and seasonal. We are looking into both types, encouraged by a study of wild voles by Steven Gaulin at the University of Pittsburgh and Randy FitzGerald at Montclair State College. They have found that sex differences on a maze task appear only in polygynous species of these rodents where males must roam a larger territory to find females. This sexually dimorphic type of vole has seasonal fluctuations in territorial range, with the range being larger in the mating season. If there is a parallel effect in humans, we might be able to detect seasonal variations in men for certain spatial abilities. This would give us another important link in understanding how individual differences in abilities evolved.

MAN'S GREATEST REFLEX

The human sexual response of erection involves your brain, your nervous system, your hormones and your spine.

Ben Pesta

Associate Publisher, Men's Fitness

Most of us don't care how erections work, as long as they work. Unfortunately, sometimes they don't. And sometimes they spring to life on occasions that might best be described as *inopportune.* If you've ever wondered what makes your erection such an imperfectly domesticated animal, read on.

Erections are completely controlled by blood pressure. Your penis contains three structures with a high concentration of blood vessels: two *corpora cavernosa* and one *corpus spongiosum.* When the sphincter surrounding the major artery leading to the penis dilates, blood flows into the capillaries of these bodies. The vessels leading *from* the penis can't handle the increased blood flow. Blood accumulates in your penis. *Voilà!* You have yourself a genuine blue-veiner.

That's *what* happens. *Why* it happens is a little—make that a lot—more complicated, involving your brain and the rest of your nervous system, your hormones and your spine.

Your erection is a reflex. That is, your nervous system signals that sphincter to dilate. Like most reflexes, it operates in a more or less automatic arc controlled by the spinal cord. This is why some people with spinal cord injuries can't get erections. This is also why you can get them from tactile stimulation in your sleep. This is also why, if you're 14 years old, you can get a spontaneous erection during algebra.

Your testosterone levels influence your erection by acting on motoneuron cells in your spinal cord. Most men's testosterone levels are highest when they awake in the morning—another reason why you may wake up throbbing. Neurologists often advise older men to have sex in the morning if they've been having trouble sustaining erections.

The human sexual response involves both parts of your autonomic nervous system, the nerves controlling your body's "automatic" functions. The *sympathetic* nervous system you already know as the system that operates the "adrenalin" (actually epinephrine) reaction, the "fight or flight" reaction that makes your heart pump faster and harder when danger is near. The *parasympathetic* system, mediated through the vagus nerve, releases the neurotransmitter acetylcholine to calm things down and return your body to a "normal" state when danger is past.

You may be surprised to learn that it's the parasympathetic nervous system that controls erections. The sympathetic system controls *orgasm.* When you think of it, this makes a great deal of sense. The sympathetic reaction sends blood to the heart and limbs to get you ready to flee. An erection requires blood in your penis, not in your legs. When it's time for your orgasm, the sympathetic nervous system kicks in, your blood pressure increases and your heart starts to pound. Once you reach orgasm, the veins around your penis dilate, blood flows out, and you get what is called *involution:* You shrink.

This process explains why stimulant

> Through the help of a kind and caring partner, anxiety is reduced and many erection problems can be solved. Communication is the key.

drugs such as cocaine increase sexual desire while interfering with the erection process. They stimulate the sympathetic nervous system, which means that they keep blood away from the penis. The worst drug of all, of course, is alcohol, which acts first as a stimulant, keeping you from *getting* an erection, and then as a sedative, keeping you from *using* it.

You can easily see why worry and anxiety make erections harder to get and harder to sustain. They trigger the sympathetic reaction, the heart pumps faster, and blood runs out of the penis and through your arms and legs. (This is also why worry makes you feel tired. Your heart works harder.) A sudden shift of attention can also activate the sympathetic system and cost you your erection.

So if this whole process is a reflex, why can you get erections by sitting around watching videotapes, or even just thinking nasty thoughts? The answer is that of course the brain gets involved in this process, too.

Conscious thought, even the kind of thinking you do while reading *Hustler* or watching an X-rated video, takes place in the brain's higher cortical centers. Sexual behavior, on the other hand, is controlled by the *hypothalamus,* a primitive part of the brain that's concerned with maintaining basic homeostatic and autonomic physical functions, such as breathing and heart rate.

These two parts of the brain communicate via the *limbic system.* The limbic system is a series of *gyri,* or convoluted ridges, that form a roughly shaped ring around the brain stem. This system includes the cingulate gyrus, the parahippocampal gyrus, the subcallosal gyrus, the fornix, the hippocampus and the amygdala.

The limbic system is a primitive system. That is, it evolved early enough in prehistory that all mammals have it. It is involved in our processes of emotional behavior and memory.

Here's the connection between sexy thoughts and sexual reactions—such as erections. Brain chemicals released by thought processes in the higher cortices affect the cingulate gyrus, which sends information to the hippocampal formation. The hippocampal formation processes this information and sends it through the fornix to the part of the hypothalamus called the *preoptic* (because it's located behind the optic tract) *nucleus.*

The hypothalamus is the origin of most human drives. Neurologists say that it controls the "four f's": fear, feeding, fighting and, uh, sexual urges. *We don't know exactly what happens there,* but we do know that the limbic system activates the parasympathetic nervous system to produce erections via the muscular and circulatory mechanism you read about above.

You can see that the neural and mechanical circuitry required for erections is so complicated that it's no wonder all systems sometimes don't fire in perfect and orderly sequence. In fact, it's a damned good thing we don't have to *think* about these processes, or there'd be no erections at all.

There are, however, some things you can do to maximize your chances of producing reliable erections in (how's this for a delicate euphemism?) *appropriate circumstances.* Since you need a good, steady flow of blood to your penis, you should get enough aerobic exercise to keep your circulation strong and steady. Hardening of the arteries will restrict blood flow to your penis (along with everywhere else), so you want to keep your diet reasonably low in fat and cholesterol and high in fiber and carbohydrates.

Low blood pressure will make it difficult to produce erections on cue. So will high blood pressure, if you're taking some of the standard prescription drugs such as Inderol. So will diabetes. And so, as you've read, will tension and anxiety, which activate your sympathetic nervous system. If you're experiencing persistent problems with any of these factors, see your urologist. It may be that all you need is to change your lifestyle to make it healthier and more active.

What do you do about the opposite problem: unwanted erections at inappropriate times? Our advice is: Think about getting your taxes audited. If that doesn't do it, think about Roseanne Barr. And if *that* doesn't do it, think about having Roseanne Barr audit your taxes.

Women and Sexuality

New research helps explain and treat the failure of women to achieve orgasm.

Melvin Konner

Melvin Konner, M.D., the author of "Why the Reckless Survive and Other Secrets of Human Nature," *is an anthropologist and a physician.*

The pulse quickens, the eyes become dilated and unfocused. . . . With some the breath comes in gasps, others become breathless . . . the powers of movement and feeling are thrown into disorder: the limbs, in the throes of convulsions and sometimes cramps, are either out of control or stretched and stiffened like bars of iron: with jaws clenched and teeth grinding together, some are so carried away by erotic frenzy that they forget the partner of their sexual ecstasy and bite the shoulder that is rashly exposed to them till they draw blood." Thus, the French physician Felix Riboud, in 1855, on orgasm. It is a description that science has improved upon in detail, but not in vividness. It has been described more favorably; yet our own postmodern reading of this passage makes us almost miss its unpleasantness— so persuaded are we of the value of this intense experience.

The source of the unpleasantness in this passage is perhaps the loss of control and hint of danger. And since the highest risks of danger here—even today, with the availability of birth control—are those associated with pregnancy and childbearing, it might not seem surprising that the failure to achieve this experience is more common in women. However, there is a substantial body of new research that explains the failure more specifically and offers significant help in treating it.

It is as if the prevalence of orgasmic failure among women were a kind of evolutionary destiny. Men, to have offspring, must have orgasms; and since they don't get pregnant, their risk in doing so is minimal. Women, conversely, can get pregnant perfectly well without orgasms, even though they face the consequences of intercourse pretty much on their own.

In Riboud's time there was little concern about or medical attention paid to the problem of orgasmic failure in women. Even a generation later, with the publication of Richard von Krafft-Ebing's "Psychopathia Sexualis"—the book that ushered in the rational study of sex—women's problems were given short shrift. Of eight cases of anesthesia sexualis (absence of sexual feeling) only one is a woman. In discussing her condition Krafft-Ebing turns to hearsay: "I have often had occasion to hear complaints from husbands about this . . . the wives have always proved to be neuropathic ab origine [from birth]."

The young Sigmund Freud (whom Krafft-Ebing didn't trust) may have taken a cue from this assessment; and he carried it to its logical conclusion—effectively defining all women as sexually impaired. In 1920, he wrote that "little girls . . . feel themselves heavily handicapped by the absence of a large visible penis. . . . the clitoris in the girl, moreover, is in every way equivalent during childhood to the penis; it is a region of especial excitability in which auto-erotic satisfaction is achieved. In the transition to womanhood very much depends upon the early and complete relegation of this sensitivity from the clitoris over to the vaginal orifice. In those women who are sexually anesthetic, as it is called, the clitoris has stubbornly retained this sensitivity." Thus, if a woman had clitoral orgasms, indeed, *because* she had them, she was considered sexually anesthetic.

Fortunately, this view did not reach most of the world's women. But it forced a generation or two of the generally better educated ones into a kind of stressful and unsatisfactory Pro-crustean bed. A famous question of Freud's was the petulant: "What does a woman want?" One of the clearest messages to emerge from the far more scientific sex research that has been conducted since his time is that Freud's answers were wrong.

In studies that in many ways remain the best research ever done on female sexuality, Alfred C. Kinsey interviewed 2,700 women throughout the United States in the early 1950's and found that, of the married women, 36 percent had never experienced orgasm when they were single. This contrasted with 99 percent of men having had it regularly by their late teens. Sexual encounters in which women did not experience orgasm declined gradually during a 20-year period of marriage, to 15 percent. Eighty-four percent of the women Kinsey interviewed who had masturbated achieved orgasm by massaging the clitoris and labia. Researchers assessed anatomical sensitivity in hundreds of women: 98 percent were sensitive to light touch on the clitoris, but only 14 percent on the walls of the vagina. Thus, Freud's "mature" transition, Kinsey concluded, was a biological impossibility: there is "no evidence that the vagina is ever the sole source of arousal, or even the primary source of erotic arousal in any female."

YET THESE OBSERVATIONS made little impact until the mid 60's, when William H. Masters and Virginia E. Johnson ushered in the era of direct physiological study of sex. Their panoply of electrodes, gauges and intravaginal cameras produced a precise description of both arousal and orgasm for nearly 700 men and women and provided the basis of modern textbook accounts. All orgasms, including those that occurred during vaginal penetration, appeared, in fact, to result from either direct or indirect stimulation of the clitoris.

Men and women could be aroused equally quickly, and (romantic accounts aside) in surprisingly similar ways. But there were also marked differences. The time from arousal to orgasm was consistently shorter in men than in women, and, unlike men, many women were capable of remarkable feats of multiple orgasm, often as their partners were drifting toward sleep. The orgasm itself was essentially the same in both sexes. In each it centered on one organ, and in this regard Freud was right: the clitoris *was* a homologue of the penis. As for vaginal orgasm, it did not appear to exist. Some women strongly disagreed; one was Doris Lessing, in "The Golden Notebook."

Recent studies show that most women can have orgasms from vaginal stimulation alone. There does not, however, appear to be any convincing evidence that a trigger on the forward vaginal wall, the so-called G spot, exists. Regardless of these details, the most common female sexual complaints continue to be inhibited sexual desire and orgasm, as shown in a comprehensive review by Sharon G. Nathan, associate director of the human sexuality program at New York Hospital-Cornell Medical Center. In most studies, at least 20 percent of women report that they have orgasms only sometimes, rarely or never, and Nathan writes that it "can be said with confidence . . . that 5 to 15 percent of women are anorgasmic."

Researchers have news, too, for many men. About two-thirds of adult women say they have faked orgasm. In one study of 805 nurses published in the Journal of Sex & Marital Therapy, many said they had done so frequently, especially in casual relationships. Men, for their part, are not always quite as dumb as they look: they sometimes find it expedient to pretend that they are fooled. But in any case, this adds up to a massive communications failure — and not a little sexual frustration for women. The old idea that women can enjoy sex without orgasm is, fortunately, believed by fewer and fewer people; yet one result is an intensity of demand for performance that can make sex more a job than a joy.

So what to do? Being human, we can't throw up our hands and accept a dismal evolutionary discordance. Consequently, we create a revolution. Over the protests of traditionalists who claim psychologists distort love and destroy privacy, sex lives are coaxed into therapy. Perhaps the greatest success in the still relatively young field of sex therapy has been in solving problems of premature ejaculation, through the use of concentration techniques, for example. Much less success has been reported with inhibited female orgasm, especially if defined as inability to achieve orgasm during intercourse, and it therefore might be right to redefine the goal.

Natural history provides some clues: anorgasmia — not having had an orgasm at all — is overcome by many women without therapy and with time and experience. Nevertheless, masturbation, an important path of learning in women's sexuality, remains taboo among a significant number of women. An article by sociologist John H. Gagnon showed that 40 percent of college-age women have never done it. Some health experts have publicly recommended it, but they apparently have had little effect so far. Homosexual women provide another clue: studies by Emily M. Coleman, Peter W. Hoon and Emily F. Hoon in The Journal of Sex Research find them more sexually satisfied — with more frequent sex and more frequent orgasms — than heterosexual women. Their greater tenderness, patience and knowledge of the female body are said to be the reasons.

Barbara L. Andersen, while at the University of Iowa, reviewed 40 studies of treatments of inhibited orgasm and found that the most successful therapies included the encouragement of masturbation, followed by efforts to transfer this newfound knowledge to relationships. Talk therapies also help. In fact, studies in the last three years have shown *both* that general couple therapy has a positive effect on sex and that sex therapy has a positive effect on a couple's overall relationship.

It is extraordinary how much ignorance there is among consenting adults. It is not rare, for instance, to find married couples who think they are having intercourse — not orgasm, intercourse — but are actually falling rather short of it. The husband of one such couple, having been duly instructed by a physician, came back a few days later and without explanation punched the doctor in the nose.

Almost equal ignorance motivates Congressional opposition to sex research — for example, Representative William E. Dannemeyer, a California Republican who is a member of the House Subcommittee on Health and the Environment, ridiculed such research in a letter to Science magazine last June. He and others like him are apparently unable to grasp that these intimate matters affect our emotional and physical health, including our risk of contracting AIDS and other sexually transmitted diseases. We urgently need a new national survey comparable to Kinsey's; the National Institutes of Health is ready to undertake it, and politicians should get out of the way. Studies of sexual satisfaction and sex therapy, for their part, may play a role in reducing risky sexual practices.

ULTIMATELY, OF COURSE, the mind is the organ of orgasm. Julian M. Davidson, a physiologist at Stanford University, has recently recognized this with his "bipolar hypothesis." Deep in the brain a convergence occurs: something must happen to touch the soul — or the high brain centers — while something else is touching the proper part of the body. This mental effect need not be noble; men and women, we now know, respond equally to pornography, as long as it does not portray the subjugation of women. Yet love also has something to do with it. And poetry. And tenderness.

It is stunning to remember that so lyric and gentle a novel as D. H. Lawrence's "Lady Chatterley's Lover" was banned in the United States just a few decades ago. This is how the lover, Mellors — his name echoes the word for "better" in Romance languages — is said to have brought about a climax in the Lady: "He had drawn her close and with infinite delicate pleasure was stroking the full, soft, voluptuous curve of her loins. She did not know which was his hand and which was her body, it was like a full bright flame, sheer loveliness. Everything in her fused down in passion, nothing but that." We should recall, as we pursue our goal of simultaneous copulatory orgasm, that this very superior, very masculine lover effected the magic with his hand; that their joining was suffused with an almost unreal grace and tenderness, and, not incidentally, that he loved her.

When Female Behavior Contributes to Premature Ejaculation

Both partners' behavior requires evaluation in the context of their entire relationship before the problem can be solved.

Constance A. Moore, MD, and Kathryn Kotrla, MD

Constance A. Moore is Director, Human Sexuality Program, and Kathryn Kotrla is Psychiatry Resident, Baylor College of Medicine, Houston.

Premature ejaculation (PE), one of the most common sexual dysfunctions, has been traditionally considered to be an exclusively male problem. Only in recent years, as treatment has become more effective, have researchers explored the key role played by the female partner in contributing to or perpetuating this dysfunction.

Premature ejaculation is best defined as a lack of voluntary control over ejaculation. Causative theories have generally focused exclusively on male factors. Early theory attributed PE to a disordered mother-son relationship, with unconscious rage against women on the man's part and fear of castration in the vagina.[1] PE would serve to defile the sexual partner or deprive her of pleasure.[2]

As more effective behavioral treatment became available for PE, however, other etiologies of the disorder were proposed. Masters and Johnson, for example, have attributed PE to learning. They believe that men learn to ejaculate quickly because of rushed, stressful initial sexual encounters. This early behavior then persists.[1-3] Other studies have shown that such conditioning may also occur in response to a partner who dislikes sexual intercourse and wants to end it quickly.[1,3,4]

Alternatively, PE has been described as a failure of the man to recognize the physical sensations immediately preceding his orgasm. Since he is unaware of impending orgasm, he cannot control ejaculation.[1,2,5] Male anxiety about sexual performance is also considered important in initiating and perpetuating such dysfunctions.[3,4]

With the development of the "stop-start" and "squeeze" techniques for treating PE (see box), the female partner's participatory role is now recognized. Numerous researchers cite the woman's cooperation as crucial to the successful treatment of PE.[1,3,5-7] Similarly, marital problems and tension between a couple, sexual or otherwise, are well known to cause or aggravate sexual dysfunction.[2,3-5,7]

It has now become clear that women can encourage and reinforce PE in their male partners through words and actions that occur during sexual intercourse, and through other communications about sex, including those that

 From *Medical Aspects of Human Sexuality*, September 1989, pp. 42, 44, 46, 48.

"Squeeze" and "stop-start" techniques

The "squeeze" and the "stop-start" techniques are a graduated series of practice exercises used to help the man gain control over the timing of ejaculation. Usually the man is told to begin with masturbation, concentrate on genital sensation, and when he is near the point of ejaculation, either stop masturbating or squeeze the glans area (whichever method is most effective for him) until the urge to ejaculate is gone. He then begins self-stimulation again. He practices in sets of three and reaches climax on the fourth period of stimulation. The next step is to do the exercises with his partner providing manual stimulation and finally to do them with intercourse.

deal with the relationship but do not refer specifically to sex.

Specific female behaviors that cause PE

A literature survey of sexual roles in PE reveals a variety of maneuvers women use to speed up sexual intercourse.

"Hurry up and finish" process. Women may convey this attitude during lovemaking with direct and disparaging remarks expressing a lack of interest in or distaste for sex.

Sexual anxiety. Women who are apprehensive about intercourse, or who experience pain on vaginal penetration, may convey this anxiety nonverbally by sexual withdrawal, passivity, or fearfulness. The man often responds to the woman's cues and learns to ejaculate quickly.

Enhancement of male arousal. Some women cause PE by using techniques that heighten the man's sexual arousal, thereby hastening ejaculation. For example, a woman may first bring her partner close to orgasm during foreplay through oral or manual stimulation of the penis. He then may ejaculate almost immediately

on penetration. Or, the woman may increase her pelvic movements at the time of penetration or during intercourse—contributing to the man's loss of ejaculatory control. She may also stimulate the man by indicating her increasing level of arousal with vocalizations, a change in breathing patterns, or intense caresses. These cues may prompt him to reach orgasm more quickly.

Case 1. A woman who rushes her partner through intercourse. Beth, age 27, entered individual psychotherapy four years ago for nonsexual problems. About two years into therapy, she began talking in depth about her sexuality. She described herself as very sexually responsive, frequently fantasizing about sex and masturbating once or twice a week. Beth also described herself as rapidly orgasmic and multiorgasmic. With masturbation she could reach orgasm within 5–10 seconds; with intercourse in about 30 seconds. This capacity had posed a problem with some partners because she was sexually satisfied after a few minutes of sexual activity and then wanted only to relax and cuddle, while her partner wanted to continue inter-

course. She talked freely about how she had encouraged a few sexual partners to ejaculate more quickly.

Beth's practice was to learn what type of sexual stimulation was most arousing to her partner during foreplay, which, in the case of her current partner, was fellatio. She would try to bring him almost to orgasm and then suggest intercourse, usually in the "missionary" position. As he would begin to penetrate her, she would signal her quick arousal and anticipation by vocalizations and by thrusting movements of the pelvis. She was aware that her action had a stimulating effect on her partner but didn't feel manipulative because of her own high level of arousal.

The first few times Beth responded this way, her partner ejaculated approximately one to two minutes after she reached orgasm. She recalled that he had apologized for not lasting longer, but she let him know that she was very pleased with their lovemaking. Soon, they developed this pattern as their usual style of intercourse, and, according to Beth, they were both very satisfied. Each was able to reach orgasm quickly and then enjoy afterplay together. Beth said that she had developed a similar style of lovemaking with a few other sexual partners.

Comment: From a psychodynamic standpoint, the importance this patient attached to her partner's reaching orgasm quickly allowed her to feel more desirable. Also, since she was so rapidly orgasmic, she felt lonely and vulnerable in being highly aroused if her partner was not. Yet she was satisfied after her quickly attained orgasm(s) and disliked prolonged intercourse beyond that.

Sexual communications other than during intercourse

When a couple talks about their sex life in a nonsexual setting, such discussions can influence subsequent lovemaking. This most often occurs during an argument about some other topic. For example, the man may complain about the woman's spending habits, and she responds with disparaging remarks about his sexual abilities. She may berate her partner for not being manly enough or for being selfish or uncaring. She may blame him directly for her own lack of responsiveness or frustration. The result is a vicious circle. Increased male anxiety leads to continued PE. This, in turn, fuels the woman's frustration and anger, resulting in more derogatory, anxiety-provoking remarks about his inadequate performance.

Arguments of this kind can arise from the woman's fear of her own sexuality. She may unconsciously promote the man's sexual failure to enhance her sense of superiority and power and to maintain control in the relationship. These disputes over sex sometimes transform the bedroom into a psychological battlefield.

Case 2. Premature ejaculation causes termination of a relationship. Anthony, a 35-year-old man, had never had a sexual relationship prior to meeting his female partner, Debra, 18 months previously. Debra, age 27, had been married and divorced twice and was sexually experienced. Her second husband had been a very satisfying sexual partner but had often bullied and berated her. She encouraged a sexual relationship with Anthony after a few months of dating, and they made five or six attempts at coitus. Each time, Anthony ejaculated quickly upon penetration. Several days after the last sexual attempt, and during an argument about her smoking, Debra called a halt to coitus and suggested he seek help.

Anthony arrived at his therapist's office alone. During this meeting he portrayed himself as a willing but inept partner. He

> **"Some women cause PE by using techniques that heighten the man's sexual arousal, thereby hastening ejaculation."**

blamed himself for the problem and defended Debra's right to a better sexual relationship. During her only individual meeting with the therapist, Debra was adamant that she would not participate in sex therapy with Anthony, saying, "I'm not his teacher."

In three visits to the office, Anthony talked about his relationship with Debra, his view of himself as inept, his sexual concerns, and his wish to learn techniques for retaining ejaculatory control. He canceled the next two appointments and did not appear again for eight weeks. When he returned, he had begun a sexual relationship with someone else. This new lover was happy to help him gain ejaculatory control; after three sessions with his new partner and the therapist (and a number of coital attempts), Anthony was able to maintain intercourse for four or five minutes before ejaculation.

Comment: This case is open to several interpretations about what led to Anthony's clinical improvement: experience, education, discussion of sexual fears. Debra, his first partner, did not want his PE to improve and therefore fought against treatment. Anthony himself was convinced that a more supportive, less demanding partner was the solution.

The relationship at large

A troubled relationship often lies at the root of PE and other sexual problems. While a woman may not specifically demean a man's sexual performance, she may be generally hostile. For example, she may complain about his personality or the lack of time spent with her, or have myriad other criticisms. At the same time, she may be positively involved during their sexual activity together. In a relationship in which personal problems are at best dealt with only indirectly, the man may respond to the woman's verbal attacks by expressing his hostility through sexual dysfunction such as PE. In this type of situation, he uses his dysfunction as a means of exerting control in the couple's struggle for power.

Case 3. A woman demands greater sexual fulfillment. Steve and Cindy, both in their late 30s, presented for treatment of Steve's PE. They had been married for 16 years. Steve had always lacked ejaculatory control (with Cindy and with other sexual partners prior to marriage). Cindy had not complained about this until after the birth of their third child two years earlier. She then found she was developing greater interest in her own sexual fulfillment.

It was soon evident that Steve's compulsive nature played a role in his sexual dysfunction. His life seemed to center on lists and schedules, and he had trouble slowing down for lovemaking. Sensate focus exercises and then the squeeze technique, with Cindy manually stimulating her husband, were prescribed. The squeeze technique failed dismally, even though Cindy had been very supportive and understanding during the exercises.

After talking with Steve, it became apparent that he was angry and confused that Cindy was so supportive in helping him develop a relaxed pace with intercourse while, at the same time, making numerous "jabs" about his time-clock approach to the rest of life. Cindy agreed to refrain from these criticisms for the time being, and Steve was counseled on how to slow down his busy schedule. The PE resolved briefly, but then returned when he took up his list-making and, again, Cindy returned to her criticism of it.

Comment: Cindy had been content with or resigned to accepting poor sexual relations during the first 14–16 years of marriage. When she demanded change, the couple's routine and the power balance in their relationship shifted. Her stored-up anger at Steve and his annoying habits made it difficult for her to stop criticism in the nonsexual arena. She could be supportive of him in bed as long as she was free to criticize him in other ways.

Conclusion

A woman may contribute to PE in her male partner in numerous ways, both in and out of bed. When a couple presents with such a complaint, the problem requires evaluation in the context of their entire relationship, taking into account conscious and unconscious contributing factors in both partners.

References

1. Levine SB: PE: Some thoughts about its pathogenesis. *J Sex Marital Ther* 1(4):326, 1975.
2. Stanley E: Premature ejaculation. *Br Med J* 282:1521, 1981.
3. Wabrek AJ, Wabrek CJ: Premature ejaculation. *Conn Med* 41(4):214, 1977.
4. Williams W: Secondary premature ejaculation. *Aust NZ J Psychiatry* 18:333, 1984.
5. Kaplan HS: *The Evaluation of Sexual Disorders*. New York, Brunner/Mazel, 1983.
6. Cooper AJ: Disorders of sexual potency in the male: A clinical and statistical study of some factors related to short-term prognosis. *Br J Psychiatry* 115:709, 1969.
7. Hawton K, Catalan J: Prognostic factors in sex therapy. *Behav Res Ther* 24(4):377, 1986.

Men Who Fake Orgasm

It's absolutely true—men fake it too! But how? And should you stop them?

Trudy Culross

Women have been faking orgasm forever on the principle that it's okay to fool some of the people some of the time—especially when you've reached the end of a long, trying day and sleep is just an anti-climax away. But has it ever occurred to you that your man might also be faking it?

I refer not to those moments when, thanks to one vodka too many, your lover's willing spirit is ambushed by his flagging flesh. I am more concerned with those men who insist after lovemaking that the earth moved for them too, when in reality it registered zero on their personal Richter scale.

According to Sue Wood, a sex therapist, men do simulate orgasm, and they usually fake it for one of three reasons.

The first is when the female partner comes to orgasm quickly, after which she is likely to lose interest in sex and her man is left thinking, "I'm just using her now." Many men are sensitive enough to feel bad about this. And they are often uncomfortably aware of their partner's sudden loss of enthusiasm, which could mean the end of their erection. So, given this situation, many men prefer to end things by pretending they've reached a climax.

The second reason is that some men suffer from what experts call retarded ejaculation. This is a sexual dysfunction in which a man reaches a state of sexual arousal and excitement but is unable to cross the threshold into orgasm. As a result, he is capable of going on and on—something his partner may not appreciate.

"In this instance," says Wood, "a man will prefer to fake orgasm, particularly in a new relationship, when any indication that he is in any way unusual or demanding may jeopardize everything.

"The fact is that such a man is only rarely—and sometimes never—able to ejaculate and his problem is almost always psychological."

The third possibility is that the man is suffering from something called retrograde ejaculation.

"With this problem, everything appears to go well during sex. Sperm is released from the testicles and proceeds to the prostate, where it comes to something not unlike a T-junction. At this point, the ejaculate should travel down through the urethra to be dispersed externally. However, if there is a problem with the prostate, the ejaculate may run back into the bladder, and the man—who feels as if he has had an orgasm and ejaculated—has nothing to show for it. So, rather than admit to his partner that something is wrong, a man with this problem may prefer to fake an ejaculation. These men usually don't realize that a very minor operation can usually put things right again."

Emission Impossible

Still surprised by the notion that men find it necessary to fake ejaculation at all, I couldn't help wonder how they managed to fool their womenfolk. Surely there are signs, physical proof, that a man has ejaculated?

Not so, says Wood.

"The mistaken idea persists that men have sex, therefore men must ejaculate. In the face of this demand, men feel obliged to complete the sexual function and feel an enormous sense of failure if they don't. Which is why some of them will go to great lengths to cover up the fact—everything from the sound effects during a feigned orgasm to the ritual cleansing with tissues afterward. And it isn't so difficult to convince women that the act has been satisfactorily completed. If you consider

that the average ejaculation is between four and six milliliters of fluid and the average teaspoon holds five milliliters, you can see that the tangible signs of orgasm aren't so obvious. Also, during lovemaking, there is usually an emission of fluid from the man's Cowper's gland. This does not contain semen and is designed to facilitate cleansing of the urethra before ejaculation, but this extra fluid can further confuse the female partner, who creates a great deal of fluid and mucus of her own."

So the "how" of faking orgasm for men seems quite straightforward. But the "why" is much more complex. According to Wood, there are many reasons.

"Some men do it partly to protect their partner's feelings, since their failure to ejaculate could make her feel that she wasn't particularly desirable. And some men fake it partly to protect their own egos, since a failure to ejaculate is regarded as not very macho. These days, people are much more informed about sex, and the more you know, the more you worry. Now that everyone's sex life is open to discussion, we have other performances to measure our own by. Inevitably, some people are going to feel inadequate. And men find it hard to admit that they can't perform."

Actually, for some couples, the man's failure to reach orgasm may not initially be regarded as a problem at all. Especially at the beginning of a relationship, when—as in the case of retarded ejaculation—the man is seen as some kind of tireless superstud who can make love night and day without losing control. But even this palls eventually.

"Sooner or later, the novelty wears off, with one or both partners becoming tired of these sexual bouts that lead

Reprinted from *Cosmopolitan*, February 1990, pp. 84, 90-91.

pretations for this behavior, a man's tendency to fake orgasm usually signifies a desire to withhold himself from his partner. "The man may appear to be emotionally giving, but on a subconscious level, there is frequently a lack of trust or even a deeply felt resentment. Something—or someone—has inflicted emotional damage somewhere in his past, and he is still reacting to it.

"I have had one sad case of a man who never ejaculated. Over a period of counseling, we discovered that he had been frequently punished as a child for wetting the bed and for other nocturnal emissions, with the result that he was incapable of 'letting go' as an adult. And this was a problem that persisted even when he was encouraged to go away and masturbate alone and in complete privacy in a darkened room."

A Private Function

Jonathan Pincus, a consulting psychologist, has encountered male clients who admit to faking orgasm. "Why do men do it? Well, orgasm serves a social function, in that it is a convenient way of bringing sex to an end. Couples rarely talk to each other during intercourse, and in fact there can be implied rejection in a partner's admission that he or she has had enough and wants the sex to stop.

"And for too many people, good sex equals orgasm—preferably, several special orgasms and at least one each—when in reality, good sex is what pleases and satisfies both partners, whether they experience orgasm or not.

"As to why some men can't achieve orgasm, I would say that it is a psychological rather than a physical problem. Sometimes there is a deep-rooted fear of losing control, and this is a pathological condition. Such a man is frequently bossy, manipulative, and unable not to be in charge. So it follows that he may have difficulty reaching orgasm, since this state brings with it a level of vulnerability and temporary loss of control that he might find unacceptable.

"On the other hand, retarded orgasm, or the inability to reach orgasm and ejaculate, is often the result of some deep underlying anger that the man is unable to express verbally."

"Often the man is angry with his partner because of something he *perceives* she has done or some offense he thinks she has caused him. Not only may his perception of her actions be incorrect, he may also be quite unaware of his negative feelings toward her. However, they manifest themselves during the sexual act, when, by feigning orgasm, he effectively denies his partner complete sexual satisfaction. He is then punishing her without appearing to be at fault. Passive aggression, if you like. So if a client came to me and said that he was faking orgasm, I think it would be very important to get down to the question 'Why?' "

Not surprisingly, most men are extremely reluctant to talk about this problem, but I found one who was prepared to describe his feelings if he could remain anonymous.

"I don't fake orgasms as a matter of habit," he says. "Most of the time sex is no problem. But there are occasions when I do fake them, and as far as I know, my wife has no idea.

"When it does happen, it's always under a very specific set of circumstances. I've usually been drinking quite a lot; often we've just arrived home very late after a party or something. I have no problems getting an erection, or keeping it, but on these occasions I know full well after a few minutes of making love that whatever we do, there isn't the remotest possibility of an orgasm. It simply isn't going to happen. It's a bit like when you think you're going to sneeze but then you suddenly realize that your nose is playing games with you.

"It becomes a vicious circle; orgasm is very much a mental thing, and if you embark on a sex session knowing that you're not going to have an orgasm, it becomes very hard to maintain your enthusiasm.

"That's why I began to fake orgasms, because otherwise we'd go on all night and my wife would become increasingly despondent and start to wonder if it was something she was doing wrong. Sex is very much geared toward orgasm. It's important to me that my wife has an orgasm (though she often insists that it

isn't the be-all and end-all), and it's terribly important to her that I have one.

"So I suppose I started doing it to keep her happy, because she does get quite upset if I don't have an orgasm. And when she gets upset, I start to wonder if she's really enjoying this, going on and on seemingly for hours. And I suppose I also do it to get a bit of peace and quiet, because although sex is pleasurable on these occasions, it can become terribly frustrating and tiring."

Happy Endings

"And I know I'm not the only one who does it," he continued. "When I was a student, I knew one woman who used to call her boyfriend 'the pumper,' because he just used to go on and on for hours without anything happening. This was marvelous at first, but after a while she started to get a bit tired of it. And so did he. And I know for a fact, because he told me, that he started to fake orgasms simply to bring things to a conclusion. She had no idea it was happening.

"As I said, sex is fine ninety-nine percent of the time for me; I have no trouble 'letting go' or anything like that. The other one percent of the time, I fake it. It may be deceitful, but my motives are pure and my intentions are honorable, so there's no harm done."

According to Wood, retarded ejaculation is one of six recognized sexual dysfunctions (one of three in men), but it doesn't account for a sixth of her clients.

"Only about five percent of my male clients admit to this, and even then we normally only uncover it during counseling. What often happens is that many couples seek us out for sex counseling and therapy because either one or both of them has switched off sex. Sometimes men convince themselves that it's because they have lost interest in sex that they aren't climaxing, when in fact it's *because* they aren't climaxing that they lose interest in sex.

"The good news," says Wood, "is that the problem can nearly always be helped once we have traced the source of the anxiety."

Sexuality Attitudes of Black Adults

This study considers the sexuality attitudes of a black middle-class sample (N = 124). Categories assessed include beliefs and attitudes in the following: communication regarding sexuality information, adolescent contraception, adolescent pregnancy, nonmarital intercourse, responsibility for contraception and pregnancy, abortion, pornography, and masturbation. ANOVAs were performed on individual questions and groupings according to sex, age, education, and marital status. Results suggest that the participants are well-informed, moderate, and consistent in their beliefs. Implications of the study are useful for both researchers and practitioners.

Constance A. Timberlake and Wayne D. Carpenter

Constance A. Timberlake is an Associate Professor and immediate past Chair, Department of Child & Family Studies, Syracuse University, Syracuse, NY 13244-1250. Wayne D. Carpenter is a Counselor, Western New England College, Springfield, MA 01119.

In the area of sexuality, liberals and conservatives are often worlds apart. Yet with regard to educating their children, both agree that parents should be the primary sexuality educators (Gordon & Snyder, 1989; Koop, 1988). This is especially true in light of the preponderance of information and concern regarding teen pregnancy. The research described in this article is directed to the family professional. Family professionals have been aggressive in their commitment to enhance the quality of family life by designing and implementing sexuality educational programs, and more thoroughly preparing future family professionals. However, a disproportionate amount of knowledge is inherited and reflects the attitudes, beliefs, and behavior of the "traditional" family which has not, by and large, reflected nor included the full spectrum of the black family (Billingsley, 1988). For example, the literature reflects that the sexuality attitudes of black adults has yet to be an area of study. Family professionals must possess information that is both relevant and current to the population being served, if they are to design and implement programs that will take into consideration nuances that may not exist in the traditional "white" model.

At present, the adolescent pregnancy rate in the United States is twice that of France, England, and Canada; three times that of Sweden; and seven times that of the Netherlands. There

Supported, in part, by the Office of Research and Graduate Studies, Syracuse University.

Key Words: adolescent pregnancy, black sexuality attitudes.

are approximately 1.3 million children now living in the United States with 1.1 million teenage mothers. Two thirds of these children were born to mothers under the age of 18. Black American adolescent females have the highest birthrate among teenagers in the developed world. When compared to white adolescents, black adolescents are four times more likely to give birth to babies from a union of unmarried parents. Of all black births today more than half are born to unwed mothers (Hill, 1989).

Often overlooked are the statistics which indicate that while pregnancy rates for minority teenagers are higher than for white teenagers, the birthrate is increasing for whites while holding relatively stable for minorities (National Center for Health Statistics, 1986). Nevertheless, these statistics are alarming, especially when one considers the long-term effects of adolescent pregnancy on the family.

The quality of family life in the United States is largely determined by education and economic resources. Adolescent parents often suffer in both these areas. Statistics indicate that among all teenagers who give birth; one third of black teen mothers and 45% of white teen mothers will not complete high school (Children's Defense Fund, 1988). An adolescent female loses 2 years of schooling as a consequence of early parenting (BOCES Regional Planning Center, 1987).

When a teen mother or father drops out of school without the skills and resources to earn a decent living, the economic costs are high to both the individual and society. The individual loses potential earning power and often becomes dependent upon society for support. Seventy-five per-

cent of all single mothers under age 25 live in poverty. Women who were teenagers when their child was born, are less than 23 years of age, and are head of households account for two thirds of the young families who live in poverty. Of the children who are poor, 80% are white and 91% are black (Children's Defense Fund, 1988). The Center for Population Options estimates that teenage childbearing cost the United States $16.65 billion in 1985 in Aid to Families with Dependent Children (AFDC), food stamps, and Medicaid benefits (BOCES Regional Planning Center, 1987).

Noting such statistics, it is clear that past and present programs to abate the problem of black adolescent pregnancy have not been effective. Such programs have often neglected to draw on the strengths of the two most important social systems available to blacks: the family and the church (Hill, 1972).

Frazier (1963) noted that the black church has historically been the most important source of support and guidance for blacks and their families, and is a major means of communication in the black community. Yet as important as the black church may be, it is parents that play the most important role in the sexual development of their children. Unaware of the teaching roles they play in such development, parents often avoid direct communication with their children regarding sexuality. However, crucial aspects of sex education are taught indirectly, so that by the time children are 3 or 4 years of age they have received considerable information about sexuality (Darling & Hicks, 1982). Walters and Walters (1983) concur stating, "Throughout childhood, parents and children elicit behaviors and respond to each other in ways that contribute to the form and substance of the growing child's sexual attitudes" (p. 11).

In Fox's (1979) review of the literature on the family's influence upon adolescent sexual behavior, several important points emerge: (a) Not many children receive direct instruction from their parents about sexuality, sexual intercourse, or fertility regulation. (b) Parental verbal communication about sex may forestall or postpone a child's sexual activity. (c) Among those daughters who are sexually active, parental verbal communication appears related to more effective contraceptive practice on the part of the child. Children also gain sexual information from school and peers, but it must be kept in mind that such information always occurs in the context of the attitudes and knowledge that already have been provided by their families (Walters & Walters, 1983).

It is clear that parental attitudes play an important role in the sexual development of children. Ladner (1971) observed that misinformation based on "folk tradition" was often disseminated by mothers and grandmothers. Therefore, she cautioned that individuals who are concerned about adolescent pregnancy broaden their interest to include parents. Fox (1979) suggests that programs likely to be inefficient and ineffective arise from policies which both ignore the familial context of teenage sexual behavior or fail to enlist the familial base of the teenager.

This being the case, some have advocated the critical importance of sex education for *parents* in order to help them be more knowledgeable and effective sexuality teachers (Darling & Hicks, 1982; Staples, 1972; Timberlake & Carpenter, 1986). However, an appreciation of the cultural, ethnic, and preexisting parental attitudes toward sexuality is necessary to develop an effective education program that meets the needs of today's parents and their children. Without such knowledge, there is the risk of developing and implementing educational programs that may attempt to mold differing ethnic groups into idealized models as suggested by Staples (1988).

In partnership with 50 black churches, the authors were interested in developing a model sexuality program for black adults. A literature review revealed a paucity of information regarding sexuality attitudes and beliefs of black adults. It is the purpose of this article to contribute to the literature, knowledge relating to a number of attitudes held by black adults regarding: adolescent birth control and pregnancy, nonmarital intercourse, responsibility for contraception and pregnancy, abortion, pornography, and masturbation.

Method

Initial contact was made with black ministers to secure permission to distribute a questionnaire to their respective parishioners. When permission was received, the researchers delivered packets to the churches for distribution. To increase the size of the sample, the packets were also distributed at the annual conference of the Association of Black Women in Higher Education, Inc., and to parents who had registered for a forthcoming sexuality training program. Thus, this is a nonrandom convenience sample.

The packets included a letter describing the purpose of the survey, the questionnaire, and instructions to complete the questionnaire independently and return the completed questionnaire anonymously via an enclosed stamped envelope. A total of 300 questionnaires were distributed with 124 usable questionnaires returned (41%).

Three fourths of the respondents were female and one fourth were male. Almost one half (46%) were married and living with their spouses; 11% were married and not living with spouse; 16% were divorced; and 3% were widowed. The remaining 24% had never married.

Participants' education was grouped into three categories: some high school to high school graduate (19%), some college to 2-year college graduate (32%), and 4-year college graduate to advanced graduate degree (51%). Annual family income was grouped into four categories: less than $10,000 (8%); $10,000 to $24,999 (29%); $25,000 to $39,999 (26%); and $40,000 or more (37%). Age of participants was grouped into five categories: under 21 years (4%), 21-29 (17%), 30-39 (38%), 40-49 (29%), and 50-59 (12%).

All of the participants had children and/or were the primary child care provider. For the purposes of data analysis, respondents were grouped into four categories: sex, age, education, and marital status. A separate ANOVA was then performed on each of the four categories.

Instrument

The instrument consisted of a questionnaire containing 38 items related to the sexuality beliefs and attitudes of adults. A review of the literature concerning black attitudes and beliefs towards various sexual issues revealed little or no information in this regard. Indeed, most research, until very recently, has focused upon the deviant sexual behavior of blacks (Brown, 1985; French & Wailes, 1982), as opposed to nondeviant behavior, attitudes, and beliefs.

To fill this void items were selected on the basis of areas of concern most frequently raised by black adults who participated in an adult sexuality education program (Timberlake & Carpenter, 1986).

The instrument designed to assess an overview of sexual beliefs and attitudes was subdivided by assigning each of the 38 items into one of the following areas: communication, adolescent birth control, adolescent pregnancy, intercourse, responsibility for birth control and pregnancy, abortion, pornography, and masturbation.

The participants responded to each item by using a 4-point Likert-type scale, reflecting the conservatism of their beliefs. Participants indicated whether they (1) *strongly agreed,* (2) *agreed,* (3) *disagreed,* or (4) *strongly disagreed* with the item statement.

To measure the reliability of the instrument, Cronbach's Alpha was sought. The Cronbach's Alpha is a measure of internal consistency and varies from 0 to 1. When there is no internal consistency in responding to the questions an $\alpha = 0$ is obtained. Whereas, when there is perfect consistency, $\alpha = 1$ is obtained. In the 38 items that were used in this study, Cronbach $\alpha = .94$ was obtained, indicating high internal reliability.

When all eight categories were examined separately, a relatively high internal consistency was established, with the highest being $\alpha = .82$ and the lowest being an $\alpha = .60$. When one takes into consideration the low number of items in each of the categories, these Cronbach Alpha's are acceptable when considering internal consistency.

Participants provided demographic information which included age, sex, marital status, education, current and/or last occupation, and gross income. Participants also provided information regarding the number, sex, and ages of their children.

Results

Do black adults believe in sharing sexual information with children?

57

When the participants of the study were asked questions as to whether they agreed or disagreed in providing children with sexuality information, an overwhelming percentage (95%) of respondents indicated that fathers should discuss sexual issues with both sons and daughters. This same belief held for mothers discussing sexual issues with their sons as well as daughters (98%). Questions raised by children to which parents do not know the answers should not be ignored (98%), and discussion should begin before the child is in first grade (74%). Moreover, 92% do not uphold the myth that increased sexual knowledge leads to sexual activity.

An ANOVA regarding sexual information and communication revealed no differences with respect to sex, education, and marital status. There was a significant difference ($F = 3.93$, $df = 4$, $p \leq .01$) found for age, with those under age 21 being more restrained in sharing sexuality information as compared with those participants 21 years of age and older.

Regarding individual questions, all respondents agreed that it was acceptable for a child under 5 years of age to hear the words "penis" and "vagina." However, those having 4 or more years of college more strongly indicated the acceptability of using such terms with younger children compared to the other two education groups ($p \leq .05$).

How do black adults feel about teenage birth control? Most black adults (74%) do not believe teenagers regularly use contraceptives when engaged in sexual intercourse. Indeed, black adults favor ready availability of contraceptives for sexually active teens and 75% believe that contraceptives should be made available without parental consent. Asked if their own children were to become sexually active, 97% would want him/her to use contraceptives. No statistical differences were found among the four groups.

Within education groups, items 9 and 12 revealed significant differences. Respondents with a high school education or less expressed a more conservative view than persons with 4 or more years of college, believing that access to contraceptives is a major reason for the increase in sexual activity among teenagers ($p \leq .02$) and that sexually active teens regularly use contraceptives ($p \leq .03$).

Within marital groups, significant differences were found in four of the items. Never Marrieds were significant-ly more conservative compared to Married With Spouse with respect to providing ready availability of contraceptives ($p \leq .01$), and the availability of contraceptives without parental consent ($p \leq .02$). Moreover, Never Marrieds compared to Married With Spouse, were more likely to believe that the ease of access to contraceptives promotes sexual activity among teenagers ($p \leq .05$).

All marital groups agreed they would want their sexually active teens to use contraceptives. However, there was a significant difference ($p \leq .01$) between the Married Without Spouse and the Never Marrieds, with the former feeling more strongly in favor of such practice.

What do black adults believe to be the reasons behind teen pregnancy? Poor communication with parents was believed to be a factor in teen pregnancy by 56% of the respondents. Seventy percent of the respondents believed the following *not* to be major factors in teenage pregnancy: involvement in ongoing love relationships, lenient standards of behavior imposed by parents, low self-esteem, or a wish to become pregnant. Overall, no significant differences were found between the groups.

Examination of individual questions did reveal significant differences within groups. Males believe more strongly than females ($p \leq .01$) that lenient standards of behavior imposed by parents is a major contributing factor to teen pregnancy. Belief that teens who become pregnant want to do so was held more strongly by those with a high school education or less, compared with those with 4 or more years of college ($p \leq .02$).

How do black adults feel about nonmarital intercourse? Seventy-two percent of the respondents believed it was permissible to engage in nonmarital intercourse; however, this percentage dropped dramatically to 45% when specifically asked about nonmarital intercourse among teens.

With regard to premarital intercourse, education was found to be a significant factor ($F = 4.04$, $df = 2$, $p \leq .02$). When given the statement, "Only married people should engage in sexual intercourse," significant differences were found according to educational background. Those with 4 or more years of college were significantly ($p \leq .001$) more accepting of nonmarital intercourse than those with some college and those with a high school education or less. A strong tendency was also found among the marital groups with the Never Marrieds being more acceptable of nonmarital intercourse than the Married Without Spouse ($p \leq .06$).

Who is responsible for birth control and pregnancy? When asked if birth control is primarily the woman's responsibility, 86% disagreed. Ninety-one percent felt that birth control should be equally shared by both the woman *and* the man. Respondents with 4 or more years of college believed more strongly than those with some college education that responsibility for birth control should be equally shared ($p \leq .02$). With regard to pregnancy, 82% disagreed with the statement "A woman has only herself to blame if she becomes pregnant." Ninety-eight percent of the respondents believed that a man who impregnates an unmarried woman should be expected to participate in any future responsibility of the child.

What are the black attitudes toward abortion? Black adults were divided on their beliefs regarding abortion. A 50–50 split occurred when respondents were asked if abortion should be allowed no matter what the circumstances. Yet only 7% believed that abortion should never be allowed regardless of circumstances. When more specific questions were asked, differences became apparent. Seventy percent of the respondents believed an abortion should be allowed if it were known that the fetus would be born with a serious birth defect or mental retardation. If the mother's life were endangered, 64% would allow an abortion to take place. Sixty-four percent also believed it is permissible for persons under age 18 to have an abortion. When a pregnancy resulted from rape or incest, the number of respondents who would allow an abortion rose to 84%.

An ANOVA revealed education to be a significant factor ($F = 4.09$, $df = 2$, $p \leq .02$). More specifically, those with 4 or more years of college were significantly more in favor of abortions for individuals under age 18 than were persons with some college education ($p \leq .04$). Differences in marital status were also found to be significant with Married With Spouse expressing more support for abortions for persons under age 18 than Married Without Spouse ($p \leq .05$).

What are the black adult attitudes toward nonviolent pornography? Black respondents were uniformly against pornography. Eight-two percent indicated it is harmful to society; 57% believed it is a major cause of incest, rape, and child molestation; and 65% feel it should not be protected by law. No significant differences were found among the major groupings, nor were there significant differences when individual questions were examined.

What are the attitudes of black adults regarding masturbation? For most blacks (76%), masturbation was perceived as acceptable, normal behavior. Regarding masturbation among children, 90% would not punish a child for masturbation in private, and 71% would not teach their children that masturbation is wrong. A close examination of the data revealed a statistical difference among the educational groups. Respondents with a high school education felt more strongly that children should be taught masturbation is wrong when compared to those with 4 or more years of college ($p \leq .03$).

Discussion

The information gathered in this study comes largely from well-educated, middle-class, urban blacks. As a whole, these participants hold moderate, well-informed, consistent views with regard to sexuality. As such, they are not inclined to believe the many myths related to sexuality that are still prevalent in today's society.

For example, the majority of blacks in this study do not uphold the myth that increased sexual knowledge leads to increased sexual activity. Three quarters of the respondents believe that discussions related to sexuality should begin *before* a child has reached first grade. Furthermore, both parents should be involved in providing sexual information. Indeed, a majority of these blacks believe that a major contributing factor in teen pregnancy is poor communication between parents and children.

Although a majority of the respondents believe it is permissible for adults to engage in nonmarital intercourse, they do not believe teenagers should engage in such activity. For those teens who are sexually active, these black adults have a strong pragmatic belief that contraceptives should be readily available. Indeed, an overwhelming majority would want their own children, if sexually active, to responsibly use contraceptives. Furthermore, the respondents do not adhere to the once dominant belief that birth control is primarily the woman's

responsibility. The vast majority believe the responsibility for birth control should be equally shared by men and women. Responsibility for any children born to unmarried parents should also be equally shared.

These blacks do not necessarily favor abortion, per se. However, a majority of them would allow abortions under certain circumstances such as endangerment to the mother's life, if the person were under the age of 18, if the fetus would be born with a serious birth defect or mental retardation, or if the person was a victim of rape or incest. Yet, even so, the degree of support varies with the situation, thus providing a further indication of the complexity of the abortion issue. Hence, it would be a mistake to state that these blacks support abortion, per se, without accounting for the circumstances under which an abortion is being contemplated.

The belief that pornography is not only harmful to society, but also a major cause of such criminal behaviors as incest, rape, and child molestation is held by a large majority of blacks in this study. Moreover, these respondents do not hold the civil libertarian view that pornography should be protected by law.

These black respondents are less conservative, however, regarding their attitudes toward masturbation. It is viewed as acceptable normal behavior. Even where children are concerned, these blacks would not administer punishment for such behavior if done in private, nor would the majority of blacks teach their children that masturbation is wrong.

Implications for Practice

The results of this study have implications for the researcher and family professional, that is, the family practitioner and the family life educator. Family professionals who are uninformed regarding the sexuality attitudes of black adults within their historical context are more likely to create programs that mirror the attitudes and beliefs of the majority population. They run the risk of creating programs that are not effective and indeed, may be in conflict with the intended population. The findings of this study are among the first to provide a knowledge base of sexuality attitudes of black adults that family professionals should consider as they plan and implement sexuality programs for blacks. The findings provide much needed information about the differences and similarities of sexuali-

ty attitudes within the black community when differentiated by sex, age, education, and marital status.

One of the more significant findings of the study is that education is a more important factor in determining differences and similarities in sexuality attitudes than are sex, age, or marital status. However, education is not a factor when responses in the area of abortion and pornography are analyzed. The information provided by the study establishes a framework from which professionals can design and implement effective programs for black parents and their children, programs that are sensitive to the difference within the black community and more accurately reflect the full spectrum of sexuality attitudes of blacks. This study provides opportunities for the researcher and family professional to reduce the misconceptions and stereotypes regarding the sexuality attitudes of black adults.

More importantly, according to the findings, the preparation and training of family professionals must increasingly reflect the nuances of racial and cultural diversity within groups. If programs are to be designed to assist black families and subsequently their progeny, family professionals must be cognizant of the similarities and differences. Because black attitudes may differ from those of whites, these differences should not be assumed to be weaknesses but rather considered to be a part of an obviously viable culture. For example, the respondents in this study do not favor abortion per se; they are strongly against pornography, with a significant majority believing pornography is harmful to society and the majority believing that it is a significant contributor to incidents of incest, rape, and child molestation; Never Marrieds are more conservative than Married With Spouse, with respect to having contraceptives readily accessible to teenagers; and black males feel that lenient standards of behavior adopted by parents significantly contribute to teen pregnancy. These findings and others need to be incorporated into sexuality training programs and research efforts relating to the sexuality attitudes of middle class blacks.

Conclusion

This study represents a first step in investigating the sexuality attitudes of today's black middle-class adult. In order to obtain findings which are more amenable to generalization, further research would need to be conducted with larger samples drawn from other geographic regions and differing socioeconomic classes. Additional studies must also investigate the relationship between the expressed attitudes and actual behaviors. The gathering of this information may be significant to the extent that current policies may be positively influenced and thereby enhance the development of more viable programs that will more closely meet the needs of blacks and our society.

REFERENCES

Billingsley, A. (1988). The impact of technology on Afro-American families. *Family Relations, 37,* 420–425.

BOCES Regional Planning Center. (1987, April). Teen pregnancy and parenting: How can schools respond? *Voice, 8,* p. 2. Albany, NY: Albany-Scholaric-Schecnectady BOCES.

Brown, S. V. (1985). Premarital sexual permissiveness among black adolescent females. *Social Psychology Quarterly, 48,* 381–387.

Children's Defense Fund. (1988, January/March). *Teen pregnancy: An advocate's guide to the numbers.* Washington, DC: Children's Defense Fund's Adolescent Pregnancy Clearing House.

Darling, C. A., & Hicks, M. W. (1982). Parental influence on adolescent sexuality: Implications for parents as educators. *Journal of Youth and Adolescent, 11,* 231–245.

Fox, G. L. (1979, May-June). The family's influence on adolescent sexual behavior. *Children Today,* pp. 21–25, 36.

Frazier, E. (1963). *The Negro church in America.* New York: Schocken Books.

French, L. A., & Wailes, S. N. (1982). Perceptions of sexual deviance: A biracial analysis. *International Journal of Offender Therapy and Comparative Criminology, 26,* 242–249.

Gordon, S., & Snyder, C. W. (1989). *Personal issues in human sexuality: A guidebook for better sexual health.* Boston: Allyn and Bacon.

Hill, R. B. (1972). *The strength of black families* (1st ed.). New York: Emerson Hall Publishers.

Hill, R. B. (1989). Critical issues for black families by the year 2000. In National Urban League (Ed.), *The state of Black America 1989* (p. 41). New York: National Urban League.

Koop, C. E. (1988). *Understanding AIDS: A message from the surgeon general?* (HHS Publication No. (CDC) HHS-88-8404). Washington, DC: U.S. Government Printing Office.

Ladner, J. (1971). *Tomorrow's tomorrow: The black woman.* New York: Doubleday.

National Center for Health Statistics. (1986). Advanced report of final natality statistics, 1984. *Monthly Vital Statistics Report,* Vol. 35, No. 4, Suppl., July 18, 1986. Hyattsville, MD: Public Health Service.

Staples, R. (1972). Research on black sexuality: Its implication for family life, sex, education, and public policy. *Family Coordinator, 21,* 183–188.

Staples, R. (1988). The Black American family. In C. H. Mindel, R. W. Haldenstein, & R. Wright, Jr. (Eds.), *Ethnic families in America* (3rd ed., pp. 303–324). New York: Elsevier.

Timberlake, C., & Carpenter, W. D. (1986). Adult sexuality training in the black church: An approach toward combatting teenage pregnancy. *Journal of Home Economics, 78,* 29–31.

Walters, J., & Walters, L. H. (1983). The role of the family in sex education. *Journal of Research & Development in Education, 16*(2), 8–15.

Americans and Their Sexual Partners

Andrew M. Greeley
Robert T. Michael
Tom W. Smith

Andrew M. Greeley is a priest, sociologist, novelist, and journalist. He is a Research Associate at the National Opinion Research Center, University of Chicago, and Professor of Sociology at the University of Arizona. His scholarly writings concentrate on religion and ethnicity. His other writings range from critiques of the Catholic church to best-selling novels.

Robert T. Michael is an economist. He is Dean of the Graduate School of Public Policy Studies, University of Chicago, and former Director of the National Opinion Research Center. His research interests center on the economics of the family.

Tom W. Smith is a survey researcher and historian. He is Director of the General Social Survey at the National Opinion Research Center. His research interests are survey methods and social change.

In the absence of responsible social research about human behavior, poor research and media-generated folk lore become conventional wisdom. The assumptions of such conventional wisdom are seldom questioned and rarely tested. In few areas of human behavior is the power of conventional wisdom so pervasive as it is when the subject is sex. In matters of research on sexual behavior, as in other arenas, Gresham's Law applies – bad research seems to drive out good research. And there is good research on sexual behavior, as the recent lengthy and informative review by the National Research Council details. It is just less sensational than much of the poorer research, and thus less successful in shaping public perceptions about the facts pertaining to our sexual behavior. Perhaps Gresham's Law should be paraphrased in this context as: sensational findings (often the result of poor or superficial research) drive out carefully balanced and less sensational findings, at least from headlines and thus from public perception.

Bad research, like the self-selected reader surveys in popular magazines and non-random samples such as those gathered for the Hite Report, and the popular metaphor of a "sexual revolution" have created a conventional wisdom that "everyone knows" to be true: marital infidelity and sexual experimentation are widespread among Americans.

But if "monogamy" is defined as having no more than one sexual partner during the past year, research based on a scientifically sound national sample indicates that Americans are a most monogamous people. Only 14 percent of all adult Americans interviewed in a 1988 nationwide survey were not monogamous in this sense; and excluding those who were not sexually active, 18 percent were not monogamous. In only one major population group – young men – were a majority not monogamous.

Our study is based on a supplement to NORC's (the National Opinion Research Center) GSS (General Social Survey) given during the winter of 1988 to about 1500 adults who were scientifically selected from a national probability frame of households in the United States. The questions about sexual behavior were included as a self-administered form during the face-to-face interview conducted in the respondent's home. The self-administered form was sealed by the respondent and returned, unopened by the interviewer, with the rest of the survey. This procedure reassured respondents that their answers were confidential and to be used only for statistical purposes such as this article. The response rate on the 1988 GSS was 77.3 percent, and 93.9 percent of those who responded did answer the questions about sexual behavior, well within the range of "item nonresponse" that is typical for a lengthy interview. There is no evidence in this survey that respondents felt the questions about sexual partners were particularly intrusive or inappropriate.

We use two definitions of monogamy. We report the percentage of sexually active people with one sexual partner (M1) and the percentage of all people with zero or one sexual partner (M2). In both definitions we exclude those few (6.1 percent) who did not

From *Society*, Vol. 27, No. 5, July/August 1990, pp. 36-42. Published by permission of Transaction Publishers. Copyright © 1990 by Transaction Publishers.

answer the question. Each of the two definitions has some appeal as a measure of the tendency for adults to be monogamous, for the sexually inactive – those who report having no sexual partner within the past twelve months – can be considered in or out of the definition depending on its purpose. They are not monogamous in the social sense of being committed to a sexual relationship with a sole partner, but from the epidemiological standpoint of risks of contracting sexually transmitted diseases such as AIDS, they belong to the category of the monogamous. We caution that as our questionnaire asked the number of partners in the preceding twelve months, we cannot distinguish serial monogamy within the year from having two or more partners in the same interval of time. Our definitions of monogamy exclude persons

Table 1

Monogamy in the United States
(Percent of Sexually Active Persons with One Partner During Previous Twelve Months)

	M1 *	M2 *		M1 *	M2 *
All	82% (1072)	86% (1390)	Divorced	62% (125)	73% (178)
			Separated	78% (36)	81% (43)
**Gender ** **			Never	52% (205)	64% (278)
Women	86% (568)	90% (793)			
Men	78% (504)	81% (597)	**Race ** **		
			Black	69% (144)	74% (170)
**Age ** **			White	84% (889)	88% (1161)
18-24	56% (144)	61% (163)			
25-29	77% (157)	79% (168)	**Religion**		
30-39	85% (283)	86% (308)	Protestant	83% (648)	87% (852)
40-49	86% (213)	88% (243)	Catholic	85% (281)	89% (364)
50-59	91% (96)	93% (132)			
60-69	93% (119)	96% (194)	**Region**		
70+	95% (59)	98% (180)	North East	82% (216)	86% (274)
			North Central	82% (288)	87% (382)
Education			South	82% (372)	86% (482)
Grammar	81% (70)	91% (146)	West	83% (196)	87% (252)
High	83% (504)	87% (644)			
College	81% (398)	84% (480)	**Size ** **		
Graduate	84% (99)	86% (116)	12 SMSA	73% (202)	79% (265)
			Other SMSA	87% (353)	90% (440)
**Marital Status ** **			Other Urb	82% (400)	86% (530)
Married	96% (672)	97% (740)	Rural	86% (117)	90% (155)
Widowed	71% (34)	93% (151)			

M1: Monogamy defined as having one partner, people with zero partners, and people who refused to answer are excluded from the sample.

M2: Monogamy defined as having zero or one partner, refusals are excluded.

** Signifies that the percentage differences within this category are significant at the .01 level for M1 and M2. Numbers in parentheses indicate the size of the cell on which the percentage is based.

with more than one partner in a twelve-month period, serially or otherwise. Thus our definition of monogamy represents a lower bound estimate of its prevalence in this respect.

Table 1 shows the basic facts. These facts indicate that a vast majority of adults report monogamous behavior. Among all adults 86 percent were monogamous (M2), while among the sexually active 82 percent were monogamous (M2). More women (90 percent) report being monogamous than men (81 percent). More older respondents report being monogamous than do younger ones with the monogamy rate rising from 61 percent among those under 25 to 96 percent and higher among those over 60. Whites (88 percent) have higher monogamy rates than blacks (74 percent), as do residents of smaller sized communities (90 percent) compared to those in large metropolitan areas (75 percent). There appears

to be no appreciable difference between Protestants and Catholics or by region of residence in the United States. Marital status has a major influence, as would be expected, with a remarkably high percentage of married persons (97 percent) reporting monogamous behavior. Among sexually active formerly married people, monogamous behavior appears to be the norm as well. Rates of monogamy appear to vary little with educational level (the anomalous high monogamy rate for M2 in Table 1 reflects the large number of elderly people with low levels of education, many of whom are widowed and have no sexual partner). It appears that sexual experimentation exists predominantly among the young and the nonmarried.

Age, gender, and marital status are powerful predictors of monogamy, as Table 2 suggests. The rates for monogamy are strikingly high for both married men and married women in all three age groups – over

Table 2

Rates of Monogamy Among the Sexually Active, by Gender, Age, and Type of Relationship

<u>Women</u>

Age	Married*	Regular Partner	No Regular Partner
< 30*	94% (80)	64% (70)	40% (15)
30-49*	100% (159)	74% (93)	50% (16)
50+*	97% (109)	91% (23)	67% (3)
Total	98% (348)	73% (186)	47% (34)

<u>Men</u>

Age	Married	Regular Partner	No Regular Partner
< 30*	91% (44)	47% (62)	23% (30)
30-49*	95% (163)	55% (53)	42% (12)
50+*	96% (117)	75% (12)	45% (11)
Total	95% (324)	53% (127)	32% (53)

* NB: Row percentages (by partnership for each age group) are statistically significant at the .01 level for all six groups; the column percentages (by age for a given partnership) are significant at the .01 level for only one group, married women.

90 percent of each group reported themselves monogamous.

For those who have a "regular" sexual partner, the rates of monogamy are decidedly lower, typically falling 25 percentage points for women under 50 and about 40 percentage points for men under 50. Other research suggests that the half-life of a cohabitational union in the United States is only about one year, so if many of those reporting a regular partner are cohabiting, it is likely that they have been in that relationship for less than a full year. Their having more than one sexual partner within a year may cover a period different from that of the regular partnership they report. Many unmarried persons with a "regular" sexual partner may have no expectation about sexual exclusivity, so the lower rates of monogamy for these men and women may not indicate any infidelity.

For those who reported having no regular sexual partner, the rates of monogamy – are much lower, about 50 percentage points for women and 60 percentage points for men. They range from 23 percent of the young men to 67 percent of the older women. The rates rise with age and are higher for women. Of the sexually active respondents in the survey who were not married and had no regular sex partner, about one-third of the men and half of the women nonetheless reported only one partner within the year.

Even among the *nonmonogamous* sexual license is limited. Fifty-seven percent of these women and 32 percent of these men report only two sexual partners. Men, more than women, are likely to report having a large number of parnters – and hence to be the primary targets for sexually transmitted diseases. (A quarter of the men who have more than one sexual partner report in fact that they have had at least five such partners and only 8 percent of women had five or more partners.) If we project to life cycle patterns from our cross sectional data, when young people marry or reach the age of thirty or so, a large majority adopt monogamy as their lifestyle.

To see which of these demographic variables had independent effects on monogamy we carried out multiple regression analysis on the M1 definition of

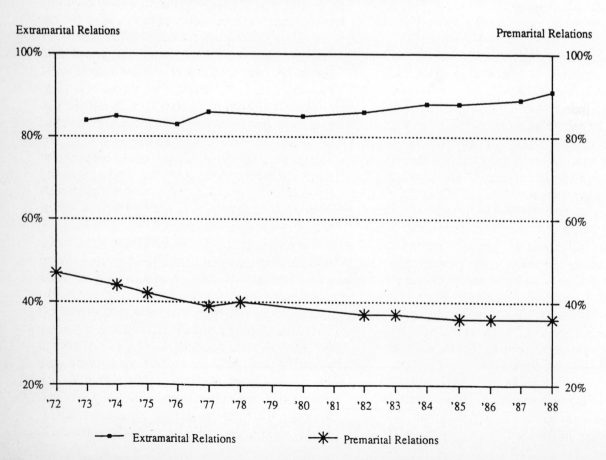

Figure 1
Attitude Toward Nonmarital Sexual Relations
GSS Annual Survey 1972-1988
(Percent Saying Always or Almost Always Wrong)

monogamy. The regressions were run separately for men and for women. They indicate that older people are more likely to be monogamous, that black men (but not black women) are less likely to be monogamous, that those in large cities are less likely to be monogamous, and that compared to the married men and women, those with and those without a regular sex partner are far less likely to be monogamous. The regressions also included information on education level, religion, household age structure, and ethnicity (Hispanics), but none of these variables had any statistically discernible effect on the rate of monogamy.

It is interesting to note, too, that when we reran these regressions on only the persons who were married, there were no significant variables for the women, and only the race variable was significant for the men. That is, marriage is the dominant determinant of the monogamy rate, and within the married population, none of the other factors we looked at — education, city size, household composition, religion, age, (except for race for men) — had an influence that was statistically notable. Again, marital status is clearly the dominant determinant of the monogamy propensity in these data.

One issue that deserves attention, but which we doubtless cannot fully address, is whether the GSS respondents are telling the truth about their sexual behavior. Might they be lying about the number of their sexual partners? Two points can be made. Survey data from the United Kingdom in 1986 reported comparable proportions of the adult population with zero, one and two or more partners. The similarity of these two quite independent surveys provides some face validity for each. The experience of those who have undertaken surveys of sexual behavior is that respondents tend to be remarkably candid. Phrases like "the new permissiveness," "the playboy philosophy," and "open marriage" have become so fashionable and discussions of marital infidelity in popular journals are so commonplace that respondents might be inclined to exaggerate their sexual accomplishments to keep up with the "trends" rather than understate them. Also, if the respondents to the GSS are falsifying accounts of their sexual behavior because of mores which demand monogamy (a circumstance we do not think is the case), then at a minimum they are demonstrating that those mores still strongly support monogamy.

Are the monogamy rates described above "high" by standards of the recent past? Might the situation of widespread monogamy described by our data reflect a response to the fears created by the AIDS epidemic? Does the high rate of monogamy represent a "retreat" from a previous state of "permissiveness" or "liberation"? Have fear and caution made sexual restraint popular?

As our data is only a snapshot about behavior in the past twelve months, it cannot help us determine directly if the fear of AIDS has affected sexual behavior. Finding that monogamy is relatively rare among young men who have never been married and who do not have a regular sexual partner does not inform us, for they might have had even more partners before they became aware of the AIDS danger.

One way our data might indirectly address this question is if we assume that knowing an AIDS victim inhibits sexual permissiveness. We can compare the sexual behavior of those who do know an AIDS victim with the behavior of those who do not know anyone with AIDS, and that can indicate the magnitude of the behavioral response. But those who do know a victim are significantly less likely to be monogamous. Among all adults 76 percent of those knowing an AIDS victim were monogamous, while 87 percent of those not knowing anyone with AIDS were monogamous. Even those who know an AIDS victim who has died are somewhat less likely to report themselves monogamous (70 percent) than those personally unaware of any AIDS fatalities (80 percent). The direction of causation here is probably that those who are not monogamous, and have a lifestyle that exposes them to greater risks of AIDS and other sexually transmitted diseases, are acquainted with more people who are also at greater risk of contracting those diseases. So this line of inquiry is not revealing.

There is, however, no evidence in our data to support a hypothesis that the current high level of monogamy is the result of fear of AIDS. The demographic correlates of monogamy suggest that sexual behavior varies greatly by gender, age, and especially marital status; these powerful predictors may explain much more of the variation in sexual behavior than does fear of AIDS.

But what might the fear of AIDS have added to the levels of monogamy that had already existed among married people? If there were a more permissive attitude among married people towards infidelity five or ten years ago, how great was this permissiveness? Data from prior years of the General Social Survey (with independent national samples of adults) can inform us about how that attitude has changed over the past 15 years. It suggests that norms against extramarital sex were strong even 15 years ago. Studying the trend in attitude toward marital infidelity in the annual GSS questionnaire since 1972, there has been a statistically significant increase in opposition to infidelity. There was an increase from 84 percent to 91 percent of the adult population saying that extramarital sex was always or almost always wrong, as Figure 1 indicates. This hardly indicates a dramatic increase in sexual restraint, especially since disapproval of extramarital sex was quite high in the early 1970s when the GSS was first conducted.

It is worth noting that this increase in opposition to extramarital sex has occurred at the same time as there has been a statistically significant increase in tolerance for premarital sex (an increase in tolerance from 53 percent to 64 percent). The notion that social change is always unidimensional and unidirectional rarely is sustained by empirical data. "Revolutions" in which there is uniformity unmarred by complexity usually exist only in newspaper articles and not in the real world.

Three independent national surveys provide data that enables us to gauge the impact of fear of AIDS on American monogamy. A CBS study in 1986 based on 823 cases reported that 11 percent of Americans said that they had changed their behavior because of AIDS. NBC studies conducted in 1986 and 1987 indicated that 7.3 and 7.4 percent, respectively, said they had modified their behavior.

These levels, when reported, were commonly seen as indicating that people were not reacting responsibly to the risks of AIDS, but our findings suggest another interpretation. If many fewer people were engaged in sexual behavior that was risky, it may be quite sensible that few altered their behavior. This is further supported by a 1987 Gallup survey in which 68 percent indicated that no change in their sexual behavior had been made because they did not need to change their behavior. We cannot be sure, and do not intend to be Pollyannas, but our findings that relatively few adults report having sex with many partners may be one reason only about 10 percent of adults report changing their behavior. Another cautionary note – we focus on only the number of partners, and there are several other dimensions of sexual behavior that one might change in response to the risks of AIDS (e.g., care in the selection of partners, avoidance of high-risk sexual practices, use of condoms, etc.), and these are beyond the scope of our survey.

The details of the reported change in behavior motivated by fear of AIDS conform quite well to the details in the GSS tables reported above about which groups are most at risk: in the Gallup survey 7 percent of the married people and 22 percent of the never married reported a change of behavior; 10 percent of

the whites and 22 percent of the blacks reported a change in behavior, as did 13 percent of the men and 9 percent of the women, 19 percent of those under 25 and 10 percent of those between 35 and 50. The changes for married people are compatible with the change in attitudes towards extramarital sex during the years Americans have been conscious of AIDS. So one can tentatively estimate that, even in the absence of AIDS, the monogamy rate for married men and women would not be less than 90 percent. For the whole population the rate, without the AIDS scare, might be between 75 percent and 80 percent. We note again the face validity here: those groups who report the lower monogamy rates in the GSS – men compared to women, nonmarried compared to married – are those who report in the Gallup survey the biggest change in behavior for fear of contracting AIDS.

The fear of AIDS may have increased monogamy especially among unmarried people and most especially if they are young, but the rates appear to us to have been quite high in any case. Despite the fear of AIDS the promiscuity rate among the young is still high, especially among young, unmarried men, with resultant dangers to themselves and their future partners.

A Sexual Revolution?

Like all metaphors the phrase "sexual revolution" is apt for some dimensions of social behavior over the past couple decades, but by no means all of it. It might be useful to review a few changes in recent years in demographic features such as marriage and divorce as well as to speculate on how they might have affected the rate of monogamy in the United States as measured by our variables M1 and M2.

Consider the changes in marital status. The divorce rate in the United States (per 1000 married women) rose from 9.2 in 1960 to 14.9 in 1970, 22.6 in 1980, and then declined slightly to 21.5 in recent years. As a result, despite a rise in remarriage rates, the proportion of the adult population currently divorced also rose dramatically from 3.2 percent in 1970 to 7.8 percent in 1986. Divorced adults are much less likely to be monogamous than are married adults, so this trend probably has decreased the number of adults with one sex partner and increased the number with more than one partner and the number with no partner, thus lowering M1 but not necessarily M2.

The median age at first marriage for women in the United States has risen over the past two decades from 20.6 in 1970 to 22.8 in 1984. As a result, the proportion of 20-24 (25-29) year-old men who have never been married rose from 54.7 percent (19.1

percent) in 1970 to 75.5 percent (41.4 percent) in 1986, and for women that proportion for the same age groups rose from 35.8 percent (10.5 percent) in 1970 to 58.5 percent (26.4 percent) in 1986. These are traditionally sexually active ages and the dramatic increases in the proportions still single probably accompany an increase in the average number of sex partners among the sexually active subsets for these growing segments of the population, thus lowering M1.

There has been a relatively large increase in the rate of cohabitation in the United States, from 0.8 percent in 1970 to 2.8 percent in 1988. This rise among young single couples and among the divorced may offset the tendency toward lower rates of monogamy somewhat, if, as the regressions above imply, the rate of monogamy among those with a "regular" sex partner is higher than among those without such a "regular" partner even though it is lower than among those who are formally married. This would tend to lower M1.

Another dimension of the issue is addressed by the earlier onset of sexual activity by teenagers in the United States. For 17-year-old urban women, the proportion who had premarital intercourse rose from 28 percent in 1971 to 41 percent by 1982. The early onset of sexual activity presumably is associated with a decrease in the monogamy rate for the population as a whole. The trends toward earlier age of beginning sexual activity and toward later age of first marriage lengthen the interval of the life cycle in which sexual activity is most associated with multiple sex partners. The resulting increase in premarital sexual activity mirrors the increased acceptance of that behavior, as reflected in the trends in attitude noted above. It probably lowers M1 and also reduces the discrepancy between M1 and M2.

The changes in fertility control through medical technology (such as the oral contraceptive) and legally accepted practices (such as abortion) have dramatically altered the risks of an unwanted birth associated with sexual behavior. That lower risk surely has had some influence, at the margin at least, on the inclination to engage in nonmarital sexual activity. This, too, may lower M1 and reduce the discrepancy between M1 and M2.

The baby boom of the fifties and early sixties resulted in a disproportionate number of young adults in their twenties over the past decade. As men and women in this age tend to exhibit less monogamy than those in older ages, that demographic bulge itself has tended to lower the overall incidence of monogamy. (This is a trend that can be anticipated with some clarity and as the size of the new cohorts of young adults for the next decade or so will be disproportionately small, this should tend to raise the incidence of monogamy over the next several years, and thus raise M1.)

As this sketchy review of demographic events indicates, there have been several social phenomena that have probably lowered the incidence of monogamy in the past decade or so. Whether these forces have helped create a "sexual revolution" or not, we cannot say. One fact is clear: the high rates of monogamous behavior in the United States exhibited in the GSS data for 1988 do not support the notion that the "revolution," if it occurred, has resulted in a society that does not value or adhere to monogamy.

READINGS SUGGESTED BY THE AUTHORS

Hofferth, S.L., F.R. Kahn, and W. Baldwin. "Premarital Sexual Activity Among U.S. Teenage Women Over the Past Three Decades," *Family Planning Perspectives* 19, (1987).

Michael, R.T., E.O. Laumann, J.H. Gagnon, and T.W. Smith. "Number of Sex Partners and Potential Risk of Sexual Exposure to HIV," *Morbidity and Mortality Weekly Report* 37, (1988).

Turner, C.F., H.G. Miller, and F.E. Moses (eds.). *AIDS: Sexual Behavior and Intravenous Drug Use.* Washington, DC: National Academy Press, 1989.

Life-Threatening Autoerotic Behavior: A Challenge for Sex Educators and Therapists

Edward J. Saunders

University of Iowa School of Social Work

Adolescents and young adults are at greatest risk for accidental deaths caused by certain life-threatening masturbatory behaviors. Sex educators and therapists can play vital roles in education, treatment, and research of little-understood, but sometimes fatal, sexual practices, including "autoerotic asphyxiation." This article reviews the kinds of masturbatory behavior that are most dangerous and discusses the psychological dynamics that may dispose youths and adults to these practices. Sex educators and therapists are challenged to learn about the problem, inform others, develop effective treatment strategies for clients at risk, and promote more research into the problem.

The AIDS epidemic in the United States has challenged sex educators and therapists in many ways. Principal among the challenges is the task of promoting safe sexual practices among clients at risk for AIDS infection. Another challenge that is less known is promoting "safe solo sex." Every year hundreds of adolescents and young adults are fatal victims of certain autoerotic, or masturbatory, behaviors that they discover by themselves, learn about from peers, or read about in pornographic magazines.

This article identifies several types of masturbatory activities that have resulted in hundreds of deaths. The discussion of these behaviors includes the estimated prevalence of cases, a profile of individuals who engage in these practices (mostly adolescent males), rationales for these life-threatening behaviors, and a brief discussion of treatment issues. Certainly, these behaviors warrant the attention of all professionals engaged in sex education or counseling of at-risk individuals or the survivors (family and friends) of fatal victims. Until recently, these behaviors have been either unknown to, or ignored by, the mental health profession. Increased research into the phenomena discussed in this article is warranted.

INTRODUCTION

Accounts of the "dangers" of masturbation have existed for centuries. In fact, only in the last several decades have professionals begun counseling youths that masturbation does NOT cause insanity, warts, pimples, insomnia, blindness, and other debilitating illnesses. Boy Scout manuals no longer carry warnings against the "unmanly" habit of masturbation as they once did. Many religious clergy, who for centuries denounced the sin of masturbation, have also recently begun counseling youths that masturbation is "natural in the sight of God" (Burg, 1987).

While youths are now assured by most parents and counselors that masturbation is not sinful or harmful, there is reason to believe, based on reviews of the medical and psychiatric literature, that certain masturbatory activities are, in fact, harmful and even life-threatening. The primary life-threatening behavior is typically referred to as "autoerotic asphyxia." Fatal asphyxia is accomplished by hanging or other oxygen-deprivation activities. In addition, there are reports of fatalities from electrocution during masturbation.

Hazelwood, Dietz, and Burgess (1981) note that the circumstances and features of autoerotic fatalities are not commonly known and, as a result, these deaths are often misinterpreted as either suicides or homicides. The majority of autoerotic fatalities are a result of accidents: failure of the victim to rescue himself or herself before the injurious agent kills. For most individuals, the agent is a rope used to compress the neck. Other injurious agents identified by Hazelwood and colleagues include: "devices for passing electrical current through the body, restrictive containers, obstruction of the breathing passages with gags; and the inhalation of toxic gases or chemicals through masks, hoses, and plastic bags" (p. 405).

Walsh, Stahl, Unger, Lilienstern, and Stephens (1977) report that producing a temporary state of as-

From *Journal of Sex Education & Therapy*, Vol. 15, No. 2, Summer 1989, pp. 82-91. Copyright © 1990 by the American Association for Sex Education, Counselors, and Therapists.

phyxia by constriction of the carotid vessels in the neck for sexual gratification has been known to anthropologists "for centuries." "The Eskimos," they write, "are known to choke each other as part of their sexual activity and it is common for their children to suspend themselves by the neck in [sex] play" (p. 158). Graphic descriptions of hanging to induce sexual sensations were provided by the Marquis de Sade in his book *Justine*, published in 1791. References to sexual hangings and other autoerotic fatalities can be found in many popular sex-oriented magazines, like *Hustler*; popular fiction; "sex manuals," including the *Joy of Sex*; and other nonfiction works. (Hazelwood, Dietz, Burgess, & Lanning, 1983).

Among popular nonfiction works that have recently described autoerotic asphyxiation to the general population is *Coroner* (Noguchi, 1983). Dr. Noguchi describes autoerotic asphyxiation as the "most dangerous sex game in the world." "The ritualists do not intend to die," writes Noguchi. "Instead they hope to achieve what they believe to be the most sublime sexual experience possible: obtaining orgasm by risking death. Almost always they handcuff themselves, or bind their hands, and sometimes they wear blindfolds or hoods. Some don transvestite clothes" (p. 216).

A popular magazine recently carried a detailed account of one teenager's death by autoerotic asphyxiation. The author called this phenomenon "the American teenager's best kept secret" (Bosworth, 1985, p. 52). The secret, of course, is often carried by families of victims who are unwilling to discuss their child's cause of death with others because the practice strikes most people as bizarre, taboo, and shameful. A current book on adolescent suicide also includes a chapter on the dangers of autoerotic hanging (Johnston, 1987). The chapter is included, writes Johnston, to put an end to the conspiracy of silence that surrounds these cases. Physicians, he suggests, also sometimes hide the real reason for the death to protect families from embarrassment. In a just-released book, Sol Gordon (1988) also counsels youths against putting a rope around their necks during masturbation: "falsely believing you get great orgasms that way." "Not true," he tells them (p. 90).

The incidence of autoerotic fatalities per year in the United States and Canada is estimated to be between 500 and 1000 (Hazelwood *et al.*, 1983). A decade earlier, Litman and Swearingen (1972) estimated the incidence at only 50 deaths yearly in the U.S. The dramatic increase in incidence can be attributed to the greater recognition of the syndrome by medical and police personnel responsible for investigating such deaths.

FATAL AUTOEROTIC PRACTICES

In eroticized hangings, Resnik (1972) reports that constriction of the neck results in (1) a disruption of the arterial blood supply resulting in a diminished oxygenation of the brain and (2) increased carbon dioxide retention. Either will heighten sensations of giddiness, lightheadedness, and exhilaration. These sensations enhance the individual's sexual gratification while masturbating during the hanging episode. Death results when an escape mechanism fails the individual or when he can no longer recover from his self-induced hypoxia. In these circumstances each fatality represents an accidental act, not one intentionally designed to result in death. Single case reports of autoerotic asphyxia from hanging have been authored in the last several years by Emson (1983) and Hiss, Rosenberg, and Adelson (1985).

The presence of protective padding between the rope and neck, the presence of sexual paraphernalia (vibrators, sexual literature, fetish items), evidence of masturbatory activity (seminal discharge), and evidence of previous activity are all indicators that the autoerotic death was accidental rather than suicide or homicide (Hazelwood *et al.*, 1981). "The practical importance of these distinctions," note Hazelwood, Dietz, and Burgess (1982), "lies in the response of family members and friends to sexual fatalities, in the life insurance benefits that may be awarded according to whether the death was an accident or a suicide, and in the potential prosecution of living persons in possible homicides" (p. 773). Miller and Milbrath (1983) provide a detailed discussion of the legal ramifications of autoerotic asphyxial death as it affects insurance settlements. The authors cite a case in which an insurer refused to pay double indemnity death benefits to a survivor, arguing that the deceased was mentally ill to engage in this practice and that the wording of the policy specifically excluded coverage of such a person.

While the majority of autoerotic fatalities are due to accidental strangulation, other deaths associated with sexual asphyxiation result from suffocation. An example of a death by suffocation is provided by Minyard (1985). He describes a case in which a man wrapped himself in plastic visquine using a snorkel tube to secure air. The victim, while masturbating inside his "cocoon," apparently lost his mouthpiece. He attempted to use a knife—his escape mechanism—to cut himself out, but he lost consciousness before he could free himself. More recently, Eriksson, Gezelius, and Bring (1987) describe a similar case: A man wrapped himself in 14 different blankets and masturbated while wrapped between them. Again, the individual died when he became too hypoxic to free himself.

Still other autoerotic fatalities result from the inhalation of asphyxiating gases. Two reports of these deaths were found in the recent medical literature. In one case, Cordner (1983) found that death had occurred during autoerotic behavior following the inhalation of an aerosol spray. In another case, death resulted from inhalation of nitrous oxide from a dental anesthetic machine by a lone individual. Evidence of an elaborate bondage fetish was found at the scene of the death (Leadbeater, 1988).

Electrocution during autoerotic activity is also documented in the medical literature. Sivaloganathan (1981) reports the case of a man who had wrapped his scrotum with an electrical wire loop and then fastened the wire to the lugs of his television loudspeaker. "Unfortunately, one of these wires had broken off, resulting in cessation of all stimulating activity. [The man] looked inside his set and came in contact with the exposed metal cap of a valve which was carrying a current of 2500 volts. It was this current that killed him" (p. 50). Tan and Choa (1983) report the fatal electrocution of a young man using a heat lamp to enhance his sexual enjoyment during masturbation. Tan hypothesizes that in the man's eagerness to place the lamp between his legs, he overextended the wire of the lamp, causing it to become energized.

In addition to the life-threatening behaviors discussed above, individuals also injure themselves using appliances and inserting objects into their urethras during masturbation. Penile injuries from vacuum cleaners, for example, are occasionally reported in the medical literature (Benson, 1985). Although not life-threatening, the penile injuries—including loss of the glans penis—can compromise later sexual functioning. Inserting objects into the urethra to enhance sexual sensation during masturbation by both men and women can also result in serious medical consequences (Bacci & Porena, 1986; Grumet, 1985).

A PROFILE OF VICTIMS

Studies of the patterns of autoerotic fatalities have been conducted by Walsh *et al.* (1977) and Burgess, Dietz, and Hazelwood (1983). In their review of 43 autoerotic deaths, gleaned from the files of the Armed Forces Institute of Pathology, Walsh and colleagues found that all but eight deaths occurred to men under age 30. The actual range of ages was 14 to 75 years. Thirteen men were married at the time of death. There was evidence of transvestism in 15 of the cases. All of the victims were white males. Although toxicological studies were performed in 21 cases, there were significant concentrations of alcohol in only 2 cases, and a toxic concentration of barbiturates was reported in 1 case.

In a larger study of 157 victims, conducted with the cooperation of the Federal Bureau of Investigation, Burgess et al. (1983) found that 132 died as a result of accidental autoerotic asphyxiation; 18 died of "atypical" behaviors resulting in electrocution, heart attacks, poisoning, or exposure; 5 died as part of sexual asphyxiation with a partner; and the remaining 2 individuals committed suicide during autoerotic activities.

Of the 132 who died as a result of autoerotic asphyxiation, the mean age of the decedents was 26.5 years.

Four victims were preadolescents, 37 were teenagers, 46 were in their twenties, 28 in their thirties, and the remaining 17 were age 40 or older.

Among the 132 victims of autoerotic asphyxiation, 127 individuals were white, Hispanic, or Native American; the remaining 5 victims were black. Where marital status was known (*n* = 112), 68 percent were single; another 27 percent were married. Given the ages of the victims, some were too young to have been married. Among the persons who died from "atypical" autoerotic behaviors (*n* = 18), 16 were white and 2 were black. Seventy-two percent of these individuals were single; 22 percent were married.

Among the 150 autoerotic deaths (both the asphyxiated group and the "atypical" group), 143 were males and 7 were females. Sass (1975) and Danto (1980) have provided rare detailed case reports of female autoerotic deaths. In both instances, the female victims had been masturbating—one with a vibrator, the other with a large bolt—while their necks were bound with rope. They died after losing consciousness during these activities. One victim was 21 years old; the other victim was 35.

RATIONALES FOR BEHAVIOR

Several theories have been presented to account for these life-threatening autoerotic behaviors. Guilt associated with masturbation, castration anxiety, oral conflicts, and risk-taking/thrill-seeking in general, have all been offered as rationales for this behavior. Each rationale is discussed in turn.

Edmondson (1972) cites a case in which an adolescent was found by his mother before fatal termination during an autoerotic hanging episode. Edmondson suggests that this youth was acting out his guilt over masturbation, exacerbated by his mother's negative attitudes toward sex. He concludes that abnormal or dangerous sexual behavior results more from the individual's "desire to punish himself than from any questionable heightening of sexual pleasure resulting from the self-induced asphyxia" (p. 438).

The suggestion that autoerotic hanging is the result of castration anxiety and/or oral conflict is made by Resnik (1972). "At the genital level," Resnik writes, "castration is feared. By repeatedly constricting the neck, symbolic amputation of the penis occurs. The simultaneous masturbation reifies the presence of the penis, thus denying castration. With the untying of the rope, the castration is undone, and the oedipal guilt is assuaged through the masochistic brush with death. . . . At the oral level, the conflict is over separation from the mother. Immobilization and asphyxia contribute to the fantasies of feeding, reunion, and rebirth. The child's conflict may well be that an erection feels good as feeding does. The gastrointestinal sensations (producing reflex erections) accompany the well-being associated with feeding and become unconsciously associated with the separation-strangle conflict" (pp. 16–17). This conflict, then, is acted out during the autoerotic bondage practice.

In a "developmental model" of sexual acting-out, Rosenblum and Faber (1979) suggest that a behavioral evolution occurs from a childhood fascination with rope to the "adolescent sexual asphyxia syndrome" and into an "adult bondage syndrome." "Basically," they suggest, "the person develops deviant sexual needs as a response to intrapsychic conflict and then must either adapt to the physiological reality imposed by his behavior (asphyxiation) or die in the process" (p. 557). Because adolescents perform the act alone, they are at greatest risk of unintentional death; therefore, Rosenblum and Faber argue that the greatest effort at intervention should be aimed at the adolescent group.

Finally, Grumley (1977) suggests that danger and risk are well employed as a means to erotic arousal. The unknown can act as an aphrodisiac, in which a person's ongoing curiosity takes him further and further along the line of experimentation, with either his own body or with another's. "Passion," he states, "is often no more than the joyous abandonment of oneself to the unknown. Not to know what to expect in a situation can be the most sexually exciting state of all. To throw oneself away from oneself to such a distance as to be no longer responsible for one's own well-being is to approach a special delirium. Thresholds only point one way, and that is on to the next" (p. 110).

This description of the fascination with masochism parallels the fascination that adolescents have with risk-taking and thrill-seeking in general. Sexual risk-taking is a challenge that takes adolescents to greater danger and to the thrill that such a risk involves. Thrill-seeking is very much associated with an "exhilarating sensation" that some individuals describe as orgasmic. "My pleasure [from autoerotic hanging activity] is closely associated with fear," Johnston (1987) quotes one youth. He continues: "I'm afraid of choking. In a state of fear, life and lust are compressed into a narrow space. The more pressure exerted by fear, the more vivid the pleasure gets inside" (p. 49). Johnston writes that in New Orleans, youths call the practice "fantasy," while another Texas teen-ager described it as "ecstasy."

TREATMENT ISSUES

While calls have been made for "greater intervention" with this at-risk population, no detailed strategies for intervention have been offered. Resnik (1972) simply advises clinicians to "question any unusual neck bruises on their male patients" (p. 19). Although Herman (1974), a pediatrician, prescribed individual and family counseling for an adolescent he saved from autoerotic hanging, he acknowledged the parents' reluctance to admit the nature of the incident and engage

fully in the treatment process. Parents, suggests Johnston (1987), must take responsibility for detecting this dangerous practice in their teenagers. He counsels them to "watch for bloodshot eyes, marks on the neck, disoriented behavior (after the youth has been alone for awhile), and possession of or fascination with ropes or chains" (p. 50).

Litman and Swearingen (1972), in their experience with nine individuals who "acted out" sexually with bondage activities—alone and with partners—were unable to discover any consistent history of specific traumata in childhood or any typical family pathology. Instead, they argue that disturbances in core family relationships, impairment in gender identity development, poor ego development, and specific conditioning experiences are all likely involved in choosing self-destructive sexual practices. They recommend treatment of such individuals "emphasizing real personal relationships to offset the overwhelming loneliness, inadequacy, and fragmentation which they have in common." A combination of individual and group treatment extending several years is recommended "for patients who are sexually deviant, isolated, depressed, and self-destructive" (p. 850).

Even the most detailed sexual history questionnaires neglect to include a question about the use of ropes or bondage devices during masturbation. Neglecting the fatal potential of certain masturbatory behaviors keeps individuals at risk. Until mental health professionals at large, and sex education/treatment professionals in particular, become more knowledgeable about these dangerous masturbation practices and, in turn, can communicate their concerns to the lay public, adolescents, in particular, will remain at greatest risk.

Responsible magazine journalism, like that of Bosworth (1985), is contributing to public awareness. It is hoped that the combination of clinical counseling for identified persons at risk, public awareness, and research will prove to be successful in their respective efforts to treat, inform, and more fully understand dangerous autoerotic activity. Each of these represent a challenge for sex educators and therapists. But these activities will occur only if individual professionals decide these are priorities.

CONCLUSION

In one of the most definitive sexual behavior surveys to date, Kinsey, Pomeroy, and Martin (1948) found that 95% of males masturbate. [More recently, Atwood and Gagnon's (1987) findings of masturbatory behavior among college males were strikingly consistent.] Every year, several hundred males die during the course of this activity. They choose, for many different reasons, a type of masturbatory activity that is life-threatening. While the experience may be sexually fulfilling, it comes with a great price: the threat of death. This threat, in fact, may be the principal cause of the behavior. In the vast majority of cases, the resultant death is unintentional.

As reflected in the above statistics, most autoerotic deaths occur during the late adolescent and early adult years (ages 17–25). Because this population is so vulnerable—relative to the risk-taking they assume in all areas of their lives, including sexual acting out—they demand special attention from the sex education/therapy profession. As discussed previously, professionals must assume more responsibility in identifying youths (and adults) at risk and respond with strategies that do not deny the seriousness of this behavior.

REFERENCES

Atwood, J. D., & Gagnon, J. (1987). Masturbatory behavior in college youth. *Journal of Sex Education and Therapy, 13*(2), 35–42.

Bacci, M., & Porena, M. (1986). Masturbatory injury resulting from intraurethral introduction of spaghetti. *The American Journal of Forensic Science and Pathology, 7*(3), 254–255.

Benson, R. C. (1985). Vacuum cleaner injury to penis: A common urologic problem? *Urology, 25*(1), 41–44.

Bosworth, P. (1985). Let's call it suicide. *Vanity Fair, 48*(3), 52–55; 108–110.

Burg, B. R. (1987). Masturbatory death and injury. *Journal of the Royal Society of Health, 107*(2), 60–61.

Burgess, A. W., Dietz, P. E., & Hazelwood, R. R. (1983). Study design and characteristics. In R. R. Hazelwood, P. E. Dietz, & A. W. Burgess (Eds.), *Autoerotic fatalities* (pp. 45–54). Lexington, Ma: Lexington Books.

Cordner, S. M. (1983). An unusual case of sudden death associated with masturbation. *Medicine, Science, and Law, 23*(1), 54–56.

Danto, B. L. (1980). A case of female autoerotic death. *The American Journal of Forensic Medicine and Pathology, 1*(2), 117–121.

Edmondson, J. S. (1972). A case of sexual asphyxia without fatal termination. *British Journal of Psychiatry, 121*, 437–438.

Emson, H. E. (1983). Accidental hanging in autoeroticism: An unusual case occurring outdoors. *The American Journal of Forensic Medicine and Pathology, 4*(4), 337–341.

Eriksson, A., Gezelius, C., & Bring, G. (1987). Rolled up to death: An unusual autoerotic fatality. *The American Journal of Forensic Medicine and Pathology, 8*(3), 263–265.

Gordon, S. (1988). *When living hurts.* New York: Dell.

Grumet, G. W. (1985). Pathological masturbation with drastic consequences: Case report. *Journal of Clinical Psychiatry, 46*(12), 537–539.

Grumley, M. (1977). *Hard corps: Studies in leather masochism.* New York: E. P. Dutton.

Hazelwood, R. R., Dietz, P. E., & Burgess, A. W. (1981). The investigation of autoerotic fatalities. *Journal of Police Science and Administration, 9*(4), 404–411.

Hazelwood, R. R., Dietz, P. E., & Burgess, A. W. (1982). Sexual fatalities: Behavioral reconstruction in equivocal cases. *Journal of Forensic Science, 27*(4), 763–774.

Hazelwood, R. R., Dietz, P. E., Burgess, A. W., & Lanning, K. V. (1983). Autoeroticism and the public visibility of autoerotic asphyxia. In R. R. Hazelwood, P. E. Dietz, & A. W. Burgess (Eds.), *Autoerotic fatalities* (pp. 1–12). Lexington, MA: Lexington Books.

Herman, S. P. (1974). Recovery from hanging in an adolescent male. *Clinical Pediatrics, 13*, 854–856.

Hiss, J., Rosenberg, S. B., & Adelson, L. (1985). "Swinging in the park": An investigation of an autoerotic death. *The American Journal of Forensic Medicine and Pathology, 6*(3), 250–255.

Johnston, J. (1987). *Why suicide?* Nashville, TN: Oliver-Nelson Books.

Kinsey, A. C., Pomeroy, W. B., & Martin, C. E. (1948). *Sexual behavior in the human male.* Philadelphia: Saunders.

Leadbeatter, S. (1988). Dental anesthetic death: An unusual autoerotic episode. *The American Journal of Forensic Medicine and Pathology, 9*(1), 60–63.

Litman, R. R., & Swearingen, C. (1972). Bondage and suicide. *Archives of General Psychiatry, 27*, 80–85.

Miller, E. C., & Milbrath, S. D. (1983). Medicine-legal ramifications of an autoerotic aphyxial death. *American Academy of Psychiatry and the Law, 11*(1), 57–68.

Minyard, F. (1985). Wrapped to death: Unusual autoerotic death. *The American Journal of Forensic Medicine and Pathology, 6*(2), 151–152.

Noguchi, T. T. (1983). *Coroner.* New York: Simon and Schuster.

Resnik, H. L. P. (1972). Erotized repetitive hangings: A form of self-destructive behavior. *American Journal of Psychotherapy, 26*(1), 4–21.

Rosenblum, S., & Faber, M. M. (1979). The adolescent sexual asphyxia syndrome. *Journal of the American Academy of Child Psychiatry, 18*(3), 546–558.

Sass, F. A. (1975). Sexual asphyxia in the female. *Journal of Forensic Science, 20*, 181–185.

Sivaloganathan, S. (1981). Curiosum Eroticum—A case of fatal electrocution during autoerotic practice. *Medicine, Science, and Law, 21*(1), 47–51.

Tan, C. T., & Choa, T. C. (1983). A case of fatal electrocution during an unusual autoerotic practice. *Medicine, Science, and Law, 23*(2), 92–95.

Walsh, F. M., Stahl, C. J., Unger, H. T., Lilienstern, O. C., & Stephens, R. G. (1977). Autoerotic asphyxial deaths: A medicolegal analysis of forty-three cases. In C. H. Wecht (Ed.), *Legal medicine annual: 1977* (pp. 155–182). New York: Appleton-Century-Crofts.

Wesselium, C. L., & Bally, R. (1983). A male with autoerotic asphyxia syndrome. *The American Journal of Forensic Medicine and Pathology, 4*(4), 341–345.

Homosexuality: Who and Why?

Melvin Konner, M.D.

Melvin Konner, an anthropologist and physician, teaches at Emory University.

In the bad old days, when homosexuality was considered a mental illness, a friend of mine was trying to go straight. He was seeing a distinguished psychoanalyst who believed (and still believes) that what some call a life style and still others call a crime is a psychiatrically treatable disorder. Through six years of anguished analysis, my friend changed his sexual orientation and married. His wife was wonderful—they had been friends for years—but he died unexpectedly of a heart attack at the age of 42, six months after the wedding. I am not superstitious, and I don't blame anyone, least of all his wife; he was happy with her. But a nagging question remains: Is it possible that my friend's doctor was trying to change something that should have been left alone?

He had been homosexual for years, and had had at least one stable long-term relationship. But he lived in a society that condemned him on religious and medical grounds. He "freely" chose to change through psychoanalysis. But this was a limited sort of freedom, and though he in fact did change—as some have—he did not live to find out how the change would work.

Those bad old days are over; yet a rising tide of bigotry against gay people has followed the AIDS epidemic. Religious fanatics point to AIDS as proof of God's wrath. Some gay men and women have begun to ponder again the nature of their sexual orientation, and parents wonder: Who becomes gay?

Neither science nor art has yet produced a single answer. Yet perhaps that in itself is an answer: that anything so complicated and various and interesting could have a single origin seems wrongheaded. Socrates and Tennessee Williams, Sappho and Adrienne Rich, to take only four people, representing only two cultures, seem certain to have come to their homosexuality in four such different ways as to make generalizations useless. In the further reaches of the anthropological universe, we find variations that knock most folk theories for a loop.

Consider the Sambia of New Guinea, described by Gilbert Herdt in "Guardians of the Flutes." They belong to a group of cultures in which homosexual practices are actually *required* of boys for several years as rites of passage into adulthood. After adolescence, the young men abandon homosexual practices, marry women, father children and continue as heterosexuals for the rest of their lives.

The lesson is threefold: first, a culture can make such a rule and get every person to conform; second, years of obligatory homosexuality apparently do not commit the average man to a lifetime of homoerotic desires. The third lesson may be drawn from the life of Kalutwo, a Sambia. He grew up stigmatized as the illegitimate son of an older widow and had no contact with his father. He showed unac-

ceptably strong homoerotic attachments, and never adjusted to a heterosexual relationship, having four marriages without issue—possibly unconsummated—by his mid-30's. According to Herdt and the psychoanalyst Robert Stoller, Kalutwo would have been homosexual anywhere.

The conclusion is reasonable. In every population, some men—most estimates say 5 to 10 percent—are drawn to homoerotic pursuits, whether they are punished, allowed or required. The percentage of strongly homoerotic women is generally estimated to be smaller, though in bisexuality women are said to outnumber men. But it should be remembered, definitions vary, and biases in such estimates are inevitable.

Some homosexuality was said to be present in all of 76 societies examined in one cross-cultural study, including the Tahitians, the Mohave Indians and a number of Amazonian tribes. In 48 (64 percent), it was condoned; in no society was it the dominant mode. Thus, all the societies had homosexuality, and the majority accepted its inevitability.

Not so our society. The Judeo-Christian tradition condemned homosexuality unequivocally, ending Greco-Roman tolerance. Yet centuries of condemnation, culminating in the Nazi attempt to physically exterminate homosexuals along with Jews and other "undesirables," have failed to make this minority acquiesce. Where do homosexuals come from, and how do they persist in the face of such persecution? In April 1935, with the Nazi's noose tightening around homosexuals, Sigmund Freud wrote to the mother of a gay man, "Homosexuality is assuredly no advantage, but it is nothing to be ashamed of, no vice, no degradation, it cannot be classified as an illness." Yet he went on to attribute it to "a certain arrest of sexual development" and then to deny that successful reorientation through psychoanalysis was possible, at least not "in the majority of cases."

Freud's sensitive formulation is remarkably close to the one we would give today. Although few accept his notion about arrested sexual development, most psychiatrists agree that sexual orientation is difficult to change, and that change is not intrinsically desirable. But a person's sexual orientation may be linked in some poorly understood way with anxiety, depression and other medically defined symptoms that can be treated, regardless of what may happen to sexual orientation.

Extensive research on the psychological development of homosexuals, by Allan Bell and others at the Kinsey Institute, found no support for most theories. The only factor implicating parents was (for both sexes) a poor relationship with the father — something shared by Kalutwo.

Yet some characteristics of the child could be predictive. For both sexes, but especially for males, gender nonconformity in childhood predicted homoerotic adaptation in adulthood. Other studies have drawn the same conclusion. The most dramatic, called "The 'Sissy Boy Syndrome' and

From *The New York Times Magazine*, April 2, 1989, pp. 60-61. Copyright © 1989 by The New York Times Company. Reprinted by permission.

Age-old questions on the subject abound. Even after many studies, there are few, if any, authoritative answers – and prejudice is rife.

the Development of Homosexuality," was published in 1987 by Richard Green, a psychiatrist at the University of California at Los Angeles. His was the first study starting with childhood and following through to adulthood, rather than asking adults about their memories. Boys dissatisfied with being boys — cross-dressing, avidly pursuing traditional girls' games to the exclusion of boys' games, and the like — had a high likelihood of growing up gay. Two-thirds to three-fourths became homosexuals. No homosexuality appeared in a control group.

GREEN'S UNEXPECTEDLY STRONG findings have been variously interpreted as showing that male homosexuality is innate or that early childhood environment is key. Either way, some gay men are *intrinsically* homoerotic. Some studies have pointed to genes. For example, identical twins are more likely to share the same sexual orientation than nonidentical twins. And in a recent study by Richard Pillard and James Weinrich, homosexual men were four times as likely to have a homosexual brother (21 percent) as were heterosexual men. Although these familial patterns could be interpreted as stemming from shared early experiences, it is at least equally likely that they are due to shared genes.

Nevertheless, the rare "sissy boy" syndrome cannot account for the majority of even male homosexuals, and for females the predictive power of "tomboyishness" is less strong. Frequently, homosexual orientation is not accompanied by these or any other departure from typical gender roles. In the last decade, one study after another — as well as the expressive literature that followed the increased tolerance of the 1970's — has shown that homosexuals differ enormously from one another. As Bell and Martin Weinberg concluded in another book: "We do not do justice to people's sexual orientation when we refer to it by a singular noun. There are 'homosexualities' and there are 'heterosexualities.' " Life styles, personalities, behaviors, hopes and dreams all show tremendous variation among people who share either of those labels. No uniformity, psychological, hormonal or genetic has been found.

Bell and Weinberg write that their "least ambiguous finding . . . is that homosexuality is not necessarily related to pathology." In 1974, the American Psychiatric Association conceded the truth of this observation, essentially made by Freud. In that year — three years after my friend's death — homosexuality was removed from the association's list of diagnostic categories. In the current official diagnostic manual, it is represented by only a vestige: "persistent and marked distress about one's sexual orientation," a subcategory under "Sexual Disorder Not Otherwise Specified." This allows homosexuals who are distressed by their sexual orientation to seek psychiatric help to change it. A good therapist will understand that the distress is not necessarily intrinsic, but may be the product of continued social prejudice. As Freud put it in his 1935 letter to the mother about her homosexual son, if he "is unhappy, neurotic, torn by conflicts, inhibited in his social life, analysis may bring him harmony, peace of mind, full efficiency, whether he remains a homosexual or gets changed."

In fact, if the psychiatrist is fair-minded, the same diagnostic subcategory will admit patients dissatisfied with their heterosexual orientation and wanting to become gay. Adrienne Rich — whose lesbian poems are perhaps the most beautiful recent love poetry — has described a syndrome she calls "compulsory heterosexuality." It refers to the requirement of universal heterosexual adaptation imposed on American women, who she believes are, like all other women, naturally bisexual.

In this realm, diagnoses will not help much. The most common recent answer to the main questions about sexual orientation has been something like "I'm O.K.; you're O.K." But, better, is the reply to that bit of psychobabble provided by Fritz Perls, the founder of Gestalt psychotherapy: "I'm not O.K.; you're not O.K. — and that's O.K." As for religious pieties, they are even less helpful than diagnoses. Fear of AIDS is understandable, but it's really beside the point. If AIDS were God's punishment for gay men, then gay women would presumably be God's chosen people, for they have the lowest rates of AIDS and other sexually transmitted diseases. Perhaps in an atmosphere of tolerance and compassion, we can all do better at finding out — and becoming — who we really are.

Variations on a Theme

Gays, single mothers and grandparents challenge the definition of what is a family

JEAN SELIGMANN

Gay and Lesbian Couples

What's in a family? A mommy, a daddy, a couple of kids and maybe a grandma, right? Well, yes, but that's not the whole picture anymore. The family tree of American society is sending forth a variety of new and fast-growing branches. Gay and lesbian couples (with or without children) and unmarried heterosexual couples are now commonplace. What's surprising is not so much that these offshoots of the main trunk are flourishing but that the public seems more and more willing to recognize them as families. Earlier this year the Massachusetts Mutual Life Insurance Co. asked 1,200 randomly selected adults to define the word "family." Only 22 percent picked the legalistic definition: "A group of people related by blood, marriage or adoption." Almost three quarters instead chose a much broader and more emotional description: "A group of people who love and care for each other." As usual, the American people are changing old perceptions much faster than the courts are. But in many parts of the country lawmakers are now finally catching up and validating the legitimacy of the nontraditional family.

Several landmark legal developments this year have greatly expanded the definition of what constitutes a family. In May, San Francisco's Board of Supervisors passed "domestic partnership" legislation recognizing homosexual and unmarried heterosexual couples as families. The ordinance, which was put on the ballot for a November referendum, defines domestic partners as "two people who have chosen to share one another's lives in an intimate and committed relationship of mutual caring." The law's intent was to extend to qualifying domestic partners some of the benefits accorded married heterosexuals. Health benefits, property and life insurance, bereavement leave, and annuity and pension rights are all under consideration.

In July the New York State Court of Appeals ruled that a gay man whose long-term lover had died qualified as family. The survivor was therefore entitled to assume the lease of his partner's rent-controlled Manhattan apartment. Similar state legislation and municipal ordinances are under consideration nationwide. Legislators, judges and elected officials in Michigan, Wisconsin, Washington, Maryland and the District of Columbia are forging efforts to reach an all-inclusive understanding of the family.

Some experts think it's no longer possible to define the family. "Family has become a fluid concept," says Arthur Leonard, professor of law at New York Law School. Others fear recognizing domestic partnerships will undermine the sanctity of the heterosexual nuclear family, reducing it to a mere abstraction. But in fact most American households today don't consist of the "traditional" family (a mother and father living with their children under 18—or stepparents and stepchildren). Many are single-parent families; others are just plain singles. The courts are acting appropriately, says Leonard, who is also chairman of the New York City Bar Association's Committee on Sex and Law. "The law must follow society and reflect reality," he maintains.

Figures from the annual census reports underscore Leonard's argument. Fewer than 27 percent of the nation's 91 million households in 1988 fit the traditional model of a family. At the same time, the bureau has counted 1.6 million same-sex couples living together, up from 1.3 million in 1970, and 2.6 million opposite-sex couples sharing a household, up from just half a million in 1970. Reasons cited for these demographic changes include divorce, delayed marriage and the growth of the gay-liberation movement. For now the Census Bureau still excludes most nontraditional arrangements from its "family" category. But Paul Glick, until 1981 the department's senior demographer, thinks the federal legal definition of family could broaden considerably in the next 20 years.

While gays are not the only beneficiaries of the new legislation, they, above all others, have been most profoundly changed by increased social acceptance of alternative lifestyles. Galen Ellis, 28, and Elaine Askari, 38, have been a couple since 1986 and this year donned white tuxedos to celebrate their "commitment ceremony" before 100 friends and family members in an Oakland, Calif., park. They exchanged vows and rings and cut a wedding cake. Ellis's mother attended the festivities, and Askari's father sent a wedding card. Since deciding they are a family, they've bought a house together and drafted a variety of legal forms designed to cement their relationship, including wills, powers of attorney and other contracts. Soon they'd like to become parents, as so many other gay couples have done already.

According to Roberta Achtenberg, executive director of the National Center for Lesbian Rights, there are more than 2 million gay mothers and fathers. Most of their children are from earlier, heterosexual relationships, but she estimates that some 5,000 to 10,000 lesbians have borne children after "coming out," and hundreds of gay and lesbian couples have adopted.

Among these nontraditional parents are Michael Pesce, 35, and Jonathan Jarnig, 36. Pesce, a social worker, and Jarnig, a maitre d' at a restaurant, live in a three-bedroom house in suburban Sacramento with their two kids, James, 7, and Carly, 5. Parenthood was always a compelling goal for both men; they even discussed it on their second date seven years ago. "I didn't feel like a whole person without kids," recalls Jarnig. "I didn't feel it was right for gay people to be robbed of a sense of family." The couple, whom the kids call Dad and Poppa, are among fewer than a dozen gay couples in the United States who have been granted "joint adoption," which means both fathers have the same secure legal relationship to the children.

"Our values really are the same as those of our parents," says Jarnig. "We just happen to be two men." "We're really quite boring," adds Pesce. "Just homebodies. We're Ozzie and Harry." Their home is one with rules and structure: no playing in the living room, cleaning up the family room after play, and no candy. But it's also one with love and understanding for the children, who are Hispanic siblings. "It's impor-

Rights of Domestic Partners

A few places that have particularly broad definitions of what constitutes a family:

■ **New York**
In July 1989 the Court of Appeals held that a longterm, live-in gay couple may be considered a family under the state's rent-control regulations.

■ **San Francisco**
In June 1989 the Board of Supervisors passed legislation recognizing homosexual and unmarried heterosexual couples as families and allowed for registration of "domestic partners."

■ **Madison**
In August 1988 the city council OK'd sick and bereavement leave to domestic partners of city employees and extended the right of domestic partners to live in single-family zones.

■ **West Hollywood**
In December 1988 the California city became "self-insured" and offered medical benefits to domestic partners, extending a 1985 ordinance permitting domestic partners official registration and hospital and prison visitation rights.

tant to tell them every night that they're valued and loved," says Pesce.

Cindy and Margie share a house on a quiet side street near Boston with their son, Jonah, who recently turned 3. (Like several others in this story, they chose not to have their last names published.) Both professionals in their mid-30s, they have been together for 12 years. Their decision to become "Mommy" and "Mama," as Jonah calls them, reflects societal changes that also affect single straight women seeking to become mothers. Medical advances have made donor insemination much safer from infection by AIDS and other sexually transmitted diseases, and activism by the feminist and gay women's movements has made it more widely available.

Despite the growing demand, many U.S. doctors still won't inseminate unmarried women. But there are some exceptions. "We opened our facility to accommodate women being turned away by sperm banks across the country," says Mary Lynn Hemphill of the Feminist Women's Health Center in Atlanta. Almost all FWHC clients are single; one third are lesbians. At Boston's Fenway Community Health Center, which expanded in 1983 to serve lesbians seeking to become mothers, the clientele is still mostly gay, with a growing straight minority.

Sperm donors at many facilities are drawn from college and graduate students, who earn about $35 each time they "give." For the most part, that's the last connection they have with the children they sire this way, but a couple of programs now offer a "yes" option, in which the donor agrees to let his offspring get in touch with him once they reach the age of 18.

Donors are thoroughly screened for a family history of inherited diseases and also for current infections, especially for the HIV virus that causes AIDS. Indeed, the AIDS epidemic has made the use of fresh semen donations obsolete. In September New York became the first state to adopt protective regulations to prevent the transmission of AIDS through donor insemination. The new rulings require that a donor be tested twice during a six-month period for antibodies to the AIDS virus, before his frozen donation can be released and used.

Some insemination programs require donors to fill out a 25-page questionnaire, mostly anticipating requests by recipients on topics like religious and academic background, hobbies and even receding hairlines. The would-be mom can specify the race and physical characteristics of her baby's father; everyone, of course, wants good health and high intelligence. At most facilities, recipients can choose the baby's sex (since it is the sperm that determines gender), but most women don't exercise the option.

In some states, insemination must be performed by a physician, but the Fenway and other centers encourage women to bring the semen home and inseminate themselves using a syringe or pipette. As with standard conception, some women get pregnant on the first try; for others, it may take a dozen or more attempts. At Fenway, the monthly cost for two vials of semen is $250.

Cindy and Margie, who had a private physician perform their insemination, meet with a group of 50 Boston-area lesbian families at least four times a year—including Mother's Day. Among their friends are Lorraine, 43, and Linda, 33, who gave birth to the couple's son, Andrew, nearly four years ago. She tries to describe the boy's relationship with Lorraine, whom he calls "Boppie." "There aren't words for it," she says. "Lorraine's not the same as a father, but she's also not a mother." Lorraine would like to legalize her relationship to Andrew through "second-parent" adoption but doesn't care about labels. "I can be 'Boppie' all his life," she says. In fact, the arrangement has worked out so well that she and Linda hope to have another child by the same donor.

Most couples who are openly gay, with and without children, acknowledge that they are still not universally accepted as families, and many have experienced some form of rejection or discrimination. Pesce and Jarnig say their biggest disappointment is that their own parents have kept their distance. "My mother lumps gay people together with child molesters," says Jarnig. "She's ashamed that I'm gay and have children—her only grandchildren—and doesn't want to get involved as a grandmother."

Linda and Lorraine worry about the effect of their nontraditional arrangement on their son. For now, "we don't have people around us that don't accept us as a family," says Linda, but she realizes that will inevitably change as Andrew grows up. "When he's a teenager," she says, "if he doesn't want both of us to go to some event, we won't go." Adds Lorraine: "We want to protect him but not get outrageous about it. We want him to know we made choices that affected him and that we tried to do it the right way."

Single Mothers by Choice

Lesbians aren't the only women taking advantage of donor insemination. A growing number of unmarried moms are heterosexual but have decided they just can't wait any longer for Mr. Right to show up. "When people hear about a woman having a baby without a man, they still kind of scratch their heads," says Lisa McDonnell of Boston's Fenway Community Health Center. During the next decade the head scratching is likely to disappear, as illegitimacy continues to lose its stigma and more women become economically independent. "Most of us wanted to be married and have children in a more traditional way, but it just didn't work out," says Noel (not her real name), 37, a Boston-area classical musician and mother of a 3-year-old daughter conceived through donor insemination. "Then we hit those age deadlines and we can either make the choice of having children on our own or never have the experience of having a family."

The typical single woman pursuing pregnancy is a middle-class professional in her mid-30s or older. Marilyn Levin, 45, trained as a psychotherapist, now spends her spare time leading workshops for the Boston chapter of Single Mothers by Choice. For Levin, like most women in her support group, putting motherhood before marriage came only after a long struggle. At 30, she reports, she caught "baby fever," then got married and divorced without having a child. As the ticking of her biological clock grew louder, she launched a last-ditch effort to start a traditional family. "I tried therapy. I did the singles scene. I gave finding a relationship top priority. It was unproductive. Finally I said, 'That's it,' and went ahead on my own."

Levin's daughter, Cate Lara, was born two and a half years ago; Levin's sister attended childbirth classes with her and was at the delivery. Initially, Levin says, her father was "worried about what society would think." Now, both her septuagenarian parents are very much involved with the new little relative. "It's probably lengthened their lives," she says.

Noel, who picked a Chinese sperm donor, often wonders about his genetic contribution to her daughter. "At times I wish she looked a little bit more like me," she admits. "But other times I just think of how beautiful she is." Noel is convinced some of her daughter's personality traits come from the father. "She tends to be much more of a neatnik and much more orderly than I am," she says.

Susan (also a pseudonym), 41, is a registered nurse in a small town in the Southwest. When she took stock at 36 of "possible life partners," her options seemed few. A year later she began inseminating and after five failed attempts became pregnant; her son is now 2. Unlike Noel and Marilyn Levin, she knows almost no one who has done what she did. She and her son have been easily accepted, however, by the largely Hispanic community they live in. Though she sometimes feels isolated and thinks of moving, Susan has no regrets. "Donor insemination was the way to do it," she says. "I didn't want to just sort of use some man and not tell him. Besides, there's no one I wanted to have as a father." She often speculates about the man who is her son's biological father. "It's interesting to wonder what the other half of his genes are, because people say he looks like me," she says. "But no one in my family has eyes that color."

For Susan, who now works just one day a week, many worries of single motherhood have been mitigated by family money. Levin, on the other hand, had to return full time to her job as an administrator at the Massachusetts Department of Mental Health when Cate was still an infant. Now Cate attends a licensed family-day-care center, run by two women who take a small number of babies and toddlers into their homes. Levin says the other kids are a good substitute for siblings. Noel's parents pay for day-care costs, but her finances are always a worry.

All three moms realize their children will soon ask about their origins or the absence of a father in the household. Levin plans to explain gradually. When her daughter is young, she says, "I'll tell her, 'Families are different. There are all kinds. Ours is the kind with just a mommy.' When she realizes that she had to have a father to be born, I will tell her that her father is a kind man who wanted to help me have her. We're grateful to him, but he's not involved in our life." At some point, Levin thinks Cate will have to grieve, and may be angry. "When she's a rebelling adolescent, she'll have an easy target."

Noel also believes her daughter may eventually feel hurt and angry. "You do wonder about the psychological ramifications later on," she says. "We're at the forefront, so we don't know how it's going to affect the children. We're just going to have to do the best we can."

'Skip-Generation' Parents

An entirely different kind of nontraditional family is born when mothers can't or won't take care of their children. Often it's Grandma who comes to the rescue. Five years ago Ruth Rench was looking forward to retirement. Her children had long since moved out of her house near Ft. Worth, and she was planning to travel, using the nest egg built up during 25 years with the local school system. That's when Rench's 3-year-old granddaughter gave her some chilling news: she had been molested by one of her mother's male friends. It would not be the last time the girl was abused. Finally, Rench filed for custody.

Two years and $25,000 later, Rench, now 65, finally won custody of her granddaughter, who is now 8. She has joined a nationwide groundswell of grandparents who are stepping in to raise their children's children. Rench and her granddaughter are one of 95 "skip-generation" families who belong to the Ft. Worth area chapter of Grandparents Raising Grandchildren (GRG).

According to family-court judges, social workers and counselors, the skip-generation phenomenon is often linked to drug and alcohol abuse. The affected parents cannot or should not assume responsibility for their children. But the problem is not limited to families of the inner city, or even to drug users. "Most of these grandparents are from good middle-class families who have never had to face anything like this before," says Ellen Hogan, 44. Hogan, who heads a 55-member Houston GRG group, and her husband, Harold, are in the middle of a court battle with their 23-year-old daughter over custody of their two grandchildren, ages 1 and 4. "It's happening to blue-collar workers, white-collar workers, blacks and whites," she says. "It's so widespread—it's happening all over."

Often frustrated by the expense and the legal hoops they must jump through to gain custody of neglected or abused grandchildren, many grandparents stand by helplessly as the youngsters are shipped off to foster homes. Others simply take on the child-rearing burden without legal custody. They may start on an informal basis: watching the grandchildren for the weekend, or while the parents are at work. Gradually, the time the children spend with them is extended as the parents lose control of their lives through drugs, financial difficulties or extreme self-absorption. This situation may go on for years until suddenly the mother decides she wants the child back—often in order to increase her welfare payments so she can buy drugs. "It often ends up in court," says one family counselor, "sometimes amicably, sometimes not."

Psychologists are just beginning to look at the long-term emotional effects skip-generation rearing has on children. California social worker Sylvie de Toledo has spent the last two years working with such families in programs she started at the Psychiatric Clinic for Youth in Long Beach and the Reiss-Davis Child Study Center in Los Angeles. Though skip-generation grandparents and parents suffer great emotional strain during these crises, it is the children who are at greatest risk. They often do poorly in school, defy authority, have problems making friends and exhibit physical aggressiveness or feelings of isolation. "It is crucial that the children be helped to understand that they are blameless," de Toledo emphasizes.

Although these children are quite attached to their grandparents, she explains, "they have a profound sense of abandonment and loss and rejection by their parents . . . They worry consciously and unconsciously that they may once again be abandoned." One of their greatest fears is that their grandparents may get sick or die, leaving them with no one else to turn to.

Quietly heroic grandmothers like Ruth Rench are sacrificing their own needs and plans to provide their "rescued" grandchildren with that precious sense of security and love that is every child's birthright. They are also struggling to keep their grandkids from perpetuating a dangerous cycle. "All I can do now is give her all the moral and spiritual training that she needs and hope that she doesn't grow up in the pattern she was born into," says Rench. "You've got to break that pattern somewhere. If you don't, we're all going down the drain."

With FARAI CHIDEYA in Boston, ELIZABETH LEONARD in New York, PETER ANNIN in Houston and NADINE JOSEPH in San Francisco

Should Gays Have Marriage Rights?

On two coasts, the growing debate produces two different answers

WALTER ISAACSON

Long-term homosexual lovers in New York State, thanks to regulations issued by Governor Mario Cuomo's housing commissioner last week, now have the same right as surviving spouses to take over rent-stabilized apartments upon the death of their partners. In San Francisco voters last Tuesday narrowly rejected—after vocal opposition from the city's archbishop and other religious leaders—a proposal entitling gay couples to register their relationships with the county clerk. In Washington and Los Angeles, task forces have been set up to investigate whether denying gay couples the benefits enjoyed by married people is a form of discrimination. It is all part of a growing national debate over whether gay couples should be allowed to declare themselves "domestic partners," or even become legally married, and thus be eligible for some of the rights accorded to married couples.

The rewards of marriage in today's society are more than merely emotional. Among the tangible benefits available to husbands and wives are coverage under their spouses' health and pension plans, rights of inheritance and community property, the joys of joint tax returns, and claims to each other's rent-controlled apartments.

Such policies have evolved as the expression of a basic social value: that the traditional family, with its economic interdependence, is the foundation of a strong society. But what about a gay couple? They might be similarly dependent on each other, economically and emotionally. Yet no state in the U.S. allows them to marry legally, and nowhere are they offered the same medical, pension, tax and legal advantages as married heterosexuals.

Since as much as 40% of a worker's compensation comes in the form of fringe benefits, the issue is partly one of economic equity: Is it fair to provide more for a married employee than for a gay colleague who does the same work? There is also a larger moral issue. Health plans, pension programs and inheritance laws are designed to accommodate the traditional family. But nowadays, only 27% of U.S. households consist of two parents with children, down from 40% in 1970. Is the goal of encouraging traditional families therefore obsolete? Is it discriminatory? Or is it now more necessary than ever?

Although the drive for domestic-partnership legislation partly reflects the changing priorities of the gay-rights movement, the new rights being proposed would be available to heterosexual couples as well. Of the nation's 91 million households, 2.6 million are inhabited by unmarried couples of the opposite sex. Only 1.6 million households involve unmarried couples of the same sex. These figures include a disparate array of personal arrangements: young male-female couples living together before getting married, elderly friends who decide to share a house, platonic roommates and romantic gay or straight lovers. Among those whose emotional and financial relationship would qualify them to be called domestic partners, only 40% or so are gay.

Still, the most ardent support for partnership rights comes from gay groups. For them the issue is more pressing: heterosexual couples at least have the option to wed if they wish to be eligible for family benefits, but gays do not. (Denmark in October became the only industrial nation to allow registered gay partnerships.) In addition, the spread of AIDS has raised

Do you think homosexual couples should be legally allowed to inherit each other's property?

Yes 65%

No 27%

Not sure 8%

Do you think homosexual couples should be permitted to receive medical- and life-insurance benefits from a partner's policies?

Yes 54%

No 37%

Not sure 9%

From a telephone poll of 1,000 adult Americans taken for TIME/CNN on Oct. 9-10 by Yankelovich Clancy Shulman. Sampling error is plus or minus 3%.

the importance for gays of medical coverage, bereavement-leave policies, pension rules, hospital visitation rights and laws giving family members the authority to make medical decisions and funeral arrangements. "We are not talking about symbols here," says Thomas Stoddard, executive director of the Lambda Legal Defense and Education Fund, a well-organized gay-rights group. "These are bread-and-butter issues of basic importance to individuals."

In an attempt to clarify the murky statistics, the Census Bureau is making a major change in family categories when its decennial count begins in April. For the first time, couples living together will have the option to designate themselves "unmarried partners." The bureau has not yet said whether it will get explicit about the precise sexual and emotional relationship that distinguishes "unmarried partners" from another category in the survey, "housemates-roommates." (Those who have to ask can perhaps be assumed to be merely roommates.)

"We are hoping that we will get at the true unmarried-couple situation where there is intimacy between partners," says Arlene Saluter, who studies marriage and family composition for the Census Bureau, "but it will depend on how people view the question."

This difficulty in defining who qualifies is one of the problems facing those who would grant new rights to domestic partners. It is important to have criteria that are strict enough to prevent just any casual lover, roommate or friendly acquaintance in need of health insurance from cashing in. But prying into private lives and requiring proofs of emotional commitment are hardly suitable activities for government.

In order to qualify as "domestic partners" in New York City, which offers bereavement leave to municipal workers, a couple must officially register their relationship with the city's personnel department, have lived together for one year and attest that they have a "close and committed personal relationship involving shared responsibilities." Thomas F. Coleman, a law professor who directs California's Family Diversity Project, proposes that live-in couples "who have assumed mutual obligation of commitment and support for each other" be allowed to apply for a "certificate of domestic partnership" that would function like a marriage certificate.

In addition to New York, five other cities provide bereavement leave for domestic partners: Los Angeles; Madison, Wis.; San Francisco; Seattle; and Takoma Park, Md. The only cities that currently offer health benefits to the domestic partners of employees are three in California: Berkeley, Santa Cruz and West Hollywood. State governments, which have the real authority to legislate family and marriage laws, have so far shied away from the issue. But across the country, major efforts are under way to change the laws:

▶ In Los Angeles a new task force on marital-status discrimination is investigating discrimination against domestic partners by insurance companies, health clubs, credit companies and airline frequent-flyer programs.

▶ In Seattle the city's human rights department ruled in June that the AAA

automobile club of Washington had illegally discriminated on the basis of marital status by refusing to grant associate membership to a gay man's domestic partner. A city law that could require health plans to provide insurance benefits to domestic partners has been shelved while officials await clarification of an Internal Revenue Service ruling that suggests that these benefits might be considered taxable.

▶ In Washington a domestic-partnership benefits commission has been established by the city council to explore extending benefits to the partners of municipal employees.

▶ In New York City three gay teachers are suing the board of education for the right to include their companions in their group health plans, citing a state law prohibiting employment discrimination based on marital status.

One large problem facing the domestic-partnership movement is a practical one: major U.S. insurance companies have thus far refused to offer group plans that include coverage for unmarried partners, partly because of the unspoken fear that the pool would include a higher proportion of gay males at risk for AIDS. In West Hollywood when the city decided to provide health coverage to its employees' domestic partners, no insurance company would underwrite the business. The city had to resort to self-insurance. So far that has resulted in a drop in costs, but it has not yet encouraged leading insurance companies to consider offering domestic-partnership plans.

The other major objection is a moral one. Social conservatives object to policies they see as sanctifying homosexuality and further threatening the traditional family. John R. Quinn, the Archbishop of San Francisco, was in the forefront of the fight against the proposal on that city's ballot last week to provide certain domestic-partnership rights to municipal workers. He called the idea a "serious blow to our society's historic commitment to supporting marriage and family life."

The domestic-partnership movement, says David Blankenhorn of the Institute for American Values, a Manhattan-based group that studies family issues, "just misses the whole point of why we confer privileges on family relationships." As Archbishop Quinn argues, "The permanent commitment of husband and wife in marriage is intrinsically tied to the procreation and raising of children." Despite the emergence of women in the workplace and changes in the traditional structure of family dependency, it is still necessary for most families to share rights and benefits in order to raise children and remain financially secure.

Thomas Stoddard of Lambda counters that "history by itself cannot justify an unduly limited definition of family,

Do you think marriages between homosexual couples should be recognized by the law?

Yes 23%

No 69%

Not sure **8%**

Do you think homosexual couples should be legally permitted to adopt children?

Yes 17%

No 75%

Not sure **8%**

particularly when people suffer as a result." Yet even within the gay-rights movement, there is some disagreement about the goal. Paula Ettelbrick, the legal director of Lambda, argues that the campaign for domestic partnership or gay marriage is misdirected because it tries to adopt traditional heterosexual institutions for gays rather than encouraging tolerance for divergent life-styles. "Marriage, as it exists today, is antithetical to my liberation as a lesbian and as a woman, because it mainstreams my life and voice," she says.

The public seems to be tolerant of the notion that gay couples should be allowed more of the rights now accorded to married couples. In a TIME/CNN poll conducted by the firm of Yankelovich Clancy Shulman, 54% agreed that "homosexual couples should be permitted to receive medical and life-insurance benefits from their partner's insurance policies." Yet there is little support for gay marriages: 69% said such arrangements should not be made legal, and 75% felt that gay couples should not be allowed to adopt children.

Despite this public resistance, legalizing some form of marriage for gay couples is probably the logical outcome of the drive for domestic-partnership rights. "Given the fact that we already allow legal gay relationships," writes Andrew Sullivan in the *New Republic,* "what possible social goal is advanced by framing the law to encourage those relationships to be unfaithful, undeveloped and insecure?" Marriage involves the obligation to support each other both in sickness and in health and to share financial benefits and burdens. It implies, at least in theory, a commitment to a long-term and monogamous relationship. The advent of the AIDS epidemic increases the stake that all of society has in promoting such relationships, for gays as well as straights.

Domestic-partnership rights and legal gay marriages, therefore, can be justified to the extent that the couples involved profess a willingness to accept the mutual financial obligations, community-property rights and shared commitments to care for each other that are the basis of family life. With this broader goal in mind, it makes sense for society to allow—indeed to encourage—domestic partners both gay and straight to take on all the rights as well as the responsibilities of marriage.

—Reported by Melissa Ludtke/Boston, Jeanne McDowell/Los Angeles and Andrea Sachs/New York

Interpersonal Relationships

- Establishing Sexual Relationships (Articles 20-22)
- Responsible Quality Relationships (Articles 23-26)

Most people are familiar with the term "sexual relationship." It denotes an important dimension of sexuality: interpersonal sexuality, or sexual interactions occurring between two (and sometimes more) individuals. This unit focuses attention on these types of relationships.

No woman is an island. No man is an island. Interpersonal contact forms the basis for self-esteem and meaningful living; conversely, isolation results in loneliness and depression for most human beings. People seek and cultivate friendships for the warmth, affection, supportiveness, and sense of trust and loyalty that such relationships can provide.

Long-term friendships may develop into intimate relationships. The qualifying word in the previous sentence is "may." Today many people, single as well as married, yearn for close or intimate interpersonal relationships but fail to find them. How and where to find potential friends, partners, lovers, and soul mates is reported to be more difficult today than in times past. Fear of rejection causes some to avoid interpersonal relationships, others to present a "false front" or illusory self that they think is more acceptable or socially desirable. This sets the stage for a "game of intimacy" that is counterfeit to genuine intimacy. For others a major dilemma may exist—the problem of balancing closeness with the preservation of individual identity in a manner that at once satisfies the need for personal and interpersonal growth and integrity. In either case, partners in a relationship should be advised that the development of interpersonal awareness (the mutual recognition and knowledge of others as they really are) rests upon trust and self-disclosure—letting the other person know who you really are and how you truly feel. In American society this has never been easy, and it is especially difficult in the area of sexuality.

The above considerations in regard to interpersonal relationships apply equally well to achieving meaningful and satisfying sexual relationships. Three basic ingredients lay the foundation for quality sexual interaction. These are self-awareness, acceptance of the partner's state of awareness, and a free and open sharing of each partner's awareness through communication of feelings, needs, and desires. Without these, misunderstandings may arise, bringing into the relationship anxiety, frustration, dissatisfaction, and/or resentment, as well as a heightened risk of contracting AIDS or another STD or experiencing an unplanned pregnancy. Indeed, these basic ingredients, taken together, may constitute sexual responsibility. Clearly, no one person is completely responsible for quality sexual relations.

As might already be apparent, there is much more to quality sexual relations than our popular culture recognizes. Such relationships are not established on penis size, beautiful figures, or correct sexual techniques. Rather, it is the quality of the interaction that makes sex a celebration of our sexuality. A person-oriented (as opposed to genitally oriented) sexual awareness coupled with a leisurely, whole body/mind sensuality and an open attitude toward exploration make for quality sexuality.

The subsection on *Establishing Sexual Relationships* opens with an article that examines some 1980s and 1990s twists to the dating scene—special interest dating services. In the next article, the double standard of premarital sexual behavior is addressed. This is followed by an article that explores intimacy, detailing our needs for and fears of this sought after state.

In the subsection *Responsible Quality Relationships* the examination of sexual and intimate relationships continues with a variety of experience-sharing and advice-giving articles. The first article ponders the risks, benefits, and patterns of friends who seek to become lovers, too. The second article takes these emotional and possibly sexual partnerships a step further by exploring the financial pros and cons of joint ownership. The next article is actually a compilation of five shorter essays on sex, love, seduction, and caution for today. The final article is the counterpart to the final article in the previous subsection. It offers advice to men who want to become "erotic virtuosos."

Looking Ahead: Challenge Questions

What do you see as the greatest barriers to satisfying intimate relationships? Are there some people who are destined to fail at establishing and/or maintaining them? If so, who and why?

What makes you most fearful of trusting or intimacy? Why?

What about sexual pursuit in the "old days"? Do you

wish it were still the same today? What are you glad has changed?

Have you ever been involved in a friendship that you (or your friend) hoped would grow into a sexual relationship? What was your perception of the risks and benefits of such a shift?

Which advice offered to your gender intrigued you? Offended you? Why?

Which advice offered to the opposite gender pleased you? Offended you? Why?

LOOKING FOR LOVE IN ALL THE RIGHT PLACES

DOES MR./MS. RIGHT HAVE TO BE VEGETARIAN? A BOOKLOVER? A SHORT PERSON? HAVE WE GOT A SINGLES CLUB FOR YOU!

Steven Kaplan

Steven Kaplan is a free-lance writer living in St. Paul, Minnesota. He is a frequent contributor to THE WORLD & I.

If you've noticed what Pepsi girls look like these days or have taken a gander at the *Sports Illustrated* swimsuit issue lately, you'll know what 5'4", 200-pound Bonny D. is up against. Bonny is an executive, a college graduate, and an attractive woman; but she's about as far from the media's idea of the ideal American woman as is possible. That fact has been brought home to her all too often in her dating life. Men avoid her in bars and other public places, and blind dates have been a nightmare. Bonny had been rejected and rudely treated so many times that she was just about ready to give up dating altogether when she discovered the Bigger and Better Dating Service, which caters to overweight men and women.

"For the first time in my life," she says, "I am able to have a social life that is normal. I don't have to worry about what my date will think when he meets me, because everybody there is either a big person or somebody who wants to date a big person. I date several times a month now, and I'm enjoying my life like never before."

Bonny is a beneficiary of an eighties trend in dating services, the special-interest dating club. Dating services in the seventies tended to be catchall affairs, a little like the singles bar scene, only more organized. But lots of people were unable to fit into the broad-based singles scene. These were people who either didn't look "right"—they were too tall or too short, too skinny or too fat—or they had particular interests or requirements that were unlikely to be met at random in a crowd.

In Palo Alto, California, the Vegetarian Dating Club connects singles who would prefer a cheese to a pepperoni pizza after their date. In Chicago, Yvonne Monte's Ebony/Ivory Society is set up for individuals interested in meeting dates of another race. And in Brooklyn, Stephanie Alexandra's Music and Art Lover's Club for Singles creates an atmosphere in which cultured young people can meet to enjoy art and music and perhaps find that perfect match.

THE SEARCH FOR A 'PERFECT MATCH'

Thousands of dating clubs have opened in the United States in the last decade. Dating services today represent a $40-billion business in the United States. There are television dating shows such as *Love Connection*; magazines and newspapers devoted to the single person's search for a mate; dating-service information bureaus that will guide you through the singles scenes of various big cities; and even "attraction researchers" —psychologists who specialize in studying the details of dating and courtship. The old neighborhood matchmaker is still around, but she's got help these days from videotapes, computers, fax machines, and just about every other high-tech gadget you can imagine. With all that, one hard fact is clear to anyone who is still playing the dating game in America: You can't always get what you want.

A major factor affecting the rise of dating clubs is the extraordinary growth in the U.S. singles population. A generation ago an unmarried person in a social gathering was the odd man out, but that situation has changed dramatically. Today almost one in five Americans —more than sixty million people —are single, and the single lifestyle has become fashionable. Since 1950, according to the U.S. Census Bureau, the number of single Americans has grown an astonishing 385 percent.

This explosion in the number of unmarried people has made it easier to be single in this country. Being single no longer carries the social stigma it did even a decade ago. But in one crucial way, things are as they always have been: Single people are still looking for love and are still having trouble finding it. The logistic and personal problems of finding a suitable partner have been, and probably will be, here forever.

However, there are many resources available to help singles find each other. They range from Bible study groups, to health and workout clubs, which *Rolling Stone* magazine dubbed as the "singles bars of the eighties." Some of the most successful ways of meeting new people are still the most traditional. About one-third of all singles are introduced to their marriage partners by family members or friends, according to Jacqueline Simanauer and David Carroll, authors of *Singles: The New Americans.* Church groups, too, continue to provide the meeting ground for many successful relationships. Many singles, though, have turned to newer methods of meeting, such as singles ads in classified advertising pages.

Dating clubs and services provide some of the best ways for singles to meet. There has been an explosive growth in their membership and in the number of such services on the market. The movement has been from broad-based dating services (such as video and computer dating clubs)

to dating services serving specific interests. The most common type of specific-interest dating service attempts to connect people with similar religious backgrounds.

CHICKEN SOUP... AND A DATE

The Jewish Dating Service (JDS) in Minneapolis typifies how these work. There's no high-tech equipment here, no leather couches or fancy waiting rooms; but upon entering there is the unmistakable smell of . . . chicken soup. "What else would you expect?" asks Bobbie Goldfarb, who has been running JDS for more than a decade. Customers are offered a cup of instant soup or coffee and then get the once-over from Goldfarb and her partners, who make all their matches based on personal knowledge of their client base.

Goldfarb has been matching couples since her college days, when she kept a box of notes filled with information about potential dates for herself and her friends. Back in 1979 she and partner Sandy Olkon identified a need for matching singles who wanted to marry inside the Jewish community and figured, quite rightly, that they were perfect for the job.

The success of JDS bears out their judgment. Goldfarb and Olkon have a clientele of more than four hundred people, with applicants from up to five hundred miles away. The service averages one engagement or marriage every month and has been responsible for more than 125 marriages since it began. More than one hundred children have been born from these marriages, and Goldfarb speaks of them as if she were the godmother of them all. "I'm very proud of those kids, and why not?" she says. "We're helping to keep a tradition going. And, after all, in fifteen or

twenty years they're apt to become customers of mine."

Another type of specialized dating service seeks to serve the needs of people who have atypical tastes in the opposite sex. Phyllis Sydney, for example, found herself bored with men her own age and much more interested in men considerably younger.

"I figured the best way to meet this thing was head-on," she recalls. "In 1984 I decided to start a club where younger men who were interested in older women would have a place to meet." Sidney moved ahead with her idea. She ran an ad in a local singles paper advising any younger men and older women who were interested in meeting for dating purposes to attend a luncheon meeting at a Beverly Hills Hotel restaurant. Much to her astonishment, five men and six women showed up at the designated restaurant.

Thus was born the DecMay Club. Today it has an active core of about thirty members, with dozens more attending its various activities. Up to five times a month the club sponsors brunches, picnics, and parties. At least one marriage has grown out of the club meetings—an executive of a major Hollywood studio married a man seventeen years her junior.

"There probably have been more marriages," Sidney says. "But when people meet each other here, they don't report back to the person who's running the club, they just go quietly off into the sunset. I do know that there's a lot of dating going on, though."

"I love this club because this is a place where what you want is completely understood," one of its newer members said recently at a Beverly Hills brunch. "When I'm with these people I don't have to deny, explain, or justify my preferences, which many people regard as odd or even distasteful. Everyone here knows exactly why we're here, and we all enjoy each other."

In New York, Debby Mellen understands those sentiments exactly. Debby was an exercise instructor, which put her in constant contact with overweight women. "These were vital, alive, and beautiful women," she says, "but they all had trouble maintaining a satisfactory dating life. They encouraged me to look for a solution to this, and so I thought of a dating service for overweight people."

Mellen began her service by placing an ad in the paper announcing a party to be held for overweight singles. "The response was astounding," she says. "Almost 150 people attended that first party, and we've been going strong ever since. Today we have over eight hundred members in the New York-New Jersey area.

"When I started the club I thought it would be for both large women and large men, but it turned out to be mostly for average-weight men who are interested in large women," Mellen says. "I think it's easier for heavy men to meet women. But society imposes on women a much stricter standard of how they should look, and that is, first of all, thin. But not all women are thin, and not all men want thin women. The men who attend our functions just naturally like larger women, like some men like blondes or taller women. In the past this has not been socially acceptable, so they just kept quiet. But our club provides an avenue where they can express those desires."

NONTHREATENING ATMOSPHERE

Probably the most common type of specialized dating club attempts to gather people of similar interests in a nonthreatening atmosphere. One of the most successful of these has taken the old-fashioned dinner date and expanded it to serve a communal meeting function. The Single Gourmet, a social club with outlets across the United States and Canada, connects single men and women through dinners at fine restaurants in their area.

Candyce Stout, who runs the Twin Cities Single Gourmet Club, understands the difficulty of meeting quality dates. Stout is a teacher working on her Ph.D. and is single herself.

"I had been frustrated with options for professionally educated singles in my area," she says. "I heard about this concept and liked the idea, so I went to New York City and to Ottawa to see how the clubs worked in those two cities. I liked what I saw and decided to open one here in the Twin Cities.

"Because of the activities we do—some cultural outings but primarily fine dining at the best restaurants—we tend to attract an upper-middle-class clientele. I would say that 90 percent of our four hundred members have at least a bachelor's degree, and many of them have advanced degrees."

The Single Gourmet sponsors several events every month, including one or more meals in a fine local restaurant. Each outing is attended by several dozen members, with every occasion an opportunity to meet a changing but friendly group of people.

"Everybody loves to eat," Stout says, "so this is a real safe place to meet. I think of it like a group date, but paying only for yourself."

Stout says as many members use the Single Gourmet to meet new people and make new friends as those who use it as a singles meeting place. But romance definitely blooms around those dinner tables. Since she began her service, several couples who have met there have married.

Among the most popular places to find romance is the two-week vacation, whether spent touring a new locale or relaxing on a cruise ship. People who enjoy traveling start out with a major interest in common, and the vacation itself tends to loosen them up and make meeting others easier.

The Travel Companion Exchange connects singles who like to travel with others of like mind. It is probably the largest of its kind in America, which means a larger membership list from which to choose potential travel mates. Members are given a changing list of two thousand singles looking for traveling companions. Every member is listed in a newsletter that details in brief their travel plans and personal interests and characteristics. Want to travel around America in an RV or hike through the Black Hills? Want to go parachute jumping in England or accompany a woman on a shark-cage diving trip? These are a few of the hundreds of travel opportunities in a recent TCE newsletter.

Not everyone in the club is looking for romance. The club has been very successful in matching singles who love to travel but hate traveling alone. But romance is definitely on the mind of most members.

"We did not start out to be a dating service, but it works very well in that respect," says Jens Jurgen, owner of the club. "We've had lots of marriages. One elderly woman met and married a gentleman through the service. A few years later I saw her name on the list again. Her husband had died during a trip on the Orient Express, so she signed up to find another one. I don't know if she's found a new husband yet, but I have gotten postcards from her from across the world. She may not have found romance again, but she's definitely having fun trying."

Has the Double Standard Disappeared? An Experimental Test

SUSAN SPRECHER
Illinois State University

KATHLEEN McKINNEY
Oklahoma State University

TERRI L. ORBUCH
University of Wisconsin

A person perception experiment was conducted to examine the possible effect of a double standard on judgments formed of others based on information about their sexual experiences. Subjects were presented with information about the first coital experience of a stimulus person, who was either male or female, age 16 or 21, and had the first sexual intercourse experience in either a casual or steady relationship. Both stage of the relationship and age of the stimulus person at first coitus were found to interact with gender of the stimulus person in affecting how he/she was judged on a number of dimensions. More negative evaluations were made of the female if the first time she had sexual intercourse was in a casual rather than in a steady relationship or as a teenager (16) rather than as a young adult (21). On the other hand, stage of the relationship and age at first coitus did not affect, to the same degree, the evaluations made about a male. The results were interpreted as providing support for a conditional (or transitional) double standard. Differences between this experimental study and recent survey research indicating that the double standard has disappeared are discussed.

Background Literature

According to a double standard of premarital sexual behavior, sexual intercourse before marriage is judged to be more acceptable for males than for females (Reiss, 1960). In general, research conducted in the 1950s and 1960s indicated that the double standard was prevalent (Ehrmann, 1959; Reiss, 1967), particularly in its transitional or conditional form

An earlier version of this paper was presented at the annual meeting of the American Sociological Association, New York, New York, August, 1986. The authors would like to thank Carrie Anderson, Anthony Cortese, John DeLamater, Nora Schaeffer, Beverly Scholer, Robert Walsh and Robert Wazienski for assistance and/or comments on an earlier draft of this paper. Address all correspondence to Susan Sprecher, Department of Sociology, Anthropology and Social Work, Illinois State University, Normal, IL 61761.

(Kaats and Davis, 1970; Reiss, 1960). According to the transitional or conditional double standard, males are allowed more freedom than females to engage in premarital sex, but females are permitted to be sexually active as long as they are in affectionate relationships (Reiss, 1960; Walsh et al., 1983). This is a more egalitarian double standard than the orthodox double standard, which condemns premarital sexual intercourse for women regardless of the circumstances.

Research conducted more recently indicates that there has been a continued waning of even the conditional double standard and an emergence of a single, egalitarian premarital sexual standard. The sexual standard most frequently endorsed is what Reiss (1967) termed "permissiveness with affection." Men and women believe that premarital intercourse is acceptable for both genders within a relationship character-ized by affection and some commitment. Those who adhere to a more permissive standard (e.g., "permissiveness without affection") also tend to apply it equally to men and women. Most of this recent research consists of survey studies using small, nonprobability samples of college stu-dents (see, for example, Ferrell et al., 1977; Harrison et al., 1974; King et al., 1977; LaBeff and Dodder, 1982; and Spreadbury, 1982), although in one study (DeLamater and Mac-Corquodale, 1979 a large probability sample of both students and nonstudents was interviewed.

Although the common proclamation is that the double standard no longer exists (DeLamater and MacCorquodale, 1979), another possibility to consider is that it has taken a more subtle form. More specifically, the results indicating that the double standard has disappeared may be an artifact of the specific scales used in survey research to assess premarital sexual standards, in combination with the influence of prevalent societal norms. Typically, the respondents are first asked if it is acceptable for a man to engage in premarital intercourse (or another sexual behavior), and then the same question is asked in reference to a woman (see, for example, the Reiss, 1960, Premarital Permissiveness scale). The purpose of cross-gender comparisons is probably fairly transparent to the respondents, which can cause them to try to appear more consistent and egalitarian than they actually are. Although the same scales were used during a previous time, when evidence was found for a double standard, societal norms have changed. Egalitarianism is now a prominent norm in our society.

If there is a single sexual standard, it should be evidenced in a methodology that is character-ized by less direct and obtrusive measures of sexual standards. The person perception experi-ment affords the opportunity to assess sexual standards more unobtrusively. Subjects can be asked to form impressions of a hypothetical person after receiving information about his/her sexual behavior. Gender of the stimulus person can be experimentally manipulated so that subjects are randomly assigned to evaluate either a male or a female, but not both. This between-subjects random assignment of gender helps to assure that when subjects react to a particular gender, their responses are not influenced by how they did or will respond to the other gender.

There is another advantage of using a person perception experiment for examining the possi-ble existence of the double standard. The person perception experiment examines the actual consequences or effects of a double standard—in the form of perceptions or evaluations that are made of others who have certain sexual histories. This methodology can more directly address the question of whether there is greater condemnation of sexually active women than of men, particularly if the sexual activity occurs in casual relationships. This was proposed several years ago by Reiss (1960), but has never been adequately tested. A double standard is evi-denced if women are more negatively evaluated than men for engaging in the same sexual behavior under the same conditions.

Recently, a few such person perception experiments have been conducted. Although these studies vary somewhat in their design and the dependent variables measured, they all indicate nonsupport for a double standard. That is, in these studies, a female stimulus person has not been judged significantly more negatively, overall, than a male stimulus person for the same sexual behavior (Garcia, 1983; Istvan and Griffitt, 1980; Jacoby and Williams, 1985; and Mark and Miller, 1986).

Perhaps the reason that more support for the double standard was not found by Garcia (1983) and Istvan and Griffitt (1980) is because only the *degree* of sexual behavior was manipulated, and not the *context* in which the sexual activity occurs. That is, information was presented about the sexual experience of the stimulus person, but no information was presented about the conditions under which the sexual activity occurred. If the double standard still exists, however, it is most likely to be in a conditional or transitional form, with differences in stan-dards for men and women minimal for affection-ate, committed relationships, but more pro-nounced for casual relationships. Subjects in these experiments may have assumed that a female stimulus person had her sexual experi-ences in (a) close relationship(s), and thus did not judge her more negatively than a man.

In two other recent person perception experi-ments (Jacoby and Williams, 1985; Mark and Miller, 1986), the emotional context of the sexual activity was considered, but in ways that were confounded with other variables. In the Jacoby and Williams (1985) study, the emo-tional context of sexual activity was manipulated by presenting information concerning the total number of sexual partners, number of partners for whom affection was felt, and the number of partners for whom love was felt. Such a manipulation requires the subjects to do calculations and it's questionable whether they actually did. Mark and Miller (1986) manipulated the emotional context of sexuality, but in combination with the degree of sexual activity. A person was presented as either a virgin, as having sexual experiences in committed relationships, as having sexual experiences in casual relationships, or no information was presented. Although the experiment was thoughtfully designed, it also does not allow for (or at least it did not present) a direct test of the interaction between gender of stimulus person and the emotional context of sexual activity. This is the particular test that is needed, however, to examine the degree of the transitional double standard.

Description of This Research

Because the previous person perception experiments have not adequately tested for the possible existence of the transitional double standard, this study was designed to do so. Gender of a stimulus person and the emotional context of his/her sexual activity are independently manipulated for the purpose of examining the significance of the interaction between them. If a transitional or conditional double standard is operating, a female will be evaluated more negatively if sex occurs in a casual than in a more serious relationship, whereas evaluations of a male will be less affected by the emotional context of the sexual activity.

Because the focus of this research is specifically on the effect of the context of the sexual experience in interaction with gender, sexual activity is not varied. For all subjects, information about the *first* sexual intercourse experience of a hypothetical person is presented. The focus is on the first coitus because of its significance in our society (Carns, 1973). The stimulus person is presented as having his/her first sexual intercourse in either a casual or a steady relationship.

In this study, gender of subject and gender of the stimulus person will not be confounded, as it was in some of the previous research (e.g., Istvan and Griffitt, 1980; Jacoby and Williams, 1985). In these previous studies, male and

female subjects judged only those of the opposite sex. Consequently, the effects they found for gender (for example, as presented by Jacoby and Williams, 1985), are difficult to interpret because they could be due to gender of subject, gender of target, or an interaction between the two. In our research, each subject is randomly assigned to judge either a male or a female, which allows for the separation of the effects of gender of stimulus person and gender of subject.

The effect of another characteristic of the stimulus person, in addition to gender, will also be considered in this study. This is the *age* at which the sexual activity occurs. Surprisingly, previous research on sexual standards has not considered how the strength or nature of the double standard, and acceptability of sexual activity more generally, might depend on the *age* of the targets for whom standards are assessed. However, because the age at first coitus is decreasing (Zelnik and Kantner, 1977; 1980), and the age at marriage is increasing (Glick, 1979), the period of premarital sexual activity is now potentially longer than it has ever been. The sexual behavior that is considered to be acceptable for a single adult may not be the same as that for a single teenager. We hypothesize that the double standard will be more pronounced in the judgments of teenagers than of young adults. This can be considered another type of a conditional double standard, with age rather than quality of the relationship as the conditional factor. As norms change and people become more accepting of the premarital sexual behavior of women, this acceptance will likely come more quickly for the sexual activity of females who have reached adulthood than of females who are still teenagers.

The subjects in this study are asked their impressions of the hypothetical person on a wide range of personality characteristics. This will allow us to examine more specifically the extent of the effect of the double standard. The two hypotheses that will be tested in this person perception experiment are the following:

(1) Evaluations of a female will be more negative if she has first coitus in a casual rather than a steady relationship, whereas the evaluations of a male will be less affected by the type of relationship in which sexual activity occurs.

(2) Evaluations of a female will be more negative if she has first coitus as a teenager

rather than as a young adult, whereas the evaluations of a male will be less affected by age at first coitus.

METHOD

Subjects

The subjects were 233 males and 320 females attending one of two universities during the spring of 1985. Of the total 553 subjects, 371 (67%) were from the University of Wisconsin-Madison, and 182 (33%) were from Oklahoma State University. A majority of the subjects were white and middle class. The mean age was approximately 21 years. All four undergraduate class levels were represented: 10% were freshmen, 31% were sophomores, 26% were juniors and 31% were seniors (1% were graduate students, and .5% were special students).

Procedure

The research was conducted during class time in several introductory and upper division sociology courses. The subjects were given a questionnaire that contained instructions, manipulations, and dependent measures, and was titled "Accuracy of Person Perception Based on Limited Information About a Person's Sexual Behavior." In the written instructions, the subjects were told that they would be reading through a page of a questionnaire completed by a high school or college "student" from another research study and then would be asked to estimate the student's personality and attitudes from the information presented. As part of the cover story, the subjects were told that the impressions they formed of the student would eventually be compared with information actually provided by him/her.

The page from the bogus survey contained questions about the person's first intercourse experience and was designed to look authentic. It was typed in a different typeface than the rest of the questionnaire and copied on a different color of paper. To make it appear as if the page was taken from a larger questionnaire, the title on top of the page was "Section III: Your First Sexual Intercourse Experience" and the page number was "7." The answers to the questions were handwritten.

All of the manipulations were contained within this page, primarily through responses to a set of questions. At the top was the student's gender, which was either *male* or *female*. The age of the student at first coitus was manipulated

by indicating either *16* or *21* in answer to the question, "At what age did you have your first sexual intercourse experience?" (The same age was given to the next question, which asked the age of the partner at the time of the experience). The stage of the relationship in which first intercourse occurred was presented as either a *steady* dating relationship that had lasted almost a year or a *casual* dating relationship that had lasted one week.[1] Each subject was randomly assigned to one of 24 versions of the "page." Several additional questions about the sexual experience were also included on the page in order to make it appear more realistic. The answers to these additional questions were identical for all subjects. For example, "no" was the response to the question "Did you tell your friends about this experience?" and "a friend's apartment" was the answer to the question "Where did you have the sexual intercourse experience?"

Measurement of the Dependent Variables

After examining the page ostensibly completed by a student in another study, the subjects were asked to indicate their impressions of him or her. Specifically, the subjects were asked to rate the "student" on 23 personality characteristics using seven-point bipolar scales. These personality characteristics included, for example, dominant-submissive, popular-unpopular, sexually inexperienced-sexually experienced, cold-warm, and intelligent-unintelligent.[2]

RESULTS

Description of Subscales that are the Dependent Variables

The 23 adjective pairs referring to personality characteristics were factor analyzed for the purpose of developing subscales to serve as dependent variables in the analysis. Principal factoring (with multiple correlations as communality estimates) was the extraction technique

---

[1] The type of contraception that was used during first coitus by the stimulus person or his/her partner was also manipulated—either nothing, the condom, or the pill was used. The results related to this variable are beyond the scope of this paper, however, and will be covered in another paper (see McKinney et al., in review).

[2] Subjects were also asked their impressions of other aspects of the relationship, such as who has the power and who contributes more to the relationship. Because these items are not directly relevant to our hypotheses, those results will not be presented in this paper.

used, and the rotation chosen was varimax. Four factors emerged from this analysis. Based on the factor loadings, each of the adjective pairs was assigned to one of the four factor scales. To be assigned to a particular factor scale, the item had to load on the factor .50 or above. One personality item (career-oriented, not career-oriented) did not meet this criterion and thus was eliminated from the analyses.

The first factor scale contains seven adjective pairs related to *Sexual and Other Values,* and is described by such adjectives as sexually experienced, sexually liberal and liberal in sex-roles. The second scale contains eight adjectives which refer to *Maturity and Intelligence*—for example, wise, responsible, careful and intelligent. Four adjectives which refer to a *Positive Personality* make up the third scale and these include the adjectives likeable, moral and warm. The last scale contains three adjectives that refer to *Dominance*—dominant, active and masculine. Cronbach's Alpha, a measure of internal consistency, was .92 for the Sexual and Other Values scale, .87 for the Maturity and Intelligence scale, .70 for the Positive Personality scale and .60 for the Dominance scale. The mean scores on these scales were the dependent variables in the analyses.

Overview of the Analysis

To examine whether a double standard is manifested in the evaluations the subjects formed of the stimulus person, the mean responses to the factor scales were subjected to an analysis of variance. The factors to be considered, singly and in interaction with each other are: gender of the stimulus person (male or female), age of the stimulus person (16 or 21), relationship type (casual or steady) and gender of subject (male or female).

With a total of 48 cells, the number of subjects in the cells ranged from 6 to 17, with a mean of 11 subjects per cell.[3] There was an unequal number of subjects per cell because there were more female than male subjects, and because the number of questionnaires planned for each class was often more than the number of students attending on that particular day. The focus of this research, however, is on examining the

---

[3] Specifically, a $2 \times 2 \times 2 \times 2 \times 3$ between analysis of variance was conducted on the data. Contraceptive behavior (none, condom, or pill) will not be discussed in this paper, however. (See McKinney et al., in review.

effects of two-way interactions (for example, between gender of stimulus person and stage of the relationship at first coitus), and the number of subjects per cell for these interactions range from 110 to 160.

Main Effects

Before the results are presented that are germane to our hypothesis that the evaluations of the stimulus person will reflect a conditional double standard, the main effects will be considered. The means and F values for these main effects are in Table 1.

Significant main effects were found for all of the manipulated independent variables:

Gender of stimulus person. Females received a significantly higher score on the Sexual and Other Values scale, and significantly lower scores on the Maturity and Intelligence, Positive Personality and Dominance scales than did males.

Age of stimulus person. Younger stimulus persons received significantly higher scores on the Sexual and Other Values and Dominance scales, and significantly lower scores on the Maturity and Intelligence and Positive Personality scales.

Stage of the relationship. Males and females who had first coitus in a casual relationship received significantly higher scores on the Sexual and Other Values and Dominance scales and significantly lower scores on the Maturity and Intelligence and Positive Personality scales.

These results indicate that there are differences in evaluations based on these characteristics (i.e., gender, age, stage of relationship) for people who have engaged in first coitus under the conditions presented. They do not, however, indicate whether these same differences would be found if information had not been presented about the individual's sexuality.

Interactions

Next, the results are presented for the interactions between gender of the stimulus person and each of the two conditional factors considered in this study—stage of the relationship in which the sexual activity occurs and age of the stimulus person at first coitus. The analyses indicated that there were no significant higher-order interactions of these variables with gender of subject, which means that male and female subjects did not significantly differ in their perceptions. Thus, the results presented below apply to both male and female subjects.

Stage of the relationship at first coitus. The interaction between gender of stimulus person and stage of the relationship in which first coitus occurs was significant for two of the four scales: the Positive Personality scale and the Dominance scale. The pattern of means presented in Table 2 and post-hoc comparisons among the cells indicated that both male and female stimulus persons were perceived to have a less positive personality if they had first coitus in a casual relationship than in a close relationship ($p<.001$). The difference between the two conditions, however, was somewhat greater for the female than for the male stimulus person.

On the Dominance scale, the male stimulus person was perceived to be more assertive if first coitus occurred in a casual relationship rather than in a close relationship ($p<.001$), whereas the opposite pattern of means was found for the female ($p=$ n.s.). Because the characteristics contained in the Dominance scale (e.g., active, dominant) are considered to be desirable traits in our society (Broverman et al., 1972), this finding also demonstrates a double standard.

Age at first coitus. The interaction between gender and age of the stimulus person at first coitus was significant for three of the four scales: Maturity and Intelligence, Positive Personality, and Dominance (see Table 3). As predicted, a female was perceived less favorably by the subjects on the dimensions of Maturity and Intelligence and Positive Personality if she had first coitus at age 16 rather than age 21 ($p<.001$). On the other hand, a male received

Table 2. Mean Scores on Four Factor Scales as a Function of the Interaction Between Gender of Stimulus Person and Stage of Relationship in which First Coitus Occurs

	Male Stimulus Person		Female Stimulus Person	
	Casual	Close	Casual	Close
(1) Sexual and Other Values	4.17	3.56	4.42	3.80
(2) Maturity and Intelligence	3.98	4.88	3.58	4.65
(3) Positive Personality	4.60	5.11	4.17	4.98
(4) Dominance	4.95	4.52	3.47	3.62

Significance of Interactions:
(1) $F (1,491) = .68$; $p =$ n.s.
(2) $F (1,491) = 1.95$; $p =$ n.s.
(3) $F (1,491) = 5.45$; $p<.05$.
(4) $F (1,491) = 14.45$; $p<.001$.

approximately the same score on the Positive Personality scale, regardless of whether he had first coitus at age 16 or 21 ($p=$ n.s.). Furthermore, although he was perceived more negatively on the Maturity and Intelligence scale if he was age 16 at first coitus rather than age 21 ($p<.05$), the difference was not as large as it was for the female stimulus person. A slightly different pattern was found for the Dominance scale. A male having first coitus at age 16 was perceived to be more dominant than a male having first coitus at age 21 ($p<.001$), whereas there was basically no difference in how a 16 versus 21 year old female stimulus person was perceived ($p=$ n.s.). These results, particularly for the Positive Personality scale, suggest that

Table 1. Main Effects for Gender and Age of Stimulus Person and Stage of the Relationship

	Sexual and Other Values		Maturity and Intelligence		Positive Personality		Dominance	
	Mean	F	Mean	F	Mean	F	Mean	F
Gender								
Male	3.86		4.44		4.86		4.73	
		15.88		24.24		16.24		241.80
Female	4.16		4.12		4.58		3.54	
Age								
16	4.50		4.08		4.60		4.30	
		189.37		53.85		16.19		20.18
21	3.48		4.50		4.85		3.96	
Relationship Stage								
Casual	4.35		3.78		4.38		4.20	
		85.00		239.02		95.13		3.89*
Close	3.68		4.77		5.05		4.07	

* All of the above F values are significant beyond the .001 level except for this last one, which is significant at the .05 level.

the double standard exists to a greater degree if standards are assessed for teenagers (i.e., age 16) than for young adults (i.e., age 21).

In sum, the results provide evidence for a conditional double standard. Although having first coitus in a noncommitted relationship or at a young age generally has a negative effect on how both a male and a female are evaluated on many personality dimensions, the negative effect is greater for the female.

DISCUSSION

Overall, this research indicates the existence of a conditional double standard. In the person perception experiment conducted, both a male and a female stimulus person received negative evaluations (especially on general personality characteristics) if first coitus occurred in a casual relationship or at the age of 16, but evaluations of a female were more negative than that of a male under these conditions. Furthermore, the male was perceived to be more dominant when he had first coitus in a casual relationship (rather than in a close relationship), or at age 16 (rather than at age 21), whereas the female was not. Although some might argue that a double standard is demonstrated only if females are more negatively evaluated while males are more positively evaluated for having sex in a casual rather than a close relationship (or age 16 rather than age 21), we consider the difference in the degree of the negative evaluations for males versus females to also demonstrate a double standard, albeit a more subtle one.

Table 3. Mean Scores on Four Factor Scales as a Function of the Interaction Between Gender and Age of Stimulus Person

	Male Stimulus Person		Female Stimulus Person	
	16	21	16	21
(1) Sexual and Other Values	4.33	3.35	4.67	3.62
(2) Maturity and Intelligence	4.29	4.59	3.86	4.41
(3) Positive Personality	4.81	4.91	4.38	4.80
(4) Dominance	5.01	4.43	3.59	3.50

Significance of Interactions:
  (1) $F (1,491) = .28$; $p =$ n.s.
  (2) $F (1,491) = 6.97$; $p < .01$.
  (3) $F (1,491) = 6.98$; $p < .01$.
  (4) $F (1,491) = 11.11$; $p < .001$.

These findings contradict some recent survey research. For example, DeLamater and Mac-Corquodale (1979, p. 227) concluded, "Our results indicate that, in the sense of accepting premarital coitus for men but not for women, the double standard has disappeared." The person perception paradigm employed in this study is different from the survey methodology in several ways, which could account for the different results.

First, measuring the double standard via a person perception experiment reduces the possibility of a social desirability bias. Because a norm of egalitarianism is pervasive, the more transparent measures typical of survey studies may elicit egalitarian responses that do not completely reflect what the individuals honestly believe. In contrast, the person perception experiment disguises, in several ways, the purpose of assessing the double standard: subjects are randomly assigned to give responses to one gender and not both, a cover story is presented that encourages honest responses, and the actual measures taken (first impressions of a specific person) are less subject to being biased by socially desirable responses.

Another difference between this experiment and the previous survey research is in how the double standard is operationalized. As stated by DeLamater and MacCorquodale, their survey research focuses on whether the double standard has disappeared in the broad sense of the "acceptance" of premarital coitus for both genders. In this experiment, on the other hand, the double standard is operationalized by asking subjects to make very specific personality evaluations of a male or female individual who has engaged in sexual intercourse. The greater specificity of this person perception experiment may present a more salient task to the respondents, which could lead to greater endorsement of the double standard. A positive association between specificity of the measurement and the endorsement of the double standard has been demonstrated in some previous survey research. Kaats and Davis (1970) examined how specificity of the referent or target in attitude statements affected the degree to which the double standard was endorsed. They found evidence for a double standard among both male and female respondents, but it was particularly strong for males when the female referent was a specific and meaningful person, such as a sister or a potential spouse.

Finally, the apparent contradictory results between the surveys and this experiment may be reflecting more subtle changes in the nature of the double standard. Perhaps the double standard is now more subtle, weaker, or more complex, and therefore contingent on many other characteristics of the person and/or situation. As was argued earlier, the person perception experiment may be able to tap this subtle, complex standard more easily than the survey.

More support for the existence of a double standard was also found in this experiment than in other, similar person perception experiments. However, it is not surprising that more support for a double standard was found in this study than in the Istvan and Griffitt (1980) and Garcia (1983) studies. The variables manipulated in their studies were appropriate for assessing the existence of an orthodox double standard, whereas this study was designed to test for a conditional or transitional double standard. Very few people still adhere to an orthodox double standard, which condemns premarital sexual behavior for women regardless of the circumstances (Reiss, 1960). We predicted, on the other hand, that women would be evaluated more negatively than men if first coitus occurred in a casual relationship (in contrast to a close relationship) or as a teenager (in contrast to as a young adult). This prediction of a conditional double standard is more in accord with the results of previous survey research than is a prediction of an orthodox double standard.

Our experiment also provides more support for a double standard than that of two other recent experiments (Jacoby and Williams, 1985; Mark and Miller, 1986). As discussed earlier, however, their manipulation of the emotional context of the sexual activity (and the confounding of gender of subject and gender of target in the Jacoby and Williams study) prohibited specifically examining the interaction between emotional context of sexual activity and gender of target.

Unlike any past experimental or survey study, our study considered how age of stimulus person affects the degree to which the double standard is evidenced. The results indicated that the double standard operates more strongly if standards are assessed for teenagers (age 16) than for young adults (age 21), at least for the limited age group that was used in this study. Future research could represent several age groups and consider how age of the stimulus person interacts with the age of the respondent.

Although this study indicates that a double standard operates under some conditions, can these results be generalized to the behavior of men and women as they actually interact with their peers and dates? Certainly, in everyday contexts, men and women are not presented with survey data on the sexual behavior of others. Evidence indicates, however, that people do gain knowledge of the sexual experiences of their peers. For example, Carns (1973) found that 44% of young women and 68% of young men had told three or more friends about their first sexual intercourse experience. The rumor mill, however inaccurate, is another source of information about the sexual behavior of others. Furthermore, people are likely to react to the information they acquire about others, by forming impressions and evaluations of these others.

The existence of a conditional double standard is not surprising if the research on sex role and sexual socialization is considered. Men and women continue to be taught two sets of standards and values about sexuality—one for men's behavior and one for women's. More specifically, men and women are socialized to different *sexual scripts* (DeLamater, 1986; Gagnon and Simon, 1973; Laws and Schwartz, 1977; Simon and Gagnon, 1983), which are norms and beliefs about the when, why, what, where and with whom sex is appropriate for a particular gender. This socialization results in men and women interpreting and evaluating the same sexual behavior differently depending on whether the actor is male or female and whether this actor is violating his/her appropriate (gender based) sexual script. The fact that both men and women hold this conditional double standard follows the notion that both men and women are socialized to know the different sexual scripts for the two genders.

The present research points to at least two of the important contextual factors in people's sexual scripts—the stage of the relationship in which the sexual activity occurs and the age of the individual. The data imply that an appropriate (positively or less negatively evaluated) sexual script for women involves delaying first intercourse until they are in a more serious relationship and have reached the age of young adulthood. Norms about the relational context of sexual activity and the age at first coitus seem to be much less stringent in scripts for men.

Part of these sexual scripts may involve making different *attributions* for sexual behavior. This may be especially true for attributions about women's sexual behavior since their scripts appear to be more constrained by contextual features. When a woman's sexual behavior matches the sexual script appropriate for her gender, such behavior may be more likely to be perceived as the result of external/contextual factors, and as appropriate. On the other hand, when her behavior violates the script, it may be seen as the result of negative, internal dispositions; that is, she is seen as a "bad girl." In this latter situation, observers may make more negative evaluations about her. Differential attributions as an intervening variable between knowledge of sexual behavior and its context, and perceptions of the target person must be directly assessed in future studies.

Further research examining the double standard and other premarital sexual standards should be continued—through person-perception experiments, as well as survey studies.

REFERENCES

Broverman, Inge K., Susan R. Vogel, Donald M. Broverman, Frank E. Clarkson and Paul Rosenkrantz. 1972. "Sex Role Stereotypes: A Current Appraisal." *Journal of Social Issues* 48:59–78.

Carns, Donald E. 1973. "Talking About Sex: Notes on First Coitus and the Double Sexual Standard." *Journal of Marriage and the Family* 35:677–88.

DeLamater, John and Patricia MacCorquodale. 1979. *Premarital Sexuality: Attitudes, Relationships, Behavior.* Madison: University of Wisconsin Press.

DeLamater, John. 1986. "Gender Differences in Sexual Scenarios." In *Females, Males and Sexuality: Theories and Research,* edited by K. Kelley. Albany, NY: SUNY Press.

Ehrmann, Winston. 1959. *Premarital Dating Behavior.* New York: Henry Holt and Company.

Ferrell, Mary Z., William H. Tolone and Robert Walsh. 1977. "Maturational and Societal Changes in the Sexual Double-Standard: A Panel Analysis (1967–1971; 1970–1974). *Journal of Marriage and the Family* 39:255–71.

Gagnon, John H. and William Simon. 1973. *Sexual Conduct: The Social Sources of Human Sexuality.* Chicago: Aldine.

Garcia, Luis T. 1983. "Sexual Stereotypes and Attributions About Sexual Arousal." *The Journal of Sex Research* 19:366–75.

Glick, Paul C. 1979. "The Future of the American Family." In *U.S. Bureau of the Census. Current Population Reports.* Washington, D.C.: Government Printing Office. Series P–23 No. 78.

Harrison, Danny E., Walter H. Bennett, Gerald Globetti and Majeed Alsikafi. 1974. "Premarital Sexual Standards of Rural Youth." *The Journal of Sex Research* 10:266–77.

Istvan, Joseph and William Griffitt. 1980. "Effects of Sexual Experience on Dating Desirability and Marriage Desirability: An Experimental Study." *Journal of Marriage and the Family* 42:377–85.

Jacoby, Arthur P. and John D. Williams. 1985. "Effects of Premarital Sexual Standards and Behavior on Dating and Marriage Desirability." *Journal of Marriage and the Family* 47:1059–65.

Kaats, Gilbert R. and Keith E. Davis. 1970. "The Dynamics of Sexual Behavior of College Students." *Journal of Marriage and the Family* 32:390–99.

King, Karl, Jack C. Balswick and Ira Robinson. 1977. "The Continuing Premarital Sexual Revolution Among College Females." *Journal of Marriage and the Family* 39:455–59.

LaBeff, Emily E. and Richard Dodder. 1982. "Attitudes Toward Sexual Permissiveness in Mexico and the United States." *Journal of Social Psychology* 116:285–86.

Laws, Judith L. and Pepper Schwartz. 1977. *Sexual Scripts.* Hinsdale, Ill: Dryden Press.

Mark, Melvin M. and Mark L. Miller. 1986. "The Effects of Sexual Permissiveness, Target Gender, Subject Gender, and Attitude Toward Women on Social Perception: In Search of the Double Standard." *Sex Roles* 15:311–22.

McKinney, Kathy, Susan Sprecher and Terri L. Orbuch. (In review). "A Person Perception Experiment Examining the Effects of Contraceptive Behavior on First Impressions." Manuscript in review. Copy can be acquired from first author at Oklahoma State University, Department of Sociology.

Reiss, Ira L. 1960. *Premarital Sexual Standards in America.* New York: Free Press.

———. 1967. *The Social Context of Premarital Sexual Permissiveness.* New York: Holt, Rinehart and Winston.

Simon, William and John Gagnon. 1983. "Sexual Scripts: Permanence and Change." Paper presented at the American Sociological Association Meetings. Detroit.

Spreadbury, Constance. 1982. "The 'Permissiveness with Affection' Norm and the Labeling of Deviants." *Personnel and Guidance Journal* 60:280–82.

Walsh, Robert, William Ganza and Tim Finefield. 1983. "A Fifteen Year Study About Sexual Permissiveness." Paper presented at the Midwest Sociological Society, April, 1983.

Zelnik, Melvin and John F. Kanter. 1977. "Sexual and Contraceptive Experience of Young Unmarried Women in the United States: 1976 and 1971." *Family Planning Perspectives* 9:55–71.

———. 1980. "Sexual Activity, Contraceptive Use, and Pregnancy Among Metropolitan Teenagers: 1971–1979. *Family Planning Perspectives* 12:230–38.

How do you build
INTIMACY
in an age of divorce?

CARYL S. AVERY

Caryl S. Avery is a New York-based free-lance writer specializing in health and psychology.

Given one wish in life, most people would wish to be loved — to be able to reveal themselves entirely to another human being and be embraced, caressed, by that acceptance. People who have successfully built an intimate relationship know its power and comfort. But they also know that taking the emotional risks that allow intimacy to happen isn't easy. Preconditioned on the sharing of feelings, intimacy requires consummate trust. And today trust is in short supply.

Few adults under 40 can remember a world without cynicism. Faith is no longer fashionable, and a quarter-century of wars and double-dealing in high places has eroded our confidence in institutions we once revered. The personal realm seems similarly shaky. With one of two new marriages ending in divorce and countless others existing in name only, trusting someone to be honest and committed over the long haul is increasingly difficult.

This isn't to say that the concept of marriage or commitment has fallen into disfavor — in fact, among certain age groups the marriage rate is up, and a new National Opinion Research Council survey finds that for Americans monogamy is still the ideal.

But ideals aside, the "till death do us part" of the marriage vow rings increasingly ironic. "Nobody goes to a wedding today without somewhere in the back of their mind wondering how long the marriage is going to last," says psychologist Judith S. Wallerstein who, with writer Sandra Blakeslee, authored the wave-making book *Second Chances: Men, Women and Children a Decade After Divorce.* Clearly, an anticipation of dissolution is not the best foundation on which to build a relationship that will be rich and meaningful. And it's the ultimate saboteur of trust, since it's the sense of continuity and permanence provided by commitment that creates an atmosphere in which trust can flourish.

Although trust in a partner means different things to different people — dependability, loyalty, honesty, fidelity — its essence is emotional safety. Trust enables you to put your deepest feelings and fears in the palm of your partner's hand, knowing they will be handled with care. While feelings of love or sexual excitement may wax and wane over time, ideally, trust is a constant. When you have it, you have it all. The challenge for most of us is not to let the spectre of deception in love interfere with finding the intimate connection we want and need.

When the world — or your own past — plants seeds of doubt, how is it possible to overlook them? Clearly, people's capacity for trust in intimate relationships varies widely, depending many factors — early upbringing, the quality of their parents' relationship, their own experiences with love. Because nobody emerges unscathed from that early infantile period when "basic trust" — the sense that the world is fundamentally a kindly place — is formed, none of us is 100% trusting, or trustworthy.

Yet the more trusting we are, the more likely we are to be trusted by others — a finding that has come out of the research of Julian Rotter, a professor of psychology at the University of Connecticut. This theory of reciprocity can be used to help build trust, Rotter believes: Take the risk of trusting, and you may be trusted in return. Initially, this requires the sophisticated skill of sensing just how far to risk your trust, what John and Kris Amodeo, authors of *Being Intimate,* call making an "intelligent leap of faith." True trust is felt, not willed, they say. It must be developed over time, by sharing your innermost thoughts and feelings gradually, and seeing how they're received.

"John made it clear from the beginning that he'd accept my feelings no matter what they were," says Kass Patterson, 28, a legal secretary who married John, 31, almost a year ago after a three-year courtship. "Since my teenage years, I'd never trusted a man; I was betrayed so often. But John proved over and over that he was true to his word. And he allowed me to be me."

Two years into the relationship, John lost his job in the oil and gas industry and remained unemployed for about a year; he didn't want just another job but a career that would make him happy. Kass, however, was ready to get married and began wondering, aloud, if John was the man for her: Was he a stable person, would he be a good provider? John's reaction: "I tried to reassure her that I was doing this for both of us. I said, 'If you can wait, thank you; if you can't, do what you must.'"

Despite the doubts, deep down Kass knew that John was a go-getter and would get back on track. So she waited. Looking back she says, "Making it through that hard time, I know I can make it through anything; I have even greater confidence in John. But I know I hurt him back then and regret having done it."

Says John, now a successful restaurateur, "It was hard when she was questioning my values, but she shouldn't regret it — she was looking for the man of her dreams."

To be able to be oneself and not have to disown one's values to please another — that's what intimate love is all about. John and Kass achieved it because they knew themselves, accepted each other and were willing to take a risk. By validating Kass's need to look for her dream man, John gave her space to find it in him.

the intelligent leap of faith it takes to get on to

the more serious business of loving another person requires that we first increase our awareness of the forces — both social and personal — that would undermine it. The divorce rate isn't the only sign flashing "danger." There are novels and films about fatal attractions and dangerous liaisons, television shows that make infidelity look positively routine, tabloids that report every relationship rift and rupture. Trash sells, trust doesn't. But trash makes trust seem increasingly improbable.

To adopt that mindset is to court trouble. Your inclination may be to trust less — but then you'll pay the price of being trusted less. Or you might be inclined to put less into the relationship, while researchers find that the more you invest, the more commitment increases.

external messages like

these can sabotage our sense of trust. And in addition, we have to grapple with internal impulses. There's the tendency to idealize others and compare their "perfect" relationship to our own. The "investment model," as defined by psychologist Caryl E. Rusbult of the University of North Carolina, asserts that we feel satisfied with what we have to the extent that it exceeds our expectations or our handy comparisons. But what can possibly compare with perfection?

Another powerful element, the flip side of idealization, is the habit of sitting in judgment of other people's relationships in a way that confirms the elusiveness of caring, intimate partnerships. What looks "bad" to us — she

takes separate vacations, he has a number of women friends — may work fine for them. Our intolerance of others' creative solutions, says one expert, leads us to draw inappropriate, negative conclusions about the quality of their love — and about the possibilities of love in general.

The tendency to lump all your past failed relationships together also can undermine present and future bondings. You can't realistically attribute a failed marriage to a breach of trust when there never was trust — or the potential for it — to begin with. The issue in this case is bad choice of partner, not bad faith. Still, it can *feel* like betrayal, so it's important to examine the causes of poor choices — and how to avoid them.

Judith Wallerstein found the question of choices particularly striking in the daughters of divorce she observed over 10 years as part of her landmark study. She believes that many of these women select wrong because they're afraid to select right. "They're so scared of abandonment or betrayal that they pick men they're sure of not losing or don't care about losing," she says. Even those who initially adjust well to parental divorce often experience a delayed reaction. "These women are afraid to risk, and you can't trust or love without risking."

To break out of their pattern, Wallerstein says, women who can't trust need to realize their anxiety has less to do with the present than with the past. "Sometimes therapy is necessary, but often these women can work through their fears themselves. Talking with others who have the same problem can be helpful, as can a good love affair where one feels heard and understood and respected."

sons of divorce fare no bet-

ter. According to Wallerstein, many of them bury the feelings that flow from their parents' divorce and become constricted emotionally. As a result, they tend to lead lonely, insular lives, dating seldom if at all, and are extremely vulnerable to rejection from women.

But children of divorce aren't the only ones who select poorly or are unusually vulnerable to hurt. Many women in particular don't see themselves as choosers and consequently are so happy to be chosen they jump too quickly, notes Rosalind Barnett, a psychologist in Weston, Massachusetts. If the relationship ends, they feel betrayed, as if they had lost their best friend. But in reality, they'd never tested the friendship to begin with.

Wendy and Steve Herstein have four children, run a business and have been married for more than 25 years. Yet until recently, each often had one foot out the door, literally or figuratively.

"Whenever we had a fight, I'd storm out of the house and Wendy would yell, 'Don't come back, I want a divorce,'" says Steve. "That made me so angry I'd shout, 'If that's what you want, that's what you'll get.'"

Since it wasn't what either of them *really* wanted, they'd eventually decide they couldn't get divorced because their lives were too intertwined — the kids, the business, etc. "But the real reason," says Wendy, "was that there was a personal commitment."

That commitment eventually led them into therapy,

where Wendy discovered that her calls for divorce were caused by fear of abandonment. "Since my parents divorced when I was four, the thought of Steve leaving me was something I couldn't handle," she says. "His storming out felt like desertion, so I'd end it. Now I've stopped threatening him with divorce just because he walks out the door; I see a fight as a disagreement that's going to end, instead of a marriage that's going to end."

the cornerstone of commitment

is exactly this attitude: the feeling on the part of both partners that the marriage will last—not because of the kids or the finances but because the relationship itself is valued and cherished. Steve and Wendy were able to harness the power of their commitment to find a solution for other problems within the marriage. And in any relationship, trust is inspired when both partners communicate that the relationship is a priority, something they want to invest in for their own benefit and their partner's.

Scott M. Stanley and Howard Markman, psychologists and co-directors of the Center for Marital and Family Studies at the University of Denver, call this kind of commitment *personal dedication* and believe that it's the key determinant of relationship stability. The other determinant they identify, *constraint commitment,* includes all the forces, internal and external—religious and moral beliefs, social pressures, children, joint possessions—that motivate a person to stay in a relationship even if not dedicated to it. Interestingly, constraints are not perceived as negative by couples so long as their dedication remains high. "In fact, happy couples barely notice them and, when they do, tend to think of them positively, as signs that they're truly connected," says Stanley.

How a couple demonstrates their dedication is, of course, a personal matter, and often nonverbal: It can be a willingness to do things for each other, spending time together, making personal sacrifices on the other's behalf, being consistent. Self-disclosure is a part of it too, because sharing what's inside—even if what's inside isn't pretty—is the supreme act of faith in another.

Love flourishes in a mutual universe of shared secrets, deep understanding, complete acceptance.

◆━━◆━━◆

building trust

also requires sharing the feelings of everyday life. Many couples find this uncomfortable, especially when the feelings are negative—whether or not they have anything to do with the relationship. But for intimacy to develop, partners must be able to express their emotions and have them heard.

If, for example, your spouse tells you she got criticized at the office and is feeling really down, "a trust-enhancing response would be, 'Sounds like you're upset. Why don't we talk about it?' " says Markman. "A trust-busting response: 'I had a tough day, too.' " The first approach validates her feelings; the second discounts them. To continue in the validation mode, he adds, "stay with discussing the problem, don't try to solve it. More than a solution, most people just want an ear."

Of course, it's one thing to listen to your partner complain about her boss, another to sit there calmly while she criticizes you. But that's exactly what pastoral psychotherapist Harville Hendrix prescribes in his book *Getting the Love You Want: A Guide for Couples.*

Hendrix, who is an ordained minister, has developed a rage-containment exercise to help couples express their anger constructively. In it, the angry or "expressive" partner briefly communicates his or her frustration, but without attacking or blaming the other. Then the "receiving" partner paraphrases the frustration, affirming the expressive partner's right to be angry but not necessarily agreeing with the reason. After this, the angry person can convert the frustration into a behavior-change request.

Scott Stanley suggests a different way of dealing with anger. By identifying the immediate underlying hurt and expressing *it* instead of rage, you can use anger to increase trust and intimacy.

For example: A woman is angry because she feels her husband doesn't spend enough time with her. She can either attack ("You don't care about anyone but yourself") or express the frustration and disappointment underneath ("I know your job is important, but spending so little time with you makes me sad").

"Most people attack because it's safer," says Stanley. "Sharing your real feelings is riskier: On the one hand, it's your only hope of getting the caring acknowledgement you want; on the other, you leave yourself open to rejection." But even that will at least tell you where you stand with your partner.

a final, vital step

toward overcoming the doubts that block intimacy is to examine the validity of your own expectations about a relationship. When expectations are unconscious, uncommunicated, unrealistic—unreasonable—we can feel we've been betrayed when we haven't been. And that perpetuates our feelings of distrust.

"Betrayal implies that someone has made a promise and broken it," says psychologist Norman Epstein of the University of Maryland in College Park. "But often we feel betrayed when no deal was ever made. We may have wanted or *expected* something from another person, but he or she never agreed to give it." For instance, a woman may marry expecting her husband to do 50% of the housework, even though she never discussed this with him.

When he fails to "follow through," her trust plummets.

In another scenario, a man accuses his wife of disloyalty when she fails to take his side in an argument with a friend. "Not only was *she* unaware of his concept of loyalty prior to this event," says Epstein, "I doubt he'd ever given the matter a thought."

Then there are the Unreasonables: Believing that if your spouse truly loves you, she should be able to read your mind; that partners in "good" relationships rarely disagree; that "being in love" feels a certain way and shouldn't change over time.

When feelings of betrayal, even subtle ones, seep in, look at your own expectations as well as your partner's shortcomings. One way, Stanley suggests, is to write down *everything* you expect from your current relationship. Include both intangibles (independence, emotional support) and tangibles (kids, a house in the country, frequent vacations). With these expectations in mind, try keeping a journal of every time your partner — or anyone else for that matter — disappoints you. Instead of stewing about those disappointments, *face* them. Ask yourself why you felt betrayed: "What did I expect that I didn't get?" And "Is it OK to expect it?"

You may find that some of your expectations don't stand up to such scrutiny, that you can let go of them. The ones that still seem reasonable to you are worth fighting for in the name of intimacy.

When Judith Wallerstein told Margaret Mead how upset she was over her early findings on children of divorce, Mead reportedly said, "There is no society in the world where people have stayed married without enormous community pressure to do so." Now that the pressure's off, you can take it as an omen — or a challenge. John Patterson, whose parents and sister are divorced, has made his choice about his marriage to Kass: "When most people say 'I do,' they regard it as 'I did.' They take it for granted that love will be easy. I intend to work at it."

Friends and Lovers?

A good man friend is hard to find. So when that friendship turns romantic, should you nip it in the bud or should you give it a whirl?

David Seeley

David Seeley is the author of *Too Cool to Get Married*, published by Harper & Row.

WHEN PAULA HAINS first kissed her good friend Humphry, she worried that she was making a big mistake. They'd been close friends for nearly a year, and Paula, a 33-year-old Manhattan account executive, had never really imagined what it would be like to kiss him—he was just a friend. Oh, he was tall and good-looking; it wasn't that. He even had a sexy accent—he was British—and he was 34, charming, and single. But Paula had decided when they first met that he wasn't her type, that she and Humphry should just be friends.

They were introduced one spring by a friend of Paula's, and soon they were pals. They began having lunches, weekend brunches, cocktail parties, and outings to the country with gangs of friends. Paula even fixed Humphry up on blind dates, telling her girlfriends, "He's sweet, sensitive, and wonderful. He's great husband material."

As the Christmas holidays approached, they were as close as childhood friends. They told each other their secrets, went gift shopping, discussed their amours. Then one lazy Sunday they were lounging around his place with a *New York Times* spread on the floor, a leg of lamb eaten, a bottle of wine opened and gone. As the afternoon sunlight waned, Humphry did something very surprising: he leaned over and said, "Paula, would you mind if I kiss you?"

"What?" she laughed. "And ruin our friendship? You're crazy!" But Humphry was serious. Somehow the blurry warmth of the wine, the tran-

quility of the stolen Sunday, and Humphry's British charm dissolved her protests, and they were kissing. It felt strange; Paula wondered whether she should stop, wondered how this had started, wondered how they could ever be just friends again. But she also thought something else. She thought: *Mmm, Humphry is one good kisser.* Was the man of her dreams right under her nose?

For many women whose best friends happen to be men, Paula's dilemma is a familiar one. What can you do if your best guy buddy really starts to look good? Sure, you're dating other men. You're a *veteran* of the dating game. You've suffered dry spells when Earth seemed like a *Star Trek* planet inhabited only by females; at other times you juggled two boyfriends, weighing their good points, trying to decide which one to drop. You usually dropped both. And when the dating game goes your way and you do fall for a guy, the same things always happen. He's afraid of commitment. He stops calling you. You catch him in bed with another woman, or worse.

So you think, *Why can't I ever meet wonderful men? Men like . . . well, like my best friend? Now* he's *a catch, a man any woman would be lucky to have.*

Maybe you work together, met at college, or come from the same town. But somehow you've always clicked. He tells you all his secrets, and you tell him yours. You find each other blind dates, laughing later at the disastrous results. He jump-starts your car on winter mornings; you rub his shoulders after he's knocked around in a touch football game.

And while you rub his shoulders, you might wonder, *Have I been looking for love in all the wrong places?*

Anthropologist Margaret Mead said that people forge their first relationship for sex, their second relationship

for having children. But the third, most meaningful and lasting relationship is based on companionship. Ultimately, people learn that friendship is the most indispensable part of true love. Indeed, a recent study of fidelity in marriage revealed that 80 percent of men and 73 percent of women say their spouse is their best friend. So if you're already friends with a man, you may be halfway home. That's what Paula and Humphry discovered—though getting there took some time.

That Sunday, Paula was momentarily lost in Humphry's arms, slightly amazed by his kisses, when she heard vague alarm bells go off in her head. Luckily, she was saved by a real bell—the doorbell. His next-door neighbors were calling to invite him to tea. Paula fled; less than a day later, Humphry flew to London for an extended Christmas holiday.

He returned on Paula's birthday, ready to take up where they left off. But Paula had decided they should forget the kisses and just be friends. At her boisterous birthday party, she exiled him to the end of the table. The next evening, she asked him to help her host a dinner party. When everyone was leaving, she asked him to stay and help with the dishes.

"That's when I was going to have a talk with him," she says, "and tell him to forget the kissing, that it didn't mean anything, it had been the heat of the moment—we should just be friends."

So how did their talk go?

Paula laughs. "We've been inseparable ever since." Instead of dismissing their momentary brush with romance, they talked seriously for hours—until long after the dishes were washed, dried, and put away—about not just kisses, but their dreams, their needs, and their futures. Just two months after that first kiss, Humphry asked Paula to marry him. Their wedding was last September.

"Now we're friends *and* lovers," Paula says. "It's a combination, a whole package deal. We didn't have to date, so we didn't have all those weeks and months of b.s. when you go out on dates and make small talk. So once we did start dating, we could get into the real meat and potatoes. The level of commitment and the openness of the communication is totally different, and that was established with the friendship. There's a certain trust. I've never had a relationship like this."

The initial stages of a relationship—falling in love, falling into bed—are usually easy. You can fall in love at a mere glance, or in the course of one party. But the hard part of romance—getting to *know* a man, learning that you can trust him, having the intimate familiarity to read his mind, understand his feelings, and know you can always depend on him—that takes time. With a close male friend, you already have all this. The question is, should you, like Paula and Humphry, have more?

The truth is—although it turned out well for Paula and Humphry—friends who become lovers don't always experience such happy endings. Not every woman should run out and ravish her best male friend—for many, it could be a mistake. You may date hundreds of men in a lifetime, but how many men will be your very close friend? It would be a shame to ruin a great friendship by ill-advisedly jumping into bed together. You run the risk of not only losing a lover, but losing a cherished friend as well. So how can you *know,* before you chance such an important relationship, whether you and your best guy friend should take things further? Here are some ideas to think about and some advice that may help you resolve your situation.

Reassess why you're just friends.

You had your reasons for becoming just friends. They may be etched in stone—you want to marry within your religion but his is different; he's your first cousin; or there's no physical attraction. But other reasons can change with time. Perhaps you discounted him as a lover because he was immature; well, since then, he has been through three long-term relationships and two therapists. He's now a model of maturity. The guy you thought was too straitlaced? He has since resigned from Merrill Lynch, doffed his suit and tie, and become an actor. One of you

may have been married, but not that happily, and not anymore. If you've both changed over time, maybe your roadblocks to being lovers are simply no longer there.

Don't break out the bubbly too soon.

Before you plunge into a serious romance, you should have some long talks, like the one Paula and Humphry had over their sinkful of dishes. Do both of you want this? Are you sure it's the right thing to do? It would be awful if you ruined your friendship because of an impetuous decision to have sex. Sex with a friend is an important step, much more so than deciding to have sex with a new boyfriend. If things don't work out with a guy you've started dating, you can simply stop seeing him. But if things don't work out with your friend, you won't want him to get lost—he's one of your best friends, he understands you in ways no one else ever could. If things work out badly, you might lose a lover *and* a friend.

Don't alter your friendship for the wrong reasons.

He's been one of your best friends for a long time, but suddenly you're thinking of him differently. Ask yourself why. You may just be stuck in a dating drought. You may hear your biological clock ticking. Or you may be stuck in a period of low self-confidence with men, and your friend seems less intimidating than all those well-heeled guys you meet at cocktail parties. If you have no better reason, you may later regret risking your friendship so impulsively.

Susan, a 30-year-old schoolteacher, says she'll always regret the affair she had with her best friend, Michael.

"We became friends when we were seniors in college," Susan says. "He was the kind of guy you could study with all night in his dorm room, and go to sleep on the other bed, and not think anything about it. He had his girlfriends, and I had my boyfriends."

Susan and Michael remained close friends after college. They lived in the same town, even worked together for two years. Susan got engaged to a man in another city, but she and Michael continued to be as close as ever.

Then Susan's fiancé broke their engagement. "I was very upset and needed comfort," Susan says. "And Michael felt the freedom to pursue me, so we just fell together. We began having sex, and after years of being my friend, he was suddenly writing me these passionate letters about how

much he loved me. He painted portraits of me. It was overwhelming."

After two months, Susan realized she didn't respond to Michael as a lover, and she broke things off. Their abortive affair wrecked their friendship as well: Michael felt rejected, while Susan felt he was pressuring her into maintaining a relationship that she no longer wanted. Eventually, they stopped seeing each other altogether.

"In a strange way, we were more intimate as friends than we were as lovers," Susan says. "Friends know your faults but love you anyway—you don't have to put on a front. I learned with Michael that once I have that good a friendship, I should be careful to protect it."

Don't mistake attraction for romance.

When you have an intimate friendship with a man, it's natural to feel attracted to him at times. True, you see friends at their worst—when he's stained with grease underneath your Nissan, or when he has a temperature of 102°—but you also see him at his best and most alluring. You may even flirt sometimes, which is common in male-female friendships. But there is always a line that friends can't cross if they want to remain just friends. Getting the hots for your pal after a party one night doesn't mean you should become lovers—it may just mean you should take a cold shower. At your place. *Alone.*

Okay, old friends can make the best lovers.

You've known him for years—and years. He's an old buddy, a longtime friend. When you've been this close this long, is it really possible to have a first date?

Ann Ware says yes. When she met her future husband, Alan, marriage was the farthest thing from her mind. After all, it was her first day of first grade. They were both 6 at the time.

Since they grew up in the tiny town of Maud, Texas, they studied in the same classrooms, fidgeted in church on Sundays, and played dodgeball on the not-very-mean streets. Their only flirtation occurred in seventh grade.

"We started going together that year," Ann says. "But it didn't last long. He was a real sloppy kisser."

For the next four years, Ann dated Alan's good friend, Gene. But she never stopped being best friends with Alan. They did everything together—during class, after school, on church trips. When Alan's girlfriend from out of town came to Maud for the weekend, she stayed at Ann's house.

After they both graduated from high school, they went their separate ways—Ann to Baylor University, Alan to Louisiana Tech. They exchanged letters and phone calls, comparing their college romances.

Then, one Christmas break, they were driving around Maud talking about their relationships. Alan said his girlfriend wanted to get too serious. Ann said her boyfriend was the same way.

"I've been wanting to talk to you about something," Alan blurted out. "I've been thinking lately that I miss you as more than just a friend."

When what he'd said sank in, Ann stared at him in amazement. "You've got to be kidding," she laughed. "Us date?"

But Alan wasn't kidding; to prove his point, he leaned over and kissed her. ("It was weird, almost *gross,*" Ann recalls. "It was like kissing your brother—something you just don't do. I told him, 'But we're friends! I shouldn't be kissing you!' ")

After a while, Ann realized that she missed Alan as more than just a friend, too. When their lips met a second time, he didn't seem so much like a brother. "He'd learned a lot about kissing since the seventh grade," she recalls, laughing.

Alan transferred to Ann's university. He proposed to her a few months later by hanging a huge sign above the Brazos River that read, "ANN, WILL YOU MARRY ME? I LOVE YOU. ALAN." They were married the summer after her senior year. They're 25 now, with a baby boy named Daniel and a home in the mountains of eastern Oklahoma, where Alan manages a farm. Ann is glad to have a husband she has been friends with nearly all her life.

"I know a lot of things about Alan I'd probably never know if I'd just married some guy from college," she says. "We've been through everything together—good and bad—all through grade school, junior high, high school, and college. He's always known he could come to me with his problems, and I could come to him with mine."

You may be like Ann: your long friendship with that certain man may enrich a possible romance. You know *everything* about him, which could lend your love a depth of closeness and familiarity no regular union could match. On the other hand, maybe you know too much. Perhaps he has revealed every juicy detail about his girlfriends, confessed frankly and candidly to the various sins he has committed against his long list of loves. If you become lovers, he'll have to find someone else to talk to about his girlfriend—and you'll wonder what he's saying. And when he's making love to you, it might be hard to forget the intimate portraits he used to paint of his past lovers.

Who makes the first move? Maybe one of you already has. Your friend may sometimes flirt with you, relying on you to good-naturedly fend him off. But is there something serious behind his flirtation? You can find out by simply flirting back the next time, letting him know you may be interested. If you want to make the first move, wait for the right moment, when the two of you are alone in some vaguely romantic setting. Then approach it gently. Say something like, "Have you ever thought what it would be like if we were . . . lovers?" If he has thought about it every night for a year, you're on your way. If he's unresponsive, you can get

your mind off him and concentrate on the earth's supply of billions of other men. And who knows? You may have planted an idea in his head, which, while he doesn't want to act on it now, may bear fruit later.

Be prepared if it doesn't work out.
Let's say you and your friend are sure that becoming lovers is the right step. Before you go further, talk about what you'll do if something goes wrong. What if it just doesn't feel right? Some women never get over the feeling that they're kissing their "brother." Some treasure the freedom, openness, and honesty they've had with a friend and discover their forthrightness becomes skewed when he's a lover. If you expect your love affair to be miraculous, you may be disappointed. Instead, take it slowly, and make sure neither of you has second thoughts along the way. If one of you decides the romance is a mistake, both of you should be prepared. That might help ease the shaky transition back to being just friends. But there's nothing "just" about being friends, is there?

Happy endings aren't guaranteed when you have a romance with a male friend. But if the two of you do take that leap, try to stay friends no matter what happens—whether you break up in two days or spend a lifetime together. Even if things don't work out, you may have added a depth and richness to your friendship you both will always treasure. And you can go back to the crazy world of dating knowing that at least you tried, that you went for something you thought could be right. Maybe you'll learn more about what kind of man is right for you, and you'll be that much closer to finding the man of your dreams.

Major Mergers

*Whenever partnerships, romantic or otherwise, are in the offing,
decide what's <u>mine</u> and what's <u>ours</u> beforehand*

Grace W. Weinstein

Joint accounts demonstrate commitment and strengthen a relationship.

Joint accounts preclude privacy and undermine independence.

OPPOSITE POINTS OF VIEW? YES. YET both statements are true. Because joint ownership has both advantages and disadvantages, deciding how to own and manage money and property demands careful consideration. Some assets probably should be owned jointly while others should not. If you're trying to decide how to handle income and assets in a new or ongoing relationship, here's what you need to know.

Legally speaking, all joint ownership is not alike. The form called "tenants in common" suits singles buying property together (see box), but is generally not appropriate for marriage partners because either can sell her or his share at any time and because the survivor does not automatically inherit the property. If you're married, "joint tenancy" or "tenancy by the entirety," depending on where you live and what kind of property you're talking about, protects you during life and also provides this vital "right of survivorship" after death.

Practically speaking, you'll want to own some assets jointly and some individually. You'll also want to differentiate between property you have before and that you acquire after marrying.

State laws differ but usually recognize that you continue to own whatever assets you bring into marriage. You can sell the property or borrow against it, as you please—so long as you keep it in your name alone. Put your husband's name on the title, however, and you're giving up a measure of control. No matter how fervent your love, think twice before you do so. We all know that true love, these days, doesn't necessarily last forever.

Assets you acquire together during marriage are a different story. In the nine "community property " states (Arizona, California, Idaho, Louisiana, Nevada, New Mexico, Texas, Washington, and Wisconsin), such property is automatically considered joint property, owned by both of you in equal measure. In the other 41 states, you have to make a decision (although property acquired while you live in a community-property state remains community property even if you later move to another state, notes Elizabeth S. Lewin, author of *Financial Fitness for Newlyweds*).

Try this course of action. Even if you want to mingle most current income, keep property that you brought to the marriage in your own name. Keep property that you inherit or that is a gift to you personally (from your parents, for example) in your own name. Then, should worst come to worst, you won't be in the position of a friend of mine. She had to scrape together the money to buy the half of her home that "belonged" to her ex-husband—even though the funds to purchase that home had come solely from her parents. Had "Joan" segregated that money so that she could prove its source in court, she would have had a stronger claim on the jointly owned home.

You *should* own the family home jointly,

partly because a home is such a powerful symbol of commitment and partly because neither of you would want the other to be able to sell the old homestead out from under. But owning other property jointly reduces each partner's control over the property in a way that makes effective money management difficult.

With stocks and bonds, for example, it will take both signatures to sell. If one of you is out of town, ill, or just plain stubborn, it can make it impossible for the other to take appropriate action. Instead, why not take turns investing, putting equivalent assets in each name? Many couples find this approach has an added benefit of reducing friction over how much risk to assume and what kind of investment to choose.

With joint bank accounts, by contrast, either partner is free to withdraw all the funds at any time. But each partner also knows exactly what the other is spending. And, with one checkbook and two checkwriters, each can scramble accounts by forgetting to make checkbook entries. I recommend three checking accounts per couple (marrieds or live-togethers)—a joint household account for convenience, plus individual accounts to give each partner financial independence.

One of the reasons for keeping separate accounts is, of course, "just in case . . . " Who owns which property isn't supposed to matter under the equitable distribution divorce laws of most states, but it does in fact make a difference to the judges who make the decisions.

If you've been through a divorce, you know this all too well. If you're entering a second marriage, you'll probably be extra careful about keeping some assets separate. Here's an additional tip from financial planner Rianne Leaf, a district manager with IDS Financial Services in Minneapolis: if you sell your house to move in with your new husband, and use the money from the sale to buy an insurance policy on his life, make sure that you are not only the beneficiary of the policy but also its owner. That way, because a life insurance policy can be borrowed against or cashed in, you keep control of your own money.

First marriage, second, or third, it's important to reach an understanding about how you will own property and how you will manage your money. You may want to consider a legally drawn prenuptial agreement, particularly if one or both of you has been married before and has children. Such agreements, once considered a threat to the institution of marriage, are now accepted by courts almost everywhere.

Perhaps you don't own enough to make a formal prenuptial agreement necessary. Even then, suggests Marjorie A. O'Connell, a Washington, D.C., attorney, you should make yourself put "what ifs" on paper. What if either of you decides to go to graduate school? To stop work? What if one of you inherits a sizable sum? Receives down payment money for a house from parents?

Contract or not, discuss (preferably in advance) whose paycheck will be used for what and whose name goes on which property. Sort out your expectations about what will happen in various money situations and you'll be less susceptible to conflict later on.

Terms of Cohabitancy

WHETHER FOR REASONS OF LOVE OR economy, more and more singles are buying houses together. If you're thinking of doing so, protect yourself by drawing up a written agreement designed to resolve any potential problem before it occurs. Martin Shenkman, a New York City real estate attorney who is the author of *The Total Real Estate Tax Planner,* suggests that your agreement include the following:
• Who owns what percentage of the house and how much each will contribute toward the down payment and monthly upkeep.
• What happens if one of you runs into financial reverses and can't meet monthly obligations; Shenkman builds a loan provision into the agreements he writes to cover this contingency.
• Who else can live in the house.
• Under what circumstances either of you can make financial commitments for the other; you don't want to come home from a trip and find that your house-mate has committed $10,000 to replacement windows, but you do want him or her to be able to make emergency repairs.
• What happens if one of you moves away, becomes disabled, or dies. If death severs the partnership (and young people, unfortunately, sometimes die), your agreement should provide the terms on which the estate will sell the half-interest to the other partner within a specified period of time. You might also want to take out an inexpensive term life insurance policy on each other, enough to buy out the other's interest. —G.W.W.

SEXUAL PURSUIT

LOVESTRUCK

Reigniting an Old Romance

Gilbert Deering Moore

WHO WOULD HAVE THOUGHT THAT LOVE COULD ENDURE, even after all this time? Even after the fighting and the fury, the betrayals on both sides, the bitterness over the babies, the rancor running wild over the money and property? Even after the depth of the rift and the terrible ugliness when everybody's dirty laundry was out in the open?

Who would have thought that you could bury love six feet under, then dig it up 10 years later, and it would still have the breath of life? Who would have dreamed that the feeling could stay so strong, so sweet like it is, so tender, even after all this time?

The woman was through with me—too through. Through with my womanizing, dope-smoking, my reckless way of living. And I was through with her—her basic bitchiness and her headstrong ways. But it turns out we're not through at all. We're just beginning.

Ten years ago we were all washed up. One harsh day in November I came home from work to find the woman packing, preparing to leave me. The children were already shipped off to stay with Grandma. The time for our third and final breakup was ripe.

People split up long before one of the parties moves out. They still "live together"—they're still under the same roof. But they sleep in separate beds, eat at separate tables. They come and they go, but they don't speak.

The handwriting was on the wall for as long as a year before. I tried very hard to prevent the breakup, but there was an inevitability about it.

Part of the problem was that I was into heavy dope-smoking, and the effects of it used to frighten her. I thought marijuana was this marvelous painkiller and bountiful source of creativity.

This was illusion: the wonderful weed took my pain and multiplied it by four, shackled my muse, drove me to the brink of paranoid madness.

But the heart of the trouble was my womanizing. All the time we were together, I was steady playing the cheating game, steady chasing after luscious females. I used to meet them on the street, on planes and trains, in bars and workplaces. And having met them, I was forever making secret arrangements to see them in the underground. None of my exploits remained much of a secret, however, because I tended to leave incriminating evidence lying about. I was careless and, perhaps, callous.

SEX TIPS

BE SMART!
Do it with someone you like.
—Molly Ivins

SEX TIPS

ARTS & CRAFTS
Using a Magic Marker, paint tiny happy faces on your partner's condom. Watch them wink and expand as he does.
—Comedian Susan Vass

Things came to a head that fall as she changed jobs. The new environment gave her fresh perspective on her life and new confidence in herself. It also put her in the company of adoring men and made her less and less tolerant of my shaky ways. Suddenly the tables were turned. Whereas she had always been the one who was jealous and insecure, worried about some "outside agitator," now it was my turn to stew.

The day of disaster finally came. The woman was leaving me. She didn't want any further discussion about it. I pleaded with her to stay and work things out. She was adamant. The woman walked out the door and she didn't look back.

So now I had to deal with the pain: the pain of jealousy and rejection and self-reproach; the pain of vain regret and irretrievable loss. Furthermore, I had to deal with it by myself, for there were no lovely ladies left to hold my hand, and no men I cared to face, given my pathetic condition.

When a woman is in pain, she can call up her sister, her girlfriend, her mother. She can tell the whole sad story, chapter and verse—how the bastard brutalized her, left her high and dry. When a woman suffers a broken heart, she can cry with dignity.

A man with a broken heart is in big trouble. There's no place to go with his humiliation and his tears. His he-man friends will laugh at him. A man has no business crying in the first place—certainly not because some witch left him. This is what my daddy might have said, had I been silly enough to unburden myself at his feet.

So I find myself alone, with a big knife sticking out of my heart. I go into a little room and close the door. I smoke my dope; I guzzle my Sneaky Pete wine. I rush to kill the pain. But the pain is powerful and nothing I do can kill it. 'Cause the knife is in me and the blade is thick. The wound is deep and the bleeding is bad. I'm stuck. I can't pull it out and I can't leave it there. So I lie and I bleed and I die . . .

I call her treacherous, I call her whore. Snatch up her pretty clothes and burn 'em. Grab her picture off the wall and burn that too. I shatter her fine crystal and her lovely looking glass. I wish deep-seated evil on the witch. I pray that she should rot in hell . . .

I get down on the floor and I wallow and I crawl and I cry like a baby. The woman is gone. And the babies are gone with her. And there is not one effing thing I can do about it . . .

The days pass. The nights come and I dream long ugly dreams. She is naked, stretched out in the bed—queen-size. Got them long legs way up in the air. And on top of her is this dude I know. The two of them are into it. The two of them are gruntin' and groanin' and sweatin' like racehorses . . .

I am made to sit there and watch. My eyes are fixed in their sockets. My skin crawls. And the two of them? They laugh, they feast, they love, and they mock me . . .

I always wanted to catch her—catch her with the stuff on her nose like she used to catch me. And the time came when I commenced to follow her 'round. And I opened her mail. And I listened in on her phone calls. And I sniffed her dirty drawers, looking for clues, hoping to trap her, but it never worked. The only time I caught her was in a dream, a long dream I had over and over. Except the times were such that my faculties were all askew. Who could tell where the border was between the world of dreams and the realm of the real?

I went underground, withdrawing from polite society to live like a monk. I left the opulent corporate world I used to work in, went where the work was hard and the pay was peanuts. Isolated, I relived my whole life in my head. Sensitized now to pain, I began to realize the terrible suffering I caused my wife and the other women I got involved with.

> *I thought every relationship would necessarily get old. It ain't necessarily so. I look at the woman sometimes and desire sweeps through me like fire through a forest.*

It was the end of an era, the death of one way of living and the birth of another. When I was younger, I played it fast and loose. I was the playboy. He struts about, flaunts his manliness, "conquers" woman after woman. He is *much* man. Yet inside beats the heart of a self-centered child whose only purpose is to gratify himself. When it comes to the gratification of his primary needs, he is ruthless and cruel and unfeeling.

He wears the mask of the great lover, but behind his disguise is a greedy little boy whose capacity for love is seriously impaired. Eager to take love, he has precious little to give. He rushes headlong to be intimate, yet real intimacy is the last thing he wants.

He wants to be known as a great lover, but by this he means not someone who feels deeply but someone who fucks well. His preoccupation is not love in the heart but technique in the head. Still, he understands the importance of love to women, and in his exploitation schemes he is always willing to feign a love he does not feel. The name "playboy" is well chosen, for the primary instinct of this Don Juan is to play. His principal plaything is the woman—her and that priceless toy between her legs.

Once upon a time I felt compelled to play the role of a Don Juan. One woman could not satisfy me, no matter how lovely her looks, how subtle her wit. No matter how fantastic she was in bed. One woman cannot satisfy the Don, nor two or three or four. He requires a *chain* of women passing through his life in endless procession. Possessed of a strange inner force (some call it demonic), the Don Juans of this world wage a lifelong war against women, endlessly moving to conquer them and bend them to their iron wills.

Don Juans come in all sizes, shapes, colors, and creeds. They hail from the four corners of the earth, though each continent produces a breed peculiar to its climate. We in the United States have, of course, our species of machismo, and produce a many-splendored breed composed of white boys as well as black, Latin boys (to whom we must give special credit for the Don Juan legend), and Jewish ones too. Among the Don Juans are rich boys who own boats and planes and emeralds, and poor boys who scarcely have pots to pee in. What they all have in common, what makes them brothers under the skin, is their burning ambition to become great playboys of the Western world.

My daddy was a "ladies' man." So was my big brother Charlie. So were a string of first cousins I once lived with. So was a certain rake of a roommate I had in college. Most of these "role models" of mine had wives and children to support. But off to the side, they had their extra ladies: women they slept with, made babies with, and frequently established semisecret homes with.

I remember, when I was a timid teenager in Jamaica, watching my big brother in action fencing with the ladies. I myself was so terribly frightened of the female—these lovely, remote creatures who held awesome powers of rejection over the male of the

SEX TIPS

PICK & PLAY!
1. Safe: Buy sex toys.
   Invite your lover.
   Use them together.
   Talk about the experience.
2. Safer: Buy sex toys.
   Invite your lover.
   Use them individually.
   Talk about the experience.
3. Safest: Buy sex toys.
   Don't invite your lover.
   Use them on yourself.
   Talk about it on the phone
   to your therapist.
   —Comedian Janice Perry,
   a.k.a. Gal

species. They could break your heart so easily. One wrong turn of the head, one baleful bat of an eyelash and they could crush you with their tender might. My brother Charlie, on the other hand, was completely unfazed by women. He always knew what to say to them and when to say it.

I used to stand there on this big veranda we had overlooking a great, busy street, and my brother used to stand there watching the women go by. When he saw the right cutie-pies, he would call out to them. Lo and behold, they would stop and Charlie would go downstairs and run his game on them, feeding them a line of his lyrical bullshit. In short order Charlie would score again.

Then I studied under Jake, this big stud I used to live with when I was going to college. Many people wondered what we could possibly have in common. I was a serious straitlaced egghead, and Jake was an ex-con, a dude of the streets. Jake used to enjoy whipping me at chess—"the intellectuals' game"—and he enjoyed teaching me how to be the great cocksman he was.

Starting with the landlady's daughter, there was a long string of women he used to cavort with, and every evening when I came home from class I would find him in the sack with someone different. Jake passed on to me the secret of his success with women. Be tough, he used to say. Let them pour their hearts out. Let them do the falling in love. You maintain your cool. When they cry, when they become hysterical, just turn your back and walk away. Never blow your cool.

Once upon a time I embraced the philosophy of hedonism that sensual pleasure is the principal good in life. And so, like the bobcat stalks the reindeer, I made it my business to track the luscious female wherever I could find her. The fact that I was in love with one particular woman, married to her and making babies, in no way restrained me.

On the surface, I'd been having a grand time sleeping in all those beautiful beds, but when you peeped behind the mask you saw a face contorted in pain. Except that, being a man conditioned to keep out of touch with feeling, I'd been a stranger to my pain and to my innermost self.

Belatedly I was learning that the endless pursuit of pleasure does not in the end bring pleasure. A man pursues the pleasures of love; he escapes the pain of love, but only for a little while. So there was more to a man than met the eye. Quite apart from his brain and his broad shoulders and his big bamboo, a man had a heart every bit as fragile as the female's—quite often, more so. A man could be stern like steel one minute and the next soft as apple jelly.

After two years of agonizing reappraisal, I made up my mind to start fresh somewhere else. I went to Chicago to visit an old

SEX TIPS

LET'S PRETEND!
You be Snow White and have your partner pretend to be each of the seven dwarfs in succession (many men have Grumpy and Sleepy down anyway).
—Comedian Janice Perry, a.k.a. Gal

friend and abruptly decided to cut the Apple loose. I lived in the Windy City with another woman for four years. The relationship was, in a word, beautiful. And yet there was some elusive something missing from it. All I knew was that I did not feel that all-consuming passion I thought would be necessary if I were ever to chance marriage again. I tried, while we were together, to be different, to be faithful in a way I never was

before. Still, after four years, we parted, continuing to be friends, if not lovers.

Meanwhile, my wife in New York was no longer my wife. She had met and married someone else. But, after four years, the marriage crumbled; she frankly admitted that the whole thing was a mistake. We were regularly in touch—writing letters, making long-distance telephone calls and the occasional visit to "pick up the kids, drop them off." Terribly civilized about the whole thing, all the rancor from the past apparently gone. We were pals now, you might say, the kind of pals who laugh and talk and reminisce about a shared past. As recently as September last, this is the way we were.

Now comes fall 1988 and our daughter Vanessa—suddenly terribly grown up—is packed and ready to go off to college. I fly in from Chicago and the four of us (Mommy and Daddy, son Justin, plus Vanessa) drive up to Connecticut where Vanessa will begin school. It's like old times having the family together and happy again, if only for this special occasion.

Conversation is congenial but still careful between the former lovers. We talk about the children—how phenomenal it is that they aren't babies anymore. We talk about the intervening relationships we've had. We swap stories and ply each other with details: what it was like living with somebody else. Nobody thinks the unthinkable. Nobody broaches the subject of how we feel about each other now. Nobody says one word about getting back together again. Who would have the nerve to propose so preposterous a thing!?

Mind you, the thought popped into my mind more than a few times on this visit, but I was not prepared to speak it. There were several moments of private crisis when I looked at the woman and secretly turned to mush—another subject I did not care to broach.

Vanessa now safely ensconced in school, I drive Mommy and Justin back to New York, get on a plane, and fly back to Chicago. And, ostensibly, the Moore family is gone back to being the way it was—split down the middle. Except that now, instead of talking once every three months or so, the woman and I are talking every day, sometimes two, three times a day. And instead of careful, abstract conversation, the talk grows ever more tender, ever more pointed. And, before you know it, the woman dares to speak of love, and the man dares to confirm it.

We begin to make plans. We must get back together again, remarry. The coming Christmas seems the perfect time. Then Christmas appears too far away. How about Thanksgiving? I quit my job in Chicago, rent a truck, pack it with all my earthly possessions, and I race cross-country, back to the Apple.

These are contradictory times we live in. On the one hand, we see love touted everywhere—plastered on billboards and made banal on TV screens. Many scoff at it, say cynical things about it, say there is no such thing. On the other hand, many are afraid to feel it, and some are leery of others feeling it for them.

Who wants to be strung out and vulnerable, have happiness depend on what someone else says and does or fails to say and do? Many of us have the memory of a double cross branded on our souls. Many of us, badly burned, are none too eager to go back for more. And so we have those who are perpetually making love, perpetually performing the act of love, yet always backing away from love.

But it turns out that love is real—every bit as exhilarating as poets promise. The woman and I have a love at once old, tested in the fire, and at the same time new, brand-new, resurrected from the dead. We are like you new lovers who can't see enough of each other and hang on each other's every word. Who hold hands and play footsie under tabletops, sit in restaurants after the food is finished, gazing into each other's eyes. Every touch tingles, every kiss lifts you off the ground. The sun goes down and you race to the sack and do it all night long, and in the daytime too. The closeness is too sweet to be believed, the excitement too heady to reckon about.

But our love is old and seasoned, too, with that certain ease not to be scoffed at. After all, we've known each other 20 years, so there are a host of pretenses we don't have to make, parlor games we don't have to play. The newly met carry the burden of being perpetually charming. We skip all that.

In our culture we prize new things—the latest model car, the most recently developed computer—and disparage everything old. Our technology breeds in us a perpetual discontent. We can never enjoy the latest gadget for we are too busy anticipating that it will shortly be made obsolete. We reach for a new relationship with the same limited expectations that we have when picking up a new ballpoint pen.

When I was younger, I thought every relationship would necessarily become old and tired. It ain't necessarily so. The passion is still there, even after all this time. I look at the woman sometimes and quiver like a schoolboy. Desire sweeps through me like fire through a forest. And, then, there are moments when passion subsides and a certain tenderness comes to the fore. I walk down the street holding the woman's hand and it thrills me. I feel complete, lacking for nothing.

This is a far cry from the old days when I was always terribly uptight while walking the street holding a woman's hand. Sometimes it was because the woman was white and I was perpetually on guard lest some angry, jealous white man leap to the attack. But no matter what color she was, I didn't want to hold her hand. I wanted to be perpetually available to the chance female who might pass us by.

In modern parlance, the word "lover" has been stripped to its barest essentials to mean hardly more than an occasional lay. It's so easy to be cynical about love and dismiss it as a ruse to rake in the gullible. Sooner or later we wake up with a bleeding heart over some unworthy somebody, and that somebody takes our bleeding heart and tosses it in the air like a Frisbee.

But if you're lucky, as I am, your love is a fortress. It protects you from the hellishness of the street and the marketplace where tenderness is for fools, brutality passes for strength, where dogs devour dogs with relish.

I do believe that nobody gets away with anything, except for a little while: not even the slickest of the slick playboys, not even the coolest of the cool dudes. As I grow older, I learn to place higher and higher premiums on friendship—the older the friendship, the higher the premium.

If you're lucky, as I am, your lover is your closest friend, maybe even your oldest. She's seen me at my lowest ebb and my times of triumph. Between us there is an invisible contract establishing the terms of our mutual affection and respect. Unlike the business contract—which takes no chances, spells out every detail, and covers all contingencies in a spirit of mutual mistrust—the love contract is eternally nonspecific. The love deal leaves everything to chance, and is willing to take incredible risks.

There is a richness in old love that no new hot flash can match. The past we share—all of it, the pain and suffering as well as the joy—is a vast treasure trove the two of us draw on. She has her scrapbook of ugly memories as I have mine. Each of us is subject to doubts and suspicions, to flashes of mistrust. But a powerful current surges through us—an overwhelming need to touch and be touched, a powerful need to love and see that love returned. A need to transcend the awful solitude of this tomb called the body. A need to reveal ourselves, to unveil the deep secrets at last. ♦

NICE GIRLS DO

Or Want To

Katie Monagle

THE "NEW MORALITY" IS GIVING ME A BAD CASE OF DÉJÀ VU, even though I'm only 23. This time the danger of AIDS is the rationale for sticking to "old-fashioned" values that create a sexual double standard and legitimate only heterosexual relationships with people of one's same race and class. However, I got these same messages during my childhood and teen years—only then there wasn't a convenient disease to mask the sexual politics. Then, the reasons for holding people, especially women, in check were based on ideas of class and respectability, religion, racism, and homophobia.

When I began my official journey into sexuality with my first real kiss at 14, I had few inhibitions other than keeping my hymen intact until I was at least in love, if not married. I was attending an all-girl, nun-run Catholic high school. When I got to see boys, what registered was the tingly possibility of a fooling-around kind of fun, and the more pragmatic goal of being socially acceptable: there was obviously something wrong about a girl without a beau.

Kissing and making out were the most fun I'd ever had. I lost my library card, forsook *The Love Boat* and *Fantasy Island*, and concentrated on the telephone and my social life. I knew my precoital sexual activity needed to be kept from my parents. They had always told me, and I knew they were sincere, that sex inside marriage is beautiful. Until I was 14, I believed them.

SEX TIPS

DON'T FORGET!
Sex is a really precious form of communication that is magical, and that we don't get in other kinds of connections with people. Perhaps this is why, even in the Age of AIDS, we are driven to communicate sexually. A particular spiritual place in ourselves is touched, a self that we don't wear out on the street, that we don't necessarily talk about, that in fact doesn't have words.
—JoAnn Loulan, author and marriage and family counselor

Later, I reinterpreted their message to fit my life: sex inside *love* is beautiful. I figured that until love knocked at my heart, anything but the actual deed could be done. To me, as to many teenagers, my parents weren't the most reliable judges of right and wrong—my peers were, and I still remember when I got the message from them that I was doing something wrong.

The day after a newly acquired "best" friend and I had double-dated, she teased me—amid a group of her old and my new friends—about how she and her date had laughed at the way my date and I shook the car with our enthusiastic "making out." Those few minutes of my life in the sunny courtyard of an old New Orleans convent and girls' school linger sharply in my memory nine years later. Instead of titters and mutual girlish confidences, my new friends looked uncomfortable, and eyed me appraisingly. I felt gross, as though—despite my "virginity"—I belonged to the ranks of the sleazy, easy girls.

Now these narrow-minded values I've spent almost half my life trying to escape are the cornerstone of "the biggest social movement since the sixties" (this information is courtesy of *Good Housekeeping*'s New Traditionalist ad campaign). Young people are more conservative now than a generation ago, we're told. Casual sex is out. Heterosexuality and monogamy are in, lauded as the only ways to have Safe Sex and Beautiful Relationships.

I feel threatened by the New Morality. It's not just sex that's under attack—it's my ability to be me, whoever I am, without being subjected to painful censure in my personal or professional life. I'm seeing not just more conventional relationships among my peers, but also a license to censure other people's decisions about how to run their sex and their lives. Although my friends in the urban Northeast are politically liberal, socially permissive, and not particularly monogamy-minded, I'm afraid I won't be very comfortable outside our circle.

Whether due to the old morality or the new, the pressure is on to be monogamous—single or married. Jane,* a 23-year-old New York woman pursuing a promising career in finance, believes, "People would think I was crazy if I just slept with someone—even if they weren't thinking in terms of AIDS." Liz, 24, an old friend who lives with her boyfriend in Queens, New York, senses condescension and pity for women who are not married or almost-married—especially from women who sowed their oats during freer days and now have naturally evolved into monogamy. "The glamour of being single is gone," Liz says.

And it's not only our sex lives that Liz sees endangered by the New Morality. "I think AIDS will just make people more prejudiced than they already are—make them think it was wrong and foolish to have been liberal in any way. There are all these people out there who aren't prejudiced against blacks or homosexuals in the stereotypical sense—don't use nasty labels—but who feel that AIDS is a 'minority problem.' People are being prejudiced in a covert way."

Mark, who is 25, a Wall Street attorney, and gay, says that in the gay community the emphasis is not on how much sex one has, but on taking precautions and communicating honestly about one's sexual and drug use history. Still, "People think I should cut down on the number of my sex partners rather than making sure I'm totally safe. Deep down, everyone wants to find one person to fall in love with, but in the meantime they would

* Names have been changed.

have casual sex. Now 'in the meantime' is gone."

But the double standard that always went along with monogamy—setting limits on women and gays but leaving promiscuous heterosexual men uncensored—is still with us. Brian, a 24-year-old San Franciscan still prowling on the singles scene, has been the lover of almost 40 women in his short lifetime. Yet he sheepishly admits to living by the double standard: "If I have sex with someone, afterward I shouldn't have to feel like, 'Wow, I don't like this person anymore' because she's had sex with me. But sometimes I do feel that, if it's a one-night stand."

Of women who carry condoms in their purses, Brian says, "I think maybe these girls sleep around a lot and that's why they're carrying these condoms." He explains that "all guys are sluts," but "when I say 'male slut' I kind of think positively. A male slut is a guy who is good with the girls, a guy who can pick up women." About female "sluts," though, Brian thinks "negatively. That's terrible, but it's true."

Yet Brian—he who doesn't like women who carry condoms—will now, because of AIDS, "always wear a condom. I used to claim I couldn't get a hard-on if I wore a rubber," he confesses. "That was my big philosophy. When I was having sex, it was like, 'Grunt, I hope you have, grunt, grunt, something. No? Okay, we'll chance it.' Now I'll use a condom. It's important. I don't want to die for it."

I used to have problems asking men to wear condoms. They'd say no, or whine and prophesy that it just "wouldn't work." I'd get embarrassed by the fact that I could produce a condom when they couldn't—it made me look so eager. Finally I got tired of the conflict with the men and myself, and blew off even suggesting prophylactic protection for a while. Hell, we lily-white and middle class aren't really in danger anyway. Right?

For that, I suffered. I suffered a minor medical problem. I suffered a blow to my personal pride: never have my feminist politics been more pertinent to my real life, and I failed myself. And my partner.

Well, I don't have a problem anymore. I want sex, I want my life, and I want to live my life with a sense of pride in myself—which means doing what I know is responsible and right, even if it makes me uncomfortable sometimes. Besides, I didn't like the fact that a little bit of sexism intimidated me enough to suppress my principles and endanger people's lives.

However, I do think AIDS is being used as an excuse for moving back into the old 1950s-style morality. I am aware of AIDS and, despite the old adage "Never say never," I will never have sex without protection before my partner and I have carefully examined each other's doctor's certificates. But I'm also determined not to allow all this hysteria and conservative social coercion to box me into believing I can't have sex again till I've picked my white-bread mate for life. Monogamy, bigotry, and homophobia won't save me from the hazards of modern life.

There have been a lot of places in my life where I didn't feel free to be me—it wasn't cool, respectable, or attractive. I wasn't happy in those places because I couldn't be part of a community. Sometimes I'm not brave enough to be different in a seemingly united world. So I don't want caution to turn into rights-reducing fanaticism that makes all sorts of people into outsiders. We still have some degrees of freedom, medically and socially, about what we do in bed, with whom, and why. I want that freedom for myself, and I endorse it for others. And I still wanna have fun.

FEARLESS FLYING
Singles on the Prowl

Maggie Rafferty

BEFORE AIDS, THERE WAS HERPES. BEFORE REAL FEAR THERE was doubt. Early in the 1980s we began to take a second look at our lifestyles. Casual sex had long been divorced from making love, but we didn't feel any loss until the cold sores began. This was something we could relate to—

paying prices. The question was still open on how high prices would go before demand peaked. The curve turned down when AIDS hit the streets.

At least you'd think that would be the case, wouldn't you? Well, actually, there's been little real change in our sexual consumerism. The three-dates-before-sex rule has become all of five dates. We're still sleeping with people we haven't met yet. Instead of closing our eyes and crossing our fingers that he isn't married, we hope he isn't contagious.

The one-night stand is down but not out. It's hot and crowded at New York City's Cafe Iguana. The bar is packed. The place is a subway station and, according to the bartender, the decision is always being made whether to take the express or the local with the attractive patron in the next seat.

"Lena" and "Sylvia" haven't planned on taking anyone home tonight, but they haven't planned against it, either. Sylvia is 26 and recently started as a registered representative for a Wall Street brokerage house. She claims a standard of ethics and a healthy respect for greed. "I've seen others in my field grab for too much too soon and too blindly. If my life was a portfolio, it would be diverse, with a broad foundation in medium- to long-term growth stocks." She starts laughing at her own joke: "A quick buck is like a quick fuck—exciting, energetic, but leaves you craving pizza at 3 A.M."

Lena has been Sylvia's roommate since they graduated from New York University. A paralegal for a midsize law firm with her sights set on going solo, Lena says, "I'm not going to live my life scared or stupid. I'll take the studied risk. The guys here have money—the drinks aren't cheap and neither are the clothes," she continues. "I mean, they're our own kind. A slut I'm not, but I've slept with a guy on the first date and I probably will again. I trust my instincts; they're going to protect me a lot better than plastic."

With a flick of her polished fingers and a smirk on her polished mouth, Lena dismisses the chances of getting AIDS from heterosex as slim or none: "Too many people being paranoid with too little evidence."

Sylvia isn't into arrogance. "I've picked up two guys in the last year—to sleep with. Honestly, I don't have a lot of experience with instant intimacy. A few months ago, I met someone here. We had a few drinks, traded some mutual experiences, and started feeling warm and cozy with one another. I let the movie studio in my head take over. We rented a room at the Pierre, bathed and drank champagne, and went to bed. The right moment to discuss safety just didn't happen. I remember thinking that I should be concerned," she adds, "but I guess I was hoping he would bring it up. The danger and surprise of it were what attracted me, though, turned me on. Sometimes I

> *Now, instead of closing our eyes and crossing our fingers that he isn't married, we hope he isn't contagious. The one-night stand is down but not out.*

get very bored with preparing, plotting, graphing, and organizing. I didn't catch anything, not even a cold."

After Sylvia leaves with a trader from a competing firm, Lena and I share a cab uptown. She tells me I'm much too paranoid about all the AIDS stuff. In New York City, she declares, we're more likely to be mugged or hit by a car.

Counselors at the New York City Department of Health reg-

ularly hear disbelief from persons who discover they are HIV-positive although they aren't in any of the well-publicized "at-risk" groups. They didn't make the distinction between at-risk *people* and at-risk *behavior*.

We women are still shy. Not wanting to ask indelicate questions or stop an embrace to tear open little wrappers, we will, nonetheless, get naked. Judy Macks, former Director of Training for the AIDS Health Project in San Francisco, has said that many women—because of low self-image and poor communication skills—are reluctant to discuss sex with their partners.

Among women who use the personals ads and dating services, there seems to be an idea that a man's status protects against his being mean, boring, or contagious. The usual personal ads or singles services clients are between 25 and 40, have white-collar professional jobs, and look for others like themselves. The main question women have is if they'll be matched with someone from similar social and economic backgrounds.

Helena Amram, owner of the international meeting service Helena, finds that few clients make the medical standing of potential dates a major issue. Amram's service is one of a few whose screening procedures include requesting a doctor's letter stating that the client is free of communicable diseases; but such letters aren't foolproof, given the possible six-month lag between exposure to the virus and the time antibodies show up in testing. The Together dating service—more typical of the genre than Helena—doesn't require proof that a client is free of STDs. That doesn't seem to worry the clientele.

"Cathy," 34, highly recommends personals ads for meeting men. She's had a number of very fun, likable dates and two short but worthwhile relationships. Talented, well read, articulate, Cathy is working on a law degree after 10 years as a reading specialist.

This tall, striking blond usually seems to be in charge, but her comments about condoms belie that impression. "Sometimes I ask the guy to use protection, sometimes not," she says. "It depends on the situation, how comfortable I feel around him. Also, some won't wear them; they feel insulted. After you go out with someone a few times you can judge what they're about."

In fact, Cathy rarely uses condoms, although she's bought quite a few. "Every so often I feel paranoid, usually after reading some article." Explaining that she was "much wilder after college and really up to a year or so ago," she asserts, "if I had AIDS, I'd know by now. I'm careful, but not deeply worried. We'll probably find a cure in a few years. A condom isn't 100 percent secure either. Nothing is, except celibacy, and I'm not ready or willing for that."

A reluctance to broach the use of condoms was mentioned by a number of women. This is ironic since, says a friend highly placed in the condom industry, women are the targets of today's condom advertising because they are more susceptible to it than men. Women have historically taken responsibility for birth control.

Some women seem to feel that dating the boy-next-door or the boy-next-desk is sufficient protection against STDs. "Barbara," a midwesterner transplanted to urban New England, has a solid job with a solid insurance firm, and a house with a porch. A self-described liberal, she feeds a fair and open mind through an exceptionally broad reading list—prompting the thought that she'd have equally solid knowledge and reasoning about so timely a topic as AIDS.

Wrong, wrong, wrong. To Barbara, AIDS is a gay/junkie disease and she's freezing her own blood, just in case. She usually dates men she meets in the neighborhood. "I know something about them before they get to my door," Barbara reasons, "their ex-wives, good and bad habits, hobbies. It's like getting a résumé prior to the interview."

Barbara doesn't sleep with every date, and never on the first date. She doesn't buy condoms at all, but will use them if her partner suggests. "I still get embarrassed buying tampons," she says. "Anyway, I don't go out with drug users, and obviously not with gays, so unless he's hemophiliac, I'm safe." Though apparently not afraid of STDs, Barbara focuses on the contaminated blood supply: "I've arranged to put aside my own blood in case I ever need a transfusion. Doesn't hurt to prepare, I guess."

Women are thinking about the "now," not the "then," when they assume that you get to know something about a man because you work with him 40 plus hours a week. Where was he last year, last job?

Elaine works so many hours that she rarely meets people in other than work-related situations. She's relaxed, has a sharp sense of humor and looks that shout high tea and scones at London's Savoy. As a financial planner for a commercial real estate firm, working an 80-hour week is common for her.

"You learn a lot about a person in a 10-hour planning session," Elaine maintains. "If you don't, you're not very bright, are you? The fact is, I don't believe it'll happen to me, or any of my friends. The closest I've come to using a condom is asking the man, 'Are you safe?' and giggling into his chest.

"Now that I have the money and am starting to get the time for a spontaneous weekend or a wild night out," Elaine continues, "I'm told to put the brakes on and approach the man with a list of questions, as if I were his prospective employer. You could be married 50 years and still not know everything about him for sure."

A 1987 survey among singles, ages 18 to 34, living in New York, measured reactions to a safe sex ad campaign. Over 80 percent of those surveyed thought sexually active people should carry condoms and *women* should get their partners to wear them. The flip side is that over 60 percent of the sexually active respondents reported not using condoms at all or only some of the time.

AIDS is a feminist issue—we are at risk. Sleeping only with those who fit a nonrisk profile is putting our health in the hands of strangers. Mary Fleming, former director of the Illinois State AIDS Hotline, feels that we underestimate the practices of the white middle class. IV heroin and cocaine use are factors in that group. Elizabeth Whelan, executive director of the American Council on Science and Health, infers that younger middle-class women aren't seriously concerned about AIDS and other STDs. An even more frightening indication of future AIDS/STD demographics is a 1986 study done in Massachusetts. Seventy percent of the 16- to 19-year-olds surveyed were found to be sexually active, but only 15 percent said they had changed to safe sex practices.

So, as yet, the AIDS plague seems not to have made much difference in our dating behavior. That's too bad—because it should. ◆

MODERN ROMANCE

A Lesson in Appetite Control

Mary Gaitskill

AT SOME POINT BETWEEN THE AGES OF 13 AND 14 I WAS BESET with romance fever. What I mean by that (and what I'll mean for my purposes here) is that excruciating hybrid of hormones and emotions that can, at any time, roar up out of the personal murk in a swollen rose-colored blur and wrap itself around anyone, however inappropriate. It can feel like love but it's different; while love has to do with who and what is being loved, romance can totally ignore such details. Romance has more to do with the person who is doing the feeling; it is the projection of some deeply subjective longing.

Being 14 and in a fever, my romanticism was ready to attach itself to even more than the usually absurd objects—my overweight cross-eyed math teacher, the pouty bleached-blond bad girl sitting in front of me, the dumpy dandruff-encrusted, pasty-faced psychiatrist my parents sent me to. Mainly, though, it pulsated around a large muscular oily boy two grades ahead of me, with whom I had had a few sweaty dates.

My feelings about him were certainly sexual, but, partly because I didn't really know what sex was, these feelings were monstrously dilated and distorted by my equally strong feelings of romance. When I fantasized having sex with him, I didn't picture anything happening below the waist: it was searing eye contact and intense jaw-setting action; there was a thunderstorm raging outside and flowers filling my dimly lit canopied boudoir. Never mind that we could barely hold a conversation; delirious with imaginings I more or less engineered the event, which finally took place on the floor of the garage, and it took several weeks for me to recover from the

shocking clash between my fantasy and the actual painful, grunting, odorous occurrence.

Many people have had an experience like this, with various gradations in the gap between the real and the romantic. Some people react by repudiating their romantic feelings as lies and illusions—in fact, *The Concise Oxford Dictionary* defines "romance" as "an exaggeration," "a picturesque falsehood," or, as a verb, to "exaggerate or distort the truth, esp. fantastically." Even those adults who describe themselves as romantics tend to append words like "hopeless" to their description as though they know they're being foolish, but that it's a nice kind of foolishness proving how idealistic they are.

At 14, I wasn't about to decide that romance was a crock. My stubborn will to romance simply burrowed underground where it continued to live, finding nurturance in the crevices and claw holds of what was, I'm afraid, a series of seedy and preposterous adolescent experiences. In other words, since I was unable to find romance in the forms I'd been taught by popular culture to expect it—Valentines, flowers, declarations of pure love, gooey theme music that came out of nowhere—I saw it in unconventional places, in those unexpected moments of tenderness and communication that can occur between people in the most superficially unromantic circumstances.

I had, for various complex reasons, learned very little about intimacy and love, about the tension between desire and personal territory, about the space between my needs and the needs of others. All this confusion was exacerbated by the way in which romance was presented to adolescent girls at that time and probably still is: as an inexplicable idealized feeling that you could have for someone you just glimpsed across the room, based mainly on their appearance, a feeling that would end in love and marriage, a feeling that was totally disconnected from and incompatible with anything else in daily life, even sex. It is this disconnection that seems to me the oddest feature of our idea of romance.

Just a few years ago, I had a romantic experience that was very different from my first. I developed an intense crush on a man I worked with, an adorable big-eyed honey who could actually carry on a conversation. The same level of fantasy was in operation as the first time around—except that this time there were no flowers, no thunderstorms, the lights were on full blast and there was major action below, above, and all around the waist. There was only one thing preventing me from luring him into the metaphorical garage; he had a live-in girlfriend.

This situation, which sounds hideously painful, became a sort of epiphany for me. Somehow, in a startling outburst of maturity, I was able to place my romantic feelings in the context of my other feelings for him. I don't mean I suppressed my romantic feelings, or tried to control them—quite the contrary. I allowed them to exist and respected their realness without throwing all of my emotional weight on them. In this way I was able to enjoy my feeling of tenderness for him while allowing space for a gentle, calm, sensitive connection between the truth of who he was and the limits of our relationship.

What I learned from this experience came in mighty handy when, further down the road, I found myself involved with a handsome sexbomb playboy who was a lot of fun but who was clearly not Mr. Right. Although I knew I wasn't in love with him and never would be, I found myself assailed in the night by enormous fanged fantasies of ultimate romantic communion, fantasies in which we performed the most incredible sex acts to the thundering sound track of our equally incredible emotions. None of this had anything to do with what was actually happening between us, but the more I tried to deny my romantic outburst the closer I got to the edge of an obsessional abyss.

Then, on some barely conscious level, I shifted gears. I stopped trying to control and contain my feelings. Instead I simply allowed myself to feel them—to respect their reality in the context of my other feelings for the guy, which ranged from friendship to

attraction to disinterest. Throughout the affair, I was able to enjoy my hot romantic feelings for him, and to see him for who he was—which, if you must know, was a charming meatball.

This of course goes against our conventional concept of romance, which is defined as incomprehensible and overwhelming; women, especially, are taught to regard it as a ferocious onset, a feeling that will render them helpless, swooning, and incapable. Whatever turns you on. But remember: to feel helpless and out of control isn't the same thing as being helpless and out of control. Romance is as real as lust, friendship, and love, but it is only part of a shifting spectrum of possible responses. There's nothing wrong with wanting to make out in a flower-filled room while a thunderstorm rages. There's also nothing wrong with wanting to rip off someone's clothes and roll around on the garage floor with them. It's when these feelings don't acknowledge each other that you court disappointment.

By fetishizing romance in the ways that we do, disconnecting it from other feelings and then placing such enormous weight on it, we make it hard for it to flower. For it is only when romance allows for and works with emotional intimacy as well as the power of gut-level sexual passion that all at once, there is loud theme music playing, the flaming sun is setting, you are bursting out of your bodice—or whatever your fantasy is. ♦

SEX TIPS

Your move . . .

THE ART OF SEX

20 ways to perfect your style

Paul Cooper

First, let us affirm that we're modern, sensitive guys; we know that having a repertoire of sexual tricks is not the same as sharing love and intimacy. On the other hand, being an erotic virtuoso never hurt love and intimacy one bit. So we've gathered facts and tips that focus on sexual delight for you and your partner. (May she call for encores.) As for intimacy, that angle was already summed up by the classical poet Ovid: "To be loved, be lovable."

ALL WORK, NO FOREPLAY

A hurry-up-and-go lifestyle can lead to speedy ejaculations, warns Sheldon Burman, M.D., director of the Male Sexual Dysfunction Institute in Chicago. "When you have an inordinate amount of stress and not enough time to meet all the demands in your life, your pattern of haste can carry over into the bedroom," Dr. Burman explains. He adds, however, that if premature ejaculation has no physical or deep emotional causes, it often goes away with a lifestyle change, such as reducing stress, quitting smoking, losing weight and exercising. For more information, call the MSD Institute's 24-hour hotline (except Saturdays) at (312) 725-7722.

TRY, TRY AGAIN

"**I** always suggest that people try something new three times," says sex counselor Robert O. Hawkins, Jr., Ph.D., a health sciences professor at the State University of New York–Stony Brook. The first time, he says, you may be worrying about bending your knees and elbows at the proper angle; by the second or third time, you may find you're able to relax and enjoy it.

GO BUY THE BOOK

Sexual handbooks "should be used the way they were intended," says Hawkins. "Sort of like cookbooks, in which you select only the suggestions that suit you."

If your erotic imagination is getting stale, read Nancy Friday's *Men in Love* (Dell). Her book describes a wide variety of men's erotic fantasies; it could jump-start your libido.

WAKE UP SEX

Sex in the middle of the night, after you've both had some sleep, can be much more intense, says Michael Morgenstern, author of *How to Make Love to a Woman* (Ballantine).

EXERCISE CONTROL

Kegels are exercises that give some men stiffer erections and more control over ejaculation by strengthening the muscles of the pelvic floor, say William Hartman, M.D., and Marilyn Fithian, codirectors of the Center for Marital and Sexual Studies in Long Beach, California. Here's the program:

First, find the right muscles, the ones you use to stop your urine flow. To exercise them, squeeze them and hold tight. Half your contractions can be brief; hold the rest for three seconds. No one will know you're doing Kegels, so you can do them anywhere. Start with a few and work toward 200 a day.

After doing Kegels for a few months, your pelvic muscles will be strong enough to prevent ejaculation if you squeeze them tight just before the urge to ejaculate reaches the "point of no return."

THE YEAR'S BEST SEX

Men have hormonal sex cycles like women's, only subtler. Male sexual potency is maintained by testosterone, secreted by cells in the testicles. The male hormone peaks daily in the early morning, and yearly in the fall, according to a study conducted in France. So those cool mornings may be the best time of the year for sex.

But you don't have to wait until fall to be full of wild oats. Regular exercise makes men feel better about themselves, more relaxed and arousable. In a study of men who began a workout program, more than half said their sex life improved. And the sexual benefits of exercise last. A survey of masters swimmers found that those in their 60s through 80s had sex more than once a week, more typical of 30-year-olds.

Of course, it's possible to overdo a good thing: In one study, male ultramarathoners who ran 100-mile races showed a *decrease* in testosterone.

WHEN YOU'RE HOT, YOU'RE HOT; WHEN YOU'RE NOT, YOU'RE NOT

If you're looking for every sexual encounter to sweep you away on a Technicolor tide of ecstasy, you've been watching too many late-night cable movies. Accept the fact that sex isn't always a fiery welding of souls, advise William Masters and Virginia Johnson in their book *Masters and Johnson on Sex and Human Loving* (Little, Brown). Sometimes sex is awkward. Sometimes even orgasms are blah. Nobody said men and women had to be sex machines, so relax about your peaks and valleys.

THE G-SPOT EXISTS

Some women do have a G-spot, a pleasure area about halfway up the front wall of the vagina, says David M. Quadagno, Ph.D., a medical sciences professor at Florida State University. These women can have intense orgasms from strong, rhythmic pressure against this area inside the vagina. G-spot stimulation in man-on-top positions is heightened by putting a pillow under your partner's hips.

MEN HAVE HOT SPOTS, TOO

Men have two hot spots that are just waiting for the right touch, says Paul Pearsall, Ph.D., author of *Super Marital Sex* (Ivy Books). One area is the small, triangular region on the underside of the head of the penis where a thin strip of skin, the *frenulum*, runs from the head to the shaft. The other area follows the *raphe*, the line you can see and feel that runs lengthwise along the center of the scrotum. Pearsall suggests asking your partner to trace her fingers along this line from behind the scrotum to the front and up the penis.

LOVE POTIONS: REAL AND FAKE

The prescription form of the drug yohimbine produces erections in about one-quarter of men suffering from impotence, say researchers.

No one knows for sure, but yohimbine, derived from a certain type of African tree bark, may work by boosting blood flow to the penis, by slowing blood flow from it, or by activating pleasure centers in the brain. Whichever, the men for whom it does work get full, sustained erections. Users also report warm spinal shivers, pelvic tingles and heightened sexual pleasure. Side effects have included increased blood pressure, raised heart rate and skin flushing, however.

A word of advice: Just because prescription yohimbine worked for the men in the studies, don't expect to gain sexual powers from over-the-counter or mail-order versions of yohimbine. The U.S. Food and Drug Administration has banned the sale of all nonprescription products that claim to arouse or increase sexual desire or improve sexual performance. Among the "aphrodisiacs" the FDA calls useless: ginseng, mandrake, minerals, sarsaparilla and vitamins. Yocon is the name of the leading prescription yohimbine.

WHAT WOMEN WISH MEN KNEW

Women don't want you to prove your manhood in bed, they want you to have fun. That was some of the good news we heard when we conducted a confidential sex survey, asking women, "What do you wish men knew about sex?" Other common themes: Don't worry about The Big "O"; women don't care about penis size; slow down, you move too fast; help her tell you what she likes; please discover the *whole* body, guys.

WHAM, BAM, THANK YOU, SIR!

Some women get an overwhelming orgasm from quick intercourse without foreplay but with deep penetration, and say it feels different from the orgasms they get from clitoral stimulation or from less vigorous intercourse, reports Alex Comfort, M.D., in *More Joy of Sex* (Crown). This sort of orgasm produces "gasping, breath-holding, and a once-for-all climax." Too much foreplay derails this special response, which, when it happens, is as rapid as a man's.

CULTIVATE A SEXUAL APPETITE

Experts say a low-fat diet may keep you sexually potent as you get older. Tubbing out on foods high in saturated fats and cholesterol may lead to clogged blood vessels, in the penis as well as in the heart, and that can leave you limp. One study showed that clogged penile blood vessels are the main cause of impotence in men over 50.

KNOWLEDGE IS BLISS

The basis of great sex is knowledge of your own body and your partner's; finding out what she likes, letting her know what you like, says Jerome Sherman, Ph.D., a Houston psychologist and president of the 3,000-member American Association of Sex Educators, Counselors and Therapists. "Then maybe you can enhance the basics with mirrors, colored lights, aromas, lotions, positions, locations—whatever you want to explore," Sherman says.

SOME MEDICINES HIT BELOW THE BELT

Some prescription drugs, such as ulcer and blood-pressure medicines, can cause temporary impotence. Even over-the-counter drugs like Dramamine (for motion sickness) and Benadryl (for allergies) can have that unpleasant side effect. "Sometimes it takes some careful detective work to pinpoint the offending medication, but it is often possible to make substitutions," says Albert McBride, M.D., national spokesperson for the Impotence Foundation (3540 Wilshire Blvd., Los Angeles, CA 90010).

FOCUS ON PLEASURE, NOT MEASURE

I get about four phone calls a week from men who want their penises enlarged or lengthened," says Chicago's Dr. Burman. The average erect human penis is about 5 to 7 inches long, he says, "but guys with normal-sized penises become dismayed because some woman says her last lover was 7½ inches." Although psychological factors may come into play, the mechanism of female orgasm has nothing to do with penis size, says Dr. Burman. "Nine out of 10 women have clitoral orgasms, caused by *external* stimulation to the clitoris. If you're physically fit and attractive and an adequate lover, a 4-inch erection is long enough."

For deeper penetration with a short penis, though, Burman recommends positions "where the woman's thighs won't get in the way." The best: "Woman-on-top, kneeling and facing the man."

FUTURE SEX ## BETTER LOVING THROUGH ELECTRONICS?

Someday, impotent men may push a button to get an instant, long-lasting erection, says Neil McAleer, author of *The Body Almanac* (Doubleday). Researchers have found nerve bundles near the prostate gland that trigger erections in monkeys when electrically stimulated. By implanting electrodes activated by radio signals, the researchers induced and maintained erections in the animals for several hours. McAleer says this same technology may be used in the near future for humans.

Then again, in a few decades, bachelors may not be as driven to find a sexual partner. Orgasms—cascades of them—may be available by direct electrical stimulation of the brain's pleasure centers, McAleer says. Once scientists have pinpointed these brain sites, a tiny electronic "orgasm box" could be rigged. Who says Woody Allen isn't a visionary?

SOOTHING THE SAVAGE BREAST

Men's breasts have the same potential for erotic pleasure as women's breasts, says Jack Morin, Ph.D., a former health-sciences teacher at Skyline College in San Bruno, California. In both sexes, the breasts are richly supplied with nerve endings, especially in the nipple area. Although only half as many men as women get hard nipples spontaneously when aroused, men's nipples are about as likely as women's to become erect when directly stimulated.

KEEPING SCORE

Pssst. Want to buy some sexy software? *Interaction* will provide you with a "personal sexual analysis" based on your answers to 100 multiple-choice questions. An optional module compares your profile with someone else's to let you know if you're compatible. Available for certain IBM, Apple, Atari, Commodore and Tandy computers, the programs cost $59.95 and $49.95, respectively, or $99.95 for both. Order from IntraCorp, Inc., 14160 S.W. 139th Court, Miami, FL 33186; (800) 468-7226.

WHEN ONCE IS NOT ENOUGH

Men with low sperm counts can improve their fertility simply by having a second ejaculation 30 to 60 minutes after the first, reports a study in the journal *Fertility and Sterility*. Researchers found that 14 of 20 men who tried the method had higher sperm counts in the second ejaculation, and five of their wives became pregnant. In men with normal sperm counts, however, the second ejaculation usually contains fewer sperm.

SILENCE IS WOODEN

"A lot of my patients complain that their partners don't say anything or are too quiet during lovemaking," says sex therapist Shirley Zussman, Ed.D., co-director of the Association for Male Sexual Dysfunction. "Telling your lover things like, 'Oh, you feel so good,' and grunting, sighing, making noise—it's all a part of lovemaking," she says. "Good sex is like a light and sound show: Leave the lights on and let out some sound."

Reproduction

- **Birth Control (Articles 27-33)**
- **Pregnancy and Childbirth (Articles 34-37)**

While human reproduction is as old as humanity, there are many aspects of it that are changing in today's society. Not only have new technologies of conception and childbirth affected the *how* of reproduction, but personal, social, and cultural forces have also affected the *who*, the *when*, and the *when not*. Abortion remains a fiercely debated topic, and legislative efforts for and against it abound. The teenage pregnancy rate in the United States is one of the highest in the Western world. The costs of teenage childbearing can be high for the parents, the child, and for society. Yet efforts to curb U.S. teenage pregnancy have not been convincingly effective.

This section also addresses the issue of birth control. In light of the change in attitude toward sex for pleasure, birth control has become a matter of prime importance. Even in our age of sexual enlightenment, some individuals, possibly in the height of passion, fail to correlate "having sex" with pregnancy. Before sex can become safe as well as enjoyable, people must receive thorough and accurate information regarding conception and contraception, birth and birth control. In addition, it is even more crucial that individuals make a mental and emotional commitment to the use and application of the available information, facts, and methods. Only this can make every child a planned and wanted one.

Despite the relative simplicity of the above assertion, abortion, and even birth control, remain emotionally charged issues in American society. While opinion surveys indicate that most of the public supports family planning and abortion at least in some circumstances, individuals who seek abortions often face stigmatization. After the 1989 *Webster v. Reproductive Health Services* Supreme Court ruling opened the door to new restrictions on abortion, several states began drafting legislation that would restrict some or all women's access to abortion. The outcome of these efforts is largely unknown as patterns in passage, constitutionality, and public reaction are not evident yet.

Many of the questions raised in this section about the new technologies of reproduction and its control are likely to remain among the most hotly debated issues for the remainder of this century. It is likely that various religio-political groups will continue to posit and challenge basic definitions of human life, as well as the rights and responsibilities of women and men associated with sex, procreation, and abortion. The very foundations of our pluralistic society may be challenged. We will have to await the outcome.

The first two articles in the *Birth Control* section focus on efforts aimed at reducing teenage sexual activity and pregnancy. The next two focus on currently available contraceptive methods and choices. Each offers important information and advice to individuals or couples seeking to safely and effectively prevent conception. The next article profiles Etienne-Emile Baulieu, the inventor of RU-486, the French drug that has met fierce opposition by pro-life forces who have labeled it "the abortion pill." The final two articles in this subsection focus on abortion. The first tells the heart-wrenching story of a young girl whose mother attributes her death to an abortion law that required parental consent. The second overviews trends in Americans beliefs, attitudes, and policies toward abortion.

The first two articles of the subsection on *Pregnancy and Childbirth* focus on teenage pregnancy, childbirth, and parenting. Each provides some different concepts and insights on these topics. The first challenges the concept that teenage childbearing is a tragedy. The second asserts that teenage parents, as well as all teenagers, are really victims of American society's conflict and failings. The final two articles address sexual intimacy and activity during pregnancy and after childbirth—two oftentimes problematic periods for couples. Each provides information, reassurance, and suggestions while dispelling common myths.

Looking Ahead: Challenge Questions

Is there hope for reducing teenage pregnancy and childbearing in this country? Why or why not?

As a teenager, who advocated abstinence to you? What was your reaction?

In your opinion, what are the most important characteristics of a contraceptive?

Do you feel you are an educated and informed consumer when it comes to condoms? Why or why not? What would make you more comfortable when purchasing condoms?

Do you expect RU-486 to become an accepted form of birth control in the United States? Why or why not? Would you use (or support your partner's use of) RU-486?

How have recent events in the abortion rights/access arena affected you? Have they changed your beliefs and/or attitudes?

DON'T GO OUT WITHOUT YOUR RUBBERS.

We're talking about condoms.
And we're talking about AIDS.

An Evaluation of an Adolescent Pregnancy Prevention Program:

Is "Just Say No" Enough?*

The current study evaluates the impact of an abstinence promotion program that targeted middle school-age children. After being exposed to six program sessions that focused on self-esteem, communication skills, peer pressure, and teaching the value that sex should be confined to marriage, the only change shown by the 191 participants but not the 129 controls is an increase in precoital sexual activity. The implications for family life education are discussed.

**F. Scott Christopher
and Mark W. Roosa**

F. Scott Christopher is an Assistant Professor and Mark W. Roosa is an Associate Professor in the Department of Family Resources and Human Development, Arizona State University, Tempe, AZ 85287–2502. Both authors contributed equally to this project.

The rate of teenage sexual involvement is at an all-time high (Trussell, 1988). As a result, there are over 800,000 pregnancies to U.S. teenagers each year, most of them unplanned and unwanted. The potential life-long outcomes and risks of this phenomenon have been well documented and include live births, abortions, and miscarriages (e.g., Center for the Study of Social Policy, CSSP, 1986; Olson, Wallace, & Miller, 1984). Further, the overwhelming majority of those teens that give birth choose to keep their child. Such teenage mothers are at risk for experiencing repeat pregnancies and for living a life of poverty (Hayes, 1987). In response to this pressing need, Congress passed the Adolescent Family Life Act (AFLA) of 1981. This Act allowed the Office of Adolescent Pregnancy Programs to establish primary prevention demonstration projects designed to promote abstinence of sexual activity

until marriage (Mecklenburg & Thompson, 1983). The present study was an evaluation of the effects of one of these projects.

Although the AFLA projects are mandated to have an evaluation component, few of the evaluation designs have been of sufficient quality to provide meaningful data (Hofferth & Hayes, 1987). In fact, only two projects have published results on the efficacy of their intervention over the history of the AFLA (Olson et al., 1984; Vincent, Clearie, & Schluchter, 1987). The first program was a high school based project conducted in three western states. It served mostly white students, with a sizable proportion of the sample affiliated with the Mormon Church.

This program was designed to be a part of the normal health, parenting, or home economics curriculum. It emphasized the involvement of the high school students' parents and promoted family discussions about sexual values and beliefs. The program brought about short-term increases in family strengths and parental discussions that focused on sexual values and decreases in permissive premarital sexual attitudes (Olson et al., 1984). However, the long-term impact of the program has not been reported. Furthermore, no information has been pro-

vided on the impact of the program on actual sexual behaviors.

Other programs that have exclusively emphasized premarital sexual abstinence have reported parallel findings (Hayes, 1987). For instance, in a preliminary report of another AFLA project, the Search Institute's "Human Sexuality: Values and Choices," Donahue (1987) reported both knowledge and attitude changes supportive of sexual abstinence, with no changes in actual sexual activity. However, the effects on knowledge and attitudes decayed over a 3-month period.

The second AFLA program that has reported its results is not truly an abstinence program (Vincent et al., 1987). Although this program was able to reduce pregnancy rates, the AFLA funded only the abstinence proportion of the program. Birth control information and services were also a part of this program but were funded by other sources. Hence, the results of this program are not directly comparable to programs that rely on an abstinence theme alone.

The program evaluated in the current study was a six-session abstinence only AFLA program entitled the "Success Express Program"

This evaluation study was supported in part by grant #APH 000319-01-1 from the Office of Adolescent Parenting Programs, National Institute of Health, Department of Health Services to the Maricopa County YWCA. The authors would like to thank Anita Petitti for her dedicated help with data entry.

Key Words: abstinence, adolescence, evaluation, pregnancy, prevention.

From *Family Relations*, Vol. 39, No. 1, January 1990, pp. 68-72. Copyright © 1990 by the National Council on Family Relations, 3989 Central Ave. N.E., Suite #550, Minneapolis, MN 55421. Reprinted by permission.

(Lucero & Clark, 1988) that targeted middle school-aged children. Five of the sessions were designed to teach behaviors, attitudes, and skills consistent with the abstinence theme of the AFLA. The sixth was used to gather posttest data and to allow participants to go through a graduation ceremony. Each program session had individual goals and objectives designed to help meet the overriding goal of the project.

The first session focused on self-esteem and family values with an emphasis on the messages adolescents receive from their social environment. Session 2 examined adolescent patterns of growth and development while highlighting reproductive knowledge. The third session analyzed pressures adolescents encounter to become sexually active. It focused on the types of media and peer pressures they are likely to experience and the effects these pressures have on values, decision-making, and behaviors. The complications of premarital sexual activity, teen pregnancy, and sexually transmitted diseases, as well as the benefits of abstinence, were also discussed in this session. Session 4 exposed participants to different communication strategies, with an emphasis on how to say "no" assertively in sexual interactions. Finally, the fifth session prompted adolescents to examine their future life goals and helped them to attain goal-setting skills.

In designing this program and its evaluation several key issues were kept in mind. First, with few published evaluations of sexual abstinence programs, replications with a variety of designs and samples are necessary to clearly determine the efficacy of such programs. Second, the abstinence only programs that have been evaluated and published their results have served primarily white, middle class, and high school-aged students; the former are less at risk for premarital sexual activity or pregnancy than minority and low-income adolescents, and the latter are more likely to have begun sexual activity before entering their respective programs (CSSP, 1986; Hayes, 1987). Thus, primary prevention of adolescent pregnancy, by definition, may need to target younger adolescents, especially when serving low-income minority groups. Third, abstinence programs rarely have asked participants to report actual sexual behaviors; most have limited their assessments to beliefs or attitudes. This is a critical shortcoming since the relationship between sexual attitudes and sexual behavior is not at all clear for this age group. When sexual

behaviors have been assessed, no changes have been reported (Donahue, 1987). Finally, because of design or analysis limitations previous evaluations have failed to report dropout analyses. This oversight makes generalization of results difficult and weakens the interpretation of any positive results reported.

In contrast, this study focuses on low-income, primarily minority, early adolescents. It utilizes a quasi-experimental pretest-posttest control group design; random assignment to conditions was not possible. This evaluation also includes a detailed analysis of program dropouts to give a clearer picture of whom the program was serving and failing to serve. Finally, this evaluation includes assessment of sexual behaviors which, although important in itself, allows for separate analyses of program effects for the entire sample as well as for participants who had not yet engaged in sexual intercourse.

Method

Sample

Three hundred and twenty adolescents participated in the program, including 191 participants and 129 controls. Sixty-one percent of the sample were female while 39% were male. Most of the adolescents were in either the sixth or seventh grade and their average age was 12.8 years. The majority of the sample were Hispanic (69%) or black (21%) with fewer Caucasians (8%) and Native Americans (2%). While the adolescents were not asked about parents' occupation and education level, an examination of census tract data from the neighborhoods where the Success Express programs were conducted indicated that the sample came from predominately lower-class families. According to these data the average median family income in the neighborhoods of the eight program sites was $12,688 and the average percent of families who lived below the poverty level was 26.4%.

Procedures

The first session of the program was divided between pretesting and instruction. Posttest data were gathered 6 weeks later in the final session. Three month and sixth month follow-up data

were also collected and will be the focus of future analyses. Pretests and posttests were administered in group settings. Each adolescent was given a questionnaire with a cover letter that informed them that their responses would be "kept secret," program leaders and school officials would not see their answers.

Prior to administering the questionnaire, participants were told that if they did not understand the meaning of any of the items, or if they had any questions, they should feel free to ask for clarification. The instructions for each measure, and the items contained in each measure, were read aloud to control for differences in reading ability. Reliability analyses on the instruments showed internal consistency in the respondents' answers indicating that the adolescents were able to comprehend and complete the questionnaire.

The Success Express program was conducted at eight sites including five schools in which it was used to supplement the health curriculum. Control group data were gathered in these same schools in classrooms where the Success Express program was not run; in most cases the control groups received the treatment at a later time. The remaining programs were conducted at community sites within the same area of the city.

Instruments

Several different variables were measured within the overall evaluation design. Only those measures directly related to the evaluation will be reported here.

Self-esteem. Self-esteem was measured with the Rosenberg (1969) self-esteem scale, a 10-item, Likert scale. Participants indicated how much items reflected their feelings. Cronbach's alpha for the pretest was .67 and for the posttest was .70.

Family communication. The quality of family communication, as perceived by the adolescents, was measured with the Parent-Adolescent Communication Scale (Barnes & Olson, 1982). This Likert scale asked participants to indicate the extent to which they agreed or disagreed with each item. The mother was used as the parent referent throughout the scale because the researchers felt that the child was not only more likely to communicate with the mother, but that the mother was more likely to remain a part of the family if the family composition had changed in the past. The scale itself is composed of two subscales:

4. REPRODUCTION: Birth Control

The Openness of Family Communication subscale (10 items; Cronbach's alpha = .85 for the pretest and .86 for the posttest) and the Family Communication Problem subscale (10 items; pretest alpha = .68; posttest alpha = .68).

Premarital sexual behaviors. Lifetime sexual behavior and perception of best friend's lifetime sexual involvement were measured with a modified version of DeLamater and MacCorquodale's (1979) premarital sexual interaction measure. The original scale was modified by using only the first seven behaviors of the scale. These behaviors started at kissing, progressed through different types of fondling, and ended at sexual intercourse. Items that measured oral-genital interaction were eliminated because the researchers felt that these items were not appropriate for this age group. Participants were asked to indicate which behaviors they had experienced and which they thought their best friend had experienced. These scales met the Guttman reliability standards for being reproducible (self lifetime behavior pretest lambda = .90, posttest lambda = .90; friend's lifetime behavior pretest lambda = .92, posttest lambda = .93).

Premarital sexual and marital attitudes. Premarital sexual and marital attitudes were assessed by an approach previously used by Miller, McCoy, Olson, & Wallace (1986). Participants were asked what was their attitude about "teen-agers having full sexual relations (sexual intercourse) before marriage." They responded on a 5-point scale from *always all right* to *always wrong*. Additionally, the participants indicated the best age to have sex for the first time, the best age to marry, and the age they expected to have sex for the first time.

Results

Program Effects

The primary purpose of this research was to evaluate the effects of the Success Express program. The first step in this process was to test the equivalence of the participant and control groups. This was done with a series of one-way ANOVAs on the pretest scores. Only those who completed both the pretest and the posttest were used in these analyses. Two significant differences emerged; participants ($\bar{X}$ =

6.98) were a half a grade more advanced than controls [$\bar{X}$ = 6.53; $F(1, 189) = 18.27, p < .0001$] and participants ($\bar{X}$ = 12.00) began dating at a slightly earlier age than did controls [$\bar{X}$ = 12.50; $F(1, 54) = 4.02, p < .05$].

It was possible that the difference in grade level could have affected the sexuality outcome measures of the study. Past research has indicated that the likelihood of engaging in sexual behavior increases with age (Hayes, 1987). It is also conceivable that premarital sexual attitudes could similarly be affected by maturation. Therefore, the effect of grade was controlled for by using it as a covariate in the evaluation analysis. It was not possible to use age at first date as a covariate since not all participants had begun dating.

The second step in the evaluation was to compare the pretest and posttest scores of the participant and control groups. This was done with a series of 2 X 2 X 2 (Participant/Control Group X Gender X Time) repeated measures analysis of covariance tests. Group and Gender served as aggregating variables while Time was a repeated measure. Only significant Group by Time interactions and Group by Time by Gender interactions are reported; either would reveal specific program effects.

No significant interactions were revealed for the variables of self-esteem, family communication problems, openness of family communication, best age for engaging in sex for the first time, age expect to have sex for the first time, best age for marriage, attitudes about premarital sexual intercourse, and best friend's lifetime sexual interaction (see Table 1). In fact, only one significant Group by Time interaction emerged; participants and controls were significantly different in their posttest lifetime sexual behavior measures [$F(1, 179) = 4.29, p < .04$]. Further, an examination of the means revealed that the participants increased their mean sexual interaction level between time 1 and time 2 while controls did not.

This finding was surprising and raised the question of what specific sexual behaviors were increasing over the six sessions of the program. The frequency of each behavior was therefore calculated for both the pretest and the posttest to allow comparisons between the two times. Furthermore, although a significant Group by Time by Gender interaction failed to emerge, it is conceivable that male and female participants may differ in their pretest to posttest changes in specific behaviors, and that these changes may

Table 1.
Pretest and Posttest Differences for Participants and Controls

Variables	Participants		Controls	
	Pretest	Posttest	Pretest	Posttest
Self-esteem	29.25	29.47	29.35	29.40
Communication problems	26.18	27.41	26.00	26.38
Open family communication	37.46	36.14	37.54	35.26
Best age for first coitus	19.90	20.27	19.13	18.81
Age expect first coitus	20.23	20.19	19.11	19.21
Best age for marriage	21.97	22.09	22.17	22.56
Lifetime sexual involvement	2.25	2.55	1.99	1.84*
Friends lifetime sexual involvement	3.13	3.18	2.73	2.77

*p < .02.

Table 2.
Sexual Behavior Frequencies

Sexual Behaviors	Participants				Controls			
	Male		Female		Male		Female	
	Pretest	Posttest	Pretest	Posttest	Pretest	Posttest	Pretest	Posttest
Kissing	78.4	78.4	76.2	74.6	78.4	78.8	62.0	60.0
French kiss	66.7	69.4	54.7	62.5	57.6	54.5	52.1	50.0
Touch breasts	44.4	63.9	11.7	13.3	25.0	25.0	22.4	14.3
Male touch female genitals	44.1	55.9	6.7	10.0	21.9	28.1	8.3	6.3
Female touch male genitals	42.4	45.5	5.0	3.3	20.0	20.0	12.5	6.3
Genital to genital	39.4	54.5	1.7	8.5	21.9	21.9	8.3	2.1
Coitus	36.4	36.4	1.7	3.3	16.7	23.3	4.2	2.1

120

not be reflected in their mean lifetime sexual involvement scores. Therefore, frequencies were calculated separately for the males and females (see Table 2).

The results revealed that both male and female participants reported increases for several sexual behaviors. However, the male participants reported far more dramatic increases across the seven sexual behaviors. There were large (greater than 10%), upward posttest shifts for the male participants for the behaviors of touching female breasts, touching female genitals, and genital to genital contact. No changes were seen, however, in the rate of males engaging in sexual intercourse.

Virgin Analysis

Olson (1987) has suggested that abstinence programs may work better for adolescents who have not yet experienced sexual intercourse. He argued that adolescents who are virgins are more likely than nonvirgins to adopt a sexual abstinence attitude after being exposed to this type of program. This hypothesis was tested by excluding nonvirgins from the data pool and making comparisons with the remaining participants using the same analysis strategy as before. Once again, the only significant Group by Time interaction to emerge was for the lifetime sexual behavior measure [$F(1, 159) = 6.08, p < .01$]. Even when the nonvirgins were removed from the analysis, participants, but not controls, reported a slight but significant increase in sexual behaviors between time 1 ($\bar{X} = 1.62$) and time 2 ($\bar{X} = 2.04$).

Dropouts

A secondary purpose of this evaluation was to report on the type of adolescent that left the program before completing all of the sessions. Forty-one percent of the participants and 30% of the controls completed a pretest, but failed to complete a posttest. Chi-square analysis indicated that these dropouts were just as likely to be males as females ($\chi^2 = .000, p < $ n.s.). Since most program sites were in middle schools, dropping out was most likely due to either absence or moving out of the area. However, since significantly more participants than controls dropped out, the possibility of "voluntary absences" must be considered.

A series of 2 X 2 (Dropout Status X Treatment/Control Group) ANOVAs

Table 3.
Significant Dropout Status by Group Interactions

Variables	Participants		Controls	
	Dropouts	Retain	Dropouts	Retain
Age expect sex	15.46	19.50	19.18	17.82
Best age for first coitus	16.79	19.36	19.27	18.21
Lifetime sexual involvement	3.42	2.46	1.63	2.07

were conducted on the variables measured within the evaluation. Only significant Status by Group interactions are reported. These interactions revealed the ways in which participant dropouts were different from control dropouts and from adolescents who were retained regardless of which group they belonged to. Three significant interactions emerged from the analyses.

The first of these was for the age the adolescents expected to have sex [$F(1, 87) = 8.05, p < .006$]. An examination of the means shows that dropout participants expected to have sex at a mean age of 15½ years (see Table 3). This was 4 years younger than the mean age indicated by participants who were retained in the program and almost 4 years younger than controls who failed to complete a posttest.

The second significant interaction revealed that, when asked what was the best age to have sex for the first time, dropout participants responded with a significantly younger age when compared to the individuals in the other groups [$F(1, 87) = 5.65, p < .02$]. They indicated a mean age that was 2½ years younger than participants who were retained and controls who dropped out of the program.

The final significant interaction was for the lifetime sexual involvement measure [$F(1, 203) = 4.29, p < .04$]. An examination of the means showed that dropout participants were significantly higher in their level of sexual experience than the adolescents from the other groups.

Discussion

The Success Express program is an Adolescent Family Life Act demonstration project that attempts to teach early adolescents from a predominantly lower-class minority population to abstain from sexual involvement, to "Just Say No" to sex. It does this through a series of six sessions that focus on instilling premarital sexual abstinence attitudes, raising self-esteem, teaching communication skills, providing reproductive knowledge, and building an awareness of

pressures to engage in sex. The present study is an evaluation of these efforts. It has two main purposes: (a) To report on the initial outcomes of the program; and (b) to report on the characteristics of the dropouts of the Success Express program.

Program Effects

The present study reveals an increase in sexual activity among participants, with a sizable increase reported by male adolescents who took part in the program. This finding is at once disturbing and perplexing. One potential explanation for the reported increase is that the males were falsely reporting that they had engaged in the sexual behaviors. At least one study indicates that male teenagers are prone to do this (Newcomer & Udry, 1988). However, two arguments can be raised against this conclusion. First, if false reporting were the problem, a similar increase should be found among both participants and controls and this was not the case. Second, increases were seen for precoital behaviors but not for intercourse for participant males. Status is gained within male adolescent groups for engaging in intercourse (Carns, 1973). Therefore it would be expected that if these teenagers were to falsely report other sexual behaviors they would be at least as likely to do so for coitus, something they did not do for the present study. Thus it appears likely that the reported increase in sexual activity is either an outcome of participating in the program or that participation interacted with a third unidentified variable to produce this effect.

This finding, coupled with the lack of positive program outcomes and the reported lack of efficacy of similar programs (CSSP, 1986; Donahue, 1987; Olson et al., 1984) raises concerns about programs that rely exclusively on a premarital sexual abstinence approach. While previous abstinence programs have been able to report positive short-term outcomes, most of these effects involve changes in attitudes rather than behaviors and these effects deteriorated over short periods of time (CSSP, 1986; Donahue, 1987; Olson et al., 1984). The long-term effects of the present program are still being evaluated. However, given the reports of other strictly abstinence programs and the findings of the present evaluation, the potential that the long-term evaluations will reveal positive outcomes is small.

This suggests that adolescent pregnancy primary prevention programs that utilize a single approach to the problem (teaching abstinence) may be ineffective (cf. Trussel, 1988). This is not overly surprising when considering the multiple influences impacting adolescent sexual behavior (e.g., CSSP, 1986; Hayes, 1987). Past research has shown that personality, family, social network, and the dating relationship itself all play a role in premarital sexual decision making (DeLamater & MacCorquodale, 1979; Hayes, 1987). Therefore, it may be simplistic to believe that a single approach to this problem would be effective. In fact, few single dimension programs have been successful at reducing the incidence of teen pregnancy (Hayes, 1987). The programs that have been successful have intervened along several different dimensions (CSSP, 1986; Vincent et al., 1987).

Dropout Analysis

The analysis of the dropouts indicates that the adolescents who may be at greatest risk failed to complete the program. The fact that dropouts expected to have sex in the early years of adolescence, indicated that the best time to first engage in sex was in the middle years of adolescence, and had a significantly higher level of sexual activity would suggest that these adolescents were more likely to encounter problems of teen pregnancy and sexually transmitted diseases than adolescents who completed the program (Trussell, 1988).

The dropout analysis offered by this study is unique among premarital sexual intervention programs that have been evaluated to date; other programs have not published reports about the dropouts from their programs. It is therefore difficult to know if this problem is unique to the Success Express Program or if it is endemic to abstinence only programs. Minimally these findings point to the importance of including dropout analyses in future evaluation reports of premarital pregnancy intervention projects. They further suggest that educationally driven, adolescent pregnancy intervention projects should make a special effort to recruit and maintain high-risk adolescents.

Implications for Intervention

The results of this study have two major implications for family life educators and policymakers. First, family life educators who are conducting adolescent pregnancy prevention programs cannot take adolescent interest for granted. The dropout rate of the current program indicated that large numbers of high-risk students were not motivated to participate and possibly "voted with their feet" even though most of the sites offered the program within regular classroom time. As is the case in most education settings, motivating student interest in the subject matter is a primary factor in program success.

Second, there may be an inherent insensitivity in programs that stress abstinence as the only alternative to adolescent pregnancy. This approach ignores students who have already experienced sexual intercourse, especially those who may have experienced coitus involuntarily as in the case of rape or incest. Those who have experienced voluntary intercourse may be turned off by a message that suggests they have done something bad or wrong; those whose experience was involuntary may find abstinence only programs particularly upsetting. A greater effort needs to be made to motivate adolescents to participate and such approaches need to encompass all adolescents in a sensitive manner. Whether abstinence only approaches can be so all encompassing remains to be seen.

An implication of a more fundamental nature is the questioning of a social policy that supports abstinence only programs exclusively over those that have demonstrated an ability to reduce teenage pregnancy. The United States has a much higher teenage pregnancy rate than other Western nations that are similar in their standard of living, their level of development, and their form of government even though the sexual activity levels are comparable. Researchers have concluded that this difference can be attributed to the irregular and ineffective use of contraception by American adolescents (Jones et al., 1986). Most other Western nations emphasize reducing adolescent pregnancy through approaches that emphasize abstinence but offer the alternative of effective contraceptive to those who choose to become sexually active; none rely solely on programs that advocate abstinence of sexual activity.

Two programs within the United States have been able to show the wisdom of this policy by demonstrating sizable reductions in the pregnancy rates in their target populations. The first of these was conducted in an urban, lower class, predominately black community (Zabin, Hirsch, Smith, Streett, & Hardy, 1986; Zabin et al., 1988). This program provided adolescents with an in-school program which consisted of classroom presentations, discussion groups, individual counseling, and an after-school clinic which provided free educational intervention, medical examinations, counseling, and contraceptives. A 3-year evaluation revealed that participating adolescents delayed first intercourse, started using effective contraception earlier in their sexual activity, and, most significantly, reduced their pregnancy rate by 30% while controls experienced a 57% increase.

The second program, also multidimensional, was conducted in a rural setting with a population composed mostly of low-income, black adolescents (Vincent et al., 1987). It included offering teachers graduate level courses in sex education, implementing a community-wide curriculum that integrated sex education within present courses (grades K through 12), educating clergy and parents, and utilizing local media. Although abstinence was emphasized, a secondary objective was to promote the consistent use of effective contraception for adolescents who chose to be sexually active. The results of this program were equally dramatic. Premarital pregnancy rates in the targeted group declined from 54.1 estimated pregnancies per 1000 females to 25.1 estimated pregnancies within 5 years while comparison data indicated controls experienced large increases in pregnancy rates (Vincent et al., 1986).

The current evaluation of an abstinence only program does not, by itself, establish the lack of efficacy of such approaches. However, the meager information that is available from over 7 years of such programs has yet to provide much promise for strictly "Just Say No" approaches. In contrast, more complex, comprehensive, multiple approach programs have clearly demonstrated their efficacy in both rural and urban settings. Thus, if reducing teenage pregnancy rates in the United States is an agreed upon primary goal, it seems clear that efforts should be made to model future programs after those that have been successful. This does not mean that the encouragement of abstinence should be dropped as a goal and forgotten; more likely, all programs should encourage abstinence but also offer an alternative for those who are already sexually active or who choose to become so.

REFERENCES

Barnes, H., & Olson, D. (1982). Parent-Adolescent communication scales. In D. H. Olson, H. J. McCubbin, H. Barnes, A. Larsen, M. Muxen, & M. Wilson (Eds.), *Family inventories* (pp. 33-48). St. Paul: University of Minnesota.

Carns, D. (1973). Talking about sex: Notes on first coitus and the double standard. *Journal of Marriage and the Family, 35,* 677-687.

Center for the Study of Social Policy. (1986). *Preventing teenage pregnancy: A literature review.* Washington, DC: Author.

Delamater, J. D., & MacCorquodale, P. (1979). *Premarital sexuality: Attitudes, relationships, behavior.* Madison: The University of Wisconsin Press.

Donahue, M. J. (1987, September). *Promoting abstinence: Is it viable?* Paper presented at an Office of Adolescent Pregnancy Programs technical workshop, Washington, DC.

Hayes, C. D. (Ed.). (1987). *Risking the future: Adolescent sexuality, pregnancy, and childbearing. Vol. 1.* Washington, DC: National Academy Press.

Hofferth, S. L., & Hayes, C. D. (Eds.). (1987). *Risking the future: Adolescent sexuality, pregnancy, and childbearing. Vol. 2 Working Papers and Statistical Appendices.* Washington, DC: National Academy Press.

Jones, E. F., Forrest, J. D., Goldman, N., Henshaw, S., Lincoln, R., Rosoff, J. I., Westoff, C. F., & Wulf, D. (1986). *Teenage pregnancy in industrialized countries.* New Haven, CT: Yale University Press.

Lucero, E., & Clark, T. (1988). *The Success Express curriculum.* Unpublished manuscript. Maricopa County YWCA, Phoenix, AZ.

Mecklenburg, M. E., & Thompson, P. G. (1983). The adolescent family life program as a preventative measure. *Public Health Reports, 98,* 21-27.

Miller, B. C., McCoy, J. K., Olson, T. D., & Wallace, C. M. (1986). Parental discipline and control attempts in relation to adolescent sexual attitudes and behavior. *Journal of Marriage and the Family, 48,* 503-512.

Newcomer, S., & Udry, J. R. (1988). Adolescents' honesty in a survey of sexual behavior. *Journal of Adolescent Research, 3,* 419-423.

Olson, T. D. (1987, September). *Adolescent pregnancy and abstinence: How far have we come?* Paper presented at an Office of Adolescent Pregnancy Programs technical workshop, Washington, DC.

Olson, T. D., Wallace, D. M., & Miller, B. C. (1984). Primary prevention of adolescent pregnancy: Promoting family involvement through a school curriculum. *Journal of Primary Prevention, 5,* 75-91.

Rosenberg, M. (1969). *Society and the adolescent self image.* Princeton: Princeton University Press.

Trussell, J. (1988). Teenage pregnancy in the United States. *Family Planning Perspectives, 20,* 262-272.

Vincent, M. L., Clearie, A. F., & Schluchter, M. D. (1987). Reducing adolescent pregnancy through school and community based education. *Journal of the American Medical Association, 257,* 3382-3386.

Zabin, L. S., Hirsch, M. B., Smith, E. A., Streett, R., & Hardy, J. B. (1986). Evaluation of a pregnancy prevention program for urban teenagers. *Family Planning Perspectives, 18,* 119-126.

Zabin, L. S., Hirsch, M. B., Streett, R., Emerson, M. R., Smith, M., Hardy, J. B., & King, T. M. (1988). The Baltimore pregnancy prevention program for urban teenagers: I. How did it work? *Family Planning Perspectives, 20,* 182-187.

Curbing Teenage Pregnancy:

A NOVEL APPROACH

*"Unlike traditional
programs designed to help
curb teenage pregnancy,
Education for Parenting is
offered well before
students become sexually
active."*

Sara Park Scattergood

*Ms. Scattergood is executive director,
Education for Parenting, Philadelphia, Pa.*

TEENAGE pregnancy and child abuse are on the rise in the U.S. Approximately 1,000,000 teenagers become pregnant in this country every year—that's one American teen in 10, compared with fewer than one in 20 in England, France, or Canada, and one in 30 in Sweden.

In terms of child abuse, more than 2,000,000 children are reported abused in the U.S. each year. (Numerous other cases go unreported.) Approximately 40% of abused and neglected children are of pre-school age and almost 25% are teenagers. The most recent data available from 34 states shows there were an estimated 1,200 child abuse and neglect fatalities in 1986—an increase of 23% over 1985.

The harmful effects of child abuse and teen pregnancy impact all levels of our society, regardless of race or socioeconomic status. For those young women who become teen parents, the promise of a viable future appears beyond reach. The sad reality for the teen mother is that she receives half the lifetime earnings of a woman who waits until age 20 to have her first child. Most teen mothers drop out of school and often become a financial drain on society. Without marketable job skills, they are unable to create opportunities for themselves to advance in our highly competitive and technological society.

Teen mothers also are more likely to be child abusers because they lack the maturity to handle parenting and have no training in basic human development. Because of this lack of preparation, these youngsters tend to follow their parents' behaviors in child rearing, which often are far from healthy. Essentially, too few children in our society are being prepared in any way to care for the next generation competently. The consequences could be devastating for their children.

In 1978, an interdisciplinary team of concerned professionals in Philadelphia joined together to create a curriculum for the teaching of parenting to children—the "parents of the future." The team was led by Henri Parens, director of the Early Child Development Program and research professor of psychiatry of the Eastern Pennsylvania Psychiatric Institute of the Medical College of Pennsylvania, and included six doctors and social workers from the Institute. The team was joined by Julie Currie and myself, teachers from Germantown Friends School in Philadelphia.

Our team's first objective was to put together a body of information that would be a basic theoretical foundation for the building of an Education for Parenting curriculum, envisioned for students in grades kindergarten through 12. It soon became apparent that the ideas generated needed to be tested so that our group might learn first-hand what could be taught to schoolchildren and at what ages.

We had to know if our curriculum could raise students' awareness of the complexity of parenting, highlight the critical issues, teach skills in child rearing, and focus on the important aspects of child development.

To test the ideas, Currie and I sought funds that would allow us to experiment in a school setting at Germantown Friends. Through these teaching experiences, our team began to identify methods and materials most appropriate for use with students at different ages. In the belief that schoolchildren learn most readily when theory is confirmed through direct observation, a central part of the curriculum is a live laboratory experience.

Babies and their parents come into the classroom on a monthly basis so that students as young as six years old can observe and track the physical, emotional, and cognitive growth and development of the infants. Students have the unique opportunity to observe the interaction between mother and/or father and child. They learn that each infant has its own distinct temperament and capabilities that influence the manner and rate in which he or she develops. Depending upon their age, they also read about babies, keep a journal on the infant they are studying, and learn how to estimate the costs of feeding, clothing, schooling, etc. Prior to the baby's visit, the students practice analytical and planning skills and then discuss how successful these proved, ultimately helping them to understand the responsibility inherent in parenting. It is this interactive learning and live observation at an age early enough to shape behavior that gives the project uniqueness and strength.

The pilot program worked so well at Germantown Friends that the curriculum was implemented in 1988 at other independent academic institutions, including Abington Friends, Baldwin, Friends Central, Friends Select, Moorestown Friends, William Penn Charter, Shipley, Springside, and Wilmington Friends schools, as well as Chestnut Hill Academy.

Convincing other schools of our program's benefits was not easy. They were hesitant to initiate some of its innovative aspects—even the relatively simple teaching tool of having an infant and parent visit the classroom. Influencing the thinking of school administrators to accept the importance of such a program required long, continuing education, advocacy, and support. Nevertheless, through the staff's diligence and the belief of those touched by the program, it has grown, and was introduced into the Philadelphia Public School System in 1985. More recently, school districts in New York City, Chicago, and Alaska have adopted the curriculum.

Education for Parenting has the purpose of bringing parenting into the school as a subject of study. In the past, mothers taught their daughters how to parent, and the daughters, in their turn, became the principal parent. Today, more than 50% of mothers with children under the age of one year work outside the home, a figure that is increasing. The parenting of today and of tomorrow must be done by both fathers and mothers, and must be taught to boys and girls in school.

Schools validate what our society considers preparation for important work. In them, you learn skills that some day will let you be a lawyer, doctor, teacher, etc. If parenting is to be viewed by children in our society as important work, then that work must be validated as vital by being made a subject of study and reflection, and developing understanding and skill from kindergarten up. If taught about parenting in school, young children will discover that it is something that can and must be learned.

American families are undergoing fundamental transformation. Mobility in search of jobs means the dismantling of the extended family support structure. Both parents working outside the home means increased need for support of families with young children. The growth in the number of single-parent households means children at risk in our society in ways we have not experienced since the days youngsters also worked outside the home for pay. This transformation of family life requires a new relationship between schools and families.

The new role of schools is to teach skills and values which will help children become competent parents in these situations. Schools now must prepare students not simply for employment outside the home for pay, but for the work—at least as valuable to the society—that is the skill and value of parenting.

In some areas where family structure is not dependable and other organizations—such as social service agencies and religious institutions—find themselves short of funds and overwhelmed, schools must become day-long family resource centers. It is acknowledged everywhere that schools must upgrade the teaching of academic skills. Often, this can be done best in an environment where young children are learning in school what it means to be cared for and to care for others. Observing the developmental stages of infants and the parenting skills which correspond with that development teach children that all life requires—and benefits from—education.

Why do teenage girls become mothers? It is not that they lack information about contraception. Why do so many minorities drop out of high school? It is not the lack of inherent intelligence. Can it be that they did not learn in their early education that parenting is a skill and a competence, not too different from reading, writing, and arithmetic? All require self-confidence, validation by adults, and a process of developing competencies. The Education for Parenting program does just what it says—educating schoolchildren in the skills, demands, rewards, and pride of parenting. It is a process involving a structured curriculum, developing analytic and reflective capacities that apply other academic skills to the fascination young children have with babies and family life. This crosses misplaced barriers in our society and brings family life into schools and education into parenting.

Our ultimate goal is to let students experience first-hand some of the pleasures, hardships, and responsibilities associated with caring for a baby. We want them to learn that parenting involves protecting and nurturing the developing person. The program stresses the importance of positive parental interaction with the baby, which provides the first ongoing, in-depth human relationship. The students are taught how important it is that parents provide an environment where the baby can explore and experiment in order to become competent and secure. Our hope is that, once students realize how much time, energy, knowledge, expense, and skill are required for healthy parenting, they will think twice before getting involved in situations they will regret later.

In addition, many of the fantasies of being a parent are dispelled, and students see the negative consequences of becoming parents before they are emotionally, developmentally, and financially ready. They learn that, in unplanned pregnancies, everyone involved is hurt, including the teenage parents, the baby, and, many times, the grandparents who often take over much of the child raising. The program also strives to increase students' sensitivity to other family members.

Importance of early intervention

Unlike traditional programs designed to help curb teenage pregnancy, Education for Parenting is offered well before students become sexually active. According to the most recent available data, of 4,200,000 girls 15-19 years old who were sexually active, 3,600,000 were not married and 1,000,000 became pregnant. Therefore, the main focus is in the elementary and junior high school years. Although we expect to have an effect on decreasing the teen pregnancy rate, we do not teach birth control or sex education. Rather, we provide children with an understanding of why they would not want to be a teen parent and how their lives would be affected adversely if they became parents prematurely.

Since the nation's teen pregnancy problem affects all of us, economically as well as socially, teaching the responsibilities involved in parenting to youngsters at an early age is critical. This is particularly important for children who come from disadvantaged backgrounds and may never have known the security and warmth of a caring household environment.

With the appropriate classroom teaching, problems such as child abuse, school dropouts, drug and alcohol use, and single-parent families can be decreased significantly. In addition, school human development programs need to be taught at a much earlier age. At present, they usually are begun on the secondary level, by which time many students already have dropped out, become unwed parents, or developed debilitating emotional problems. The solution very well may lie in early intervention—before any serious damage takes place.

Birth control

Women have good reason to rethink their contraceptive options. Newly approved Norplant offers five years of no-fuss, 99.8 percent-reliable protection. A special report

STEVEN FINDLAY

Women throughout the country last week went silent as they turned up the volume on the TV or intently read the newspaper stories. What they were captivated by was news of the approval, after years of testing, of the first major new contraceptive to come on the market since the Pill arrived in 1960. Norplant, though unlikely to have the Pill's seminal social and cultural impact, will almost surely prompt millions of American women and their partners to rethink their birth-control options. The under-the-skin implant confers a higher degree of pregnancy protection than any other method except sterilization, does so for five years—and with "no gook and no fuss," says Dr. Gabriel Bialy, director of contraceptive development at the National Institutes of Health.

Norplant is also certain to add heat to the debate over the role of contraception in a society increasingly burdened with the social and emotional costs of accidental pregnancies and out-of-wedlock babies—especially those born to teens. Already, voices have been heard recommending that Norplant be urged on young, sexually active women whose use of less reliable methods, or no method at all, leads to 1 million accidental pregnancies each year. "We ought to do everything we can to promote Norplant for younger women, for whom other methods aren't appropriate or often fail," argues Isabel Sawhill, a senior fellow at the Washington, D.C.-based Urban Institute. But some worry that Norplant could end up being imposed rather than just promoted.

The human factor. Norplant should be especially welcomed by women who, troubled by the health risks associated with estrogen in the Pill and by the intrauterine device's (IUD) link to pelvic inflammatory disease and sterility, have turned to less reliable alternatives like the diaphragm, condom and spermicides. While the epidemic of teen pregnancies has drawn plenty of attention, fewer people realize that a third of all pregnancies in women age 30 to 45 are also unplanned. Many of these couples simply use no birth control. But most of the pregnancies are due to "user failure," the human tendency to leave the diaphragm, condom or sponge tucked in the pocketbook or sitting on the night stand or to use these methods sloppily. Norplant eliminates the human factor, as well as glitches inherent in the devices themselves: Condoms often slip off or break and diaphragms become dislodged. Once implanted, Norplant "does the job," says Jacqueline Forrest, vice president for research at New York's Alan Guttmacher Institute, which studies birth control and sexual behavior. About 1 Norplant user in 100 will become pregnant over a three-year period; 3 to 4 in 100 over five years. By comparison, of 100 users of the Pill, 6 will become pregnant in the first year of use and 10 to 14 over five years. Fourteen in 100 women who rely on condoms can expect to be pregnant within a year (see page 128 for details on all the methods).

Using Norplant calls for surgery, but about on the level of removing a mole. In a usually painless 10-to-15-minute procedure that requires a 1/8-inch incision and a local anesthetic, six tiny silicone capsules are implanted beneath the skin on the inside of the upper arm. Each capsule, a little over an inch long and about as thick as a matchstick, contains levonorgestrel, a synthetic progesterone identical to the one used in birth-control pills. The progesterone trickles into the bloodstream and finds its way to the pituitary gland in the brain, signaling the gland within a day or two to stop releasing two hormones necessary for ovulation. The mucus that lines the cervix also thickens, trapping sperm trying to enter the cervical canal. After five years, the levonorgestrel runs low—there is actually a six-month to one-year margin of safety—and the capsules must be removed. A new batch can be inserted immediately at the same site. The capsules can be taken out at any time, and fertility generally resumes with the next menstrual cycle.

Clean record. Norplant's safety record is especially reassuring: None of the roughly 500,000 women in 15 countries who rely on Norplant have reported life-threatening problems, and the FDA's approval follows 20 years of testing on some 55,000 women. That is not to suggest, however, that Norplant carries zero risk. To be on the safe side, women who already have heart problems, acute liver disease, diabetes, high cholesterol, high blood pressure, breast cancer or a history of blood clots are cautioned against using Norplant—as they are against using the Pill—though no signs have surfaced that Norplant either causes or aggravates any of these conditions. Generally, it has been the estrogen in birth-control pills that has been implicated, not the progesterone, and Norplant contains no estrogen. Moreover, a woman who uses Norplant for five years gets a much lower dose of progesterone over time than she would with the Pill. There is also no direct evidence that Norplant capsules add to a smoker's risks for heart ailments and cancer, but smokers are warned off, too.

Minor side effects are Norplant's biggest limitation. Most users—82 percent in one study—experience menstrual changes that plague Pill users to a lesser extent: Prolonged periods, spotting between periods or an end to periods altogether. The changes are not dangerous and tend to disappear after the first year about half the time, but about 30 percent of women are sufficiently bothered to have the implants removed. Norplant can also wreak the same hormonal havoc as the Pill can: Headaches, nausea, dizziness, acne, weight gain or loss, breast tenderness and mood changes. In a Norplant study involving 205 women in the San Francisco area, 95 percent reported experiencing at least one of these side effects.

Many women are happy to pay the price. "I feel totally safe with Norplant," says Kathleen Rañeses, 31, a divorced mother of two from San Francisco who has used many methods in the past, and whose second daughter was conceived, she says, while she was on the Pill. Rañeses, who had the capsules put in last summer in a clinical trial, says she had a dull headache for about a month afterwards, and has gained 11 pounds—a welcome addition in her case.

Some women are clearly better candidates for Norplant than others. The surgical procedure probably isn't worthwhile for women who might want to become pregnant within two or three years, and women in their late 30s or 40s who are certain they want no more children may be happier with sterilization than with Norplant's possible side effects. Monogamous married women who are comfortable assuming a greater risk of pregnancy may also prefer to stick with the familiar. Norplant is somewhat less effective in women who weigh more than about 150 pounds. Eight in 100 heavier women will conceive over five years, compared with the typical three or four.

Norplant is most obviously appropriate for sexually active singles, though the fact that the capsules' outline is sometimes visible through the skin of thin women may deter those reluctant to advertise their birth-control method. Women over age 35 who cannot or do not want to take the Pill because it contains estrogen and couples finished with childbearing but uncomfortable with the finality of sterilization might also give Norplant serious thought.

For some, cost may determine the decision. Norplant is expected to run half or less of the five-year cost of the Pill—the annual bill for the Pill comes to $200 to $250—but the hit comes all at once. The doctor's fee alone is likely to be $150 to $200. Wyeth-Ayerst Laboratories, the

Philadelphia company that will distribute Finnish-made Norplant in the U.S., hasn't yet set a price for the device itself, but women can probably plan on another $200 to $400. Wyeth-Ayerst is negotiating with Planned Parenthood to provide Norplant at a discount to its clinics. It will be marketed beginning in February, but only about 100 U.S. doctors have been trained to implant the capsules. Wyeth-Ayerst hopes to bring the number to 8,000 by June. Meanwhile, the Association of Reproductive Health Professionals in Washington, D.C., (202) 863-2475, can refer women to trained doctors.

Anyone weighing a switch to Norplant should be armed with the latest information on other contraceptives, the Pill in particular. Reported links to heart disease, stroke, blood clots and breast and cervical cancer led millions of women to abandon the Pill in the early 1980s. Manufacturers have since lowered the doses of estrogen and progesterone to reduce the risks, which were slight for most women anyway. The facts as of 1990 are these: The Pill does *not* increase the risk of heart disease in healthy women of any age who don't smoke. Only smokers and women with such medical conditions as heart disease, any cancer or diabetes are told in no uncertain terms to bypass the Pill. While the final answer is not yet in on the Pill's link to breast cancer, nine studies since the 1960s have failed to show any solid connection, and a 10-year World Health Organization review released last week showed no link between the Pill and breast, cervical or liver cancer. "Today's Pill is far safer," says Dr. David Grimes of the University of Southern California, a leading birth-control researcher. "And many women don't know about its noncontraceptive benefits."

Pill pluses. Strong evidence shows that Pill users have about one fifth the risk of ovarian and endometrial cancer of women who have never used the Pill. Norplant may also confer this benefit, but it's too soon to be sure. To be safest, women should make sure they are taking a Pill with the lowest level of estrogen and progesterone. (The "minipill," which contains only progesterone, is available for women who cannot take the regular Pill for health reasons, but it is a somewhat less effective birth-control method.) One recent study indicated an argument for low progesterone levels: High-progesterone pills tended to lower levels of the "good" cholesterol in the blood, increasing heart-disease risk. Norplant meters out its progesterone at a low enough dose that this should not be a concern.

Barrier contraceptives have gained new respect, too. Numerous studies have shown that the diaphragm, condom, cervical cap, contraceptive sponge

and spermicides used alone help protect against sexually transmitted diseases, including the virus that causes AIDS. A barrier method plus a spermicide is even safer. Neither Norplant nor the Pill gives that protection. Many doctors advise women with multiple sex partners to use a barrier method even if they are on the Pill and will press women who try Norplant to do the same. Teenagers have apparently heard the message: The number of 15-to-19-year-old girls saying their partner used a condom the first time they had intercourse rose to 47 percent in 1988 from 22 percent in 1982, a Guttmacher study found.

A steady decline. The IUD, by contrast, has steadily lost favor over the past decade. A number of studies have shown a link to pelvic inflammatory disease, sterility and even death, especially in women with many sex partners. The only people for whom the IUD remains an option are monogamous women who have used the IUD in the past without any ill effects.

Given drug-company reluctance to devote significant resources to developing contraceptives and the painstaking FDA review of new methods, Norplant could well be the last radically different contraceptive in this country until the turn of the century at least. (The next innovation, now under review by the FDA, could be a woman's condom that works on the same principle as a male condom, but is inserted into the vagina.)

But research at universities and small companies is producing intriguing possibilities. Several work on the same principle as Norplant. These include a progesterone-laced vaginal ring, the size and shape of a diaphragm, that would be inserted for up to three months to suppress ovulation; rice-size pellets implanted under the skin of the arm or hip that release the same hormone as Norplant and prevent conception for up to 18 months, and skin patches with a week's worth of hormone protection. A two-capsule version of Norplant is also under study; it works the same way as the six-capsule version but is simpler for doctors to insert.

The controversial "morning after" pill, RU-486, approved in France and China, may have a better shot at approval in this country now that the drug shows promise in treating ovarian and breast cancers. RU-486, which causes a miscarriage if taken during the first few weeks of pregnancy, has yet to be submitted to the FDA because of pressure from anti-abortion activists. While it has proved safe in France, the drug's side effects include heavy cramping and bleeding. Even if RU-486 is approved here, it will never be the drug of choice to counter conception in the 72 hours after an unprotected act of intercourse. That drug is Ovral, a high-dose estrogen birth-control pill that keeps a fertilized egg from taking root in the uterine wall. Ovral is approved as an oral contraceptive, not specifically as a "morning after" pill, but its use for that purpose is widely accepted. Depo-Provera, an injectable steroid available in 90 countries that suppresses ovulation, may never reach American shores. The FDA has rejected the drug because tests suggested it may have caused mammary cancers in dogs and uterine cancers in monkeys.

The two methods that promise to alter the birth-control landscape most profoundly should they ever come to market are a reliable, reversible and nonsurgical male contraceptive and a vaccine against pregnancy for women. After years of trial and error, the former appears within reach. A World Health Organization study, conducted in seven countries including the U.S. and reported in October, found that weekly injections of synthetic testosterone safely halted sperm production in 157 of 271 men over a period of six months. For the next six months, the 157 men's wives stopped using all contraception. Only one pregnancy resulted. The prospect of weekly injections limits the practicality of this approach, and for now it looks as if the injections could not be safely turned into a pill; the amount of hormone required can damage the liver if taken orally. The method is years away from even being submitted to the FDA for scrutiny.

The antibody approach. A birth-control vaccine also must clear many research hurdles, but three are in early stages of development in the U.S. and abroad. All aim to induce the body to produce antibodies that will thwart pregnancy. One vaccine is designed to trigger antibodies that latch onto the surface of the egg, preventing sperm from doing so. The second produces antibodies against human chorionic gonadotrophin, the hormone that supports early pregnancy; the third, against sperm themselves. Animal research confirms that all three approaches are feasible and, because the vaccine's effects are temporary, reversible.

As effective as such methods may be, they are products of the next millennium. Today's challenge is to get people to use what is available. Norplant could be up to the task.

A user's guide to 14 methods

Many couples choose a contraceptive based only on how well it works and how hassle-free it is. But health-related risks and benefits should be weighed, too. This guide summarizes the pros and cons of all major methods. In "pregnancy/failure rates," the first number is the percentage of women expected to conceive in a year assuming they always use the method correctly; the second is the percentage who actually conceive the first year.

IMPLANT

■ **Norplant**
Pregnancy/failure rates: 0.2%, 0.2%
Cost: Projected at $150-$200 for insertion plus $200-$400 for the device
Advantages: Allows sexual spontaneity. Protection lasts five years. Fertility returns by next menstrual cycle after removal. May reduce risk of endometrial cancer.
Disadvantages: Frequent menstrual irregularities: Spotting, prolonged bleeding and missed periods. Can cause weight gain, headaches, mood changes. Insertion and removal require minor surgery. No protection against sexually transmitted diseases.

ORAL CONTRACEPTIVE

■ **Pill** (combined estrogen and progesterone)
Pregnancy/failure rates: 0.1%, 3-6%
Cost: $235 per year
Advantages: Allows sexual spontaneity. De-creases menstrual pain, discomfort and blood flow. Protects against ovarian and endometrial cancer. Lowers risk of pelvic inflammatory disease.
Disadvantages: Must be taken daily, and a prescription is needed. Can cause weight gain, headaches, mood changes, breast tenderness and spotting between periods. Increases the risk of heart attack, stroke and high blood pressure in women over age 35 who smoke. May suppress lactation in nursing mothers. Confers no protection against sexually transmitted diseases.

■ **"Minipill"** (progesterone only)
Pregnancy/failure rates: 0.5%, 3-9%
Cost: $235 per year
Advantages: Allows sexual spontaneity. Produces fewer side effects than combined pill. Decreases menstrual pain and bleeding. Does not suppress lactation. May lessen risk of developing endometrial cancer. Since no link has been shown to cardiovascular disease, may be a better option than the combined pill for women over 35 who smoke.
Disadvantages: Effectiveness is reduced if the pill is taken even a few hours late one day. Causes more spotting than the combined pill. Increases the risk of ectopic pregnancy and of benign ovarian cysts. No protection against sexually transmitted diseases.

STERILIZATION

■ **Female sterilization** (tubal ligation)
Pregnancy/failure rates: 0.2%, 0.4%
Cost: $1,500-$2,500
Advantages: Allows sexual spontaneity. Safe, with below 1 percent complication rate.
Disadvantages: Surgery carries small risk of infection and complications. As many as 70 percent of women are not candidates for reversal, since fallopian tube often cannot be successfully reconnected. After reversal, pregnancy rate varies from 43 to 88 percent depending on sterilization technique.

■ **Male sterilization** (vasectomy)
Pregnancy/failure rate: 0.1%, 0.15%

Cost: $350-$750
Advantages: Allows sexual spontaneity. Minor surgery compared with tubal ligation and fewer complications.
Disadvantages: Slight risk of infection. Some postsurgical discomfort. Reversal requires major, costly surgery and succeeds about 50 percent of the time.

BARRIER METHODS

■ **Diaphragm** (*used with spermicide*)
Pregnancy/failure rates: 6%, 16%
Cost: $120-$180 per year
Advantages: Can be inserted up to 6 hours before intercourse. Protects against sexually transmitted diseases, including chlamydia, gonorrhea and AIDS. Users have half the risk of developing pelvic inflammatory disease as sexually active women who use no contraception at all.
Disadvantages: Reduces sexual spontaneity, since spermicide must be reapplied for each act of intercourse. The diaphragm must be left in place 6 to 8 hours after intercourse. Failure rate approaches 20 to 25 percent for women under age 25 who have intercourse four or more times per week. Heightens risk of urinary-tract and bladder infections.

■ **Condom**
Pregnancy/failure rates: 2%, 14%

Cost: 50 cents for each condom
Advantages: Inexpensive, easy to obtain and use. Can be teamed with a spermicide for greater protection, particularly since condoms occasionally slip off or break. Protects against sexually transmitted diseases.
Disadvantages: Reduces sexual spontaneity. Also reduces sensation for most men and women. Breaks at a rate of about 1 in 160 acts of intercourse. Cannot be used with lubricants, which weaken the latex.

■ **Cervical cap**
Pregnancy/failure rates: 6%, 8-27%
Cost: $50-$150 per year
Advantages: Up to 48-hour protection is provided with no need to reapply spermicide, which allows spontaneity once the device is in place. Reduces risk of sexually transmitted diseases.
Disadvantages: Requires a prescription and a pap smear. More difficult to insert than a diaphragm and dislodges more readily. Must be inserted at least a half-hour before intercourse to allow adherence to cervix, and it must be left in place 6 hours after intercourse. The failure rate reaches 20 to 25 percent in women under age 30 and in women who engage in sex four or more times weekly.

■ **Sponge**
Pregnancy/failure rates: 6-9%, 18-28%

Cost: About $1.50 for each sponge
Advantages: No prescription is needed, and sponge is easy to use. Provides 24-hour protection, regardless of how often intercourse occurs. Reduces the risk of sexually transmitted diseases.
Disadvantages: Can be used one time only. Absorbs vaginal secretions, so can cause dryness. Increases the risk of yeast infections. Failure rates approach 25 percent in women under age 30, or in women who have intercourse four or more times a week. Also is less effective in women who have previously had children.

"NATURAL" FAMILY PLANNING

■ **Periodic abstinence** (*rhythm*)
Pregnancy/failure rate: 1-9%, 20%
Cost: None
Advantages: Totally safe. Effective if intercourse is strictly limited to infertile days of menstrual cycle.
Disadvantages: Requires high degree of motivation, detailed knowledge of reproductive cycle and precise record keeping to pinpoint ovulation and identify the interval when intercourse is safe. Unreliable for women whose menstrual cycles are irregular. Confers no protection against sexually transmitted diseases.

INTRAUTERINE DEVICE (IUD)

■ **Medicated Cu-T 380A** (*ParaGard, "Copper T"*)
Pregnancy/failure rates: 0.8%, 6%
Cost: $300 for device and insertion
Advantages: Allows sexual spontaneity. Effective for up to six years.
Disadvantages: May be expelled without user's awareness; thus, the relatively high failure rate. Increases menstrual flow, can cause cramping. Greatly increases risk of pelvic infection in women with a history of sexually transmitted disease or multiple sexual partners. Increases risk of ectopic pregnancy.

■ **Progestasert**
Pregnancy/failure rate: 2.0%, 6%
Cost: $90 per year
Advantages: Allows sexual spontaneity. Less likely to cause heavy menstrual flow and pain than Cu-T 380A.
Disadvantages: Can be used for only one year; the Cu-T 380A can be used six years. Multiplies risk of ectopic pregnancy six to 10 times over Cu-T 380A. Otherwise same drawbacks as Cu-T 380A.

SPERMICIDE

■ **Vaginal suppositories**
Pregnancy/failure rates: 3%, 21%

Cost: 67 cents per insert/10 inserts per package
Advantages: No prescription is needed. Can be used in combination with barrier methods for greater effectiveness. Protects against some sexually transmitted diseases, including chlamydia and gonorrhea.
Disadvantages: A wait of at least 15 minutes is necessary before intercourse begins. Only 1 hour of protection is provided; another suppository is necessary if intercourse is repeated. May not completely dissolve, which may lower reliability. Effervescence of foaming vaginal suppositories may be unpleasant. May increase risk of urinary-tract infection.

■ **Foams, creams, gels**
Pregnancy/failure rates: 3%, 21%
Cost: About $1.25 per application/six applications per tube
Advantages: No prescription is needed. Can be used with barrier methods for greater effectiveness. Protects against some sexually transmitted diseases.
Disadvantages: A wait of 10 to 15 minutes is necessary before intercourse begins. Must be reapplied for repeated intercourse. Can be messy; may lessen sensation. Can cause genital irritation. May increase risk of urinary-tract infection.

COMPILED BY STEVEN FINDLAY AND MUADI MUKENGE

Can you rely on
CONDOMS?

Close to half of some 3300 readers surveyed for this report told us that they had changed their sexual habits in response to AIDS. "More condoms, more consistently" was one of the major themes. Heeding public-health warnings, Americans have helped boost condom sales more than 60 percent over the past 2½ years. People who had never considered condoms before—women and gay men, especially—are now buying and using them. Women, for example, purchase 40 to 50 percent of condoms today, up from 10 percent a few years ago. Often the women are single, and often it's disease—not birth control—that's on their mind.

Just how good are condoms for preventing sexually transmitted disease? How effective a product are the condom manufacturers sending to market? And how often do condoms break?

Condom manufacturers say they get one or two consumer complaints per million condoms sold—and not all of those involve breakage. When we asked readers, however, about one in four said that a condom had broken in the past year. Nearly one in eight reported at least two incidents of breakage. On the basis of those reports and the number of condoms readers estimated using, we calculated that about one condom in 140 broke. But they break more often in some activities than in others.

Anal intercourse, one of the riskiest activities for contracting AIDS, is also one of the most punishing for a condom. (Anal sex isn't limited to gay or bisexual readers: One in 10 of the heterosexual men surveyed reported having engaged in heterosexual anal intercourse using a condom.) We calculated the breakage rate for anal sex among survey respondents at one condom in 105, compared with one in 165 for vaginal sex.

The disparity could result from such factors as differences in brands or lubricants used. But just as likely, it's due to the nature of anal sex itself. Indeed, many condoms now carry a disclaimer that they're solely for vaginal sex; that other uses can result in breakage.

When condoms are intact, though, how good are they? In principle, latex condoms can be close to 100 percent effective. (Most condoms are made of latex; fewer than 5 percent are fashioned from lamb intestine. See the box on page 132.) Under a scanning electron microscope at 30,000

More people are counting on condoms for protection against AIDS. We tested some 40 varieties for defects and strength.

power, the surface of a latex condom appears somewhat bumpy but shows no pores. When stretched, the latex remains a continuous pore-free membrane. It won't even let water—one of the tiniest of molecules—filter through.

Such an intact barrier shields the wearer's penis from exposure to germs in cervical, vaginal, or rectal secretions or lesions. For the partner, the condom prevents contact with potentially infectious semen and any lesions on the wearer's penis.

A number of laboratory experiments have explored whether various sexually transmitted germs—some less than one-fiftieth the size of a sperm cell—can get through latex condoms. Condoms filled with a solution containing high concentrations of a sexually transmitted microbe are suspended in a sterile liquid medium. Then the medium is cultured to determine whether any microbes have passed through the latex. Some experiments use an apparatus to simulate intercourse, to check if mechanical stress affects porosity.

Such experiments have confirmed that intact latex condoms won't let even the smallest microbes through. So compelling is the evidence that since 1987 the U.S. Food and Drug Administration has let manufacturers list a roster of diseases that condoms, when used properly, can help prevent: syphilis, gonorrhea, chlamydia, genital herpes, and AIDS.

Outside the lab

Data gathered since World War I also

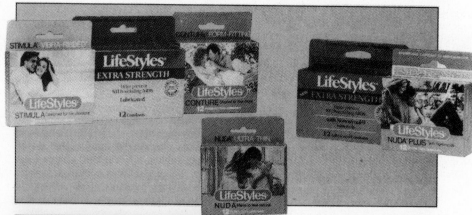

Of six LifeStyles lines, above, three models performed well in our airburst test—Conture, Extra Strength Lubricated, and Stimula Vibra-Ribbed. A fourth, Nuda, failed somewhat more often. But many samples of two brandmates—LifeStyles Extra Strength with Nonoxynol-9 (a spermicide) and LifeStyles Nuda Plus—were grossly defective. When they were filled with water (see photo at left), bulges sometimes appeared, revealing thin spots. The same lines did poorly in airburst testing.

In airburst testing, condoms are inflated until they break, as the maximum pressure and volume they can withstand are monitored. Condoms can burst in various ways. Below, high-speed photography records two possibilities. The burst happens so quickly that it takes a stroboscopic flash, firing at one-millionth of a second, to capture the event.

Photographs by Andrew Davidhazy

confirm the condom's value in disease prevention. The rates of sexually transmitted disease among condom users are typically a fraction of the rates among nonusers. Most times, condoms help cut risks substantially, though not quite to zero.

Scientists also gauge the condom's effectiveness from its performance as a contraceptive. A contraceptive's failure rate is calculated as the percentage of women who have an unwanted pregnancy while using the method over one year's time. For condom users, failure rates have ranged from roughly 5 to 15 percent.

But experts often point out that many contraceptive failures stem from human error, not defective condoms. A couple may not use condoms every time, from start to finish, or may not use them correctly.

Motivation may also play a role. Married women who rely on condoms because they don't want a child under any circumstances have fewer failures than married women who turn to condoms to delay an otherwise wanted pregnancy. Researchers say that strong motivation to use condoms properly could theoretically cut failure rates to 1 or 2 percent.

The FDA's role

When they became popular in the 1930s, many latex condoms—one report estimates as many as three-fourths—were in some way defective. That prompted Congress to ask the FDA to start testing condoms, which the agency has done for 50 years. Until recently, testing had been a low priority. But in the face of AIDS, the FDA has dramatically stepped up its program, putting more than 100 staffers into the effort.

Since April 1987, inspectors have shown up unannounced at condom factories to review records and sample condoms at random, checking for cracks, mold, dry or sticky rubber, and the like. Chiefly, however, the agents run a standard water test—filling condoms with about 10 ounces of water—to spot pinholes. If they find leaks in the equivalent of more than four per 1000 condoms in a production run, that entire lot must be destroyed—often tens of thousands of condoms or more. Imports are inspected, too, at their port of entry.

Over the first 15 months of the program, FDA inspectors checked more than 150,000 samples from lots representing 120 million condoms. The agents had to reject about one lot in 10 of domestic condoms because too many leaked. Imports turned out to be worse—one in five lots were rejected.

Condom quality has been improving, though. Since the new FDA program's inception, defect rates have been cut in half, and far fewer lots are currently being

scrapped. Apparently, the Government presence acts as a strong incentive to improve quality control. And most companies themselves are testing every condom for pinholes electrically.

Gauging condom strength

For this report, we checked some 16,000 condoms in all, either at CU or at a contract laboratory that specializes in testing contraceptive devices. Our samples included 37 varieties of latex condoms from all major U.S. manufacturers and three imports from Japan. Like the FDA, we ran the standard water test on most, examining a total of 250 samples of each.

We turned up one or two leaky samples in 18 different models, products of all major manufacturers. But the overall leakage rate for each model, projected from the failures, fell well within the Government's tolerance of four failures per 1000 condoms.

The leakage test did highlight potential problems with two *LifeStyles* models, however. When we filled them, bulges appeared at thin spots near the tip of some samples (see photo on preceding page). The condoms didn't leak, but the bulges suggested a potential for breakage in use—a potential underscored by a different test on samples from the same lots.

Strength—or resistance to breakage—is related to the ability of the latex to withstand stresses and remain intact. One test of strength involves cutting a band of latex from a condom's shaft and stretching it to the breaking point. That test is part of the voluntary standard domestic producers comply with. But condoms can have problems elsewhere that the test won't pick up. We instead turned to airburst testing, a method used routinely in Canada, Australia, and several European countries.

The airburst test

In airburst testing, condoms are inflated under controlled conditions until they break—often with a loud bang after having reached watermelon size. The volume and pressure of air a condom withstands before bursting are both recorded. We believe those values are likely to be related to a condom's potential to resist breakage in actual use.

Although an airburst test isn't required in the U.S., it is all but certain to be adopted into U.S. standards in the future. In fact, a number of American manufacturers already use such a test, because they export to countries that demand it.

To pass our airburst test, a condom had to withstand a minimum volume of 15 liters of air and a minimum pressure of 0.9 kiloPascal (roughly 0.13 pounds per square inch), two values proposed for an international standard now under discus-

131

sion. For most models, we tested 100 samples, 20 from each of five lots, in an attempt to examine lot-to-lot consistency. In instances where we didn't obtain five lots, we took the total number of condoms sampled from each brand model into account statistically in projecting a model's overall failure rate in the test.

Some flunked too often

Our results produced three performance groups. We project that only about 1.5 percent (or fewer) of the condoms in the top group of the Ratings would fail the airburst test. We judge that to be a realistic quality level—in line with the proposed international standard.

Generally, condoms toward the top of the first Ratings group took the most volume, pressure, or both. On average, they withstood double the minimum values for pressure and volume. Some took triple the required pressure or triple the volume. But even condoms toward the bottom of the group exceeded the minimum values, typically by at least 40 percent.

For condoms in the middle Ratings group, we project a maximum airburst failure rate of 4 percent, higher than we'd prefer to see.

The two condoms in the worst group— *LifeStyles Extra Strength with Nonoxynol-9* (a spermicide) and *LifeStyles Nuda Plus*— flunked, with more than 10 percent projected failures. In some lots, up to half the tested samples failed. (Note that the *LifeStyles Extra Strength* model without spermicide performed so well that it earned the number two spot in the best group.)

Last October, the manufacturer of *Life-Styles*, Ansell Inc., issued a voluntary recall for defective lots of *LifeStyles Extra Strength with Nonoxynol-9*, including several of the lots we tested. The recall, prompted by health officials in Hawaii, covered about 6 million condoms manufactured more than a year earlier. The problem, according to the manufacturer, arose from a machine intermittently contaminated with oil, a substance that can weaken latex. Very little of the stock remains in stores, the company said.

There was no recall of Ansell's *LifeStyles Nuda Plus* line. Like the *Extra Strength with Nonoxynol-9*, some samples of *Life-Styles Nuda Plus* condoms showed bulges during the water tests, a result of thin spots. But it was impossible to tell from our airburst test whether the thin spots or some other factor was the reason samples

Skin condoms: Unresolved questions

Skin condoms are made from lamb cecum, a pouch forming part of the animal's large intestine. They typically cost several times what latex condoms cost; but as an alternative, "skins" have several things to offer.

They're promoted as more "natural feeling" than latex, and indeed many survey respondents who prefer skins noted the condoms' "greater sensation." Skins are also strong. The brands we checked— *Fourex Natural Skins* and *Trojan Kling-Tite Naturalambs*—withstood more than 10 times the pressure that typical latex condoms took in airburst testing.

For the one or two percent of people allergic to latex, such condoms may be the only choice. (Some allergic reactions stem from the chemicals used on certain latex condoms and may disappear if you try another brand.)

Skin condoms are packed wet, so we had to devise a leakage test different from the standard water test. We inflated the condoms under water and looked for bubbles, as you might check an inner tube for leaks. We found no problems. But that's not to say skin condoms aren't porous at all.

Under a scanning electron microscope, the membranes reveal layers of fibers crisscrossing in various patterns. That latticework endows the skins with strength but also makes for an occasional pore, sometimes up to 1.5 microns wide. That's

smaller than a sperm, a white blood cell, or even some gonorrhea bacteria. But it's more than 10 times the size of the AIDS virus, and more than 25 times the size of the hepatitis-B virus.

The pores aren't tunnels through the skin's wall. They occur in individual layers of the skin's multilayered membrane. So some experts believe that skin condoms can still offer protection against small viruses. To get to the outside, such a virus would have to zigzag through each layer's tortuous fiber structure, somewhat like negotiating a maze. But, given enough time, the virus might be able to do so. Since skin condoms are a natural product, they can also have thin spots, which might contribute to porosity.

Laboratory evidence on whether the AIDS virus can pass through skin condoms is limited to only a few small studies. One study has demonstrated passage; three others have not. Similar studies show that skin condoms do pass the smaller hepatitis-B virus but usually not the herpes virus, which is slightly larger than the AIDS virus.

The relevance of these results to condoms in actual use isn't known. For example, lab studies typically use virus suspended in blood serum or tissue-culture media, not real semen. Semen has greater surface tension—it forms a glob—so any suspended material may have a harder time migrating outward.

Skin condoms work well as contraceptives. But, apparently because of the skins' possible porosity, the FDA doesn't allow their packages to carry the disease-prevention labeling that latex condoms may carry. It remains an open question whether the skins' relative strength outweighs their potential to pass small microbes. In view of the uncertainty, CU's medical consultants advise latex condoms for disease prevention.

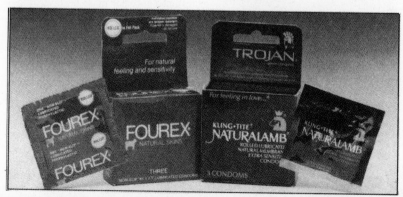

Readers report on condoms

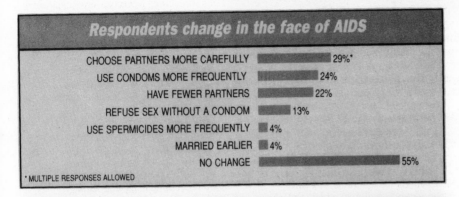

Respondents change in the face of AIDS

CHOOSE PARTNERS MORE CAREFULLY	29%*
USE CONDOMS MORE FREQUENTLY	24%
HAVE FEWER PARTNERS	22%
REFUSE SEX WITHOUT A CONDOM	13%
USE SPERMICIDES MORE FREQUENTLY	4%
MARRIED EARLIER	4%
NO CHANGE	55%

* MULTIPLE RESPONSES ALLOWED

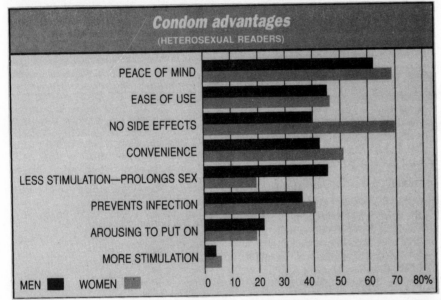

Condom advantages
(HETEROSEXUAL READERS)

- PEACE OF MIND
- EASE OF USE
- NO SIDE EFFECTS
- CONVENIENCE
- LESS STIMULATION—PROLONGS SEX
- PREVENTS INFECTION
- AROUSING TO PUT ON
- MORE STIMULATION

MEN ■ WOMEN ▨ 0 10 20 30 40 50 60 70 80%

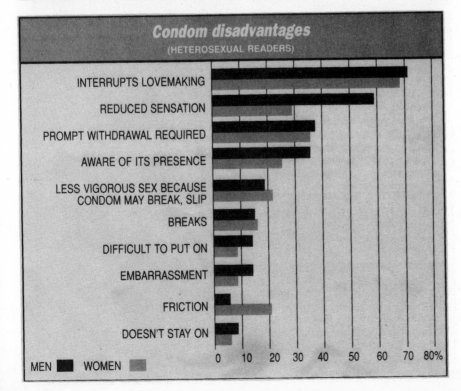

Condom disadvantages
(HETEROSEXUAL READERS)

- INTERRUPTS LOVEMAKING
- REDUCED SENSATION
- PROMPT WITHDRAWAL REQUIRED
- AWARE OF ITS PRESENCE
- LESS VIGOROUS SEX BECAUSE CONDOM MAY BREAK, SLIP
- BREAKS
- DIFFICULT TO PUT ON
- EMBARRASSMENT
- FRICTION
- DOESN'T STAY ON

MEN ■ WOMEN ▨ 0 10 20 30 40 50 60 70 80%

In response to a query last year in CON-SUMER REPORTS, almost 3300 readers participated in a survey about their use of condoms. They filled in an eight-page questionnaire, which also included questions about their knowledge of AIDS.

As a group, these readers were younger than the average mix of CONSUMER REPORTS subscribers (most were between 25 and 45). And 80 percent were men, compared with some 60 percent for our readership. Because of such differences (and the volunteer aspect of the survey), we can't generalize our findings to all subscribers. But the information we received was still instructive.

Two-thirds of the respondents were currently using condoms for birth control (sometimes along with another method). But disease—AIDS in particular—also had a major impact on condom use. In 1979, when we last reported on condoms, only 8 percent of the respondents checked "avoidance of venereal disease" as a reason for using condoms. Now 26 percent cited diseases such as AIDS and herpes as a reason for using condoms with their regular partner. Of the respondents who had "occasional partners"—about a quarter of the sample did—two out of three mentioned disease prevention.

Ten percent of the respondents reported being gay or bisexual, about the same as what's estimated for the U.S. overall. Most gay readers—85 percent—told us they personally knew someone with AIDS. Among exclusively heterosexual readers, 19 percent personally knew a person with AIDS.

Forty-one percent of heterosexuals living alone said they used condoms as protection against AIDS. Only 7 percent of married readers said they did. Among gay and bisexual respondents, the figure soared to 77 percent. Some readers used condoms for oral sex, too.

Condoms chiefly confer peace of mind, their greatest advantage, readers said. But condoms also interrupt lovemaking, their biggest drawback. About two-thirds of our respondents noted that major advantage and that major disadvantage.

Heterosexual men and women were pretty much alike in reporting the condom's pluses and minuses. Men, however, were twice as likely to complain about reduced sensation. (Yet nearly half the men praised condoms precisely because less stimulation allowed them to prolong sex.) Women were far more likely to favor condoms for the lack of side effects.

of those condoms tested so poorly.

Across most brands, we were surprised at the variability we sometimes observed either between packages or within a single package: A brightly colored condom in a box of plain ones, or vice versa; differences in the shape of the same product; unlubricated condoms mixed in with lubricated ones; or textured condoms showing up among plain ones. Mistakes like that point to an industry-wide sloppiness in some aspects of quality control.

The role of spermicides

Nonoxynol-9, the active ingredient in most over-the-counter spermicides, kills sperm cells through a detergent action that attacks the cell membrane. Nonoxynol-9 also kills various organisms that cause sexually transmitted disease, including AIDS, gonorrhea, syphilis, chlamydia, herpes, and hepatitis B. Even concentrations well under 1 percent have inactivated the AIDS virus in the lab. So nonoxynol-9 spermicides, used with a condom, can provide something of an extra safety net, should the condom break.

Some condoms now come with a spermicide in their lubricant. However, the amount of nonoxynol-9 in condoms is no

Readers judge the brands

Two condoms tested—one *Sheik* and one *Trojan*—come closest to a no-frills model: They're not lubricated, textured, tinted, contoured, or equipped with a reservoir tip. For the rest, though, you can find every conceivable permutation of those features. Store shelves are stocked with dozens of varieties.

According to our survey, the features readers appreciate most are lubrication and the reservoir tip, preferred by about three in four. Substantial minorities—some 35 to 40 percent—liked extra-thin, extra-strong, or spermicidally lubricated condoms. For each of those three features, though, at least 10 percent of the readers said they *wouldn't* use condoms that had them.

Condom strength, important to many readers, was even more favored among women and gay men. Both of those groups also leaned toward spermicide lubrication. Textured (ribbed) condoms, often touted as enhancing a woman's pleasure, got a mixed reaction from women: A little more than one-fourth preferred the texture but nearly an equal number said they wouldn't use such condoms. Gay men tended to avoid skin condoms, presumably because such condoms may offer less protection against viruses (see the box on page 132).

Most readers have used a variety of condoms. We asked for preferences from respondents who had experiences with particular brand models. We've charted the percent of heterosexual respondents who told us they prefer a specific brand versus those who say they would not want to use it again. (Gay respondents appeared to have different opinions but were too few to provide a brand-by-brand listing.) All brands listed were rated by at least 150 respondents—in most cases by more than 300. We also note the advantages and disadvantages readers reported.

Respondents as a group expressed ambivalence about a number of brands, often with a large split in pro and con votes. The most extreme case: *Mentor* condoms, which almost 30 percent liked and almost 40 percent vetoed.

Mentor is unique among all models tested. It features a special applicator "hood" and an inner ring of adhesive to hold the condom on the penis. That helps prevent slipping and leakage. Readers told us: *Mentor* stays on (correct); is difficult to don (right again—instructions are more complex than a regular condom's); and costs too much (right, too—we paid more than $18 a dozen).

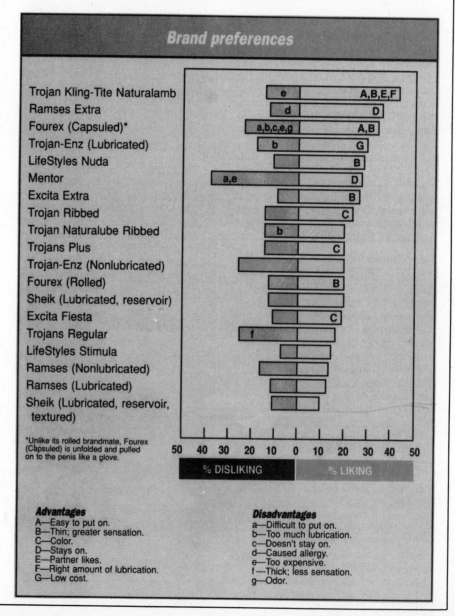

Brand preferences

Brand	% Disliking	% Liking
Trojan Kling-Tite Naturalamb	e	A,B,E,F
Ramses Extra	d	D
Fourex (Capsuled)*	a,b,c,e,g	A,B
Trojan-Enz (Lubricated)	b	G
LifeStyles Nuda		B
Mentor	a,e	D
Excita Extra		B
Trojan Ribbed		C
Trojan Naturalube Ribbed	b	
Trojans Plus		C
Trojan-Enz (Nonlubricated)		
Fourex (Rolled)		B
Sheik (Lubricated, reservoir)		
Excita Fiesta		C
Trojans Regular	f	
LifeStyles Stimula		
Ramses (Nonlubricated)		
Ramses (Lubricated)		
Sheik (Lubricated, reservoir, textured)		

*Unlike its rolled brandmate, Fourex (Capsuled) is unfolded and pulled on to the penis like a glove.

50 40 30 20 10 0 10 20 30 40 50

% DISLIKING   % LIKING

Advantages
A—Easy to put on.
B—Thin; greater sensation.
C—Color.
D—Stays on.
E—Partner likes.
F—Right amount of lubrication.
G—Low cost.

Disadvantages
a—Difficult to put on.
b—Too much lubrication.
c—Doesn't stay on.
d—Caused allergy.
e—Too expensive.
f—Thick; less sensation.
g—Odor.

substitute for a vaginal spermicide, which can be applied more copiously. The nonoxynol-9 in spermicides varies in concentration from about 1 to 12 percent. If a high concentration causes irritation, try a product with a lower one.

Spermicides are formulated so that they can be used with latex diaphragms and thus shouldn't damage latex condoms. As yet, the safety and efficacy of spermicides for preventing disease transmission in anal sex remains unknown.

Precautions with condoms

Air pollution, heat, and light can all spoil latex condoms. So never open one until you're ready to use it, and store condoms in a dark, cool, dry place.

Condom packets should be opened gently to avoid damaging the contents. If the condom shows any signs of deterioration—sticky, discolored, or dried-out latex—discard it.

Some condoms come in translucent or transparent packets, which could hasten aging. We also found some individual packets not quite sealed, which could also hasten aging. And some packets were hard to tear apart. The Ratings give details.

Stored properly, condoms can last up to five years. Most brands tell the manufacturing date. Spermicide condoms give an expiration date for their nonoxynol-9.

If a condom breaks, having a foam spermicide handy to apply quickly may help. It's no guarantee against pregnancy, because sperm cells travel very fast; but it still might help to kill disease organisms. Douching is unreliable, because it might push semen up through the cervix.

Recommendations

Using condoms is part of what public-health authorities now call "safer sex"—practices that can reduce your risk of exposure to AIDS and other sexually transmitted diseases. For that purpose, it makes sense to choose from among condoms that performed well in our airburst test. No in-use research has yet shown conclusively that the better a condom performs in a laboratory test, the more it will resist breakage in actual use. But we think it's only prudent to make that assumption.

The first group of condoms in the Ratings had the fewest failures in our airburst test. The models in that group are listed in order of how much they exceeded the minimum values of pressure and volume. Although we would consider any of them safe by current standards, we suggest you choose from the upper portion of the group if you, like many of our survey respondents, encounter broken condoms as often as once or twice a year.

Our tests did not address other aspects of condom use, perhaps most importantly

that of sensitivity. Still, the variety of condoms in the top Ratings group offer just about any mix of features you and your partner may prefer.

To be effective, condoms must be used consistently, not just some of the time. Surprisingly, among the readers surveyed who have "occasional partners," less than half say they use condoms every time. The notion that it's possible to guess when protection is or isn't needed invites disaster. As one AIDS researcher put it, trying to "take someone's sexual history" is far more fallible than using a condom.

There's a right way to use condoms. Place the rolled condom over the tip of the erect penis. If the condom has a reservoir tip, squeeze out the air. Otherwise, leave a half-inch space at the end (and squeeze out the air). Unroll the condom down the length of the penis (uncircumcised men should first pull back the foreskin). Right after ejaculation, grasp the condom firmly at the ring and withdraw before losing the erection; that will prevent spillage. Use a new condom for each act of intercourse, and avoid any genital contact before putting the condom on.

A condom lubricated with spermicide may offer some extra protection against disease. But using a separate vaginal spermicide with a condom is more effective.

Safe use of lubricants

Lubricants to use with latex condoms

Most readers who responded to our survey preferred prelubricated condoms (see preceding page). But just over half supplied their own lubrication or supplemented that already on the condom. That can lessen chances of breakage. But it can also *increase* the risk of breakage if you use an oil-based lubricant, as one in eight readers did.

Oil-based lubricants weaken latex considerably. Mineral oil, baby oil, vegetable oil, petroleum jelly, cold cream, and hand lotions containing such oils can all affect latex. We tried some of those lubricants on latex condoms and saw condom performance suffer markedly in airburst testing: At least half of the samples of each condom tested failed. At body temperature, oiled latex will weaken in minutes.

The lubricants safe for condoms are water-based. They include surgical jellies, such as *K-Y Lubricating Jelly* and *Today Personal Lubricant*, both of which we tested. But don't confuse water-based with water-soluble products, which may not be safe for latex. Lotions that wash off easily can still contain damaging oils. Check the label or ask a pharmacist.

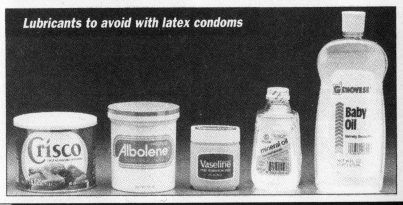

Lubricants to avoid with latex condoms

Guide to the Ratings

Grouped by projected failure rate in airburst testing, adjusted statistically for number of samples tested; within groups, listed in order of decreasing volume and pressure withstood in test. Differences between closely ranked models are not significant.

1 Price. Average price CU shoppers paid in New York City area stores for one dozen condoms.

2 Lubrication. Some models come with "dry" lubrication (D), typically a silicon-based oil. Others are wet-lubricated (W), with a water-based surgical jelly.

3 Spermicide. These models contain the spermicide nonoxynol-9, but concentrations and amounts vary. Most labels say that their spermicide lubricant is no substitute for the use of vaginal spermicide.

4 Texture. Ribbing or stippling around the shaft.

5 Contour. Shapes varied considerably. Some condoms are flared, others tapered, yet others have contouring for more snug fit.

6 Variability. Inconsistencies included: large differences in airburst performance among lots tested (A); color variations among or within packages (C); lubrication variations within packages (L); shape variations among or within packages (S); and texture variations among or within packages (T). Some models come in strips, and in some lots it was hard to separate the individual packets (P). For some models, we didn't test enough lots to check lot-to-lot differences in airburst results (X).

Specifications and Features
Except as noted, all: • Have reservoir tip. • Showed small lot-to-lot variation in strength. • Did not vary among or within packages in color, lubrication, or texture. • Had opaque individual packet. • Were sealed in individual packets, packed in strips, and easy to separate and open. • Had a slight odor. • Have a natural latex color.

Key to Comments
A—Instructions judged better than most.
B—Instructions judged worse than most.
C—Packets translucent; could hasten aging.
D—Packets transparent; could hasten aging.
E—Individual packets not sealed; could hasten aging.
F—Many packets not airtight; could hasten aging.
G—Individual packets hard to open.
H—Has unpleasant odor.
I—Had thin spots.
J—Comes in assorted colors (*Excita Fiesta, Wrinkle Zero-0 2000, Yamabuki No. 2*); comes in pink (*Protex Arouse*); comes in golden yellow (*Trojans Plus, Trojan Ribbed*).
K—Comes with wallet for purse or pocket.
L—Has plain tip.
M—Thinner than most (roughly, 0.05 mm).
N—Thicker than most (roughly, 0.08 mm or more).
O—Has applicator and adhesive to hold condom on penis.

Ratings

Latex condoms

Brand and model	1 Price	2 Lubrication	3 Spermicide	4 Texture	5 Contour	6 Variability	Comments
The following models had a projected maximum failure rate of 1.5 percent.							
Gold Circle Coin	$2.75	—	—	—	—	X	A,E,N
LifeStyles Extra Strength Lubricated	5.63	D	—	—	—	—	N
Saxon Wet Lubricated	4.47	W	—	—	—	X	B,G
Ramses Non-Lubricated Reservoir End	5.96	—	—	—	—	S,X	F
Sheik Non-Lubricated Reservoir End	3.43	—	—	—	—	P,X	F
Excita Extra	6.60	D	✔	✔	—	P	A,C
Kimono	7.64	D	—	—	✔	X	A,D,G
Sheik Elite	4.83	D	✔	—	—	—	A,C,M
Koromex with Nonoxynol-9	6.56	D	✔	✔	—	—	C,K
Excita Fiesta	6.77	D	—	✔	—	P,X	C,J
Embrace Ultra-Thin	3.36	D	—	—	✔	L	B,C,F
LifeStyles Stimula Vibra-Ribbed	5.08	D	—	✔	—	P	B,C
Ramses Extra with Spermicidal Lubricant	5.80	D	✔	—	—	P	A,C
Lady Trojan	5.25	W	✔	—	—	X	A,F,H
Trojan Plus 2	5.25	W	✔	—	✔	X	A
Protex Secure	4.32	D	—	—	—	C,S	C,F,H
Protex Touch	3.87	D	—	—	—	—	C,H
Protex Arouse	4.00	D	—	✔	✔	C,S,T	C,J
Trojan-Enz	3.56		—	—	—	—	—
Lady Protex with Spermicidal Lubricant	4.14	D	✔	—	—	C	C,H
Sheik Fetherlite Snug-Fit	5.42	D	—	—	✔	P,X	C
Trojan Naturalube Ribbed	5.30	W	—	✔	✔	—	H
Protex Contracept Plus with Spermicidal Lubricant	4.61	D	✔	—	—	C	C,H
Lady Protex Ultra-Thin	3.97	D	—	—	—	C,X	C,H
Trojan-Enz Lubricated	4.41	W	—	—	—	—	H
Trojan Ribbed	5.15	D	—	✔	—	—	D,J
Today with Spermicidal Lubricant	6.16	D	✔	—	✔	X	A,G,I
LifeStyles Conture	4.28	D	—	—	✔	—	B,C
Trojans	3.74	—	—	—	—	—	L
Trojans Plus	5.07	D	—	—	✔	—	D,J
Yamabuki No. 2 Lubricated	7.32	D	—	—	✔	X	A,C,J,M
Wrinkle Zero-0 2000	7.32	D	—	✔	✔	—	A,C,J
The following models had a projected maximum failure rate of 4 percent.							
Sheik Non-Lubricated Plain End	4.08	—	—	—	—	—	L
Ramses Sensitol Lubricated	5.82	D	—	—	✔	P,S,X	C
Pleaser Ribbed Lubricated [1]	3.46	D	—	✔	✔	—	C,F
Ramses NuFORM	6.26	D	—	—	✔	P	C
Mentor	18.62	D	—	—	—	—	A,O
LifeStyles Nuda	4.69	D	—	—	✔	—	B,C
The following models had a projected maximum failure rate of more than 10 percent.							
LifeStyles Extra Strength with Nonoxynol-9	8.07	D	✔	—	—	A	F,I,N
LifeStyles Nuda Plus	5.40	D	✔	—	✔	A	A,C,I

[1] Now called **Saxon Ribbed Lubricated**.

Reluctant Crusader

Etienne-Emile Baulieu

RU 486 may do much more than end the abortion debate in America, says its inventor.

Mark Dowie

Mark Dowie, *author of* We Have a Donor, *profiled surgeon Thomas Starzl for* American Health *in June 1989.*

When I arrived to meet Professor Etienne-Emile Baulieu, I was surprised to find the door to his hotel room wide open. He is, after all, the inventor and primary promoter of what American anti-abortionists call "the death pill," RU 486, and thus a targeted enemy of an increasingly angry and militant movement. Anti-abortion leaders fear that his invention will close the debate on abortion for good.

He sat in plain view of the entrance, one leg slung over the arm of an easy chair, talking to a friend on the phone. He spoke casually, as if discussing baseball or the weather, of "norprogestagens," "hormone receptors" and "steroid antagonists." Such is the small talk of endocrinologists.

I had come to discuss his discovery of RU 486, an antiprogesterone agent that, if taken shortly after missing a period, has a 96% chance of inducing miscarriage. But Baulieu prefers not to call it miscarriage, abortion nor even contraception. "What is really happening," he says, "is 'contragestion,'" a word he coined in response to strong opposition to his invention. "My aim is to get rid of the word abortion. It is

almost as traumatic as the procedure itself."

He waved me in casually, indifferent to who I was or what might be in my large black briefcase. Later he told me he was unconcerned because abortion is barely an issue outside the U.S. "It was not mentioned once in our last national elections—and France is a Catholic country." (After a brief bout of controversy, RU 486 has been approved and is widely used in France. Despite initial public outcry, the government declared it "the moral property of women" and forced its manufacturer, Roussel-Uclaf, to keep it on the market.)

"But this is America," I explain. "Anti-abortionists here are. . . ."

"Even if American anti-abortionists are angry with me," he interrupts in a thick Parisian accent, "they are not violent. They are for *life*, are they not?" He laughs aloud. It is pointless to argue with his logic.

Baulieu is disappointed with my agenda. He'd rather discuss a rare steroid hormone produced in the brain that he discovered, which California researchers believe helps restore memory. According to experiments on rats in Baulieu's lab, it may even return comatose people to consciousness. He seems exhausted by the fame RU 486 has brought him, and eager to move on. "I don't like abortion," he says, "and I don't like talking about it. I am a physician and would rather talk about saving life."

Later Baulieu argues that RU 486 may save lives: Each year, the World Health Organization (WHO) estimates about 200,000 women die the world over from botched surgical abortions. "I am not really for abortion, you see," he says. "I am for women."

Born in 1926, the son of a physician named Léon Blum (no relation to the French prime minister), young Etienne-Emile took a new surname in 1942 after the Nazis occupied Paris and began rounding up Jews. At 15 he joined the French resistance and fought in the countryside until 1944.

After the war he began to study medicine. His first mentor was a blind physician/biologist named Max-Fernand Jayle. Although they were complete opposites in politics, they liked each other very much. The leftist Baulieu followed Jayle's example and became a physician and a scientist, obtaining his M.D. and Ph.D. degrees at about the same time. Today he is still not certain in his own mind whether he is primarily a doctor or a scientist. It was for his research, however, not his treatment of patients, that Baulieu received the 1989 Albert Lasker award for his lifelong work with steroid hormones—which led, of course, to his discovery of RU 486.

The presentation of such a prestigious award to Baulieu (46 Lasker winners have gone on to win Nobels) deeply angered leaders of the American right-to-life movement, who expressed their disgust in letters and editorials. "I really would be very alarmed," said Beverly LaHaye, founder of Concerned Women for America, "if we allowed [RU 486] to be legally used in the United States."

Baulieu's plush suite overlooks one of two 18-hole golf courses at the Silverado Country Club and Resort, a tony corporate retreat in Northern California where world-class neuroendocrinologists have gathered for five days to read papers, show slides and play a little golf.

"I don't play golf," scowls Baulieu. "It takes too much time." But he seems to enjoy the other perks of fame, and politely offers "champagne, Perrier or beer, whatever you like," before we begin our discussion.

American Health: Were you looking for a contraceptive when you discovered RU 486?

Etienne-Emile Baulieu: No. Basic research doesn't work that way. I was working with steroids and, among other things, with antagonists to hormones and progesterone receptors. Progesterone is vital to fertility and pregnancy. If you remove it from the wall of the uterus in pregnancy, the embryo will detach itself and die. So when I saw that the Roussel chemists had a compound that inhibited progesterone action, I knew I had something that could terminate a pregnancy.

AH: So it was an accident?

EEB: Not really. I have been interested in reproductive controls for 25 years—ever since I met Gregory Pincus [inventor of the Pill]. So it was natural that I should interpret RU 486's properties as I did. No scientific discovery is purely accidental. Louis Pasteur said it better than I can: *"Le hasard ne favorise que les esprits préparés."* [Chance favors only the prepared mind.]

AH: So at some level of your consciousness you were searching for something that would terminate a pregnancy?

EEB: Sure. I have thought a lot about reproduction and sex hormones. That prepared my mind, as Pasteur might have said, to find something related to pregnancy. So when the Ford Foundation gave me a large grant to research receptors (molecules that recognize specific hormones, the way a lock recognizes a key, triggering a response in the cell), I naturally began to work with receptors and sex steroids. Then we found the receptor for progesterone, which led to the possibility of a simple antipregnancy pill.

Another thing that prepared me to discover RU 486 happened during the 1950s, when I was a resident at medical school. There I witnessed a number of D and C's [dilation and curettage]. Although they were and still are a standard medical activity, I didn't like them. It was hard to watch.

AH: Why?

EEB: Because it was so painful for the patient.

AH: But weren't they anesthetized?

EEB: Not always. You see, it was forbidden in France to abort then. So a D and C was often performed to achieve the termination of unwanted pregnancies women had started to interrupt themselves. Some of our bosses believed that women who aborted their pregnancies should suffer for their sins, so they would do the procedure without anesthesia, much the way abortion is still performed at many clinics in the Third World.

The memory of those painful abortions never left me. So when I saw what RU 486 could do, I knew I had found a relatively painless way to terminate a pregnancy.

AH: So the compound belongs to Roussel-Uclaf [the second largest pharmaceutical house in France]?

EEB: Yes. I was, and still am, a consultant to Roussel.

AH: How does RU 486 actually work?

EEB: During the second [luteal] phase of a woman's cycle, progesterone is essential for reproductive function. In the uterus, this hormone protects the developing embryo and fetus. RU 486 is a progesterone antagonist. By binding in uterine cells it prevents progesterone from attaching itself to the wall of the uterus. Without progesterone, the uterus simply cannot keep a fertilized egg.

The procedure involves taking a single dose [600 mg] of RU 486 within three weeks of a missed period. Then, 48 hours after taking RU 486, the patient is given a small dose of prostaglandin (in the form of a shot or vaginal suppository). That helps eliminate the contents of the uterus, just as if she were having a heavy period.

AH: So it is not literally a "morning after" pill.

EEB: No, although it is still sometimes called that. The process is a little more complex.

AH: Do you think that at some point down the road you or another scientist will be able to find a simpler abortifacient than RU 486?

EEB: Yes. In fact, I just mailed a letter this week to Professor Sune Bergstrom, WHO's chief advisor on birth control. He has been at the forefront of prostaglandin research. Prostaglandin is the complicating factor in this whole method because it has to be so carefully administered by a physician. So the patient has to return. I suggested to Professor Bergstrom that a 72-hour time release prostaglandin would be useful, since it could be taken with the RU 486. One visit.

AH: What has been the response in France to your discovery?

EEB: There was some early opposition from anti-abortionists. The Catholic Church reacted immediately, saying that they like the fact that RU 486 decreased suffering but did not like anything else about it because it is something in between contraception and abortion. And of course, they are against both. It's too easy, they said. And that has been a common criticism, which is an antiwomen opinion when you think of it. Why shouldn't abortion be less painful?

But the whole debate has calmed down in France. From the extreme right to the extreme left, the people of France have accepted abortion and RU 486. I believe this will happen one day in the United States.

AH: But the moral debate is different in this country. Abortion is a very central issue in electoral politics.

EEB: I know, and that's too bad. It's a social debate which should not be politicized.

AH: Have you seen any signs of a black market for RU 486 forming anywhere in the world?

EEB: No. A black market would be disastrous.

AH: Why?

EEB: A black market would lead to nonmedically supervised administration of RU 486. To have a medical examination is the right of any woman who thinks she is pregnant, whether or not she decides to interrupt the pregnancy. Medical supervision is needed in particular to exclude ectopic pregnancies.

AH: Did you know that it's legal in the U.S. to mail-order a drug that is not approved for use in this country if a physician is willing to prescribe it?

EEB: Really? No, I didn't know that. But it doesn't matter. I don't think Roussel-Uclaf would mail RU 486 anywhere and I approve of that attitude.

AH: With all your scientific accomplishments, why have you made RU 486 your personal crusade?

EEB: No, no, no. I haven't made it a crusade. The crusade came by itself.

I have done many things which I would rather crusade for, particularly in the field of cancer. The media have made me a crusader for RU 486. What I like about science is the fact that most of us forget who invented things, with some exceptions of course. Even the people in my own lab forget that they are working with compounds that I discovered. That's okay. It's the way it should be. Painters put their initials on their work, not scientists.

But RU 486 has attracted a lot of attention, being attached to a human problem that is centuries old. And I am identified with it, whether I like it or not.

AH: Are there other uses for RU 486 you'd rather promote or be identified with?

EEB: Yes, there are many other uses. First, RU 486 can be used in other ways in the field of pregnancy. It might even one day be used as a standard contraceptive. Since RU 486 blocks progesterone, if you take it constantly you'll stop ovulating—a sort of estrogen contraception. It isn't used this way now because the drug needs to be tested for long-term use. It may be too toxic.

Second, RU 486 may prevent implantation when given just after ovulation. We (and others in England and Sweden) have studied that. The problem is it would have to be administered at an exact moment after ovulation, and we usually do not know when ovulation occurs, because cycles are too irregular. So I don't think it will become a widely used contraceptive for that reason.

RU 486 may also be used at the end of the cycle, whether or not a woman knows she's pregnant. This morning, for example, I got a call from a friend, a very famous American doctor. He said his daughter had had sex last week

. . . just one time . . . she doesn't know yet whether she will miss her period . . . so my friend wants to know if RU 486 will work as a sort of "morning after" pill? It does, so I said yes . . . except, of course, it is not really the morning after. Nevertheless, it could be very useful for teenagers or single women.

RU 486 can also be used to assist the delivery of a full-term, normal baby when the cervix doesn't open well. So it may constitute an alternative to some Caesarean sections.

Outside the pregnancy field there are other potential uses for RU 486. We don't know yet whether it cures endometriosis, but it definitely reduces the pain it causes. Some breast cancer tumors have responded well to RU 486. And with at least one category of Cushing's disease, associated with excess adrenal function, it has worked by inhibiting cortisone. Glaucoma, when linked to excessive corticosteroids, may be successfully treated with RU 486. Experiments have also been initiated to apply RU 486 locally in wound or burn repair.

AH: Would it be safe to say, then, that because of public opposition to RU 486, Americans suffering from endometriosis, breast cancer, meningioma, Cushing's disease, glaucoma and burn injuries are being deprived of a possible cure?

EEB: I think that's a reasonable possibility. RU 486 may be treated like morphine—a very active drug for pain that is also addictive and therefore has to be placed in a very special category. Patients should not be deprived of RU 486 just because people oppose abortion. Therefore, why not also put RU 486 in a special category, with well-controlled use? I hope the situation will soon be defused, because if you look at it on a global basis, you may find many people suffering because of an insignificant minority.

AH: A recent op-ed piece in *The Wall Street Journal* mentioned the possibility of birth defects in infants that are not aborted by RU 486 and go to term.

EEB: There has never been a single case of that sort. In fact, there are three children born in England to mothers who took RU 486. They are all normal. We have run extensive trials with monkeys and the babies are perfect.

But I like the fact that there is still a

little fear about abnormalities because I think that when a woman has made a decision she should go through with it. If RU 486 combined with prostaglandin doesn't work (and it doesn't 4% of the time) she should then have a surgical abortion.

AH: *The Wall Street Journal* referred to some rabbit studies that showed birth defects.

EEB: Oh yes, that's another story. Those studies are not applicable to the human situation because when you partially deprive a pregnant rabbit of progesterone, its uterus contracts powerfully and crushes the skulls of the kits. The few that live through it are born deformed. The same partial deficit of progesterone does not provoke any fetal abnormality in other species.

AH: So you are confident that treatment with RU 486 is preferable to a surgical abortion?

EEB: Women have to decide. And 80% of the women who have terminated pregnancies both ways say they prefer RU 486.

AH: David Grimes, professor of obstetrics and gynecology at USC and the principal researcher of RU 486 in this country, says that you are "heroic" for representing the drug in the U.S., where there is such strong opposition to it. Don't you think Dr. Grimes is also taking some risks?

EEB: It is a different world here. I forget that sometimes. Actually, I think that David Grimes is very courageous.

AH: You have said publicly that you believe the FDA will soon approve RU 486. What makes you so confident?

EEB: Well, I have the highest esteem for FDA scientists. They know the compound, they know about the trials, and they tell me they like what they have seen.

AH: But don't you think the Bush administration will stop it?

EEB: I guess I don't know how things work here. In my country, politics and medical science are kept separate.

AH: Our FDA director is appointed by the President, and this President ran on a strong anti-abortion platform.

EEB: Well, you spoke of heroism. Perhaps the FDA director needs to be heroic. I think the wind is blowing differently now. There are literally dozens of venture capitalists in this country willing to invest millions in this product. Eventually the drug will make its way.

AH: Do you have any financial interests in Roussel or RU 486?

EEB: I am paid a fixed consulting fee by Roussel-Uclaf. It doesn't matter how many meetings I attend or how many ideas I give them, good or bad. The fee is the same.

AH: You call yourself a physician and a scientist. Which first?

EEB: Difficult question. Technically, I am a physician who does science. I must admit I love science; the beauty of nature and its mechanisms is very inspiring. And I like beauty, so I like research.

But I am also a physician. One day when I was in residence, I was 20, I stood next to the bed of a patient. At that moment I knew I would be a physician for the rest of my life. That happened before I began doing research. So it came first. But I really don't know which comes first in my heart today.

AH: But if you were to have a single mission in life, in terms of your work, how would you describe it? As a scientific mission or a healing mission?

EEB: That's a very good question. I think I would choose research because ultimately research leads to healing.

AH: And what currently interests you most in the world of healing?

EEB: Steroid hormones in the brain, mostly because we have only just discovered them. But what excites me most is that these hormones appear to be related to memory. I believe human life is meaningless without memory. No memory, no life.

AH: Do you believe it's possible to revive patients from a coma with synthetic steroid hormones?

EEB: In fact, we have performed experiments on anesthetized animals. But that's a small aspect of our work. The larger potential involves arresting the aging process in the brain—by helping the growth and healing of brain cells.

AH: Sounds like you may come up with something even more exciting than RU 486?

EEB: Maybe. Or maybe zero. Who knows? That's what is fascinating about research. You really don't know where you will end up until you get there. Although you cannot predict very much, you feel you must go on. I do love this work. My only regret is that I can't do everything at once.

Making Its Way
AN RU 486 BLACK MARKET?

Etienne-Emile Baulieu's belief that a black market in RU 486 would be "disastrous" doesn't assure that there won't be one. At this point, however, all known attempts to bring the drug into the U.S. have been legitimate. Import schemes range from the numerous proposals devised by venture capitalists who have approached Baulieu in his travels, to Every Child A Wanted Child. A nonprofit organization in San Francisco, Every Child's purpose is to educate the public about the benefits of RU 486 and eventually market the drug in the U.S.

Cofounded by a former member of the city's Board of Supervisors, Carol Ruth Silver, Every Child has announced its intention to apply for a single-product federal import license.

"American pharmaceutical companies fear that their whole product line would be boycotted by anti-abortionists if they import RU 486," says Silver. "So despite the enormous profit potential of the drug, they will not apply for a clearance. Our firm will have only one product, so a boycott can't hurt us."

However, if abortion rights are further eroded and President George Bush stands by his right-to-life platform, Silver's license will certainly be denied. If that happens, women's organizations have hinted they will take matters into their own hands. Some speak openly of performing their own abortions, a few admitting that they have already helped others do so. A few centers are even training women to become skilled abortionists.

There is also talk in feminist health care circles of smuggling RU 486 across the Atlantic. Since smuggling is illegal and abortion is not, women will not go on the record announcing their intention to traffic in contraband. But until the Customs Department's drug-sniffing dogs are trained to bark at RU 486's distinctive aroma, it would seem almost impossible to contain a moderate trade in the pill. Responds Baulieu: "The best way to avoid an uncontrolled, and thus dangerous, use of RU 486 is to ask Hoechst-Roussel [Roussel-Uclaf's American counterpart] to sell it in the U.S."

"She Died Because of a Law"

A mother denounces parental consent

Rochelle Sharpe

Rochelle Sharpe is a national reporter at Gannett News Service, covering social issues. She was the first to break the story of Rebecca Bell nationally.

At the age of 46, Karen Bell was flying on an airplane by herself for the first time in her life. She looked at the speech her husband had written for her and decided she could not deliver it.

Karen wasn't sure what she wanted to say to the National Women's Political Caucus about laws requiring parental consent for abortion, but she knew that speech just didn't sound like her. So when she finally talked to the crowd, she merely described how she felt about the law that destroyed her family: "My life was over when my little girl died."

Karen explained how her daughter became the first teenager in the nation known to die because of a parental consent law. She described 17-year-old Rebecca's desire to keep her pregnancy secret, her futile attempts to get a legal abortion near her home in Indianapolis, Indiana, and her death from an abortion-related infection. By the time Karen was finished, women were wiping tears from their eyes; many approached her to discuss how they could work together to defeat parental consent legislation—an area of the reproductive rights struggle that even some pro-choice activists seem willing to compromise.

Karen's life as a full-time housewife had ended, but her work as an activist had just begun. Although she does not always enjoy her new role, she is committed to it. And she is unusually effective because her story is so genuine. She can do what seems impossible in the debate on abortion: she can change people's minds.

"She made an impact on me," said Ginger Barr, a Republican legislator in Kansas who was wavering on parental consent until she heard Karen Bell and her husband testify at a committee hearing. "Everybody was just spellbound," she said. The committee eventually voted down three parental notification and consent bills by a 12 to 8 margin.

In Albany, New York, the Bells had a similar effect, galvanizing four aides to Governor Mario Cuomo into a sympathetic group. Karen's question to them was intensely personal: "Do you remember the first time you were in love?" Then she described her daughter's first boyfriend and showed pictures of the smiling, blond-haired girl. "My little girl was my life and she died because of a law I didn't know existed." Lobbyists try to explain to her the power and impact she brings to the abortion debate, but she scoffs and says, "Oh, no, I'm just a mom. That's all I know how to do."

All Karen Bell ever wanted was to be a good mother. For years, she lived in a Leave It to Beaver world; when she wasn't playing hostess, Karen often volunteered as a teacher's aide for special education students and baby-sat at a local church during Bible study meetings. She never read the newspaper. Until last year, she had never heard of the National Organization for Women. She lived in a quiet neighborhood near the Indianapolis Motor Speedway until she married her husband, William, when she was 24. After the wedding, the couple moved into a house three doors away from her parents, and started a family. Once her son, Bill, and Rebecca had been born, she thought, "We've got the perfect family."

In Karen's view, she and her daughter were like best friends, talking about everything—including sex. They almost always got along until Rebecca met her first boyfriend. After that, their relationship was strained. Before long, Karen heard through a family friend that Rebecca feared she was pregnant and that she was using drugs as well. Mortified, she rushed her daughter to Planned Parenthood for pregnancy tests, which proved negative. Later, she and her husband put Rebecca in a detoxification center to rid her of her new drug habit.

"Becky, I don't want to go through this again," William Bell recalls telling his daughter while she was recovering. Neither he nor his wife realized the impact of that statement; Rebecca repeatedly told her best friend she would be thrown out of the house if she got into trouble again. And Karen had no idea that Rebecca resumed seeing her boyfriend and became pregnant.

Rebecca tried to deal with her unwanted pregnancy by herself. She returned to Planned Parenthood and asked for an abortion, only to be told she would need her parents' consent. She talked with a friend about driving to an abortion clinic in Kentucky, where parental consent wasn't required, but she kept postponing the trip.

Karen still has no idea what Rebecca did to end her pregnancy. All she remembers of her daughter's last week of life is that a mysterious illness began to afflict her one Saturday night. In hindsight, Karen believes her daughter had someone try to induce an illegal abortion that night. But at the time, she believed Rebecca's story that she had the flu—a likely scenario since relatives were just recovering from it. The illness, however, was really pneumonia, triggered by the infection in her womb.

All the while, Karen couldn't understand why Rebecca would go to the bathroom and mutter, "Nothing's happening." By the following Friday, she was puzzled when her daughter reported with glee that she had started her period, an event Rebecca usually dreaded since she got such bad cramps. Now, Karen realizes, her daughter was awaiting the onset of a miscarriage.

Once the bleeding began, Rebecca agreed to go to a doctor, but it was too late. Neither Karen nor her husband learned about the pregnancy until they talked to a doctor who emerged from their daughter's room saying, "I don't know whether we're going to be able to save the baby." Only after Karen opened her daughter's purse did she discover a list of abortion clinics outside of Indiana that did not require parental consent.

When she and her husband were planning their daughter's funeral, they decided they did not want abortion mentioned during the service at all. But the minister convinced them they might help other teenage girls by discussing Rebecca's pregnancy in the eulogy.

At the funeral, Karen "felt kind of ashamed. I kind of held my head down, wondering, 'Oh, what are they thinking?' " But before long she was glad the minister had told the teenagers that she would help anyone afraid to talk to her parents. "At least fifteen kids came to tell me about their abortions," she said. One girl left a note on Rebecca's grave: "I did exactly what you did, Becky, but I lived."

For more than a year Karen grieved, and did not speak publicly of her daughter's death. It wasn't until she heard from Rebecca's teacher that Indiana NOW was circulating a flier about her daughter's death that Karen began to understand why Rebecca died. When a TV reporter called, she discovered that Indiana had a parental consent law. Then she started getting mad. Before long, the Bells agreed to talk to reporters and state legislators. They decided to help pro-choice groups make documentaries and commercials about parental consent.

Karen usually makes public appearances with her husband, letting him do most of the talking. "I always get up and tell the story of Becky. I can't go out and quote statistics. He's the toughie and I'm the big fluffie." She believes public speaking has helped them both. It has transformed her husband, she says, making him act more alive because he feels he is avenging Rebecca's death. And for her part, she says, "I feel happy when I speak because I feel like I have my daughter with me."

At times the public appearances are scary for Karen, who still is happiest staying at home. But she says: "Nothing really frightens me anymore. Nothing can hurt me now because I hurt the most when my little girl died."

Although most people are supportive, she occasionally meets someone who wants to debate abortion. She's learned to give a terse reply: "If you're against abortion, then don't have one. But don't take it away from me or anyone else." Karen respects feminist organizations now, but says she has little desire to become politically active in them—except to speak out against parental consent. "I don't want to make a career out of this," she says. "I don't like this world, if you want to know the truth. I just want what was, but it can never be.

"Now, if I can help somebody or some family, I'll do it."

ABORTION IN A NEW LIGHT

Treating abortion as a public health problem, rather than a criminal act or ideological flashpoint, will actually reduce its incidence.

JODI L. JACOBSON

Jodi L. Jacobson is a senior researcher working on population, family planning, and women and development at the Worldwatch Institute.

Among the first actions taken by Romania's provisional government following the execution of dictator Nicolae Ceausescu in December 1989 was a repeal of the ban on abortion. The 14-year-old edict, created by Ceausescu in a fruitless attempt to raise the nation's birthrate, outlawed contraceptives and made abortion a criminal offense punishable in some instances by death.

Some six months earlier, the United States, a country with one of the world's most liberal abortion policies, took a step backward on reproductive rights. Last July's U.S. Supreme Court ruling on *Webster v. Reproductive Services* in effect flashed a green light to those states seeking to strictly regulate abortion procedures. In *Webster,* the court threw out the trimester framework established in the landmark 1973 *Roe v. Wade* decision, which permitted states to regulate abortions only after the first trimester, and to ban them only in the last. The case upholds Missouri's law declaring that life begins at conception and that physicians must carry out extensive tests before performing many second trimes-

ter abortions. Furthermore, *Webster* extended government control of private abortion facilities by upholding Missouri's ban on the use of public facilities for abortion.

Not since the Vietnam era has a single issue so polarized public opinion in the United States. For abortion-rights activists, *Webster* has been the equivalent of the Tet Offensive, galvanizing supporters in much the same way that battle rallied opponents of the Vietnam War. State election gains in November 1989 by candidates supporting abortion rights indicate that the long-somnolent pro-choice majority may finally have awakened. But, the zeal and dedication of a highly organized pro-life minority ensures that the fight over reproductive freedom is far from over.

A careful examination of trends in Romania, the United States, and other countries illuminates several important points about the global abortion debate. One is that, against the backdrop of a general liberalization of abortion laws, events in several countries reveal an ominous undertow eroding recently codified reproductive rights. Two, abortion politics has become deadlocked in a no-win dispute over the ideology and criminology of abortion procedures, resulting in a tug-of-war over laws that don't even begin to address the complex social phenomenon of abortion. Three, this dispute postpones the day when the energies of both the pro-choice and pro-life camps can be directed

From *World•Watch,* March/April 1990, pp. 31-38. *World•Watch,* published by Worldwatch Institute, Washington, D.C.

fully toward improving the health and welfare of women and children worldwide.

The Issue that Knows No Compromise

In legalizing abortion, Romania joins some 35 other countries that have made similar changes since the late-1970s. In fact, a 30-year tide of liberalization in laws governing family planning has increased access to contraceptives and made abortions safer for millions of women worldwide. As a result, the relative number of unintended pregnancies and deaths due to illegal abortion procedures has dropped in many countries.

But groups vociferously opposed to abortion—and, in many cases, to family planning methods altogether—have kept up their fight to reverse these policies. The U.S. decision, the first major success of the "pro-life" movement, sent shock waves through the ranks of activists in Western Europe, where the abortion debate has been far less emotional than in the United States but is becoming more polarized. Europeans from both camps have described the decision as a "wind from the west." While European pro-life groups have been "in the doldrums for a number of years . . . supporters are [now] heartened by what has taken place in the United States [and are] back in business," declares Bill Sherwin, executive secretary of the International Right to Life Federation in Rome.

The struggle over abortion rights is now a cross-border affair, with money and anti-abortion protestors crossing the Atlantic from the U.S. to Europe. According to Leonora Lloyd, director of the pro-choice National Abortion Campaign in London, Operation Rescue, a group that has been linked to violent tactics, is sending its organizers to England and elsewhere. Abortion-rights activists in Canada, France, Italy, Spain, and West Germany are gearing up for renewed battle.

Pro-life activists from the U.S. and Europe are supporting the growth of parallel movements in developing countries. Their agenda focuses on maintaining or reinstating restrictive abortion laws rather than providing couples with the means to prevent unintended pregnancy. However, studies show that millions of Third World couples still lack access to birth control. Not surprisingly, poor women suffer the highest rates of death due to complications of pregnancy and illegal abortion. In 1989, the anti-abortion group Human Life International held its first international conference in Zambia, a country with one of Africa's most liberal reproductive rights policies. Representatives of this group are suspected of starting a widespread disinformation campaign about locally available contraceptives, causing a great deal of confusion and anguish on the part of women relying on these methods.

Unanswered Questions

In many ways, the goals of pro-life activists raise more questions than they answer. For example, why are so-called pro-life forces so blind to the public health toll of illegal abortion?

Illegal abortion represents a global public health problem of tremendous proportions. Estimates indicate that about 55 million unwanted pregnancies end in abortion every year, nearly half of which are illegal operations carried out mostly in the Third World. The World Health Organization (WHO) attributes the loss of roughly 200,000 women's lives annually to illegal abortions, most of which are performed by unskilled attendants under unsanitary conditions, or are self-inflicted with hangers, knitting needles, toxic herbal teas and the like. What is more, for every woman who dies, many others suffer serious, often long-term health consequences.

By contrast, modern abortion procedures performed under proper medical supervision in countries where they are legal are among the safest of all medical procedures. In the United States, for instance, an early abortion procedure is 11 times safer than a tonsillectomy or childbirth.

Why focus on banning abortions when evidence overwhelmingly indicates that this is not the answer to the problem? History has proven that laws cannot eliminate abortions, they can only make them more or less safe and costly. Try as it might, no government has ever legislated abortion out of existence.

In Ceausescu's Romania, for example, reproductive repression was as widespread as economic privation. No woman under the age of 45 with less than five children could obtain a legal abortion. A special arm of the secret police force Securitate, dubbed the "Pregnancy Police," administered monthly checkups to female workers. Pregnant women were monitored, married women who did not conceive were kept under surveillance, and a special tax was levied on unmarried people over 25 and childless couples that could not give a medical reason for infertility.

Despite the law, data show that in the 1980s Romania's birthrate fell before rising again later, and that the country outranked virtually all other European nations on rates of abortion and abortion-related maternal mortality. One survey showed that Bucharest Municipal Hospital alone dealt with 3,000 failed abortions last year; still other sources indicate that well over 1,000 women died within that city each year due to complications of botched abortions. Legalization of abortion in Western Europe, by contrast, has produced the world's lowest abortion-related mortality rates. In several of these countries, public education efforts on planned

---

*G*iven
*pro-life groups' desire to
ban or restrict contraceptives,
how do they propose to
reduce the incidence
of abortion?*

---

parenthood have precipitated a fall in the number of abortions.

Why are pro-life groups opposed to programs most likely to prevent the greatest number of abortions? The best way to reduce the number of abortions and unintended pregnancies is to support a comprehensive family planning and health program that educates couples about birth control and lets them know where to get it. Epidemiological and social studies show conclusively that family planning improves the health of women and families most effectively by preventing the most dangerous pregnancies — those that occur in women too young or too old to carry safely to term, and those that come within 24 months of a prior birth.

Family planning also affords people the means with which to exercise their basic human right to determine the number and spacing of their children. The benefits extend to children because infants who are

adequately spaced tend to be better nourished and cared for than those following close on the heels of their siblings. These facts notwithstanding, pro-life groups in the United States and elsewhere have been the most vocal opponents of strategies that would reduce the number of unintended pregnancies and abortions and improve overall family health.

Politicking by pro-life groups led the United States to dramatically restructure and limit its involvement in international family planning efforts. The Reagan administration ended U.S. leadership on international family planning efforts with the announcement of a new policy stance at the 1984 International Conference on Population in Mexico City. This policy, developed under heavy lobbying from groups opposed to family planning in general, cut off U.S. funds to any private voluntary group that provides abortion services or counseling, even though a law banning the use of U.S. funds for abortions abroad was already on the books and had been stringently enforced since 1973. Blacklisted agencies include the well-respected International Planned Parenthood Federation (IPPF) and United Nations Population Fund.

Unfortunately, this turnabout has curtailed IPPF plans to expand the number of family planning clinics around the world to cope with a growing number of couples of reproductive age. At the same time, the research, development and marketing of low-cost, long-acting contraceptives, such as implants and injectables, has also been slowed. Similar efforts in the United States and Europe have resulted in costly legal battles over family planning funds, as well as research and development of drugs such as RU-486, which terminates pregnancy in its earliest stages, when abortions are least controversial.

Given the fact that many pro-life groups harbor a strong desire to ban or restrict contraceptive methods now on the market, eliminate contraceptive research and development, and scuttle family planning altogether, just how would they propose to reduce the incidence of abortion?

If the pro-life lobby were successful in severely restricting birth control and abortion in many countries, how would it propose to deal with the regional disparities between population and resources? Without abortion as a backup to the failure, ineffective use, or total lack of birth control methods, just how would the world deal with 55 million additional (and unwanted) pregnancies each year? More fundamental to the debate perhaps is the question of how will women, forced to bear children they do not want, ever really achieve their potential as individuals?

Abortion Laws, Worldwide

"Pro-choice" or "pro-life," few people would disagree with the idea that reducing the number of unintended pregnancies and abortions worldwide, and attempting to ensure that the largest share of abortions are carried out in the first trimester, when they are safest and least controversial, is a desirable public policy goal. Ironically, few countries have worked wholeheartedly towards this end.

The majority of the world's people now live in countries that have moved from blanket prohibition of abortion to a more reasoned acceptance of its role as a backup to contraceptive failure and unwanted pregnancy. The debate in these countries has evolved from whether or not to legalize abortions to just under what circumstances they should be available. Still, most countries relegate abortion to the criminal code, rather than dealing with it comprehensively as a public health problem.

The trend toward liberalization began in full force in the 1950s, as recognition of the need to reduce maternal mortality and promote reproductive freedom became widespread. Social justice was also an issue. Bringing abortion into the public domain reduced the disparity between those who could afford adequate medical care and those forced to resort to unsafe practitioners.

Most countries have enacted abortion laws within their criminal codes, using traditional legal justifications to indicate the actual circumstances under which abortions can be legally performed. Countries with the narrowest laws restrict abortion to cases where pregnancy poses a risk to a woman's life, although most include cases of rape or incest. Other laws consider risks to physical and mental health; still others the case of a severely impaired fetus. Some societies condone abortion for what are known as "social" reasons, as in cases where an additional childbirth will inflict undue burdens on a woman's existing family. Broadest are the laws that recognize contraceptive failure, or a simple request (usually within the first trimester), as

sound basis for abortion. Most governments leave specific interpretations (how to define "health") up to the discretion of the medical community.

According to Rebecca Cook, professor of law at the University of Toronto, several of the 35 countries that liberalized their laws since 1977 created new categories, such as adolescence, advanced maternal age, or infection with the AIDS virus, as a basis for legal abortion. Cyprus, Italy and Taiwan, for example, all broadened their laws to consider "family welfare," while Hong Kong recognized adolescence. France and the Netherlands have included clauses pertaining to pregnancy-related distress. In Hungary, one of the first Eastern European countries to liberalize abortion laws, abortion rights are extended to pregnant women who are single or have been separated from their husbands for a period of six months, to women over the age of 35 with at least three previous deliveries, and to women caught in economic hardship, such as the lack of appropriate housing.

Even countries with the most liberal laws recognize some constraints on a woman's right to abortion. Generally speaking, abortions are least regulated during the first trimester of pregnancy, during which most liberal codes permit abortion on-request. In Singapore, for example, abortions are available upon request until the 24th week of pregnancy, while in Turkey only until the 10th week. A woman seeking to terminate a pregnancy after this period must show just cause under the law.

A recent review of international abortion policy data by the Washington-based Population Crisis Committee indicates that about 75 percent of the world's population (3.9 billion out of 5.2 billion people) live in countries that permit abortion on medical or broader social and economic grounds. In Ethiopia and Costa Rica, for example, abortion is legal only in cases of risk to the woman's health, while in Tunisia it is available on-request until the 12th week of pregnancy and in Taiwan on-request until the fetus can live outside the womb (otherwise known as viability, the stage between the 24th and 28th weeks of pregnancy). Another 20 percent live in 49 countries in which abortion is totally prohibited or is legal only to save the life of the mother. The category includes much of Africa, Latin America and Muslim Asia. Unfortunately, these are also countries where women have the least access to safe, affordable means of contraception. The remaining 5 percent of the world's people are governed by laws that have added rape and incest to this fairly restrictive list.

Bucking the liberalization trend are Finland, Honduras, Iran, Ireland, Israel, New Zealand and now the United States. Abortion laws in this group have become more restrictive since 1977. A Honduran law permitting abortions in cases where they would protect the life and health of the mother and in cases of rape and fetal deformity was rejected because it was perceived to conflict with constitutional provisions stating that the "right to life is inviolable."

Likewise, changes in the constitutions of Ecuador (1978) and the Philippines (1986) incorporated provisions according the right to life "from the moment of conception." Some of these changes have ambiguous implications. Chile's constitution, for example, protects not only the right to life and to physical and psychic integrity of individuals, but also of those "about to be born." Whether or not an embryo or 10-week-old fetus is "about to be born" remains unclear.

Because many nations' legal codes reflect social ambivalence about abortion, what happens in practice often does not reflect the law on the books. In some countries where abortion is illegal in principle, it is carried out quite freely in practice. Conversely, in other countries where women hold the legal right to abortion on demand, they find it difficult to actually procure one because of local opposition or reluctance to carry out national laws. Such is the case in the Bavarian region of West Germany, where local officials have sought to circumvent national abortion rights laws.

"Liberal" laws themselves do not always safeguard a woman's ability to exercise abortion rights. A pervasive problem is that while many countries have liberalized their laws, they have not gone so far as to commit public resources to providing safe abortion services, nor do most countries mandate widespread access.

Some laws work against the goal of ensuring that when abortions do occur they are carried out at the earliest possible point. New laws in Bermuda, Kuwait, the Seychelles and Qatar include hospital committee authorization requirements before an abortion can be performed. Yet, in most cases,

these regulations, strongly supported by the pro-life community, act only to delay abortions until later stages of pregnancy, when procedures are riskier and the fetus is more developed. Such institutional and third-party authorization requirements have come under legal attack in many countries and been struck down in several, including Canada and Czechoslovakia. Unfortunately, several U.S. states may soon enact such restrictions.

The resolution of other issues under debate in countries throughout the world could have a negative effect on abortion rights. They are: when and to what extent government health-care programs should cover the costs of legal abortion; whether or not a husband's consent or notification should be required before a married woman can obtain an abortion; and whether or not laws should condition adolescent abortions on parental notification.

The question is, Will the same forces responsible for the U.S. *Webster* decision be successful in turning back the clock in other countries? The social impacts of setting limits on family planning options are likely to be staggering. Apart from the immediate health impacts of illegal abortion, experience in a number of countries shows that forcing women to carry pregnancies to term results in higher rates of infanticide, greater numbers of abandoned and neglected children, and, particularly in the Third World, a decline in health and nutritional standards. In Romania, the numbers of abandoned and neglected children soared after abortion and contraception were outlawed. Similar trends have been documented in African and Latin American countries.

A Prescription to Reduce Abortion

Only by making contraceptives safer and more available, increasing access to family planning information and supplies, and teaching children the concept of responsible parenthood will the number of unintended pregnancies and abortions be reduced. Abortion, however, will never disappear. Activists and policymakers need to begin rejecting fixed but unfounded notions about the ideology and criminality of abortion in favor of a more rational understanding of its role in the spectrum of choices within a comprehensive family planning program. In effect, this would be a strategy based on the notion that prevention is better than cure.

The first step is to remove abortion from the criminal code and address it as a public health problem. A few countries—China, Togo and Vietnam—have already done so. In Cuba, abortion is considered a criminal offense only when it is performed for profit, by an unqualified person, in an unofficial place, or without the woman's consent.

Second, mobilize support for family planning programs. According to Rebecca Cook, a number of countries have taken this positive step by setting up programs aimed at reducing the incidence of unwanted pregnancy. Some countries now require post-abortion contraceptive counseling and education, and some mandate programs for men, too. Italy now requires local and regional health authorities to promote contraceptive services and other measures to reduce demand for abortion, while Czech law aims to prevent abortion through sex education in schools and health facilities and provides for free contraceptive and associated care. Turkish law provides access to voluntary sterilization as well as to abortion.

These efforts have been successful. On the Swedish island of Gotland, abortions were almost halved in an intensive three-year program to provide information and improved family planning services. Similar results have been shown in France and elsewhere.

Third, provide support and funding for international contraceptive research and development. Making contraceptives safer, more affordable, and more widely available will reduce the need for abortions around the world.

Fourth, target high-risk groups with education programs. In the United States, for example, lack of education on family planning methods leads to one of the highest rates of unintended pregnancy among teenagers in the industrial world. That group undergoes about one-third of all abortions each year. It's no coincidence that U.S. teens lag far behind their Western European counterparts in knowledge of contraception. A common myth perpetuated by the pro-life movement is that sex education, including family planning information, leads to teen promiscuity. Data from the Alan Guttmacher Institute and elsewhere show the reverse is true.

The impact of unwanted pregnancies extends beyond the individual to encompass public health and the question of sustainable development. An international consensus among a diverse body of policymakers already exists on the adverse effects of rapid population growth on economic performance, the environment, family welfare, health, and political stability. If minimizing population-related problems is an international priority, as has been accepted by a number of U.N. legal conventions, then it is essential that abortion be available as a birth control method of last resort.

The success of abortion-rights activists throughout the world will depend on their ability to make clear that abortion is a social reality that cannot be erased by legal code. Obviously, the ideal situation would be to eliminate all unintended pregnancies. In the real world, though, limited access to birth control and the inevitability of contraceptive failure, either through imperfect technologies or human error, means that unplanned pregnancies will continue to occur.

Teenage Birth's New Conceptions

SUMMARY: There's no denying teenage pregnancy is a problem, but new studies show that many notions about the problem may be wrong. A famous study found, for example, that most young mothers adapt well to parenthood. The real problem may not be teen births but out-of-wedlock births. These and other findings raise the issue of whether public policy regarding family planning needs to be refocused. Some scholars say it would be better to give young families more support.

The girl who has an illegitimate child at the age of 16 suddenly has 90 percent of her life's script written for her. She will probably drop out of school; even if someone else in her family helps to take care of the baby, she will probably not be able to find a steady job that pays enough to provide for herself and her child; she may feel impelled to marry someone she might not otherwise have chosen. Her life choices are few, and most of them are bad.

These three sentences, from a 1968 article by sociologist Arthur A. Campbell, are the most famous words ever written about teenage pregnancy. Widely disseminated, they formed the philosophical basis for more than two decades of efforts of education, subsidization, exhortation and persuasion to get teenage girls not to have babies.

A massive 1987 report by the National Research Council, "Risking the Future: Adolescent Sexuality, Pregnancy and Childbearing," listed a litany of the "personal and public costs" of adolescent pregnancy; they included "discontinued education," "reduced employment opportunities," "unstable marriages," "low income," "frustration" and "hopelessness." The report called for intensifying a variety of preventive strategies, from promotion of contraceptives to the now-popular concept of "life options" or self-esteem programs designed to encourage teenagers to delay sex. Other reports appear periodically that try to calculate the cost to taxpayers of adolescent childbearing in terms of welfare and Medicaid benefits.

A network of advocacy organizations has grown up around the issue: the Urban Institute, the Children's Defense Fund, the Center for Population Options, the Planned Parenthood Federation of America and its research affiliate, the Alan Guttmacher Institute. The position shared by most members of these groups is that what teenagers need is the right kind of information and access to contraceptive technology — "getting to them," in the words of Martha Burt, a researcher for the Washington-based Urban Institute. The answer, to Burt and others, is a program or series of programs that would get birth control into teenagers' hands, show them how to use it and make sure they follow through.

A 1976 pamphlet from the Guttmacher Institute added the word "epidemic" to the national vocabulary as a way of talking about teenage pregnancy. It was titled "11 Million Teenagers: What Can Be Done About the Epidemic of Adolescent Pregnancy in the United States." The 11 million represented the 4 million girls and 7 million boys the institute believed were "sexually active" — that is, who had had sexual intercourse at some time between ages 15 and 19. "Adolescent pregnancy is a problem our nation can no longer afford to ignore," the pamphlet declared. More Guttmacher reports appeared: "Teenage Pregnancy: The Problem That Hasn't Gone Away" in 1981, and "Teenage Pregnancy in the United States: The Scope of the Problem and State Responses" last year.

The publications spawned a spate of media accounts of "babies having babies." In 1974, only five states and the District of Columbia mandated sex education in public schools. By 1989, 16 states and the District required the courses and 24 others encouraged school districts to offer them. In an effort to make contraception even more accessible to adolescents, about 150 junior and senior high schools since the early 1980s have set up school-based clinics that either dispense birth control or refer youngsters to off-premises sources.

The federal government has similarly responded. In 1970, two years after Campbell wrote his famous words, Congress passed Title 10 of the Family Planning Services and Population Research Act, providing for federally subsidized birth control; Title 10 funds now go mostly for minors. A 1974 law denied federal funds to school districts that discriminated against pregnant girls.

The Adolescent Health Care, Services and Pregnancy Prevention Act of 1978, passed after Health, Education and Welfare Secretary Joseph Califano declared teenage pregnancy the nation's top domestic policy priority, funded a range of support systems for teenage mothers, along with more family planning funding, and set up the Office of Adolescent Pregnancy Programs as a new government agency. The Adolescent Family Life Act of 1980 also subsidizes services for pregnant teenagers as well as prevention programs that mostly stress abstinence from sex. During the peak years of federal support for teenage pregnancy programs, the late 1970s and early 1980s, the government spent about $300 million a year on such programs. The spending level has since dropped to about $150 million.

There is only one problem, a number of scholars have argued: None of these commonly held assumptions is exactly true. Just for starters, the peak year for teenage childbearing was not in the 1960s or 1970s. It was in 1957. That year, the fertility rate was 97.3 births per 1,000 females 19 or younger. By 1977, it had fallen to 52.8 births, and to 51.1 births in 1987 — a fertility decline of almost 50 percent over 30 years. The gross number of such births has also shrunk each year as the number of teenagers has declined with the passing of the baby boom. In 1987, 462,312 teenagers gave birth, and by 1992, the U.S. Census Bureau estimates, there will be 420,000 births to teens if the fertility rate continues at present levels. About 10 percent of girls get pregnant at some time between age 13 and 19; half give birth, 40 percent have abortions and the rest miscarry. This has

coincided with a general decline in fertility for all age groups and races. (The teen fertility rate for blacks in particular has also declined, though far more slowly than for whites, and it remains, at 89.7, twice as high as that for whites.) At the current fertility rate, a woman can expect to have 1.9 children, which is lower than the population replacement level of 2.1.

Of the births to younger teenagers, only

10,000 each year are to girls younger than 15, a number that has stayed constant for about a decade. Research shows that these births reflect a significant number of pregnancies brought about by rape or incest. All 462,312 adolescent births in 1987 represented just 12 percent of the total number of births in the United States that year (in 1973, 20 percent of births were to teens).

The other demographic fact is that two-

An Assignment Leads to a Surprising Conclusion

In 1984, a journalist named Leon Dash got an assignment to write about teenage pregnancy. Like most people, he thought that ignorance about reproduction and contraception was at the root of it. To do his research, the Washington Post reporter spent a year living in Washington Highlands, a neighborhood he selected because a census map showed that it had more teenage parents than almost any other neighborhood in the District of Columbia.

Few even among city natives have ever heard of Washington Highlands, which is separated physically from the rest of the District by the Anacostia River and a series of winding roads. The chief architectural feature of this Southeast Washington neighborhood is the run-down public housing project in a variety of styles dating from the late 1940s, each project building separated from the other by vast expanses of overgrown grass and bare ground.

"I began my research into adolescent childbearing burdened with adult preconceptions," Dash wrote in "When Children Want Children: The Urban Crisis of Teenage Childbearing," the 1989 book about his experiences. He continued: "I assumed that the high incidence of teenage pregnancy among poor, black urban youths nationwide grew out of youthful ignorance both about birth control methods and adolescent reproductive capabilities. . . . I was wrong on all counts."

Ignorance, contraceptive failure, seduction by more sophisticated older boys — those were the stories the girls gave adults they encountered in official contexts, including Dash himself. But after interviewing his subjects for more than 30 hours apiece over the course of a year, during which he won their trust, the young mothers started pouring out different stories. They had wanted to get pregnant, they confessed, sometimes playing the sexual aggressor to lure bashful boyfriends into bed, sometimes deceiving them into thinking they were using birth control.

"They were all very well-versed in sex education, and those who didn't want children didn't have them," says Dash. The District of Columbia is one of 17 jurisdictions that make sex education mandatory in

public schools and one of four that require teachers to pass a course in human sexuality as a prerequisite for teaching it.

"These girls became mothers to be affirmed as women," says Dash. "In my estimate, it was not a wise decision, but it doesn't have anything to do with sex education. It has to do with the poor academic education they were receiving. Most were doing very poorly in school, and they had been told they had a poor chance of finishing. In their perception, there was no need to postpone motherhood and fatherhood. Being a mother meant becoming a woman, and being a father meant becoming a man."

"Mr. Dash, will you please stop asking me about birth control?" an exasperated 16-year-old Tauscha Vaughn begged him. "Girls out here know all about birth control. There's too many birth control pills out here. All of them know about it. Even when they twelve, they know what [birth control] is."

Dash's book depicts its youthful subjects not as hapless points on a graph of social trends but as functioning moral agents, even though many of the decisions they made would be considered wrong, unwise and immature by most people's standards.

Growing up amid poverty, poor education, family disorder and degradation, they were not themselves degraded. One girl, Sherita Dreher, at 14 saw her mother die of cancer and at 15 gave birth to a son. She then found herself at 16 abandoned by her entire family including her father and two brothers. The father of her child was in a youth detention center; his next stop was a six-year prison term for armed robbery. In a gesture of generosity, Sherita's father's ex-wife took the girl and her son into her already overcrowded apartment, giving them a home.

Dash's interviews provide an explanation why, although black teenagers have an abortion rate twice as high as that of white teenagers because of an overall higher pregnancy rate, the percentage of pregnant teenagers who have abortions is far lower for blacks than for whites (44 percent for nonwhites vs. 64 percent for whites, according to a 1989 report from the Alan

Guttmacher Institute). "If I could breathe into dirt like God does and make a life, then I feel I would have the authority to take a life," declared Sheila Matthews, age 15 and six months pregnant.

After another year of research, Dash sought to trace these underclass patterns of childbearing to the backbreaking exigencies of life for their sharecropper ancestors in the South. Early fertility and large families were essential for sharecroppers as in all peasant cultures, where children take on adult responsibilities early, where there is little premium on formal education and where all hands are needed to help in the fields. Dash believes these cultural patterns persist to this day.

Dash's book, recently reissued as a paperback, has received mixed reviews from social scientists.

"It's interesting journalism, but it's not scholarly research," says Maris Vinovskis, a history professor at the University of Michigan who served as an adolescent-pregnancy consultant for the Reagan administration. "I don't think the scholarship supports his conclusions," he says. "I don't think that sex and family life education deters pregnancy, and I think we put too much faith in education. But most teenagers don't want to get pregnant."

"He's raised an age-old issue," says Donna Franklin, a professor of social services administration at the University of Chicago. Franklin has made Dash's book required reading in her classes. "His results need to be addressed with a more rigorous methodology. We need to know to what extent women get pregnant by choice before we take all our money and put it into a massive family planning campaign as we did during the Sixties and Seventies. If pregnancy is a function of poverty or the culture of poverty, then the policy implications are very different."

Dash is unfazed at the so-so reception his book has received in the world of teenage-pregnancy professionals. "I find that academics generally write for each other, using the language and jargon of their disciplines," he says. "I wrote my book for the public."

thirds of all teenage births are to young women age 18 and 19, women who have graduated from high school (or dropped out), are old enough to vote and are legally adults. Half of all teenagers who give birth are married; in rural areas and among Hispanics, youthful marriages are common. Those marriages can be fragile, but a 1986 study showed that after 10 years, three-fourths of teenage marriages to legitimate babies were intact among whites and half among blacks.

And, it is likely that almost every American had a mother, grandmother or great-grandmother who first gave birth as a teenager and turned out just fine. During the 1920s, the adolescent childbearing rate was exactly what it is today, and few teenage mothers finished high school; no one worried about them. Rosalynn Carter was 18 when she bore her first child.

The reason teenage childbearing today looks like an "epidemic" and a major social problem but did not in 1957 or 1937 may be due to one crucial difference: the fact that nearly all teenage births 30 years ago took place in marriage. Of babies born out of wedlock, 50 percent were relinquished for adoption in 1970; now, 90 percent of unmarried mothers raise their babies.

There is very little research correlating a mother's marital status to social and medical problems for her children such as poor nutrition, low school attainment, delinquency and crime. One scholar who has looked at the numbers, Nick Eberstadt of the American Enterprise Institute, says birth out of wedlock is the key predictor for later trouble, whether the mother is in her teens, her early 20s — the peak fertility years in which childbearing occurs — or even older.

"It doesn't matter what the mother's socioeconomic status is or her race," says Eberstadt. Ninety percent of teenage births to blacks now take place out of wedlock (compared with 47 percent 20 years ago). But the fastest rise in out-of-wedlock births has been among whites. In general, illegitimate births rose 40 percent from 1980 to 1987, accompanied by a decline in the marriage rate during the same period; the number of cohabiting unmarried couples quintupled as a proportion of all couples in 1970-1988. Furthermore, a number of sociological studies have shown Campbell's deterministic assumptions — that having a baby as a teenager automatically ruins a woman's life — to be far from the mark.

The most famous work of scholarship on teen pregnancy is an ongoing longitudinal study of 400 teenage mothers in Baltimore from the late 1960s to date by Frank F. Furstenberg Jr., a sociology professor at the University of Pennsylvania. Although he described adolescent pregnancy as "a social problem," he also found that most of the mothers adapted successfully to motherhood and that 70 percent were married five years later. Their children lagged in

school, but Furstenberg suggested that might be due to economic disadvantage. He also found relatively low rates of long-term welfare dependency among teenage mothers. Only one-fourth were on welfare when their children were born, and most were back in the work force by the time their youngest child was 3. Furthermore, Furstenberg found that only one-third of the daughters of women who bore their first child as teens became teenage mothers.

More recent studies further bolster the notion that teenage pregnancy per se is not the precipitator of social problems. Dawn M. Upchurch, a health policy professor at Johns Hopkins University, and James McCarthy, a public health professor at Columbia University, issued a paper early this year concluding that teenage mothers are no more likely to drop out of school than teens who did not have babies, although girls who bore a child after dropping out of school were less likely to return than their childless peers. In November, Steven D. McLaughlin, a researcher at the Battelle Human Affairs Research Centers in Seattle, issued results of a longitudinal study showing that the self-esteem of adolescent mothers who kept their babies was about the same as that of teens who relinquished their infants for adoption (the mothers who relinquished did somewhat better financially and educationally, however).

In March, two University of Washington researchers, Shelly Lundberg and Robert D. Plotnick, delivered a paper to a Health and Human Services Department-sponsored forum on the underclass reporting that for black women, having a child before age 19 has no effect on earning potential. In fact, black women, married or not, who start having children in adolescence can expect to earn 14 percent more during their 20s than black women who postpone childbirth until that decade. For disadvantaged black women, the earnings gap is 21 percent if the child is out of wedlock, 29 percent if the woman is married when she has her first child. "Our study is still ongoing, and it's still too early to say why this is," says Lundberg. For whites, bearing a child out of wedlock during adolescence does carry an earnings penalty — but a low 14 percent.

On Feb. 16, a grenade landed in the debate. A 33-year-old assistant professor of public health policy at the University of Michigan, Arline T. Geronimus, made a three-hour presentation to the American Association for the Advancement of Science. Her findings reflected research on the health of adolescent mothers and their infants that she had already published in two papers and expects to publish soon in two more. She declared that, because poor women, especially poor black women, are healthier in their adolescence than they are during their 20s and very poor women have little to lose by having babies early — indeed, might have a network of kinfolk to

help them — teenage childbearing makes adaptive sense for the impoverished, just as it does in poor countries where life expectancy is short (in Bangladesh, more than 85 percent of women bear their first child while in their teens).

"I would like to go on the record today in opposition to the view that teen childbearing is self-destructive, irrational or antisocial," Geronimus declared. "Stopping teen pregnancies buys them nothing. In fact, it may even harm them."

Her presentation drew quick and hostile responses from the advocacy establishment. "Her facts are misrepresentative, her premise is wrong and the policy implications of her arguments are perverse," Karen Pittman of the Children's Defense Fund told The New York Times. "She might be right from the teenager's point of view, but the public costs are still there," says researcher Burt of the Urban Institute. In a letter to The Washington Post, Rosann Wisman, executive director of Planned Parenthood's District of Columbia office, accused Geronimus of ignoring "uncontradicted data" showing that "for most adolescent families, becoming a parent is detrimental to the health and welfare of both the teenage mother and her child."

"We have an almost ideological disapproval of teen childbirth," says Geronimus. "We don't as a society have a meaningful role for young people to play. We think that the meaningful role for them is to be in college, but for poor women, college is not a meaningful option. They talk about having children in very positive terms. I've found from talking to them that they find raising children to be very meaningful work. They have grown up having to care for younger children, and they know how to take care of babies."

What Geronimus is saying is that adolescent childbearing is a phenomenon of the poor and the very poor, of young women who grow up early and look their best when they are young, have little interest in higher education, do not see themselves as having careers and live in communities where health starts deteriorating quickly. The "opportunity costs" — forgone earnings potential — of having a child early are close to nil, and life expectancy is short.

Teenage girls with college and career aspirations typically choose abortion — or their mothers choose it for them — when they get pregnant, and they are from the same highly motivated socioeconomic group that uses contraception faithfully. If the United States had the same social homogeneity as, say, Canada, it is likely the nation would have the same teenage fertility rate as well, which is one-half that of the United States.

If Geronimus and others such as Upchurch, McCarthy and Lundberg are right, teenage childbearing does not so much cause poverty as grow out of poverty. The rate for blacks is twice that for whites because blacks constitute the highest proportion of the urban underclass. And if early childbearing is associated with such negative consequences as drugs and low-birth-weight infants, it is because such things are endemic in poverty as well. In fact, the difference in the neonatal death rate — the rate of babies who die between birth and four weeks — for infants born to teenage mothers and to mothers age 25 to 29 disappears when the numbers are adjusted for socioeconomic status, Geronimus says.

If this research is correct, a public policy overwhelmingly oriented toward teaching high school students how to use birth control — viewing teen pregnancy as a problem of ignorance that information can solve — may be on the wrong track. A series of research papers in the mid-1980s by Douglas Kirby of the Washington-based Center for Population Options concluded that sex education in school had no effect on adolescent contraceptive use, and a report last year by Kirby on school-based clinics showed similar findings. Only one experiment, by Johns Hopkins University demographer Laurie Schwab Zabin, indicated that an off-the-premises clinic for high school and junior high school students produced dramatic decreases in pregnancy. But Zabin's research has been faulted as using a hit-or-miss approach that did not follow through on specific populations.

Even at the New York City-based Guttmacher Institute, a leading proponent of education and contraception as the way to reduce adolescent pregnancy, there has been some rethinking. "Most of the programs we have had have been preaching sex education," says Jeannie I. Rosoff, the institute's president. "We now know that increasing knowledge does not necessarily affect behavior. But sex education is something we know how to do."

A better approach, some scholars say, would be to focus on policies to strengthen young families. One theory, by Maris Vinovskis, a University of Michigan professor and adolescent-pregnancy consultant during the Carter and Reagan years, is not to discourage pregnant teens from getting married (now, the prevailing wisdom is against youthful marriages on the theory that they will not last). "It's too easy to give up on fathers and say, 'What's the use?'" says P. Lindsay Chase-Lansdale, a researcher at the University of Chicago's Chapin Hall Center for Children, who collaborated with Vinovskis on a policy paper encouraging stronger efforts to collect child support from young fathers (1988 welfare reforms went in this direction).

The boys who father children with teens tend to be a few years older than the girls — and thus higher earners. Most are in their 20s, with an average earning capacity that is above the poverty level and steadily rises, according to a study by Robert Lerman, a sociologist at American University.

Preaching "morality" at teenagers as a way to reduce pregnancy is also frowned upon in these nonjudgmental days; young people are supposed to find the very idea of morality laughable. But the best indicator these days for not getting pregnant as a teenager is membership in a fundamentalist Protestant church that teaches in no-nonsense fashion that sex outside marriage is a sin. A study by Sandra Hofferth, an Urban Institute researcher, shows a direct correlation between weekly attendance at religious services and delayed sexual activity.

Finally, says Lerman, making a place for teens as productive members of society — perhaps via apprenticeships — would encourage them to think of themselves more maturely. After all, the 19th century sculptor Vinnie Ream was 18 when she chiseled a statue of Abraham Lincoln for the U.S. Capitol, and Joan of Arc was burned at the stake at 19. But today, many middle-class young people do not consider themselves grown-up and ready for adult responsibilities until they reach 30 or so. "I read a study that described a 25-year-old as an adolescent," says Joseph Adelson, a University of Michigan psychologist. That leaves lower-income teenagers without anything at all that is socially acceptable to do.

"People project on poor teenagers what a middle-class teenager would want — going to the senior prom, getting into the best college," says Geronimus. "We have sort of assumed that no teenager would ever want to have a child. In fact, most teenagers at this point in history don't want to become mothers, and for those teens, sex education and contraception may be the best approach. But bear in mind that poor men die much younger — I think the life expectancy in Harlem is lower than it is in Bangladesh — and there are high rates of joblessness. You just can't postpone forever the bearing of children.

"I think that people ought to stop focusing on teen childbearing as the cause of all the problems of the underclass," she says. "These are young women who are trying to do the best they can under adverse hardships in a dangerous community. We can't just sit back and say to them that it's their fault for having babies young."

— *Charlotte Low Allen*

Teenage pregnancy in New York

César A. Chelala

Argentine-born medical scientist writing from New York

An article in the Journal of the American Medical Association three years ago gave some welcome news on the adolescent pregnancy issue in the United States. Although the teenage pregnancy rate increased between 1974 and 1980, it declined between 1980 and 1983; there was a concomitant decline in the overall birth rate during that same period.

Compared to other developed countries, however, the US still has an unwelcome primacy. The teenage pregnancy rate in the United States is more than twice as high as that of Canada and the United Kingdom, and this difference is even more marked in comparison with the Netherlands. Although the pregnancy rates among black teenagers in the US are higher than among whites, these contrasts with other countries remain, even when only the white teenage population is considered. It is estimated that every year more than one million US teenagers become pregnant, and 30,000 among them are below 15 years of age.

The US also has primacy, over other countries at a similar stage of economic development, in respect of two other related indicators: the adolescent birth and abortion rates. The number of US adolescents per 1000 who give birth exceeds comparable figures in Canada, France, the Netherlands, Sweden and the United Kingdom. This fact is especially notable among younger teenagers. The adolescent abortion rate is increasing in the US, and close to 400,000 teenage pregnancies now end this way.

Several studies have identified a series of circumstances that place adolescents in a "high risk" category for becoming pregnant. They include not only individual factors but also those relating to the family, institutions and society. The analysis of these factors is important if we are to arrive at a better understanding of the problem, and to design effective prevention strategies.

Such an analysis is of importance not just to policy-makers in the US but to those in other countries too, since they are found to be similar whatever the context. Any variations are of a quantitative rather than a qualitative nature. Studying these factors can help to address specific policies aimed at alleviating the problem of teenage pregnancy, not only in industrialised countries but in the developing world as well.

Among the reasons that explain risk-taking behaviours among adolescents are a combination of many factors, which include lifestyles, individual circumstances, lack of experience to accurately measure risks and peer influence.

When parents are more involved with their children and have better communication with them, there is a delay in the initiation of sexual activity among teenagers. Two specialists in this field, S.L. Jessor and R. Jessor, have indicated that youngsters are more prone to fulfil their parents' expectations when their mutual relationship is rewarding and loving. Experts also believe that trust between adolescents and adults whom they love and respect can function as an effective deterrent to risk-taking behaviours.

Another important factor related to pregnancy in adolescents is the use of effective contraceptives. The Alan Guttmacher Institute in New York reports that in England and Wales, the Netherlands and Sweden contraceptive services are more accessible and contraceptive use is more widespread than in the US. Sweden was also the first country in the world with an official sex education curriculum in its schools, and there is a close connection between the schools and contraceptive services for adolescents.

Sexual activity in adolescents is related to other risk-taking behaviours as well; for instance, the abuse of alcohol or other drugs is likely to result in a greater level of sexual activity.

Poverty a factor

There is some evidence that poverty is another factor that may be associated with higher pregnancy rates for girls under 18. According to statistics reported in *Preventing adolescent pregnancies: what schools can do*, a publication of the Children's Defense Fund in Washington D.C., mothers aged 16 to 19 whose income levels and skills were below average considerably outnumbered those with average or above average incomes. Although there were differences according to ethnic background, the results were broadly similar.

Many adolescents of low social and economic level who become pregnant find themselves launched into a vicious cycle of poverty and cultural deprivation that tends to perpetuate their personal insecurity and despair.

Considering the multiple factors outlined above, adolescent pregnancy can be seen as a part of a larger group of problems some of which at least can be mitigated or even prevented.

Specifically in the case of adolescent pregnancy we now know that we need to include programmes and services for adolescent males, since their behaviour, motivation and attitudes are as crucial to the solution as that of their female partners. In general, boys are more ignorant than girls about sexuality, contraception and pregnancy.

One study found that teenage fathers themselves are often afflicted with a variety of personal problems that include unemployment, lack of housing and poor health. New strategies have to be devised by health educationists to reach them, especially since young men seem to be less aware of the implications of early parenthood than adolescent girls, and are less careful about trying to avoid it. In the particular context of New York, there are sensitive cultural and ethnic factors to be taken into account in trying to influence adolescent behaviour.

Similarly, we have to be cautious about blaming teenagers, even male teenagers. "I feel society has made victims out of these kids," says Alice Radosh, the Coordinator in the Office of the Mayor on Adolescent Pregnancy and Parenting Services in New York City. "They are scared, they are embarrassed, and they need all the help we can give them," she says.

One of the critical issues in dealing with adolescents today is how to approach the problems related to their sexuality. "The difficulty is adolescence, in which nature authorises what society forbids," said the French paediatrician Jean-Pierre Deschamps. Shall we ignore their sexual drives or shall we accept them as part of normal development? If we choose the latter, it follows that they should be taught how to integrate their sexuality in a healthy manner with other aspects of their developing sense of self. What we want for our children is that – whatever decision they take regarding their sex life – it should be as informed, mature and responsible as possible. Thus, rather than minimising adolescents' needs, we should apply proven strategies and plan new ones for the prevention of adolescent pregnancy.

For many years, there have been too few efforts specifically directed at the care of adolescents. Too young to be treated by the general practitioner, and believing themselves too old to seek the advice of the paediatrician, adolescents seemed to constitute an isolated generation. It is only in the past few decades that health and health-related personnel have been specially trained to deal with young people's problems. Because of the complexity of these problems, they require a variety of approaches that should have as a focus the development of a more positive and caring attitude of society towards adolescents.

Sex education is rarely given in US schools. Teachers need to be trained to convey the "right" messages to youngsters. School courses aimed at increasing young people's motivation towards responsible family behaviour should be added to more traditional approaches to education on sexual reproduction. Also important is the need to include appropriate recreational, job training and employment programmes that make use of the energy and enthusiasm of the youngsters.

Constancia Warren, from the Center for Public Advocacy Research in New York City, remarks: "Any long-term solution should be seen in the broader context of quality of youth life." Related to this approach is the need to offer youngsters possibilities for personal achievement, a fact that would bolster their confidence and self-esteem, and would take them away from a vicious cycle of despair. That is one of the conclusions of the Panel on Adolescent Pregnancy and Childbearing of the US National Research Council.

Challenge the teenagers

John A. Calhoun, executive director of the National Crime Prevention Council in Washington, D.C., suggests: "We should challenge teenagers, make them feel part of their communities and channel their energies to positive ends. What is needed is an approach that gives them the message that they are responsible and are needed."

Whether or not this approach of involving youngsters in community work has had any direct effect on pregnancy rates, it has already proved its worth. It has resulted in their participation in programmes such as the one in the South Bronx in New York City where, through a work-study programme, youngsters have rehabilitated a once drug-ridden park or are now working in anti-drug programmes or with the homeless. The Atlanta public school system now requires 75 hours of public service before graduation. Integrating adolescents as active participants in meaningful community work may give them a sense of value in society.

Adolescent pregnancy is a problem for New York and the United States that will not go away. It is one that will increasingly confront other countries, both rich and poor. However much the cultural circumstances differ from country to country, pursuing adequate policies and drawing up strategies in good time can significantly lessen the magnitude of the problem. Such policies and strategies will be not only the responsibility of the teenagers' parents but should involve the work of community, social and political leaders. Only by taking into consideration all the factors in this multi-faceted problem, and by acting with imagination and compassion, can we have hopes for a less troubled future.

sex during pregnancy

KIM BROWN FADER

Kim Brown Fader frequently writes on family topics for national magazines.

Isabelle and Kevin first met in a New York flower shop, and went home with more than roses. The intense physical attraction they felt lasted through several years of dating and the first few years of marriage. Then Isabelle got pregnant. "Suddenly—almost from the moment the pregnancy was confirmed—the sexual closeness we'd felt just evaporated," said Isabelle, twenty-six, then in the seventh month of her term. "It was as if someone turned a switch, and the attraction was gone."

"At first, we were both frightened that sex might cause a miscarriage, or somehow hurt the baby," she explained. "But by my tenth or twelfth week, when it was clear that the baby was okay, I thought things would get back to normal. They haven't. We make love sometimes, but Kevin is only going through the motions—the passion just isn't there."

It wasn't only in the bedroom that Isabelle felt deserted. She began to feel that she and her husband were in two different worlds. "In the evenings, I'm reading about childbirth and infant care, and he's reading about sailing in the South Seas," she said. "I thought that just as we used to go sailing together, we would now be preparing for the baby together. But instead I'm doing it alone."

Kevin, twenty-eight, felt equally deserted: "I used to be number one with Isabelle, and now I'm not. When it comes to anything having to do with the baby, she trusts the opinions of her mother, her friends and the authors of those books she's always reading more than she trusts mine. She's so wrapped up in herself, she doesn't even realize how much she's turned away from me."

Pregnancy produces sexual shock waves in many marriages, giving rise to unpredictable highs of lust and lows of disgust, new abandon and new inhibitions along with new concerns and preoccupations. And even if the couple is having a child precisely because their marriage is going well, pregnancy's barrage of unsettling emotions may upset the status quo, or even blow apart their sexual relationship.

The problem, one new father claims, is that both partners feel they deserve to be pampered—the woman because she's carrying the load, the man because he feels deprived of his wife's customary involvement in his life. "These stresses make it very difficult for either partner to be generous—in bed or out of it," this father says.

On the other hand, he says, a wife's pregnancy can also bring tremendous exhilaration and a new sexual high to the relationship. "There was a wonderful, luxurious feeling to my wife's body during her pregnancy; her hair was thicker and her breasts fuller. I felt possessive of her in a unique way, and proud to be responsible for her round stomach. These feelings tended to refuel our sexuality and bridge the distance we sometimes felt."

While some couples glide through pregnancy without a moment's bad temper, and others do nothing but suffer for nine months, most find that their experience falls somewhere in between: There are good weeks and bad. As the pregnancy progresses, many must constantly adjust and readjust to an ebb and flow of sexual desire.

"One week belly-patting nauseated me and the next week it didn't," says Helen, thirty-five. "After my initial seasickness finally subsided, I felt sexier and more passionate than ever. Usually, my husband's sex drive is a little stronger than mine, but during the middle trimester, I initiated sex more often than he did. That was a pleasant surprise for both of us."

Toward the end of her pregnancy, though, Helen was less eager: "I was preoccupied, huge and hot—it was the middle of August. Hugging, fondling and stroking each other was enough for me," she recalls. "My husband minded, but I didn't even notice."

Nancy, thirty, also experienced sexual ups and downs. "In my second and third months, I was sick to my stomach on and off all day long. At work, in the back of my mind I was constantly measuring the distance between my body and the nearest ladies' room." Despite the nausea, Nancy's desire for sex increased, and she often longed for an afternoon in bed with her husband. "By the time evening rolled around, though, sex was the last thing I wanted," she recalls ruefully. "I was so fatigued I could barely keep my eyes open." Timing was easier on weekends, when the schedule was looser, and then the couple's lovemaking was very passionate. After Nancy's sixteenth week, when the nausea passed, they made love more frequently than ever.

The honeymoon ended abruptly in Nancy's last trimester. "There were nights I tried to initiate sex, but Eric just wasn't interested," she recalls. "I felt miserable. Finally, we talked, and Eric reassured me that he loved me; making love to a large pregnant woman just wasn't an erotic experience for him."

It surprised Nancy that Eric, usually sensual and earthy, would be turned off by her blossoming body. Eric, thirty-four, says he found his wife's pregnancy visually shocking. "I was used to seeing her look one way, and she rapidly changed to look almost like a different person," he says. "The transformation was kind of surreal, and it put me off sexually."

The couples apt to be hardest hit by sexual incompatibility are those who haven't been together long enough to have experienced the normal ups and downs of married sex. Marilyn, thirty-one, had been married only a few months when she got pregnant, and her sexual desire rapidly dwindled to zero. "There was so much going on physically—what with the baby kicking and other sensations—that my sexuality was overshadowed completely. I like sexual experiences to be purely erotic and that wasn't possible given my state of mind as a pregnant person."

Not having a long history of sexual experience with Gary, thirty-seven, to help her put their current problems in perspective, Marilyn wondered if her marriage would ever recover. "Gary was disappointed and hurt; I was panicked," she says. "But I was also consumed by what was going on with my body. And in a way, I blamed him for not trying harder to bring my desire back. We became so sexually estranged that even after the baby was born it took us a long time to work things out."

"She used to snuggle up to me..." says Mark. "Now I feel a bit like a tugboat pushing an ocean liner."

What tends most powerfully to erode a pregnant woman's sexual confidence is her increasing size—the "beached whale" syndrome. And indeed, some men have a definite distaste for their wives' new bulk. "She used to snuggle up to me and press her smaller body against me," says Mark, thirty-nine. "Now I feel a bit like a tugboat pushing an ocean liner."

Says one woman in her sixth month of pregnancy, "I look at myself and the last thing I think of is sex. This body isn't appealing to *me*, and unless I'm turned on to myself, it's hard to get a charge out of sex."

Some women's self-image suffers most in the early months, when the world at large doesn't yet attribute their thickening middles to pregnancy. "I felt *fat*," one woman says, "not lush and pregnant."

The weight gain in pregnancy may be a blessing in one respect; larger, fuller breasts are sometimes eagerly anticipated by both men and women. For Helen, the change produced a surprising affirmation of her husband's appreciation of her body. "When I was a teenager, I always wanted larger breasts," she says. "I got them and that was nice. But what I liked even more was that my husband then said he loved me the old way; he couldn't wait to get my smaller breasts back."

Some husbands arouse their wives' resentment by seeming to ignore the ballooning of their bellies. The avoidance may have complex roots: Some men find it virtually impossible to overcome the "mommy taboo" in our culture. Other men are fascinated by their wives' bellies, but they're scared to rub or pat them, for fear of harming the fetus.

And still other men feel the opposite. "My husband loves to talk and sing to the baby, rubbing my tummy," says Sally, thirty-two, in her eighth month of pregnancy. "He thinks the baby responds and that makes him excited and emotional."

In the advanced stages of pregnancy, overcoming the awkwardness of intercourse can become a private joke between mates. "The fun of it is trying to innovate," says Marsha, twenty-nine. "With our bad backs, it's tricky." Many couples are most comfortable with the woman on top, or lying side by side—either facing each other or spoon-style. "During my first pregnancy, I didn't want my husband on top, even at the beginning," says Joanna, thirty-one. "I was afraid he was going to squish the baby. When I was pregnant the second time, my earlier fears seemed funny to me; I loved having my husband on top, as long as he kept his weight off my belly."

The latter months may also bring renewed closeness. As the pregnancy progresses, and the baby becomes more of a reality to the father-to-be, the mother is less likely to feel that she's going it alone. Isabelle notes that it wasn't until her ninth month, when Kevin saw the baby on an ultrasound test, that they experienced any of their old intimacy. "Ever since, Kevin has been paying more attention to my tummy, rubbing it, feeling the baby move, even falling asleep holding my belly," Isabelle says. "Although we still aren't sexually close, this physical contact is very special; we know that the romance is back."

For some couples, pregnancy produces a surprising feeling of sexual abandon. "My husband was dead set against having children for the first five years of our marriage, since we were having such a rough time financially," says Janice, thirty-two. "I was so paranoid that our birth control would fail us that anxiety really interfered with my sexuality. When we finally decided to have a child, it was an immense load off my mind. Our sexual relationship became much freer and more experimental; we got out of a rut we didn't even know we were in. I enjoyed oral sex for the first time in my life."

Unlike Janice and her husband, most couples won't find pregnancy an outright aphrodisiac. Most report, though, that the progress of pregnancy creates a pleasant, positive effect on mood. As Sally put it, "There's always something new to be excited about. I feel a little like I'm on a second honeymoon."

Sex After the Baby

It can take months before a couple feels in sync sexually. But there are ways to make the adjustment easier.

Leslie Bennetts

Leslie Bennetts is a contributing editor of *Vanity Fair.* She lives in Manhattan with her husband and one-year-old.

The books make it sound so easy. Just wait six weeks after delivery, they assure you brightly, and then you can resume your normal sexual relationship as if nothing had ever happened. All those cheerful childbirth manuals give you the impression that everyone waits the prescribed month and a half, heals neatly on schedule, then resumes an active sex life with her eager husband. There may be people for whom this is the case, but you could look a long time before you met any.

The reality is far more complicated and tends to be obscured by embarrassed secrecy. Giving birth may be the most transcendent experience a woman can ever have, but joy and elation are only part of the picture. Some women manage to be quite chipper within a couple of days, but others feel more like victims of a train wreck: weepy, overwhelmed by powerful emotions, and bruised and battered in parts of their bodies they didn't even know existed. A difficult labor can be emotionally traumatic, and women whose pregnancy ended in a cesarean section are recuperating from major surgery; it will be weeks before they can even imagine feeling normal again. Then there's sleep deprivation: Every night, that angelic little bundle seems to howl for hours, demanding to be fed with a frequency you didn't think possible. Who knew such a tiny creature could eat so much, not to mention so often? Between the feeding and the burping and the changing, it can easily get to be four o'clock in the afternoon before you realize you're still in your flannel nightgown because you haven't yet had a chance to grab a shower and brush your hair, which is glued together with baby spit-up. This is a sex object?

Conflicting emotions.

For many women, the prospect of making love again is initially horrifying. "A friend had warned me that the doctor would come sidling up after I had my baby and want to talk about sex," says Stephanie,* a Texas writer and mother of two. "I remember lying there in my hospital bed. Every erogenous zone in my body hurt." When the doctor told her she could resume sexual relations after six weeks, she was appalled. "I said, 'You don't understand—no one is going to touch me *for the rest of my life!'* After I got out of the hospital, I felt as if my husband were following me around clicking off the days, which to my mind were going all too quickly. Just the thought of sex was absolutely traumatic."

Needless to say, Stephanie's second child is proof that such feelings don't last forever. Still, even after a woman heals physically, the psychological adjustments can take time. Some women feel a certain distance from their partners because of what they've been through. "I felt my husband just didn't understand that no matter how much a man and woman go into this together, certain things had happened to me alone," says Stephanie. "A baby changes everything. Pregnancy and childbirth give you a redefinition of your body; all those sexual parts of your body are being used in a very different way, first to give birth, and then to breastfeed. It makes you think very differently about sex for a while."

Even the method of giving birth can have long-term repercussions. "Having a cesarean made me feel like less of a woman on some level," admits Susan, a psychologist who lives in Chicago. "It confirmed all my negative feelings about myself as a woman, and I'm sure it made me feel less desirable." A stunning, auburn-haired woman with the figure of an eighteen-year-old, Susan might seem an unlikely candidate for such doubts, but they affected her for months after the birth of each of her two children. The fact that she was breast-feeding also had a major impact. "It made me feel more married, more connected in a physical way, to my baby than to my husband," she confesses. "I fell in love with both my

*Parent's names are pseudonyms.

babies in a way I never dreamed was possible, and I'm sure the fact that they're both boys had significance, in terms of feeling less sexual toward my husband. I got a tremendous amount of gratification and intimacy from breast-feeding, and in some ways that replaced sex."

Although many women are ashamed to talk about such conflicts, they are quite common. "I feel very torn between my loyalty to my husband and my loyalty to the baby," says Alice, a Florida social worker who is currently nursing her second child. "I feel very drawn to the baby, and it's as though anything sexual is a violation of trust. Once the breast-feeding stops it gets easier, but for a while you feel like your body's being used and used and used and you just want a little private time. It's a wonderful luxury just to be left alone."

For a new mother who's feeling overwhelmed by her baby's demands, the additional pressure of her partner's needs may breed resentment and anger. And a man who is used to being his wife's first priority may find her attachment to the baby a rude shock. "The husband has to take second place for a while," says Roy Whitman, M.D., a psychiatrist who specializes in sex therapy at the University of Cincinnati College of Medicine. "The woman may try to satisfy her husband, but it can seem more like she's placating him; I think her heart tends to be with the baby at this point. Bonding with the infant is uppermost for the mother, and the father may be seen as an intruder," Whitman says. "Some fathers are jealous of the baby, and if they start to interfere with the mother-child bonding in an envious, intrusive way, the mother will push them away. Bottle-feeding mothers may be more receptive because the breast becomes an erotic source again rather than a nurturant source—but if you're breast-feeding, the breast belongs to the baby."

Such changes have been known to cause enormous stress. "This is a dangerous time for a marriage," warns Domeena Renshaw, M.D., a professor of psychiatry and director of the Sexual Dysfunction Clinic at Loyola University Medical Center, in Maywood, Illinois. "There are some husbands who cheat during pregnancy and afterward because the mother has a romance with the baby and they feel left out."

New fathers may be just as exhausted as mothers, which doesn't enhance their interest in sex either. My baby has never been a good sleeper. My husband clocked her one night when she was about eight months old; the longest she slept without waking us was 40 minutes, so we were up approximately every half hour all through the night. Sleep deprivation can definitely alter your sense of priorities. "For me the most erotic, pleasurable thing I can think of for the first six months after a baby is born is ten hours of sleep," says Elaine, a computer programmer with four small children.

What fathers feel.

Although new mothers get most of the attention, husbands have to make their own psychological adjustments. Many men had a hard enough time with their wives' pregnancies, and when the baby arrives, any sexual problems can be compounded; the fact that a man's partner has just become a mother may present a real sexual hurdle that experts generally attribute to subconscious incest taboos. "My husband basically doesn't like to have sex with a pregnant woman," confides Elaine, who lives in San Jose, California. "He's not crazy about breast-feeding from a sexual point of view, either. He thinks breast-feeding is the greatest for the baby, and he would feel very put out if I didn't nurse, but at the same time, I think he finds it a turnoff. Breast-feeding keeps me tied to the baby longer, and it keeps me more mother than wife—and with four kids, I'm often more mother than wife."

People vary tremendously, of course; one man may find his wife's swollen breasts tremendously sexy, while another is turned off by the leaking and spraying a nursing mother may experience when she is sexually aroused. Women's reactions run the gamut as well, and some feel a strong need to reassert their own sexuality after a baby is born. "The classic scenario is, Dad's howling at the door of the cage and Mom's not in the mood for months, but sometimes it's the opposite," observes one mother. "After I had my baby, it was very important for me to feel I wasn't just this lactating mommy." However, her husband seemed to feel that if he touched her, she might break. "I felt as if he was treating me like some giant egg," she says.

When both partners are ready and willing, sometimes they can resume an active sex life with little delay, particularly if they have a cooperative baby. "I was very interested in sex during pregnancy, and I didn't wait for six weeks after either of my children were born," says Marcy, a Philadelphia mother of two. "I found childbirth very exciting and sexy, and I thought nursing was absolutely sexual. My first kid slept through the night ridiculously early, so I wasn't having the kind of fatigue a lot of people have. There was no reason not to have sex."

Some new fathers find that parenthood strengthens their feelings of love for and sexual attraction to their mates. "Having a child deepened my love for my wife and made her special in a new way," says Steven, a New York City lawyer. "Our sex was made better by the baby, not worse."

Easing physical discomfort.

This situation is the ideal, of course, but you can enhance your prospects of achieving it by taking note of some practical advice. If you're experiencing acute pain, you should consult your doctor to make sure you're healing properly and that there's no infection. If you receive a clean bill of health but find that sex remains difficult, don't worry—it's quite normal. Women who are postpartum have diminished estrogen levels, resulting in lessened lubrication and a thinning of the vaginal walls—both of which are exacerbated by nursing and can cause discomfort during intercourse. Simply using additional lubrication for a while can improve the situation significantly. "Sex was not pleasurable for me after I had my first child, and I didn't know how to make it feel better," one mother admits. "If someone had just said to me, 'It's going to be painful and dry now, so just use a lot of K-Y Jelly,' things would have been much easier. As it was, I took my nonlubricated status as a statement about my womanliness."

When his wife is in such a tender state, a man can help matters immeasurably by being sensitive to her discomfort. Doctors and sex therapists say that longer periods of foreplay may make intercourse more pleasurable, and they also recommend experimenting with different positions. For example, although penetration can be deeper with the woman on top, she also may be able to control contact better and avoid any pain.

If it seems for a while that no position is comfortable, consider other ways of satisfying your husband and maintaining a sense of emotional and sexual intimacy.

The experts offer a variety of additional suggestions to new parents who may be having trouble with their sex lives. "Some people keep the baby in their room, so there's a third person there, which may be a factor," observes Renshaw. If you find yourself listening for every rustle of the baby's bed covers rather than thinking sexy thoughts, it might be a good idea to reclaim your bedroom for yourselves.

Realizing you're not alone in this can also help; having the mistaken notion that other people aren't troubled by any of these problems can make you feel even worse. "It's like some kind of dirty little secret. You assume you're the only one on earth who feels this way," says one woman.

Indeed, it sometimes seems as if there's a conspiracy to keep new parents in the dark. "Why doesn't anybody level with you about this?" asks the writer Dan Greenburg in his book *Confessions of a Pregnant Father* (Fawcett). "Why do the obstetricians and the guidebooks imply that you'll be having sex right up to the time you're fully dilated, and that the longest it ever takes any normal couple to get back to regular sex is six weeks? If there could be a bit more candor in this area, new parents might feel they were within the mainstream of human experience rather than candidates for the Masters and Johnson clinic."

Maintain an open dialogue.

Whatever you're feeling, talking about it with your mate will help; even without sex, sharing your thoughts will make you feel closer and may clear up any misunderstandings. Don't wait for him to make the first move; tell him what you're going through, and ask him how he feels about it all. Sometimes people act as if their spouses read their minds, which isn't fair no matter how long they've been married. It also leaves room for all kinds of missed signals. One woman was eager to resume a lusty sex life, but her husband kept acting as if she were some kind of invalid. When they finally talked about it, she learned that he had been preoccupied with her episiotomy and had been terrified of hurting her.

Other than communication, the best therapy is simply time. As the weeks pass, you'll start feeling better, life will seem more manageable, and eventually you'll find yourself thinking that making love sounds like fun instead of the worst idea anyone ever had. How long this takes may vary widely, and just because you have a friend who felt great three weeks after delivery, or you read in some book that everything should be fine in six weeks, doesn't mean you need to feel bad if it takes you as much as a year to adjust.

No matter how long it takes, don't panic. "Women put so much pressure on themselves," Elaine observes. "They say, 'So I haven't gotten a decent night's sleep in six months, I'm stressed out, I'm fifteen pounds overweight, my body organs still haven't gone back to where they're supposed to be, and my hormones are all over the map. So what's the problem with me?' There are so many pressures. I think that a good sex life is really cyclical, anyway. There can be dry periods, and then things will get real hot and heavy again. I think we tend not to be patient enough with ourselves."

Sexuality Through the Life Cycle

- Youth and Their Sexuality (Articles 38-40)
- Sexuality in Adult Years (Articles 41-44)

Individual sexual development is a lifelong process that begins at birth and terminates at death. Contrary to popular notions of this process, there are no latent periods during which the individual is nonsexual or noncognizant of sexuality. The growing process of a sexual being does, however, reveal qualitative differences through various life stages. This section devotes attention to these stages of the life cycle and their relation to sexuality.

As children gain self-awareness, they naturally explore their own bodies, masturbate, display curiosity for the bodies of the opposite sex, and show interest in the bodies of mature individuals such as their parents. Such exploration and curiosity are important and healthy aspects of human development. Yet it is often difficult for adults (who live in a society that is not comfortable with sexuality in general) to avoid making their children ashamed of being sexual or showing interest in sexuality. When adults impose their ambivalence upon a child's innocuous explorations into sexuality, or behave toward children in sexually inappropriate ways, distortion of an indispensable and formative stage of development occurs. This often leaves profound emotional scars that hinder full acceptance of self and sexuality later in the child's life.

Adolescence, the social status accompanying puberty and the transition to adulthood, proves to be a very stressful period of life for many individuals as they attempt to develop an adult identity and force relationships with others. Because of the physiological capacity of adolescents for reproduction, sexuality tends to be heavily censured by parents and society at this stage of life. Yet individuals and societal attitudes place tremendous emphasis on sexual attractiveness—especially for females, and sexual competency—especially for males. These physical, emotional, and cultural pressures combine to create confusion and anxiety in adolescents and young adults about whether they are okay or normal. Information and assurances from adults can alleviate these stresses and facilitate positive and responsible sexual maturity if there is mutual trust and willingness in both generations.

Sexuality finally becomes socially acceptable in adulthood, at least within marriage. Yet routine, boredom, stress, pressures, the pace of life, and/or a lack of communication can exact heavy tolls on the quantity and quality of sexual interaction. Sexual misinformation, myths, and unanswered questions, especially about emotional and/or physiological changes in sexual arousal/response, or functioning, can also undermine or hinder intimacy and sexual interaction in the middle years.

Sexuality in the later years of life is again socially and culturally stigmatized because of the prevailing misconception that sex is for young married adults. Such an attitude is primarily responsible for the apparent decline in sexual interest and activity as one grows older. Physiological changes in the aging process are not, in and of themselves, detrimental to sexual expression. A life history of experience, health, and growth can make sexual expression in the later years a most rewarding and fulfilling experience.

Youth and Their Sexuality begins with an article about toddlers and their sexuality. It is an article written for parents about accepting and utilizing the natural curiosity and openness of their child to begin positive and healthy communication about sex. The second article explores perceptions and distortions of body image and sexuality, especially in young women. This author advocates early sex education and self-esteem building as preventives for sexual derogation.

Sexuality in Adult Years contains four articles that seek to combat myths, especially about aging, disease, and familiarity being detrimental to sexual enjoyment, functioning, and intimacy. Suggestions and advice while replacing myths and inhibitions with facts and permission are offered. The final article in the subsection focuses on the sexual complaint of the 1980s and 1990s—loss of interest or desire now labeled hypoactive sexual desire. It distinguishes this problem from other dysfunctions and discusses a range of treatments and their effectiveness.

Looking Ahead: Challenge Questions

Have you been around younger siblings, nieces, nephews, or the children of friends who embarrassed the adults in the vicinity with candid questions or behaviors about sex or their bodies? How did you respond to the children? To what the adults did?

How distorted is your body image? To what extent do you worry about being sexy? Are you concerned about measuring up to the ideal for your gender?

Close your eyes and image a couple having a pleasurable sexual interlude. When you are done, open your eyes. How old were they? If they were younger than middle age, can you replay your vision with middle age or older people? Why or why not? How does this relate to your expectations regarding your own romantic and/or sexual life a few decades from now?

Have you experienced times of decreased interest in sex? If so, have they corresponded with emotional, relationship, physical, or other difficulties or traumas? How would (or have) you respond(ed) to declining interest?

My Body, My Self:
The Age of Exploration

Lisa Feder-Feitel

Lisa Feder-Feitel, a freelance writer, lives in New York City with her husband and two children.

Two-year-old Nick loves to rip off his diaper and yell "Ta da!" to anyone and everyone present. During her nightly bath, 2½-year-old Jennifer unconsciously fondles her genitals. Four-year-old Daniel, on the other hand, likes to examine his friend Tammy—in the nude with a toy stethoscope. What's a parent to do?

If the same children were playing with their toes, stroking their earlobes, or rubbing their bellies, their parents wouldn't even blink. However, once parents have answered the question "Is it a boy or a girl?" on the day of their child's birth, most would prefer to shut the door to further discussion of their children's sexuality. But such exploration of their bodies, whether it be their toes or their genitals, is a natural part of all children's development.

It may not be easy, but most experts agree that the first step parents should take when they see their child involved in sex play and self exploration is to relax. "I urge parents not to prohibit, divert, or otherwise try to interfere," writes pediatrician Dr. T. Berry Brazelton in *Toddlers and Parents* (Dell). "It's fun for a little boy to find out about his penis, a little girl about her vagina. Having been hidden by diapers heretofore, these are like new toys. The period of exploration and investigation will pass, unless someone makes a child feel guilty for his normal interest."

According to Dr. Ronald Moglia, director of the human sexuality program at New York University, "There are no rigid rules for normalcy. Whatever children do as they explore their bodies—*every* part of their bodies—is normal. What isn't normal is how some parents react to it."

You're the Teacher

Beginning at your child's birth, you are her primary sex educator. Your response to your child's behavior will shape both her values and her self-esteem.

In *The Magic Years: Understanding & Handling the Problems of Early Childhood* (Scribner's), Selma H. Fraiberg, a pioneer in the field of child development, wrote: "How a child feels about himself, how he values himself, will also be tied up with his feelings about his own body. The child who discovers that his sex play arouses disgust in his parent may come to feel that his body is bad and that he, as a person, is bad."

While no caring parent would willfully create shame in a child, parents can unconsciously transmit the idea that sexuality is shameful by overreacting to their child's sexual curiosity. It's important, therefore, for parents to act and react in a way that will reassure their child as well as give her a sense of respect for herself and others. As she grows up, her parents will impart to her

their own values about sexuality in general, in much the same way that they transmit their feelings about honesty or good table manners. And while there is a wide range of values that are acceptable among adults, parents should be aware that their values—if they fall at extremes of privacy and openness—can upset a child.

For instance, if a child opens the bathroom door, surprising the usually very private parent inside, it would serve everyone best for the parent to keep from overreacting. On the other hand, parents who are quite comfortable walking around in the nude may notice that their behavior may overstimulate their child. For their child's sake, it would be a good idea for the parents to remain dressed when around him. As with any situation, the key for parents is to watch children carefully for any signs of discomfort and to adjust their own behavior accordingly.

It Feels Good, But...

Remember when your daughter first discovered her ears, or the hours your son spent finding out what his fingers and toes could do? Watching your child explore these body parts probably delighted you as much as it did your child. But somehow, as infants become toddlers and their hands and curiosities go south, many parents—even those who tend to be open in matters of sexuality—grow uncomfortable with their child's sex play.

Why do children masturbate? Child-development experts agree that masturbation is a normal and natural act for children. Psychologist Dr. Lawrence Balter suggests four possible reasons why young children masturbate. "First of all," he says, "it feels good. Second, it is a self-soothing activity that reduces tension. Third, it's sometimes a sign of overexcitation from having witnessed a lot of sex. Finally, occasionally kids masturbate in order to deal with a specific fear, such as a little boy's fear that he might lose his penis. Reaching for it reassures him that he's still 'okay.'"

Many doctors point out that masturbation is for some children not a source of pleasure but a sign of underlying anxiety. Since there is no way to tell this from the act of self-stimulation alone, parents must observe the child's behavior in other realms to determine if her masturbation is excessive or a symptom of some other trouble. What else is the child doing or saying? Is she cranky or throwing tantrums? Is she wetting the bed? It's important to re-member that masturbation, which is comforting and a normal part of a child's development, is not in itself a problem.

In *The Growing Years* by the New York Hospital/Cornell Medical Center, with Mark Rubinstein, M.D. (Fireside/Simon & Schuster), child psychiatrist Dr. Theodore Shapiro says, "I wouldn't be so concerned about a child fondling his genitals; rather, [I would be concerned] that tension and anxiety are prominent in his life. Frequent masturbation may be a symptom of underlying difficulties."

In most situations, however, children masturbate not because something is wrong but because it is part of their growing process. "All toddlers masturbate at times," notes Dr. Brazelton. And as a self-soothing device it can be regarded not only as acceptable but helpful. "The word [*masturbation*]," he suggests, "carries such ugly implications for many people that perhaps a new one should be coined." In addition, he says, it may be "better for a child to use this way of handling tension, for he'll 'grow out of it' if he's left alone."

Even though it's normal for a child to fondle himself occasionally, there are times when it is socially unacceptable and when the parent must take responsibility to redirect the child's attention. Dr. Balter advises addressing the situation gently when it arises: "If you're shopping, ask the child to hold one of your groceries for you. If you're at Grandma's, engage him in a game that requires the use of his hands. Distract him."

The Bare Facts

At around age two, children also start to form a definition of their gender roles and their need to explore their bodies takes on added dimension. And though they've been "playing doctor" for centuries—probably well before Hippocrates took his oath—this kind of interaction can be particularly troublesome for parents. Unless parents put their kids under a 24-hour-a-day watch, it's unlikely that they can squelch the curiosity that prompts it. But parents who encounter their children involved in this kind of play feel compelled to react. Dr. Sol Gordon, director of the Institute of Family Research and Edu-

My Heart Belongs to Daddy

Figuring out their relationship with their parents is part of the process children go through as they define their gender roles. Jenna and her three-year-old daughter, Marie, used to have a beautiful friendship. "She never went through the terrible twos. In fact, she was delightful. Then on her third birthday she looked me straight in the eye and said, 'I don't love you anymore!'" Her heart at this point belonged to Daddy.

Around the age of three, children often "fall in love" with their opposite-sex parent. Some even announce their intentions at the dinner table: "Guess what?" Jack tells his dad. "I'm going to marry Mom!"

According to child psychiatrist Dr. Theodore Shapiro, when contemplating their child's wishes and desires, parents should remember that their child's thinking is magical and not nearly so sophisticated as adult logic. "She wants the same loving attention from her father that mother already has," he explains. "She knows that her parents have a private life together; she wants to take part in it and have her father to herself."

Educator and psychoanalyst Selma H. Fraiberg has pointed out that children are not always so blatant about their feelings. They are much more likely to mask them in a piece of puzzling behavior, such as a tantrum, a verbal attack, or a bad dream. Whether we puzzle it out or not, the outcome remains the same. As Fraiberg has noted, "It's an impossible daydream which must end in disappointment and renunciation for all children."

On the receiving end, you may be amazed at your own emotional reactions to a child's seductive behavior. Parents need to be very aware of their own sexuality during this highly charged time, advises human-sexuality expert Dr. Ronald Moglia. "It's important to recognize your feelings, positive and negative, and to be aware of their impact on your child."

All normal children experience a romantic phase, and most pass through it without emotional scars. In a few years, this impossible dream of taking the parent's place fades, and it may never be remembered. In fact, the child's chief rival, the same-sex parent, soon turns into the hero or heroine. It's as if the child says, "Since I can't take my parent's place, I will be like him [or her]." Through your understanding and care, you and your child can survive this stage, and build a foundation for a happier future.

—*L.F.F.*

cation at Syracuse University in New York, suggests that parents try to stifle their taboos and address the questions raised by this behavior.

If, for example, you find your four-year-old examining her friend, Dr. Gordon suggests that you calmly ask both children to get dressed and direct them to another activity. "Later, explain to your child that it isn't a good idea to touch the sexual parts of anyone else's body or to allow anyone else to touch hers," says Dr. Gordon. "Add that you are aware that she has questions and that you can show her pictures or answer any question to satisfy her curiosity."

Dr. Balter adds that finding your child playing doctor gives you an opportunity to teach him about decorum and restraint. If you notice, for instance, that your son's playmate seems unhappy with their game, it's important to point this out to him. "You might say to your son," suggests Dr. Balter, "'Mary doesn't seem to want to play. I think we should respect her wishes. If you didn't want to show your body, I wouldn't force you to. After all, it's your body and you can decide if you want to show it to somebody else or not.'"

It's hard not to feel embarrassed and alarmed when you first discover your child wearing a stethoscope and little else. But most kids will be secretly relieved to be "caught," and if you can remain calm, you can use it as an opportunity to teach and reassure your very curious child.

One Discovery Leads to Another

During the preschool years, your curious child discovers the world, as well as her body and identity, through a variety of ways, including sex play. Your preschooler will imitate, adopt, discard, and identify with your actions and the values you share with her. Before your child asks you the "big" questions about the meaning of life and where babies come from, before you answer her with facts, she has already learned a lot about your attitude toward sex—from watching you and noting your reactions to *her* sexuality.

Then all too soon the world begins to intrude: social influences, including peers, preschool, and television, feed your child thoughts and images that can influence his attitudes. With all the information that bombards children every day, how can parents be sure that the values that are getting through to them are the ones that they want them to have?

Dr. Stanley Greenspan, clinical professor of psychiatry and child health and development at George Washington University Medical School in Washington, D.C., and author of *First Feelings* (Viking/Penguin), suggests that parents examine and decide what messages they want to send their child and also show their child that they respect each other. "What is most important," he says, "is that members of the family recognize the child's need to feel natural and comfortable with them and this topic."

Parents can start implementing these ideas in the comfort of their living rooms, notes Dr. Moglia. "Set a tone; establish a sense of constant availability and trust in your home," he says. "Let your children know that you want to hear them and help them learn. It's like setting up a long-term insurance policy. Start it now, and it'll pay back in years to come."

Double Vision

PENNY WARD MOSER

Why do we never match up to our mind's ideal?

IN 1959, I WAS THE BEST TEN-year-old baton twirler at the Dundee, Illinois, Fall Festival. I was also the skinniest baton twirler. In my sequined leotard, I resembled nothing more than a sparkly red clothespin. All through my childhood, I looked like one of the orphans in "You can help feed this child" ads. Except for my frizzy Tonette-waved hair, my knees were my most outstanding feature.

For the first eighteen years of my life, I was a human Cuisinart. I simply processed huge quantities of food and grew taller without changing very much at all. I was thirteen, 5'5" and 110 pounds when the horror of my predicament struck. There I was, awash in a sea of angora sweaters, nylon stockings and slow-dance parties, and I found myself without a body. I had arms and legs and all, but other girls were acquiring soft, round body parts that I lacked. Annette Funicello betrayed me when she suddenly sprouted huge breasts that made her name jiggle on her Mouseketeer T-shirt. Full-page ads for high-calorie potions cried out, "Don't let them call you skinny!" We all knew that what men wanted was Marilyn Monroe, Jayne Mansfield or Sandra Dee. I can still remember choking down triple helpings of mashed potatoes, butter and milk, trying to round out my body. I wasn't very successful, but did remain a hell of a baton twirler.

My how times have changed. Today, at 124 pounds, I think I'm too heavy, even though I barely make the low-normal weight range on standard height/weight charts. In the last twenty years, something has influenced me to believe that the ideal body is very, very thin. Indeed, the quest for a perfect, lean body has become a sort of national pastime. In one survey, 81 percent of adults said they were dieting to lose weight. Seven hundred thousand attend weekly Weight Watchers meetings. We trot dutifully to exercise classes and buy millions of copies of diet books, no matter how far-fetched the concept. We jam tapes into our VCRs: tapes from the fit and famous, from weight trainers, even from diet specialists who, at the push of the Play button, pop onto the TV screen and yell for twenty minutes.

There's nothing wrong with sensible dieting to keep obesity at bay. But today, for normal-weight and even slender people, dieting has taken on the aspect of war. The enemy is the stuff that scientists call adipose tissue and that the rest of the population knows as fat. Although there are growing numbers of men in the battalions, most of the foot soldiers are women. (Some studies show men tend to have positive images of themselves, even when they're overweight; women tend to look at themselves with a more negative eye.) In an effort to be thin, women are ignoring signals from their bodies, fighting against their genes and—increasingly—become casualties.

At the University of South Florida, associate professor of psychology Kevin Thompson, Ph.D., thinks he's figured out part of the problem: Our mind's eye makes us bigger than we really are. And the more we worry about our body images, the more we tend to mentally blow ourselves up. He's designed a test to show us how we see ourselves.

This is how I've come to be standing in a darkened little lab room, wearing a spiffy hot-pink leotard and tights. I am going to take Dr. Thompson's body-image test.

A graduate student fiddles with some little wooden dowels that slide on a board atop an overhead projector. When I move the dowels, I can narrow or widen the light beams projected onto the wall ten feet in front of me. To take the test, I stare at the wall and move the beams until I think I have projected my own body size. I am going to estimate the widths of key points on my body—the ones Thompson thinks people worry about the most: my face (across the cheekbones), waist, hips and thighs.

This should be easy. "Let's see," I think. "If I were standing there...." I move the light beams in and out. "Hmmm. My waist is—no, it's bigger. Not that big. Ah, this is right. But hey, my thighs aren't that wide, at least not if I push my knees together real hard. Now my hips...."

When I finish positioning the light beams, the grad student measures me with body calipers. At that moment, I officially fall into the legion of 95 percent of Thompson's "normal" women subjects—I had overestimated my body size. Only by about 4 percent, mind you, but still, my imagination had added about five pounds. Even so, I didn't do badly. Consider this: A study Thompson did showed that not only did 95 percent of women overestimate their body size, they overestimated by an average of 25 percent. Smaller women did the most overestimating. The most extreme overestimations, up to 75 percent, are among young women with eating disorders—anorexia and/or bulimia.

It was such a person who first led Thompson to his field of research. "In 1978, my first patient as a student therapist was a young woman who was 5′8″ and weighed 85 pounds. She pulled at the skin on her arms and said, 'Look! Don't you see how fat I am?' She was a nutrition major. That sort of hit me in the face." So what does this all mean? Thompson recently completed several studies to detail the causes of body-image distortion. He says, "It seems to be largely correlated with a lack of self-esteem. The better people feel about themselves, the less they tend to overestimate their size."

One psychiatrist I talked with suggested the Barbie doll first exposes our young psyches to slim-think. Barbie is impossibly long-legged and slim, with large, high, perky breasts. But nobody is going to grow up to look like Barbie. To prove this, I measured a Barbie doll, then measured myself. I used our hips as the constant, and with a little math found that for me to look like Barbie, my bust would have to grow twelve inches, my waist would have to shrink ten inches and I would have to be 7′2″.

Each person has, after all, about ten

Proof that self-image begins in our heads: Nine out of ten women studied overestimate their own body size

thousand taste buds that are on the side of the enemy. Early man, sitting around tearing apart a ground sloth with his bare hands, trying to stuff it down before a tiger came along and made dinner of it and dessert of him, probably didn't stop to think it would be better sautéed with onions. Man used to live quite nicely on a few handfuls of insects a day. If a woman had a few locusts for breakfast, a few more for lunch, and was looking forward to her husband throwing a few locusts on the grill for dinner, she probably wouldn't get up from her desk at three o'clock and pace around the office having a locust attack.

Why can't men and women just be happy being a little on the round side? Not health-hazard fat, but soft and cuddly? One reason may be that we have made sex into an art form. Something people do for a good time without, for the most part, making babies. A plump body, psychologists say, has historically been associated with maternity. To bear a healthy child, lug it around the field and nurse it—maybe through hard times—would take a woman with some adipose tissue reserve. In many cultures men still like their mates a little heavy to downright fat.

Women still have babies today, but American society thinks of sex as more recreational than procreational. And our lower infant/child mortality rate means a woman doesn't have to have ten kids to see that one lives.

It's theorized, then, that the lean woman symbolizes sex for fun, not sex for motherhood. The problem is that nobody has told her genes about this. A woman's biological systems are still primarily geared up for baby-making.

In the last few weeks before a baby is born, and during about the first year after, its body makes fat cells. Some people make fat cells during puberty; but, for the most part, a cute toddler has most of the fat cells she's going to have. Then—and here's the problem—as a girl grows and develops a lifestyle, so do her fat cells. Although science is only beginning to unravel the mysteries of fat cells, it is clear they vary from person to person, behaving as if they have minds—or, it seems to me, appetites—of their own.

A friend of mine, a retired physician, says we have all simply "entered an age of total narcissism." I'd like to think I'm not a part of that. But I am. The thin cues dance in my mind. They're ballerinas. Now that I'm forty, my body wants to gain weight I don't want it to. My mouth would like to send my hips and thighs more M&M's and french fries. Now if Thompson's body-image test is right, I'm not as big as I think I am, and I still have that five pounds to play around with. But in the back of my mind is the knowledge that I do not come from skinny people. And the rest of my life will be a contest between my genes and my jeans.

What College Students Want to Know About Sex

Everything that they don't know yet, which, according to the authors, amounts to more than you would think possible.

Sandra L. Caron, PhD,
and
Rosemarie M. Bertran, MSW

Sandra L. Caron is a health educator, Cornell University, Ithaca, NY. Rosemarie M. Bertran is a therapist at Fairmount Children's Center, Solvay, NY.

"Do you have to have sex to have a baby?" "Is sex habit-forming?" "Is cunnilingus good for your teeth?" "Can you get pregnant from swallowing semen?" These and many other questions are commonly asked by young adults attending college, and they may come with these questions to your office, too.* Contrary to the widely held belief that college students know all about sex, the fact is that despite the widely available sexual literature, and explicit sex on television and in popular films, many students know very little about their sexuality. While some are reasonably knowledgeable and comfortable with their own sexuality, others, far more typically, are not. Worse, they're often embarrassed by what they perceive as their excessive ignorance, and fear ridicule if they openly seek the information they need.

Most typically, students come to college with many misconceptions and a host of questions about human sexuality, which reflect their particular stages of psychosexual development. Thus, if you quickly review the typical college student's levels of development, you'll better understand the source of these young adults' questions, and provide the answers and sexual information they seek.

College students' psychosocial/sexual stages of development

New choices and values. As a result of geographical separation from their parents and living in a new environment that invites and encourages reevaluation of values, most college students are suddenly confronted by many new social and sexual issues. They are thus forced to come to grips very quickly with such questions as "Who am I?" "What is my role in life?" and "What value systems do I want to align with?" If they can't answer these satisfactorily, they become confused, and may experience a psychological crisis. They realize that they are no longer subject to their parents' definition of their role, but this may heighten their bewilderment. Typically, issues of identity are presented in questions about sexual behavior, heterosexuality/homosexuality, and body image.

---

*The questions quoted in this article are selected from among those raised by students in a human sexuality course at a large eastern university, and are in the students' own words. The course is popular and always over-registered; thus, the majority of students were juniors and seniors. Questions were collected anonymously on 3″ × 5″ cards on the first day of class during 1983–1986, and are generally representative of commonly asked questions.

Common questions and their answers

Q: *Is it true that it is harder for a woman to orgasm than a man?*
A: I'm assuming you are referring to sexual intercourse versus masturbation. Although it may take a woman longer to become aroused, she tends to stay aroused longer than the man. Awareness and consideration of individual differences enhance lovemaking. Most women need stimulation of the clitoris. Intercourse is usually not the most effective way to get it. The vagina is often too far from the clitoris for intercourse alone to provide sufficient stimulation for orgasm.

Q: *Is it normal for a man, on occasion, not to be able to get an erection while being stimulated?*
A: Yes. Physical and emotional factors may interfere. A man who is overtired or overstressed is not at his best in anything. Be understanding and patient.

Q: *I have never had sex with someone of the same sex, but have often admired their bodies. Is this unusual?*
A: No, this is not unusual. All of us can admire both male and female human bodies with pleasure. A trip to an art museum demonstrates that the human body has great beauty. It would be sad if one could see beauty only in one sex.

Q: *Which is better in a penis—length or width?*
A: The vagina is quite adept at accommodating to penis size, and many women actually prefer stimulation around the clitoris and vaginal opening to deep thrusting, which some women find painful. Pleasant stimulation doesn't require a large penis (in width or length).

Q: *I have heard that each time a man ejaculates his sperm count decreases. Can a man become sterile from a ultra-active sex life?*
A: Sperm are continually being produced in the testes. Barring severe injury, you're likely to have a lifelong supply.

Q: *How can I tell if a woman is ready to make love?*
A: Women's bodies usually signal readiness with lubrication, pelvic motion, and greater intensity. Many women feel comfortable telling their partner when they are ready. If you are not sure, gently ask your partner to tell you when she is ready.

Q: *I am a virgin and my boyfriend isn't. He says it's okay that we're not having sex, but my friends say our relationship will never last. Should I be concerned?*
A: Since every person is unique, every relationship is unique. If you and your boyfriend are comfortable with your relationship why worry about what your friends say? If you're not comfortable, I suggest you talk it over with your boyfriend rather than your friends. It's ultimately up to you and him to decide.

Q: *How important are simultaneous orgasms?*
A: Not very. In fact, "separate turns" may be even more pleasurable, especially in a new relationship where you are getting to know each other. Most people find they are unable to fully experience their own sensations while trying to give pleasure to their partner.

Q: *Do men really enjoy giving oral sex, or do they do it just to please their partner?*
A: Some men (and some women) enjoy oral sex and some do not. That's a decision for you and your partner to talk about. Why don't you ask him?

Q: *Is it possible to become aroused and/or have an orgasm while under the influence of alcohol?*
A: Most drugs, including alcohol, numb sexual feelings and depress sexual function unless taken in very small amounts. Alcohol may loosen inhibitions or tensions to make intimacy more approachable, but at the same time may diminish physical awareness and make orgasm unlikely. Many a partygoer has been dismayed to find his performance impaired after an evening of heavy drinking.

Learning about intimacy. One of the tasks of young adulthood is to develop the capability of *intimacy*, the giving of oneself to another believed worthy of trust. Without intimacy in a relationship, the individual feels a sense of *isolation*, which leads to despair and loneliness. Typical areas of con-

Questions about body image, virginity, thoughts/fantasies, STDs, and body functions

Body image
Can a penis be curved and still be normal?
Why do womens' genitals differ so much from one woman to the next?
Which is better in a penis—length or width? How big is the normal penis?
Do big-breasted women get aroused quicker than others?
One of my breasts is definitely bigger than the other—is this a deformity?
What is a circumcised penis? Is it better?
Why do we have pubic hair?

Virginity
What exactly is a virgin? Can guys be virgins too?
Is being a virgin at my age (21-years-old) psychologically damaging?
Is a female virgin scared of sex or of the size of a big man's penis?
Is being a virgin the same thing as being frigid?
I'm a virgin and my boyfriend isn't. He says it's okay that we're not having sex, but my friends say it
   will never last. Are they right?

Thoughts/fantasies
Is it strange to think about having sex with my brother?
Is my relationship in trouble if I think of other people when I have sex with my partner?
I've never had sex with someone of the same sex, but have often admired their bodies. Is this
   unusual?

Sexually transmitted diseases (STDs)
What is a sexually transmitted disease? What is gonorrhea?
Can you tell the type of person who gets sexually transmitted diseases?
How is AIDS contracted?
Would I know if I had a sexually transmitted disease?
Can a sexually transmitted disease kill you?
Can you really get a sexually transmitted disease from a toilet seat?
Can oral sex cause you to get an infection?
Who do you go to see if you think you might have a sexually transmitted infection?
I got a vaginal infection, but I didn't have sex. How is that possible?

Body functions/parts
Why do I have a moist spot on my underwear?
Do guys menstruate?
What's the purpose of menstruation?
Should women douche? How is it done?
Why do vaginas smell differently?
Does the G-spot exist? Where is it?
Does it hurt when a guy has an erection?
I don't get anything out of having my breasts touched—is there something wrong?
Do you really "lose it" if you don't "use it"?
What is the most sensitive part of the penis?
Is it normal for a man, on occasion, not to be able to get an erection while being stimulated?
How and where do you locate a woman's clitoris?

cern therefore focus on relationships, social issues, and the mysterious "opposite sex."

The physician's essential role in sexual counseling
   College students' questions directly reflect their success (or lack) in mastering these stages of development. They involve rela-

tionships, masturbation, virginity, homosexuality, intercourse, orgasm and ejaculation, birth control and pregnancy, and sexually transmitted diseases.

A review of questions commonly asked by college students indicates that they fall into two broad categories: those based on the need for specific factual information, and those that reflect the students' intense concern with their physical/sexual normality. While you may well be surprised at the often enormous lack of factual knowledge, you'll need to present a review of basic facts about reproductive physiology and sexuality in such a way that you don't point out the student's ignorance and so threaten his/her self-esteem. For example, you can use such phrases "As you probably already know . . . " and "As you may be aware . . . " as tactful introductions to factual information. If you have any doubts about the extent of the student's knowledge, it's best to err on the side of giving too much rather than too little information.

Fears concerning "normality." The gnawing fear of adolescence, "Am I normal?" often haunts college students as well. In this age group, however, the fear focuses specifically on sexual concerns and intimate relationships. For despite the generally more liberal attitudes about sex, prevailing social customs and sexual taboos continue to prohibit the free exchange of information about sexual topics. Thus, aside from hasty comparisons in the locker room, few young people have the opportunity to compare their bodies to those of others. Such questions as "Am I normal?" most often refer to "Am I the right shape and size?" Still another concern for normality relates to sexual experience, eg, "Am I the last

---

Questions about masturbation, anal sex, homosexuality, and oral sex

Masturbation

Exactly what is masturbation?

Do girls masturbate?

What is mutual masturbation?

Is masturbation considered abnormal if it continues into adulthood?

Is it bad to still masturbate if you have a girlfriend?

Is it normal to masturbate every day since age 13?

How often do college men masturbate on the average? College women?

Why do some women masturbate with cucumbers?

Do girls who masturbate ejaculate like boys?

Anal sex

What is anal sex?

How safe is anal sex? Is it dangerous?

Can you get diseases from anal sex?

Is it normal to enjoy anal sex with a woman?

How did man get the idea for anal sex?

Homosexuality

Is a guy who masturbates a homosexual?

Can homosexuals identify other homosexuals in a crowd?

When I masturbate I think of my friend. I just picture him and think about him. I don't want to have sex with him, or with any man. Does my masturbation fantasy mean that I'm gay?

How can two people of the same sex be attracted to each other sexually?

Besides oral sex, what do lesbians do in bed?

What causes homosexuality? Is there a cure?

Oral sex

What is oral sex?

Do men really enjoy giving oral sex, or do they do it just to please their partner?

What do people mean when they talk about body fluids being exchanged during oral sex? Are these fluids harmless if ingested?

Is cunnilingus good for your teeth?

What percentage of sexually active women enjoy swallowing during fellatio?

Describe oral sex—is it painful or dangerous?

Is semen good for acne if swallowed?

Is oral sex unhealthy?

---

virgin in the universe?," "Is it okay not to want sex all the time?," and "I never pass up a sexual opportunity—is this unusual?"

Sexual techniques. Students

Questions concerning pregnancy/birth control

Can you become pregnant before/during/after your period?

Can you get pregnant the first time you have sex with someone?

When is the best (safest) time for a woman to have sex without the worry of pregnancy?

Can you get pregnant from swallowing semen?

Is it possible to get pregnant without actually having sex, and if so, how close can you come?

Do you have to have sex to have a baby?

How long does the penis have to stay in the woman's vagina to let sperm out?

What is a rubber?

What is the safest method of birth control?

How do you use the Pill? How does it work?

How do you put a condom on?

Do you swallow foam? Before or after sex?

What is a diaphragm? What does it look like?

How soon after conception does a woman know if she is pregnant?

Questions about relationships and the other sex

How do you French kiss?

How far can a "good girl" go on a date?

Do guys know where a woman's clitoris is?

Do guys get turned on as much by girls with small breasts as opposed to girls with big ones?

Is it possible to be in love with two people at once?

How do you know when you're in love?

How long does it take to fall in love?

What do guys look for in a girl?

Do guys really have friendships like girls (or do they just talk about cars/sports/etc)?

How can you tell if your partner is responding to your touch without having a running commentary?

Can a guy who you date rape you?

Why can't men ever take "No" for an answer?

When my boyfriend won't take "No" he goes ahead and has sex with me anyway. It upsets me; he says it's OK. Is it?

and over again: "Is it okay if she's on top?," "What's the right way to get a woman ready for intercourse?," and "Is it okay that I enjoy masturbating with a vibrator?" Finally, many young people need to be reassured that their thoughts and fantasies are within normal limits. Generally speaking, all thoughts and fantasies may be regarded as normal, unless they are obsessive.

Confidentiality. This is a crucial issue for college-age students, who are now entitled to the confidential status given to adults. If you have known and treated these students since they were infants, you may find it difficult to see them as the adults they now are.

Guiding the student toward sexual maturity

Young people in general and college students in particular are sensitive about their need for adequate information and their newly achieved status as adults. It will take tact and warmth—essential qualities in the delicate balancing act of recognizing that a young person's questions may reveal a shocking lack of information and providing that information without condescension. Similarly, it is important to use correct terms for body parts and functions. Accurate terminology not only permits more precise communication; it also enables people to talk more freely and with less embarrassment.

In order to make the student feel that you are "approachable," try to convey the attitude that all questions are permitted, and that "There's no such thing as a dumb question." Commend the student for seeking accurate information in a straightforward way.

If you prefer to counsel students only about physical facts, and feel uncomfortable talking

are insatiable in their attempts to learn about sexual techniques, reflecting a prolific interest in reading how-to books and viewing steamy films. Amazingly, the same questions are asked over

Common questions about intercourse

Is it true that during sex people get stuck together like dogs?

Does it hurt to have sex?

How is the penis put into the woman? Where?

Can a guy's penis be too big for a girl?

Are you supposed to only have sex in the dark?

What is the most enjoyable sexual activity?

Do my parents still have sex? I find this hard to believe.

Is too much sex bad for your penis?

Can too much sex endanger your health?

Do certain foods make you horny?

Until what age can you have sex?

Can you have sex after age 100?

Is sex during a girl's period messy? Does the tampon get in the way?

Can you jeopardize your longevity by having too much sex?

Does the average woman think about sex as much as the average guy, or do guys just verbalize thoughts more?

Do girls really need foreplay?

Are certain positions better than others?

How do you know if you are ready to have sex?

Is sex the most important thing to college guys? Why?

Does penis size matter in having sex?

How come I'm always horny or thinking about sex?

During sex, how can I tell if the man is ejaculating if he doesn't tell me?

What's the youngest age one can have sex?

Is it possible to have sex once you become pregnant?

Is it unusual that I don't always need sex?

about relational issues and the psychological dynamics of sex, you may wish to refer the student in need of this information to the college health service or a local family planning agency, such as Planned Parenthood.

Remember: the most predictable fact about college students' questions about sex is that they will have them. If you are familiar with these students' psychosocial/sexual stages of development, are approachable, and anticipate their frequently surprising questions, they will also feel free to ask them, and with your advice, progress more contentedly along the road of healthy sexual development.

Recommended readings

Boston Women's Collective: *Our Bodies, Our Selves*. New York, Simon and Schuster, 1984.

Calderone MS, Johnson EW: *The Family Book About Sexuality*. New York, Simon and Schuster, 1980.

Carrera M: *Sex: The Facts, The Acts, and Your Feelings*. New York, Crown, 1981.

Erikson EH: *Identity: Youth and Crisis*. New York, Norton, 1968.

Zilbergeld B: *Male Sexuality. A Guide to Sexual Fulfillment*. Boston, Little, Brown & Co, 1978.

Questions about orgasm/ejaculation

I've heard that each time a male ejaculates his sperm count decreases. Can a man become sterile from an ultra-active sex life?

Is it true that men must have ejaculations fairly regularly for physical reasons?

If you have too many ejaculations can you run out of sperm quicker? At what age?

Can you ever hit bottom?

Is it possible to become sexually aroused and/or have an orgasm while under the influence of alcohol?

Why do guys reach orgasm after 30 seconds? Is it my fault?

Can orgasm be reached just by holding hands/being with someone you love?

Why do girls hold off having an orgasm longer than guys?

Is there such a thing as multiple orgasm?

I think I've had an orgasm, but I'm not sure. How do I know?

Do men ever really "come in their pants"?

What's the difference between the terms "coming" and "orgasm"?

Is it unhealthy for a male to have several orgasms within a limited amount of time?

How long should a male take to come?

Is it true that once you've reached a certain point or have gone so far, a guy must ejaculate? Does it hurt?

What is the maximum number of times a guy can come in one night?

How important are simultaneous orgasms?

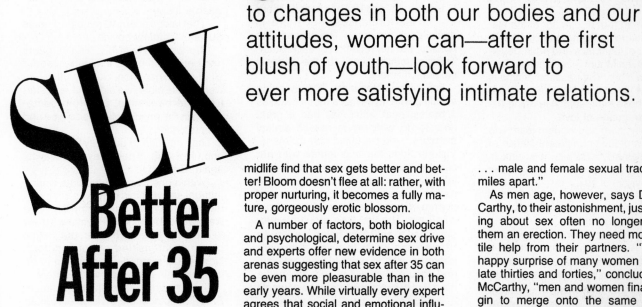

● Experts have discovered that, thanks to changes in both our bodies and our attitudes, women can—after the first blush of youth—look forward to ever more satisfying intimate relations.

SEX Better After 35

BY SHERRY SUIB COHEN

My mother-in-law worried incessantly about her daughter's lack of interest in marriage at an early age.

"You'd better meet a man before you lose your bloom," she daily and direly warned. "Bloom" to all who knew my mother-in-law was her euphemism for an irresistibly appealing state of youthful and romantic sexuality. My mother-in-law was no dope about sexuality: she met her man when she was in full bloom at 18, and held his interest for more than 50 years of marriage.

It was clear to my mother-in-law that the "losing of bloom" occurred somewhere in the early twenties, but it wasn't nearly as clear to the rest of the family, who indulged in spirited arguments about when the loss of bloom really occurred. You lost your best bloom at 25, thought a cousin. Bloom definitely lasted till 30, claimed another. It was my husband who settled the matter one day, to our infinite relief.

"You don't even *find* your bloom until you're thirty-five," he pronounced with the air of one who knows. I could only smile a self-satisfied (but modest) smile.

Because he's right. So many women over 35—even considerably over 35—overwhelmingly concur that their sex lives are more richly textured and satisfying than ever before. More in touch with their bodies, less inhibited about expressing desires to partners, infinitely more confident, women beyond midlife find that sex gets better and better! Bloom doesn't flee at all: rather, with proper nurturing, it becomes a fully mature, gorgeously erotic blossom.

A number of factors, both biological and psychological, determine sex drive and experts offer new evidence in both arenas suggesting that sex after 35 can be even more pleasurable than in the early years. While virtually every expert agrees that social and emotional influences bear far greater responsibility than physical influences for intensified sexual interest, the biological players in the passion game are, nonetheless, compelling.

● **Hormones are in our favor**

The higher the level of the sex hormone testosterone in the body, the stronger the sex drive for both men and women, maintains Niels Lauersen, M.D., associate professor of obstetrics and gynecology at the Mount Sinai School of Medicine in New York. Estrogen, the female hormone, naturally suppresses or counteracts the effects of testosterone in young women. But as a woman ages, her estrogen level gradually diminishes while her testosterone level stays constant. The fortunate result: Since there's less estrogen to suppress the testosterone, says Dr. Lauersen, "it's definitely possible that many women will feel sexier and more passionate as the years pass."

● **Only as men and women pass their mid-thirties do their mismatched sex drives operate in tandem**

"Biology has planned that girls are far less sexual than boys . . .," says Barry McCarthy, Ph.D., a professor of psychology at American University in Washington, DC, clinical psychologist at the Washington Psychological Center. "[young men] don't need much from their partners; their primary aim is to score and achieve ejaculation. Women, on the other hand, need more intimacy and touching to connect deeply, but often, in their early sexual experiences, they simply don't get what they crave.

. . . male and female sexual tracks are miles apart."

As men age, however, says Dr. McCarthy, to their astonishment, just thinking about sex often no longer gives them an erection. They need more tactile help from their partners. "To the happy surprise of many women in their late thirties and forties," concludes Dr. McCarthy, "men and women finally begin to merge onto the same sexual track. They need each other's attentive stimulation, caring and tenderness for successful lovemaking. Since the best aphrodisiac is an involved and aroused partner, sex after thirty-five becomes a slower, more foreplay-rich kind of lovemaking."

● **Females also reach orgasm more readily when they're older**

Many women say they have had to grow into deeply orgasmic pleasure by trial-and-error sexual relations over the years. As they get used to *expecting* arousal, it becomes easier to achieve orgasm. Jerry Lanoil, Ph.D., assistant professor at New York Hospital, Cornell Medical Center, Westchester Division, and a psychologist in private practice in Manhattan who leads sex-therapy programs, says, "it's sort of a self-fulfilling prophecy. If you have confidence that pleasure will come, it usually does.

"Some women report a certain bodily relaxation after childbirth that appears to make it easier for them to achieve orgasm," Dr. Lanoil adds. "This new easiness melds with their partners' lessening need to prove themselves 'studs' or sexual athletes. Because an over-forty male is not so obsessed with ejaculation, part of his attention can be transferred from his penis to his partner."

Self-worth Encourages Satisfaction

Of far greater consequence than the biological factors that pave the way for better sex after 35 are the enormous psychological influences. Sex no longer exists as the secretive, frantic gropings of adolescence or the often selfish, conquest-driven sessions of early adulthood. Perhaps most significant, men and women, graduated from the first blush of young-adult sexuality, tend to take more time for lovemaking.

And "time" is the operative word, says Robert N. Butler, M.D., a Pulitzer Prize winner, former director of the National Institute on Aging and Brookdale Professor of Geriatrics and Adult Development at the Mount Sinai Medical Center in New York. The passage of time is what acts as a comprehensive dictionary for those interested in learning the sensual language of love.

"Actually, men and women learn two languages of love at different stages of life," explains Dr. Butler. "The first is biological and instinctive and occurs in the early years of sex. It is a tumultuous language, volatile, urgent, explorative and bent on self-discovery. But, ah—the second language of love . . .

"It is a far more lyric expression," says Dr. Butler, "that is not instinctive and must be learned as people mature. It means clearing up old grudges and irritations so you don't waste your sexual energy in negativity. The secret of learning the second language of love lies in learning how to give, how to listen. It implies sensitivity and playfulness as well as passion; laughing, teasing, sharing secrets as well as fears. It involves a responsibility to maintain romance—even soupy romance. It is gloriously sexual."

And, continues Dr. Butler, sometimes "it need not involve the sex act at all."

Sex without the sex act?

Absolutely, says Laura Shapiro Kramer, 39, and married to the same man for ten years.

"Intercourse alone is not how I think of sex anymore," she says. "I think of sex as the warm embrace before we go out. Or the way, sometimes in bed, we kiss and rub those places on each other that we know ache after a long day. Or feet touching in a restaurant, or holding hands when we walk, or—best of all—the way he gets up from a chair for me when he's been waiting and I arrive. I find that irresistibly sexual.

"Before I was married I had a fairly extensive sexual life," she continues. "Then I married. At first, having kids was frightening to me. I was trying to work too, and it threw my professional life off balance. That really affected our sex life. Also, in my twenties and early thirties I didn't know how I wanted life to be so I never paid attention to the moment in which I lived. We were both pretty fragmented."

But in this past year, Laura says, something changed. "I started to focus in, really pay attention to all my riches. I think I fell in love with my life and that made it easy to find romance with my husband. We grew up this year and be-

gan to pay attention. It's like a muscle we're trying to stretch.

"For the first time," she says, "it's very important to me to be beautiful in his presence. He's learned to say, 'you look fantastic' and I love to hear it. There are no performances, but there is heavy-duty romance. The kisses, the holding, the appreciation of each other: There's nothing like it for the deepest sexual fulfillment."

For Victoria Secunda, "Finally being satisfied with myself as a mother and as a professional writer has had a great deal to do with my increased sexual pleasure." After a failed first marriage, Victoria finds her late forties with her second husband, Shel, a photographer, infinitely more sexually exciting than her earlier years. "I have greater control over my life and feel more secure about who I am. The first time around, I suddenly had to shift from being the world's oldest living virgin to being a sexually informed wife. In reality, I was awkward and unsure of myself in bed, and had a hard time expressing my own wants and needs."

Victoria is tall, beautifully elegant, and she can't help but be aware of her magnetic personal presence. Is she worried about the physical effects of aging on her looks, on her sexuality?

"I'm in much better shape now than I was fifteen or twenty years ago because I don't take my good health for granted as I used to. I eat sensibly, work out and know that when I come in from a three-mile run covered with mud, my husband will still find me sexy."

Her husband has been listening to her say this. "She's *particularly* sexy when she's covered with mud," he says.

Taking the Time for Pleasure

One of the psychological pluses of sex after 35 is the increased aptitude for *patience* that many women develop. Susan Brody is in her mid-forties and has learned the virtues of 'try, try again.' A legal secretary when she was married at 20, she found herself in a marriage where it was clear that she was more interested in sex than her husband was.

"Nothing like that for giving one a secure self-image," she comments. "I remember fantasizing about sex constantly, but the reality was that I was sleep-deprived and often in bed by eight-thirty. My children were small and made enormous demands on me. Privacy was often nonexistent."

After she was divorced at 41, Susan took more control of her life. She left her job, which gave little chance for independent action, and became an entrepreneur in the personnel business. And she met a terrific guy. Was the sex terrific? No. Very far from terrific.

"Twenty, even ten years before, I wouldn't have given him a second chance. But, in my forties, I tried harder to make it work."

"See him, but forego the sex," advised a friend.

"That lasted about 10 minutes," notes Susan. "Crummy advice."

"We were new at this singles game and both of us pretty inexperienced for all of our experience. Still, because we were a little older, we didn't have to start from the beginning, but from somewhere in the middle. He was so nice and so interesting."

They decided to go away for a weekend. Not bad. Then they went away again. Better.

"Within one month of the time when I thought sex with this man was so unsatisfying," says Susan, grinning, "we were wonderful together. Once we grew to like, then love each other, our sexual pleasure intensified a thousandfold. Now, we're married—and expect to be marvelous in bed when we're ninety."

"It's amazing," says Sheila Jackman, Ph.D., director of the Division of Human Sexuality at the Albert Einstein College of Medicine in New York, "how the mid- and post-childrearing ages often bring a sexual rejuvenation to women who were just too busy to bother much before. It's almost as if women, having done a decent job with their families, feel more competent to trust themselves in the sexual arena. They no longer have to look to friends and mates to ask, sometimes silently, 'am I OK?' "

This ability to relax extends to the bedroom. A playful quality in lovemaking often eludes many men and women when they are young and green. They take their sexuality too seriously. Many are trapped in a cinema version of what sex is supposed to be, darkly mysterious, even a lot of work to preserve all that mystery, all that pressing of the right buttons. No one ever told them that you could laugh when you were making love—in fact, that mirth was both provocative and sensual. As one woman in her sixties puts it, it seems ironic that the farther one gets from childhood, the freer one feels to "horse around."

And finally, we come to a ticklish subject: menopause. According to Joseph W. Goldzieher, director of endocrine research and a professor in the department of obstetrics and gynecology at the Baylor College of Medicine in Houston, Texas, "This is a time when women burst free from previous sexual stresses because they are liberated from worry about contraceptives, cramps, missed periods and childrearing."

As one lusty 58-year-old put it, "I consider menopause God's reward for a lifetime of service." Yet another woman referred to her postmenopausal years as a "magical bank account: the more it was drawn upon, the higher the balance of pleasure in the account."

Certainly, there are some physical effects of female aging that are not quite such a reward to enhanced sexuality. In addition to the fabled hot flashes, when ovaries stop manufacturing estrogen, decreased vaginal lubrication and thinning vaginal walls may lead to coital discomfort. Still, estrogen-replacement therapy is available and many specialists, Dr. Goldzieher among them, feel that most women of menopausal age

not only benefit sexually but also substantially cut their risks for developing osteoporosis and heart disease later in life if they opt for such treatment.

Still, uneasiness about aging lingers. I was unable to find a woman who would have it in print that she's gone through the "Big M." There was nothing left to do but come out of the closet myself. My husband and I are both in our fifties, and I have just gone through menopause. Nothing to it, mashed potatoes, has been my experience. Talk about an overrated event.

Our bodies, to look at them closely,

may be a tad lumpy, and we are sometimes surely a trifle creaky. But when we climb into bed, these same bodies, familiar with each other and with making love, can anticipate every cue and respond to it. We have learned to trust each other, not to steal the scene or hog the stage. Every now and then we throw in a new trick to keep the act fresh.

These bodies dive into the act of love with more grace and confidence than ever before. Is there sex, better sex, after 35? You better believe it. And it just keeps getting better.

YOUR SEXUAL NEEDS

Erotic Play

How *do* you rediscover that heady, exhilarated feeling when you first fell in love? All you need is the desire and a few "magic touches" . . .

Putting the Passion Back Into Your Love Life

Connie Berman

Too many people dream about the "perfect" sexual relationship, using scenes from romantic movies and novels to fuel the fires of their private fantasies. Unfortunately, real-life sex is seldom anything like that found in film or fiction, but with a little effort, you and your lover can become stars in your sexual extravaganza . . .

The Players

The goal of good sex is giving and receiving pleasure, but before you can do either you have to know your body: **Take a warm bath.** Make sure you're alone in the house and in a relaxed mood. Run a warm tub, including bath oil or bubbles, if desired. Lie back and allow your hands to travel down your body. Touch yourself as if for the first time. Feel the smoothness of your skin and explore your curves and contours. Close your eyes and concentrate on feeling and sensation. Touch your body with your fingertips and then with the flat of your hands, with a stronger pressure. Note the kind of touching that gives you the most pleasure. Allow yourself to respond with all your senses. **Message your naked body with oil.** Place a towel under you on either the bed or the floor. Use baby oil or a lubricant made specifically for messages. Rub the oil all over your body, from neck to feet. Focus your mind on your body and notice the different textures and sensations that arise as you oil and stroke every part of yourself, even your toes and armpits. What feels good, and what feels wonderful? Take note.

Look at yourself in the mirror, naked. Please suspend all judgments, such as "I'm too fat" or "my breasts are too small." Look at your body from all angles; grow accustomed to it; accept it. Look at your good points and ignore the less-than-perfect ones. Put your inhibitions aside and get to know the most intimate parts of your body visually. Look at yourself in terms of being sexy and desirable.

Now that you have explored your own body and have taken note of its responses, it's time to share this knowledge with your partner. Try and put your shy feelings aside. Bear in mind that your partner *wants* to share intimacy and pleasure with you.

In working toward the goal of good sex, there are three main principles to keep in mind.

1. Good sex does not revolve around the act of intercourse alone. Sexuality takes in sight, sound, taste, smell and touch, as well as kissing, holding, speaking, stroking and feeling. Satisfying, loving sex can take place without intercourse and without orgasm. It has to do with your whole body, not just the sex organs. It has to do with your mind and emotions as well.

2. Good sex takes time. We're not talking about an hour here and there, a hurried act of sex sandwiched between putting the kids to bed and the 11 o'clock news. Good sex involves intimacy between you and your partner, and whatever it takes to bring true intimacy about—time to talk, time to share feelings, time to cuddle and hold hands, time to bring you close to each other both physically and emotionally.

3. Good sex involves pleasure, not performance. Quite simply, what is erotically pleasing to one couple may not be to another. In bringing about a better sex life, the emphasis should always be on what feels good to the two of you.

The Setting

"Somewhere there's a place for us," the love song goes, but is there a place where you and your lover can enjoy intimacy and closeness undisturbed? You need a place where you can come down from the stresses of the day and relax without the threat of intrusions. **Get rid of distractions.** A TV set is hardly conducive to true intimacy; in fact, it can be a barrier against a couple doing some meaningful talking. Similarly, it might be a good idea to clear books and magazines—unless they're the kind you want to look at together. Other distractions to get rid of include: piles of laundry; stacks of unpaid bills (if your desk has to be in the bedroom, close it up at night); toys; dirty dishes and ashtrays; and any other clutter that is an eyesore. Design the place where you make love for that purpose only and keep it free of visual and mental distractions. Aim for softness and rounded edges. Fill your space with pillows of all sizes, down comforters, diaphanous curtains, fabric-covered walls, canopied ceilings (you can drape them with sheets); plush, upholstered chairs; thick, padded rugs. **Choose warm colors** (red, yellow and orange) rather than cool ones (blues and greens). If you prefer blue or green, make sure to use a warm accent color such as rose, melon, or gold. But if you and your partner both think a black and white color scheme is sexy, by all means go for it.

Light up your love life. It can't be stressed enough how the proper lighting affects lovemaking. Virtually no one wants to make love under harsh, glaring lights. By the same token, lighting that is too dim or non-existent depersonalizes sex since you can't even see your lover's face, let alone the expression on it. When it comes to lighting up your love life:

Do Use	Don't Use
red or pink	naked light bulbs
moonlight	overhead lighting
low-watt bulbs	75-watt bulbs or
candlelight	more
adjustable track	fluorescent lights
lighting	

The Mood

Once you've designated and decorated your intimate hideaway and equipped it with lighting that is conducive to lovemaking, there are still some "extras" that can add romance and sensuality to any environment.

Here are some "magic touches."

Satin sheets. These are a luxury item to be sure, but nothing can match the sensuous feeling of slithering and sliding all over the inimitable sleekness of satin.

Flowers. If you live in a rural or suburban area, you can pick them wild. But even off-season or in the city, fresh flowers in all varieties of colors and scents are readily available. A bunch of them placed near the bed is sure to add beauty and romance to your lovemaking.

Potted plants and trees. No matter what size your bedroom, plants hanging around the bed will add freshness and life to your environment. If you have the space, you can create an exotic jungle atmosphere in your lovenest.

Wind chimes. Available for a few dollars at any Oriental import store, wind chimes both look and sound beautiful. Hang them near your window and be lulled and soothed by their musical tinkling sound.

Floor pillows. If you have the space, a pile of these in colorful coverings can

be pleasing to the eye and can also be used as an erotic accoutrement. For variety, prop your bodies and facilitate some new positions.

Incense and scented candles. An exotic scent wafting through the air can definitely be sensually arousing.

Music. There's nothing like music to appeal to the emotions, and certain beats, voices and rhythms are guaranteed to put you in the mood for lovemaking:

• Jazz (try Charles Mingus, Miles Davis, or Horace Silver).

• Frank Sinatra (any album, but especially *In the Wee Small Hours*).

It's Showtime!

You can turn an ordinary lover into a partner who knows exactly what you need.

• **Guide your partner's hand to where you want it.** Joanna's boyfriend

---

5 SURE WAYS TO SPARK HOT (LOVING) SEX

Perhaps you've come finally to discover your true erotic needs and how to satisfy them. But, you're thinking, what about passion and romance? How can we rediscover that heady, exhilarated feeling of a couple when they first fall in love? All you need is the desire—and a generous amount of time.

• **Plan a candlelit dinner.** Have it either at home or in a nice restaurant, and either prepare or order all your favorite foods, washed down with your favorite wine. Eat in a leisurely fashion, with plenty of eye contact, handholding, and romantic toasts. We guarantee that your dessert will be each other!

• **Take a vacation together.** Even if it's just for a weekend, get away—just the two of you. Look for package deals—maybe a weekend in the city seeing shows in winter. The point is, you'll be alone together in a hotel room with no distractions.

• **Pretend it's your first time.** This can happen anywhere, but a good start is a cocktail lounge, where the two of you make believe you're meeting for the first time. Ask questions as if you're both strangers, and carry the "unknown" element through all the way to going to bed together.

• **Viewing X-rated movies.** For the best erotic effect, we recommend home viewing. If you watch them together, in the privacy of your boudoir, we bet that you won't be able to keep your hands off each other. You might get some fresh erotic ideas as well. . . .

• **Kissing and petting in public.** Yes, going this far sexually outside of the home can have a definite aphrodisiac effect. We're not advising you to "do it" in the middle of Main Street, but there's nothing wrong with getting amorous in a park, a car, a drive-in, on a beach, even in a restaurant or movie theater. After all, didn't you do it as teenagers? The point is to feel attracted and turned on to each other spontaneously—not just when you're in bed together.

Alan had the best intentions as a lover but the worse sense of direction. Every time he tried to arouse her, his finger ended up everywhere but where she literally ached to feel it. So now when he starts to fondle her, her finger lightly presses on his.

• **Tell him what really turns you on.** A simple way of letting your mate know when he pleases you is by murmuring sounds of approval. Those "oohs" and "aahs" and one-word superlatives ("Great," "Wonderful!," "Terrific!") not only let someone he is on the right track—they're a boon to the ego.

• **Don't be afraid to laugh in bed.** Years ago, Elizabeth Taylor was asked to explain what drew her so strongly to Richard Burton that she married him twice. Confided Liz: "He makes me laugh in bed." Take it from that sex symbol: laughter *does* belong in the bedroom. Gentle humor and playfulness pave the way to super sex.

The most-asked sex questions

Do you long for a happier and more fulfilling lovelife? Here's everything you need to know to put passion and sensuality back in your marriage. In the process, you and your mate can make sex better than ever!

Dr. Dagmar O'Connor with Nelly Edmondson Gupta

Dr. Dagmar O'Connor is director of the sex-therapy clinic at St. Luke's/Roosevelt Hospital Center, in New York City. She is also the author of How to Put the Love Back Into Making Love *(Doubleday, 1989) and* How to Make Love to the Same Person for the Rest of Your Life *(Doubleday, 1985).*

During seventeen years as a practicing sex therapist, I have been asked thousands of questions about sex. That's partly because communicating about sex can be very difficult; saying "I like this" or "Please don't do that" makes many people acutely uncomfortable. Therefore, most of us keep our sexual wants and needs secret. Sometimes, we don't even know ourselves how to achieve sexual satisfaction. Some of the most frequently asked questions are listed below. In my answers I have been frank and explicit about the techniques sex therapists use to help women and men conquer sexual difficulties. An astonishing number of people are unable to deal comfortably with the physiology of sex. Yet part of improving one's sex life is learning to be forthright about ones needs. Husbands and wives can improve their sex lives by sharing without embarrassment both physical and emotional intimacy. The techniques I suggest have enriched many marriages.

Q My husband and I love each other, but we rarely have time for sex these days. What's the solution?

A There are always underlying reasons that lovemaking is given short shrift, and each couple must examine these for themselves. However, the cure is always the same. You must *make* time for sex. It's a matter of setting priorities: You will make time and space for whatever is at the top of your list.

Once you've decided sex is important, put it on your schedule: Draw a red circle around Wednesday—or whatever day you choose. That night, send the kids to Grandma's house, get a baby-sitter to take them to a movie, or splurge and go to a hotel. You can also simply put a lock on the bedroom door. Remember, you're *not* locking the kids out, you're locking your privacy in.

And instead of spending time cooking, pick up sandwiches or other takeout food on the way home. The idea is to set the stage so you and your mate can spend the evening together in bed, nude. You may not even want to have sex—you might just want to give each other back rubs or read the newspaper together. The point is that you have actually made the time to enjoy each other physically.

Q My husband doesn't have trouble getting an erection, but right before we have intercourse, he loses it. What can I do to help him get turned on again?

A Be supportive, but don't put more pressure on him by being too helpful. Simply reassure him that it's okay, that you'd like more foreplay anyway, and focus on yourself. Make sure, too, that you're satisfied in this encounter so he doesn't feel it's up to him and his erection to satisfy you. If a woman knows how to have an orgasm only one way—through intercourse—she will be at a complete loss when her mate has difficulty maintaining an erection. Therefore, it's important to vary the ways you have orgasm. Experiment with oral and manual sex, and try different positions and locations, too. Intercourse is not the only option.

Q I've never had an orgasm. What can I do to have one?

A About 10 percent of all women report never having had an orgasm. However, one of every six women I see discovers, after sex therapy, that they've *always* had orgasms—they just never recognized them! Either way, the first step toward increasing sexual pleasure is to take responsibility for your own arousal. Sex therapists agree that it's very important to familiarize yourself with your own feelings through self-stimulation. Get comfortable—perhaps in a hot, relaxing bath—and caress your entire body, including the clitoral area. Try to stimulate yourself without expecting to have any feelings at all at first. If you're not used to touching yourself, you must get used to the sensations.

Conscious or unconscious anxiety about sex can also inhibit pleasure. If you feel uncomfortable, you may find yourself thinking about other things: unpaid bills or chores, for example. When this happens, you may find yourself turning off sexually. Each time your mind wanders, mentally pull yourself back into the situation and arousal will increase.

You might find it helpful to read the book *For Yourself*, by Lonnie G. Barbach (Doubleday, 1975). Many hospitals also run self-help groups for pre-orgasmic women; they have an 80 to 90 percent success rate.

Q I'm able to have an orgasm only during oral sex or masturbation. What can I do to reach climax during intercourse?

A Some women believe stimulating the clitoris is the only way they can climax. Nonsense! If you want to, you can become more flexible. At St. Luke's Hospital, we suggest the following technique for women who have this problem: Insert one or two fingers in the vagina and at the same time stimulate yourself a quarter of an inch *below* the clitoris. It may take many tries before you finally have an orgasm this way, and at first, the orgasm may not feel very strong. But this only reflects ambivalence about changing your ways.

Once you learn to have an orgasm in this way on your own, try having intercourse in the woman-on-top position. Many women find it easier to

climax this way because they have more control and freedom of movement.

Some women's orgasmic responses are blocked by suppressed feelings—such as anger or resentment toward their mate. If you're really angry, you can go through the motions of sex without feeling a thing. That's because whenever we suppress one feeling, we suppress all feelings. Therefore, you must learn to verbalize angry feelings in a constructive, nonblaming way.

If you find yourself feeling angry or resentful toward your husband during sex—and yet you don't want to break the romantic mood—say something like, "Honey, I need to lie still for a few minutes." Then silently think about how angry you are. Spend some time feeling those negative feelings as strongly as you can. Very often, after this exercise, they will diminish and sexual pleasure may increase.

Q When my husband has a few drinks, he invariably wants sex. He rarely has trouble getting an erection, but he doesn't ejaculate. I get uncomfortable and tired after a while, but when I want to stop he gets angry. He ejaculates normally when he's sober, but I'm getting turned off to sex even then. What can we do?

A Many people overcome sexual inhibitions with alcohol or drugs, but if he's so high he can't ejaculate, you need outside help. While many people think they're more interested in sex while they're high, alcohol—and other drugs—actually dulls responsiveness. If your husband is unwilling to get counseling or join Alcoholics Anonymous, I suggest *you* go to Al-Anon, a program for family members of alcoholics. (Check your phone book for local listings.)

In the meantime, try to get as much sexual satisfaction for yourself as you can. It's perfectly okay to say you'll have sex only when he's sober; doing this could also help him by making him aware that he has a real problem.

Q My husband is a real go-getter. He's also a loving husband and father. The only problem is, when we make love, I can't have an orgasm fast enough to please him. As a result, I often feel frustrated after sex. Any advice?

A Your husband sounds like someone who's good at reaching goals very fast but has trouble slowing down long enough to enjoy the process. This pattern is typical of people who have difficulty with arousal; being sexually turned on makes them feel anxious and vulnerable, and they deal with their discomfort by trying to get sex over with as quickly as possible.

The best way for your husband to deal with this is to slow down by using a technique sex therapists often recommend to men who ejaculate quickly: He needs to stimulate himself just until he achieves an erection, then he should stop and think about something completely unsexy—the mortgage or who's going to do the dishes, for example—until he loses his erection. Even if this feels a bit strange, he should do this several times before continuing on to orgasm. After he has spent time practicing by himself, you two can incorporate this into your lovemaking. Once he gets used to losing and then regaining erections without ejaculating, your husband should feel much less anxious about being in a state of arousal, and in no hurry to finish things off.

Q My husband is a macho guy who thinks he knows everything—especially when it comes to sex. How can I get him to try something new in bed without threatening his masculinity?

A You don't threaten his masculinity, he feels insecure. Although you can't force your partner to do things he doesn't want to do, you can figure out what you want and need when it comes to sex. Once you know this—and feel entitled to sexual pleasure—negotiation becomes very important.

For example, if you want to try a new position and he refuses, don't give up. You know your partner's personality; there are lots of nice ways to persuade him to do the things you want him to do. You might offer to do something he especially likes in bed, or you can even offer a playful trade like ''I'll pick up your shirts at the laundry if you'll give me twenty minutes of foreplay.'' I tell my patients never to be embarrassed by making this kind of swap; being able to bargain with your partner for what you want indicates you feel very secure in your relationship and in yourself.

Q My husband is always buying me black underwear, stiletto heels and other crazy things. He wants me to dress up and parade around, which makes me feel cheap. Shouldn't he be able to get turned on without props?

A Yes, he should. But there are two things going on here: He wants to relate sexually to a woman who looks like a ''bad girl,'' and you have a problem with looking like a bad girl. Let's start by looking at your end of the situation: Why is it so difficult for you to play his game at least a little bit?

At the same time, he should think about why it's so difficult for him to enjoy having sex with a woman he views as a good girl. It may have to do with his childhood. For example, when parents are too seductive or just too emotionally dependent on their children, sexual conflict may develop. In your husband's case, it may be that having sex with a woman who resembles Mom—that is, a woman he views as good and virtuous—feels very threatening. He may

need therapy to work through such feelings. In the meantime, if you can meet him halfway by dressing the way he likes occasionally, your sex life will probably improve. A little bit of game playing makes sex more exciting for many couples!

Q My husband confessed to me that he had an extramarital affair. I don't want to end my marriage, but I refuse to sleep with him until he gets an AIDS test. Now he's angry at me. I have to stick to my guns on this issue, don't I?

A It seems there's a lot of unresolved anger—yours and his—in this relationship. An extramarital affair often serves to displace tension in a relationship by making a triangle out of it. In most cases, both parties are responsible.

Your demand that your husband take an AIDS test may be an indication of rage, but it's also a realistic concern. Your husband has had sex with someone else, and you know nothing about this woman's lifestyle. Therefore, I believe he should comply with this request.

I suggest you and your husband seek counseling together to get past the anger that remains on both sides.

Q I love my husband but can't bring myself to perform oral sex on him. Is he asking too much—or am I a prude?

A Lots of women—and men—have reservations about oral sex. Often that's because they view semen as a body waste, and body wastes are considered dirty. Actually, semen is very clean—much cleaner than the mouth itself. Other women avoid oral sex because they don't feel they're in control of the situation.

If you are in a committed and mo-

nogamous relationship and want to learn to enjoy oral sex, you must first decide to do it because you want to grow sexually, not just to please your partner.

Next, ease into the activity. In my practice, I suggest this strategy: During the first few sessions, try giving your husband a little oral stimulation as part of foreplay. Next, as you continue sex, practice holding his penis at the base so you'll have control over whatever thrusting movements he makes. Third, tell him when you want him to stop, or ask him to stop before he ejaculates if you prefer. Many women find that they feel much more comfortable about oral sex when they have some control.

Q My husband loves to caress my breasts, but I don't enjoy it at all. Is something wrong with me?

A Many women don't feel anything when their breasts are touched. On the other hand, lots of women experience immense pleasure—and even reach orgasm—through breast stimulation. You can develop numbness—or a high degree of sensitivity—in *any* part of your body.

One problem is that many men grab or stimulate the nipples too harshly. Some are also unaware that women's breasts may swell and become extra sensitive during the menstrual period. For this reason, when your husband caresses your breasts, I suggest you put your hand over his to show him exactly how you like to be touched. This will make you feel you're in control. You do have the right to ask your partner to touch your body in a way that pleases you. Then you can work on the experience together—which is, after all, what good sex is really all about!

In therapists' offices today, the big dark secret is lack of desire

DEATH OF A SEX LIFE

Daniel Goleman

DANIEL GOLEMAN *is a psychologist who covers the behavioral sciences for* The New York Times. *Additional research for this article was completed by Marion Asnes.*

When Jane and Len*, both age 30, became engaged they were a typical happy couple. He was an engineer on the fast track and she had just left her copywriting job to pursue a serious freelance writing career. But soon after they decided to marry, Jane completely lost interest in sex. By the time she and Len walked into sex therapist Gayle Beck's office, they had not made love in five months.

Modern American culture is so highly sexualized that a visiting stranger who did nothing but watch our films and listen to our music might wonder whether people ever did anything other than seek out sexual partners and make love. But all of this sexual suggestiveness hides a dark little secret: Today, low desire such as Jane's is the most common problem bringing couples to sex therapists. In fact, the number of couples requesting treatment for low desire has increased exponentially since the sexual dysfunction was first described a decade ago, says Beck, associate professor of psychology at the University of Houston.

It is normal for partners in a committed relationship to differ somewhat in their ideal frequencies of lovemaking, Beck says, but in healthy pairings, couples manage to compromise. And as long as both are satisfied, there is no "correct" rate of sexual activity—once a month is as normal as once a day. But for people like Jane and Len, desire problems go beyond the common no-time-for-sex complaint of many two-career marriages. Such couples don't make love even when they're vacationing on a romantic tropical isle while the kids are home with Grandma.

When researchers like Masters and Johnson pioneered the study of sexual activity in the 1960s, their focus was not on desire but on arousal—the physical aspects of sexual intimacy, from the first

*The names of the couples in this article have been changed.

stirrings of excitement to orgasm. Difficulties with arousal, such as premature ejaculation or failure to reach orgasm, used to be the most common reason couples sought assistance. Sex therapists began to pay attention to lack of desire after Helen Singer Kaplan, M.D., now director of human sexuality at New York Hospital-Cornell Medical Center, published her landmark book, *Disorders of Sexual Desire* (Brunner/Mazel), in 1979.

Kaplan's book explained that desire, unlike arousal, is in the mind. It is a subjective state, more difficult to conjure and control—and therefore to treat—than arousal. A person's desire, or lack of it, may not manifest itself in behavior. In fact, a man can have an erection and people of either gender can reach orgasm even if their desire is low. "Desire and arousal are entirely different processes, each influenced by different factors," observes Beck. "Emotions affect desire more strongly than they do arousal. For example, if a woman has an argument with her partner, it may extinguish her desire for him. But if she does make love with him that night, her residual unhappiness would not impair her ability to become aroused. Only her desire is affected."

Libido Lost

The clinical definition of low sexual desire, now called *hypoactive sexual desire* (HSD) by therapists, is engaging in sexual activity (including masturbation) or having sexual thoughts, fantasies or urges less than twice a month. According to this definition, one could be celibate for years and not be diagnosed with HSD. One also could consistently reject sexual advances—as often happens among single people concerned about safe sex—and not lack desire. Unlike individuals who are unwilling to make love even though they'd like to, such as those who abstain for religious reasons, people with HSD just aren't interested. If Kim Basinger were to saunter over to a man with HSD and purr a proposition, his most likely response would be, "Not this year, dear, I have a headache."

Though therapists say they are seeing a glut of patients with desire problems, little wide-ranging research has been done to substantiate their accounts. However, in a 1986 study of the troubles patients brought to 289 sex therapists, the number one complaint was partners' discrepant levels of passion. In the early '80s, researchers at the Sex Therapy Center at the State University of New York at Stony Brook rediagnosed cases dating back to 1974. They found that the incidence of low desire grew from 32 percent of couples seeking treatment in 1974–76 to 55 percent in 1981–82. And although in early years women suffered more frequently, the sex ratio gradually shifted: The percentage of males with low levels of lust rose from 30 percent in 1974–76 to 55 percent in 1982–83.

Therapists agree that HSD has a complex range of causes and manifestations. Typically, couples seek help because one partner is no longer willing to have sex, leaving the other hurt, angry, humiliated and frustrated. Whereas once such a pair might have parted, each seeking a more sexually compatible mate, now concerns about AIDS and other sexually transmitted diseases are causing many couples to try to improve their sexual relationships.

Though lust originates in the mind, a lack of desire can still have a physical cause. Research shows that the male hormone testosterone triggers emotional desire (but is not directly linked to physical arousal) in both sexes. A lack of testosterone can squelch it, which leads some researchers to suggest extra doses of testosterone as a treatment for the condition (see "Hope in a Hormone," p. 183). Many medications, including drugs used to treat hypertension, anxiety and depression, can also reduce desire (in these cases, changing prescriptions may work a cure). Diabetes can give men erection problems that may lead to depressed desire. Among women, hysterectomy and menopause cause drops in androgens and estrogen that can shift the sex drive into low gear. In either sex, alcohol and drug abuse can suppress libido, particularly when they are long-lasting.

....

Even to Kim Basinger, men with chronic low desire would say, "Not this year, dear, I have a headache."

....

What Went Wrong?

More often, however, the issues underlying HSD are emotional, ranging from long-simmering resentment to trauma from past abuse. For example, when Dot and her husband Gary, both in their early 30s, consulted Oakland, California, psychologist Bernie Zilbergeld, they had been married six years; during that time Dot never had much interest in sex, rarely became highly aroused and never experienced orgasm. Although the two loved each other, Gary took his wife's lack of interest personally. Only after therapy enabled Dot to come to terms with a suppressed childhood horror—she had been sub-

jected to incest for five years—was she able to enjoy sexual intimacy with her husband.

Most instances of HSD owe their existence to an intricate combination of factors. According to Harold Lief, M.D., professor emeritus of psychiatry at the University of Pennsylvania, marital dissatisfaction is the culprit in about 50 percent of the HSD couples he sees. Many of these clients discover in therapy that they have lost not their sexual feeling but their feeling for their spouses. For them, sex acts as a lightning rod for anger that actually stems from very different slights, hurts and betrayals.

"One of the first questions I ask couples is whether they have an active fantasy life involving other people," Lief says. "If they do, it means that the loss of desire is situational, not a general problem." In some such cases, Lief reports, the partner who seems to lack passion may reveal in therapy that he or she is having an affair; and the couple will have to heal the emotional relationship, if possible, before working on the sexual one.

When long-established couples seek therapy for dwindling desire, Kaplan says, most often the problem has to do with long-hidden anger—or intimacy problems. Resolving the closeted anger and giving sex a higher priority are the common solutions.

In many cases of HSD, a person's sex drive may be muffled by stress or depression, then altogether squelched by a major life change. According to Kaplan, developments such as marriage or buying a house can precipitate a loss of desire because they dramatically deepen a couple's commitment. "Among these couples, diminished sexual longing is the external manifestation of a fear of intimacy," says Kaplan. "One or both members of the pair cannot reconcile a new stage of intensified emotional closeness with sexual passion." Withdrawing from sexual intimacy becomes a way of maintaining emotional distance, preserving one's sense of personal integrity and independence. In such a case, Kaplan explains, a therapist would first try sex therapy, such as having the couple share erotica and fantasies or experiment with new sexual techniques; if this didn't work, the next step would be traditional psychotherapy to alleviate the partners' anxieties about intimacy.

Beck used both sex therapy and interpersonal communication training to help Len and Jane. Over the course of their treatment, the real causes of their trouble slowly surfaced. When Jane agreed to marry Len and simultaneously started working from home, he expected her to act more like a traditional housewife. He had grown up in a Hindu family in which men and women held highly circumscribed roles. Jane wanted an egalitarian relationship. After the couple became engaged, their cultural differences led to conflicts Jane didn't know how to handle. She panicked, and as a result lost interest in sex.

In therapy, Beck taught the couple to communicate and resolve conflicts through discussion. Then, in a private session, Jane confided to Beck that Len was an inexperienced lover. "All Len really needed

Hope in a hormone

DESIRE MAY BE ROOTED in the mind, but that doesn't mean it lacks physical traces. In fact, the "chemistry" that draws one person to another is truly chemical. Testosterone, called the male sex hormone but present in both men and women, is the substance now known to directly influence desire by stimulating the brain. What's more, testosterone therapy may be a promising way to replenish flagging passion in men and women alike.

For years, testosterone had been assumed to regulate sexual behavior, but recent studies have shown that it actually drives desire. When various researchers administered testosterone to men with underactive gonads, study subjects reported increased desire and more frequent sexual fantasies. Women whose ovaries have been removed surgically are now treated with testosterone to stimulate desire. Today, some sex therapists recommend that patients with hypoactive desire consult an endocrinologist to assess whether some physical problem is reducing their testosterone levels.

For people with normal hormone levels and low desire, however, testosterone's usefulness is controversial. A study published last year by Dr. Patricia Schreiner-Engel and colleagues at New York's Mount Sinai School of Medicine and at the University of Siena in Italy found no measurable difference in testosterone levels of normal women and those with hypoactive sexual desire (HSD). (The study also ruled out another suspected culprit—the hormone prolactin, which stimulates lactation. Excessive amounts of it can suppress desire, but the HSD women had normal levels.)

Nevertheless, Dr. Harold Lief, professor emeritus of psychiatry at the University of Pennsylvania, is experimentally treating a small number of premenopausal women with intramuscular testosterone injections. Although his data are still preliminary, he does report that half the women under treatment have shown some increase in sexual desire.

Research points to other potential aphrodisiacs as well. It's known that testosterone triggers the brain with the help of certain neurotransmitters, including dopamine. Some researchers believe that drugs affecting dopamine may hold promise as kindlers of desire, but so far none have proved reliable.—*D.G.*

was some sex education," Beck said. After six weeks, Len and Jane came to therapy giggling; they were making love again, and enjoying it. They are now happily married.

Like other dramatic life changes, childbirth may provoke a retreat from sex, but not necessarily because it increases the new parents' sense of commitment. Aside from fatigue, which could dampen anyone's ardor, a couple may now view sex as solely for reproduction rather than as mutual pleasuring. In addition, the expanded role of the woman—from lover to mother as well—may leave both partners anxious about her sexuality. A new mother may be so enraptured with her child, or so engulfed by her new responsibilities, that she closes out her husband for a spell. A new father, too, may be so overwhelmed by his new role that he ignores the needs of his wife. Recognizing the causes of these feelings can help couples adjust to becoming a family without losing each other.

Perhaps the most insidious reason for loss of desire—even though it may be the easiest to remedy—is the stress of an overloaded life. For so many people who live out multiple roles—worker, spouse, parent, caretaker of an aging parent—making the earth move at night may seem like just too much. "Some couples work too hard to have sex during the week, spend the weekend taking care of the kids and seem to give up on sex," says Lief. These couples may not have true HSD, but their anhedonic, all-work-and-no-play lifestyle may be just as destructive to their libidos. The goal for them is to find time for each other before they drift too far apart. In rare instances, individuals report long-standing low sexual desire for no apparent reason—they are relaxed, physically healthy, psychically fit and love their partners without ambivalence. These HSD cases are the most mystifying, and are least likely to be treated successfully. Perhaps, for these asexual few, the best way to cope with HSD is to find a partner with the same condition. "When neither member of a couple wants to engage in sex, we don't say they lack desire," says Lief. "We call them 'ideal mates.' "

Old/New Sexual Concerns

- **Sexual Hygiene (Articles 45-49)**
- **Sexual Abuse and Violence (Articles 50-53)**
- **Focus: Gender Roles (Articles 54-58)**

This final unit deals with several topics that are of interest or concern for different reasons. In one respect, however, these topics have a common denominator—they have all recently emerged in the public's awareness as "social issues." Unfortunately, public awareness of issues is often a fertile ground for misinformation and misconceptions. In recognition of this, it is the overall goal of this section to provide some objective insights into pressing sexual concerns.

Health consciousness has increased through the 1970s and 1980s. In the past decade the term wellness has been coined to represent healthiness encompassing physical and emotional factors. Sexual health or wellness is often incorporated into this sought-after ideal. In order to accomplish sexual health we must learn about sexual hygiene, normative sexual processes, and the effects of diseases on our sexual functioning. Of particular concern in this area are diseases misappropriately labeled "social diseases." This stigmatization may reflect a still prevalent negative aura that surrounds sexuality. We can achieve sexual health only when we can learn about and be responsible for our sexual selfs in a positive and accepting way.

The *Sexual Hygiene* subsection of this unit strives to help readers achieve sexual health by providing articles on sexually transmitted diseases, one each on premenstrual syndrome, menopause, and impotence.

Sexual abuse and violence is another topic of ongoing concern. These acts of violence are especially pernicious when an acquaintance, a relative, or a parent is involved. The trust that may have existed is destroyed and the relationship may be damaged beyond repair. The psychological scars of child sexual abuse and incest may last for years and may not heal without professional help. It is "the hurt that keeps on hurting."

Some of the most devastating and flagrant violations of individual sexual and personal integrity arise from the misuse of sex as a means of humiliation and violence. Rape is an example of this. Public awareness of the threat and incidence of rape must increase in order to dispel long-held myths about this crime. It must be emphasized that rape is not a sex act; it is a crime of violence.

Another kind of sexual abuse or misuse that has begun receiving media attention is sexual harassment. Like sexual abuse, incest, and rape, sexual harassment has existed for some time prior to its gaining media attention. Also like its related abusive behaviors, sexual harassment is surrounded by myths, misinformation, and tendencies to "blame the victim."

The first article in the *Sexual Abuse and Violence* subsection deals with sexual harassment. It is informative and counters many commonly held myths about the incidence, types, and effects of this abuse of sexuality in the 1980s. The next article profiles the youngest New York City prostitutes and finds common patterns of abuse and trauma. The last two articles comprise a point-counterpoint on the most prevalent kind of rape—date rape. The first sensitizes readers to this traumatic occurrence and provides guides for responding to and assisting victims. The second questions the appropriateness of current definitions of rape especially date rape. It raised issues of intent, consent, force, and others.

The focus section of this year's edition is on gender differences and similarities. Over two decades after the women's liberation movement began challenging women's roles, there is still question, disagreement, and high emotions associated with male or female roles. What is the ideal woman or man for the 1990s?

The final five articles focus on today's changing and unchanging personal, societal, and cultural perceptions of maleness and femaleness. In addition to image and role issues, several of the articles address how gender identities affect relations between the sexes, including sex and marriage. These articles also seek to enhance the sensuality and sexual pleasure of males, females, and couples.

Looking Ahead: Challenge Questions

How knowledgeable are you about sexual health issues such as sexually transmitted diseases, infections, and related problems? What keeps you from being more informed and involved in your own sexual wellness?

How would you have defined sexual harassment before reading the article in this section? In what ways has your view changed after reading it?

Is date or acquaintance rape a problem for many college women? What are some of its causes and what relationship changes may prevent it? What are some long-lasting effects of rape?

What do you dislike about society's expectations of your gender role? Do you wish, like Henry Higgins of *My Fair Lady,* that women were more like men? Or men more like women?

If the gender gap is closing as one author predicts, what do you see as the effects?

CHLAMYDIA
IS NOT A FLOWER.

*It's a Sexually Transmitted Disease
with Devastating Effects.*

Predictors of Risky Adolescent Sexual Behavior

Ralph DiClemente, PhD

Ralph DiClemente is Research Psychologist, Department of Epidemiology and Biostatistics, University of California, San Francisco, School of Medicine.

Adolescents have recently emerged as a risk group for acquisition of the human immunodeficiency virus (HIV), based on epidemiologic data describing the frequency of sexual intercourse, number of sexual partners, and prevalence of sexually transmitted diseases in this age group.[1,2] Currently, adolescents between the ages of 13 and 21 account for approximately 1.2% of the total number of AIDS cases in the United States.[3] However, relying on prevalence data as a marker for assessing the threat of AIDS for this population severely underestimates the potential for infection. In view of the variable and lengthy latency period between HIV infection and appearance of AIDS symptoms,[4] many of the persons diagnosed with AIDS at age 20–29 may have acquired their infection as teenagers.

At present, there are no representative population-based studies for estimating seroprevalence among adolescents. Screening of potential military applicants, who are typically in their late adolescence, has identified an overall seroprevalence of approximately 1.5 per 100,000, with ethnic/racial-specific rates of 0.8, 4.1, and 2.3 per 100,000 for whites, blacks, and Hispanics,

respectively.[5] The unrepresentative nature of the samples studied, especially the potential for high-risk individuals to self-defer, suggests that actual rates may be substantially higher.

A key research objective in preventing the spread of HIV in the adolescent population is to identify those factors associated with the adoption or maintenance of health-promoting sexual behavior (eg, condom use during intercourse) that may reduce the risk of exposure.

Knowledge of disease prevention

There is no evidence to suggest that knowledge about AIDS *per se*, especially routes of HIV transmission, motivates adolescents to adopt or maintain health-promoting behaviors.[6]

In a recent study of 1,127 college students from across the United States, we evaluated the relative effect of knowledge about AIDS-prevention behaviors and perceived susceptibility to HIV infection on the reduction of sexual risk behaviors.[7] We found that while level of AIDS knowledge was not associated with behavior change, the perception of personal susceptibility to HIV acquisition was strongly associated with reduction in high-risk behaviors (unprotected sexual intercourse, anal intercourse, and many different sex partners).

Not only was AIDS knowledge not associated with positive behavior change, but those adolescents with lower levels of knowledge about disease transmission and prevention reported slightly less sexual risk-taking behavior. Of those reporting behavioral changes, very few selected abstinence as a risk-reduction strategy.

Clearly, AIDS knowledge is necessary for adolescents to identify effective risk-reduction strategies and, equally important, to recognize those strategies that are ineffective. However, this knowledge, in and of itself, is not sufficient to motivate behavior change. One possible explanation: Although adolescents are knowledgeable about the threat of HIV infection, their decision-making processes may be mediated by such factors as a sense of personal invulnerability[8] and optimistic bias[9] about the likely consequences of risk-taking. Adolescents apparently discount their risk, with the result that they do not view the actual risk objectively. Perhaps as a direct consequence of lack of experience, many youths consider themselves invulnerable and are therefore less likely to adopt preventive behaviors.

Peer-related behavior

A second factor that determines whether adolescents will practice AIDS-preventive behavior is their perception of normal, peer-group sanctioned behavior.[10] Adolescents are generally more susceptible than adults to the influence of peer-group values, given their lack of experiences and their limited exposure to other age groups.

In another as yet unpublished study, we investigated factors affecting condom use in 802 adolescents (mean age, 16 years). The adolescents completed a self-administered questionnaire in which they reported (1) what they consider normal peer behavior, (2) other factors that might affect sexual behavior (eg, respondent's number of sexual partners, age, race, gender, age of sex debut, and knowledge about HIV transmission and prevention), and (3) their frequency of engaging in condom-protected sexual intercourse. Condom use was characterized as "always-sometimes" or "rarely-never."

Of all the factors under investigation, the only significant one was perception of normal peer behavior. Thus, the teenagers who felt that their peer group believed in using condoms were almost twice as likely to report using a condom during sexual intercourse.[11] Peer group identification and its resulting social influence thus appears to be a powerful force in shaping behavior among adolescents, particularly minority adolescents.

Conclusion

Behavior is the outcome of a multifactorial decision-making process in which many influences—biological, social, developmental, and psychological—underlie the willingness of adolescents to tolerate, accept, and seek risks. While much more remains to be learned about the factors that motivate teenagers to adopt or continue health-promoting sexual practices, the evidence to date suggests two important predictors of adolescent risk-taking behavior: (1) their perception of their risk of contracting HIV infection and (2) whether or not their respective peer group supports health-promoting behaviors. Future studies will need to more clearly define the interrelationships between determinants of risk-reduction behavior and the magnitude of behavioral change associated with these determinants.

References

1. DiClemente RJ: The emergence of adolescents as a risk group for human immunodeficiency virus infection. *Journal of Adolescent Research* 5:7, 1990.
2. Hein K: AIDS in adolescents: A rationale for concern. *New York State Journal of Medicine* 88:290,1987.
3. Centers for Disease Control: AIDS Weekly Surveillance Report, United States. Atlanta, GA, CDC AIDS Program, January 14, 1990.
4. Curran JW, Morgan WM, Hardy AM, et al: The epidemiology of AIDS: Current status and future prospects. *Science* 229:1352, 1985.
5. Burke DS, Brundage JF, Herbold JR, et al: Human immunodeficiency virus infection among civilian applicants for United States military service, October 1985 to March 1986; demographic factors associated with seropositivity. *N Engl J Med* 316:131, 1987.
6. Becker MH, Joseph JG: AIDS and behavioral change to reduce risk: A review. *Am J Public Health,* 78:394, 1988.
7. DiClemente RJ, Forrest K, Mickler S: College students' knowledge and attitudes about AIDS and changes in AIDS-preventive behaviors. *Journal of AIDS Education and Prevention,* in press.
8. Gruber E, Chambers CV: Cognitive development and adolescent contraception: Integrating theory and practice. *Adolescence* 22:211, 1987.
9. Weinstein ND: Why it won't happen to me: Perceptions of risk factors and susceptibility. *Health Psychology* 3:431, 1984.
10. Fisher JD: Possible effects of reference group-based social influence of AIDS-risk behavior and AIDS prevention. *American Psychologist* 43:914, 1988.
11. DiClemente RJ: Psychosocial determinants of adolescents' HIV-related risk-taking behavior, in D'Angelo L, Ma T (eds): *HIV and Youth: The Greatest Challenge.* New York, Elsevier Press, in press.

DANGEROUS LIAISON

A Mysterious, Sexually Transmitted Virus Threatens to Trigger a New Epidemic

Janny Scott

Janny Scott is a Times *medical writer.*

There is something pure and innocent about Patty and Victor Vurpillat. She was 18 and he was 19 when they met in 1988. They fell in love. She moved in. Within 10 months, they were married. Everybody freaked, as Victor tells it; it was like the 1950s.

The newlyweds found a sunny little apartment in Pacific Palisades. She stocked the refrigerator with health food and began training for a marathon. He enrolled at Santa Monica College, bringing home A's and B's. Conversation turned to babies.

But then Patty and Victor came down with a most un-1950s disease—a condition fraught with all the uneasiness of sexual relations in the age of AIDS, caused by a virus with disturbing links to cancer that threatens to become the venereal disease of the 1990s.

It all started with some bumps on Patty's cervix. Genital warts, the nurse-practitioner at the clinic pronounced them. A closer examination turned up an area of abnormal tissue. The clinic recommended a biopsy to check for signs of cancer.

Suddenly Patty was on her back with a microscope perched between her thighs. A nurse peered in and snipped away at her insides. Later, Patty returned to have the warts frozen off. It was creepy: She could feel her cervix defrost.

Victor, too, had to be vetted. There he lay in a women's clinic, surrounded by women. They put his feet up in stirrups; there were little mittens on the stirrups. Two nurses set about removing tiny warts, one by one.

Back at home panic colored Patty's thoughts: She would get cancer; she would have a hysterectomy; there would never be any children. She tried reminding herself that the risk was small. But fear ached in her gut.

"It was just awful—not knowing what's going on with your body and if you're going to be OK or not," she said recently. "There's a certain percent chance you're going to be all right. But then, maybe you're not."

Patty and Victor Vurpillat are infected with a strain of human papilloma virus—HPV—the virus that lurks behind one of the country's fastest-spreading sexually transmitted diseases and is rapidly becoming a prime suspect in the search for the causes of cervical cancer.

As much as 15% of the population may already be carrying the virus—a fact that many health officials view with alarm. It is estimated that 750,000 people become infected every year—most of them teen-agers and young adults who are healthy, sexually active and entering their peak reproductive years.

For most of them, HPV infection will mean nothing more than a frustrating struggle with the virus's most common visible symptom, genital warts—small, cauliflower-like growths that usually can be removed with various disconcerting and less-than-perfect treatments.

But, for a few, HPV may contribute to a profoundly disturbing form of cancer—cancer of the genitals, and in particular, cervical cancer, a condition that threatens the core of one's sexuality, the ability to reproduce and, occasionally, life itself.

The difficulty is, it is impossible to predict who will fall into which group.

As a result, millions of Americans find themselves condemned to a sentence of life beneath the cloud of HPV, carrying in their tissues an incurable and highly infectious virus that may eventually unleash a devastating cancer.

The burden falls especially hard on women. Both sexes can carry and spread the virus, but symptoms are more pronounced in women. Although the virus has been associated with cancers of the penis and anus, the greater risk appears to be cancer of the cervix.

What's more, some people are spreading the virus unknowingly: It is transmitted by contact with warts, and warts often go unnoticed. Some physicians suspect that HPV may even occasionally be spread indirectly—perhaps on a tanning bed, toilet or washcloth.

For that reason, it may not be possible to protect oneself completely. Physicians strongly recommend condoms. But they acknowledge that even condoms are not foolproof; some warts remain exposed, and contact can occur before or after the condom is used.

What are the long-term implications of the spread of such a virus?

Many researchers insist that HPV is unlikely to produce a significant increase in the number of deaths from invasive cervical cancer in the United States, because cervical cancer is highly treatable and, in most cases, even preventable if women are screened regularly.

Nevertheless, some have noticed a worrisome trend—an apparent rise in the incidence of cervical dysplasia, abnormalities in the cells on the surface of the cervix that, although treatable, in some cases turn out to be antecedents of cancer.

Some physicians also have reported an increase in adenocarcinomas, a particularly nasty subset of cervical tumors. Those tumors now seem to strike younger women in particular, researchers say; and they may be especially difficult to detect early and cure.

Both of those trends, which some researchers believe may be linked to HPV, suggest a startling shift in the demographics of cervical cancer: A disease that in the past has afflicted mostly women in their late 40s and beyond is now threatening women in their prime.

"My guess is that the teen-age cervix is phenomenally sensitive, in that there is a tremendous amount of cell division," says Dr. Stephen L. Curry of Tufts University. "If they are exposed to whatever carcinogens there are, there will be a higher incidence of cancer."

Even more troubling is the fact that as many as half of all women in the United States don't undergo annual cervical cancer screening, without which it is impossible to detect and treat the cancer's precursors, staving off more serious disease.

At a large public-health clinic near downtown Los Angeles that serves mostly low-income Latinos, women are turning up with the earliest stages of cervical cancer at twice the national rate, and their average age is just 24.

HPV infection is rampant among her clients, says Catherine Wylie, who oversees the family-planning program at the H. Claude Hudson Comprehensive Health Center at Adams Boulevard and South Grand Avenue. The spread will continue, she says, until the law requires that partners of people who have HPV be tracked down and treated.

"Our women have sex early because they marry at 16 to 18," Wylie said recently. "As long as this disease is not reportable, and there's no partner follow-up and treatment, I think we're going to have an epidemic of cervical cancer."

There is nothing new about warts—on the genitals or elsewhere. They have been around for millennia. As early as the 1st Century AD, physicians described the more ignominious form—warts on the genitals and anus, also known as condylomata.

But it was not known until this century that warts came from viruses—a specific family of viruses called human papilloma viruses. (It is now known that some strains cause common warts on the hands and feet and other strains cause genital warts.)

That discovery led to an intriguing glimpse of HPV's mysterious links to cancer.

In the early 1930s, researchers discovered that a form of papilloma virus caused benign tumors (also known as papillomas) in cottontail rabbits. When exposed to certain chemicals that were otherwise innocuous, those tumors quickly turned malignant.

Even today, those initial animal experiments remain a model for examining the way papilloma virus-induced abnormalities can progress to cancer, researchers say. But the links between HPV and human cancers would remain unrecognized for another 40 years.

In the meantime, it became clear how HPV is spread.

The first report of sexual transmission of HPV came in 1954. Twenty-four women came down with genital warts after their husbands returned from the Far East. All 24 husbands admitted to having had sex overseas, and all had recently had penile warts.

Sex with a partner who has untreated warts is known now to be extremely risky, since the virus is highly concentrated in warts. In studies, most partners of people with warts developed warts themselves within weeks or months. Cuts and abrasions appear to increase one's infection with the virus.

There is at least one other form of transmission: HPV can be spread to an infant during childbirth. In rare cases, the infection produces a life-threatening condition in which warts on the infant's larynx interfere with his or her ability to breathe.

And because physicians have seen instances of HPV spreading in cases in which no sexual contact is believed to have occurred—for instance, among non-intimate members of the same household—some wonder whether HPV is spread in other ways. Those cases, however, are difficult to prove.

By whatever routes, genital warts began proliferating in the 1960s under the influence of increased sexual freedom and declining use of barrier contraceptives. Statistics on visits to U.S. physicians indicate a 12-fold increase in cases in just 20 years.

According to the National Disease and Therapeutic Index, the number of visits for treatment of genital warts leaped from 160,000 in 1966 to 1 million just a decade later. By 1988, that number had reached 1.2 million.

In the meantime, HPV research languished, in part because of an obstacle that has yet to be overcome. Scientists had never managed to grow HPV in the laboratory, making it difficult to study its transmission, its treatment and how the virus affects cells.

Then in the mid-1970s, a pathologist working in a laboratory in Canada began noticing a peculiar pattern under his microscope: He found striking similarities between cells from genital warts and cells from pre-malignant lesions on the cervix.

The pathologist, Alexander Meisels, a professor at Quebec's LaVal University, was intrigued by two features in particular. The cells he was studying seemed to have in common an unusual cavity around the nucleus and an overabundance of a protein called keratin.

Suddenly, it dawned on Meisels: The lesions must have come from the same source as the warts. If HPV caused not just warts but cervical lesions as well, and lesions were known in some cases to develop into cancer, then HPV had a role in the process leading to cervical cancer.

"The cells seem to have to be infected [with HPV] first," says Meisels, who is also head of the department of pathology and cytology at Saint-Sacrement Hospital. "But that is not sufficient. Something else is acting on them."

Cervical cancer has long been thought to be caused at least in part by a sexually transmitted infectious agent. Among the most important risk factors for the disease is simply the number of sexual partners a woman has had and the number of partners her partner has had.

Worldwide, cervical cancer is a top cancer killer. Half a million women come down with it annually. Half of those women will die within 2½ years, mostly in countries with poor access to health care and inadequate cervical cancer screening.

In the United States, the death rate has plummeted since the Papanicolaou smear made it possible to identify and treat the precursors of cervical cancer. This year, there will be about 13,500 new cases of invasive cancer and 6,000 deaths—down nearly 70% since the 1950s.

Even so, some researchers are worried by recent reports of an increase in the especially virulent adenocarcinomas—an apparent rise that some believe may come from a sexually transmitted infectious agent, perhaps HPV.

Twenty years ago, this particularly aggressive type of tumor made up just 5% of all invasive cervical cancers. Now that figure is 30%, says Dr. Alex Ferenczy, a professor of pathology and obstetrics and gynecology at McGill University in Montreal.

Sex with a partner who has untreated warts is risky, since that's where the virus is concentrated.

There are also signs that invasive cancer is striking at a younger age. According to Ferenczy, 22% of all invasive cancers in developed countries are now diagnosed in women aged 35 and younger. That figure is up from less than 10% just 15 years ago.

"That's a heavy-duty increase," Ferenczy says. "This has major clinical implications for whoever screens women for cervical cancers. They have to remember that invasive cancer is no longer and not necessarily a disease for elderly women."

That lesson is not lost on Dr. Louise H. Connolly, medical director of the Manhattan Beach Women's Health Center, a full-service medical clinic operated by Centinela Hospital on a busy South Bay thoroughfare a few miles from the beach.

A graduate of Yale Medical School, Connolly opted for a career in obstetrics and gynecology. What appealed to her was the possibility of practicing preventive medicine—as she puts it, protecting a woman's right to sexuality without harmful consequences.

But these days, harmful consequences walk into the office every day. About one in five of Connolly's patients is infected with HPV. The average age of those women, Connolly figures, is 22. News of the diagnosis, and the risk of cancer, comes as a rude shock.

"When you're 18 to 25, you feel that your health is guaranteed. You feel invulnerable to major disease," Connolly says. "I think initially they're shocked and frightened

that they're 18 or 20 years old and they have something that might lead to cancer.

"Right behind that, they feel they have a sexually transmitted disease and they may feel dirty," she added. "So it's fear and shame together. It cuts them off from asking people for support—from family, boyfriends and friends."

One woman, who asked to be identified simply as Annie, was in her mid-40s when she discovered that she had genital warts. She was divorced at the time, sexually active and in a relationship with a man she has since married.

Annie had no gynecologist, so she told her family doctor. For a year and a half, they fought a losing battle against the warts. Annie would go in for treatment with various ointments, the warts would disappear, and within several months they would be back.

"It's emotionally painful and it's demeaning," Annie says. "You've got a sexually transmitted disease and someone is fooling with your bottom. And to be honest, one of the hardest parts about the whole thing was my husband's lack of understanding.

"He just didn't understand what I was going through emotionally," she says. "It was more like an imposition to him. He'd see me going for another treatment and he'd think, 'She's going to be out of commission for a week.' "

After eight or 10 episodes, even the physician was becoming impatient. So when the next wart arrived, Annie went to see Connolly. "When she examined me, she said, 'This is not a wart,' " Annie recalls. "It's something else, and I want to remove it.' "

Connolly cut off the growth and sent it in for a biopsy. The results came back: Annie had early cancer of the vulva. (Vulval cancer is another genital cancer that has been linked to HPV but is less common than cervical cancer.)

Fortunately, Annie's cancer was at its earliest stage. It was confined to the top layer of the skin and could be cut off easily. Simply removing it and a surrounding margin of normal tissue for a pathologist's scrutiny would probably be sufficient treatment.

But Connolly had Annie return for colposcopy, an extensive internal examination with a binocular microscope that magnifies and illuminates the vagina and cervix. Through the scope, Connolly would be able to detect any warts or more troubling changes.

"It was horrible, just horrible," Annie remembers, referring to her fear of what Connolly might find. "There you are, spread-eagle, for [nearly half] an hour. None of it really hurts. . . . But every time she'd stop and look at something, I'd think, 'Oh God, oh God, oh God.' "

HPV infection contributes to a range of manifestations in women. They fall along a continuum from barely significant to severe. Some people suffer no symptoms, some suffer just one. Others proceed at varying rates of speed from one to the next.

The least serious are warts and so-called subclinical infections—barely perceptible changes in the cells that cover the cervix. A specialist scrutinizing cells scraped off during a Pap smear might detect the virus's distinctive footprint—

clumps of oddly misshapen cells.

More-extensive cell changes create a condition known as dysplasia, or cervical intraepithelial neoplasia (CIN). Those abnormalities can be detected through Pap smears or colposcopy, where they appear as areas of white tissue where it should be smooth and pink.

Dysplasia can range from mild to severe. Many cases will clear up spontaneously, some become worse. A small minority seem to advance to become carcinoma *in situ,* an early and highly treatable form of cancer confined to the top layer of tissue of the affected organ.

Finally, there can be invasive, or malignant, cancer.

Deep in the vastness of Los Angeles County USC Medical Center, Carol Carriere peers through a microscope at a small glass slide. Thousands of cells from a woman's cervix are smeared on the slide, clustered like dense constellations of stars.

Carriere is chief cytotechnologist in the Department of Cytology at County USC. Some 30,000 slides pass through her lab every year. Most are from Pap smears, and many carry the tell-tale signs that HPV has invaded the cells.

Scanning the slide, Carriere looks for subtle changes—say, a cell with an oversized nucleus or cells in abnormal patterns of clumping. A key tip-off to HPV's presence is that enlarged and irregularly shaped nucleus, often surrounded by a widening cavity.

In moderation, she says, those changes suggest subclinical infection or warts. More extensive abnormalities may indicate pre-malignant cells.

Treatment of HPV-related diseases depends upon the symptoms. There are do drugs that can rid the body of the virus, just as there is no vaccine. So physicians such as Connolly treat the manifestations: They freeze or vaporize or slice off the warts and areas with abnormal cells.

The first line of attack is a variety of chemicals, administered either by the patient or physician. For persistent warts and warts on the cervix, many physicians use cryosurgery, freezing the wart and surrounding tissue with a low-temperature probe.

Another option for extensive warts and dysplasia is laser surgery, in which a concentrated beam of light serves as a scalpel. Finally, a so-called cone biopsy is occasionally used to slice a cone-shaped chunk of abnormal tissue from the cervix.

It is not really known why such approaches work, but they seem to. Many people treated for warts and dysplasia never experience a recurrence. By removing a repository of virus, the treatments may be diminishing the load of virus in the body. Or, they may be triggering an immune response.

Nevertheless, there are limitations.

"It's clear that you can't cure a viral infection by burning the skin off," says Dr. Kenneth L. Noller, chairman of the department of obstetrics and gynecology at the University of Massachusetts Medical School. "It would be like trying to cure a cold by burning off the lining of the lungs."

Connolly, for one, also prescribes what she discreetly terms "pelvic rest" until the warts or areas of dysplasia have

been treated and have healed. She advises frequent Pap smears—as often as every three to six months—a repeat colposcopy in a year and examination and treatment of any partners.

"Most of them drag their feet," Connolly says. "Some couples break up: She gets angry, they have a fight, he leaves."

Genital warts are common in men as well as women. They can occur on the penis, anus, scrotum and in the urethra. But they are often less visible than on women, noticeable only with close examination. So, many men unknowingly infect their partners.

There may also be certain "high-risk males"—men for whom a succession of partners or wives develop cervical cancer. Some researchers have speculated that such men are

---

There are no drugs that can rid the body of the HPV virus, just as there is no vaccine.

---

transmitting some carcinogen, probably an infectious agent, perhaps a strain of HPV.

Gynecologists say many men's physicians are unfamiliar with HPV infection.

"Some of them will just go to their family practitioner, who just eyeballs them and says, 'No, you don't have it,' " says Dr. Virginia A. Siegfried of Los Angeles. "That may be part of the problem in some of the patients we seem to keep getting back again: They're just re-exposed."

"You need a urologist or dermatologist who will go over the entire penis, urethra, scrotum and peri-anal area carefully," Connolly says. "They should check the opening of the urethra to make sure there isn't one tiny wart sitting in there that's going to infect someone."

Nan Singer (not her real name) discovered in her early 30s that her husband had warts on his anus. When she asked him about them, he conceded that he had had them for seven months. But he had neglected to tell her and had neglected to have them treated.

Even after she confronted him, her husband was reluctant to see a doctor. Then he expected Nan to be responsible for seeing that he used the medication, and even for administering it. Nan felt betrayed and disgusted; their sexual relationship deteriorated. Existing problems in their marriage grew worse.

"The thing that shocked me was that he was so uninformed," says Nan, who believes her husband's response to the disease contributed significantly to their subsequent divorce. "He knew what they were, but he made no effort to understand what it could mean to me."

Nan began having Pap smears every four to six months. One after another, they came back normal, or Class 1. Then, during one four-month period, the results switched suddenly from Class 1 to Class 3, signifying cell changes consistent with dysplasia.

Nan's gynecologist recommended laser surgery, a process Nan likens to "taking napalm to your insides." She describes her recovery as protracted and painful, sloughing off dead tissue for days. The smell seemed so foul, she feared co-workers noticed.

Neither Nan nor Annie has had any further problems. But both are familiar with their gynecologists' waiting rooms. They go in every few months and have tried to make peace with the unsettling knowledge that trouble could surface any time.

Nan has become one of those women Connolly set out to protect: She is now a veteran of HPV, herpes infection, three ectopic pregnancies and pelvic inflammatory disease; but at 34, she remains determined to preserve her ability one day to conceive and bear a child.

"I've lived with a lot of pain and this bad equipment for years," Nan said bitterly one morning recently, in an interview at her home near Los Angeles. "I [am not] about to lose it for venereal warts."

Unfortunately, there are as many questions as there are answers about HPV.

Many more people are infected than come down with any visible symptoms. What percentage will develop symptoms remains unknown. "People are flipping up figures," Ferenczy says. "Probably 5% to 15% will show up with some sort of HPV-related disease."

Of those who do, most will develop warts or dysplasia. In many of those, the conditions might clear spontaneously if left alone. In a small percentage, HPV infection will lead to cancer. What percentage that will be, and who they are, is impossible to say.

"I'm not sure now we know what the true risk is to a woman who has HPV infection," says Dr. John Curtin, a gynecologic oncologist at the USC School of Medicine.

The infection can remain hidden for long periods, surfacing at any time. One 65-year-old woman in Minnesota recently developed genital warts inexplicably, leaving her physician, Dr. Leo B. Twiggs, wondering why her symptoms emerged when they did.

According to Twiggs, director of the Women's Cancer Center at the University of Minnesota Hospital, research suggests that symptoms may surface when a patient's immunity is down. Other factors probably cause the immune suppression, he says; but maybe the virus can, too.

"Once the virus is interlocked into the cells, it's like a small computer program or a mini-computer hooking into a mainframe," Twiggs says. "The question is, where does it sit? Next to what operations systems? What's it doing there?" No one really knows what turns the program on.

Another question is one foreshadowed a half-century ago in the initial experiments with papilloma virus infection in rabbits: What are the so-called co-factors that encourage the progression to cancer? Are there ways women can minimize their risk?

One prime suspected co-factor is cigarette smoking. Opinion is divided on oral contraceptives. Other possible co-factors include additional infectious agents, such as the herpes virus, hormonal influences, genetic background and environmental and dietary factors.

The National Cancer Institute is preparing to try to answer the co-factor and risk questions with the help of a study of 15,000 to 20,000 women. Researchers will track them for several years to determine who among them develops the kinds of abnormalities known to precede cervical cancer.

They will then screen the women for HPV infection and those possible co-factors that might have played a role in their symptoms. Thus, researchers hope to be better able to predict the consequences of HPV infection and what puts people at greatest risk.

"What's certain is if you have an abnormal Pap smear or dysplasia, you are more likely to have the virus detected," says Dr. Mark Schiffman of the National Cancer Institute. "But if you have HPV today but are normal, does that mean you will get an abnormal smear?

"People assume that women with the virus will go on and get dysplasia," Schiffman says. "Maybe the answer is no. Maybe most women can fight off the virus with their immune system. . . . We are trying to determine for physicians and women the meaning of infection."

It is also possible that, in some women, warts and mild dysplasia will disappear without treatment. For that reason, there is disagreement among physicians about when treatment is warranted and how much difference it makes.

Dr. Jonathan S. Berek, director of gynecologic oncology at the UCLA School of Medicine, believes that some women are being over-treated—at considerable pain and expense and with limited evidence that the therapy really helps.

But other physicians argue that they cannot afford to wait. If even a small minority of patients risk developing cancer, they suggest that it would be irresponsible to not do everything possible to protect those patients.

"Since we don't have the tools to say which will progress . . . you're almost forced to over-treat the others,"

Physicians disagree about when treatment is warranted and how much difference it makes.

Connolly says. Furthermore, many patients are anxious to be rid of their warts.

There is similar controversy about the value of a new form of HPV testing.

There are now some 60 known strains of the virus. (In 1987, they were being identified at a rate of three a month.) Some are found primarily in benign warts; some turn up in connection with dysplasia. A few seem to be linked primarily to invasive cancers.

But the associations are not hard and fast.

Several companies have developed tests capable of identifying the strain with which a person is infected. The first test on the market appeared in the United States early last year and is being offered by some commercial labs.

The manufacturer suggests that the test be used with the Pap smear to alert physicians to the presence of a potentially cancer-causing virus. The company claims that once physicians know the strains involved, they can monitor their patients accordingly.

But some physicians counter that all patients should be closely monitored anyway. They say the association between specific strains and symptoms is not yet sufficiently clear to justify alarming, or reassuring, patients on the basis of the test.

"I'm not sure how to use it, to tell you the truth," says Siegfried of Los Angeles. "It doesn't change how we treat the patients, and I'm concerned that it might cause more anxiety if the patients are told they have the type that is more closely linked to cancer."

In the end, researchers say that panic about HPV is counterproductive.

Most people never will develop cervical cancer, they repeatedly point out. The disease's antecedents are easily detected and treated. And in most cases, the rate of progression is slow enough that a single missed Pap smear will not be crucial.

But with nearly half the women in the United States not undergoing regular screenings, says Berek of UCLA, attention should be focused on encouraging those women to change their lifestyles and get regular checkups.

Berek would like to see more public resources devoted to comprehensive cancer screening of all Americans—an approach he and others point out repeatedly has been proven cost-effective but rarely attracts much political support.

"So I think the broader issue here is not so much that we've identified a virus that causes warts—a small proportion of which are virulent and probably are associated with the development of genital cancers," Berek says. "The issue is who's getting screened and why can't we save those other 6,000 lives?"

But statistics offer little comfort to people such as Patty Vurpillat.

In Patty's case, the warts on her cervix returned within a few months of treatment. When the clinic advised a second biopsy, she balked. She feared the pain of another biopsy and was losing confidence in the clinic where she was being treated.

Unsatisfied and anxious, she sought a second opinion. In December, the new physician suggested waiting three months. Warts sometimes regress. If they don't go away, the physician said, she might try once more freezing them off.

So these days, Patty Vurpillat is waiting.

"I've been worried," she said sadly one recent afternoon. "It's always in the back of your mind: I'm thinking, 'Could something really be messing up my reproductive system?' I'm going to turn 20 this week. And I feel like I'm going to turn 40."

PMS: Proof or Promises?

BONNIE LIEBMAN

I was in the library, searching for an article on (what else?) saturated fats, when the headline caught my eye: "Efficacy of Alpha-Tocopherol in the Treatment of the Premenstrual Syndrome."

Could a simple, safe supplement like vitamin E put an end to PMS—those monthly bouts of misery that afflict millions of otherwise normal women, and, indirectly, the men and children who have to live or work with them?

I've never had a particularly bad case of PMS. Usually it's only a day or two of feeling irritable and unable to cope. My response to the problem is not exactly high-tech: I try not to cry in public or say anything I'll later regret, and I wait for the day to end.

But what if vitamin E, vitamin B-6, or one of those "PMS Formula" supplements could end all that? I abandoned saturated fats and read on.

Dr. Jekyll/Ms Hyde. The scientific literature on PMS is a mess. That's because no one is quite sure what it is. In 1983, investigators at the National Institute of Mental Health (NIMH) agreed that only women who met two criteria should participate in studies on PMS:

▪ The women had to record their symptoms daily for three months, rather than fill out questionnaires about how they usually feel the week before their menstrual periods.

▪ For at least two of the three months, they had to report at least a 30-percent change in symptoms between the pre- and post-menstrual weeks of their monthly cycles.

"Only about one-third of the women who seek help from health professionals actually have PMS according to these criteria," says the NIMH's Peter Schmidt.

"The way these women feel, the way they perceive themselves and others and their life activities, undergoes a profound change," says Schmidt. "It's really a Dr. Jekyll/Mr. Hyde phenomenon."

Using the NIMH's criteria, four to seven percent of all women suffer from PMS, says Schmidt. But in response to other surveys, many more women— perhaps 30 to 40 percent—report premenstrual *symptoms*. There are well over 100, including mood swings, food cravings, temper outbursts, breast tenderness, bloating, and—my husband will love this one—a "tendency to nag."

Like me, these women may not have what the NIMH calls PMS. But they're often the ones taking the PMS supplements, buying the self-help PMS books, and visiting the PMS clinics. I decided to start with studies on this poorly defined group, knowing that their uncertain diagnosis makes the results somewhat questionable.

Folk Remedies? In a recent survey of 630 nursing-school graduates who said they had premenstrual symptoms, one out of four said they had "changed their diet" to help relieve their discomfort.[1] "The changes recommended most commonly are decreasing the intake of fat, sugar, salt, alcohol, and caffeine," says the study's co-author, Susan Johnson, of the University of Iowa.

But no one's ever tested those changes to see if they help.

Johnson also found that 19 percent of the nurses took vitamins and 42 percent exercised. Studies have tested those remedies, but the evidence, I soon discovered, is rather skimpy.

"E" for "Equivocal." Robert London, director of Reproductive Medicine at North Charles Hospital in Baltimore, was testing vitamin E's ability to alleviate discomfort caused by benign breast lumps (it didn't) when he decided to investigate the vitamin's effects on premenstrual symptoms.

Every day for three menstrual cycles, 22 women took 400 International Units (IU) of vitamin E, while 19 others took an inactive, look-alike placebo.[2] (London didn't use the NIMH's criteria to screen the women, so chances are they had premenstrual *symptoms*, not the more severe *syndrome*.)

But the results did not bear out the "efficacy" promised in his study's title. The vitamin-E-takers reported statistically significant improvements only in motor coordination and a few physical symptoms (bloating, breast tenderness, finger or ankle swelling, and weight gain).

Irritability, tension, depression, impaired social interactions, diminished mental ability, inefficiency, distorted eating habits, headaches, confusion, dizziness, and reduced sexual drive did not get significantly better.

Yet an earlier study by London found

just the opposite: vitamin E improved all symptoms *except* bloating, breast tenderness, swelling, and weight gain.[3] Hmm.

London argues that you can't look only at improvements that met the scientific definition of "significant."

"If a symptom goes from 'severe'— where the woman wants to kill herself— to 'mild' or 'moderate,' that's clinically important," he says.

True, but if you don't reach statistical significance, it's more likely that the results were due to chance. Until someone does a larger study, the evidence on vitamin E remains in limbo.

Optivite: Disappointing . . . and Dangerous! PMS was first described in the medical literature in 1931, but it wasn't until the early 1980s that most researchers began to explore its possible link with vitamins and minerals. One reason was Guy Abraham.

Abraham is the medical director of Optimox, Inc., which sells Optivite, a nutritional supplement for PMS sufferers. Optivite is a multi-vitamin-and-mineral that's especially rich in vitamin B-6, magnesium, zinc, and vitamin A.

Frankly, it made me suspicious to see a full-page ad for Optivite wedged between the articles on PMS in a 1987 issue of *The Journal of Reproductive Medicine* devoted to the subject. Still, Abraham's financial interest doesn't disqualify his theories.

In early, poorly designed studies, Abraham reported that Optivite offered dramatic relief for PMS. But there have been only three "double-blind" studies, in which neither the participants nor the researchers know *who's* getting a placebo and *who's* getting the vitamins. And one of those studies was flawed.[4] "Technically, I don't think it's a good study," admits Abraham.

He does stand behind a study he co-authored with Zaven Chakmajian, now in private practice in Dallas, and a new study by North Charles Hospital's Robert London, which hasn't been published yet.

But the women in Chakmajian's study weren't exactly cured. They weren't significantly less depressed, and breast tenderness or other signs of water retention didn't improve.[5] Anxiety did drop slightly-but-significantly (16 percent on average), and the participants' appetites and craving for sweets diminished by an impressive 31 percent. (At least that's what they said. The study didn't

attempt to find out if they actually ate any less.)

But I'm not convinced that an increased appetite and a craving for sweets is such a problem. In one recent study, women ate about 200 to 300 extra calories—and a teaspoon or two more sugar—per day the week before menstruating.[6] So what? They returned to a lower calorie and sugar intake during the following weeks.

Burning for B-6. I might have been tempted to try Optivite, to see if it curbed my "anxiety". . . if it weren't for the hazards of vitamin B-6.

The six Optivites taken every day by Chakmajian's patients supplied a total of 300 mg of the vitamin. Women who have taken 500 mg or more of B-6 (often for PMS) for two months or longer have developed burning, shooting, or tingling pains or numbness in their hands and feet, clumsiness, or unstable gait—a condition known as sensory neuropathy.[7]

Fortunately, it goes away when the victims stop taking B-6. One report says that doses as low as 50 mg can cause the disorder in sensitive people.[8]

"At doses less than 500 mg, neuropathy is not a problem," says Abraham, arguing that the report was not well-documented. But most B-6 experts are not that cavalier.

"I consider 300 mg to be in a gray area," says Robert Reynolds, of the U.S. Department of Agriculture. "We don't have sufficient data to say whether that dose can be taken with complete confidence or complete panic."

Until someone gets sufficient data, 300 mg is too close to the danger dose for me. Especially when I'm not convinced that B-6 works.

Three earlier double-blind studies on vitamin B-6 alone (not Optivite) showed that it failed to alleviate the symptoms of PMS. Abraham says that's because the doses (50 to 200 mg) were too low.

In his own study, 500 mg relieved symptoms in 21 out of 25 patients.[9] But that study has been heavily criticized.

"Abraham didn't diagnose his patients properly," says David Rubinow, clinical director of the NIMH. Samuel Smith, of Sinai Hospital in Baltimore, agrees. "Forty percent of his patients didn't have PMS," he says. "They had symptoms during the [post-menstrual] phase."

Nevertheless, the NIMH hasn't given up on B-6. It's testing 200 mg a day on

women with confirmed premenstrual *syndrome* (so far, none of the participants has had problems with that dose). The results, says the NIMH's Peter Schmidt, "should be available in the next year or so."

Down the Primrose Path. Samuel Smith's solution, at least for PMS-sufferers who have breast tenderness or water retention, is now illegal.

The supplement—evening primrose oil—is 72 percent linoleic acid (the major component of safflower, corn, and soybean oil). Nine percent is gamma-linolenic acid, the so-called "active" ingredient.

The Food and Drug Administration recently won a lawsuit to prohibit the sale of evening primrose oil, on the grounds that the oil is not generally recognized as safe and is not approved for use as a food additive.

(I asked the FDA's John Thomas why this now-illegal supplement is still widely available in health food stores and through the mails. His answer: "The police can't catch everyone who goes through a red light.")

So far, only one well-designed study has tested evening primrose oil as a treatment for PMS.[10] The women taking the oil reported 11 percent less depression. Water retention, irritability, insomnia, and headaches did not improve.

Nevertheless, Smith recommends it for PMS patients who have breast tenderness, because of an earlier study on women who had breast pain (not necessarily from PMS), and because of his own "clinical experience." In other words, it works for *his* patients.

That's what worries me. When I asked Smith about vitamin E, he said, "Anecdotally, I can tell you it doesn't work with my patients."

That phrase sounded vaguely familiar. Ah yes. Vitamin-E-and-Optivite-researcher Robert London said the same thing about evening primrose oil.

Run It Off? You can't blame Jerilynn Prior for trying to test exercise's ability to prevent premenstrual symptoms. The researcher from the University of British Columbia got eight sedentary women to run an average of 32 miles per menstrual cycle. After three months, the women reported significantly less breast discomfort and "puffiness" than six women who did not participate.[11]

In a later study that lasted six months, eight other sedentary women who ran an average of 47 miles per cycle reported the same improvements, plus significantly less "personal stress" than six ordinarily active women who were not in training.[12]

But these studies were small, and weren't well-designed. What's more, Prior's—or anyone's—studies on exercise have an inherent problem: you can't give one group a placebo. If you're not exercising, you know it. So it's possible that the women who exercised felt better because they expected to.

Are Carbs the Cure? I was about to give up. So far, only a few studies had relieved any symptoms, and none of those had used women the National Institute of Mental Health would consider true PMS-sufferers.

Then I heard of a new study on carbohydrates by Judith Wurtman, of the Massachusetts Institute of Technology (MIT).[13]

Wurtman screened her participants with excruciating care. Each filled out questionnaires, recorded symptoms, sat through interviews with psychiatrists, took personality and depression tests, and gave blood and urine samples. "We rejected more than 90 percent of the applicants because their PMS wasn't severe enough," she says.

The surviving 19 PMS-sufferers and nine non-sufferers ("controls") lived at an MIT research center for three to five days during the premenstrual and two days during the postmenstrual weeks of their monthly cycles. That way, Wurtman could monitor everything they ate.

"The women with severe PMS ate significantly more food, primarily carbohydrates—not just sweets, but rolls, pasta, and potato salad—but only when they were premenstrual," she reports. "The controls had no change in food intake."

But Wurtman didn't stop there. In a second phase of the study, she fed each woman a high-carbohydrate meal consisting of "a very big, banal, bland bowl of corn flakes with low-protein, artificial milk."

One hour after the women with severe PMS consumed the cornflakes, they reported 43 percent less depression, 38 percent less confusion, 47 percent less fatigue, 42 percent less tension, and 69 percent less anger. "The effects were gigantic," says Wurtman. "The sort of thing you'd see with women on Valium."

The cornflakes had no effect on the controls' moods or on the PMS-sufferers' moods during their postmenstrual week.

Cornflakes, Not Snickers. But once again, it's possible that the women felt better because they expected to. To really test her theory, Wurtman would have to feed half the participants a high-carbohydrate meal and half a low-carbohydrate meal that looked and tasted identical.

Still, Wurtman's work pokes a hole in the popular advice to cut back on carbs. "The anecdotal reasoning went something like this," she explains. "Women who have PMS crave carbohydrates and throw knives at their husbands, so they shouldn't eat carbohydrates. But the advice has never been tested."

Instead of avoiding carbohydrates, she says, PMS-sufferers should eat more of them. "And they don't have to be Snickers," she adds. "Try pasta salad with vegetables, oatmeal with honey, sweet potatoes with marmalade, or breakfast cereals."

Back to the Drawing Board. I would be exaggerating if I said I can't wait to try out Wurtman's advice. (And I'm a bit skeptical, since I already eat lots of carbohydrates.)

Still, it's encouraging to think that Wurtman may be on to something, because no one else has found anything to lessen the symptoms of PMS.

Most of the PMS supplements on the market are either high-dose multivitamins and minerals or B-6 with a few other ingredients, such as herbs, a sprinkling of vitamins, or the amino acid DL-phenylalanine.

Interestingly, whenever I asked their manufacturers for evidence that the products work, I got the same answer: "We make no claims."

"PMS Formula" sure sounds like a claim to me.

Even prescription drugs have failed to alleviate PMS. "There are no pharmacological agents that have been consistently and convincingly superior to placebo except for those that cause cessation of ovarian function," says NIMH clinical director David Rubinow.

Those drugs (like Danocrine or Synarel) cause side effects that mimic menopause, including hot flashes, headache, decreased breast size, weight gain, vaginal atrophy, and bone loss.

That's what we have to look forward to when PMS ends? I'm depressed already.

[1] J. Reprod. Med. 33: 340, 1988.
[2] J. Reprod. Med. 32: 400, 1987.
[3] J. Am. Coll. Nutr. 2: 115, 1983.
[4] J. Reprod. Med. 32: 435, 1987.
[5] J. Appl. Nutr. 37: 12, 1985.
[6] Am. J. Clin. Nutr. 49: 252, 1989.
[7] N. Eng. J. Med. 309: 445, 1983.
[8] Lancet i: 1168, 1985.
[9] Infertil. 3: 155, 1980.
[10] J. Reprod. Med. 30: 149, 1985.
[11] Eur. J. Appl. Physiol. 55: 349, 1986.
[12] Fertil. Steril. 47: 402, 1987.
[13] Am. J. Obstet. Gynecol. 161: 1228, 1989.

Chronic Disease and Impotence

Erectile failure due to chronic disease is frequently reversible or treatable.

Thomas Mulligan, MD

Thomas Mulligan is Assistant Professor of Geriatric Medicine and Gerontology, Medical College of Virginia, and Associate Chief of Staff for Extended Care and Chief, Geriatric Medicine, Hunter Holmes McGuire Veterans Affairs Medical Center, Richmond.

Aging begins at the moment of conception. Virtually all body systems change with the passage of time, even in individuals who are in excellent health. During the early years of growth and development, muscle strength increases and motor skills improve. As the decades pass, however, most organ systems become less efficient; maximum aerobic capacity declines, and nerve conduction velocity slows. While most of these normal changes of healthy aging do not cause disability, age-associated change in sexual function is often a serious problem. Thus, when an older man presents with sexual complaints, it is essential to determine if the patient's sexual decline is simply a part of normal healthy aging or due to age-related disease.

Normal aging versus chronic disease

As men and women advance in age, sexual interest gradually declines but rarely disappears entirely, even in the oldest old.[1] The frequency of sexual intercourse, however, declines more precipitously than libido.[2] Although many factors may contribute to declining frequency of intercourse, it is most often due to male sexual dysfunction, usually erectile failure. This discrepancy between sexual interest and ability in the aged male is known as the "libido-potency gap." The causes of erectile failure in the elderly can be categorized as those that are a part of normal aging and those that represent disease.

Normal aging. With normal aging, there is a gradual decline in the conduction velocity of the penile nerves. Thus, greater penile stimulation is required for the release of penile vasodilatory neurotransmitters (acetylcholine and vasoactive intestinal polypeptide).[3] In addition, the penile vasculature in older individuals is less able to deliver arterial blood to the penis and trap the penile blood volume needed to achieve a rigid erection.[4] As a result, the elderly man's penis takes longer to become erect, is less rigid in that state, and remains erect for a shorter period of time than when he was younger.[5]

Even with these changes, completely healthy older men are usually able to achieve penile rigidity adequate to permit sexual intercourse into old age.[6]

Age-related disease. When health problems complicate aging, various chronic diseases develop. Some of these common disorders, such as vascular disease (eg, hypertension, ischemic arterial disease) and metabolic disease (eg, diabetes mellitus), have a profound impact on sexuality through their effect on erectile function. Moreover, the treatment of these diseases may cause sexual dysfunction, as in the case of medication-induced impotence. When chronic disease is superimposed on the aging process, the patient is 47 times more likely than a young, healthy man to be sexually disabled.[7]

The most common causes of erectile failure in aged men are the development of either penile vascular disease or penile neuropathy.[8] Although not as frequently a cause of geriatric impotence, psychogenic factors, adverse drug reactions, and hypogonadism each account for approximately 5% of cases. It is important to bear in mind that some men with ischemic heart disease may develop psychogenic impotence because they and their partners fear the exertion of sexual intercourse. Similarly, a patient with a life-threatening illness (eg, cancer) may develop psychogenic impotence due to depression. Appropriate counseling may restore potency in both cases.

Evaluating the patient

History and physical. The most effective approach to evaluating an older man's complaint of inadequate erections is to first determine whether the changes are due to normal aging or disease. If the patient reports that his erections are less rigid than when he was younger and require greater stimulation to achieve, but are adequate for intercourse, then education and reassurance are all that is needed. On the other hand, when erections are inadequate for vaginal penetration, despite additional stimulation and patience, aging is unlikely to be the sole cause. In these patients, the medical history and physical examination may reveal the underlying etiology (see table). In the absence of a single, easily attributable cause (eg, diabetes with known peripheral neuropathy), a laboratory evaluation may be indicated.

Laboratory work-up. One of the most helpful laboratory tests for evaluating impotence in an older man is direct injection of papaverine into one of the corpora cavernosa.[9] Although viewed as invasive by some physicians, this test will induce erection in virtually all men who have an intact vascular system. Because vascular disease is one of the most common causes of impotence in old age, a poor response to injected papaverine often obviates the need for further evaluation. On the other hand, when papaverine injection induces a rigid erection, further testing is usually required. Penile electromyography and testosterone assays may be helpful in diagnosing penile neuropathy or hypogonadism.

Although psychogenic impo-

Table. Causes of erectile failure in a study of 121 men (mean age, 68 years)

Cause	% of patients
Multifactorial	30.3
Vascular	21.1
Diabetic neuropathy	17.1
Nondiabetic neuropathy	10.5
Psychogenic	9.2
Drug effects	3.9
Hypogonadism	2.6
Peyronie's disease	1.3
Idiopathic	3.9

Adapted, with permission, from Mulligan T, Katz PG: Why aged men become impotent. *Arch Intern Med* 149:1365, 1989.

tence is less common in older than in younger men, the diagnosis, when suspected, can be confirmed with sleep laboratory monitoring or the less specific Snap Gauge test.

Treatment

Once the underlying disease causing the impotence has been determined, the most appropriate treatment options can be prescribed. In some cases, the treatment of choice is obvious. For example, when an adverse drug reaction causes impotence, the drug should be discontinued or changed. When depression is the culprit, counseling is most effective. However, the most common problems in geriatric impotence are of neurovascular origin. Therefore, treatment with negative pressure devices, penile injection, or a penile prosthesis may be needed.

Negative pressure device. The least invasive approach involves use of a negative pressure device. There are two basic types: The first is a hollow cylinder into which the flaccid penis is

placed. The cylinder is attached to a vacuum pump that pulls blood into the penis and creates an erection-like state that can be maintained with a constricting band around the base of the penis. This device is best for men with venous or neurogenic impotence, and is totally noninvasive.

The second device is silastic, condom-shaped, and remains on the penis during intercourse. The vacuum is used primarily to draw the penis into the condom. The condom itself is relatively rigid; hence the combined rigidity of the condom and penis is adequate for vaginal penetration. This device is useful for impotence of virtually any etiology. However, penile sensitivity is diminished, and an understanding partner is necessary.

Penile injection. Self-injection of the penis with vasoactive agents bypasses the usual neural pathways and mimics physiologic erections in appearance and function. Papaverine, phentolamine, and prostaglandin E_1 are all effective, with response dependent upon the cause of impotence. Pa-

"I'd give anything to be a man again"

Robert, a 72-year-old man, comes to your office complaining of difficulty falling asleep and lack of interest in activities that he used to find enjoyable (eg, traveling with his wife). He has a history of exertional angina and noninsulin-dependent diabetes mellitus. The former condition is well controlled with a beta blocker, and the latter is treated with an oral hypoglycemic agent. Robert has been married for 40 years, has three grown children, and often brags about his attractive wife who is 12 years his junior. He used to smoke but quit five years ago after being told that he had mild emphysema. He has never been more than a social drinker and has never used illicit drugs.

When questioned about his bowel and bladder habits, Robert jokingly says of his penis, "Passing water is the only thing it's good for anymore." When the physician asks if his lack of erections bothers him, Robert becomes obviously distressed and says, "Doc, I'd give anything if you could make me a man again."

On further questioning, Robert reports that he first noticed the problem two years ago when he found that he couldn't maintain an erection for satisfactory intercourse. It gradually became more and more difficult for him to achieve an erection at all. Although both he and his wife joked that he was "just getting old," attempts at sex became a source of conflict. Six months ago, the couple ceased trying altogether.

The physician explains that although aging may play a role in Robert's erectile problem, the primary cause may be his medications, vascular disease, diabetes, or some other chronic problem. Together, they discuss the options for evaluation and possible treatment of his sexual dysfunction. Robert is obviously relieved and eager to begin the evaluation.

tients with neurogenic impotence may be hyperresponsive, whereas patients with vascular disease may not develop a firm erection. Prostaglandin E_1 causes a burning sensation in some cases, but is safer for long-term use because it causes less penile fibrosis.

Penile prosthesis. Penile prosthesis implantation is currently often utilized after other, less invasive options have failed. Available prostheses include malleable, inflatable, and self-contained inflatable devices. The malleable prosthesis provides permanent rigidity, but can be bent for concealment. The inflatable prosthesis consists of paired, fluid-filled cylinders implanted in the corpora cavernosa, a scrotal pump, and an abdominal reservoir. The pump controls erection and flaccidity, but manual dexterity is required and mechanical problems are frequent. The newer self-contained inflatable prostheses allow for variable degrees of penile rigidity, but long-term reliability is unknown.

Surgery. Penile revascularization may correct the underlying problem, but has met with limited success overall. The high prevalence of distal vessel disease in the elderly usually precludes successful arterial revascularization. Penile venous ligation has been performed in patients with abnormal venous drainage, but has also met with a disappointing success rate of less than 50%.

Summary

Aging has a significant impact on the sexual interest, ability, and activity of most individuals. If health is maintained as the years pass, however, satisfying sexual activity may continue. Unfortunately, many people develop chronic disease as they age. Chronic disease in a man often brings with it impotence and eventually the cessation of sexual intercourse. The diagnosis of chronic disease responsible for impotence often leads to more rational treatment and the return of an active sex life for both partners.

References

1. Verwoerdt A, Pfeiffer E, Wang HS: Sexual behavior in senescence: Patterns of sexual activity and interest. *Geriatrics* 24:137, 1969.
2. Pearlman CK, Kobashi LI: Frequency of intercourse in men. *J Urol* 107:298, 1972.
3. Newman HF: Vibratory sensitivity of the penis. *Fertil Steril* 21:791, 1970.
4. Ruzbarsky V, Michal V: Morphologic changes in the arterial bed of the penis with aging. *Investigative Urology* 15:194, 1977.
5. Masters WH, Johnson VE: Sex and the aging process. *J Am Geriatr Soc* 29:385, 1981.
6. Bretschneider J, McCoy NL: Sexual interest and behavior in healthy 80- to 102-years-olds. *Arch Sex Behav* 17:109, 1988.
7. Mulligan T, Retchin SM, Chinchilli VM, et al: The role of aging and chronic disease in sexual dysfunction. *J Am Geriatr Soc* 36:520, 1988.
8. Mulligan T, Katz PG: Why aged men become impotent. *Arch Intern Med* 149:1365, 1989
9. Abber JC, Lue TF, Orvis BR, et al: Diagnostic tests for impotence: A comparison of papaverine injection with the penile-brachial index and nocturnal penile tumescence monitoring. *J Urol* 135:923, 1986.

AIDS

THE NEXT TEN YEARS

SPECIAL REPORT A sense of crisis is hard to sustain. It thrives on earthquakes and tornadoes, plane crashes and terrorist bombings. But forces that kill people one at a time have a way of fading into the psychic landscape. So, if you've stopped thinking of AIDS as an emergency, consider a few numbers. In 1984, when scientists identified the virus that causes the illness, fewer than 4,500 Americans had been stricken. Today more than 3,000 cases of AIDS are reported every month in this country;

the total tops 130,000. An estimated 1 million Americans are infected with the virus—and by the end of the decade, most of those people will be sick.

The AIDS epidemic is far from over. It's not even under control. "The worldwide situation is deteriorating," says Dr. Jonathan Mann, former director of the World Health Organization's Global Program on AIDS. "We are facing a decade in the 1990s that will be far more difficult than anything we saw in the 1980s." The WHO estimates that as of this year 700,000 people have developed AIDS worldwide and 6 million to 8 million have contracted the virus that causes it. By the end of the decade, an estimated 5 million to 6 million will be sick, and the total number infected may approach 20 million. Worse still, the situation isn't expected to stabilize for several more decades.

Already, the AIDS virus infects a third of the population in some parts of Africa. This nation's most desperate neighborhoods appear headed in the same direction. Regional surveys have turned up infection rates of 5 to 12 percent among pregnant women in the Bronx, 25 percent among young men surveyed in Newark, N.J. But the poor aren't the only ones suffering. Dr. June Osborn, chairman of the National Commission on AIDS, foresees a time when most Americans may know someone with AIDS. "By the end of the 1990s," she says, "people will be shaking their fists and saying, 'Why didn't you tell us?' That's going to hurt, because we did."

This week thousands of people from throughout the world will converge on San Francisco for the Sixth International Conference on AIDS. What once served as a quiet forum for sharing technical insights will look more like a political convention, as the affected segments of society—not just scientists but patients and caregivers, public officials and angry activists—unfurl their flags. No longer just a medical problem, AIDS has become a pock on the social

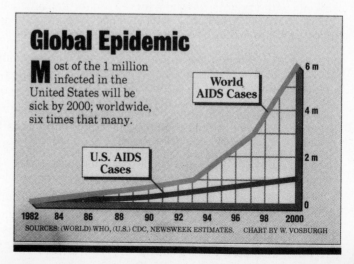

Global Epidemic

Most of the 1 million infected in the United States will be sick by 2000; worldwide, six times that many.

World AIDS Cases

U.S. AIDS Cases

6 m
4 m
2 m
0

1982 84 86 88 90 92 94 96 98 2000

SOURCES: (WORLD) WHO, (U.S.) CDC, NEWSWEEK ESTIMATES.   CHART BY W. VOSBURGH

order, a festering emblem of countless other ills. Federal spending for AIDS research and treatment has climbed to $1.6 billion in just nine years. Scientific progress has been brisk. Yet for many of the afflicted, here and throughout the world, minimal health care is still a distant hope.

Though AIDS is spread solely through the exchange of blood or other body fluids, local conditions have a lot to do with who gets sick and how. In Africa, the virus is transmitted almost exclusively through heterosexual contact. In Thailand—where the number of infected people has shot from 1,000 to roughly 50,000 in just three years—the epidemic apparently started among intravenous drug users and spread into the heterosexual community. In Eastern Europe, AIDS has been spreading mainly through unsafe medical practices.

The U.S. epidemic has always been concentrated in major cities, among gay men and IV drug users. But that pattern is changing as the epidemic matures. Last year AIDS incidence rose nearly four times as fast in the nation's smallest cities as in its largest ones. And while the number of new cases rose by 11 percent among gay males, it increased by 36 percent or more among heterosexuals and newborns. By the year 2000, says Dr. James Chin, an epidemiologist in charge of AIDS surveillance at the WHO, "heterosexual transmission will predominate in most industrial countries." The growth of the epidemic may be slower among heterosexuals than it has been among gays or IV drug users, but it will be implacable nonetheless. "AIDS is a sexually transmitted disease," says Dr.

> Last year newborns got AIDS at a faster rate than gays or IV drug users. Many got it prenatally; in Romania, bad medical conditions also caused hundreds of infants to be infected.

Robert Redfield of the Walter Reed Army Medical Center, "and the fact is that most of us in society are heterosexual."

Monogamous couples are not at risk, but there's no evidence that Americans are about to become wholly monogamous. Syphilis and gonorrhea—diseases that not only indicate unsafe sexual practices but facilitate the spread of the AIDS virus—have skyrocketed in recent years. At the same time, the crack epidemic has created a whole new class of high-risk heterosexuals: women who trade sex directly for the drug. "We've seen the rate of syphilis in various parts of the country quadruple because of sex associated with crack," says Don Des Jarlais of the Chemical Dependency Institute at New York's Beth Israel Hospital. "The same thing could happen with AIDS."

With or without crack, American teenagers are ripe targets for AIDS: they're already experiencing 2.5 million cases of sexually transmitted disease every year, and nearly a million unintended pregnancies. "We know their sexual behavior results in significant risk for infection," says Dr. Gary Noble of the federal Centers for Disease Control. Indeed, at least 20 percent of today's AIDS patients were probably infected as teens.

How the Virus Attacks, and How to Attack the Virus

The AIDS virus turns cells into factories that produce more viruses. New drugs show hope of bringing the process under control.

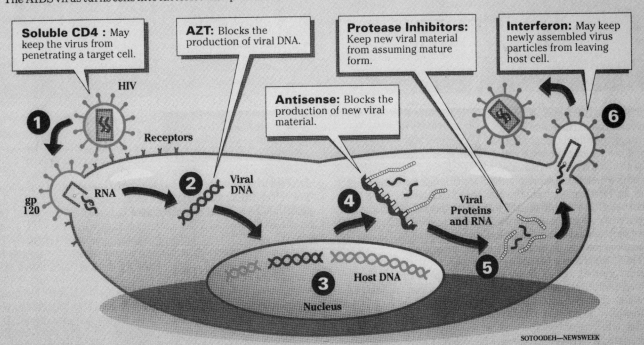

SOTOODEH—NEWSWEEK

The viral production cycle involves six basic steps. **(1)** The virus attaches to receptors on a host cell, injecting pieces of genetic material (RNA) and enzymes. **(2)** A viral enzyme transcribes the RNA into the same form as the host cell's genetic material (DNA). **(3)** The viral DNA is integrated into the chromosomes in the nucleus of the host cell. This integrated DNA is called provirus.

(4) After a long, idle period, the provirus directs enzymes in the host cell to produce new strands of viral RNA. The new viral RNA serves as a blueprint. Other enzymes use it to produce proteins that will become new virus capsules. **(5)** An enzyme called protease cuts the long, unmilled proteins into shorter pieces, which clip together to form new capsules. **(6)** The completed capsules bud from the surface of the cell.

As long as we fail at sex education and drug-abuse treatment, millions of Americans will remain at risk. And clearly we are failing. Medically, though, the past decade has brought remarkable successes. No one had heard of AIDS when doctors started describing the syndrome in 1981. Since then, scientists have not only identified the human immunodeficiency virus (HIV) but learned a great deal about how it infects cells and ruins the immune system. The 1980s brought a diagnostic test, a safe blood supply and several useful treatments. Thanks to drugs like AZT and pentamidine, patients who would once have died within months of developing AIDS are now surviving a year or more.

In the short run, treating the myriad infections and cancers that actually kill AIDS patients is the surest way to extend their lives. Activists have long accused scientists, drug companies and federal agencies of neglecting these secondary complications, of preferring the higher drama of fighting the virus itself. The criticism has had an effect. Dr. Anthony Fauci, director of the National Institute of Allergy and Infectious Diseases (NIAID), says the proportion of federally funded AIDS studies relating to opportunistic infections has risen from 10 to 20 percent during the past year and may eventually grow to 30 or 40 percent. Yet treating symptoms won't solve the problem. AIDS patients who survive early bouts with *pneumocystis carinii* pneumonia and other once lethal infections are now falling prey to an array of other maladies. Among San Francisco AIDS patients, the number of lymphomas rose by 48 percent in 1987 alone. Until the AIDS virus can be locked out of the body, or paralyzed from within, the plague will spread and the afflicted will die.

The epidemic has prompted a resurgence in the study of infectious disease. Antiviral drug research, long stagnant before AIDS struck, is now among the hottest fields in medicine. And the quest for a vaccine, though far from fruition, is proceeding briskly. Can this virus be stopped? What are the strategies? What are the obstacles? These turn out not to be simple questions, for the battle against AIDS is being fought inside the cell, amid genes and proteins and enzymes and antibodies. But the questions are worth grappling with. All of humanity has a stake in the answers.

■ WHAT HIV DOES TO CELLS

Just nine years ago, epidemic diseases were a thing of the past. Modern medicine, having subdued The Germ with vaccines and antibiotics, was busy saving us all from cancer and heart disease. Then came AIDS, and the realization that a devious bug could still cause a worldwide plague. At first no one knew what was causing the mysterious illness, but scientists in Paris and Washington soon linked it to an infectious agent known as a retrovirus. Today there are still unanswered questions about the human immunodeficiency virus, such as why it causes illness so much faster in some people than in others. But its basic mechanisms are now well understood.

HIV has no life of its own. Unlike a bacterium, it doesn't absorb nutrients, generate waste or reproduce by dividing. It's just a protein capsule containing two short strands of genetic material (RNA) and a few enzymes. It happens to use human cells to perpetuate itself. After infecting someone, HIV may spend 10 years or more quietly ensconced within various tissues and organs. But when activated, it turns certain immune cells into virus factories, which produce a flurry of new virus capsules and die. Other cells become infected in the process, and the immune system falls like a house of cards.

The immune system is an elaborate, internal defense network that includes different types of blood cells. Among these immune cells, the ones that identify an intruder and authorize an attack on it are called T4 lymphocytes, or (imprecisely) "helper T cells." Every T4 cell has appendages called CD4 receptors, through which it exchanges information with other immune cells. And it is through these CD4 receptors that HIV attacks. The outer shell of the HIV capsule (known as the envelope) is equipped with an appendage called gp120. This distinctive protein molecule happens to fit the CD4 receptor as a plug fits a socket. When the two molecules dock, the contents of the viral capsule—the RNA and the enzymes—flow freely into the cell's interior.

Once inside, HIV becomes a permanent feature of the cell. First, an enzyme called reverse transcriptase uses information encoded in the RNA to manufacture a double strand of DNA—a piece of software that can direct the cell to manufacture more virus. This DNA, known as the provirus, then integrates itself into the host cell's chromosomes. It represents just a tiny segment of the cell's genetic code. Once activated, however, it's the only segment that counts.

The trouble begins when the provirus starts directing enzymes in the host cell to produce new strands of viral RNA. These rogue pieces of RNA serve as a blueprint, from which other enzymes start churning out the raw material for new virus capsules. These raw materials (long protein molecules) get chopped into shorter pieces by an enzyme called protease. Those pieces then clip together to form new HIV particles, which burst from the surface of the host cell and float off to infect others. The host cell is killed in the process.

One reason HIV poses such a challenge is that the infection itself is not even theoretically curable: modern biologists, for all their ingenuity, are far from knowing how to purge unwanted DNA sequences from human chromosomes. Still, scientists are hopeful that by keeping the virus from replicating so wildly, they will gradually make it less deadly. Scores of researchers are working on drugs to interfere with HIV's production cycle at one stage or another. Twenty-one such drugs are now under development in this country alone. The hope is that they'll work, in some felicitous blend, to make AIDS a chronic, manageable condition, much like diabetes or high blood pressure.

■ ONE DRUG THAT HELPS

So far, only one of these drugs has been approved as a treatment for AIDS. Zidovudine, or AZT, attacks the virus after it has wormed its way into the cell but before it has integrated itself into the host cell's chromosomes. Specifically, it impedes the "reverse transcription" of viral RNA into DNA. The only way HIV's reverse transcriptase enzyme can manufacture DNA is by gathering up chemical units called nucleosides and matching them to the pattern on the viral RNA. AZT looks just like one of these nucleosides. In fact, reverse transcriptase prefers it to the real thing. But AZT turns out to have a slightly different structure. When it's clipped on to a growing chain of DNA, the next link doesn't fit and the whole production is foiled.

Conceived as a cancer treatment back in the 1960s, AZT found no use until 1986. It now earns the Burroughs Wellcome Co. well over $100 million a year. The big comeback started when scientists noted a decline in infection and death among AIDS patients taking a daily dose of 1,200 milligrams. Despite a number of side effects—ranging from headaches, vomiting and malaise to bone-marrow suppression and anemia—AZT sped through the drug-approval process in record time. In March 1987, the Food and Drug Administration approved it as a treatment for patients with symptoms of AIDS or with T4 counts below 200 (the normal range is 600 to 1,200). Since then, AZT has been found to work just as well at half the original dose, and federal guidelines have been changed to recommend the drug for any infected person whose T4 count dips below 500—even if no sickness has set in.

That may sound like a minor adjustment, but it pushes the number of potential AZT users in this country from 40,000 to more than 600,000. A panel convened by the National Institutes of Health made the early-treatment recommendation this spring, after two studies showed that AZT could delay the initial appearance of AIDS. But many experts consider the move premature and potentially dangerous. They note that several ongoing studies have so far failed to show the same beneficial effect. Moreover, they say, the NIH studies didn't compare the advantages of early and late treatment. They compared early treatment with no treatment. "We don't know that it ultimately does you any good to delay crossing the 200 mark by a few months," says Dr. John Hamilton, chief of infectious diseases at the Durham, N.C., VA Medical Center and cochair of an AZT trial designed to answer that question. "If you're building up resistance to AZT by taking it early, when you're still feeling fine, you may be losing a crutch you could use later."

Even the proponents of early treatment agree that AZT leaves much to be desired. First, it's quite toxic: even with lower doses, nearly a third of those taking the drug develop grave bone-marrow problems within a year. Second, it's not cheap. Burroughs Wellcome has twice reduced the price but still charges $1.20 for every 100-mg capsule—more than $200 for a month's supply. Third, while it does help ward off opportunistic infections in AIDS patients, it doesn't prevent the outbreak of lymphomas or tumors such as Kaposi's sarcoma. Most important, it seems to become less effective as the virus mutates out of its range of action.

Researchers are hopeful that AZT's close relatives DDI and DDC, both now in clinical trials, will help address some of these problems. DDI and, especially, DDC are toxic in their own right: both cause a painful nerve irritation called peripheral neuropathy, and DDI can damage the pancreas. But they could provide alternatives for people who can't tolerate AZT or who develop resistance to it. Both drugs are also being tested in low-dose combinations with AZT. The hope is that patients will get cumulative benefits but, because of the lower doses, experience less toxicity and resistance. "The way to go," says Dr. Samuel Broder, head of the National Cancer Institute, "is not to discard drugs that show promise, even with side effects, but to find ways to use them more creatively."

■ BREAKING THE CYCLE

AZT and its kin all attack HIV at the second stage of its life cycle—after it has entered the host cell but before it has integrated itself into the cell's DNA. But there are several other possibilities. One is to keep the virus from entering the cell in the first place. To do that, one would have to keep HIV from plugging its distinctive appendage—the gp120 envelope protein—into the CD4 receptors on target cells. Several laboratories have designed synthetic, free-floating CD4 receptors with just that thought in mind. In principle, flooding the blood with this "soluble CD4" should inactivate the virus by covering all its plugs before they find real sockets. That's exactly what happens in a test tube. There is no evidence yet on whether soluble CD4 will help infected people, but toxicity tests have shown no serious side effects. In an interesting variation on this same approach, the Upjohn Co. and others are now working on molecules that combine CD4 and a potent synthetic toxin. When the CD4 binds to the viral envelope proteins protruding from infected T4 cells, it's supposed to release the poison and kill them. Unfortunately, there is at least one large drawback to the whole CD4 approach. The molecule is very expensive to make, and it breaks down so fast that it has to be taken—by injection—every few hours.

Suppose the virus eludes both CD4 and AZT, penetrating the cell and infiltrating the local DNA. There are still possibilities for checking its growth. Opportunity No. 3 arises shortly after the provirus (the integrated viral DNA) starts running off RNA copies of itself. The enzymes that manufacture the raw materials for new virus particles from this RNA use its chemical sequence as a blueprint. If the enzymes can't read the blueprint, they can't do their work. And it's possible—using genetically engineered "antisense" molecules—to make the blueprint illegible. By zipping itself onto a crucial segment of the viral RNA, an antisense molecule blots out vital information, and protein production grinds to a halt.

Antisense represents a whole new approach to drug design, and HIV is not its only potential target. Traditionally, notes biochemist Jack Cohen of Georgetown University Laboratories, researchers

have treated people with various organic compounds in the hope that one would prove therapeutic. With antisense, he says, "you figure out exactly what genetic process you need to alter and design a molecule accordingly." In test-tube experiments, antisense molecules have slowed production of the AIDS virus by 90 percent. The catch is that they're still difficult—and exceedingly expensive—to make. "We've been working on [an antisense drug] for a year," says Dr. Jeffrey Laurence of the Laboratory for AIDS Virus Research at Cornell University Medical College. "I'm promised that by the end of the summer we'll have enough to treat one mouse."

While awaiting affordable antisense, researchers are targeting still later stages in the viral life cycle. A fourth possible strategy is to keep HIV's protease enzyme from milling the construction materials into pieces that can form new virus particles. A number of companies have developed drugs that work at this stage, and human trials are expected to start within the next year. These "protease inhibitors" have performed well in test-tube experiments, and animal tests have turned up no serious side effects. That's not surprising. For unlike AZT and its kin, which disrupt a number of cellular processes, the protease inhibitors affect only a single enzyme. As a result, researchers expect them to be far less toxic.

In other labs, scientists are working with a fifth group of antiviral agents, known as interferons. These are antiviral chemicals produced naturally by cells. Drugs that step up production of interferons can help control the growth of tumors—and at high doses, the same drugs seem to impede the budding of new virus particles from infected cells. In a study published this month, NIH researchers conclude that alpha interferon can have a "significant antiviral effect" in patients whose immune systems are still largely intact. In a small trial involving asymptomatic patients, the investigators found that 41 percent of those getting the drug became "culture negative," meaning the virus dropped temporarily out of sight in their blood samples. Only 13 percent of the untreated subjects became culture negative (a common but temporary occurrence). Moreover, T4 counts held steady in the treated patients but declined slightly in the others. There is a catch, of course: the treatment was so toxic that a third of those receiving it dropped out of the trial.

■ A VACCINE IN THE '90S?

Antiviral drugs aren't the only hope for eliminating AIDS. If we could vaccinate everyone, the epidemic might really be stopped. Vaccines have triumphed famously over other viral diseases, from measles to smallpox to polio. The approach consists of exposing people to a virus in some harmless form to provoke a natural immune response without causing serious illness. Unfortunately, the AIDS virus is well designed to foil that approach. One problem is that no one knows what natural immunity would consist of. Infected people produce a flurry of antibodies directed at different parts of the virus, but those people don't end up safe from future infection. They end up dead, as the virus destroys the system producing the antibodies. It's possible that one or more of those antibodies *would* prevent infection in healthy people, but there's no guarantee. A second problem is that HIV is not a single, well-identified target. Like a cold virus, it varies widely and changes fast. There are dozens of strains of HIV, and a vaccine that worked against one might prove worthless against another.

Despite these and other obstacles, the quest for a vaccine is gaining momentum. "A year ago I wouldn't have been able to say whether we would ever have a vaccine," says Fauci, of the NIAID. "I think most scientists are now reasonably optimistic that some time, hopefully in the 1990s, we will." The change of heart stems from a handful of recent experiments. Two research teams have succeeded at protecting monkeys from SIV (the simian AIDS virus), and two other groups have protected chimpanzees from HIV itself. Still other scientists have shown that infected women who produce large amounts of a particular antibody are less likely to bear infected children—a finding that could lead directly to a prenatal vaccine.

In the monkey trials, conducted at primate-research centers in Massachusetts and Louisiana, scientists injected animals with whole, inactivated SIV to produce an immune response and then challenged them with unadulterated virus to see what would happen. The New England researchers managed to protect two out of six monkeys from infection, the Louisiana group eight out of nine.

The chimpanzee experiments involved a different approach. Researchers at two biotechnology companies—Pasteur-Vaccins in Paris and Genentech in South San Francisco—inoculated their animals with "subunits" of the human AIDS virus before injecting them with the whole agent. (HIV infects chimps but doesn't cause illness.) In the Pasteur experiments, two chimps resisted infection after receiving cocktails of several HIV fragments. The Genentech vaccine, based on a fragment of HIV's gp120 envelope protein, also protected both of the chimps that received it.

However impressive, none of these feats means that school kids will soon be lining up for inoculations against AIDS. To be of real use, a preventive AIDS vaccine would need to have a lasting effect against a wide range of virus strains. The animals in these experiments were tested at the peak of their immune responses, and they received the same strains of virus they had encountered in their vaccines. "If we had a simple vaccine that worked in chimps," says Marc Girard, the virologist who directed the French experiments, "it would be five years before it could be used in man, with toxicity tests and all that. And we're very far from that takeoff point." Even a vaccine that proved effective in chimps might perform miserably in people. And finding out would be a challenge in itself, since human subjects can't be purposely exposed.

■ SAVING THE BABIES

One virtue of trying to block mother-to-child transmission is that success is easier to gauge. Since 30 to 40 percent of the children born to infected women are themselves HIV positive, a vaccine that changed that ratio would clearly be making a difference. No one has yet tested such an agent, but Dr. Arye Rubinstein, director of the Center for AIDS Research at New York's Albert Einstein College of Medicine, is rapidly laying the groundwork.

Intrigued by the fact that many infected mothers *don't* bear infected children, Rubinstein and his colleagues set out to identify specific antibodies that might set those women apart. Last month, in a study of 15 AIDS pregnancies, the researchers described such an antibody. Of the 11 women in the study who bore infected babies, not one was producing an antibody directed at the HIV envelope protein's so-called principal neutralizing domain (PND), a short molecular segment that is common to many different strains of the virus. By contrast, the PND antibody was present in three of the four mothers who bore healthy babies. "We suspect the fourth mother had the antibody," Rubinstein says, "because it showed up in the baby."

The PND antibody doesn't seem to help people once they're infected; the mothers who produce it suffer the same fate as those who don't. But if that antibody is the reason some babies are born uninfected, then protecting others might be fairly simple: you would simply inoculate mothers with the tiny piece of the virus that engenders it. Dr. Yair Devash of Ortho Diagnostics has already fabricated the viral fragment, and Rubinstein has incorporated it into a vaccine that could be given to pregnant patients. He's now testing it for toxicity in animals and expects to start a human trial later this year. If the vaccine were to succeed at protecting babies, he notes, it might protect other uninfected people as well.

Preventing infection is not the only goal of vaccine research. Scientists are also testing vaccinelike agents designed to boost the defenses of people who are already infected. These researchers study the body's production of antibodies to different parts of HIV,

then try to amplify the most useful responses. Several preliminary studies show promise. Dr. Robert Redfield of the Walter Reed Army Medical Center has observed that when some patients are exposed to a synthetic fragment of gp160 (a large envelope protein that includes gp120), they produce antibodies directed specifically at that fragment and their T4 cells die less quickly. Allan Goldstein of George Washington University has sparked potentially useful immune activity by exposing people to a piece of the virus core. And Jonas Salk, inventor of the polio vaccine, has reported beneficial effects in about half of the patients he has treated with whole virus stripped of its envelope.

Again, because HIV can hide in places that are beyond the reach of the immune system, none of these therapeutic vaccines could root out the infection completely. But as Salk observed recently, winning and losing are not the only alternatives in the battle against AIDS. A negotiated settlement may still be possible.

■ THIS WILL HAPPEN AGAIN

AIDS, unfortunately, is not just a medical challenge. Science will eventually produce better treatments, maybe even a vaccine. The question is whether these costly advances will reach the populations most in need. It's clear that the burden of sick people will rise steeply during the 1990s, but not at all clear that the world's health systems are prepared to respond. "My fear," says Dr. June Osborn, of the National Commission on AIDS, "is that [scientific progress] will be overwhelmed by a health-care disaster."

All over the world, the epidemic is raging most fiercely within groups that are most removed from education and health care. One major exception is the U.S. gay population. Since the epidemic began, homosexual men have fought discrimination, demanded treatment and research, and reaped the rewards of safe sex and blood testing. In large groups that have been followed over the past decade, the proportion becoming infected each year (not developing AIDS but contracting the virus) has fallen from 7.5 percent in the early 1980s to 1 or 2 percent today. Studies also suggest that infected gay men are living longer thanks to AZT and new treatments for secondary infections.

The experience of inner-city minorities could hardly be more different. Infection rates have not declined substantially among intravenous drug users. And as the epidemic spreads to their sex partners and children, new treatments are making little difference. "These people are intensely poor, alienated, powerless," says Dr. Harold Freeman of Columbia University and Harlem Hospital. Last fall Freeman coauthored a study showing that black men in Harlem were less likely to reach 65 than men in Bangladesh. The data were collected before AIDS even struck. "This is a disaster on top of a disaster," he says. "The people who are suffering need to cry out. But the people involved in this problem have no voice."

Minority women who are infected by their partners may *avoid* seeking treatment for fear they will lose their children to foster homes if their illness is discovered. Maria, a 31-year-old Hispanic woman in Chicago, is the widow of the man who infected her after contracting the virus through his own drug use. Now, with three children to care for (one of them HIV positive), she is suffering full-blown AIDS. Yet she and her family keep her illness a secret. They fear that if others knew, the children would be excluded from school and they from their jobs and their church congregation. Maria's family *curandera,* a traditional healer who treats patients with herbs, incantations and prayer, believes persistent illness is a sign that the sufferer has strayed too far from Latino culture and is being punished by God.

Inner cities aren't the only places health care is lagging. Consider rural Georgia, where AIDS rates have soared in recent years. None of the 14 hospitals in the Southeast Health Unit, a 16-county area roughly the size of Massachusetts, can afford to buy the $80,000 machine needed to test patients' T4 counts. "The problem is real critical now," says Dr. Ted Holloway, director of the Southeast Health Unit. "There is a limited amount of AZT that

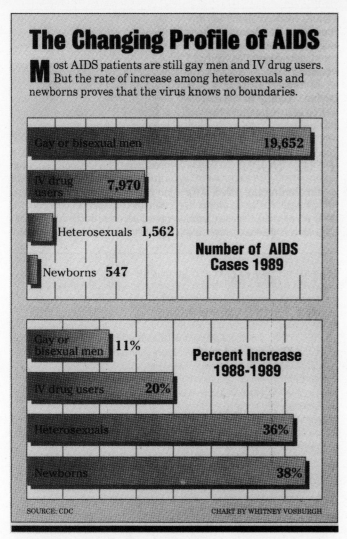

The Changing Profile of AIDS

Most AIDS patients are still gay men and IV drug users. But the rate of increase among heterosexuals and newborns proves that the virus knows no boundaries.

Gay or bisexual men — 19,652

IV drug users — 7,970

Heterosexuals — 1,562

Newborns — 547

Number of AIDS Cases 1989

Gay or bisexual men — 11%

IV drug users — 20%

Heterosexuals — 36%

Newborns — 38%

Percent Increase 1988-1989

SOURCE: CDC   CHART BY WHITNEY VOSBURGH

we can give to indigent patients, but we have to have a T-cell count." The problem is compounded by a lack of physicians willing to treat the disease. "No one wants to be the AIDS doctor," says Halloway.

"If you set up a service, people are going to come from miles away."

Because people who are infected with HIV can't buy private insurance, Medicaid has become a major source of care. Roughly 40 percent of AIDS patients end up on Medicaid, and the federal portion of AIDS-related Medicaid spending has soared from $10 million in 1983 to an anticipated $670 million this year. Yet many infected people who need the assistance don't qualify: besides being poor, one has to be over 65 or a member of a family with dependent children or totally disabled. For many people, that means no medical care until total disability sets in. When AIDS patients finally do qualify for Medicaid, they're often hospitalized for illnesses that might have been prevented through earlier intervention.

To eliminate the Catch-22, Congress is now considering legislation that would let states approve outpatient services for infected people as soon as treatment is needed to prevent a decline in health. And the House and Senate have recently passed bills that, if signed into law, would provide an additional $600 million to $700 million for AIDS care each year. To June Osborn, head of the National Commission on AIDS, such efforts are mere "fingers in the dike." This spring the federally appointed commission issued a report to the president, decrying a lack of leadership from the federal government and repeating its demand for a national AIDS plan with clear roles for federal agencies, state governments and the private sector. To date the report has elicited a *pro forma* letter of appreciation.

No single government initiative is going to solve the AIDS crisis. The crisis is global, and it is magnifying social problems that were already enormous. But complacency would be a mistake. Jonathan Mann, the former WHO official, argues that the world has actually been lucky with the AIDS epidemic so far. Had the virus had a longer latency, the disease might just now be coming to light, in a much greater number of people. The next such virus—and there will most assuredly be others—may be more devious than this one. What HIV teaches us about retroviruses, and about the necessity of education and basic health care for all, could turn out to be valuable. "It takes a lot of hubris to imagine that this couldn't happen again," says Mann. "It could be happening right now."

GEOFFREY COWLEY *with* MARY HAGER *in Washington*, RUTH MARSHALL *in Paris and bureau reports*

SEXUAL HARASSMENT
'80s-STYLE

More subtle now—and more costly.

Brian S. Moskal

This is a quiz. Read each incident and answer "Yes" or "No" as to whether you think the situation presents a case of sexual harassment.

• Jackie thinks Bob is very well-built. She often stares at his body when she thinks he isn't looking. Although he hasn't told her, Bob has noticed Jackie looking and, frankly, it makes him uncomfortable. Sexual harassment?

• At a Christmas party, Barbara's boss has too much to drink. He tells her how beautiful she is and that she understands him better than his wife. He says he intends to make an obvious token of his appreciation of her and her work. Then he asks to drive her home. Is this sexual harassment?

• Sylvia hates the days when she has to work with Jeremy, a co-worker with whom she once had a stormy and romantic relationship. Jeremy hasn't gotten over Sylvia and persistently asks her to come back to him. Sylvia tells her manager about the situation, and he replies that they should try to work it out, reasoning that it is best for

him to stay out of Sylvia's personal business. Is this sexual harassment? Is the manager liable?

• A new clerical-support person in your area of responsibility tells you that she feels uncomfortable during breaks. She says the men who are in the designated break area tell crude jokes and pass around girlie magazines while she is there. Sexual harassment or not?

• Your manager and one of your colleagues are having an affair. Since the affair started, your colleague has received better and easier work assignments, a bigger raise, and a recent promotion. Until their relationship began, you had been the star of the department. Sexual harassment?

The answer to all five questions is "Yes." All five could result in sexual-harassment charges being brought against individuals and the company.

In the first example, Jackie is creating what's called a hostile working environment for Bob. He could file a sexual-harassment charge without even telling Jackie that her looks are unwelcome.

Barbara's partying boss likely is in deep trouble. This is an example of quid pro quo (something for something) sexual harassment. Sex in exchange for raises or promotions are other forms of actionable sexual-harassment cases.

Jeremy had better get the message from Sylvia that their affair is over. Both he and Sylvia's manager are liable under sexual-harassment laws. If the manager does nothing, Sylvia would not only have a case against both, but also the corporation would be legally liable for perhaps millions of dollars in claims.

The new clerical-support person is being subjected to a hostile environment. Sexually suggestive posters hanging on the walls, even in a private office, can offend someone and make the poster owner liable for his or her actions.

The affair between your manager and your colleague is an example of third-party sexual harassment. Your status has been diminished not because of a change in your work ability but because your colleague has gained an unfair advantage.

This is sexual harassment, '80s-style, more subtle than the boss chasing his secretary around the desk. It's also more pervasive, and more expensive, than many may be aware of.

Here's a shocking statistic: Sexual-harassment complaints by female employees were reported at 90% of the nation's largest corporations last year, according to a survey by *Working Woman* magazine. In addition, more than one-third of the companies were sued by alleged victims, a quarter had been sued repeatedly, and each spent an average of $6.7 million a year in sex-harassment related costs (based on absenteeism, low productivity, and employee turnover).

Two-thirds of the complaints, the survey reports, were made against immediate supervisors and upper management. The overwhelming number of incidents were reported by women complaining about unwanted and unwelcomed attention from men.

The survey suggests that many companies are responding to the problem, partly because they fear the adverse publicity and litigation costs associated with harassment complaints. Two out of ten sexual harassers are eventually fired, and others are given written or oral warnings.

It's an expensive issue. In 1987 a record $3.2 million was paid by one company, K mart Corp., to settle a single case. A court settlement, bad publicity, and damaged recruitment can cost more than a company spends annually for employee health and medical benefits.

Under Title VII of the Civil Rights Act, sexual harassment is a form of sex discrimination, and the usual remedies apply—back pay, reinstatement or front-pay injunctive relief, and attorney's fees.

But just what is sexual harassment? In short, unwelcomed sexual advances, requests for sexual favors, and other verbal (sexual jokes) or physical conduct (pinching, arms wrapped around

HOW MUCH DO I KNOW ABOUT SEXUAL HARASSMENT?

A TEST FOR EMPLOYEES
TRUE OR FALSE?

1. If I just ignore unwanted sexual attention, it will usually stop. [T] [F]

2. If I don't mean to sexually harass another employee, there's no way my behavior can be perceived by him or her as sexually harassing. [T] [F]

3. Some employees don't complain about unwanted sexual attention from another worker because they don't want to get that person in trouble. [T] [F]

4. If I make sexual comments to someone and that person doesn't ask me to stop, then I guess my behavior is welcome. [T] [F]

5. To avoid sexually harassing a woman who comes to work in a traditionally male workplace, the men simply should not haze her. [T] [F]

6. A sexual harasser may be told by a court to pay part of a judgment to the employee he or she harassed. [T] [F]

7. A sexually harassed man does not have the same legal rights as a woman who is sexually harassed. [T] [F]

8. About 90% of all sexual harassment in today's workplace is done by males to females. [T] [F]

9. Sexually suggestive pictures or objects in a workplace don't create a liability unless someone complains. [T] [F]

10. Telling someone to stop his or her unwanted sexual behavior usually doesn't do any good. [T] [F]

Answers: 1) FALSE. 2) FALSE. 3) TRUE. 4) FALSE. 5) FALSE. 6) TRUE. 7) FALSE. 8) TRUE. 9) FALSE. 10) FALSE.

A TEST FOR MANAGEMENT PERSONNEL

1. Men in male-dominated workplaces usually have to change their behavior when a woman begins working there. [T] [F]

2. An employer is not liable for the sexual harassment of one of its employees unless that employee loses specific job benefits or is fired. [T] [F]

3. A court can require a sexual harasser to pay part of the judgment to the employee he or she has sexually harassed. [T] [F]

4. A supervisor can be liable for sexual harassment committed by one of his or her employees against another. [T] [F]

5. An employer can be liable for the sexually harassing behavior of management personnel even if it is unaware of that behavior and has a policy forbidding it. [T] [F]

6. It is appropriate for a supervisor, when initially receiving a sexual-harassment complaint, to determine if the alleged recipient overreacted or misunderstood the alleged harasser. [T] [F]

7. When a supervisor is talking with an employee about an allegation of sexual harassment against him or her, it is best to ease into the allegation instead of being direct. [T] [F]

8. Sexually suggestive visuals or objects in a workplace don't create a liability unless an employee complains about them and management allows them to remain. [T] [F]

9. The lack of sexual-harassment complaints is a good indication that sexual harassment is not occurring. [T] [F]

10. It is appropriate for a supervisor to tell an employee to handle unwelcome sexual behavior if he or she thinks that the employee is misunderstanding the behavior. [T] [F]

11. The *intent* behind employee A's sexual behavior is more important than the *impact* of that behavior on employee B when determining if sexual harassment has occurred. [T] [F]

Source: ©1988 by Anderson-davis.

Answers: 1) FALSE. 2) FALSE. 3) TRUE. 4) TRUE. 5) TRUE. 6) FALSE. 7) FALSE. 8) FALSE. 9) FALSE. 10) FALSE. 11) FALSE.

the shoulders) of a sexual nature when (1) submission to such conduct is made either explicitly or implicitly a term or condition of employment; (2) submission to or rejection of such conduct by an individual is used as a basis for employment decisions affecting that individual or third parties; or (3) such conduct has the purpose, in effect, of unreasonably interfering with an individual's work performance or creating an intimidating, hostile, or offensive working environment.

In the '80s a greater proportion of cases involves co-workers rather than boss-subordinate incidents. In addition, sexual harassment today can be more subtle and even more threatening to women than ever before.

There's the member of upper, upper management and part owner of a 650-person business who was fond of checking out the women's locker room at the company's physical-fitness center in the early afternoon. That's when a certain female employee would often exercise and shower so that she would miss the peak hours of fitness-center use. He would not so innocently knock on the locker room door and quickly push it open in the hope of seeing her in the buff. After the woman complained to a human-resources professional, a lock was placed on the door. The next time Mr. Big tried to get in he was stymied. The woman, without ever confronting one of her ultimate bosses, resolved the situation. And Mr. Big got the message when he found the lock on the door.

"I sometimes think we haven't touched the real issue," says Neil E. Schermitzler, Chicago-based director of human resources, central region, Wang Laboratories Inc. "I sense there continues to be a need for management and employees to really understand what sexual harassment is and get with the 1980s. There is still a lot of confusion over the subject. It's an issue of power and exclusion.

Many women continue to feel unempowered or disenfranchised in the workforce. They feel their livelihoods are in jeopardy. In a day of visible litigation, many sexually harassed people are hesitant to go through company procedures to resolve the issue or through the legal process because they might feel like lepers or it will take too long. The predominant number of sexually harassed women are still afraid of retribution from their immediate manager," adds Mr. Schermitzler.

For the most part, males are still downright ignorant about what constitutes sexual harassment. "It's hard for some men to realize that what they might get away with in a single's bar or other social situations isn't acceptable behavior in the business environment," observes Mr. Schermitzler.

"There isn't a good understanding or comprehension that people's jobs and careers are on the line. I blame it on the lack of education and training at the corporation. It's a hard lesson to learn. Men still think sexual harassment is a joking matter."

Supervisors, management, and the corporation itself can be held legally liable for tacitly approving, condoning, or ignoring cases of sexual harassment. It's surprising that, with so many women in the workforce believing they are subjected to major and minor forms of sexual harassment, more legal cases aren't filed.

"It's so rampant and so devastating that if people don't address the issue, it could mean the downfall of a company," asserts Anthony M. Micolo, vice president, human resources, Dime Savings Bank of New York. "Sexual harassment is very widespread. In a way, it's like rape—it happens much more often than it's ever reported. A lot of people are harassed, yet they don't initiate formal complaints because they feel they will be blamed for instigating it or will become outcasts in the company."

In addition, "sexual-harassment verdicts against companies create bad press and can hurt a company in its future recruitment efforts. It's a negative, and if a company has a negative reputation for sexual harassment, people don't want to work there. Outside of the bottom line, the intangibles are just huge," says Mr. Micolo, who is the author of several books on the human-resources function.

Sexual harassment isn't a joke, even though many harassers see it that way. Nor is it a compliment to women. Even a comment that may sound innocent to many men—"that's a nice dress"—can be a form of sexual harassment.

"Men say they are complimenting women, but women don't take it as a compliment," observes Odessa Komer, United Auto Workers' vice president and director of the Women's Dept. In the case of union workers involved in sexual-harassment cases, the local, the national, and even the international union can be sued.

Who gets harassed? After examining sexual-harassment charges filed with the Illinois Equal Employment Opportunity Commission over a two-year period, David E. Terpstra, a professor of business at the University of Idaho, found that "less serious" rather than "more serious" forms of behavior prompted the filing of charges. "We found that most of the charges were based on unwanted physical contact, offensive language, sexual propositions unlinked to threats or promises, and socialization or date requests."

The age of the filers ranged from 18 to 50; however, the majority were clustered in the 20-to-35 age group. Of the 81 people who filed charges, 95% were women. By education, 41% of the filers had a high-school education, 38% had a college degree. By occupation, 25% were secretarial/clerical, 26% were semiskilled or unskilled, 18% were paraprofessional/technical, 5% were skilled craft, 3% were professional, 12% were in sales, and 11% were administrative/managerial.

The percentage of filers by salary were: less than $10,000—39%; $10,000 to $14,999—25%; $15,000 to $19,999—25%; and $20,000 or more—10%.

How does a company protect itself from cases of sexual harassment? First and foremost, there should be a strict company policy banning any forms of sexual harassment. Second, there ought to be a training and education program that outlines examples, subtle and not so subtle, of sexual harassment.

"Once a company has a corporate policy, men are much more careful. Policies make every employee, supervisor, and member of management aware," says Kathy B. Willingham, personnel director at AnSon Gas Corp., Oklahoma City. "Policies are a first step a company can take to protect itself. The second is to have an outlet for sexually harassed people to use as a complaint route." It can be a human-resources professional, ombudsman, ombudswoman, or a member of management who is sensitive to issues of harassment and isn't the alleged victim's immediate supervisor. It's usually best to have a member of the same sex listen to the complaint.

"It's much better for a company to handle sexual-harassment complaints inside the company rather than going outside for solutions and resolution. If it goes outside, it increases the corporation's liability and you can bet you'll lose money," says Ms. Willingham.

Once companies are made aware of a complaint, they should investigate it on a thorough and prompt basis—"a couple of days, not weeks or months. You must literally investigate 'as soon as possible,'" stresses Ellen J. Wagner Esq., president of Creative Solutions Inc., Red Bank, N. J. Her firm specializes in the legal aspects of the human-resources function.

The corporate policy must state that the company will take action based on its findings. That action must be spelled out and could include a verbal warning, a suspension, a departmental transfer, or dismissal.

"People must be put on notice that this is serious business," states Ms. Wagner.

Adolescent Female Prostitutes: A Growing National Concern

Ivan D. Gibson Ainyette, PhD

Dr. Ivan D. Gibson Ainyette is Senior Psychologist, Department of Psychiatry, Harlem Hospital Center, and Adjunct Instructor of Psychology, College of New Rochelle at The New York Theological Seminary Campus, both in New York City.

Prostitution, termed the world's oldest profession, has been recorded since ancient times. Most references, however, focus on adult female prostitutes, with little discussion of adolescents. Since the mid-1960s, the number of juveniles entering "the life," as it's commonly called, has increased. Between 1967 and 1976, for example, there was a 242% rise in adolescent female prostitution. The average age of initiation is approximately 14.[1]

We interviewed 23 adolescent New York City prostitutes in parks, old abandoned buildings, restaurants, bus terminals, and over the telephone, to find out the traits, or constellation of traits, that characterize these teenagers.[2] Although they proved to be a diverse population, many shared certain characteristics.

Family background

In most instances, researchers find that adolescent prostitutes come from abusive homes.[3,4] The present study substantiates these findings. All of the teenagers questioned reported an immense degree of family tension, resulting from conflicts, arguments, and physical, verbal, and sexual abuse. Such conditions occurred equally in single- and double-parent households. The adolescents complained of receiving little love or caring from either parents or siblings. Parents were described as not having, or not taking, the time to positively interact and communicate with them. When the girls tried to approach their parent(s), they were often met with indifference or rejection.

Sharon. One prostitute, Sharon, described her father and his live-in girlfriend as always arguing, with herself often the focus of their disagreements. On other occasions, drugs or financial matters received the family's principal attention. Sharon ultimately found the courage to confront her father and was told that "the sooner she left the better." At age 13, she did leave and has not returned.

Sharon's family had had frequent encounters with the law. Police officers had been repeatedly summoned by family members or neighbors because of altercations, disturbances of the peace, or drug-related activities. Similarly, 14 of the 23 adolescents studied had at least one relative who was incarcerated.

The young victim

Adolescent prostitutes reveal an early history of sexual abuse. Twenty of the study's adolescents reported having been coerced into sex, usually with an older man or male member of their household, and seven reported incestuous relationships. Other investigators have found various early erotization patterns in teenage prostitutes.[3–6] In one study, most adolescent prostitutes had been sexually abused by an older person

From *Medical Aspects of Human Sexuality*, October 1989, pp. 57-60. Copyright © 1989 by Reed Publishing.

(more than 10 years older) prior to their first sexual intercourse.[3] In another investigation, 57% of adolescent prostitutes studied had been raped at least once; 35% more than once.[6] (In our study, 40% had been raped at least once and 25% more than once.) These researchers also reported that most prostitutes had no further intercourse with their first partner, which often seems to initiate a pattern of short-term sexual relationships.[6] (Only 20% in our study had another sexual relationship with their first partner.) They suggest that the adolescent may feel manipulated by or rejected from these short-term relationships,[6] a finding that our research supports.

The pattern of sexual abuse, as described by the youngsters in our study, is particularly noteworthy. According to their experience, once a rape becomes known, it seems to set the stage for other men to make advances.

Alice. Alice described such an ordeal. Her first rape by a stranger, when she was 13, became public knowledge. Weeks later, she was approached and raped by a member of her church. Two months afterward, a second church member raped her. Alice stated that she was afraid to tell her parents or the authorities about either rape.

Rosa. This same pattern also occurs in the family setting. Rosa, another teenage prostitute, had been repeatedly raped by her father, cousin, and brother. When Rosa informed her mother, the woman punched and slapped her daughter, instead of offering comfort and support. Neither Alice nor Rosa received any medical or psychological treatment after being raped.

Low self-esteem

Initially, when interviewed, adolescent prostitutes project a deceptively positive self-image. Eventually, however, this pretense gives way to obvious low self-esteem, in their view a direct consequence of poor family relationships prior to entering prostitution. Almost without exception, these girls describe their first sexual experience as a prostitute as provoking disgust and loathing. Some report that they refused to acknowledge what was taking place at the time.

Nine of the 23 teenagers studied expressed regrets about participating in such degrading behavior and became tearful as they spoke. After months of working the streets, up to 15 hours a day, the youngsters' appearance began to deteriorate, and, not surprisingly, they frequently seemed older than their chronologic age. Several

mentioned incidents of scars, bruises, and disfigurement, and even the death of some of their peers at the hands of pimps, customers, robbers, and fellow prostitutes. These conditions, coupled with an already low self-image, often led the victim to contemplate suicide. Even in our relatively small sample, seven subjects knew at least one adolescent prostitute who had taken her own life.

Confusion and lack of alternatives

Confusion and the lack of alternatives (and money) seem to play a major role in the dynamics of adolescent prostitution. Eleven admitted they were perplexed and upset. Leaving home voluntarily or frequently by force, with few or no skills, they found themselves on the city streets hungry, cold, and desperate. They had to begin immediately searching for a place to stay in a bus terminal or public park. Often they were approached by persons already involved in prostitution who subtly invited homeless girls to enter their line of work. Contrary to popular belief, many teenagers are recruited not by male pimps but by other prostitutes. In our study group of 23 girls, 21 had such an experience.

Cookie. A 14-year-old girl called Cookie illustrates a typical scenario. Leaving an abusive home in Alabama, she came to New York City with only $34 in her pocket. She had expected to find many employment opportunities in a metropolis. But her fantasies ended as soon as she arrived by bus. With no particular plan, she began roaming the streets and sleeping in the bus terminal. Two adolescent prostitutes approached her after her second night. At first, they helped her purchase food. When Cookie's funds were depleted, they gave her money. They wore expensive clothing, carried large sums of money, and made their profession known. Cookie realized only later that the teenagers' clothes were stolen, and the money was provided by their pimp to lure her and other naïve adolescent recruits into prostitution. Several days afterward, these young women urged her to meet their "man." Initially apprehensive but finally persuaded, she accepted their invitation.

Cookie has now been a prostitute for almost two years. Once every month it's her turn to patrol the bus terminal—searching for young girls to bring to her "man."

Pregnancy and venereal disease

When asked what precautions they took to prevent pregnancy, 17 of our subjects cited use of an IUD or diaphragm with, or frequently without, contraceptive jelly. They had received few instructions on how to use these devices, and none was told of any adverse side effects. Although 19 of the adolescents regularly asked customers to use condoms, the men generally refused and became indignant. A small number of teenagers (four) contended that they could not become pregnant and as a result used no birth control.

Several of these adolescents, moreover, did not consider themselves at risk for contracting any sexually transmitted disease (STD), including AIDS. They felt that only homosexual men and intravenous drug users were likely to contract AIDS. Asked about the possibility of being infected with AIDS by bisexual clients, they were at a loss for words. Apparently, they rarely, if ever, considered that they might contract AIDS from bisexual clients. One of these girls responded, "Why would a bisexual man come to us for sex?" Nearly all attempted to rationalize their behavior by stating, "If your number is up, it's up." Most alarming, two of the prostitutes thought AIDS was a fallacy and simply denied its existence, claiming the government just wanted to "scare people."

Six girls agreed to be examined for STDs. The two who admitted testing positive for AIDS continued to work. When asked about spreading the deadly disease, they declared it was not their concern. On the contrary, they felt it was the customer's responsibility to wear a condom.

Since entering "the life," only seven of the 23 adolescents studied had received a gynecologic examination. Although all complained of pain and discomfort, they were reluctant or not permitted to visit a doctor. One girl who had a vaginal discharge and itching described a typical situation: "My man said there ain't enough time for me to get looked at. He said to me, 'Just wash yourself at the end of the day, and you'll be okay.' " She had been a prostitute for over two years.

Attitude toward men

Studies offer various perspectives concerning the adult prostitute's attitudes toward men.[7,8] Some prostitutes hate their customers while others feel neutral. In our group of adolescents, 18 disliked their clients. They were especially infuriated by men who sexually desired partners the same age as their daughters, granddaughters, or nieces. At times, customers displayed photographs of their families sitting around a table or Christmas tree. These pictures often caused jealousy and anger in the adolescent prostitute who wished to be part of such a family group. Other men verbally abused and spat on the teenagers during their sessions.

Although most of the girls' customers desired "traditional" intercourse, many others preferred bizarre and unusual sexual acts. The prostitutes complained bitterly about such matters as their clients' poor personal hygiene and physical threats by some men who, after engaging in sex, wanted their money returned.

Educational background

While all the adolescent prostitutes interviewed had completed grammar school, most had difficulty with basic language skills and arithmetic. After gaining rapport, we asked each girl to take the Reitan-Indiana Aphasia Screening Test, a 15-minute written test that screens for various language disorders. (The test was administered only on "slow" afternoons, usually in an isolated section of a restaurant or on a park bench.)

All but three subjects displayed evidence of dysnomia, dyscalculia, and reading dyspraxia. Their construction of various geometric designs, however, appeared to be within normal limits. Inquiry revealed that 13 of the girls had been placed in special education classes or held back a grade.

Behavioral diversity

Adolescents enter prostitution for a variety of reasons. More than half in this study were runaways who had no place to go.

All the adolescent prostitutes interviewed use drugs. Many have experimented with amphetamines, opiates, cocaine, crack, or phencyclidine. Periodically, some of them take barbiturates or tricyclics. A few have tried benzodiazepines. Most consume small amounts of alcohol (one or two beers a week). The five prostitutes addicted to such drugs as heroin, cocaine, or crack had all resorted to streetwalking to maintain their habits.

Four of the girls are young mothers supplementing their public assistance stipend. Some of these girls live at home, go to school, and prostitute themselves without their parents' knowledge. Still others are only active periodically to raise money for Christmas, other holiday expenses, and school clothes. Fifteen of the girls are heterosexual, five are bisexual, and three are homosexual.

Almost without exception, the girls complain that prostitution limits their leisure activities.

Most have not gone to a movie or out to dinner except fast-food restaurants since entering "the life." Most of these adolescents feel lonely and depressed, with no insight into the future.

Gail. Gail's situation is typical. Although engaged in prostitution for 3½ years, she has saved only $200; most earnings went to her pimp. Basically, Gail has no more now than when she started. Asked where she expects to be five years hence, she drearily responded, "I don't know. I don't think about it."

Conclusion

This limited study indicates that adolescent prostitutes usually come from abusive, uncaring households. They tend to be poorly educated, have low self-esteem, show negative attitudes toward customers, and express confusion about personal goals. Some of them rationalize and even deny the dangers of their profession.

Although most of the adolescent prostitutes interviewed came from abusive homes, many came not from poor but from middle-class working families. Almost 60% had at least one parent/guardian working, and approximately 25% had two parents/guardians working. In fact, 34% had attended parochial schools. Most of these adolescents were runaways from six different states. Thus, adolescent prostitution is not a middle- or lower-class problem; it is a human problem that pervades every socioeconomic class.

Physicians who take the time to obtain a detailed history of each young patient's sexual, familial, and educational background can often identify adolescents at risk of turning to prostitution. Prompt intervention may prevent them from taking this self-destructive course, and help to reverse this dangerous social phenomenon.

Moreover, public health personnel should become involved in meeting the medical needs of these adolescents, and in helping them take preventive measures to reduce and eventually halt the rapid spread of STDs, especially AIDS, in this population.

The author wishes to thank his secretary, Gloria Maldonado, for her help in preparing the manuscript.

References

1. *Juvenile Prostitution: A Federal Strategy for Combating its Causes and Consequences.* Washington, DC, US Dept of Health, Education, and Welfare publication 105-77-2100, 1978.
2. Gibson-Ainyette I, Templer DI, Brown R, et al: Adolescent female prostitutes. *Arch Sex Behav* 17:431, 1988.
3. James J: Motivations for entrance into prostitution, in Crites L (ed): *The Female Offender.* Lexington, MA, Lexington Books, DC Heath and Co, 1976, pp 190-204.
4. Bracey D: *"Baby Pros": Preliminary Profiles of Juvenile Prostitution.* New York, John Wiley and Sons, 1979, p 48.
5. Bracey D: The juvenile prostitute: Victim *and* offender. *Victimology* 8:151, 1983.
6. James J, Meyerding D: Early sexual experience as a factor in prostitution. *Arch Sex Behav* 7:31, 1978.
7. Hollander X: *The Happy Hooker.* New York, Dell Publishing Co, 1972.
8. Goldstein P: *Prostitution and Drugs.* Lexington, MA, Lexington Books, DC Heath and Co, 1979.

Date Rape

You can help the victim to regain a sense of control over her life, improve self-esteem, and avoid future acquaintance rapes.

Andrea Parrot, PhD

Andrea Parrot is Assistant Professor, Department of Human Service Studies, Cornell University, Ithaca, NY.

As many as 15%–25% of college age women have been sexually assaulted or raped by an acquaintance, recent studies show.[1,2] An even higher rate probably occurs in the general population, and marital rape occurs as well.[3,4] Not all acquaintance rape victims are female: The FBI estimates that 10% of all sexual assault victims are male. (The pronoun "she" will be used in this article to refer to victims of date rape since most are female.) Men rarely report this crime unless they are physically injured. In fact, most date rape victims do not report the crime to the police or any other authority since they may not define their experience as rape or may feel partly responsible and therefore guilty.

Most date rape victims believe the myth that a sexual attack is a rape *only* when a stranger violently attacks a woman and injures or kills her while she is fighting him off. In fact, rape is what happens anytime a victim is forced to have sex (usually vaginal intercourse) against her will. Moreover, if sex takes place when the woman is unconscious, or if she is under the age of consent or is physically or mentally incapacitated, the act meets the legal definition of rape in most jurisdictions. Similarly, rape occurs if the victim capitulates to sex out of fear for his or her physical safety.

Identifying the victim

The date rape victim who believes her action or behavior "caused" the rape may tell you only that she "got into a bad situation." She may feel guilty and responsible for the rape and therefore probably will not report it. Instead, it'll be your task to determine whether the patient has indeed been raped. You can do this by taking a particularly careful history and looking for symptoms of the rape trauma syndrome (Table).[5,6] Since it is such a common occurrence, it is advisable to discuss date rape with every adolescent patient during an office visit, since date rape occurs most often between the ages of 15 and 25 years.

What to ask. Getting the truth out of the patient may be difficult. The following questions will help:
• Have you ever had sex when you didn't want to?
• Have you ever been forced to have sex?
• Do you have difficulty saying "no" when you don't want to have sex?

What not to ask. Don't discredit the victim by subtly placing unfair blame on her. Avoid questions such as:
• Have you had sex with this person before?
• Are you married to the man who forced you to have sex?
• Did you fight back or sustain any injuries during the unwanted sexual encounter?
• Were you drunk at the time?

Preventive teaching for adolescent boys/men. All patients, male as well as female, need relevant medical and legal information about rape. Adolescent boys need this information

 From *Medical Aspects of Human Sexuality*, April 1990, pp. 28-31. Copyright © 1990 by Reed Publishing.

especially urgently, since they may commit date/acquaintance rape without thinking they are doing anything wrong. Many grow up believing that a woman's "no" never really means "no" and that if the man persists, he will get what he wants.

Effects of date rape

Three typical behavior patterns may be observed in acquaintance rape victims, either immediately after the rape or years afterwards, according to one researcher[7]:

• Withdrawal from social interactions. The victim does not feel she can trust her own judgment, because she once chose to date a rapist. Therefore, she stops making any decisions requiring judgment and withdraws from social interactions.

• Repression of the rape memory. In the attempt to get back to normal, the victim may repress her memory of the rape; once under stress and reminded of the rape, however, she may explode emotionally. Such a reaction may be triggered by an act as simple as being touched on the shoulder by a man or being examined by a male gynecologist. This reaction to reminders of the rape may precipitate recurring crises.

• Nondiscriminatory sexual behavior. If the victim was a virgin before the rape, she may conclude that she is now "a bad person" and has no legitimate reason to refuse any requests for sex. She may therefore adopt a sexually promiscuous behavior pattern.

If the victim shows any of these behavior patterns, she needs counseling that will help her to overcome feelings of guilt and self-blame. Such feelings often play havoc with the woman's interpersonal relationships and her self-esteem.

Table. Rape trauma syndrome[5,6]

Acute phase (may last for several weeks)

Expressive reaction	Controlled reaction
Angry	Composed
Fearful	Calm
Anxious	Subdued
Tense	

Long-term reorganization phase (may last for years)

Sleep disturbances
Exaggerated startle response
Guilt
Impaired memory or power of concentration
Avoidance of others and social situations
Mistrust of men
Defensiveness, both physical and emotional
Rapid mood swings
Self-blame
Headaches
Feeling that she is "going crazy"

The physician's role

Believe the victim. If you counsel a patient who is a date rape victim, start by believing her. Such patients stand to gain little from lying and in fact may lose the support and friendship of family and friends by reporting an acquaintance rape. This is particularly true if the family and friends know the assailant and feel forced to choose whom to believe: him or the victim. Indeed, the false report rate for date rape is very low.[8] Emotionally healthy people do not falsely accuse others of crimes. Thus, if a patient reports what turns out to be an imaginary rape, she needs a psychiatric referral.

Refer for counseling. You can help the rape-traumatized woman regain a sense of control over her life, improve self-es-teem, and avoid future acquaintance/date rapes by referring her to specially trained counselors at a local rape crisis center. Caution: Counselors trained to help victims raped by a *stranger* may do more harm than good if they have not been taught how to counsel *acquaintance rape* victims. Regardless of what led to the date rape—even if the woman went to the apartment of a man she did not know very well—she should never be blamed for having caused the rape to occur.

Let the victim choose the best options. Your patient can overcome her rape experience by taking some of the following actions:

• Tell her family.
• Tell her friends.
• Seek therapy.
• Confront her assailant.

- Report the rape to the police.
- Press criminal charges.
- Sue the assailant in civil court.
- Report the rape to school authorities.

Your patient may want to confront the assailant after the event (when she is feeling stronger) to tell him her reactions to what he did to her. (She may prefer to do this in a safe, public place and with a support person present.) She can give information to the police without being obliged to give her name or press charges, or she can press criminal charges against her assailant. She may also sue him in civil court for pain and suffering and for the recovery of therapy costs. She may, in fact, have a better chance of winning in civil than in criminal court.

If the rapist is a student, the victim can report the rape to the school authorities. If both victim and assailant attend the same institution, the rapist may be transferred, suspended, or expelled so she will not have to see him every day in her classes.

Teach avoidance tactics. Regardless of what the victim decides to do about reporting the assault or seeking help, she needs to learn how to become less vulnerable so that she can avoid situations likely to end in date rape in the future. She must learn to assess potentially dangerous situations and exercise assertive behavior to get out of them or avoid them completely. For instance, she can learn to use her voice as a weapon by yelling or saying when threatened, "Stop it. This is rape." She can also defend herself verbally against a date who tries to exploit her.

To succeed, she must have enough self-esteem to believe in her right to defend herself against someone she knows and likes but who is trying to force her to do something against her will. However, even if she does not defend herself by any of these means and is raped, she is not to blame. The rapist is the one who is guilty of the crime, not the victim.

Conclusion

The most important thing a victim can do to regain control over her life is to place blame and responsibility for the rape where it belongs—with the rapist. Since date rape is usually nonviolent, the woman is not likely to have any physical evidence of trauma. The psychological trauma of rape, however, may lead to other symptoms such as depression, eating disorders, or acting out sexually (a response requiring medical intervention). You can best aid your patient's recovery when you promptly identify the woman who has been raped, treat her physical symptoms, help her determine a course of action, and refer her to a specially trained counselor. If the woman is involved in a sexual relationship, it may be advisable for both partners to enter counseling jointly.

References

1. Koss M, Gidycz C: Sexual experiences survey: Reliability and validity. *J Consult Clin Psychol* 53(3):422, 1985.
2. Parrot A: Comparison of acquaintance rape patterns among college students in a large co-ed university and a small women's college. Read before the 1985 National Society for the Scientific Study of Sex Convention. November 1985, San Diego.
3. Koss MP, Gidycz CA, Wisinewski N: The scope of rape: Incidence and prevalence of sexual aggression and victimization in a national sample of higher education students. *J Consult Clin Psychol* 55(2):162, 1987.
4. Russell DEH: The prevalence and incidence of rape and attempted rape of females. *Victimology* 7:81, 1982.
5. Burgess AW, Holstrom LL: Rape trauma syndrome. *Am J Psychiatry* 131:981, 1974.
6. Nadelson C, Nortman M, Zackson H, et al: A follow-up study of rape victims. *Am J Psychiatry* 139:1226, 1982.
7. Burkhart B: Acquaintance rape statistics and prevention. Read before the Acquaintance Rape and Prevention on Campus Conference. December 1983, Louisville, KY.
8. Warshaw R: *I Never Called It Rape.* New York, Harper and Row, 1988.

Rape hotlines

Help for rape victims is just a phone call away. All large cities, and most small ones, have crisis centers that provide information, counseling, emotional support, and sometimes legal assistance to sexual assault victims. To find a hotline in your area, contact your local YWCA, police department, or health department; or call one of these clearinghouses:

National Organization for Victim Assistance (202) 393-6682
National Coalition Against Sexual Assault   (202) 483-7165
National Criminal Justice Reference Service (800) 851-3420

"It sounds like I raped you!"

How date-rape "education" fosters confusion, undermines personal responsibility, and trivializes sexual violence.

Stephanie Gutmann

Stephanie Gutmann is a recent graduate of the Columbia School of Journalism.

Judging by the news and entertainment media, the problems of date and acquaintance rape have reached crisis proportions in recent years. A search in the database Nexis turns up 54 mentions of date or acquaintance rape in the *New York Times* during the past two decades—nearly half of them in the last year. Television shows such as "A Different World," "21 Jump Street" and numerous made-for-TV movies have featured date-rape themes. Oprah, Phil, Geraldo, and Sally have each taken a crack at the subject.

But although the barrage of media coverage has driven date and acquaintance rape into the public consciousness, the meaning of these terms is not at all clear. Hearing the phrase *date rape*, the average person probably imagines a scenario something like this: A man and a woman who have recently met go to dinner and a movie. He takes her back to her apartment afterward. She is tired and wants to get to sleep, but he wants to come in for some coffee. She lets him in out of politeness and sits next to him on the couch as he drinks his coffee. He overpowers her, pins her to the couch, and rapes her.

The experts whose research and warnings feed the alarming publicity have quite a different idea of date and acquaintance rape. Their definition, which goes far beyond both the legal and popular understandings of rape, would encompass a host of ambiguous situations that involve neither the use nor threat of violence. Under some versions of the new definition, a man who whined until his girlfriend agreed to have sex with him would be guilty of rape.

"Any sexual intercourse without mutual desire is a form of rape," writes Dr. Andrea Parrot, a psychiatry professor at Cornell University who specializes in studying date rape. "Anyone who is psychologically or physically pressured into sexual contact is as much a victim of rape as the person who is attacked on the streets."

The training manual for Swarthmore College's Acquaintance Rape Prevention Workshop states: "Acquaintance rape...spans a spectrum of incidents and behaviors ranging from crimes legally defined as rape to verbal harrassment and *inappropriate innuendo*." (Emphasis added.)

A former director of Columbia University's date-rape education program says: "Every time you have an act of intercourse there must be explicit consent, and if there's no explicit consent, then it's rape. Almost every woman I've ever talked to has had an experience where she's been in a situation where she's had intercourse where she's not really been a fully willing participant—I would call that rape. People don't have the right to use other people's bodies assuming anything. Stone silence throughout an entire physical encounter with someone is not explicit consent."

Although largely driven by feminist ideology, this redefinition of rape casts women as eternal victims, undermines personal responsibility, and trivializes the very idea of sexual violence. Combined with misleading statistics from weak studies, it fosters unrealistic fear and distrust. Nowhere are the effects of rape revisionism more pronounced than on college campuses.

"Colleges work to solve—and stop—a shockingly frequent, often hidden outrage," the subhead of a *Newsweek* story announces. "Fear Makes Women Campus Prisoners," howls a *Chicago Tribune* article describing students who, because of the "prevalence of date rape," stay in their rooms at night, cringe when classmates make "sexist" remarks, and keep "themselves out of threatening situations at parties."

Colleges throughout the country have announced large increases in reports of rape, usually from female students under

20 and generally involving friends or acquaintances. Meanwhile, date-rape education programs run by administrators or students have proliferated like amoebae in a jar.

Many schools have instituted Rape Awareness Weeks and appointed special deans to deal with sexual assault. In annual marches to "Take Back the Night," young women leap up, give frenzied testimony about their experiences as victims, and entreat members of the audience to testify as well, so that "others will have the courage to come forward." Educational videos, pamphlets, training manuals, and posters teach students about the dangers of date rape.

On a wall of Columbia University's student health service building is a bright red poster resembling a warning about radioactive material that announces: "Date Rape is Violence; Not a Difference of Opinion." A university program trains students for 10 weeks as date-rape educators and dispatches them to dorms to conduct seminars, video screenings, and discussion groups. The program is mandatory for all new fraternity and sorority pledges. At a recent gathering at Barnard College, an employee of New York City's Task Force Against Sexual Assault drew a group of young women into a circle and gravely informed them that "one in five dates end up in assault."

Since last fall, when five female students at Syracuse University reported being raped by acquaintances, the school has seen the creation of a student-organized group called SCARE (Students Concerned About Rape Education), a Rape Awareness Week, a Rape Task Force, plans for a Rape Education Center, and Speak Out rallies attracting as many as 200 members of the university community. "The epidemic of rape must come to an end on this campus," thundered an editorial in the student newspaper that fall. "This crime is running rampant at Syracuse University...other [campus issues] pale in comparison to the apparent crime wave of rape striking all parts of this university."

By at least one measure—reports to campus security and police—all this alarm is puzzling. At Irvine, for example, campus security received only one report of rape in 1989—the year in which 60 rapes and sexual assaults were reported to the campus women's center. Columbia University's security department says it has received no reports of rape in the last five years, although in 1986 Ellen Doherty, a rape counselor at a hospital near Columbia, told *Newsweek* that acquaintance rape is "the single largest problem on college campuses today."

Those who perceive an acquaintance-rape crisis explain that women, understandably afraid of callous treatment by campus security and the police, are more willing to tell their stories to the sympathetic people at the local women's center. This explanation raises another issue, however. The people staffing these centers and similar institutions tend to assume that most acquaintance rapes go unreported and that, given skepticism in the past, believing the victim is of utmost importance. Since reporting challenges the system, encourages others to come forward, and empowers the individual, they consider it a positive good that should be encouraged.

Hence Parrot, the Cornell date-rape specialist, writes in a 1987 paper: "If the prevention strategies presented in the program are employed as suggested, participants should be at reduced risk for acquaintance rape involvement, and the report rate of acquaintance rape in your community should increase." Increasing the number of reports is thus an end in itself.

"People respond to numbers," the aforementioned employee of New York's Task Force Against Sexual Assault told her Barnard charges. The bigger the numbers, she explained, the bigger the indictment of a society in which sexual assault is rampant and condoned. Attempts to verify reports through investigation or clarify them through in-depth interviews would therefore be counterproductive.

The reliability of report figures is not the only source of doubt about the alleged rape crisis. The broader statistical foundation for acquaintance-rape alarm, including the survey data that college administrators solemnly invoke, is also deeply flawed.

The University of Illinois provides a good example of how flimsy studies and dubious research conclusions are embraced by the press and become the basis for campus policy. Once again, the university was primarily concerned with acquaintance rape. Although the Urbana campus had been haunted twice in the previous five years by a nonstudent serial rapist, the school's Rape Awareness and Prevention Committee had concluded that "the greater risk to women students involv[es] sexual assault by their male friends, boyfriends, and acquaintances."

Following reports of increases in date rape at other schools, the University of Illinois created a Campus Task Force on Sexual Assault, Abuse, and Violence in 1989. The task force attempted to measure the school's date rape problem with a survey that was mailed to 1,460 women on the 35,000-student campus. It classified 16.4 percent of the 537 students who replied as victims of "criminal sexual assault," defined as intercourse with a clearly expressed lack of consent.

Last winter the task force issued a report offering recommendations based on the survey's evidence that the university environment "engenders sexual abuse." The report advocated abolishing the school's intramural, all-female pom-pom squad, "instituting a mandatory human relations program" for all undergraduates covering "the risk of and responsibility for sexual misconduct," and adding provisions covering sexual misconduct to the school's code of behavior. Punishable by expulsion, sexual misconduct would be defined as intercourse without the female's knowing consent.

"A person who is intoxicated is incapable of giving knowing consent...a person who is under any form of coercion (including physical, psychological, academic, or professional) is not free to give consent," the report stated. Finally, the task force recommended "investigating and seeking to eliminate the prevalent philosophies, cultures and attitudes of fraternities and other organizations that are built on sexism, lack of respect for women, and that lead to violence against women."

The task force's recommendations and the results of its

survey were soon picked up by the local press and aired on National Public Radio's "All Things Considered." The *Chicago Tribune*'s story began with the pithy factoid, "16.4 percent of female students who responded to a questionnaire had been raped"—suggesting that this finding was representative of the entire student population.

The reporter failed to address important shortcomings of the survey. For example, the sample was self-selected, a significant problem since the questionnaire was rather lengthy. "If people have never had any experience with this, they're not going to even bother" with the survey, says Kalman Kaplan, a psychologist at Wayne State University.

The bias was compounded by the title of the questionnaire, "Survey of Sexually Stressful Events," which may have predisposed respondents to view ambiguous situations in a particular light. Kalman adds that it's not clear what meaning respondents attached to key terms used in the survey. For example, the survey includes a question asking whether the parties had been sexually intimate before, but it does not try to determine what kind of signals would have constituted "resistance" in the context of the relationship. Even Vice Chancellor Stanley Levy, who defends the survey, admits that "you have difficulty in extrapolation" from its findings.

The *Chicago Tribune* bolstered the University of Illinois study with figures from another, highly influential poll. The story declared that women at the university "apparently have good reason" to be scared because "a nationwide survey...by Mary Koss, a psychiatry professor at the University of Arizona, found that one in four women reported having been the victims of rape or attempted rape, usually by acquaintances."

Koss's numbers, especially the one-in-four firgure, are widely cited. They come from the *Ms.* Campus Project on Sexual Assault, considered the most comprehensive study of campus sex crimes. In 1982, using a $267,500 National Institute of Mental Health grant procured by the magazine, Koss and a platoon of assistants fanned out across the country to administer a "Sexual Experiences Survey" to college students. After three years of data collection and tabulation, Koss announced her findings: "25 percent of women in college have been the victims of rape or attempted rape," and "84 percent of these victims knew their assailants."

Koss went to great lengths to obtain a representative, sufficiently large sample. Still, there are obvious problems with her study.

Koss obtained her data on the "incidence and prevalence of sexual aggression" with a 10-item survey featuring questions such as, "Have you given in to sexual intercourse when you didn't want to because you were overwhelmed by a man's continual arguments and pressure?" (number 6) and "Have you had sexual intercourse when you didn't want to because a man threatened or used some degree of physical force (twisting your arm, holding you down, etc.) to make you?" (number 9). A positive answer to question 6 or question 7 (which asks whether the subject has been pressured into sex by someone in a position of authority) labeled the respondent a victim of sexual coercion.

A positive answer to any of questions 8 through 10 put a respondent in the rape category.

Question 9 and question 10 (which also refers to the use of force or threats of violence) seem to fit the conventional picture of rape, but consider question 8: "Have you had sexual intercourse when you didn't want to because a man gave you alcohol or drugs?" In the terminology of psychological testing, this question is considered "double-barreled": Exactly what it's asking is not clear. For example, it might be interpreted as asking if the respondent has exchanged sex for alcohol or drugs. Koss was probably trying to identify respondents who had been raped while incapacitated. Still, the question's wording clearly invites respondents to put the blame for an unpleasant or ambiguous event on alcohol or drugs, mysterious forces over which one has no control.

Another problem with the survey is its leading quality. In a properly designed survey, important or more meaningful questions should be interspersed with filler items, Kaplan says, not grouped together in order of ascending seriousness as Koss did. "If a person answers yes to the first question you're almost preparing them to answer yes to a later one," he says "If they came at you with questions 8, 9, 10 to begin with, you'd probably have fewer positive responses to those questions."

In general, surveys such as Koss's encourage women to reinterpret sexual experiences after the fact. University of Chicago psychologist Catherine Nye notes that 43 percent of the women classified as rape victims by the Koss study *had not realized they'd been raped.* "Well, I think if you don't know you've been raped," Nye says, "then probably you're talking about a situation which has to be redefined, reconstructed."

Indeed, Parrot, the Cornell psychiatrist, has said that "only one [rape] incident in 100 to 150 is reported to police, sometimes because women don't recognize the sexual assaults as rape. Education is necessary to sensitize both men and women to what constitutes rape."

And here is the crux of the matter: If you have to convince a woman that she has been raped, how meaningful is that conclusion? Her "education" requires her to adopt a different understanding of rape. Consider how the new definition is applied.

Columbia University uses a scene from the movie *She's Gotta Have It* to illustrate the dynamics of date rape: The female protagonist is at home, depressed after having broken up with her boyfriend. She calls him and begs him to come see her. Bitter over the fact that she has been unable to be faithful to him (which he has taken as a rejection), he at first refuses. She continues to plead, and eventually he relents—obviously apprehensive about getting sucked into the vortex again with this seductive but capricious woman.

When he arrives she throws her arms around him and pleads with him to make love to her. They argue. She tries intermittently to embrace him; he is furious, shaking her off, but perhaps enjoying the fact that the role of the needy one in the relationship is now reversed. Finally, still suffused with bitterness and fury, he pushes her coarsely onto the bed, and—saying, "You want it; you've got it!"—takes her from behind, violently and angrily. She whimpers, "What are you doing?" or some such protestation a couple of times, but she submits—making no effort to resist—in an exhausted, masochistic way.

It isn't pretty—but it isn't rape.

Not, at least, according to Richard Uviller and Vivian Berger, two Columbia University law professors. "This is certainly not rape," says Uviller, a criminal law specialist. "It just seems like seduction to me."

"It certainly doesn't seem like rape to me," agrees Berger, who has studied rape law extensively. "Under the more technical definition in New York, it seems to me that she doesn't fear any kind of injury."

In the effort to distinguish between rape and seduction, sex offense and offensive sex, most rape laws have set the same basic criteria: There must be an expressed lack of consent and/or coercion by force or threat of force. In New York, "forcible compulsion" is defined as "to compel by either the use of physical force or a threat express or implied which places a person in fear of immediate death or physical injury to himself, herself, or another person."

Intent is another important ingredient of criminal law. "A man cannot be guilty of a crime he doesn't know he's committed," Uviller says.

Some legal scholars, however, are building a philosophical base for a change in the law that would dramatically affect the way judges and juries are obliged to think about sexual relations. In her 1987 book *Real Rape*, Susan Estrich, a law professor at the University of Southern California and former campaign manager for Michael Dukakis, discusses the "reasonable woman" standard frequently invoked in ambiguous rape cases. The judge's view "of a reasonable person is one who does not scare easily, one who does not feel vulnerable, one who is not passive, one who fights back, not cries," she writes. "The reasonable woman...is a man."

Estrich would eliminate the defense that the man charged with rape honestly believed there was consent. "Consent should be defined so that no means no," she writes. Women should be "empower[ed] in potentially consensual situations with the weapon of a rape charge."

But in many sexual encounters, things are not so clear-cut, especially when the man and woman have deep feelings for each other or have engaged in sex previously. The picture is further clouded by the tradition that men should take the sexual initiative, the inclination of some women to voice resistance in order to avoid appearing "easy," and the prevalent belief that saying no is a mere convention, part of foreplay.

Other legal scholars see dangers in the direction that Estrich recommends: "We don't want the law to patronize women," Berger wrote, reviewing Estrich's book in *Criminal Justice Ethics*. "To treat as victims in a legal sense all of the female victims of life is at some point to cheapen, not celebrate, the rights to self-determination, sexual autonomy, and self and societal respect of women."

Legal definitions change as society changes and after sus-

tained pressure from interest groups. The law is not written in stone, and sometimes it is wrong. But comparing the legal meaning of rape to the new definition helps measure the gap between the thinking of the rape revisionists and community standards, which have slowly shaped our current laws. Moreover, the comparison demonstrates the difficulty of estimating how many of the women who are classified as rape victims based on the meager information provided by surveys would be considered rape victims under the law.

Legal reform aside, many feminists see value in broader use of the word *rape*, even if they don't seriously propose to prosecute anyone on that basis. "In terms of making men nervous or worried that they might be overstepping their bounds, I don't think that's a bad thing," Parrot says. "Our culture has given men permission to ignore womens' wishes, to disregard appropriate responses to sexual interactions."

Leaving aside the question of whether such an approach is fair to men, what effect does the redefinition of rape have on women? In addition to generating inappropriate alarm, it encourages young women to isolate troubling and ambivalent feelings in a cell called rape—far away from honest examination. The story of "Jane," a student at a prestigious midwestern university, is illustrative.

Jane and a girlfriend have been pressuring their dean of students "to do something about date rape on campus." Action is needed, Jane says, because the "experience has affected people close in my life and I've seen what it's done to them. All of it could be prevented if people knew what they could do about it and really believed that it was wrong." Jane eventually agreed to talk about what she described as her own experience of date rape.

She had been living upstairs from a young man in a co-ed dorm for about six months. They talked often, hung out in each other's rooms, had pet names for each other, propped each other up during stressful times, and occasionally necked. One night just before spring break, the boy called Jane and asked if he could come up. Jane had just gone to bed, but she reluctantly agreed because she knew her friend had been feeling bad lately and wasn't looking forward to going home on break.

When he came in she could tell that he was very drunk. Then, she says, he "was all over" her. She squirmed in protest and said "c'mon...no," but he didn't seem to listen. She didn't scream or push him off, or, as she puts it, "have this big fit."

She's not sure why. "Partly it didn't really seem necessary—I thought, 'Well, he's my friend....I guess whatever happens, it's not going to be that bad.' I was afraid of making him mad. I was just, 'Well, let's keep the situation under control.'...I wasn't aware of the problem then or really what was happening....After it had happened, I thought, 'OK, I didn't want that, but it's not that bad 'cause he's a friend of mine'—you know, no big deal."

Jane went home for spring break and didn't think about the incident. Then, two weeks into the next term, she saw a presentation on date rape. She says she started realizing, "Oh my God, that's what happened to me!"

Jane and the boy eventually talked about that evening (their relationship had been awkward and strained ever since), but she didn't use the word *rape*—instead telling him, "I didn't want that; that was wrong." He filled in the blanks, she says. "God! It sounds like I raped you," he eventually stammered.

"He was totally speechless," she recalls. "He stared straight ahead for so long. He said, 'Oh my God, I can't believe I did this. I can't believe I hurt you. Don't hate me.'" He said he'd misinterpreted her squirming, thinking that she wanted to do it because that's what he wanted to believe.

"Looking back on it now," she says. "that's such an interesting thing: Date rape is such a real thing. It's not something made up because the media tells you it happens; it's not something you create. It's something that really is and really affects you without your knowing it."

Catherine Nye says she and her colleagues at the University of Chicago's student counseling service see many "Janes"—young women who are essentially troubled about sex, unclear in their own minds about what they want, and sometimes guilty about sexual desires—who lately have begun to use the term *date rape* to describe their sexual experiences. She laments the psychological effect of such evasion.

"It's so much more useful to deal with these things before they've gotten put in this box of date rape, because then . . . it's not all stuck over on this guy who did this bad thing to me," she says. "If they say 'date raped,' they don't have to think about their own behavior; they don't have to think about their feelings. There's no complicity, there's no responsibility, and that's the nonfeminist piece of it as far as I am concerned."

An almost Victorian denial of complicity—of woman's emotional stake in the sexual relationship—is a big feature of the date-rape *oevre*. Man is entirely predatory; woman is entirely passive, a hapless victim, there by accident. Nye, asked by students to conduct a workshop on date rape, recently reviewed much of the training material available from Cornell and Swarthmore. "There was stuff in there that made my skin crawl," she says. "This training manual said things like, 'Don't let down your guard until you know a man really well—if at all.' I mean, talk about The Other!"

Man as "The Other" makes an appearance on the cover of Parrot's 1988 book *Coping with Date Rape and Acquaintance Rape*. The illustration portrays a couple on a date. The male figure is drawn as a devil, with horns, a Van Dyke beard, and a pitchfork tail pointing upward lasciviously. A leering, evil gleam in his eye, he stares slaveringly at the woman. She is blonde, with eyes cast demurely downward, almost closed.

The figures of the Machiavellian, predatory, demonic male and the innocent, asexual, passive, vulnerable female appear again in Parrot's description of a date:

"First, a rapist engages in intimate behaviors which make a female feel uncomfortable (for instance, by putting his hand on her thigh, or kissing her in a public place after knowing her for only a short time). This is common in party and bar situations when the music is so loud that the couple must be very close to each other to hear. In such situations it is not possible to maintain a comfortable distance from others.

"If the victim does not clearly object, the rapist proceeds to the second stage, in which he desensitizes the victim to the intrusion by escalating the behavior (moving his hand to her buttocks, for example.) She may feel increasingly uneasy as a result of this behavior, and suggest going outside for "fresh air" hoping that she can create physical distance from him. Unless she actually tells him that she is uncomfortable with his 'roaming hands,' he may misinterpret her suggestion as meaning she wants to be alone with him. The third stage occurs when they are in an isolated place (such as outside, in his apartment, in his car, etc.) and the rapist insists on intercourse."

Clearly, this situation is one in which more assertiveness on the woman's part could make a crucial difference. But date-rape rhetoric and literature, Nye says, is often implicitly about "defining yourself as a victim and blaming the men, as opposed to saying we have a responsibility to take control here and to improve communication."

As Nye's experience indicates, this message appeals strongly to many young women. In the wake of the sexual revolution—in our brave new world of co-ed living, dorm condom dispensers, and hip health-service gynecologists who smile sunnily while asking their young clients if they've had any rough sex or group sex recently—college-age women may be trying to put some limits back on sexual behavior.

In an earlier era, there were various socially supported ways to say no, as well as all kinds of controls—segregated dorms, dorm mothers, curfew laws, *in loco parentis* policies in general—to give women greater room for delay and reflection. Women also had a perfectly respectable pretext for avoiding the complications of sex—"I might get pregnant"—that has been largely eliminated by readily available birth control.

Perhaps young women are looking for an "out" acceptable in the new campus environment, where sexual openness and enthusiasm are *de rigeur*. Given feminism's reigning orthodoxies, it's more acceptable to say that men are monsters, or that sex is fraught with potential violence to women, than to say, "I don't feel like it right now."

More fundamentally, the new definition of rape gives women a simple way of thinking about sex that externalizes guilt, remorse, or conflict. Bad or confused feelings after sex become someone else's fault. A sexual encounter is transformed into a one-way event in which the woman has no stake, no interest, and no active role. Assuming the status of victim is in many ways an easy answer—but not one befitting supposedly liberated women.

Study Defines Major Sources of Conflict Between Sexes

Differences are found in what disturbs men and women.

Daniel Goleman

In the war between the sexes, virtually all combatants consider themselves experts on the causes of conflict. But now a systematic research project has defined, more precisely than ever before, the points of conflict that arise between men and women in a wide range of relationships.

The new studies are showing that the things that anger men about women, and women about men, are just about the same whether the couple are only dating, are newlyweds or are unhappily married.

The research is the most sophisticated yet conducted, and some findings are surprising. Although a vast body of literature cites heated arguments over money, child-rearing or relatives as frequent factors in disintegrating marriages, those conflicts seldom emerged in the new studies.

Instead, the research often found more subtle differences, like women's feelings of being neglected and men's irritations over women being too self-absorbed. There were also more pointed complaints about men's condescension and women's moodiness.

Upset by Unfaithfulness and Abuse

Some forms of behavior bothered both sexes about equally. Both men and women were deeply upset by unfaithfulness and physical or verbal abuse. But the most interesting findings were several marked differences between men and women in the behaviors that most disturbed them.

Sex, not surprisingly, was a major problem, but men and women had diametrically opposed views of what the problem was. Men complained strongly that women too often turned down their sexual overtures.

In contrast, the most consistent complaint among women was that men were too aggressive sexually. This conflict may be rooted deep in the impact of human evolution on reproductive strategies, according to one theory, or it may simply reflect current power struggles or psychological needs, various experts say.

Help in Counseling Couples

Understanding the sources of trouble between the sexes, psychologists say, could do much to help couples soften the impact of persistent problems in their relationships, and help therapists in counseling couples having difficulties.

"Little empirical work has been done on precisely what men and women do that leads to conflict," said David M. Buss, a psychologist at the University of Michigan who conducted the studies. The results were published in May in the *Journal of Personality and Social Psychology*.

Dr. Buss conducted four different studies with nearly 600 men and women. In the first, he simply asked men and women in dating relationships about the things their partners did that made them upset, hurt or angry.

The survey yielded 147 distinct sources of conflict, ranging from being disheveled or insulting to flirting with others or forcing sex on a partner.

In the second study, Dr. Buss asked men and women who were dating or who were newlyweds how often they had been irked by their partner's doing any of those things. From these results, Dr. Buss determined that the complaints fell into 15 specific groups. He then had another group of men and women rate just how bothersome those traits were.

Men said they were most troubled by women who were unfaithful, abusive, self-centered, condescending, sexually withholding, neglectful or moody.

Many men were bothered, for example, if their partner was self-absorbed with her appearance, spending too much money on clothes, and being overly concerned with how her face and hair looked.

Women complained most about men who were sexually aggressive, unfaithful, abusive, condescending, emotionally constricted, and those who insulted the woman's appearance, neglected them, or openly admired other women.

Many women were also bothered by inconsiderate men. For instance, they complained about a man who teases his partner about how long it takes to get dressed, or who does not help clean up the home or who leaves the toilet seat up.

'Basic Differences in Outlook'

Other research has produced supporting findings. "We've seen similar points of conflicts in marital fights," said John Gottman, a psychologist at the University of Washington whose research involves observations of married couples while they fight.

"Many of these complaints seem to be due to basic differences in outlook between the sexes," Dr. Gottman added, citing men's complaints that women are too moody, or that women dwelled too much on the feelings.

"That is the flip side of one of women's biggest complaints about men, that they're too emotionally constricted, too quick to offer an action solution to an emotional problem," he said.

"Generally for women, the natural way to deal with emotions is to explore them, to stay with them," he continued. "Men, though, are stoic in discussing their emotions; they don't talk about their feelings as readily as women. So conflict over handling emotions is almost inevitable, especially in marriages that are going bad."

For couples in the first year of marriage, Dr. Buss found the sexual issues to be far less of a problem than for most other couples. Instead, women tended to complain that their new husbands were inconsiderate and disheveled.

"You'd expect that sex would be the least troubling issue for a couple during the honeymoon year," Dr. Buss said. "Even so, newlywed men were still bothered somewhat about their wives' sexual withholding, but the wives didn't complain much about their husbands being sexually aggressive."

Nevertheless, the overall finding that men tend to see women as being sexually withholding, while women see men as too demanding, also fits with other findings. Researchers at the University of New York at Stony Brook found in a survey of close to 100 married couples that the husbands on average wanted to have sex more often than did the wives.

Problems Compounded

In the last of Dr. Buss's series of tests, married men and women were asked about their main sources of marital and sexual dissatisfaction. A new set of complaints emerged, along with the previous ones cited by dating couples and newlyweds. The more dissatisfied with the relationship, the longer the list of complaints.

For example, the more troubled the couple, the more likely the husband was angered by his wife being too possessive, neglecting him and openly admiring other men.

The dissatisfied wives, by contrast, added to their list of complaints that their husbands were possessive, moody and were openly attracted to other women.

Sex was especially problematic for unhappy married men and women.

"The sexual complaints are standard in unhappy marriages," Dr. Gottman said. "But it tends to crop up even in otherwise happy marriages. Generally, women have more prerequisites for sex than men do. They have more expectations about what makes love-making O.K. They want emotional closeness, warmth, conversation, a sense of empathy."

He added: "Sex has a different meaning for women than for men. Women see sex as following from emotional intimacy, while men see sex itself as a road to intimacy. So it follows that men should complain more that women are withholding, or women say men are too aggressive."

Investment in Reproduction

Dr. Buss sees his results as affirming the importance of evolution in shaping human behavior. "The evolutionary model that I use holds that conflicts occur when one sex does something that interferes with the other's strategy for reproduction," he said.

His view is based on the theory put forth by Robert Trivers, a social scientist at the University of California at Santa Cruz, who proposed that women are more discriminating than men about their sexual partners because biologically women have to invest more time and energy in reproduction than do men.

Men on the other hand stand to gain in terms of reproductive success for having sexual relations with as many women as possible, the theory holds.

"To some degree the sexes are inevitably at odds, given the differences in their strategies," Dr. Buss said.

Even so, Dr. Buss does not see evolution as explaining all his findings. "The sources of conflict between men and women are much more diverse than I predicted," he said.

Some of that diversity may be caused by sex roles. "Men and women are socialized differently as children," said Nancy Cantor, a social psychologist at the University of Michigan. "Men, for example, are not expected to be as open with their emotions as women, while women are expected to be less aggressive than men. So you'd expect a list very much like he found."

Dr. Gottman offered another explanation, saying: "The categories sound like much of what we see in couples' fights. But they miss what underlies all that: whether people feel loved and respected. Those are the two most important dimensions in marital happiness."

Woman vs. Man
Vive la différence

MAN | WOMAN

MAN

On average, boy babies **stay in the womb** a total of 279 days before they're born.

By age 13, boys have reached 87.3 percent of their **mature height**.

Men reach their **sexual peak** by age 20.

After **lovemaking**, men usually can't be sexually aroused again for two to thirty minutes.

The average man can expect to **live to** age 72.

At age 70, 70 percent of men still have **erections**. Provided a man's sperm count is adequate, he can remain **fertile** well into old age.

The average man's **testes** measure 1½ inches long and ¾ inch across each. His **penis** measures 3¼ to 4¾ inches long when limp; when erect, it ranges from 6¼ to 7¾ inches.

During a single **ejaculation**, a man releases 200 to 500 million sperm.

A man's body has one fifth as much **estrogen** as a woman's, one tenth as much **progesterone** and 15 times as much **testosterone**.

The average man is 30 percent **stronger** than the average woman.

A man's **brain measures** 87.4 cubic inches.

The average man is wrapped in 20 square feet of **skin**.

A man's body is about 60 percent **water**.

Fat constitutes 15 to 18 percent of a man's weight.

Twenty-four percent of men are **overweight**.

WOMAN

On average, girl babies **remain in the womb** for 279.9 days before they're born—almost a day longer than males.

By age 13, girls have reached 96.5 percent of their **mature height**.

Women reach their **sexual peak** by age 35.

After **lovemaking**, women can be sexually aroused again immediately.

The average woman **lives to** age 78.

A woman is most **fertile** at age 24 and loses the ability to conceive upon menopause.

The average woman's **vagina** measures 3 to 4 inches in length but has the capacity to expand.

It takes only one sperm penetrating a mature egg for **conception** to occur.

A woman's body has 5 times as much **estrogen**, 10 times as much **progesterone** and one fifteenth the amount of **testosterone** as a man's.

Women may not be as strong as men, but a woman holds the speed record for **swimming** the English Channel.

A woman's **brain measures** 76.8 cubic inches. (Caveat: In this instance, size is not relevant to power.)

The average woman is wrapped in 17 square feet of **skin**.

A woman's body is about 55 percent **water**.

Fat makes up 25 to 28 percent of an average woman's weight.

Twenty-seven percent of women are **overweight**.

MAN | WOMAN

MAN	WOMAN
The average man's **heart beats** 72 times per minute. During orgasm his heart rate can climb to as high as 180.	The average woman's **heart beats** 78 times per minute—faster than a man's because it's smaller. During orgasm her heart rate can climb to above 180.
By age 25, 25 percent of men show signs of a receding hairline and a **balding** crown; by age 50, 50 percent of men are balding.	**Baldness** is exceedingly rare in women prior to age 70.
Only 8.7 percent of men surveyed say they feel a strong sense of guilt about having had **premarital sex**. According to 66.5 percent of men, **extramarital sex** is always wrong.	Almost one quarter—23.4 percent—of women who've had **premarital sex** feel very guilty about the experience. According to 78.4 percent of women, **extramarital sex** is always wrong.
Forty-seven percent of **husbands say their wife is a skilled lover**; 26 percent say she's imaginative about sex; 81 percent believe she is attractive; and 55 percent say she's a romantic.	Fifty-three percent of **wives say their husband is a skilled lover**; 32 percent say he's imaginative about sex; 72 percent believe he's good-looking; and 47 percent say he's a romantic.
When they cry, men get lumps in their throats 29 percent of the time.	**When they cry**, women get lumps in their throats 50 percent of the time. And although male children cry as much as female children, women cry four times more often than men.
Men tend to use humor more often than women to **influence people**.	Women tend to use facial expression and body language more often than men **to influence others**.
Four percent of men are **color-blind**.	A fifth of one percent of women are **color-blind**.
Angular shapes, such as the diamond, are **most pleasing to a man's eye**.	Curved shapes, such as the heart, are **most pleasing to a woman's eye**.
Men **miss five days of work** per year due to illness.	Women **miss six days of work** per year due to illness.
Eating a **high-carbohydrate meal** makes men feel calm.	Eating a **high-carbohydrate meal** makes women feel sleepy.
An average man's "true **pelvis**" (the male version of the birth canal) is 13 centimeters wide.	An average woman's true **pelvis** is 13.4 centimeters wide—wider than an average man's to allow a baby to pass through the birth canal.
Men suffer more fractures, dislocations, wounds and other **injuries** than women do.	Women endure more acute and chronic **illnesses** than men, including colds, headaches, digestive and bone disorders.
Half as many men as women are afflicted by **phobias**.	**Phobias** affect twice as many women as men.
The American man has a 20 percent chance of having a **heart attack** before age 60.	For American women under 60, the risk of **heart attack** is 1 in 17.
	—Trisha Thompson

Sources:

William H. Frey II, Ph.D., St. Paul—Ramsey Medical Center, Minnesota. Pamela Hartzband, M.D., Harvard Medical School. Bruce Latimer, Ph.D., Cleveland Museum of Natural History. C. Owen Lovejoy, Ph.D., Kent State University. Wayne Sinning, Ph.D., Kent State University. Robert Tague, Ph.D., Louisiana State University. Theodore B. VanItallie, M.D., St. Lukes—Roosevelt Hospital, NYC. Anxiety Disorders Association of America. National Center for Health Statistics. American Heart Association. Sex Information and Education Council of the U.S. *Dermatology*, by Donald M.

Pillsbury, M.D., et al. *Human Sexual Response*, by William H. Masters, M.D., and Virginia E. Johnson. *Sex and Morality in the U.S.* by Albert D. Klassen, et al. *The Opposite Sex: The Complete Illustrated Guide to Differences Between the Sexes*, by Anne Campbell, M.D. *Your Vital Statistics: The Ultimate Book About the Average Human Being*, by Gyles Brandreth. *1990 Guinness Book of World Records.* Gallup Poll, "Present Status of Love and Marriage," for *Psychology Today*, January 1990. *Marketing to Women*, February 1990, Vol. 3, No. 5. *Contemporary Nutrition*, Vol. 14, No. 7, 1989.

SENSUALITY SCALE

Test your responses, enhance your desire

It can make us feel wonderful— or guilty, even out of control.

Anthony Pietropinto, M.D., and Jacqueline Simenauer

Anthony Pietropinto, M.D., a New York City psychiatrist, and Jacqueline Simenauer, a medical writer, have also written Beyond the Male Myth *and* Husbands and Wives.

It can lead to some of life's most exhilarating moments, but it can also disrupt our concentration on important matters or influence us to do things that go against our better judgment.

The greatest paradox in sexual desire is that it seems to arise effortlessly when we first meet someone yet *decreases* in intensity the longer we stay with that person. Experts declare that while desire can atrophy with time, love increases. Desire draws us together, but it's love that cements the relationship, giving it permanency. Of course, this is scant consolation if loss of sexual pleasure is part of the trade.

Yet some partners *do* continue to feel a high level of sexual desire for each other, even after years together. Invariably these couples have a genuine liking for, and attachment to, each other. They've developed true intimacy, and it is this deep connectedness that increases desire.

People often confuse familiarity with intimacy. An astronomer who peers nightly at the heavens is familiar with them, but only the astronaut, floating in space, is intimate with the heavens. People say they are bored because there are no surprises—because they know everything there is to know about their partners. When you talk to them a while, it turns out they haven't had a meaningful conversation with that partner in years.

One woman in therapy, who had been married for ten years, was strongly attracted to a male coworker. She didn't succumb to the temptation of an extramarital affair, but she agonized over the much greater emotional compatibility she found with the other man. Even his favorite movie was hers. Then the therapist asked what her *husband's* favorite movie was. She didn't know.

You may come as close as you can to possessing another in the physical act of love, but the true union is *outside* the act. Physical proximity alone is not enough.

Desire, fortunately, resides in the mind. An ailing stomach or heart cannot analyze its condition and can repair itself only in certain ways, but a mind with a problem can find its way to a solution. To understand or strengthen your sexual desire, you must remember that desire is a *mental* phenomenon.

The first step to increased desire is the desire to desire.

The second step is the willingness to explore and nurture your own sensuality.

Sensuality is not the same thing as *sexuality*. Any type of pleasurable sensual stimulus can contribute to desire, even if the stimulus itself isn't specifically sexual. Its sexual implications ultimately lie in the eye, ear, nose, tongue or touch of the beholder.

The sensory experiences that can make you desire someone are
● Sensual
● Erotic
● Romantic

Sensual experiences give pleasure to the body but don't necessarily involve a partner.

Erotic experiences occur in specifically sexual situations.

Romantic experiences arise in a loving and caring, but not frankly sexual, situation.

Some people are equally responsive to sensual, erotic and romantic stimuli. Others may respond more strongly to one type of stimulus than to others. The following Sensuality Scale was developed to help you better understand your—and your partner's—responses to sensual, erotic and romantic cues. Knowing which experiences you respond to most can help you to develop and sustain desire and the pleasure of intimacy.

You can take the test alone or with your partner. Rate each of the activities described from 0 to 3, depending on whether you would find the experience unenjoyable or unpleasant (0), mildly enjoyable (1), moderately enjoyable (2) or very enjoyable (3).

● Sensual

1. Dancing by yourself.
2. Engaging in a short period of vigorous exercise.
3. Taking a long, warm and fragrant bath.
4. Listening to music.
5. Putting on perfume/cologne, even if you're going to be alone all day.
6. Walking in a summer drizzle.
7. Hugging a friend.
8. Watching the waves and listening to the sound of the ocean.
9. Picking out an object that's your favorite color.
10. Riding in the country to see the fall foliage.

● Erotic

1. Wearing silk lingerie/nightclothes to bed.
2. Putting soft music on in the bedroom.
3. Reading erotic material with your partner.
4. Watching an erotic videocassette with your partner.
5. Having your partner give you a massage.
6. Dancing closely and slowly with your partner.
7. Taking a bath or a shower with your partner.
8. Smelling your partner's perfume/cologne.
9. Talking with your partner late into the night.
10. Cuddling with your partner.

● Romantic

1. Receiving flowers from someone you care about.
2. Writing a poem or letter to someone you love.
3. Having someone you love compliment you.
4. Sharing a problem with someone you love.
5. Talking to someone you love on the telephone during your lunch hour.
6. Picking out a gift for someone you love.
7. Calling someone you love by a pet name used only by you.
8. Sharing a task with someone you love.
9. Dressing up specially for someone you care about.
10. Having someone you love say, "I love you."

SCORING:

For each of the three areas, the maximum possible score is 30. Consider a score of more than 15 as "high," 15 or under "low." You should now have either a high or low rating for the sensual (S), erotic (E) and romantic (R) areas.

ANALYSIS:

High S, High E, High R. You enjoy sex and give it top priority in your life. If you run into desire problems, it's probably because you have high expectations and feel disappointed when even one element in your sexual relationship seems lacking. The best remedy for boosting or restoring desire is for you to figure out exactly what is missing from your love life and help your partner to supply it. Perhaps you yearn for more private time together out of bed; say so. The second-best remedy is to realize that you can't always have everything all the time and to appreciate your sex life for the many delights it *can* supply.

High S, High E, Low R. You enjoy physical pleasures and a creative sex life but have difficulty showing affection through nonphysical means. If you have desire problems, chances are your partner is pressuring you to show affection outside the bedroom. "You don't bring me flowers" is probably a prevailing refrain, with a chorus

of "All you want from me is sex!" You may never fill the house with scented candles, but you might want to hide the occasional love note in his coat pocket.

High S, Low E, High R. You generally make your partner feel loved, and you're capable of physical pleasure, but you may be somewhat uptight or perfunctory in bed. If there's a desire problem, listen for the echo of some puritanical prohibition from your childhood or adolescence. You might not even be conscious of some old guilt that is interfering. To enhance desire, carry some of that romance in your nature into the bedroom, emphasizing that love and sex make compatible bedfellows.

High S, Low E, Low R. You enjoy physical pleasures but sometimes have difficulty sharing them. Low desire may stem from anxiety about being intimate. When alone, you enjoy the sensual pleasures the world around you offers, but the presence of a partner seems to interfere with your receptive powers. Include your partner in some of those physical delights you experience *outside* the bedroom. Get used to the idea that shared pleasure doesn't mean *less* pleasure for you.

Low S, High E, High R. You usually have a high sex drive, placing emphasis on both the sensual and personal aspects of the relationship rather than on the simple bodily pleasures sex can afford. This is fine until some conflict develops in your relationship. Then "drive" alone can't be counted on to keep the sexual activity on schedule, and desire problems may arise. You may be overly concerned with your partner's satisfaction. Focusing on your own sensations and preferences during sex would probably enhance the experience for *both* of you.

Low S, High E, Low R. You're probably a "no-frills" lovemaker, interested in getting down to sex without wasting much time on preliminaries. But equating sexual pleasure exclusively with intercourse is like putting all your eggs in one basket; and who wants their sex life to be a basket case?

Low S, Low E, High R. If your partner criticizes you for lacking passion, you might vehemently retort that *you're* brimming with hot-blooded romantic feelings, only a certain critical party is inept at flame-fanning. Connecting romantic to erotic energy is not easy. The most likely route to sexual enjoyment is to first awaken your body's ability to enjoy simple sensual pleasures, preferably in a romantic atmosphere.

Low S, Low E, Low R. "It's all in your mind" might well apply to your entire sexuality. You may be out of touch with touch—and the other four senses as well. You probably feel sex is something you *should* do, from a rational, intellectual viewpoint. You may be doing it to please your partner, because it reassures you that you're normal or because you want to cement a relationship. You rarely do it simply because it feels good. If your desire is based on believing you *should* have sex, a lack of desire will probably stem from an equally strong counterconviction that you *shouldn't*. A turnoff of desire will probably relate to anger or dissatisfaction with your partner. Working through the conflict will help, but a trip together to some place you enjoy—an art gallery, concert hall or botanical garden—might lay the groundwork for relating cerebral aesthetic pleasure to the tangible physical world. Letting your partner stimulate you while you relax may reduce some of your concern about performing well and allow you to focus your attention on enjoyable sensory experiences.

YOUR DESIRE POTENTIAL

Your sexual history, personality type, attitudes and sensuality all contribute—positively or negatively—to your desire level. Good past experiences, lack of inhibitions, a taste for variety and flexibility tend to add up to a high desire level—the wish for frequent sex, making sex a high priority and more intense enjoyment of sexual experience. Of course, people with a low desire level can also be very happy with their sex lives. A good sex life depends not so much on fulfilling a strong level of desire but on fulfilling your own particular level of desire.

A loss of sexual desire can affect people with high as well as low desire levels and may be *more* traumatic for those who are accustomed to strong desire. People at any desire level can be adversely affected by personal problems, unhappy situations or conflicted relationships, but there are specifically vulnerable areas for each desire level.

If you usually have a high level of desire, a decrease can often be best overcome by working on nonsexual methods of gratification and communication. Learning to enjoy simple touching, getting accustomed to putting your feelings into words instead of sexual actions and learning more about your partner's sexual needs can add dimensions to your sexuality that transcend the purely physical aspects.

If you have a medium desire potential, you might heighten desire by improving the interpersonal aspects of your relationship. Learning how to cope when your partner declines sex, as well as mastering fair-fight techniques, can swing your equilibrium back to a higher level of desire.

If you have a low potential, you will probably want to concentrate on ways to increase your fantasies and sensual experiences and to share your new interests with your partner.

Self-evaluation is crucial to understanding and improving sexual desire. Before you can fix something, you have to understand how it works, whether you're a doctor healing a body, a mechanic repairing a car or a psychiatrist treating a troubled psyche. Once you understand where you are and how you arrived there, it's far easier to find the road that will take you where you want to be.

SEXUAL SECRETS

MEN ARE AFRAID TO SHARE

When he's tense and upset, he wants sex—not love. In bed he doesn't say the sweet things you'd like him to say. Or he rolls away when sex is over—just when you want cuddles and kisses. Why? He's afraid to tell you—but our expert will.

Barbara De Angelis, Ph.D.

Barbara De Angelis, Ph.D., is a best-selling author, lecturer and counseling therapist. She is executive director of the Los Angeles Personal Growth Center.

For the past 15 years I have worked as a therapist, counseling thousands of men and women and learning, in the process, what it is that makes relationships succeed—and what makes them fail. I've also gained invaluable insights into what makes men behave as they do, particularly when it comes to lovemaking. Now I want to share with you the secrets I've learned—and I'm not exaggerating when I say that these revelations have changed my life and can change yours, too.

❶ Men often express themselves sexually when they can't express themselves emotionally.

Has this ever happened to you? Your husband approaches you and wants to make love, but he isn't acting very loving. In fact, he seems tense and preoccupied. You try to engage him in conversation, but he's obviously not interested in anything but sex.

What's going on in a case like this is that your husband is looking for relief from the intensity of some emotion he's feeling. Most men are brought up to believe that it's not okay to verbally express vulnerability

in the form of fear, helplessness, disappointment or regret. Consequently, men often convert this emotional energy into sexual energy which is a "safer" outlet for them.

What complicates matters more is that most women function in precisely the opposite way, finding it difficult to feel sexual when they are not emotionally at ease. That's why it's so important for women to understand that, for men, sex is almost a language they use to communicate their repressed emotions. Not surprisingly, this fact can cause problems in your relationship in at least two ways:
● Your husband experiences physical release during the sexual act, but doesn't resolve his emotional tension.
● You feel offended when you sense that he's using your body as a dumping ground for his frustrations.

A couple I'll call Gary and Fran were a perfect example of this pattern. They came to me complaining about sexual incompatibility. "Sometimes I think Gary is upset about something," Fran confessed, "but he won't talk. He just starts being sexually aggressive, and yet I don't even think he's enjoying himself. All I know is that this doesn't satisfy either one of us."

Gary, who is the president of a construction firm, acknowledged that his wife was right, that he did sometimes have what I called "release sex" with Fran. I asked

him to think back to the last time it had happened and tell me about any events that had disturbed him that day.

"Well," he began, "last Thursday I had a run-in with my operations manager. He's been sloppy with his reports lately, and I was dreading having to reprimand him again. Sure enough, there was a scene. Then that afternoon, I found out we'd been outbid by another firm for a job. That was a real disappointment. I had worked two months to get that contract. All in all, it was a pretty terrible day."

"Okay," I responded. "Now I'd like you to picture yourself in the bedroom with Fran, beginning to come on to her sexually. How were you feeling just then?"

Gary thought for a moment and then answered: "Tired, angry, discouraged. I guess I was feeling kind of like a failure because I didn't get that contract."

"Were you feeling romantic or turned on?" I asked.

"Now that you mention it, I guess not," Gary admitted.

"Well, if it wasn't sex that you wanted, what was it you *did* need?" I pressed.

"I guess I just wanted to feel close to Fran, to feel as though she still loved me, that she wasn't let down, that at least somebody was on my side."

"What if Fran had just lain down beside you and stroked you and told you how much she loved you? What if she had listened to you describe those same feelings you just told me about? How would that have felt?"

"Great," Gary said with a shy smile. "Probably a lot better than how we both ended up feeling after sex."

Clearly, like so many men, Gary had been reaching out to his wife for reassurance and comfort, and being sexual was the only way he knew how. For Fran, this insight came as a great relief. She went over and gave Gary a big hug and said, "Honey, I knew something was bothering you that night, but I thought maybe it had something to do with *me*!"

If you think you and your husband fall into this pattern, here are my suggestions:

Acknowledge the problem. Try to talk your husband through the same conversation I had with Gary. The time to do this is *not* when your husband is preoccupied with the problem; he'll only insist he doesn't want to talk or that nothing is wrong. Wait for a time when he appears relaxed and say something like, "Our sex life is wonderful, but I think I've found a way to make it even better." What you don't want to do is say, "You're making problems for us in bed and you'd better fix it."

Second, whenever you sense that your partner's sexual advances are covering up suppressed emotions, make it safe for him to share his feelings with you. Be gentle. Don't say "Listen, I know you're upset about something, and until you tell me what it is, we're not having sex." Do say, "Honey, I'd love it if you'd lie here with me and hold me for a little while. I want us to feel close." Then see if you can get him started by suggesting what you think might be on his mind. ("Boy, it's sure been a hectic week for you at the office, hasn't it?" . . . "I know you must be upset about your Mom's operation.")

With practice, you can learn to make it safe for him to fully experience and then clearly express his own emotions by showing him that you understand how he feels, and that you don't think he's a failure for being vulnerable. And the payoff is that when you make it possible for him to release his tension verbally, you'll be much more intimate, and the sex that follows will be truly passionate.

❷ **For men, sexual rejection is total rejection.**

Sex is a very primal form of giving for men—a way to offer themselves emotionally and physically. When your husband makes a sexual overture to you, he is doing more than asking for sex. He is saying, "Please accept me." He may be unaware of this subconscious motivation, but if you turn him down, he won't hear "I'm tired" or "Not now." He'll hear, "I don't love you. I don't want you. You're not desirable." If you turn him down often enough, he may simply stop making advances or,

worse, seek sex—and personal acceptance—elsewhere. Yet the solutions to this problem are fairly simple.

Don't totally reject your husband's sexual advances. This does *not* mean that you should always say yes, but simply that you need to understand his vulnerability.

You might say something such as, "I love you, but I'm so tense from work that I wouldn't be able to make love to you the way I want to right now. Could we just cuddle for a while, and see how I feel a little later?" In other words, if you aren't in the mood, say no to sex, but say yes to loving him. He'll feel better, and who knows? After sharing some affection, you might find you're in the mood after all!

Be the sexual aggressor now and then. Men love it when a woman isn't afraid to show that she loves sex. Besides, when a man always has to be the initiator, he's always the one who has to risk rejection. He'll love you for being willing to put yourself on the line the same way. And you'll learn why it's so important for him to have his overtures sensitively received.

❸ **When a man has an erection, it doesn't *always* mean he's turned on.**

A great many otherwise sophisticated women don't realize that when a man has an erection, he isn't necessarily turned on or ready for sex. This is what I call the "erection illusion."

An erection is caused by a flow of blood to the penis. The stimulus *might* be sexual arousal, but it could also be the physiological transition from sleep to a waking state in the morning, a full bladder, friction from tight clothing, or stress.

Automatically assuming that your husband's erection means he is sexually turned on can cause problems in your relationship. For instance, you may feel pressured to satisfy him, even though he may not be in the mood for sex. When in doubt, simply ask your husband whether he's turned on. For example, if he rolls over and hugs you in the morning, ask him if he's in the mood for making love or if he wants to lie in bed and cuddle. He'll be relieved to have a choice, and so will you.

❹ **Your man will make love with you more often if you have sex with him more often.**

There is a difference between having sex and making love. Making love is an emotional act, a way of expressing your affection and commitment. Having sex is a physical act of sharing pleasure. In my interviews with hundreds of men and women, the results were clear: women prefer lovemaking—that is, slow foreplay, long kisses, cuddling—while men prefer spontaneity, physical passion and playful, lusty sex. These differences in sexual tastes have their roots in the basic differences between men and women: men are more fo-

cused on achieving a goal, while women are more focused on creating an emotional connection. This is why it's easier for men to have sex than to make love. But the truth is, if you give your husband permission to have sex with you sometimes, he will be a better lover over the long run. Also, if your husband seems to be rushing foreplay, ask him if he's in the mood for just sex. If he is, and if you feel up to it, give it a try. But if you feel the time is not right, explain your feelings to him. You'll spare yourself unproductive resentment later, and he will at least understand why you're not responding to his overtures. Believe me, most men won't take advantage of having quick, passionate sex, but knowing that it's sometimes okay will make your husband even more seductive on other occasions.

❺ **Oral sex is more than just a sexual pleasure—it's complete acceptance.**

For men, receiving oral sex is a favorite sexual activity. What's so secret about this, you say? The secret lies not in knowing that men love it, but in understanding why it gives them so much pleasure.

For some women, performing oral sex creates anxiety and discomfort. But wives may find that they'll overcome their discomfort by considering this: Not only is a man's penis the most sensitive and vulnerable part of his body, it is also the outward sign of his maleness and identity. As a result, having oral sex performed on him makes a man feel totally received and accepted.

No woman should *ever* do something she finds sexually objectionable. But in understanding what oral sex means to a man, perhaps you'll be able to view it differently. There may be times when you feel comfortable loving your husband this way, and times when you don't. Either way, the two of you should discuss how you both feel about giving and receiving oral sex. Such a conversation is an important step in creating more sexual intimacy between you.

❻ **Men often don't like to talk while they're having sex.**

Have you ever tried to get a man to talk to you while he's writing out bills or reading the sports page? Chances are he'll bark: "Stop talking to me! I can't concentrate on what I'm doing!" On the other hand, most women have no trouble doing more than one thing at a time—talking on the phone while watching a TV news report, or following a recipe while arbitrating the kids' fight. In fact, research has shown that men tend to use one hemisphere of the brain at a time—either the left side, which controls verbal functioning, or the right, which controls visual and spatial functions. In women, both sides of the brain work concurrently. This explains why talking during lovemaking comes naturally to you and not to him. You're lying there saying, "Oh, darling, that feels wonderful. I love being this close to you," and all you get in response is a few grunts and groans. You may feel rejected or used, but the truth is, he may be so involved with his right-brain activity that the actual words you say don't even register. What to do?

Discuss this observation with your husband. Ask him how he feels about talking in bed. He'll likely say that when you talk or ask him questions, he feels pressured to respond but, since conversation interrupts the passionate experience for him, he'd really rather stay quiet. That doesn't, of course, mean that you shouldn't talk as much as you want, but don't be disappointed if you don't get a response.

7. After sex, men want time alone to regain control of themselves.

Countless women have complained to me that their husbands seem to withdraw after lovemaking, lying there with a blank expression, or vaulting out of bed to raid the refrigerator. There's a reason for this behavior—and it *isn't* that they don't love you. Men retreat after sex in an attempt to regain the control they lost during orgasm. Remember, a powerful self-image is so important to most men that the idea of dropping their defenses so totally is threatening. Complete surrender of the sexual kind leaves them open, they fear, to exposing a whole host of vulnerabilities. Therefore, from a psychological point of view, experiencing an orgasm is as frightening as it is blissful for men.

One of my clients, a highly successful dentist I'll call Jim, put this very well. "Most of the time, I'm the guy in charge. I rarely let my guard down. Sex is one of the only times when I really find myself letting go. But afterwards, I almost always

feel embarrassed, as if I had been caught being too needy, too emotional. I feel like I have to pull myself together, and get back to being a man."

If you suspect your husband feels this way, describe this phenomenon to him and ask him if it rings true for him. Many men have told me that they noticed their tendency to pull away after sex, and feared that it meant they didn't love their wives enough. Chances are, your husband will feel relieved after this explanation.

Next, agree on some form of afterplay that will satisfy both of you. Some couples find that a man needs at least a few minutes to "recover," and then he'll be happy to cuddle, nuzzle and talk, if that's what you're in the mood for.

8. Men are easily turned on by visual stimulation.

Men are more visually oriented and women more verbally oriented. That's why boys look at erotic magazines for sexual stimulation, while girls read romance novels. This translates into the fact that your husband's primary source of sexual arousal is your appearance. You may not like hearing that, but it's true. And it explains why men fixate on a woman's body or what she's wearing. It also explains why even happily married, sexually satisfied men can't seem to help but look at other women. I don't mean a man who leers, just one who admires. But that can make a wife feel that her husband doesn't love her. He, on the other hand, views his wife's objection as a sign that she's being unreasonably possessive.

This is a touchy subject, but the more I work with men, the more I understand their point of view. Men can feel physically attracted to a woman without feeling the slightest emotional stirring. It's natural, after all, for them to notice and admire

beautiful faces and bodies. However, I am *not* saying that it's okay for your husband to flirt or come on to other women. This is disrespectful and potentially destructive to your relationship.

If you want to turn your husband on in new and different ways, consider leaving your sweatsuit in the drawer, and try experimenting with some sexy lingerie every once in while. Also, if you are in the habit of making love with the lights out, try keeping them on, or placing lit candles around the room. Remember that your husband is turned on by what he *sees*. Being able to let his eyes roam all over your body may be the single most passionate gesture you can make. For both your sake, let there be light!

Finally, talk with your husband about how he feels when he looks at other women. Unless your marriage is in serious trouble, your husband probably looks without having any intention or desire to do anything more. Get this out in the open. And if you really want to be bold, admire other women with him. If you say, "She has great legs, doesn't she?" he may be shocked at first and a little embarrassed at being "caught," but he will end up feeling closer to you and appreciate your "permission" to look. The basic agreement should be that he can look at other women with admiration—as long as he looks at you that way, too. He should be thinking, "There's a beautiful woman. Aren't women lovely? And gee, right next to me I have a lovely woman who is all mine. What a lucky guy I am!"

I am convinced that knowing these eight secrets about men and sex will help you and your husband create a much richer and more satisfying love life—and that, in turn, is sure to make your marriage as a whole more fulfilling. Now that the secrets are out, what are you waiting for? Enjoy!

Mind Sex

Do human brains have gender?

New research findings suggest male minds and female minds are becoming more alike

Madeline Chinnici

Madeline Chinnici, a science writer, is a frequent contributor to SELF.

It's a deceptively simple question: Are the minds of men and women different? Experience may suggest at times that men are analytical, rational, competitive and sexually aggressive; that women, by contrast, are intuitive, emotional, instinctual, people-oriented and caring. But do the minds of men and women differ "naturally" or just reflect a sex-stereotyped society? And do men and women really behave differently, or do we only *think* they do?

Nature or nurture?

For decades, scientists have been trying to answer these questions by teasing apart nature from nurture. "The very first question you ask about a new baby is 'Is it a boy or a girl?'" says Joey Sprague, Ph.D., assistant professor of sociology at the University of Kansas, in Lawrence. "The answer suggests how you will respond to that person forever."

Admittedly, there are some "sex" differences—those rooted in biology—that shape the masculine and feminine psyches. But social norms and cultural expectations may account for more of the perceived differences than does biology. Men's aggressiveness, long credited to their higher testosterone levels, may be tied to upbringing—boys learn it's okay to act that way and girls that it's not. In certain contexts, women might actually be *more* aggressive than men. "If a woman is being battered by her husband, she won't hit back because she's been taught not to," says Estelle Ramey, M.D., professor emeritus of physiology at Georgetown University, in Washington, D.C. "She has learned that men have bigger muscles and more physical power." But put her in a situation where female aggressiveness is sanctioned by society—say, protecting her child—"and you'll see a kind of female behavior that would make Attila the Hun blush."

Says Cynthia Fuchs Epstein, Ph. D., author of *Deceptive Distinctions* and professor of sociology at the City University of New York, "Most differences are those we create—differences of opportunity, status and division of labor—that wouldn't necessarily be there naturally."

The female personality: is it fact or myth?

Over the years, many attempts have been made to link male-female behavior to the fact that while men and women have the same sex hormones, they have them in different amounts. Males have more androgens, such as testosterone, and females more estrogens. A long-held theory is that an abundance of androgens accounts for such male traits as competitiveness, their relative absence in females for qualities such as passivity. Although studies have been done on everything from rats injected with hormones to humans with hormonal abnormalities, no consistent picture has emerged. Recent studies show that daily fluctuations in hormones may have more effect on behavior than absolute levels. And although a particular sex hormone might stimulate one type of behavior in males, it can have no effect—or even the opposite one—in females.

What biology can't explain, psychoanalytic theory has tried to. Women, it's suggested, exhibit more people-oriented behavior because girls develop their sense of femininity by identifying with their mothers. Boys establish that they're "not like mommy" to become masculine. In effect, males learn early on to distance themselves from relationships. "By the time children are one and a half years old," says psychiatrist Carol Nadelson, M.D., of Tufts University School of Medicine, "they've already established their gender identity." Sociologists also reason that women have had to develop special skills—such as intuition—to survive as underdogs in a male-dominated society and that they've been groomed all their lives for jobs, such as mothering, that demand nurturance.

The heart of the debate, however, is not so much what causes a female personality, but to what extent it exists. In 1974, psychologists Eleanor Maccoby, Ph.D., of Stanford University, and Carol Nagy Jacklin, Ph.D., of the University of Southern California, reviewed more than a thousand studies of differences between men and women. Their conclusion? There is no hard evidence for differences in any type of social behavior except aggression. Their work was considered by many to be the final word.

But the notion of feminine traits was revived during the 1980s by Carol Gilligan, Ph.D., a professor of education at Harvard University. In her book, *In a Different Voice*, Dr. Gilligan popularized the idea that men and women have different forms of moral reasoning. In three studies in which she interviewed close to two hundred people, ages six to sixty, she found that women tend to operate primarily from an "ethic of care." For them, every dilemma must be solved by taking into account both the circumstances and people involved; there is no single right or wrong. Men, however, tend to reason from an "ethic of justice," applying universal rules to all situations.

Gilligan's work has been criticized by researchers who charge that her studies were too small and not scientific enough, but Gilligan claims the reason her findings are controversial is that until now the accepted dogma has been that there is only one way to think about moral problems—the male way.

The sexier sex?
Conventional wisdom has it that in matters of love and sex, men and women really don't have much in common. Men are assumed to be motivated by the physical, women by the emotional. The reason men and women ever get together, it's thought, is that men "play" at love to get sex; and women "play" at sex to get

love. But the numerous studies supporting that stereotype were done largely on teenagers. In 1989, when Dr. Sprague and biologist David Quadagno, Ph.D., studied adults ages twenty-two to fifty-seven, they found younger people did fit the stereotype; but, as people got older, the roles *reversed*, with men identifying an emotional motive, women a physical one. What's more, men and women voiced a *common* ideal benefit of sex—getting emotionally close to another person.

Sprague suggests that young people may act out the stereotypes because they get their ideas from popular culture—such as TV—which promotes the images of the macho man and the emotional woman. But as people age, they find they can't fit that mold and begin to look for the part of themselves that's been missing.

Who has the better brain?
Nowhere has the nature-versus-nurture debate been argued more strongly than in the arena of intellectual abilities.

For years, women have scored higher on tests that measure certain kinds of verbal skills; men have taken the lead in math and spatial acuity, such as the ability to rotate an imaginary 3-D object in the mind. The controversial results have been read by some as proof of men's superior rational and analytic abilities and women's greater communication skills.

"Unfortunately, any differences that have been found have also been assigned a value," says Dr. Ramey. "If a man and a woman differ in their approach to a problem, then her approach is not seen as valuable." In short, some people read the results to mean that men are the smarter sex.

Other researchers have tried to explain the test results by looking for differences in brain anatomy. Neuroscientist Melissa Hines, Ph.D., of the University of California, Los Angeles, has already found that in women, the bigger the splenium is, the better the verbal-fluency skills are. Still controversial is whether there's a difference in the size of the splenium in men and women. In ad-

dition, there's evidence—also hotly debated—that a bundle of nerve fibers called the corpus callosum, that allows the brain's right (or artistic) and left (analytical) hemispheres to communicate is larger in women, and that the female brain is symmetrical while in the male, the right side is depended on more than the left.

But Ramey says this is not the point. "There *are* brain differences, but they represent the averages of all males and all females," she explains. Therefore, you can't say that because the spatial-perception area of the right brain is used more in men, then a particular man will make a better air-traffic controller than a particular female. "The only useful answer to the question, 'Who is smarter, a man or a woman?'" says Ramey, "is, 'Which man and *which* woman?'"

Finding a link between differences in brain anatomy and mental abilities doesn't automatically distinguish cause and effect. It's a two-way street, says Dr. Hines; brain structure can change throughout life. Learning can affect brain anatomy, just as brain anatomy can affect learning.

The shrinking gender gap
Lately, the smarter-sex debate has taken an unexpected turn. There's now evidence that in the past two decades the "gender gap" in cognitive skills—those related to thinking and perception—has all but closed.

Many earlier studies purporting to show differences used tests that were themselves sex-biased, for instance. When researchers analyzed hundreds of studies of math, verbal and spatial skills, they discovered that male and female scores have come close together in almost every instance. (Only in late teen years do males still outscore females in problem-solving and one aspect of spatial ability.)

Why has the picture changed? Psychologist Janet Hyde, Ph.D., director of the Women's Studies Research Center at the University of Wisconsin, in Madison, says she's not sure but thinks one reason is that the women's movement sensitized parents and teachers to giving more equal opportunity to boys and girls. But whatever the cause, the new findings don't bode well for biological theories. "Those theories," says Dr. Hyde, "presuppose a difference that's not there anymore."

If allowed, would the mind of a woman become indistinguishable from the mind of a man? No, say researchers. It's not that in a perfect society there would be no differences—it's just that they don't need to be drawn along the lines of the sexes. A man should be able to express emotion or be awful at math without his masculinity being threatened. And a woman should be allowed to be assertive or scientific or emotional if that's her nature. In short, people should be permitted to become whoever they are, regardless of what their sex is.

— A —

abnormal: anything considered not normal, i.e., not conforming to the subjective standards a social group has established as the norm

abortifacients: substances that cause termination of pregnancy

acquaintance (date) rape: when a sexual encounter is forced by someone who is known to the victim

acquired immunodeficiency syndrome: fatal disease caused by a virus that is transmitted through the exchange of bodily fluids primarily in sexual activity, and intravenous drug use

activating effect: the direct influence some hormones can have on activating or deactivating sexual behavior

actual use failure rate: a measure of how often a birth control method can be expected to fail when human error and technical failure are considered

adolescence: period of emotional, social, and physical transition from childhood to adulthood

adultery toleration: marriage partners extend the freedom to each other to have sex with others

affectional: relating to feelings or emotions, such as romantic attachments

afterbirth: the tissues expelled after childbirth including the placenta, the remains of the umbilical cord and fetal membranes

agenesis (absence) of the penis (ae-JEN-a-ses): a congenital condition in which the penis is undersized and nonfunctional

AIDS: acquired immunodeficiency syndrome

ambisexual: alternate term for bisexual

amniocentesis: a process whereby medical problems with a fetus can be determined while it is still in the womb; a needle is inserted into the amniotic sac, amniotic fluid is withdrawn, and its cells examined

amnion (AM-nee-on): a thin membrane that forms a closed sac to enclose the embryo; the sac is filled with amniotic fluid that protects and cushions the embryo

anal intercourse: insertion of the penis into the rectum of a partner

androgen: a male hormone, such as testosterone, that affects physical development, sexual desire, and behavior. It is produced by both male and female sex glands and influences each sex in varying degrees

androgyny (an-DROJ-a-nee): combination of traditional feminine and masculine traits in a single individual

anejaculation: lack of ejaculation at the time of orgasm

anorchism (a-NOR-kiz-um): rare birth defect in which both testes are lacking

aphrodisiacs (af-ro-DEE-zee-aks): foods or chemicals purported to foster sexual arousal; they are believed to be more myth than fact

apotemnophilia: a rare condition characterized by the desire to function sexually after having a leg amputated

areola (a-REE-a-la): darkened, circular area of skin surrounding the nipple

artificial embryonation: a process in which the developing embryo is flushed from the uterus of the donor woman 5 days after fertilization and placed in another woman's uterus

artificial insemination: injecting the sperm cells of a male into a woman's vagina, with the intention of conceiving a child

asceticism (a-SET-a-siz-um): usually characterized by celibacy, this philosophy emphasizes spiritual purity through self-denial and self-discipline

asexuality: characterized by a low interest in sex

autoerotic asphyxiation: accidental death from pressure placed around the neck during masturbatory behavior

autofellatio (fe-LAY-she-o): a male providing oral stimulation to his own penis, an act most males do not have the physical agility to perform

— B —

Bartholin's glands (BAR-tha-lenz): small glands located in the opening through the minor lips that produce some secretion during sexual arousal

behavior therapy: used of techniques to learn new patterns of behavior, often employed in sex therapy

berdache (bare-DAHSH): anthropological term for cross-dressing in other cultures

bestiality (beest-ee-AL-i-tee): a human being having sexual contact with an animal

birth canal: term applied to the vagina during the birth process

birthing rooms: special areas in the hospital, decorated and furnished in a nonhospital way, set aside for giving birth; the woman remains here to give birth rather than being taken to a separate delivery room

bisexual: refers to some degree of sexual attraction to or activities with members of both sexes

blastocyst: the morula, after five days of cell division—has developed a fluid-filled cavity in its interior and entered the uterine cavity

bond: the emotional link between parent and child created by cuddling, cooing, physical and eye contact early in the newborn's life

bondage: tying, restraining, or applying pressure to body parts for sexual arousal

brachioproctic activity (brake-ee-o-PRAHK-tik): known in slang as "fisting"; a hand is inserted into the rectum of a partner

brothels: houses of prostitution

bulbourethral glands: also called Cowper's glands

— C —

call boys: highly paid male prostitutes

call girls: more highly paid prostitutes who work by appointment with a more exclusive clientele

cantharides (kan-THAR-a-deez): a chemical extracted from a beetle that, when taken internally, creates irritation of blood vessels in the genital region; it can cause physical harm

case studies: an in-depth look at a particular individual and how he or she might have been helped to solve a sexual or other problem. They may offer new and useful ideas for counselors to use with other patients

catharsis theory: suggests that viewing pornography provides a release for sexual tension, thus preventing antisocial behavior

celibacy (SELL-a-ba-see): choosing not to share sexual activity with others

cervical cap: a device that is shaped like a large thimble and fits over the cervix; not a particularly effective contraceptive because it can dislodge easily during intercourse

cervical intraepithelial neoplasia (CIN) (ep-a-THEE-lee-al nee-a-PLAY-zhee-a): abnormal, precancerous cells sometimes identified in a Pap smear

cervix (SERV-ix): lower "neck" of the uterus that extends into the back part of the vagina

cesarian section: a surgical method of childbirth in which delivery occurs through an incision in the abdominal wall and uterus

chancroid (SHAN-kroyd): a venereal disease caused by the bacterium *Hemophilus ducreyi*: and characterized by sores on the genitals which, if left untreated, could result in pain and rupture of the sores

child molesting: sexual abuse of a child by an adult

chlamydia (kluh-MID-ee-uh): now known to be a common STD, this organism is a major cause of urethritis in males; in females it often presents no symptoms

chorion (KOR-ee-on): the outermost extra-embryonic membrane essential in the formation of the placenta

chorionic villi sampling (CVS): a technique for diagnosing medical problems in the fetus as early as the 8th week of pregnancy; a sample of the chorionic membrane is removed through the cervix and studied

cilia: microscopic hair-like projections that help move the ovum through the fallopian tube

circumcision: in the male, surgical removal of the foreskin from the penis; in the female, surgical procedure that cuts the prepuce, exposing the clitoral shaft

climacteric: mid-life period experienced by both men and women when there is greater emotional stress than usual and sometimes physical symptoms

climax: another term for orgasm

clinical research: the study of the cause, treatment or prevention of a disease or condition by testing large numbers of people

clitoridectomy: surgical removal of the clitoris; practiced routinely in some cultures

clitoris (KLIT-a-rus): sexually sensitive organ found in the female vulva; it becomes engorged with blood during arousal

clone: the genetic duplicate organism produced by the cloning process

cloning: a process involving the transfer of a full complement of chromosomes from a body cell of an organism into an ovum from which the chromosomal material has been removed; if allowed to develop into a new organism, it is an exact genetic duplicate of the one from which the original body cell was taken; the process is not yet used for humans, but has been performed in lower animal species

cohabitation: living together and sharing sex without marrying

coitus (KO-at-us *or* ko-EET-us): heterosexual, penis-in-vagina intercourse

coitus interruptus (ko-EET-us *or* KO-ut-us): a method of birth control in which the penis is withdrawn from the vagina prior to ejaculation

comarital sex: also called mate-swapping, a couple swaps sexual partners with another couple

combining of chromosomes: occurs when a sperm unites with an egg, normally joining 23 pairs of chromosomes to establish the genetic "blueprint" for a new individual. The sex chromosomes establish its sex: XX for female and XY for male

coming out: to acknowledge to oneself and to others that one is sexually attracted to others of the same sex

Comstock Laws: enacted in the 1870s, this federal legislation prohibited mailing information about contraception

condom: a sheath worn over the penis during intercourse to collect semen and prevent disease transmission

consensual adultery: permission given to at least one partner within the marital relationship to participate in extramarital sexual activity

controlled experiment: research in which the investigator examines what is happening to one variable while all other variables are kept constant

conventional adultery; extramarital sex without the knowledge of the spouse

coprophilia: sexual arousal connected with feces

core gender-identity/role: a child's early sense and expression of its maleness, femaleness, or ambivalence, prior to puberty

corona: the ridge around the penile glans

corpus luteum: follicle cell cluster that remains after the ovum is released, secreting hormones that help regulate the menstrual cycle

Cowper's glands: two small glands in the male which secrete alkaline fluid into the urethra during sexual arousal

cross-genderists: transgenderists

cryptorchidism (krip-TOR-ka-diz-um): condition in which the testes have not descended into the scrotum prior to birth

cunnilingus (kun-a-LEAN-gus): oral stimulation of the clitoris, vaginal opening, or other parts of the vulva

cystitis (sis-TITE-us): a nonsexually transmitted infection of the urinary bladder

— D —

decriminalization: reducing the legal sanctions for particular acts while maintaining the possibility of legally regulating behavior through testing, licensing, and reporting of financial gain

deoxyribonucleic acid (DNA) (dee-AK-see-rye-bow-new-KLEE-ik): the chemical in each cell that carries the genetic code

deprivation homosexuality: can occur when members of the opposite sex are unavailable

desire phase: Kaplan's term for the psychological interest in sex that precedes a physiological, sexual arousal

deviation: term applied to behavior or orientations that do not conform to a society's accepted norms; it often has negative connotations

diaphragm (DY-a-fram): a latex rubber cup, filled with spermicide, that is fitted to the cervix by a clinician; the woman must learn to insert it properly for full contraceptive effectiveness

diethylstilbestrol (DES) (dye-eth-a-stil-BES-trole): synthetic estrogen compound given to mothers whose pregnancies are at high risk of miscarrying

dilation and curettage (D & C): a method of induced abortion in the second trimester of pregnancy that involves a scraping of the uterine wall

dilation and evacuation (D & E): a method of induced abortion in the second trimester of pregnancy; it combines suction with a scraping of the inner wall of the uterus

discrimination: the process by which an individual extinguishes a response to one stimulus while preserving it for other stimuli

dysfunction: when the body does not function as expected or desired during sex

dysmenorrhea (dis-men-a-REE-a): painful menstruation

— E —

E. coli: bacteria naturally living in the human colon, often causes urinary tract infection

ectopic pregnancy (ek-TOP-ik): the implantation of a blastocyst somewhere other than in the uterus, usually in the fallopian tube

ejaculation: muscular expulsion of semen from the penis

ejaculatory inevitability: the sensation in the male that ejaculation is imminent

ELISA: the primary test used to determine the presence of AIDS in humans

embryo (EM-bree-o): the term applied to the developing cells, when about a week after fertilization, the blastocyst implants itself in the uterine wall

endometrial hyperplasia (hy-per-PLAY-zhee-a): excessive growth of the inner lining of the uterus (endometrium)

endometriosis (en-doe-mee-tree-O-sus): growth of the endometrium out of the uterus into surrounding organs

endometrium: interior lining of the uterus, innermost of three layers

epidemiology (e-pe-dee-mee-A-la-jee): the branch of medical science that deals with the incidence, distribution, and control of disease in a population

epididymis (ep-a-DID-a-mus): tubular structure on each testis in which sperm cells mature

epididymitis (ep-a-did-a-MITE-us): inflammation of the epididymis of the testis

episiotomy (ee-piz-ee-OTT-a-mee): a surgical incision in the vaginal opening made by the clinician or obstetrician if it appears that the baby will tear the opening in the process of being born

epispadias (ep-a-SPADE-ee-as): birth defect in which the urinary bladder empties through an abdominal opening, and the urethera is malformed

erectile dysfunction: difficulty achieving or maintaining penile erection (impotence)

erection: enlargement and stiffening of the penis as blood engorges the columns of spongy tissue, and internal muscles contract

erogenous zone (a-RAJ-a-nus): any area of the body that is sensitive to sexual arousal

erotica: artistic representations of nudity or sexual activity

estrogen (ES-tro-jen): hormone produced abundantly by the ovaries; it plays an important role in the menstrual cycle

estrogen replacement therapy (ERT): controversial treatment of the physical changes of menopause by administering dosages of the hormone estrogen

ethnocentricity: the tendency of the members of one culture to assume that their values and norms of behavior are the "right" ones in comparison to other cultures

excitement: the arousal phase of Masters and Johnson's 4-phase model of the sexual response cycle

exhibitionism: exposing the genitals to others for sexual pleasure

external values: the belief systems available from one's society and culture

extramarital sex: married person having sexual intercourse with someone other than her or his spouse; adultery

— F —

fallopian tubes: structures that are connected to the uterus and lead the ovum from an ovary to the inner cavity of the uterus

fellatio: oral stimulation of the penis

fetal alcohol syndrome (FAS): a condition in a fetus characterized by abnormal growth, neurological damage, and facial distortion caused by the mother's heavy alcohol consumption

fetal surgery: a surgical procedure performed on the fetus while it is still in the uterus

fetishism (FET-a-shizm): sexual arousal triggered by objects or materials not usually considered to be sexual

fetus: the term given to the embryo after two months of development in the womb

fibrous hymen: unnaturally thick, tough tissue composing the hymen

follicles: capsule of cells in which an ovum matures

follicle-stimulating hormone (FSH): pituitary hormone that stimulates the ovaries or testes

foreplay: sexual activities shared in early stages of sexual arousal, with the term implying that they are leading to a more intense, orgasm-oriented form of activity such as intercourse

foreskin: fold of skin covering the penile glans; also called prepuce

fraternal: a twin formed from two separate ova which were fertilized by two separate sperm

frenulum (FREN-yu-lum): thin, tightly-drawn fold of skin on the underside of the penile glans; it is highly sensitive

frottage (fro-TAZH): gaining sexual gratification from anonymously pressing or rubbing against others, usually in crowded settings

frotteur: one who practices frottage

—G—

gamete intra-fallopian transfer (GIFT): direct placement of ovum and concentrated sperm cells into the woman's fallopian tube, increasing the chances of fertilization

gay: slang term referring to homosexual persons and behaviors

gender dysphoria (dis-FOR-ee-a): term to describe gender-identity/role that does not conform to the norm considered appropriate for one's physical sex

gender transposition: gender dysphoria

gender-identity/role (G-I/R): a person's inner experience and outward expression of maleness, femaleness, or some ambivalent position between the two

general sexual dysfunction: difficulty for a woman in achieving sexual arousal

generalization: application of specific learned responses to other, similar situations or experiences

genetic engineering: the modification of the gene structure of cells to change cellular functioning

genital herpes (HER-peez): viral STD characterized by painful sores on the sex organs

genital warts: small lesions on genital skin caused by papilloma virus, this STD increases later risks of certain malignancies

glans: in the male, the sensitive head of the penis; in the female, sensitive head of the clitoris, visible between the upper folds of the minor lips

gonadotropin releasing hormone (GnRH) (go-nad-a-TRO-pen): hormone from the hypothalamus that stimulates the release of FSH and LH by the pituitary

gonorrhea (gon-uh-REE-uh): bacterial STD causing urethral pain and discharge in males; often no symptoms in females

granuloma inguinale (gran-ya-LOW-ma in-gwa-NAL-ee or -NALE): venereal disease characterized by ulcerations and granulations beginning in the groin and spreading to the buttocks and genitals

group marriage: three or more people in a committed relationship who share sex with one another

G spot: a vaginal area that some researchers feel is particularly sensitive to sexual stimulation

—H—

hard-core pornography: pornography that makes use of highly explicit depictions of sexual activity or shows lengthy scenes of genitals

hedonists: believers that pleasure is the highest good

hemophiliac (hee-mo-FIL-ee-ak): someone with the hereditary sex-linked blood defect hemophilia, affecting males primarily and characterized by difficulty in clotting

heterosexual: attractions or activities between members of opposite sexes

HIV: human immunodeficiency virus

homophobia (ho-mo-PHO-bee-a): strongly held negative attitudes and irrational fears relating to homosexuals

homosexual: term applied to romantic and sexual attractions and activities between members of the same sex

homosexualities: a term that reminds us there is not a single pattern of homosexuality, but a wide range of same-sex orientations

hookers: street name for female prostitutes

hormone implants: contraceptive method in which hormone-releasing plastic containers are surgically inserted under the skin

hot flash: a flushed, sweaty feeling in the skin caused by dilated blood vessels, often associated with menopause

human chorionic gonadotropin (HCG): a hormone detectable in the urine of a pregnant woman

human immunodeficiency virus: the virus that initially attacks the human immune system, eventually causing AIDS

hustlers: male street prostitutes

H-Y antigen: a biochemical produced in an embryo when the Y chromosome is present; it causes fetal gonads to develop into testes

hymen: membranous tissue that can cover part of the vaginal opening

hypersexuality: exaggeratedly high level of interest in and drive for sex

hyposexuality: an especially low level of sexual interest and drive

hypospadias (hye-pa-SPADE-ee-as): birth defect caused by incomplete closure of the urethra during fetal development

—I—

identical: a twin formed by a single ovum which was fertilized by a single sperm before the cell divided in two

imperforate hymen: lack of any openings in the hymen

impotence (IM-pa-tens): difficulty achieving or maintaining erection of the penis

in loco parentis: a Latin phrase meaning in the place of the parent

in vitro fertilization (IVF): a process whereby the union of the sperm and egg occurs outside the mother's body

incest (IN-sest): sexual activity between closely related family members

incest taboo: cultural prohibitions against incest, typical of most societies

induced abortion: a termination of pregnancy by artificial means

infertility: the inability to produce offspring

infibulation: surgical procedure, performed in some cultures, that seals the opening of the vagina

informed consent: complete information about the purpose of a study and how they will be asked to perform given to prospective human research subjects

inhibited sexual desire (ISD): loss of interest and pleasure in formerly arousing sexual stimuli

internal values: the individualized beliefs and attitudes that a person develops by sorting through external values and personal needs

interstitial cells: cells between the seminiferous tubules that secrete testosterone and other male hormones

interstitial-cell-stimulating hormone (ICSH): pituitary hormone that stimulates the testes to secrete testosterone; known as luteinizing hormone (LH) in females

intrauterine devices (IUDs): birth control method involving insertion of a small plastic device into the uterus

introitus (in-TROID-us): outer opening of the vagina

invasive cancer of the cervix (ICC): advanced and dangerous malignancy requiring prompt treatment

—K—

Kaposi's sarcoma: a rare form of cancer of the blood vessels, characterized by small, purple skin lesions

kiddie porn: term used to describe the distribution and sale of photographs and films of children or younger teenagers engaging in some form of sexual activity

kleptomania: extreme form of fetishism, in which sexual arousal is generated by stealing

—L—

labor: uterine contractions in a pregnant woman; an indication that the birth process is beginning

lactation: production of milk by the milk glands of the breasts

Lamaze method (la-MAHZ): a birthing process based on relaxation techniques practiced by the expectant mother; her partner coaches her throughout the birth

laminaria (lam-a-NER-ee-a): a dried seaweed sometimes used in dilating the cervical opening prior to vacuum curettage

laparoscopy: simpler procedure for tubal ligation, involving the insertion of a small scope into the abdomen, through which the surgeon can see the fallopian tubes and close them off

laparotomy: operation to perform a tubal ligation, or female sterilization, involving an abdominal incision

latency period: Freudian concept that during middle childhood, sexual energies are dormant; recent research tends to suggest that latency does not exist

lesbian (LEZ-bee-un): refers to female homosexuals

libido (la-BEED-o or LIB-a-do): a term first used by Freud to define human sexual longing, or sex drive

lumpectomy: surgical removal of a breast lump, along with a small amount of surrounding tissue

luteinizing hormone (LH): pituitary hormone that triggers ovulation in the ovaries and stimulates sperm production in the testes

lymphogranuloma venereum (LGV) (lim-foe-gran-yu-LOW-ma-va-NEAR-ee-um): contagious venereal disease caused by several strains of *Chlamydia* and marked by swelling and ulceration of lymph nodes in the groin

—M—

major lips: two outer folds of skin covering the minor lips, clitoris, urethral opening, and vaginal opening

mammography: sensitive X-ray technique used to discover small breast tumors

marital rape: a woman being forced to have sex by her husband

masochist: the individual in a sadomasochistic sexual relationship who takes the submissive role

massage parlors: places where women can be hired to perform sexual acts

mastectomy: surgical removal of all or part of a breast

menage à trois (may-NAZH-ah-TRWAH): troilism

menarche (MEN-are-kee): onset of menstruation at puberty

menopause (MEN-a-poz): time in midlife when menstruation ceases

menstrual cycle: the hormonal interactions that prepare a woman's body for possible pregnancy at roughly monthly intervals

menstruation (men-stru-AY-shun): phase of menstrual cycle in which the inner uterine lining breaks down and sloughs off; the tissue, along with some blood, flows out through the vagina; also called the period

midwives: medical professionals, both women and men, trained to assist with the birthing process

minor lips: two inner folds of skin that join above the clitoris and extend along the sides of the vaginal and urethral openings

miscarriage: a natural termination of pregnancy

modeling theory: suggests that people will copy behavior they view in pornography

molluscum contagiosum (ma-LUS-kum kan-taje-ee-O-sum): a skin disease transmitted by direct bodily contact, not necessarily sexual, that is characterized by eruptions on the skin that appear similar to whiteheads with a hard seed-like core

monogamous: sharing sexual relations with only one person

monorchidism (ma-NOR-ka-dizm): presence of only one testis in the scrotum

mons: cushion of fatty tissue located over the female's pubic bone

moral values: beliefs associated with ethical issues, or rights and wrongs; they are often a part of sexual decision making

morula (MOR-yul-a): a spherical, solid mass of cells formed by 3 days of embryonic cell division

Müllerian ducts (myul-EAR-ee-an): embryonic structures that develop into female sexual and reproductive organs unless inhibited by male hormones

Müllerian inhibiting substance: hormone produced by fetal testes that prevents further development of female structures from the Müllerian ducts

myometrium: middle, muscular layer of the uterine wall

— N —

National Birth Control League: an organization founded in 1914 by Margaret Sanger to promote use of contraceptives

natural childbirth: a birthing process that encourages the mother to take control thus minimizing medical intervention

necrophilia (nek-ro-FILL-ee-a): having sexual activity with a dead body

nongonococcal urethritis (NGU) (non-gon-uh-KOK-ul yur-i-THRYT-us): urethral infection or irritation in the male urethra caused by bacteria or local irritants

normal: a subjective term used to describe sexual behaviors and orientations. Standards of normalcy are determined by social, cultural, and historical standards

normal asexuality: an absence or low level of sexual desire considered normal for a particular person

normalization: integration of mentally retarded persons into the social mainstream as much as possible

nymphomania (nim-fa-MANE-ee-a): compulsive need for sex in women; apparently quite rare

— O —

obscenity: depiction of sexual activity in a repulsive or disgusting manner

onanism (O-na-niz-um): a term sometimes used to describe masturbation; it comes from the biblical story of Onan who practiced coitus interruptus and "spilled his seed on the ground"

oocytes (OH-a-sites): cells that mature to become ova

open-ended marriage: each partner in the primary relationship grants the other freedom to have emotional and sexual relationships with others

opportunistic infection: a disease resulting from lowered resistance of a weakened immune system

organic disorder: physical disorder caused by the organs and organ systems of the human body

organizing effect: manner in which hormones control patterns of early development in the body

orgasm: (OR-gaz-em) pleasurable sensations and series of contractions that release sexual tension, usually accompanied by ejaculation in men

orgasmic release: reversal of the vasocongestion and muscular tension of sexual arousal, triggered by orgasm

orgy (OR-jee): group sex

os: opening in the cervix that leads into the hollow interior of the uterus

osteoporosis (ah-stee-o-po-ROW-sus): disease caused by loss of calcium from the bones in post-menopausal women, leading to brittle bone structure and stooped posture

ova: egg cells produced in the ovary; in reproduction, it is fertilized by a sperm cell; one cell is an ovum

ovaries: pair of female gonads, located in the abdominal cavity, that produce ova and female hormones

ovulation: release of a mature ovum through the wall of an ovary

ovum transfer: use of an egg from another woman for conception, with the fertilized ovum being implanted in the uterus of the woman wanting to become pregnant

oxytocin: pituitary hormone that plays a role in lactation and in uterine contractions

— P —

pansexual: lacking highly specific sexual orientations or preferences; open to a range of sexual activities

PAP smear: medical test that examines a smear of cervical cells, to detect any cellular abnormalities

paraphilia (pair-a-FIL-ee-a): a newer term used to describe sexual orientations and behaviors that vary from the norm; it means "a love beside"

paraplegic: a person paralyzed in the legs, and sometimes pelvic areas, as the result of injury to the spinal cord

partial zone dissection (PZD): a technique used to increase the chances of fertilization by making a microscopic incision in the zona pellucida of an ovum. This creates a passageway through which sperm may enter the egg more easily

pedophilia (peed-a-FIL-ee-a): another term for child sexual abuse

pelvic inflammatory disease (PID): a chronic internal infection associated with certain types of IUDs

penis: male sexual organ that can become erect when stimulated; it leads urine and sperm to the outside of the body

perimetrium: outer covering of the uterus

perinatally: a term used to describe things related to pregnancy, birth, or the period immediately following the birth

perineal areas (pair-a-NEE-al): the sensitive skin between the genitals and the anus

Peyronie's disease (pay-ra-NEEZ): development of fibrous tissue in spongy erectile columns within the penis

phimosis (fy-MOS-us): a condition in which the penile foreskin is too tight to retract easily

pimps: men who have female prostitutes working for them

placenta (pla-SENT-a): the organ that unites the fetus to the mother by bringing their blood vessels closer together; it provides nourishment and removes waste for the developing baby

plateau phase: the stable, leveled-off phase of Masters and Johnson's 4-phase model of the sexual response cycle

polygamy: practice, in some cultures, of being married to more than one spouse

pornography: photographs, films, or literature intended to be sexually arousing through explicit depictions of sexual activity

potentiation: establishment of stimuli early in life that form ranges of response for later in life

pregnancy-induced hypertension: a disorder that can occur in the latter half of pregnancy marked by a swelling in the ankles and other parts of the body, high blood pressure, and protein in the urine; can progress to coma and death if not treated

premature birth: a birth that takes place prior to the 36th week of pregnancy

premature ejaculation: difficulty that some men experience in controlling the ejaculatory reflex, resulting in rapid ejaculation

premenstrual syndrome (PMS): symptoms of physical discomfort, moodiness, and emotional tensions that occur in some women for a few days prior to menstruation

preorgasmic: a term often applied to women who have not yet been able to reach orgasm during sexual response

prepuce (PREE-peus): in the female, tissue of the upper vulva that covers the clitoral shaft

priapism (pry-AE-pizm): continual, undesired, and painful erection of the penis

primary dysfunction: a difficulty with sexual functioning that has always existed for a particular person

progesterone (pro-JES-ter-one): ovarian hormone that causes uterine lining to thicken

progestin injection: use of injected hormone that can prevent pregnancy for several months; not yet approved for use in the United States

prolactin: pituitary hormone that stimulates the process of lactation

prolapse of the uterus: weakening of the supportive ligaments of the uterus, causing it to protrude into the vagina

promiscuity (prah-mis-KIU-i-tee): sharing casual sexual activity with many different partners

prostaglandin: hormone-like chemical whose concentrations increase in a woman's body just prior to menstruation

prostaglandin or saline-induced abortion: used in the 16-24th weeks of pregnancy, prostaglandins, salt solutions, or urea is injected into the amniotic sac, administered intravenously, or inserted into the vagina in suppository form, to induce contractions and fetal delivery

prostate: gland located beneath the urinary bladder in the male; it produces some of the secretions in semen

prostatitis (pras-tuh-TITE-us): inflammation of the prostate gland

pseudonecrophilia: a fantasy about having sex with the dead

psychosexual development: complex interaction of factors that form a person's sexual feelings, orientations, and patterns of behavior

psychosocial development: the cultural and social influences that help shape human sexual identity

puberty: time of life when reproductive capacity develops and secondary sex characteristics appear

pubic lice: small insects that can infect skin in the pubic area, causing a rash and severe itching

pubococcygeus (PC) muscle (pyub-o-kox-a-JEE-us): part of the supporting musculature of the vagina that is involved in orgasmic response and over which a woman can exert some control

pyromania: sexual arousal generated by setting fires

—Q—

quadriplegic: a person paralyzed in the upper body, including the arms, and lower body as the result of spinal cord injury

—R—

random sample: a representative group of the larger population that is the focus of a scientific poll or study

rape trauma syndrome: the predictable sequence of reactions that a victim experiences following a rape

recreational marriage: extramarital sex with a low level of emotional commitment performed for fun and variety

refractory period: time following orgasm during which a man cannot be restimulated to orgasm

reinforcement: in conditioning theory, any influence that helps shape future behavior as a punishment or reward stimulus

resolution phase: the term for the return of a body to its unexcited state following orgasm

retarded ejaculation: a male who has never been able to reach an orgasm

retrograde ejaculation: abnormal passage of semen into the urinary bladder at the time of ejaculation

retrovirus (RE-tro-vi-rus): a class of viruses that reproduces with the aid of the enzyme reverse transcriptase, which allows the virus to integrate its genetic code into that of the host cell, thus establishing permanent infection

Rh incompatibility: condition in which a blood protein of the infant is not the same as the mother's; antibodies formed in the mother can destroy red blood cells in the fetus

Rho GAM: medication administered to a baby soon after delivery to prevent formation of antibodies when the baby is Rh positive and its mother Rh negative

rhythm method: a natural method of birth control that depends on an awareness of the woman's menstrual-fertility cycle

RU-486: a progesterone antagonist used as a postcoital contraceptive

rubber dam: small square sheet of latex used to cover the vulva, vagina, or anus to help prevent transmission of HIV during sexual activity

—S—

sadist: the individual in a sadomasochistic sexual relationship who takes the dominant role

sadomasochism (sade-o-MASS-o-kiz-um): refers to sexual themes or activities involving bondage, pain, domination, or humiliation of one partner by the other

sample: a small representative group of a population that is the focus of a scientific poll or study

satyriasis (sate-a-RYE-a-sus): compulsive need for sex in men; apparently rare

scabies (SKAY-beez): a skin disease caused by a mite that burrows under the skin to lay its eggs causing redness and itching; transmitted by bodily contact that may or may not be sexual

scrotum (SKROTE-um): pouch of skin in which the testes are contained

secondary dysfunction: develops after some period of normal sexual function

selective reduction: use of abortion techniques to reduce the number of fetuses when there are more than three in a pregnancy, thus increasing the chances of survival for the remaining fetuses

self-gratification: giving oneself pleasure, as in masturbation; a term typically used today instead of more negative descriptors

self-pleasuring: self-gratification; masturbation

semen: (SEE-men): mixture of fluids and sperm cells ejaculated through the penis

seminal vesicle (SEM-un-al): gland at the end of each vas deferens that secretes a chemical that helps sperm to become mobile

seminiferous tubules (sem-a-NIF-a-rus): tightly coiled tubules in the testes in which sperm cells are formed

sensate focus: early phase of sex therapy treatment, in which the partners pleasure each other without involving direct stimulation of sex organs

sex therapist: professional trained in the treatment of sexual dysfunctions

sexual addiction: inability to regulate sexual behavior

sexual dysfunctions: difficulties people have in achieving sexual arousal

sexual harassment: unwanted sexual advances or coercion that can occur in the workplace or academic settings

sexual individuality: the unique set of sexual needs, orientations, fantasies, feelings, and activities that develops in each human being

sexual phobias and aversions: exaggerated fears of forms of sexual expression

sexual revolution: the changes in thinking about sexuality and sexual behavior in society that occurred in the 1960s and 1970s

sexual surrogates: paid partners used during sex therapy with clients lacking their own partners; only rarely used today

shaft: in the female, the longer body of the clitoris, containing erectile tissue; in the male, cylindrical base of penis that contains 3 columns of spongy tissue: 2 corpora cavernosa and a corpus spongiosum

shunga: ancient scrolls used in Japan to instruct couples in sexual practices through the use of paintings

situational homosexuality: deprivation homosexuality

Skene's glands: secretory cells located inside the female urethra

smegma: thick, oily substance that may accumulate under the prepuce of the clitoris or penis

social learning theory: suggests that human learning is influenced by observation of and identification with other people

social scripts: a complex set of learned responses to a particular situation that is formed by social influences

sodomy laws: prohibit a variety of sexual behaviors in some states, that have been considered abnormal or antisocial by legislatures. These laws are often enforced discriminatorily against particular groups, such as homosexuals

sonograms: ultrasonic rays used to project a picture of internal structures such as the fetus; often used in conjunction with amniocentesis or fetal surgery

spectatoring: term used by Masters and Johnson to describe self-consciousness and self-observation during sex

sperm: reproductive cells produced in the testes; in fertilization, one sperm unites with an ovum

spermatocytes (sper-MAT-o-sites): cells lining the seminiferous tubules from which sperm cells are produced

spermicidal jelly (cream): sperm-killing chemical in a gel base or cream, used with other contraceptives such as diaphragms

spermicides: chemicals that kill sperm; available as foams, creams, jellies, or implants in sponges or suppositories

sponge: a thick polyurethane disc that holds a spermicide and fits over the cervix to prevent conception

spontaneous abortion: another term for miscarriage

Staphylococcus aureus (staf-a-low-KAK-us): the bacteria that can cause toxic shock syndrome

statutory rape: a legal term used to indicate sexual activity when one partner is under the age of consent; in most states that age is 18

sterilization: rendering a person incapable of conceiving, usually by interrupting passage of the egg or sperm

straight: slang term for heterosexual

streetwalkers: female prostitutes who work on the streets

suppositories: contraceptive devices designed to distribute their spermicide by melting or foaming in the vagina

syndrome (SIN-drome): a group of signs or symptoms that occur together and characterize a given condition

syphilis (SIF-uh-lus): sexually transmitted disease (STD) characterized by four stages, beginning with the appearance of a chancre

systematic desensitization: step-by-step approaches to unlearning tension-producing behaviors and developing new behavior patterns

— T —

testes (TEST-ees): pair of male gonads that produce sperm and male hormones

testicular cancer: malignancy on the testis that may be detected by testicular self examination

testicular failure: lack of sperm and/or hormone production by the testes

testosterone (tes-TAS-ter-one): major male hormone produced by the testes; it helps to produce male secondary sex characteristics

testosterone replacement therapy: administering testosterone injections to increase sexual interest or potency in older men; not considered safe for routine use

theoretical failure rate: a measure of how often a birth control method can be expected to fail, when used without error or technical problems

thrush: a disease caused by a fungus and characterized by white patches in the oral cavity

toxic shock syndrome (TSS): an acute disease characterized by fever and sore

throat, and caused by normal bacteria in the vagina which are activated if tampons or some contraceptive devices such as diaphragms or sponges are left in for long periods of time

transgenderists: people who live in clothing and roles considered appropriate for the opposite sex for sustained periods of time

transsexuals: feel as though they should have the body of the opposite sex

transvestism: dressing in clothes appropriate to the opposite sex, usually for sexual gratification

transvestite: an individual who dresses in clothing considered appropriate for the opposite sex, and adopts similar mannerisms, often for sexual pleasure

trichomoniasis (trik-uh-ma-NEE-uh-sis): a vaginal infection caused by the *Trichomonas* organism

troilism (TROY-i-lizm): sexual activity shared by three people

tubal ligation: a surgical separation of the fallopian tubes to induce permanent female sterilization

— U —

umbilical cord: tubelike tissues and blood vessels arising from the embryo's navel connecting it to the placenta

urethra (yu-REE-thrah): tube that passes from the urinary bladder to the outside of the body

urethral opening: opening through which urine passes to the outside of the body

urophilia: sexual arousal connected with urine or urination

uterus (YUTE-a-rus): muscular organ of the female reproductive system; a fertilized egg implants itself within the uterus

— V —

vacuum curettage: (kyur-a-TAZH): a method of induced abortion performed with a suction pump

vagina (vu-JI-na): muscular canal in the female that is responsive to sexual arousal; it receives semen during heterosexual intercourse for reproduction

vaginal atresia (a-TREE-zha): birth defect in which the vagina is absent or closed

vaginal atrophy: shrinking and deterioration of vaginal lining, usually the result of low estrogen levels during aging

vaginal fistulae (FISH-cha-lee *or* -lie): abnormal channels that can develop between the vagina and other internal organs

vaginismus (vaj-uh-NIZ-mus): involuntary spasm of the outer vaginal musculature, making penetration of the vagina difficult or impossible

vaginitis (vaj-uh-NITE-us): general term for inflammation of the vagina

values: system of beliefs with which people view life and make decisions, including their sexual decisions

variable: an aspect of a scientific study that is subject to change

variation: a less pejorative term to describe nonconformity to accepted norms

varicose veins: overexpanded blood vessels; can occur in veins surrounding the vagina

vas deferens: tube that leads sperm upward from each testis to the seminal vesicles

vasectomy (va-SEK-ta-mee *or* vay-ZEK-ta-mee): a surgical division of the vas deferens to induce permanent male sterilization

villi: the fingerlike projections of the chorion that form a major part of the placenta

viral hepatitis: inflammation of the liver caused by a virus

voyeurism (VOI-yur-izm): gaining sexual gratification from seeing others nude or involved in sexual acts

vulva: external sex organs of the female, including the mons, major and minor lips, clitoris, and opening of the vagina

— W —

Western blot: test used to verify positive AIDS virus detected first by the ELISA

Wolffian ducts (WOOL-fee-an): embryonic structures that develop into male sexual and reproductive organs if male hormones are present

— Y —

yeast infection: a type of vaginitis caused by an overgrowth of a fungus normally found in an inactive state in the vagina

— Z —

zona pellucida (ZO-nah pe-LOO-sa-da): transparent, outer membrane of an ovum

zoophilia (zoo-a-FILL-ee-a): bestiality

Index

Credits/ Acknowledgments

Cover design by Charles Vitelli

1. Sexuality and Society

Facing overview—United Nations photo by John Isaac.

2. Sexual Biology and Health

Facing overview—United Nations photo by Bedrich Grunzweig.

3. Interpersonal Relationships

Facing overview—United Nations photo by John Isaac.

4. Reproduction

Facing overview—New York City Department of Health.

5. Sexuality Through the Life Cycle

Facing overview—Courtesy of Marcuss Oslander.

6. Old/New Sexual Concerns

Facing overview—Abbott Laboratories.

ANNUAL EDITIONS ARTICLE REVIEW FORM

■ NAME: _____ DATE: _____

■ TITLE AND NUMBER OF ARTICLE: _____

■ BRIEFLY STATE THE MAIN IDEA OF THIS ARTICLE: _____

_____

_____

_____

_____

■ LIST THREE IMPORTANT FACTS THAT THE AUTHOR USES TO SUPPORT THE MAIN IDEA:

_____

_____

_____

_____

_____

■ WHAT INFORMATION OR IDEAS DISCUSSED IN THIS ARTICLE ARE ALSO DISCUSSED IN YOUR
TEXTBOOK OR OTHER READING YOU HAVE DONE? LIST THE TEXTBOOK CHAPTERS AND PAGE
NUMBERS:

_____

_____

_____

_____

_____

_____

_____

■ LIST ANY EXAMPLES OF BIAS OR FAULTY REASONING THAT YOU FOUND IN THE ARTICLE:

_____

_____

_____

_____

■ LIST ANY NEW TERMS/CONCEPTS THAT WERE DISCUSSED IN THE ARTICLE AND WRITE A
SHORT DEFINITION:

_____

_____

_____

_____

_____

*Your instructor may require you to use this Annual Editions Article Review Form in any number of ways:
for articles that are assigned, for extra credit, as a tool to assist in developing assigned papers, or simply
for your own reference. Even if it is not required, we encourage you to photocopy and use this page;
you'll find that reflecting on the articles will greatly enhance the information from your text.

ANNUAL EDITIONS: HUMAN SEXUALITY 91/92
Article Rating Form

Here is an opportunity for you to have direct input into the next revision of this volume. We would like you to rate each of the 58 articles listed below, using the following scale:

1. **Excellent: should definitely be retained**
2. **Above average: should probably be retained**
3. **Below average: should probably be deleted**
4. **Poor: should definitely be deleted**

Your ratings will play a vital part in the next revision. So please mail this prepaid form to us just as soon as you complete it.
Thanks for your help!

Rating	Article	Rating	Article
	1. Sex in China		29. Birth Control
	2. Latino Culture and Sex Education		30. Can You Rely on Condoms?
	3. Manhood		31. Reluctant Crusader: Etienne-Emile Baulieu
	4. AIDS News, Highlights: Fifth International AIDS Conference: Montreal, June 4–9		32. "She Died Because of a Law"
	5. Sexuality Education in the 1900s		33. Abortion in a New Light
	6. AIDS and STD Education: What's Really Happening in Our Schools?		34. Teenage Birth's New Conceptions
	7. Abortion Policy and Medical Practice		35. Teenage Pregnancy in New York
	8. Censorship and the Fear of Sexuality		36. Sex During Pregnancy
	9. How Sex Hormones Boost—or Cut—Intellectual Abilities		37. Sex After the Baby
	10. Man's Greatest Reflex		38. My Body, My Self
	11. Women and Sexuality		39. Double Vision
	12. When Female Behavior Contributes to Premature Ejaculation		40. What College Students Want to Know About Sex
	13. Men Who Fake Orgasm		41. Sex: Better After 35
	14. Sexuality Attitudes of Black Adults		42. Erotic Play
	15. Americans and Their Sexual Partners		43. The Most-Asked Sex Questions
	16. Life-Threatening Autoerotic Behavior: A Challenge for Sex Educators and Therapists		44. Death of a Sex Life
	17. Homosexuality: Who and Why?		45. Predictors of Risky Adolescent Sexual Behavior
	18. Variations on a Theme		46. Dangerous Liaison
	19. Should Gays Have Marriage Rights?		47. PMS: Proof or Promises?
	20. Looking for Love in All the Right Places		48. Chronic Disease and Impotence
	21. Has the Double Standard Disappeared? An Experimental Test		49. AIDS: The Next Ten Years
	22. How Do You Build Intimacy in an Age of Divorce?		50. Sexual Harassment, '80s-Style
	23. Friends and Lovers?		51. Adolescent Female Prostitutes: A Growing National Concern
	24. Major Mergers		52. Date Rape
	25. Sexual Pursuit		53. "It Sounds Like I Raped You!"
	26. The Art of Sex		54. Study Defines Major Sources of Conflict Between Sexes
	27. An Evaluation of an Adolescent Pregnancy Prevention Program: Is "Just Say No" Enough?		55. Vive la . . . différence
			56. Sensuality Scale
	28. Curbing Teenage Pregnancy: A Novel Approach		57. Sexual Secrets Men Are Afraid to Share
			58. Mind Sex: Do Human Brains Have Gender?

(Continued on next page)

ABOUT YOU

Name_____ Date_____

Are you a teacher? ☐ Or student? ☐

Your School Name _____

Department _____

Address _____

City_____ State _____ Zip _____

School Telephone # _____

YOUR COMMENTS ARE IMPORTANT TO US!

Please fill in the following information:

For which course did you use this book? _____

Did you use a text with this Annual Edition?   ☐ yes   ☐ no

The title of the text? _____

What are your general reactions to the Annual Editions concept?

Have you read any particular articles recently that you think should be included in the next edition?

Are there any articles you feel should be replaced in the next edition? Why?

Are there other areas that you feel would utilize an Annual Edition?

May we contact you for editorial input?

May we quote you from above?